THE GREEK PLAYS

THE
GREEK PLAYS

SIXTEEN PLAYS BY
AESCHYLUS, SOPHOCLES, AND EURIPIDES

NEW TRANSLATIONS EDITED BY
MARY LEFKOWITZ AND JAMES ROMM

MODERN LIBRARY
NEW YORK

2017 Modern Library Trade Paperback Edition

Preface, general introduction, play introductions, and compilation copyright © 2016 by Mary Lefkowitz and James Romm

" 'Saving the City': Tragedy in Its Civic Context" copyright © 2016 by Daniel Mendelsohn
"Material Elements and Visual Meaning" copyright © 2016 by David Rosenbloom
"Plato and Tragedy" copyright © 2016 by Joshua Billings
"Aristotle's *Poetics* and Greek Tragedy" copyright © 2016 by Gregory Hays
"The Postclassical Reception of Greek Tragedy" copyright © 2016 by Mary-Kay Gamel

Copyright information for the individual play translations can be found on page 829.
All rights reserved.

Published in the United States by Modern Library, an imprint of Random House, a division of Penguin Random House LLC, New York.

MODERN LIBRARY and the TORCHBEARER colophon are registered trademarks of Penguin Random House LLC.

Originally published in hardcover in the United States by Modern Library, an imprint of Random House, a division of Penguin Random House LLC, in 2016.

Library of Congress Cataloging-in-Publication Data

Names: Lefkowitz, Mary R., | Romm, James S. | Aeschylus. Plays. English. Selections. 2016. | Sophocles. Plays. English. Selections. 2016. | Euripides. Plays. English. Selections. 2016.
Title: The Greek plays: sixteen plays by Aeschylus, Sophocles, and Euripides / new translations edited by Mary Lefkowitz and James Romm.
Description: New York: The Modern Library, 2016. | Plays include: Aeschylus: the Persians, Oresteia, Prometheus bound; Sophocles: Oedipus the king, Antigone, Electra, Oedipus at Colonus; Euripides: Alcestis, Medea, Hippolytus, Electra, Trojan women, Helen, Bacchae.
Identifiers: LCCN 2015037031| ISBN 9780812983098 | ISBN 9780679644484 (ebook)
Subjects: LCSH: Greek drama. | Greek drama—History and criticism. | Aeschylus. | Sophocles. | Euripides.
Classification: LCC PA3463 .G74 2016 | DDC 882/.0108—dc23 LC record available at https://protect-us.mimecast.com/s/ZpJmBwtDwo8ix

Printed in the United States of America on acid-free paper

randomhousebooks.com
modernlibrary.com

10th Printing

CONTENTS

Time Line (Life Spans of the Three Leading Greek
    Tragedians)   *vii*
Maps   *viii*
Preface   *xiii*
General Introduction   *xvii*

AESCHYLUS

Biographical Note   *3*
Introduction to Aeschylus' *Persians*   *5*
    Persians, translated by James Romm   *9*
General Introduction to Aeschylus' *Oresteia*   *45*
Introduction to Aeschylus' *Agamemnon*   *47*
    The *Oresteia: Agamemnon*, translated by Sarah Ruden   *51*
Introduction to Aeschylus' *Libation Bearers*   *101*
    The *Oresteia: Libation Bearers*,
        translated by Sarah Ruden   *105*
Introduction to Aeschylus' *Eumenides*   *139*
    The *Oresteia: Eumenides*, translated by Sarah Ruden   *143*
Introduction to *Prometheus Bound* (possibly by Aeschylus)   *179*
    Prometheus Bound, translated by James Romm   *183*

SOPHOCLES

Biographical Note   *219*
Introduction to Sophocles' *Oedipus the King*   *221*
    Oedipus the King, translated by Frank Nisetich   *225*
Introduction to Sophocles' *Antigone*   *275*
    Antigone, translated by Frank Nisetich   *279*
Introduction to Sophocles' *Electra*   *327*
    Electra, translated by Mary Lefkowitz   *331*

Introduction to Sophocles' *Oedipus at Colonus*   *377*
   Oedipus at Colonus, translated by Frank Nisetich   *381*

EURIPIDES

Biographical Note   *437*
Introduction to Euripides' *Alcestis*   *439*
   Alcestis, translated by Rachel Kitzinger   *443*
Introduction to Euripides' *Medea*   *483*
   Medea, translated by Rachel Kitzinger   *487*
Introduction to Euripides' *Hippolytus*   *533*
   Hippolytus, translated by Rachel Kitzinger   *537*
Introduction to Euripides' *Electra*   *585*
   Electra, translated by Emily Wilson   *589*
Introduction to Euripides' *Trojan Women*   *633*
   Trojan Women, translated by Emily Wilson   *637*
Introduction to Euripides' *Helen*   *683*
   Helen, translated by Emily Wilson   *687*
Introduction to Euripides' *Bacchae*   *737*
   Bacchae, translated by Emily Wilson   *741*

APPENDICES

A. "Saving the City": Tragedy in Its Civic Context
   by Daniel Mendelsohn   *789*
B. Material Elements and Visual Meaning
   by David Rosenbloom   *799*
C. Plato and Tragedy *by Joshua Billings*   *805*
D. Aristotle's *Poetics* and Greek Tragedy
   by Gregory Hays   *809*
E. The Postclassical Reception of Greek Tragedy
   by Mary-Kay Gamel   *815*

Life Spans of the Three Leading Greek Tragedians

Aeschylus (525–456)

- First Victory (484)
- Persians (472)
- Seven Against Thebes (467)
- Suppliants (463)
- Oresteia (458)

Sophocles (487/6–405/4)

- First Victory (469/8)
- Sophocles = State Treasurer (443/2)
- Sophocles = General (441/0)
- Oedipus at Colonus (406–5)

Euripides (480–406/5)

- Alcestis (438)
- Medea (431)
- Hippolytus (428)
- Electra (420?)
- Trojan Women (415)
- Helen (412)
- Bacchae (406)

Historical Events

- Battle of Marathon (490)
- Second Persian War (481–479)
- Peloponnesian War (432–404)
- Plague in Athens (430)
- Death of Pericles (429)
- Sicilian Expedition (415–413)
- Death of Socrates (399)

530 520 510 500 490 480 470 460 450 440 430 420 410 400 390 380

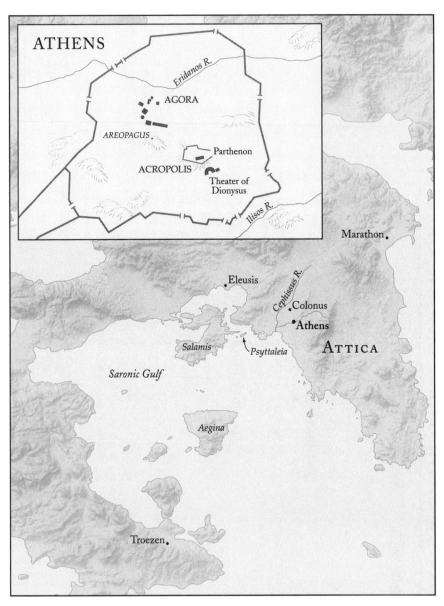

Athens and Attica in the Fifth Century B.C.

Mainland Greece and Asia Minor

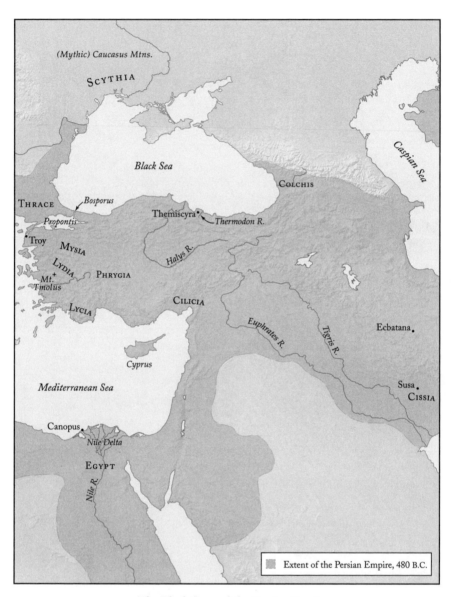

The Black Sea and the Persian Empire

Possible reconstruction of the theater of Dionysus in the early fifth century.

Possible reconstruction of the theater of Dionysus in the second half of the fifth century, with wooden seats and wooden stage buildings.

PREFACE

Almost half a century ago, Robert F. Kennedy, announcing to a crowd of followers the killing of Martin Luther King Jr., and speaking without a written text, recited words from a tragedy of Aeschylus (here quoted in Sarah Ruden's translation):

In the heart is no sleep; there drips instead
pain that remembers wounds ...

The fact that at such a moment of crisis his mind went out to verses spoken in Athens on an early spring day in 458 B.C. demonstrates the enduring power of Greek tragedy to move us, comfort our sorrows, and help us explore the deepest levels of human experience. In the modern age, when Greco-Roman antiquity is often asked to prove its relevance, the surviving plays of Aeschylus, Sophocles, and Euripides continue to speak with an urgent voice to readers, playgoers, and spectators of opera, dance, and film. In the U.S. educational curriculum, these plays are often the first works of premodern literature read by high school and college students, and their encounter with a mythic world millennia old, yet compellingly alive, is often a memorable one.

Readers of today who seek to understand these plays are faced with a paradox. Their themes are timeless and universal, yet they belong to a very precise and circumscribed historical context, the city of Athens in the fifth century B.C. In this volume we strive to retain an awareness of that context, while also acknowledging the ways in which the dramas transcend it.

To that end, the general introduction, the first two appendices, and many of the notes are designed to illuminate the original productions of these plays and the concerns (as far as can be judged from contemporary sources) of the Athenians who attended them. The short introductions that precede each play deal in part with these historical issues but also discuss the characters, themes, and poetic motifs in which the broader meanings of these works reside. Three further appendices treat the late- or postclassical reception of Greek tragedy, and many of the short introductions highlight important recent productions, adaptations, and responses to individual plays.

Our volume also includes several maps, as well as a time line showing how the life spans and careers of the playwrights correlate with the events of their times. These resources, too, are designed to allow, but not insist on, a historically contextualized reading of the plays, and to permit readers to familiarize themselves with the geography in which they are set. Orestes' journey in the *Oresteia*, for example, which takes him from Phocis to Argos to Delphi and finally to Athens, will make better sense to those who can imagine the relative distance of these places and the ruggedness of the landscape in between. Likewise, the great expanse that separates Susa—the scene of Aeschylus' *Persians*—from Athens can only be understood by way of a map of the entire Near East. An inset map of Athens is designed to show the location of the Theater of Dionysus, the site at which all these plays were originally performed, on the south slope of the Athenian Acropolis.

Of the thirty-three dramas that have survived into modern times, we have selected sixteen—approximately half—for this volume: five from the work of Aeschylus, four from Sophocles, and seven from Euripides. No collection of this kind will escape criticism that one work or another ought to have been included, but we have given priority to works that are most often taught in college classes (including our own) or are otherwise deemed most current or most resonant in the modern world.

Translations of Greek tragedy have proliferated in recent years, and many styles are available today, some of which depart far from the Greek originals in an effort to avoid foreignness or to capture the feel of modern poetry. Our translators, by contrast, have tried to preserve some of the foreignness of the original, without making the texts opaque or obscure. They avoid colloquialism, using instead a more formal style to give some impression of the elevated, non-natural feel of the Greek. As editors we have also tried to make this volume reflect the distinctions between the styles of the three tragedians, so far as English will allow us to do so. Thus each translator, including the two editors, has worked on only one ancient playwright.

To judge from the many lines in our surviving plays that are quoted by Greek or Roman authors, who had access to more definitive versions of the texts, it seems probable that our printed editions of these plays largely represent what was written, on perishable papyrus, by the original authors. But we do not want our readers to suppose that we can always be sure of this. Lines that, to judge by their content, are either garbled or inserted by later hands appear in all surviving manuscripts of any particular play, indicating that they must have been introduced quite early in the process of transmission. Other mistakes and additions, because they occurred further on in that process, survive only in certain "families" of manuscripts but not in others. In the footnotes to the plays we have let readers know why we have chosen among several possible readings in the various surviving manuscripts, or why on occasion we believe a line or lines to be inauthentic. Suspect lines have been included in the text, with or without brackets, or relegated to the footnotes, at the discretion of the translator, based on how likely it is that these are insertions by a later hand. Gaps in the text, where words or lines have evidently fallen out, are indicated by bracketed ellipses.

In addition to staying close to the diction of the original plays, we have tried, both visually and metrically, to give our readers some idea of their variations in rhythm, even though we can at best offer only an approximation. Lines that, in Greek, use the standard meter of speech and dialogue, iambic trimeter, are here rendered as iambic pentameter and run out to the farthest edge of the left-hand margin. The more complex lyric meters, typically used for choral odes and highly emotional "arias" by individual characters, are in this volume set off by an indent and rendered with various non-iambic rhythms. It has not been possible to correlate English meters with Greek ones, and the lack of such correlation is a serious loss to students of Greek tragedy, but in the footnotes the translators have tried to give some sense of metrical variations and the shifts in mood or changes of dance step they indicate. (The general introduction offers further insight into Greek poetic meter and its role in the tragic dramas.)

A word should be said about this volume's use of an iambic pentameter line for most passages of speech and dialogue set in Greek iambic trimeter. Aristotle, in the *Poetics*, said that Athenian dramatists used iambic trimeter for dialogue because it was closest of all meters to natural speech. But it is poetry nonetheless, the mark of the elevation of mythic figures and the distance that separates their world from that of the audience. Similarly, Shakespeare and his contemporaries made noble, aristocratic characters speak in verse, in iambic pentameter (while sometimes giving prose lines to more ordinary people, such as commoners and clowns). We have adopted iambic pentameter wherever the Greek plays have iambic trimeter, in part because it has Aristotle's "speechlike" feel, but also because the familiarity of English readers with Shakespearean verse makes this meter a natural way to evoke the grandeur and solemnity of mythic drama.

The translators have used various approaches to solve one of the most intractable of all translation problems: the inarticulate sounds, groans, and cries found in the original texts of the tragedies. We can usually tell from context what these exclamations meant. The cry *oimoi* (literally "oh me") expresses sorrow and despair on the part of the speaker, or sometimes outraged anger; it can represent a protracted wail, or an exclamation that fits into the metrical pattern of the line that is being spoken, like "alas" in Shakespeare. *Pheu* (pronounced "feh-ooh" but in one syllable) seems to represent a sigh or expression of regret not quite as powerful as *oimoi*. Then there are strings of vowels or vowel-consonant combinations such as *aiai*, *popoi*, or a repeated *eā* and *ē* (pronounced "eh-ah" and "ay" as in *hay*) for emotions so intense that they could not be expressed in words or gestures. There are no equivalents for these exclamations in modern English; in this volume our translators have in some cases simply transliterated them, in others they have used stage directions or linguistic emphasis to convey their tone.

Finally, we have given our translators, and ourselves, the stern task of keeping to the lineation of the Greek texts in these English versions, rather than expanding them as most recent editions have done. It is always our hope that those who connect to Greek drama will feel inspired to learn Greek, or that those who already know some Greek will use it to better understand these plays. We want such readers to be able to easily find their way to a corresponding Greek passage when using this volume, or, better still, to find the corresponding English while reading the Greek. Readers not familiar with the conventions of Greek texts should note that the line numberings their editors have added are not always regular; in places where lines have been deleted from or added to the text, or (especially) where the lineation of choral passages has been revised, there may be more than ten lines, or fewer, between line numbers spaced ten digits apart. Line numbers in our translations follow those of the Greek and therefore preserve these occasional irregularities.

We would like to thank Glen Hartley of Writers' Representatives, our agent, as well as our editors at Random House, Sam Nicholson, Vincent La Scala, and Emily DeHuff. Among the friends, family, and colleagues who have lent their help and advice, we want to especially acknowledge Steve Coates, Lauren Curtis, Wyatt Mason, and Eve Romm.

GENERAL INTRODUCTION

Human beings have always sought to be something other than themselves, informally when they are young, in formal rituals as adults. But it was the ancient Athenians who gave to posterity the idea of role playing before a large audience, with trained actors reciting and singing written texts to musical accompaniment. Their words for such performances have become part of our ordinary vocabulary; tragedy, drama, theater. *Tragōidia* originally meant a song (*ōidē*) performed in a singing competition in which the winner took home a goat (*tragos*)—a significant prize in an agricultural society. *Drama* meant "something done," an action. A theater (*theatron*) was a place where one viewed a *drama* or a *tragōidia.* Those words have a wide range of meanings today, but in the fifth century B.C. they were connected to an annual festival in one particular place: the City, or Great, Dionysia in Athens. The festival was sacred to the god Dionysus and filled with processions and feasts, but its most distinctive features were the dramatic competitions held in the Theater of Dionysus on the south slope of the Acropolis. The winners took home prizes that were much more substantial than the goat that originally gave the dramatic performances their name. The Athenians regarded the tragedies as something more than entertainments. The dramas were staged and actors and choruses trained at considerable public expense, along with private contributions from the wealthiest citizens. The festival took place at the beginning of the sailing season, when the ships were launched that helped to bring Athens her wealth and enforce her military power. The citizens appear to have thought that the performances were essential for the welfare of everyone who saw them, and for the life of the city itself.

Even after Athens had been defeated by Sparta in the Peloponnesian War at the end of the fifth century B.C., dramas continued to be performed in the Theater of Dionysus. Some were revivals of the plays by the fifth-century dramatists whose works survive to this day; others were newly composed. Starting in the fourth century, theaters were constructed and dramas were staged throughout the Mediterranean world, wherever Greek was spoken. Some plays were even written by authors for whom Greek was a second language. The Romans translated Greek dramas into Latin and used them as models for new dramas of their own, and those works in turn influenced and inspired dramas throughout Europe and the European diaspora.

What made Athenian fifth-century drama so powerful a medium that neither time nor change of language has managed to render it obsolete? The fundamental reason, certainly, is that the dramas deal with the most intractable aspects of human existence: uncertainty about the future, fear of injury, deprivation, suffering, and death. In the ancient world, war, instability, and untimely death were constants of everyday existence; it was necessary always to be on guard, against either military attack, sudden outbursts of anger or insanity, or diseases and infirmities for which there were no cures. No terrifying possibility is omitted: sudden death, suicide, terminal illness, betrayal, loss of a loved one or of many loved ones. The tragedies helped their ancient audiences to see how it might be possible to face and survive such challenges, and there is still much that modern readers can learn from them. They not only speak to the causes of human despair; they also provide the words that can bring at least a partial remedy. And they still can help us understand how to endure many of the burdens that modern medicine cannot cure, not least the isolation imposed by loss and defeat. The tragedies provide illustrations of the solace that can be offered by friends and even strangers. Alongside humanity's greatest weaknesses, the tragedies also allow us to see its most remarkable strengths: empathy, compassion, and the ability to endure even in the face of physical suffering and deprivation.

But ancient audiences were able to learn more from the tragedies than we can today, because of their connection to traditional Greek religion. Rituals held in honor of Dionysus could require worshippers to wear disguises and play roles, to abandon routines, to leave the safety of their homes to go out into the wilderness, to expect the unexpected. It was Dionysus in particular who could make mortals see what was not there, or prevent them from seeing what was right before their eyes. Tragedies, like other Dionysiac rituals, are by nature illusory and unreal, fictive representations of actions in the past. But the illusions that they created helped to remind the audience of the insufficiency of human knowledge, and of the contrast between human understanding and that of the immortal gods. Athenians liked to believe that their city was dear to the gods, and that the gods would protect them from their enemies. But the dramas warned them not to count on retaining the gods' favor, and not to suppose that they could understand what might be done by forces beyond their control in order to change the courses of their lives. The mortals who fared best in such a hostile world were those who sought the advice of seers in order to determine what the gods might wish them to do, and who were scrupulously pious in honoring them. But the dramas demonstrated that even such proper actions did not always produce the results that the petitioners sought to obtain.

The dramas were exciting to watch, even though many members of the audience would already have known how the stories they depicted would end. Most of the plots were based on material from the *Iliad*, the *Odyssey*, and other epics now surviving only in fragments. The dramatists did not seek to change the outcomes of the traditional myths, because these stories were for them a kind of history; but they were free to refashion the old narratives in any way they chose, and the ingenuity with which they devised new plots brought excitement even to familiar narratives. We still possess four dramas that offer different versions of a story outlined in the *Odyssey*, about how Orestes, returning home from exile to avenge the death of his father, Agamemnon, killed his mother, Clytemnestra, and her lover, Aegisthus. Each of the dramatists puts a different emphasis on this narrative, adds new characters, and comes up with a distinctive ending. Aeschylus in his drama *Libation Bearers* and Sophocles in his drama *Electra* characterize Orestes as a dutiful son who follows the orders of the god Apollo and returns home to Argos to avenge the death of his father. But in Euripides' *Electra*, Orestes is as keen to recover his patrimony as he is to avenge his father's death. In Euripides' *Orestes* (not included in this volume), Orestes believes he has been abandoned by Apollo and so is prepared to kill Helen and her daughter, Hermione, until Apollo himself intervenes to stop him.

The four dramas about Orestes' revenge, as does virtually every other surviving Greek drama, describe a crisis that affects the family of a royal house. The dramatists appear to have been particularly interested in the plots and murders that plagued the house of Atreus in Argos: Atreus; his brother, Thyestes; their sons, Agamemnon, Menelaus, and Aegisthus; and Agamemnon's children, Orestes and Electra. Another favorite narrative (mentioned only briefly in the *Odyssey*) concerns the house of Laius in Thebes: Laius' wife, Jocasta; her son/husband, Oedipus; and Oedipus' children by Jocasta, Antigone, Ismene, Eteocles, and Polynices. Aeschylus' drama *Persians*, although based on recent history rather than myth, describes the suffering of the family of Xerxes, king of Persia, whose great army was defeated by the Greeks in the battle of Salamis. Perhaps the Athenians believed that the autocratic power wielded by royal families was more likely to bring about disaster than was their own democracy, in which officials were elected instead of obtaining their office by inheritance, and authority was shared among the male citizens. But it also would have been easier for audiences to understand the effects of disaster on individuals within a family than on an undifferentiated group, if only because each of them was a member of a family and so potentially able to understand the conflicts and rivalries that arise among close relatives.

Most dramas involve a reversal of expectations and of fortune, a shift either from prosperity to disaster or from misery to happiness, as Aristotle saw (see appendix D). More often than not, good fortune is the result of divine rather than human action. But humans bear some measure of responsibility in the case of changes for the worse, usually because of a misjudgment on the part of some individual. Aristotle called such errors in judgment *hamartia*. That word is often mistranslated as "tragic flaw," which suggests that the mistake arises from a character fault on the part of the hero of the tragedy. A person with a calm temperament might not have struck the old man who roughly pushed him off the road, but Oedipus' quick temper led him to strike back and kill the old man who (unknown to him) was his own father. Oedipus' *hamartia*, however, was not his violent response, but his assumption that he could avoid the prophecy that he had just heard at Delphi, that he would kill his father and marry his mother. In the process of evasion, he made the prophecy come true by taking the road to Thebes, encountering the old man who was his father, and marrying the old man's widow after he arrived in Thebes. Greek tragedy teaches that human error is inevitable, and even though a person's character can make him or her more likely to err in judgment, the gods either ensure that mortals will make mistakes or fail to prevent them from doing so.

Like Oedipus, the mortal characters in the dramas at first believe that they know what they are doing and presume that they have some control over their destinies. But soon they learn that their plans will not succeed, or begin to suspect that their present prosperity will be replaced by suffering or even death. Oedipus, whose courage and intelligence allowed him to solve the riddle of the Sphinx, supposes that he can also determine who murdered his predecessor, King Laius, only to discover that the culprit is himself. In other cases the principal characters think that there is no way for them to escape from their present predicament but suddenly discover that there is a solution, often provided by the intervention of a god, as in the case of Helen and Menelaus in Euripides' *Helen*, in which Helen's brothers, the twin gods Castor and Polydeuces (Pollux), arrive just in time to guarantee them a safe voyage from Egypt to Sparta. Gods appear suddenly at the ends of some dramas to explain what the characters could not know about the past or the future. Such information can also be conveyed by a seer who can interpret the omens, dramas, and other signs that the gods have sent to him, a role often played in dramas set in Thebes by Tiresias, the seer who was said to have lived through seven generations of men.

Even when the gods choose not to send direct signals, there are clear indications that they are present, although the characters often do not seem to be aware of them. Perfect timing is often a sign of divine intervention. In Euripides' *Medea*, for example, Aegeus, the king of Athens, shows up and offers Medea a place of refuge, just when she most needs it. The heroes and heroines of the dramas in which the gods do not intervene are in particular need of compassion, like Hecuba in the *Trojan Women*, since no one comes to tell her whether she will be able to find any release from her suffering in the future.

In surviving dramas, the gods who intervene are almost always the children of Zeus, most often his daughter Athena, but never Zeus himself. Invariably the gods arrive without warning, adding to the excitement. But with the possible exception of Athena, as characters, the gods seem cold and distant. When they come to help or to punish, their interactions with mortals are brief, even when the people they have come to advise are close relatives, like Helen, or special friends, like Hippolytus—in Euripides' drama, the goddess Artemis speaks to him as he is dying but leaves in time not to be polluted by his actual death. In this way the dramatists remind the audience that mortals cannot expect much sympathy from the gods, or anything more than an intermittent and evanescent happiness. Only a few extraordinary individuals (who also happen to be children of gods, such as Heracles, a son of Zeus) could attain immortality, and then only after extraordinary loss and hardship. The best that anyone else can expect is some kind of lasting memorial, some remembrance in the form of ritual and song.

But the brief interactions between gods and mortals portrayed in Greek drama are always set in the remote past. In the fifth century, few Athenians would have supposed that a god had any reason to take the kind of direct interest in their lives that he or she showed for the royal families of the past, many of whom were the gods' close relatives. Nonetheless, by setting the dramas in the past, the dramatists could allow their audiences to step briefly outside themselves and away from the particular problems of their own lives. That remoteness has the advantage of making the dramas relevant to any time or place, including the times and places that we live in now.

Not only do the settings of the dramas seem unfamiliar and even strange; in the dramas, women in the royal families are often the central figures in the action, displaying great heroism and speaking eloquently about political and moral issues. When they are wronged (like Medea or Electra), the dramatists showed how these women could find ways to punish their enemies, or devise clever plots to escape from them, like Helen in the Euripides drama that is named for her. They could display the greatest courage, like Alcestis, who volunteers to die so her husband can live, or like Hecuba and Andromache, who manage to endure the loss of all their loved ones. Women's prominence and eloquence onstage contrast notably with the more limited roles played in real life by women in Athens, who could not own property, had no training in rhetoric, and played no role in public life. We do not even know whether they were allowed to watch the performances of the dramas in the Theater of Dionysus.

The conventions of Greek drama also helped to emphasize the distance between the action onstage and the daily existence of the members of the audience. The architecture of the theater, with its circular orchestra, separated the actors and chorus from the spectators. No one could see the actors' faces because they wore masks. Heavy costumes and specially elevated shoes kept the actors from moving easily around the stage. All the roles in any drama were played by two or three male actors, who indicated who they were by changing masks that marked them as young or old, male or female. Since there were no program notes, all the characters (including the Chorus) needed to identify themselves or be identified when they first came onstage. Violent action never took place in view of the audience. Instead, the audience learned of such events from messengers who described in animated detail what had happened offstage. The static nature of this type of presentation meant that the actors needed to generate excitement by words and gestures.

In many dramas the action occurs in one place on a single day; in others, there are longer lapses of time, which are not precisely indicated. The actors stood on a raised platform in front of the stage building, the *skēnē*, which is where the modern word "scene" comes from. The *skēnē* represented a palace or other building, with doors that could open and reveal what was inside. By the end of the fifth century B.C. a rotating device known as the *ekkyklēma* made quick scene changes possible (see appendix B). The actors who played the role of a god were placed on a different plane of action, out of reach of mortals. They were brought into view by a crane, which the Athenians simply called a device (*mēchanē*), that lifted them to the top of the stage building. The Latin term for such sudden and miraculous appearances of gods was *deus ex machina*, "the god from the device."

In addition to the actors, all dramas had a Chorus that sang, danced, observed the plight of the characters, and from time to time conversed with them. These choruses, composed of male actors, always represented a group of people who were not related by blood to the principal characters and who therefore could comment on their actions with some objectivity. They were also members of a group that did not have the power to intervene in the action, such as old men or women, and who sometimes shared the fortune, good or bad, of the principal characters in the play. Their role was to reflect, observe, advise, or sympathize, with whatever authority their assigned character might be thought to possess. They sang songs that reflected on the action of the drama, comparing it to other myths or events in the past. In Aeschylus' day the Chorus had twelve members; Sophocles apparently increased the number to fifteen (we do not know why or to what effect).

Dialogue and action took place between the choral songs, in long intervals known as *episōdia*, "additions," which were the precursors of what we now call scenes. The idea of alternation between the Chorus and a speaker may originally have come from ritual songs in honor of Dionysus known as dithyrambs, in which a soloist and a chorus would sing in alternate stanzas. The important roles assigned to individual speakers in drama may have been inspired by a long-standing tradition in Athenian politics in which speakers assumed roles to arouse the interest and support of their audience. Some of Solon's famous speeches were written in iambic verse, which was the principal metrical pattern used in speeches and dialogue in the episodes between choral songs.

The diction of the dramas was formal, almost never colloquial, and always in verse. Both actors and Chorus delivered their lines to the accompaniment of an *aulos* (pipe). Most of the dialogue and speeches were composed of three double iambic feet (indicated by the notation ˘ ˉ ˘ ˉ , where the ˘ denotes a metrically short syllable and ˉ a long one, with the long syllables held twice as long as the shorts). When heightened intensity was required, both actors and Chorus could speak in anapests (˘ ˘ ˉ ˘ ˘ ˉ) or in a longer line of four double trochaic feet (ˉ ˘ ˉ ˘). Along with the dactylic (ˉ ˘ ˘) hexameter used in Greek epic poetry, these metrical patterns were later used for poems in Latin. Eventually the same patterns were adapted for use in European languages, but instead with stress on what originally had been the long syllables. Roughly speaking, the iambic meters of Greek verse became the ancestors of the iambic pentameter familiar to us from Shakespeare's sonnets and plays.

But European poets never succeeded in imitating the metrical patterns of the choral songs in the Greek. These songs were composed in more complex metrical patterns and were set out in stanzas that followed a repeating pattern; hence the terms *strophē* ("turn") and *antistrophē* ("counterturn"), denoting two metrically identical stanzas. Sometimes the pairs of strophe and antistrophe were followed by a closing third stanza or epode (*epōidos*) in a related metrical pattern. On occasion the actors might also sing, either solo or in conjunction with the Chorus. Most unfortunately, only one specimen of the music that accompanied choral song has come down to us, a few lines from a choral song in Euripides' *Orestes* (a play not included in this volume). This fragment, despite its brevity, indicates that the music would have heightened the emotional effect of the mournful words that it accompanied. It is written in syncopated iambics called "slanting" (*dochmiac*), which were often used to express sorrow.

Even without the music we can recognize some significant rhythmic patterns in other dramas. The old men who form the Chorus of Aeschylus' *Agamemnon* begin their long narrative about the sacrifice of Iphigenia with several lines in dactylic (¯ ˘ ˘) hexameter, the meter of the *Iliad* and other epic poems. Their references to vengeance are often expressed in an iambic meter in which two short syllables replace one long syllable (˘ ˘ ˘ ¯ instead of ˘ ¯ ˘ ¯), a distinctive metrical pattern that surfaces again in the last play of the trilogy, the *Eumenides*, in the terrifying song of the Erinyes who have come to punish Orestes for killing his mother, Clytemnestra. The metrical pattern behind the phrase *ite Bakchai* ("come, Bacchants," ˘ ˘ ¯ ¯ ˘ ˘ ¯ ¯) is frequently repeated in the choral songs of Euripides' exciting drama the *Bacchae.*

In fifth-century Athens, three poets were chosen to compete against one another each year at the City Dionysia; we do not know on what grounds or by whom the selection was made. Each of the three who were chosen presented a series of three tragedies, followed by a satyr play, a lighter entertainment that usually featured a chorus of half-man, half-goat followers of Dionysus. The prizes seem to have been awarded on the basis of the best production rather than the best script. As far as we know, Aeschylus was the only playwright to base the plots of his three tragedies on the same myth; the one surviving example of such a connected trilogy is Aeschylus' *Oresteia.* The first drama in the trilogy, the *Agamemnon*, tells the story of Agamemnon's return and his murder by his wife, Clytemnestra, and her lover, Aegisthus; the second drama, *Libation Bearers*, depicts Orestes' revenge against his father's murderers; the third drama, *Eumenides*, describes Orestes' acquittal in Athens for the murder of his mother. Dramas by Sophocles and Euripides, however, all seem to have been included in sets of three in which each drama was based on a different myth. We have no way of knowing if there were other connections—thematic or tonal, for example—among the different dramas in these sets of three, because we now have only one complete play from any of them.

We know the names of more than sixty dramatists who were active in the fifth century, though in most cases, only fragments of their work survive. Aeschylus' *Persians* (472) is the earliest drama that has come down to us. Sophocles won his first tragic competition in 469; Aeschylus' *Oresteia* trilogy was produced in 458. Euripides had his first success in 441, three years before he produced the *Alcestis* (see time line). By the end of the fifth century it became clear that most people considered Aeschylus (c.525–456 B.C.), Sophocles (497/6–405/4), and Euripides (485/4–406/5) to have been the greatest playwrights. In his comedy the *Frogs*, which was first performed in 405, the poet Aristophanes imagines that those three poets are the only dramatists the god Hades had considered eligible to hold the chair of tragic poetry in the Underworld.

Euripides appears as a character in three of Aristophanes' surviving comedies (the *Acharnians*, *Women at the Thesmophoria*, and *Frogs*). Aristophanes knew Euripides' plays well, and he made fun of him by making him espouse and embody the most radical statements in his dramas, all expertly taken out of context for maximum comic effect. In the *Frogs*, which was first performed just after Euripides' death in 405 B.C., Aristophanes portrays the god Dionysus as a great admirer of Euripides' trendiness. Dionysus goes to the Underworld with the intention of bringing Euripides back from the dead. After he gets there, he is asked to judge whether Euripides should be allowed to take over the chair of tragedy, which Aeschylus had held until Euripides arrived. Aristophanes has Euripides with great insouciance and facility pray to absurdly different gods and question traditional morality. But Aristophanes' Aeschylus respects traditional religious practices, and he speaks in ponderous and sententious phrases, using cumbrous compound words, like the Choruses in some of his dramas. He boasts that he wrote plays about weighty issues like war and justice and accuses Euripides of being interested in ordinary life and trivial household affairs. After witnessing the competition between the two poets, Dionysus decides to bring Aeschylus back from the world of the dead, on the grounds that his presence would do more to help save Athens from being defeated by Sparta than would that of Euripides, who (as Aristophanes suggests) is responsible for the moral deterioration that has led to their military failures.

Because Aristophanes was a contemporary of Euripides, his portraits of the two poets have often been regarded as essentially accurate, even if exaggerated for comic purposes. But in his comedy the *Clouds*, Aristophanes turns Socrates into a pedantic sophist, suspended in a basket, claiming he is walking in the air and contemplating the sky—a caricature that didn't resemble him in the least (or so Plato has Socrates say in his *Apology*). There seem to have been few limits to what a comic poet could say about his contemporaries, and portrayals even of living persons were not expected to be fair-minded or accurate. Nonetheless, that caricature appears to have encouraged many of Socrates' contemporaries to believe that he had a corrupting influence on his young male followers. Why should we suppose that he was inclined to treat Euripides with greater respect? In reality we do not know what Aeschylus, Sophocles, Euripides, or any other ancient poet intended his dramas to convey to his audiences, and virtually nothing about how or why they became poets or how or by whom they were taught to write verses and the music that accompanied it. At best we can suppose that most poets came from propertied families, if only because they had been taught to read and write and had the time to compose verses and music.

It is almost miraculous, and a testament to their continuing cultural importance, that some of the works of these great dramatists have survived to the present day. At first the poets probably used a stylus to write down drafts of their work on wood tablets coated with wax. The finished works then were copied by hand onto papyrus scrolls, a medium on which longer texts could be written down with pen and ink. But because papyrus eventually deteriorates in variable climates, the texts of the dramas needed to be copied and recopied over the centuries. Inevitably in the course of transmission, mistakes and omissions were introduced; also, actors and editors altered the texts and added new lines of their own. In the fourth and third centuries B.C., texts of the dramas were stored in the library of the Greek city of Alexandria in Egypt, where the dry climate helped to preserve the papyrus rolls on which the dramas had been copied. But that library was destroyed at the end of the fourth century A.D., and still more copies of the dramas were lost after the fifth century, when Christianity had become the official religion of the Roman Empire. In the end, copies continued to be made of only a relatively small number of texts, most likely because they were judged suitable for reading and study of rhetoric.

As a result of the process of attrition and selection, we now have only a small fraction of what the three great poets produced. Roughly speaking, in the case of Aeschylus, we have six complete dramas (not counting the *Prometheus Bound*, which was probably by another poet) out of as many as 90, seven out of as many as 123 for Sophocles, and eighteen out of as many as 92 for Euripides (not counting the *Rhesus*, which was almost certainly by another poet). These totals, however, are not exact, because the same play could be known by different titles. Of the nineteen surviving plays attributed to Euripides, ten (including the *Rhesus*) were preserved in multiple copies because they were selected for reading in schools of rhetoric. The other nine were preserved in a single manuscript that, in addition to the ten plays selected for school use, also contained nine other complete plays whose names begin with the letters epsilon, eta, iota, and kappa; the dramas *Electra* and *Helen* in this volume come from that manuscript. We also have some fragmentary texts of dramas on papyrus that were preserved in Egypt, but the texts of the complete plays come from parchment codices, or books, starting around the fifth century A.D.

But even though the texts of the dramas that we still have contain some textual gaps, later additions, and other imperfections, and even though we have only partial information about the paraphernalia and music that accompanied the original performances, Greek dramas continue to be discussed, revived, restaged, and quoted, as they have been for generations. Even in modern languages with different sound patterns and forms of versification, reading the dramas is a transformative experience, disturbing, inspiring, puzzling, never irrelevant or boring. They have survived because they portray essential truths about the real nature of human life, our ultimate powerlessness, and the limits of our understanding.

It is said that after the Athenians were defeated by the Syracusans in Sicily in 414 B.C., wandering Athenian soldiers were given food and drink in return for reciting lyric passages from Euripides' dramas, and that some Athenian slaves working in the mines in Syracuse were freed because they could recite passages from his plays to their captors. For those soldiers and the captors it was not the props, costuming, sound effects, or staging that mattered most; for them, as for us, it was what the poets thought and wrote that they wanted to hear again and again, and, however imperfectly, to remember.

THE GREEK PLAYS

AESCHYLUS

Aeschylus (c.525–456 B.C.) came from a propertied family in Eleusis. His first tragedies were performed in the early 490s, but it was not until 484 that he won his first victory in the competition at the City Dionysia. He fought against the Persians at Marathon in 490 and probably also at Salamis in 480. In 472 he described the battle at Salamis in his *Persians*, the earliest of his surviving tragedies. In 470, Hieron, the tyrant of the Greek city of Syracuse, invited Aeschylus to Sicily to stage a performance of his *Women of Aetna* (now lost). After returning to Athens, Aeschylus won first prize at the Great Dionysia with five of his other extant tragedies, the *Seven Against Thebes* (467), the *Suppliants* (463), and the trilogy, translated in this volume, known as the *Oresteia* (458), consisting of the *Agamemnon, Libation Bearers*, and *Eumenides*.

Although Aristophanes, in his comedy the *Frogs* (405 B.C.), satirizes Aeschylus' style as pompous, bombastic, and sententious, in his extant dramas Aeschylus writes in a variety of modes, ranging from straightforward exposition to densely poetic language characterized by distinctive combinations of words and metaphors. The old men in the choruses of *Persians* and the *Agamemnon* use sonorous words and speak in complex rhythms that bring profundity and emotional depth to their reflections on the human condition and the inscrutability of the gods. Metrical motifs carried over from the *Agamemnon* reappear in the terrifying songs of the Furies in the final play of the *Oresteia* trilogy, the *Eumenides*.

In 456, Aeschylus was invited back to Sicily, and he died there. But the Athenians did not forget about him. Half a century later his dramas were so well remembered that even while making fun of his writing style, Aristophanes endorsed his work for its ethical and patriotic values, wishing that Aeschylus could be brought back to life.

Introduction to Aeschylus' *Persians*

So far as we know, only three Greek tragedies dealt with recent history rather than age-old myths, and all three portrayed episodes from what we now call the Persian Wars: the twenty-year stretch of armed conflict (499–479 B.C.) that pitted various coalitions of Greek cities against the vast, wealthy, monarchic Persian Empire. The first two of these dramatic experiments were the work of Phrynichus, but both are now lost; Aeschylus' *Persians* came third, in 472 B.C. It follows by only eight years the event at its core, the surprising, seemingly miraculous Greek victory over the Persian navy at the island of Salamis, off the west coast of Attica. That victory, achieved despite long odds, had saved most of Greece, and especially Athens, from a fearsome choice between annihilation and subjection to the might of imperial Persia.

It's no accident that the Persian Wars provided the subject matter for all three of these known Greek historical dramas. The magnitude and scope of this conflict, which appeared to the Greeks to pit the manpower and wealth of all Asia against a much poorer and less populous Europe, gave it mythic dimensions even as it took place, and these only became amplified with the passage of time. Herodotus, writing about the same struggle perhaps half a century after it ended, saw it as the culmination of a millennium-long contest for supremacy between two great ethnopolitical blocs, and therefore as a major turning point in human history.

In dramatizing the naval battle off Salamis—an event he himself, and many members of his audience, had taken part in—Aeschylus closed the chronological gap that gives most Greek plays their sense of otherworldliness, but opened up a gulf of cultural distance instead. The play takes place before the palace at Susa, one of the capitals of the Persian Empire, in what is today western Iran—a place Athenians could neither visit nor visualize, a city they imagined as replete with fantastic wealth and ruled by immensely powerful monarchs. The exotic robes and soft slippers worn by the actors helped convey this distance to the original audience, perhaps along with musical phrases and choral dance steps suggesting the Far East. It has even been suggested by a modern scholar[*]

---

[*] Oscar Broneer, *The Tent of Xerxes and the Greek Theater* (Berkeley: University of California Publications in Classical Archaeology, vol. 1. no. 12, 1944).

that the backdrop for the play's production was the ornate tent-cloth beneath which the Persian king, Xerxes, camped during his invasion of Greece—one of the proudest spoils of Athenian victory. If true, this story explains how the word *skēnē*, originally meaning "tent," came to denote the stage on which the dramas were played, eventually coming into English in a Latinate spelling, "scene."

But though the play is ostensibly set at a far remove from Athens, the moral and religious ideas around which it revolves are unmistakably those central to archaic and early classical Greece. Aeschylus uses the plight of Xerxes, a defeated king stripped of both his army and his royal robes, to explore the role of *hybris* and *atē*, unsanctioned overreach and the blindness that leads to it, in the rises and falls of individuals and of nations. The Chorus of Persian elders confide their fears about *atē* in the play's unique opening ode:

> *Kindly and wheedling at first comes reckless Atē,*
> *but then she leads men into nets and snares;*
> *no mortal man can jump over, or hope to escape.* (96–100)

If the placement of these lines by modern editors is correct (they have been moved from their position as found in the manuscripts), they follow directly after a proud recitation of Persia's long string of military victories, capped by the recent creation of a Persian navy. That navy, as the Chorus does not yet know but Aeschylus' audience does, has already been smashed by the Athenian-led Greek fleet at Salamis. The "fine-stranded [ships'] cables" of which the Chorus boast have become the woven "nets" in which the gods trap those hungry for conquest.

"Cables" in the context of this play has a wider resonance than mere ships' riggings. As Herodotus' account of Xerxes' invasion makes clear, the Persian land army marched into Europe by way of an enormous pontoon bridge stretched across the Straits of Hellespont (the modern Dardanelles), the place at which a mile-wide stream of salt water separated Europe from Asia. Enormous flax ropes, stretched between anchored ships, held this bridge together and effectively joined the continents. Aeschylus uses the double meaning of *zeugma* and related Greek words—both a "link" between two things and a "yoke" thrust upon a team of animals to subdue them—to connect this bridge to notions of enslavement and subjugation. A chariot that Atossa has dreamed of, and that she describes to the Chorus in her opening speech, is pulled by another kind of *zeugma*—the forcible "yoking" of two enslaved sisters, dressed to represent the peoples of Asia and Europe respectively (the European one, significantly, throws off her yoke, while the Asian one accepts it). A typically dense Aeschylean mesh of motifs begins to form around these *zeug-* words. Ropes, nets, ships, bridges, and yokes are woven together in this poetic tapestry, all evoking the expansionism of imperial Persia, the nation that sought (in Herodotus' words) "to make all lands one land" (*Histories* 7.8γ).

The long stretch of time over which these themes are traced is also typically Aeschylean, reminiscent of the panhistorical scope of the *Oresteia*. Two generations are represented onstage, an older one to which the Chorus and queen belong, and a younger one represented by Xerxes. But Xerxes' father, Darius, who rises spectacularly from the Underworld in ghost form at the play's climax, seems to transcend time with his omniscience about both the past and the future. He looks back over five generations of rule that preceded his own, describing Persia's gradual conquest of Asia as a mandate handed down from Zeus. Xerxes, in his view, has rashly exceeded that mandate by entering Europe, offending not only Zeus but Poseidon—here virtually a personification of the straits that Xerxes had bridged, the Hellespont. Aeschylus obscures the fact (or perhaps did not know) that Darius, too, in reality had built an intercontinental bridge (across the Bosporus, according to Herodotus) and campaigned in Europe, against the Scythians north of the Black Sea. The dead king is not a historical portrait so much as an incarnation of all of Persia's past, a past that Xerxes has, in the view of the play, betrayed and partly undone.

Though Darius rages at his son's arrogance, he also speaks of oracles that foretold the present catastrophe. Xerxes' downfall, like that of Agamemnon and other Aeschylean heroes, is the result of both error and fate. On the whole, the *Persians* suggests that Xerxes is more deserving of pity than blame. The Chorus only rarely express anger toward him, and the solemn, dirgelike procession they share with him in the play's last scene is a moving evocation of shared sorrow. Atossa's anxiety for her child allows us to see Xerxes as a frail and vulnerable creature, a mother's son as well as an army's chief. The queen exits the stage (at line 851) on a touchingly domestic mission, seeking to bring her son a new robe to replace the rags he now wears. When Xerxes enters shortly thereafter, we see that her mission remains incomplete. The tattered glory of the Persian royal house cannot be restored easily, if at all.

At the heart of the play (from lines 302 to 514) stand the reports of the first Persian soldier to return from Greece, grim catalogs of horror that rank among the finest of surviving Greek messenger speeches. Aeschylus, who had himself fought at Salamis on board an Athenian ship, here demonstrates a remarkable ability to see the battle through the eyes of the enemy. Though the gods are clearly on the side of the Greeks (as signaled by the supernatural voice bidding

them to charge and win their freedom), the sufferings of the Persians, both during the battle and in the retreat afterward, are presented with deep compassion
and superb artistry. Here and throughout the play, Aeschylus uses sonorous roll
calls of Persian casualties, their names resonant with exotic Iranian phonemes,
to construct a kind of verbal memorial to the valiant dead. Though he wrote for
Athenians, whose city had been razed by the Persians and who had reasons to
celebrate the outcome of Salamis, Aeschylus did not indulge in triumphalism
or vainglory. There is no irony in the Chorus's final wails of woe.

The date at which the *Persians* was produced, 472 B.C., makes it the earliest
play in this volume and, quite possibly, the earliest play among all surviving
Greek tragedies. Despite this antiquity, the *Persians* has had great resonance in
recent decades, especially as Western military engagement with the Middle
East has become a more central issue. Important productions were mounted in
Edinburgh in 1993 and New York in 2003, in response to the first and second
Gulf Wars.

Persians

Translated by James Romm

This translation is based on the text of A. F. Garvie's edition, *Aeschylus: Persae* (Oxford: Oxford University Press, 2009).

Cast of Characters (in order of appearance)

Chorus of Persian elders
Atossa, queen of the Persians; mother of Xerxes; widow of Darius
Messenger from the retreating Persian army
Ghost of Darius, former king of the Persians; father of Xerxes
Xerxes, king of Persia

Setting: The play takes place somewhere in the city of Susa, one of the royal seats of the Persian Empire. In the background is a council chamber. A group of old men enter, marching to the anapestic rhythm of their opening lines.

CHORUS: Here are we, the trusted ones *
    of the Persians gone to the land of Greece;
    we, guards of the wealthy, gold-decked places,
    chosen, as fits our age and rank,
    by Xerxes himself, our lord and king,
    the son of Darius,
    to steward this land.
    But my heart, a prophet of evil, is troubled
    over the homeward return of the king
    and of the army bright with gold.   10
    All of the might that Asia has spawned
    has departed. Howling for a young husband,
    […]†
    No messengers—riders nor runners—
    have come to the Persian city.
    The men of Susa and Ecbatana,
    and of the ancient Kissian stronghold,‡
    have set forth and left, some on horseback,
    others on shipboard, and others, foot-soldiers,
    forming the tight array of war;   20
    Men like Amistres, Artaphrenes,
    Megabates and Astaspes,
    chieftains of Persia,
    under-kings of the one Great King;

---

* The Chorus call themselves the *pista*, trustworthy ones, evidently a Greek version of a name the Persians gave to their council of advisers.

† The bracketed ellipsis indicates that a line of text seems to be missing from the manuscripts, to judge by the incomplete sentence in the previous line. Probably the missing text made clear that it was a widowed bride thus bewailing her loss.

‡ Kissia was a region of Persia of which Susa was the capital, though Aeschylus, here and at line 121, seems to think it was a city.

they are sped, heads of a mighty army,
horsemen and conquerors with the bow,
fearsome to look on, awesome in battle,
with steadfast resolve in their souls;
Artembares, stirred by the chariot's onrush,
and Masistres, and the bow-master,   30
noble Imaeus; and Pharandaces,
and Sosthanes, the driver of horses.
Others have gone, sent forth by the Nile,*
that great and much-nurturing stream: Sousicanes,
Pegastagon, the scion of Egypt,
and lofty Arsames, who governs
in holy Memphis; Ariomardus,
overseer of ancient Thebes;
and treaders of marshes,† now rowers of ships,
fearsome, numberless in their throng.   40
Following these went the host of the Lydians,
soft-living men, who control those who dwell
on a continent's shores;‡ these Mitragathes
and noble Arcteus, royal commanders,
and the gold-covered city of Sardis sent out,
riding on chariots, some pulled by two teams,
others by three, dread weapons of war,
a fearsome sight to behold.
Dwellers on sacred Tmolus,§ they hasten
to throw a slavish yoke upon Greece;   50
Mardon, Tharubis—anvils to spearheads—¶
and javelin-hurling Mysians.
Babylon, too,
the gold-covered city, sends forth a mixed throng
in a straggling line; these are stationed on ships,
stalwart with strength that draws back the bow.

---

* Egypt was at this time a province of the Persian empire.

† The marshes referred to are those of the Nile delta.

‡ Apparently a reference to the Greeks whose cities dotted the west coast of Asia Minor and were at one time under Lydian control. They, too, accompanied Xerxes' army, forced to fight against their fellow Greeks, though Aeschylus tactfully turns a blind eye to that fact.

§ A river in Lydia.

¶ A vivid metaphor. Anvils, thick masses of iron, could not be penetrated by the blades forged upon them.

From all of Asia there follows the race
that wields the dagger,*
heeding the awesome call of the king.
Such is the flower of men now gone
from Persian land,   60
for whom every corner of Asia, their nursemaid,
groans and laments with terrible longing.
Parents and wives are trembling in fear
at the long stretch of time, the accounting of days.†

strophe

By now the royal, city-sacking host
has crossed the straits and gone to lands adjacent,
linking with hemp-bound raft the gap that Helle swam,‡   70
throwing a many-bolted yoke on the neck of the sea, a new
  roadway.

antistrophe

Bold in assault, the leader of much-peopled Asia§
drives his divine flock over the entire earth
in double advance, on foot and by sea,¶ trusting commanders
who stay firm and true—a godlike man from a race of gold.   80

strophe

He casts with his eyes the dark-blue glance of a murderous serpent;
he has great throngs of men and of ships, and he drives a Syrian
  chariot;
onto spear-famed men he hurls the bow-wielding war-god, Ares.**

antistrophe

No one, we think, will stand up against the vast human river,
or keep out invincible waves of the sea by using stout bulwarks;   90

---

* It is unclear what nation is meant.

† The chorus now divide into halves and sing responsively (as indicated by the rubrics "strophe" and "antistrophe" below). The meter changes to one based on ionics (˘ ˘ ‾ ‾) from the preceding anapests.

‡ The Hellespont (modern Dardanelles), named for the princess Helle, who (according to myth) crossed it on the back of a ram, had been bridged by Xerxes to bring his army from Asia into Europe. The bridge was built of two lines of ships, anchored side by side and linked by long cables of hempen rope. The bridge thus formed is often termed a "yoke" by Aeschylus, both because it linked two continents together and because it aided the Persian effort to put a "yoke" of subjection on Greece.

§ A reference to Xerxes, Great King of Persia and leader of the invasion, who is not named explicitly between lines 5 and 144.

¶ The Persian invasion force consisted of both land troops and navy. The fleet sailed along shore so as to stay in contact with the land army.

** The Asian troops commanded by Xerxes relied on the archery bow as their primary weapon, whereas Greek hoplites, with armor and tactics designed for hand-to-hand combat, favored the thrusting spear.

the host of the Persians cannot be attacked; strong of heart is our
race.

strophe

Our god-sent Fate, from long ago,
sends victory; it charges the Persians
with tower-toppling wars,
with whirling swarms of horsemen, and with smashings of cities.   105

antistrophe

And they have learned to look upon
the briny grove of the far-faring sea   110
as the raging storm-wind whips it white,
relying on fine-stranded cables, and inventions for carrying
        troops.*   114

epode†

What mortal man can dodge the trick-filled deceptions of god?   93
Who thus has mastered the easy leap with a nimble foot?
Kindly and wheedling at first comes reckless Atē,‡
but then she leads men into nets and snares;
no mortal man can jump over, or hope to escape.   100

strophe

Thus is my heart robed in black and torn by terror.
"*Oā!*§ for the Persian army"—   117
I dread that the city may hear this and learn
that Susa's great fortress is emptied,

antistrophe

and the Kissians' city will sing in reply
"*Oā!*"   122
while throngings of women hear this word
and the rending of linen clothes begins.   125

strophe

All the horse-borne host and all the foot-borne host
went out like a swarm of bees, following the army's chieftain,

---

* These lines refer to Persia's recent addition of a navy to its armed forces. Originally a landlocked people who had no experience of the sea, the Persians relied on Phoenicians and Egyptians to captain their warships.

† As the out-of-sequence line numbers indicate, this stanza has been moved by Garvie and other editors from the position it occupies in the manuscripts.

‡ A divine force that spurs mortals toward rash and morally arrogant actions.

§ Greek sounds of lamentation, like this two-syllable cry, are used richly and musically in this play. These sounds and exclamations have been closely transliterated here, and in some other plays in this volume, so as to convey something of their original musicality.

passing the headland that juts in the sea, land shared by two lands, 130
a double yoke bridging them both.*

antistrophe

Beds that once held husbands now hold longing and tears;
the women of Persia, soft in their grief, are left alone,
each bidding farewell to her bedmate, the charging spear-man, with
    longing.
They're yoke-mates alone in the yoke.
Persians!† Dwellers beneath   140
this ancient roof,‡
let us take thought, careful and deep;
the need has arrived:
How will he fare, Xerxes our king,
the son of Darius?
Is it the twang of the bow that has won,
or the might of the blade
that tips the spear?§
But look! A light like the eyes of the gods,   150
the mother of our king, is coming,
my queen; I kneel before her.
We all must address her
with words of greeting.

    (Atossa enters, on a chariot, finely arrayed.)

Hail, majesty, loftiest of deep-girt Persian women,
ancient mother of Xerxes, wife of Darius that was.
You are the spouse of one Persian god,¶ and a second one's mother—
unless the divinity's gone that has always guided the army.

ATOSSA: That's it—That's why I've left my gold-decked palace and come
    here,
left the bedroom of Darius, the room he and I once shared.   160
For worries are tearing my heart. I'll confide it in you, my friends.
I can't escape the warnings, the growing sense of fear—the fear that
our great wealth, with a cloud of dust, may upset with a kick

---

* The language is obscure but refers to the straits of Hellespont.

† The Chorus here revert briefly to the anapestic meter of their entrance, before breaking into trochaic tetrameters—lines of four trochaic feet, used with unique frequency in this play—at 155.

‡ Pointing to the council chamber before which the scene is set.

§ See note to line 85.

¶ Aeschylus here has the Chorus speak of the Great Kings as gods, though the Persians did not in fact believe their monarchs to be divine.

the success my husband, Darius, brought us—he, and one of the gods.
I cannot express this double concern that troubles my mind:
a great store of wealth, without men to guard it, has no place of honor,
yet the light does not shine on men who lack wealth to match their power.
We have wealth enough, no fault there. Yet fear sits before my eyes.
The master's presence, to my mind, is like the eye of the house.
Therefore, since this is the state of things, take counsel with me   170
on what I'm about to say, you Persians, my old, trusted friends.
All my plans are in your hands; help make them wise.

CHORUS: Know this well, my country's queen: you only need ask once
for any word or deed that lies within my power to grant.
The counselors you call in this matter are well-disposed to help you.

ATOSSA:* I've often been beset by dreams at night,
ever since the day my son dispatched the army
to the land of the Ionians,† hoping to take it.
But never yet did I see one so vivid
as the dream I had last night. Let me describe it.   180
Two women appeared to me, both finely dressed,
one in the robes that Persian women wear,
the other in Doric dress.‡ They seemed to be
far taller than the women one sees today,
and flawless in their beauty. They were sisters,
born from the same race; one dwelt in Greece,
her home by lot; the other, non-Greek land.§
A discord then arose between these two,
or so I seemed to see; my son saw this
and tried to get control and calm them down;   190
he yoked them to a chariot, put halter-straps
below their necks. One gloried in this gear;

---

* Here the meter switches, for the first time in this play, to iambic trimeter. In most surviving dramas iambic trimeter is almost universal in dialogue and speeches, but the *Persians* is a very early play and more varied in its use of meter. It often employs longer trochaic tetrameter lines for dialogue; the chorus and Atossa, for example, return to this meter at line 215 below.

† The term Ionians normally refers to one subgroup of the Greek people, but Aeschylus has the Persian queen, in her ignorance of Europeans, apply it more broadly.

‡ "Doric" refers to the Greek subgroup dwelling primarily in the Peloponnese, known for a spare, unadorned style of clothing.

§ At several points Aeschylus has the Persians refer to themselves as *barbaroi* or (as here) to their land as *barbarē*—illogically adopting a Greek perspective, according to which they were foreigners. To translate these terms as "barbarian" would be misleading, as the word clearly would not have a pejorative sense when applied by the Persians to themselves.

her mouth was pacified by bit and reins;
the other grew unquiet, and with her hands
she smashed the chariot's gear and dragged it off
by force, now free of reins; she breaks the yoke
in two. Out falls my son; his father, standing there,
Darius, pities him; when Xerxes sees him,
he tears the robes he wears about his body.

That was what I saw in sleep last night.   200
When I awoke I dipped my hands in a spring
of sweet water; then, prompt with offerings,
I went to an altar, bringing a honey-meal cake,
a sacrifice for the gods who turn away evils.
But I glimpsed an eagle fleeing toward Phoebus' shrine;
I stopped right there, friends, and stood speechless with fright:
for the next thing I saw was a falcon, flying full speed,
harassing the eagle with wings and tearing its head
with talons; the eagle had no defense but to cower,
surrendering itself. This bred terror in me as I watched,   210
now in you as you hear.
                          You can be certain of this:
If my son fares well, he will be a man worthy of wonder.
If he fares ill—But he *can't* be held to account.*
If he gets out alive, either way, he'll still rule this land.
CHORUS: Mother of our king, we urge you to have neither too much fear
    nor too much confidence. Beseech the gods with offerings,
    ask them to avert the dream, if you've seen some meaningless phantom.
    Pray that good things come to pass for yourself, for your children,
    for the city, and for all your friends. Next, you must pour libations
    to Earth, and to souls of the dead. Seek their favor, and ask them this: 220
    that your husband, Darius, the one whom you say you see in your dream,
    send blessings for you and your son, from below ground up to the daylight,
    and that things without blessing stay fast in the earth and covered by
        shadow.
    I advise this out of goodwill for you; I'm a prophet who sees with the heart.
    We think that the outcome of all this for you will be nothing but good.

---

* The language Atossa uses here borrows from Athenian political vocabulary; she says that Xerxes will
not undergo a *euthunos*, the audit to which Athenian magistrates were subjected after their terms of office
were up.

ATOSSA: Yes! You, the first to interpret these dreams, the one who delivered this prophecy, you show kindness to both my son and my household. May all turn out well.

        (Indicating the offerings she has brought)

    All of these we shall set out, as you counsel,
for the gods and for our loved ones who died and went below ground,
as soon as we return home.

                     Friends, here's something I'd like to know: 230
Where's this Athens they talk of? In what part of the earth does it lie?

CHORUS: Far away, in the direction of where lord Helios sets.

ATOSSA: Really? And yet my son longs to bring down this faraway city?

CHORUS: Yes, for if he succeeds, all of Greece would be under the King.

ATOSSA: They have such an army, such numbers of men, to accomplish all that?

CHORUS: [...]

ATOSSA: [...]*

CHORUS: Yes, and such a large army as once did much harm to the Medes.

ATOSSA: Is it the bow-drawn blade in their hands that gives them
    such glory?   239

CHORUS: No, indeed. It's their shields and the spears that they wield,
    standing firm.   240

ATOSSA: What else besides this? Do their royal houses hold adequate
    measures of wealth?   237

CHORUS: They have some fountain of silver, a treasury straight from the
    earth.†   238

ATOSSA: Who is the shepherd that drives their army? What master compels
    them?   241

CHORUS: It is said they are neither subject nor slaves of any such man.

ATOSSA: What? But then how could they hold their own against warlike
    invaders?

CHORUS: They do—they destroyed the fine and full-numbered host of Darius.‡

ATOSSA: Your words bring fear to the minds of the parents of those on the
    march.

---

* Many editors assume a gap in the text here. Atossa was last heard discussing the Persian army, but when the Chorus speak at line 238, the army they refer to is that of *Athens*, victors over Persian invaders at the Battle of Marathon, ten years before the time in which this play is set. Editors have also resequenced some of the lines that follow.

† A reference to the silver deposits on Athenian land. The state-run silver mines had furnished the revenue that built most of the Athenian navy.

‡ See note above, line 238.

CHORUS: (*looking offstage*) But it seems that soon you will know the entire
    truth of this matter.
  This man who comes here on the run distinctly looks to be Persian.
  He brings some clear news of events, whether fine things, or evils, to hear.
MESSENGER:* (*entering on the run*) You cities all across the land of Asia,
  And you, my Persis, reservoir of wealth,   250
  how great is the success that's been brought down
  by a single blow. The flower of Persian youth
  is fallen. Cry Oh! It's an evil to first announce evils.
  And yet, necessity bids me unfold the whole woe.
  Persians: our entire army has been destroyed.

strophe

    CHORUS: Agony, agony—fresh wounds, and
      deep ones. *aiai!* Weep,
      Persians, as you hear them.
    MESSENGER: Yes, since all we had is brought to ruin.   260
      Beyond my hopes, I see the light of home.

antistrophe

    CHORUS: Too long the time of life
      for us old men, who hear
      of this unlooked-for woe.
    MESSENGER: I tell you, I was *there*. My tale of evils
      did not arise from other men's reports.

strophe

    CHORUS: (*lamenting*) *otototoi!*†
      In vain the varied weapons
      went out from Asian land   270
      to attack implacable Hellas.
    MESSENGER: The shores of Salamis and nearby lands
      are heaped with bodies of the ill-fated dead.

antistrophe

    CHORUS: *otototoi!* You tell of
      corpses of friends, rock-smashed, sea-dipped,
      life departed, carried about
      in robes that drift with the tide.

---

* The meter here switches briefly to iambic trimeter, before the Chorus breaks into a lyric lament; the
trimeters then resume at 290.

† See note to line 117.

MESSENGER: Their archery failed them. The whole force was destroyed
  and mastered by rammings made by ships.

strophe

CHORUS: Call out the mournful cry,   280
  the cry of ill fate for our fighters;
  the gods have made everything wretched.
  aiai, for the loss of the army.

MESSENGER: Hateful the name of Salamis, hateful to hear!
  I groan as I bring *Athens* back to mind.

antistrophe

CHORUS: Athens! Reviled by her foes!
  We remember as well.
  Athens made many Persian women
  husbandless, uselessly wed.*

ATOSSA: I've held my tongue till now, struck dumb by evils.   290
  Beyond all limit stretches our disaster—
  sufferings too great to speak or ask about.
  And yet, necessity makes us mortals bear
  the pains the gods bestow. Stand and speak;
  disclose, though groaningly, what they endured.
  Who's not yet dead? Or who among the leaders
  are we to mourn for—men picked out for rule,
  whose deaths would leave their office tenantless?

MESSENGER: Lord Xerxes lives and looks upon the light.

ATOSSA: That word you spoke—a great light to my house.   300
  Bright day bursts forth from out of black-cloaked night.

MESSENGER: But Artembares, head of a host of horsemen,
  was battered there along the Silenian shore.†
  And Dadaces, squadron-leader, at a spear's thrust
  performed a graceful leap from his ship's deck.
  And noble Tenagon, of high Bactrian blood,
  was pounded on the sea-smashed isle of Ajax.‡
  Lilaeus, Arsames, and, third, Argestes,
  mixed up together, butt the stony ground   310

---

* The Chorus are thinking back to Athens' victory over Persian troops at the battle of Marathon ten years earlier.

† Sileniae was apparently a stretch of the coast of Salamis.

‡ In mythic times, Ajax was a ruler of Salamis.

around the island famed for breeding doves,*
as does Pharnouchus, neighbor to the springs
of the Egyptian Nile, and also Arcteus,
Adeus, Pheresseues, three from one ship.
Matallus of Chrysa, captain of ten thousand,
in death has dyed his beard, changing its color
by dipping its bushy fullness into red.
And Arab Magus, and Bactrian Artabes,
who led a troop of thirty thousand horse,
has died, a settler in a cruel land.
Amistris, and Amphistreus, he who wielded
a busy spear, and noble Ariomardus,
the scourge of Sardis, and Mysian Seisames,
and Tharybis, of five times fifty ships
the master, a Lyrnaean, fair of face,
lies dead and wretched there, an unfair fate.
Syennesis, the first in bravery,
the captain of Cilicians, one single man
who gave his foes much trouble, died with glory.
So much for recollections. Many evils
took place there. I have mentioned but a few.
ATOSSA: *aiai!* Your words report the height of sorrows,
shame for the Persians, cause for wails and shrieks.
But take your story back to its beginning,
and tell me, did the Greeks have such great numbers
of ships as to assail the Persian navy,
to dare begin the clash of ramming beaks?
MESSENGER: In numbers, we of Asia† far excelled,
enough to win. In fact the whole Greek number
came to three hundred ships, including ten
that made up a picked squadron, their elite.
Xerxes, as I well know, possessed a thousand,
plus twice a hundred and another seven
that had exceeding speed; such was the tally.
No disadvantage, then, would you not think?
Some god contrived destruction for our army,

313
312

316

320

330

340

---

* Yet another reference to Salamis, or perhaps an adjacent island.
† See note to line 187.

tilting the scales with an unequal chance.
The gods protect divine Athena's city.

ATOSSA: You mean that Athens has not yet been sacked?

MESSENGER: Its people still live on, a sure defense.*

ATOSSA: How did it all begin, the clash of warships?   350
Who offered battle first—was it the Greeks,
or my son Xerxes, too proud in throngs of ships?

MESSENGER: It was some spirit of vengeance, some evil spirit,
that started this whole woe, my sovereign lady.
A Greek came from the camp of the Athenians†
and gave this message to your son Xerxes:
"As soon as night with gloomy shadow falls,
the Greeks will not stand fast. They'll leap upon
the decks of ships and sail now here, now there,
preserving life by fleeing in the dark."   360
He heard these words, but did not understand
the trickery of the Greek, or spite of god.
To all commanders he announces this:
When the sun no longer broils the earth with rays,
when darkness fills the temple of the sky,
they must arrange the navy in three squadrons,
to guard the roaring straits and passageways,
while other ships encircle Ajax' isle;‡
and if the Greeks escaped the waiting evil,
finding some hidden path for ships to flee,   370
the orders were: "All captains lose their heads."
Such words he spoke, with cheerful disposition,
not understanding what the gods would bring.

The captains took their dinner, in good order,
obedient in mind; their crews meanwhile
fastened their oars to thole-pins, ready for rowing.

---

* The phrasing here tactfully avoids stating the truth, that Athens had indeed been sacked before the battle of Salamis. Its population, however, had largely fled before the sack occurred, and this is the point Aeschylus stresses, for the benefit of his Athenian audience.

† The story of the deceitful message is also told by Herodotus, who explains that Themistocles, the Athenian admiral, contrived the trick as a way to lure Xerxes into an attack and force the reluctant Greek navy to give battle.

‡ This fourth detachment was sent around to the western side of the island, to guard a second channel connecting the Bay of Salamis to the sea. It is not clear why the ships on the eastern side were divided into three groups.

The light of day declined, and night arrived.
Onto their ships went rulers of the oar
along with those who governed soldiers' weapons.
Squadron to squadron, the crews cheered one another.   380
Each sailor keeps his place and follows orders.
All night the admirals maintain the fleet
in constant action, sailing here and there.

Night moved along, but still the ships of Greece
made no attempt at a disguised escape.
And when bright day rode in on shining steeds
and everywhere the land was clear to see,
then first a cry rang out resoundingly,
songlike, amid the Greeks, and high and shrill
an echo answered back from the island's rocks.   390
Our side was gripped by fear, for now we knew
we had been tricked. No song of flight
the Greeks were singing there, but a battle hymn
to urge them on to war with zeal and courage;
the trumpet, too, was setting them all aflame.
They beat the salty sea as criers bid them,
striking together with a splash of oars;
then suddenly they all were there, unhidden.
Their right wing came on first, and kept good order,
leading formation; next, the entire navy   400
advanced against us. A great shout could be heard:
"Go forward, all you children of the Greeks!
Free your homeland! Free your wives and children,
the shrines of gods that your forefathers worshipped,
the tombs of ancestors. Now it's a fight for all."

An answer came from our side—Persian words,
a babble of voices. Now the time had come.

In an instant, ships were driving metal prows
in other ships. The ramming was begun
by a Greek ship that smashed apart the stern   410
of a Phoenician vessel. Then all took aim at all.
At first the Persian line, a floating wave,
bore up. But when our multitude of ships

got crowded in the straits, could not give help
to allies, struck each other with bronze-beak rams—
they shattered their own oars with their collisions,
and Greek ships, not unmindful of their plight,
began to strike, sailing round them in a circle.
Ships rolled, hulls up. You couldn't see the water
beneath a layer of wrecks and butchered men. 420
The shores and reefs around were filled with corpses.
Whatever ships were left from our great host
now fled with a disordered pull of oars.
The Greeks kept striking, spearing men like fish,
some tunas they had caught; with splintered oars
they skewered them. A mournful wail arose,
groans of lament that filled the sea, until
an end at last arrived with dark-eyed night.

A host of evils—I could not tell them all,
not even if I spoke for ten days' time. 430
Of this be certain: never, in one day,
did men in such great numbers meet their deaths.
ATOSSA: *aiai!* A sea of evils! Its wave breaks
on Persians and on every Asian nation.
MESSENGER: But the evil has not even reached its midpoint.
Know this: their so great weight of sufferings
will drag the scales of woe down twice as far.
ATOSSA: What fate could have beset them worse than this?
Recount for us what ills befell the army,
tilting the balance further down toward pain. 440
MESSENGER: The Persians who were in the peak of strength,
stalwart of spirit, born of noble blood,
foremost in trusted service to their king,
are dead—and by a shameful, ill-famed death.
ATOSSA: *Aaahh!* My wretched fate undoes me, friends.
In what way do you say that these men died?
MESSENGER: There is an island hard by Salamis,
a small place, lacking harbors;* the god Pan,
lover of dances, lurks about its headlands.

---

* Psyttaleia.

There Xerxes sent these men. The plan was this: 450
When shipwrecked foes swam safely to this island,
our men would kill these undefended Greeks,
but also save our allies from the waters.
He was a bad judge of what lay in store.
For when the god gave victory to the Greeks,
on that same day, they donned their metal armor
and leaped out of their ships, drawing a noose
around the entire island. Nowhere to turn
for our men. Many were smashed by pelting stones
thrown by Greek hands, while elsewhere arrows fell,   460
launched from the bowstring, killing as they flew.
At last the Greeks rushed forth in one great wave,
striking, butchering, hacking off their limbs,
till they'd snuffed out the life of every man.

Xerxes perceived the depth of ruin, and groaned.
His perch allowed a view of the whole army—
a hilltop high above the briny sea.[*]
He tore his robes and let out a shrill wail,
then straightway gave out orders to the land force[†]
and fled pell-mell for home. So there you have   470
another woe to mourn, beside the first.

ATOSSA: You hateful deity, who stole the sense
from out of Persian minds! Revenge on Athens
has cost my son a bitter price. Too few,
were they, the ones whom Marathon destroyed?
My son set out to gain their recompense
but brought back rather this great host of woes.
But tell about the ships that fled their fate.
Where were they when you left them? Can you say?

MESSENGER: The captains of surviving ships took sail,   480
their flight both hurried and disorderly.

---

[*] As confirmed by Herodotus (*Histories* 8.90.4), Xerxes observed the battle of Salamis from a throne set up on Mount Aigaleus, overlooking the straits.

[†] While the Persian navy suffered defeat at Salamis, the vastly larger land army remained intact, not having taken part in the engagement. These troops were left in Greece when the navy fled, in hopes they could later subdue the Greeks in a land battle.

Their crews began to perish in Boeotia,*
some mad with thirst, in sight of gleaming wells,
others gasping but not getting breath.
We pressed on to the country of the Phocians
and Doric land, the gulf called Malian,
where waters of the Spercheus brought relief.
Next the Achaean plain received our troops,
the towns of Thessaly—but these had little
for us to eat. Hunger and thirst they offered,   490
and these killed many of us. We arrived
in Macedonian land and in Magnesia,
the place where river Axius is forded,
the reedy swamp of Bolbe, Mount Pangaeus,
and the land of the Edones. This was the night
the god blew in an early blast of cold
and froze the holy Strymon.† Even those
who never revered the gods now offered prayers,
falling on their knees before Earth and Sky.
After the army showed its piety,   500
we started to cross the ice-bound waterway.
Whoever set out before the rays of the god
began to spread, came safe to the other side.
For the eye of the sun, ablaze with burning beams,
warmed and dissolved the center of the pathway;
they tumbled on one another, and happiest then
was he who swiftest lost the breath of life.
Those who survived and made their way to safety
struggled through Thrace, their progress slow and labored,
and now they're here. A few, not many,   510
have reached their homes and hearths, the land of Persia
that now can groan for its lost flower of youth.

All that you've heard is true. Much else I've left
unsaid—the woes god hurled upon the Persians.

---

* The route described here takes the Persians through northern Greece and Thrace, not across the
Aegean as one might have expected (see map of Mainland Greece and Asia Minor). Ancient warships
had no room to store food or water, and had to travel along coasts except in dire emergencies (in fact this
was such an emergency, and many ships did sail direct for Asia, but Aeschylus ignores this).
† A river flowing through Thrace.

CHORUS: God who brings pains! Too heavily you jumped
with trampling feet on all the Persian race.
ATOSSA: Woe upon me, woe for the shattered army.
You—dream that brought me visions in the night—
you showed me clearly all the ills in store,
(*to Chorus*) while *you* interpreted too emptily.   520
But nonetheless I'll follow your advice
and first beseech the gods with suppliant prayers;
and next I'll bring gift-offerings for the dead
and for the Earth—a meal-cake from my larder.
These cannot alter what's already happened,
but maybe something better yet may come.
As for you: in light of our misfortunes,
you must pool all your trusty plans together.
And if my son should reach this spot before me,
Give comfort to him, take him to my house,   530
lest he contrive more woe on top of woes. (*Atossa exits.*)

    CHORUS: Zeus, our king: you have destroyed
the proud and teeming army
of the Persians.
You have plunged our cities in dark grief,
Susa and Ecbatana.
Many the women who've torn their veils
with tender hands
while soaking the folds of their robes with tears,
sharing a common pain.   540
Persian brides, tender in mourning, long
to see their new-married men;
they've lost their soft-fleeced nights in the bed,
the joy of their flourishing youth,
and they grieve with insatiable wailing.
And I, the fate of those who are gone
[...]*

---

* A line has become damaged here.

strophe

> Now the whole land of Asia
> groans, its populace emptied.
> Xerxes led them—*popoi,**   550
> Xerxes wrecked them—*totoi.*
> Xerxes handled it all foolishly
> with his seagoing ships.†
> How is it Darius did so little harm,
> when he ruled the city as bow-lord,
> the dear overseer of Susa?

antistrophe

> Land and sea forces together
> sailed in the dark-eyed and flaxen-winged
> warships that brought them there—*popoi,*   560
> warships that wrecked them there—*totoi,*
> warships with doom-bringing rammings,
> steered by Ionian hands.‡
> Even the king, we hear, barely escaped
> by way of the plains of Thrace,
> the roadways that bear hard winters.

strophe

> Seized by necessity
> *pheu*
> of being the first to die
> *ēe*
> along the Cychreian shores.
> *oā*
> Groan and weep,   570
> cry out for the woes
> that come from the sky,
> *oā,*
> strain the voice of mourning with clamorous calls.

antistrophe

> Wracked by the terrible ocean
> *pheu*

---

* See note to line 117.

† The word here translated "ships," *barides*, refers specifically to Asian or Egyptian vessels.

‡ See note to line 178.

they are mangled by the mute offspring*

ēe

of the great undefiled place, the sea

oā.

The houses, bereft, mourn their masters;

the parents now childless 580

lamenting for woes from the gods

oā,

hear the whole tale of pain, and grow old.

strophe

Those living in Asia, long since,

are no longer Persian-controlled,†

and don't any longer pay tribute

to lordly necessities;

nor do they fall to the ground

in dread of their rulers.‡ For power,

the power of our king, has been broken. 590

antistrophe

Nor are men's tongues any longer

bound fast in fetters; the people

are free to speak as they wish,

since the yoke of strength has been parted.

The isle of Ajax,§ its fields

now bloodied, and beaten by waves,

holds Persia's might in its grasp.

    (Atossa enters, on foot, plainly dressed. With her come servants
    carrying vials of offerings.)

ATOSSA: *(to Chorus)* All those who have known ills will understand

how when a wave of troubles breaks upon us

we tend to look on everything with fear, 600

but when the gods show favor, we believe

the same fair wind of luck will always blow.

---

* A poetic description of fish.

† Either the statement is an extreme hyperbole, or the term "Asia" is used to mean only Asia Minor, as is often the case. In fact only a small portion of Persia's Asian holdings, the Greek cities of the eastern Aegean, had been liberated.

‡ A reference to *proskynesis*, a deep ritual bow by which subjects showed reverence to the Persian king.

§ Salamis.

Just so for me. There's terror everywhere;
the gods' gifts have been utterly reversed;
the roaring in my ears is not a war-cry.
So sharp a blow of evils smites my wits.
Thus have I left my finery behind
and made this journey, without chariot,
bringing libations to pour for my son's father,
offerings that propitiate the dead.   610
First sweet white milk that came from a pure cow,
then shining honey, the flower-reaper's drops;
next, draughts of water from a virgin stream;
an unmixed liquid, born from a wild mother,
the shining gladness of the ancient grapevine;
and, from a tree that always stays in leaf,
the harvest of the fragrant yellow olive.
Then woven flowers, the sons of fertile earth.
My friends, with these libations to the dead,
sing hymns of reverence, call forth the god*   620
Darius, while I send these earth-drunk honors
as offerings to please the gods below.
CHORUS: Royal wife whom the Persians honor,
pour your offerings down to the halls of the earth;
while we, with our songs, shall request
those who escort the dead
to be gracious under the ground.
You, sacred divinities of the world below,
Earth and Hermes, and you, lord of the Underworld,
send up a spirit into the daylight;   630
for if he knows any cure for our troubles,
he alone among mortals could tell us their end.
          (As Atossa takes the vials and pours their contents onto the
          ground, the Chorus address themselves to the tomb of Darius.)
strophe
          Does he hear? Our blessed king, now like a god;
          does he hear me sending forth
          my many doleful, sad cries, in their clear Asian tones?

---

* Atossa does not exactly call Darius a "god" but a divine being of lesser power, a *daimōn*. The Greek word has no good English equivalent.

I shall cry out aloud
our all-wretched woes;
does he hear me, from under the ground?   640

antistrophe

You, holy Earth, and other lords of the buried,
allow him out of your dwelling,
that high-boasting spirit, the Susa-born god of the Persians;
send him up from below,
a man such as never
Persian soil ever covered.

strophe

Beloved is the man, belovèd his tomb;
for the heart that it hides is beloved.
Lord Hades, I beg, send him up and release him,   650
our king, the godlike Darius—
ēe.
Never did *he* incur losses of men
with war-ravaged follies.
Godlike in counsel the Persians called him, for godlike
he was, a sure hand at the helm of the army.
ēe.
Great shah,* shah who once was, come forth;
arise, from the peak of your funeral mound;
step forward on saffron-slippered foot,   660
revealing the peak of your royal tiara.
Blameless father, Darius, come; *oi.*

antistrophe

Master of masters, appear,
that you may hear of new woes, shared by all;
for a gloom from the Styx has descended.
Our young men are destroyed, a whole generation.   670
Blameless father, Darius, come; *oi.*

epode

aiai aiai
You whose death brought grief to your friends,
[... †

---

* This translation is an attempt to capture the exotic flavor of a foreign word, *ballēn*, the Chorus use here.

† Three lines of the epode are corrupted such that Garvie and others find them impossible to interpret.

. . .

...] the ships with their triple oar-banks
are destroyed; ships no longer, no longer.   680

(The ghost of Darius appears, rising up from the burial mound.)

GHOST OF DARIUS: Companions of my youth, most trusted counselors,
you aged Persians: What does my city suffer?
It groans and beats its breast; its soil is trampled.
Seeing my wife draw near my tomb, I'm frightened.
Yet graciously I take her offerings.
And you who stand beside my tomb, you chant
your spirit-drawing spells, in high, clear voices,
wretchedly summoning me. But my arrival
has not been easy; the gods below the earth
are better at seizing than at letting go.   690
Yet I, a king among them, have prevailed.
Be quick, lest I be blamed for tardiness.
What new and weighty evil ails the Persians?
  CHORUS: I dread to look on you.
     I dread to speak face to face,
        stirred by my old fear of you.
DARIUS:* I've come from down below, obedient to your chants.
Don't drag things out at length, but keep to the essentials
and tell me everything. Forget your dread of me.   700
  CHORUS: I fear to indulge what you ask.
     I fear to speak to your face
        words hard for a friend to pronounce.
DARIUS: I see that ancient fear has blocked your wits; and so,
(to Atossa) my noble wife, the aged sharer of my bedroom,
leave off your wails and groans, say clearly what has happened.
It's clear that ills are mankind's lot; they fall upon us all.
Some come from the sea to trouble us, while others
arrive by land, if life goes on and waxes long.
ATOSSA: Most fortunate of mortals! With your lucky destiny,
You were much envied while you lived and saw the sun's light,   710
bringing a happy lifetime for the Persians, as a god does.

---

* Darius here begins speaking in trochaic tetrameters (see note to line 176), and he and Atossa both use this meter through line 758.

I envy you also now—dead, before this abyss of evils.

I'll tell you the whole story in a brief space of time:

Persian might has been annihilated, or nearly so.

DARIUS: But how? Some blast of plague attacked the city, or civil war?

ATOSSA: Neither. But near Athens our entire army perished.

DARIUS: Which one of my children* led an expedition *there*?

ATOSSA: Impetuous Xerxes. He emptied out the continent to do it.

DARIUS: Was it by land or sea he undertook this reckless folly?

ATOSSA: By both. He used two forces, making a double assault.　　　720

DARIUS: But how did so great an army cross the straits on foot?

ATOSSA: He used contrivances to bridge the Hellespont.

DARIUS: And with that effort he sealed off great Bosporus?†

ATOSSA: Just so. Surely some god had got hold of his wits.

DARIUS: A mighty god indeed—to judge by the delusion.

ATOSSA: True. We can see at last the evil he's accomplished.

DARIUS: What fate was theirs—those for whom you're groaning so?

ATOSSA: The navy came to grief, and that destroyed the army.

DARIUS: And so the entire host has been laid low by enemy spears?

ATOSSA: Indeed. The Sousans' city now bewails its lack of men ...　　　730

DARIUS: (*in shock and sorrow*) *O popoi!* Not the army—our steadfast aid, our succor!

ATOSSA: ... and all the Bactrians, too, are gone. [...]‡

DARIUS: Oh, wretched son! The host of allied youth he has destroyed!

ATOSSA: They say that he alone, Xerxes, and only a few others—

DARIUS: How, and where, did he end up? Did he find safety somewhere?

ATOSSA: —arrived in joy at the bridge, the one yoke of the two lands.

DARIUS: So he's come safely back to Asian land—is that so?

ATOSSA: Yes. This is the story that prevails, no conflict.

DARIUS: Cry woe! The oracles came swiftly to completion.

Zeus hurled their grim fulfillment on my son. I must have thought　　　740
the gods would bring them to pass a long, long time from now.
But a man who strives in haste has the god, too, hastening him on.
A font of evils, it seems, has been unveiled for our allies.

---

* According to Herodotus (*Histories* 7.1–2), Darius had seven children by two different wives, and the succession of Xerxes was by no means a certainty at the time Darius died.

† Unlike later Greek writers who used "Bosporus" and "Hellespont" to refer to different straits, Aeschylus, both here and at line 746, conflates the two names.

‡ The line is damaged, and it is not clear why Atossa thus singles out the Bactrians, one of many Persian subject peoples.

My son, in ignorance, with youthful zeal, has done this.
He hoped to hold the holy Hellespont in fetters
as though enslaving it—Bosporus, stream of the god—
and tried to rearrange the straits. With chains that hammers forged
he compassed it and made a great path for a great host,*
wrongly believing, though mortal, he could control the gods,
even Poseidon. What else but a disease of mind was this   750
that took hold of my son? And now, I fear, the wealth
I labored for will only be the first invader's spoils.

ATOSSA: Reckless Xerxes—but his bad companions taught him this.
They kept on telling him that *you* attained great riches
at spearpoint, for your children, while *he's* been playing the coward,
campaigning close to home, not adding to his father's wealth.
Again and again he heard such taunts from evil counselors.
And so he planned this journey and this great attack on Greece.

DARIUS:† That's why this deed of his is catastrophic,
always to be remembered. Never has such a deed   760
emptied this city, Susa, of its manpower,
not since the time King Zeus established this:
one man should rule all Asia, rich in flocks,
and wield the scepter that brings order to it.
Medus was the first leader of our host,‡
and then another, his son, took up the task.
Third of this line was Cyrus,§ a lucky man,
who came to power and brought our allies peace,
for wisdom was the steersman of his passions.
He conquered the Lydians and the Phrygians,   770
and harried all Ionia with his power;
he felt no hate from god, for he had sense.
The son of Cyrus was our host's fourth leader;
Next Mardus, fifth in line, who brought great shame

---

* Referring to the bridge Xerxes built across the Hellespont.

† From here to the end of the scene the meter returns to iambic trimeter.

‡ This account of Persia's royal dynasty is partly historical, partly unique to Aeschylus. Medus is not mentioned elsewhere, though the name seems connected to the Medes, the people from whom the Persians wrested sovereignty in the mid-sixth century B.C.

§ With Cyrus and his son—known to the Greeks as Cambyses—Aeschylus' account of Persian history begins to dovetail with that of Herodotus and other historical sources. The ruler whom Aeschylus calls Mardus (see footnote on next page) is probably to be identified with Herodotus' Smerdis, an impostor who briefly usurped the throne before a team of conspirators overthrew him.

to country and to throne; Artaphrenes
conspired to kill this man, along with friends,*
the men who knew their duty, and I among them.
Then I received by lot the rule I wanted.
I campaigned many times with many soldiers,   780
yet never brought such woe upon my country.
Xerxes, my son, is young; his thoughts are young.
He does not keep in mind what I enjoined.
I here proclaim to you, aged companions,
that all of us who held this rule before him
have not, together, caused his sum of sorrows.

CHORUS: Then what comes next, my king? Or toward what end
do you conduct this speech? How, from here on,
shall we, the Persian people, do what's best?

DARIUS: Don't make campaigns against the home of Greeks,   790
not even with a greater Persian host.
Their very land's their ally and defender.

CHORUS: What do you mean? How does their land defend them?

DARIUS: It kills with hunger those who are too many.

CHORUS: But we'll equip a fleet with much provision.

DARIUS: But even the force that tarries now in Hellas
will never find the safety of homecoming.

CHORUS: What's *this* you say? The *entire* Persian army
will not recross the straits, depart from Europe?

DARIUS: Few will cross of many, if one trusts   800
the oracles of the gods, and judges how
some have come true already; the rest must follow.
If it be so, then he believes false hopes
and leaves behind a corps of chosen soldiers.
They camp beside the plain Asopus waters,
the river that gives sweet drink to the Boeotians.
The pitch of suffering awaits them there,
a scourge to punish their ungodly thinking.
For those who went to Greece were not ashamed
to rob the shrines of gods and burn their temples.   810
Altars have been destroyed, and sacred buildings

---

* A line that intrudes here in the manuscripts is clearly not genuine: "Mardus the sixth, Artaphrenes the seventh." The conspirator here called Artaphrenes is the same man Herodotus calls Intaphrenes in his account of the conspiracy that unseated "Mardus" (whom Herodotus calls Smerdis); see *Histories* 3.70.

have been wrenched up and toppled from their bases.
And so the doers of wrong shall suffer wrongs
no less than they inflict. More are to come.
The bricks that build our doom are still being laid.
Plataea's land will see a blood-soaked slush
of clotted gore, caused by a Dorian spear;*
the heaps of corpses there will wordless show
to eyes of men, for two more generations,
that mortals must not cast their thoughts too high.   820
For pride will flower and bear the fruit of folly,
from which one reaps a much-bemoanèd harvest.
Look on the punishments you see before you;
remember Athens, remember Greece. Let no one
allow his thoughts to pass his present fortune,
or, lusting for others' wealth, let slip his own.
For Zeus, the grim chastiser, will be at hand,
with recompense for over-boastful minds.
Tell *him* all this. [...]†
With soothing words, upbraid him; make him stop   830
offending god with his too-boastful daring.

(*to Atossa*) And as for you, dear, agèd mother of Xerxes,
go fetch from home the trappings fit for kingship
and bring them to your son. For rags surround him—
the tattered remnants of his splendid robes,
all torn to shreds in grief at his misfortunes.
Give comfort to him with your gentle words;
yours is the only voice that can uplift him.

I go now, down below the gloomy darkness.
(*to Chorus*) Farewell, you elders. Even amid your woes   840
your spirits must take delight in daily joys.
For wealth is useless, down among the dead.
        (*He sinks below the earth.*)
CHORUS: I grieve to hear the Persians' many woes,
    those happening now, and those that are still coming.

---

* Plataea, on the plains of Boeotia, was the site of the battle that destroyed the Persian land forces, in the year after Salamis. The Spartans took the lead role in the Greek victory there, which explains Aeschylus' reference to the "Dorian spear."

† The second part of the line is garbled.

ATOSSA: Oh, spirit! So many painful woes beset me.
　　But most of all, it's this mischance that stings:
　　your tale of the disgrace to my son's clothing,
　　disgrace that he's now wrapped in. I am going.
　　I'll fetch fine raiment from the palace halls
　　and try to meet my son as he comes homeward.　　　　　　850
　　Amid these woes, I won't desert what's dearest.
　　　　　(Atossa exits.)

strophe

　　CHORUS: *O popoi.* Great and good was the life we had,
　　　　a life under rules of the city, back when the agèd,
　　　　blameless, all-providing, unconquerable king,
　　　　Darius, the equal of god, ruled the land.

antistrophe

　　　　First we can cite the glorious deeds of our army,
　　　　[...]*　　　　　　860
　　　　Homeward journeys from war, unwearied, unhurt,
　　　　brought men back to prosperous houses.

strophe

　　　　How many the cities he captured, without crossing the river Halys,
　　　　nor leaving behind his own hearth;†
　　　　among them the cities of Achelous, by the marsh of the Strymon,‡
　　　　the country houses of the Thracians,　　　　　　870

antistrophe

　　　　and the cities with towering walls, on the mainland, outside the lake,§
　　　　obeyed this great king,
　　　　those scattered¶ around the broad ford of Helle, the embayed
　　　　　　Propontis,
　　　　and the mouth of the Pontus.**

---

* This line is unintelligible in the manuscripts.

† The point made by the Chorus is that Darius did not accompany his army on its invasions, by contrast with Xerxes, who risked his own person in Greece. The river Halys (today called Kizilirmak) runs south from Turkey's northern coast, and had to be crossed on journeys westward toward Europe.

‡ Here begins a catalog of Darius' conquests in the West, beginning with Thrace and moving eastward. Achelous was the name of several rivers and seems to have been used, by metonymy, for freshwater generally; on the Strymon, see line 497 and following.

§ If (as Garvie and others believe) by "lake" Aeschylus means the Aegean, then the cities "outside" it might be those of the Hellespont region.

¶ I have preferred Broadhead's emendation here to the manuscript reading.

** The places described are, respectively, the Hellespont, or Dardanelles, the Sea of Marmora, and the Bosporus, entrance to the Pontus (Black Sea).

strophe

> Then the islands beside the sea's headland,* girt round by the
> > waves, 880
> neighbors to our continent,
> like Lesbos, Samos with its olive groves, and Chios, and Paros,
> Naxos, Myconos, and Andros, which borders closely on Tenos.

antistrophe

> And he ruled the islands between the two shores,
> Lemnos, and the place where Icarus dwelt,†
> and Rhodes, and Cnidos, and the Cyprian cities of Paphos and Soli,
> and Salamis,‡ whose mother city gave cause for all of our groanings.

epode

> And the flourishing, populous cities in lands the Ionians got,§
> the cities of Greeks, he controlled by the strength of his mind;   900
> at his beck he had tireless strength of his warrior corps
> and of all-varied allies.
> But now—without doubt, we have had all this turned upside down by
> > the god.
> We are greatly brought low, by the blows that came from the sea.

> *(Xerxes enters, dressed in rags, his mother having failed to
> intercept him and bring him his new robe. In the long exchange
> that follows, he trades laments with the Chorus, both chanting in
> anapestic meter.)*

XERXES: *iō.*

> Wretched me! Hateful fate,
> impossible to foretell. How cruelly   910
> the god set his foot on the Persian race!
> What now lies ahead, what must I suffer?
> My knees give way as I behold
> this crowd of elder citizens.
> Zeus! If only the fate of death
> had hidden me beneath the earth,
> along with those that are gone.

---

* It's not clear what "the sea's headland" refers to, but the stanza goes on to make a broad sweep of the Aegean.

† The reference is unclear.

‡ Not the site of the recent battle but a city on Cyprus, supposedly founded by colonists from the other Salamis.

§ The coast of Asia Minor.

CHORUS: *Ototoi!* Oh, king! Our noble army,
the honor of our Persian rule,
the men in their glory   920
whom the god has cut down!
The land itself laments the dead,
its native youth, whom Xerxes killed—
and thus stuffed Hades with corpses. [...]*
Many are the men who have died,
a numberless multitude,
the flower of youth, the wielders of bows.
Aiai aiai! Our sure defense!
All Asia, O king who rules this land,
has gone down hard upon its knees.   930

strophe

XERXES: *Oioi!* I am here, fit for weeping;
A woe and bane, that's what I am,
to family and to fatherland.
CHORUS: I'll send, I'll send a tearful cry
to salute your return home,
an ill-omened wail that tends to woes,
like that of Mariandyan mourners.†   940

antistrophe

XERXES: Send out your all-lamenting voice,
long-lingering, harsh; for the god, in turn,
has reversed course against me.
CHORUS: I shall. [... ‡

      ...

...] of the city's mourner.
I'll sound again my tearful keen.   950

strophe

XERXES: An Ionian has robbed us—
Ionian Ares, ship-girt, battle-turning,
sweeping clear the gloomy plain and the hard-fated shore.
CHORUS: *Oioioi,* chant, and learn the whole truth.
Where have they gone, your cohort of allies?

---

* There is an unintelligible word in this line.

† The people of Mariandya, a region on the south shore of the Black Sea, were famous in antiquity for their wild lamentations.

‡ Much of this line and the next two have become garbled.

> Where are those who stood beside you—
> those like Pharandaces,
> Susas, Pelagon, Datamas,
> Psammis, and Sousicanes   960
> who left Ecbatana behind?

antistrophe

> XERXES: I left them perishing,
> tumbling from a Tyrian* ship, on the bluffs
> of Salamis, dashed against those cruel bluffs.
> CHORUS: *Oioioi*, where is Pharnouchus, where?
> Or noble Ariomardus?
> Where is lord Seualces
> or high-born Lilaeus,   970
> Memphis, Tharubis, Masistras,
> Artembares, and Hystaechmas?
> We ask you again to tell us.

strophe

> XERXES: *iō iō moi.*
> They got a glimpse of Athens,
> that ancient, hateful city; then with one oar-sweep†
> they all were gasping for life on the beach.
> CHORUS: Then you left, left behind
> even the flower of the Persians,
> your all-trusted man, your Eye,‡
> who numbers his army in thousands,   980
> Alpistus, Batanochus' son?
> [...]§
> You left Sesames, son of Megabates?
> and Parthus, and Oebarus the great?
> Oh, woe, for our troubles. You tell of
> evils surpassing evils for noble Persians.

antistrophe

> XERXES: You stir up a longing in me
> for those brave comrades I lost

---

* Tyrians, Phoenicians from Tyre, supplied much of the manpower and vessels for the Persian navy.

† The Greek word translated "oar-sweep" denotes any kind of rhythmic or circling movement, and could refer here to the flailing arms of the drowning Persians, metaphorically associated with the oars they once rowed.

‡ The King's Eye was a high official charged with overseeing the administration of the empire.

§ A single line has fallen out of the manuscript text.

when you tell of these hateful, unending woes.   990
My heart cries out, cries out from inside my body.
CHORUS: Yes, and there's others we yearn for,
the marshal of ten thousand Mardians,
Xanthes, and Anchares of Aria,
Diaxis, and also Arsaces,
the masters of horses,
and Kegdadatas, and Lythimnas,
and Tolmus, insatiable spearman.
I'm amazed—amazed—that they follow not   1000
behind the tented royal cart.

strophe

XERXES: They're gone, those who were the army's chiefs.
CHORUS: Gone, and nameless now.
XERXES: *iē iē, iō iō.*
CHORUS: *iō iō,* you gods,
how you've beset us with evil,
unlooked for, yet plain to see—the gaze of Atē.*

antistrophe

XERXES: We are battered [...]†
CHORUS: Yes, we are battered, that's clear—
XERXES: —by a fresh pain, a fresh pain.   1010
CHORUS: Not lucky was their encounter
with seafarers of the Greeks.
Hard is the fate of the Persian race in war.

strophe

XERXES: That's so. I've been struck a blow in my vast army.
CHORUS: What's left unruined of Persian might, deluded man?
XERXES: (*showing his torn clothes*) You see this sad remainder of my finery?
CHORUS: I see, I see.
XERXES: And this, the arrow-holding—   1020
CHORUS: What's this? You say something was saved?
XERXES: —storehouse of darts?‡
CHORUS: Little enough, out of much.
XERXES: We had too few aids to fall back on.
CHORUS: The Greek race is not frightened by the spear.

---

* See line 98 and note.
† The end of the line is mangled.
‡ Xerxes' quiver, rescued from the debacle. The term "arrow-holding" does not imply it is full.

antistrophe

> **XERXES:** Yes, too brave. I've seen a grief unlooked-for.
>
> **CHORUS:** You mean the rout of our host hedged round by ships.
>
> **XERXES:** I tore my robe at the woe that came upon us.   1030
>
> **CHORUS:** *papai papai.*
>
> **XERXES:** Yes, and more than just that *papai.*
>
> **CHORUS:** Twice and three times as much.
>
> **XERXES:** Pains, but our enemies' joys.
>
> **CHORUS:** Our might has been brought down—
>
> **XERXES:** I'm stripped of my royal train.
>
> **CHORUS:** —by the sea-borne ruin of your allies.
>
> **XERXES:** Let tears flow over the pain; set out for the palace.
>
> *(The Chorus have by now formed up into a procession, with Xerxes at the head. In what follows, the whole line marches funereally across the stage, chanting in anapestic meter and beating their breasts.)*

strophe

> **CHORUS:** *aiai aiai*, the pain the pain.
>
> **XERXES:** Shout, and beat in response to me.   1040
>
> **CHORUS:** An evil gift of evils, returned for evils.
>
> **XERXES:** Wail the song along with me.
>
> **CHORUS:** *otototoi.*
>
> Weighty comes this disaster.
>
> *oi*, this, too, I much grieve for.*

antistrophe

> **XERXES:** Ply your grief like oars; your groans bring relief.
>
> **CHORUS:** I'm drenched in tears of lament.
>
> **XERXES:** Shout, and beat in response to me.
>
> **CHORUS:** This is our task, my sovereign.
>
> **XERXES:** Raise up your voices in wails.   1050
>
> **CHORUS:** *otototoi.*
>
> And amid my wails will be mingled
>
> *oi*, the black blow of mourning.
>
> **XERXES:** Beat your breasts, and cry out the Mysian song.†
>
> **CHORUS:** Agony, agony.
>
> **XERXES:** Pull the gray hair of your beard; rip it out.

---

* It's not clear what the Chorus means by "this, too."

† Mysia is a region in western Anatolia. The Greeks thought of the music from western Asia, especially from Phrygia, as ecstatic, shrill, and emotional.

CHORUS: In handfuls, in handfuls, with sorrowful cry.

XERXES: Give a shrill wail.

CHORUS: I'll do this as well.

strophe

XERXES: Rend your gathered robe with the tips of your fingers. 1060

CHORUS: Agony, agony.

XERXES: Pluck out your hair as you lament for the army.

CHORUS: In handfuls, in handfuls, with sorrowful cry.

XERXES: Let your eyes flow with tears.

CHORUS: I am weeping indeed.

epode

XERXES: Shout, and beat in response to me.

CHORUS: *oioi, oioi.*

XERXES: Mourn, and move on to the palace.

CHORUS: *iō, iō.* 1070

XERXES: That's the cry through the city.

CHORUS: Yes, yes, that's the cry.

XERXES: Step softly as you lament.

CHORUS: *iō iō*, on the hard Persian soil.

XERXES: *ē ē ē ē*, Destroyed

　　ē ē ē ē, by triple-oared ships.*

CHORUS: With shrill laments we shall escort you home.

　　(The procession slowly moves offstage.)

---

* With his last words, accompanied by inarticulate cries of pain, Xerxes recalls his defeat at Salamis, where Greek triremes—here obliquely referred to as "triple-oared ships"—bested his navy.

GENERAL INTRODUCTION TO
AESCHYLUS' ORESTEIA

Each of the three plays that make up the *Oresteia*—the *Agamemnon*, the *Libation Bearers*, and the *Eumenides*—can be read separately, and each will be introduced separately, but it's also important to consider them, and if possible read them, together. For Aeschylus wrote them to be seen together, on a single day in 458 B.C., in effect making them into one long drama with three constituent parts. Of the surviving tragic playwrights, only Aeschylus, to our knowledge, created such connected trilogies, adapting the three-tragedy format of the City Dionysia at Athens to triple his scope and range; and the *Oresteia* is the only such triptych that survives.

Scope was what Aeschylus needed in the *Oresteia*, for its story, as he conceived it, spans all of human, and even divine, evolution. Though its dramatic action occupies perhaps only a decade, its central question—whether justice is to be administered by way of retribution and revenge, or some other, less violent process—goes back to the beginning of time, to the sequence of overthrows by which Cronus took power from his father Uranus and then Zeus from Cronus. Aeschylus effectively brings these primeval usurpations onstage, first in the sweeping, soaring poetry of *Agamemnon*'s opening choral ode, then, in *Eumenides*, in the person of the Erinyes or Furies, ancient creatures aligned with the pre-Olympian order that Zeus has displaced. That order is not yet at peace with Olympian rule; the question of justice has not yet been settled among the gods. The *Oresteia* will see it settled, for gods and for humans alike, and so resolve a dilemma as old as the cosmos itself.

Just as it stretches backward into mythic prehistory, so the *Oresteia* stretches forward, far past the Trojan War era in which it is set, into the very time and place of the original performance. Its final scene is staged in Athens and depicts a murder trial, played out before a board of nameless jurors. These jurors represent the court of the Areopagus, an Athenian political institution that, thanks to reforms enacted only a few years before performance took place, now held a newly confirmed jurisdiction over murder trials. For Aeschylus' audience, the setting was modern, the issues contemporary. The world of myth had become transposed onto that of the *polis*, the social unit in which (as the Greeks believed) justice, the highest marker of human progress, could best flourish.

Only ancient Athenian spectators, for whom tragic theater was an all-day, nonstop event on a festival day when all business had ceased, could have the experience Aeschylus intended when he composed the *Oresteia*. Most modern productions break up the trilogy into three separate plays, staged at different times or on different days, or drastically truncate them to fit the whole sequence into a single evening. The first play, *Agamemnon*, suffers particularly from this truncation, since Aeschylus made it more than half again as long as the other two and, to the frustration of many a modern director, set a giant choral ode, more than two hundred lines long, right at its outset—an ordeal for audiences anticipating speech and action, not dance and verse.

Paradoxically it is the reader, rather than the playgoer, who today can best take in the totalizing vision of the *Oresteia*. On the printed page it can remain whole and unsegmented, a monument to the unique moment, in 458 B.C., when the Theater of Dionysus was made to encompass the cosmos itself.

Introduction to
Aeschylus' *Agamemnon*

The *Oresteia* trilogy begins and ends with the kindling of fires. Its final scene, at the end of the *Eumenides*, will be a torchlight procession that mimics the festivities of an Athenian marriage. The flame seen at the start of the *Agamemnon*, by contrast, is a beacon signifying military conquest: a signal fire, the last in a chain of such fires, bringing news back to the Greek city of Argos (sometimes also called Mycenae) that Troy had fallen. Hundreds of miles away, the beacon signifies, other fires are blazing. A great city is burning, and the corpses of its warriors lie atop funeral pyres. The flames that, in the trilogy's third play, will celebrate a joyous union arrive here as messengers of downfall and death, but also of victory for the Greeks.

The beacon relay has been set up by Clytemnestra, queen of Argos, and she describes its operation in nearly ecstatic tones in her first long speech (lines 281–316). She is fiercely proud of the mastery it demonstrates, the capacity of royal power to overcome time and distance and even bridge the divide between Europe and Asia. Her husband, too, had crossed that divide, when he led an army of invasion across the Aegean ten years before. But the crossing required a blood sacrifice: trapped by contrary winds on the shores of Aulis, on the island of Euboea, Agamemnon, instructed by the seer Calchas, had killed his own daughter Iphigenia to appease the goddess Artemis. Only then had the winds turned and the fleet set sail.

The tale of that killing is retold in this play's opening choral ode, the longest and most ambitious ode found in any extant Greek play. The old men of Argos—left behind, like the Chorus of *Persians*, after the departure of the troops—describe a bird omen that was seen by the army: two eagles ripped apart a pregnant hare, representing, in the reading of the seer Calchas, the coming sack of Troy by the two sons of Atreus, Agamemnon and Menelaus. Seers often demanded that special sacrifices be made before battle; it was said that some young Persian captives were sacrificed before the battle of Salamis. But here Agamemnon must sacrifice his own child. The Chorus describe, in horrific detail, the agony of a father as he makes his horrendous choice, the desperate last struggles of Iphigenia, the gag thrust in her mouth to keep her from utter-ing curses and ruining the rite—all except the final knife thrust. They seem, for a while, to sympathize with Agamemnon, until the moment he resolves to kill his own daughter:

> *Her pleading, her shrieking for her father,*
> *the girl's short life—these were worth nothing*
> *to the lovers of battle, her judges.* (228–30)

Woven into the Chorus's account of the murder at Aulis are meditations on more ancient events, going back to the beginning of time. Over three genera-tions of gods, the cosmos has been ruled by Uranus, then Cronus, then Zeus. The victory of Zeus deserves celebration, the Chorus claim, though they are not sure what Zeus is or how to address him. But Zeus gives mortals the ulti-mate gift, the ability to find meaning in the tragic universe around them:

> *Zeus puts us on the road*
> *to mindfulness, Zeus decrees*
> *we learn by suffering.*
> *In the heart is no sleep; there drips instead*
> *pain that remembers wounds. And to unwilling*
> *minds circumspection comes.* (176–81)

Aeschylus will return throughout the *Oresteia* to Zeus' triumph in the third generation of gods, implicitly comparing it to other three-part movements: the three generations leading from Atreus to Agamemnon to Orestes, the three murders of Iphigenia, Agamemnon, and Clytemnestra. The *Oresteia* itself forms a tercet that parallels these others, telescoping into a daylong drama the differ-ent time scales of cosmogony, myth, and history.

As the Chorus conclude their great ode—in a sense, the overture to the en-tire *Oresteia*—they greet Clytemnestra, emerging from the palace, as "the chief-tain's wife." There is palpable tension in their dialogue with her, partly stemming from their obvious discomfort with female rule. But there is also an unspoken worry on their minds. Like the watchman who opened the play, they are aware of an interloper in the royal house: Aegisthus, the last surviving son of Agamemnon's uncle, Thyestes. In the long years the army has been at Troy, Clytemnestra has taken Aegisthus as lover, a move that portends nothing good for her husband. Because of a long-ago quarrel between his own father, Thyes-tes, and Agamemnon's father, Atreus, Aegisthus has been exiled from Argos and the sovereignty he might have enjoyed there.

Aegisthus stays hidden while Clytemnestra goes out to greet her returning husband, though "greet" hardly seems the right word; both spouses coldly talk past each other and make formal speeches to the Chorus. When wife finally addresses husband, it is to urge him to step from his chariot onto a purple-dyed cloth she has spread—a delicate tapestry he is reluctant to walk on, but his wife insists. In a trilogy in which colored cloths of all kinds have special meanings, this luxury item, stained with the precious secretions of a marine snail, is especially meaningful. It evokes the wealth of Asia, much of which the Greek armies have just plundered, as well as the blood they have shed and the sea they have crossed. As he steps onto it, Agamemnon reenacts the many roles he has had to play as leader of a great invasion, and he behaves, as he himself observes, more like a god than a man.

As he walks this tapestry of doom, Agamemnon gestures to the silent woman accompanying him, bidding the servants bring her inside. This is Cassandra, a daughter of King Priam, a seer fated to utter prophecies that will not be understood or believed. The army has given her to him as a prize of war, meaning in this case a concubine. A foreigner, she seems unable to speak or understand Greek, and the audience must have assumed she was only a *muta persona* (nonspeaking character), though later she bursts into frenzied, hallucinatory speech.

As he goes inside the palace, Agamemnon has earned *dikē*, punishment, on multiple counts: the murder of Iphigenia; the sack of Troy with its attendant atrocities; and, by the Greek notion that guilt can be inherited, the crimes of his father, Atreus, who butchered his brother Thyestes' children (all except Aegisthus) and fed them to him in a cannibal stew. The question is how he can be punished *syn dikēi*, with justice. *Dikē* can be translated as either "punishment" or "justice," reflecting two different phases of Greek social evolution: a prelegal stage in which victims exacted their own revenge on wrongdoers, and the world of the *polis*, or city-state, in which law courts and juries took charge of such matters. At the start of the *Oresteia*, the code of eye-for-an-eye vengeance still prevails, but its inadequacies are becoming glaringly apparent. Clytemnestra and Aegisthus, both wronged by Agamemnon or his father, can enact only punishment, not justice. The brutal pleasure they take in their murder—especially Clytemnestra, who compares the shower of her husband's spurting blood to the warm rain of spring that nourishes the fertile earth (lines 1388–92)—and the power and wealth they gain by it taint their deed with impiety.

By the conventions of Greek theater, the murder of Agamemnon could not be shown onstage. Aeschylus allows us to hear rather than see it, as Agamemnon cries out under the blows of his wife's blade. In a unique moment among surviving tragedies, the Chorus divide into small groups and the members agonize over whether to intervene—the audience knows they cannot, but their indecision adds tension to this taut scene. Then the doors are opened and Clytemnestra emerges, with *two* bloodied corpses on the *ekkyklēma* that now rolls forward. Cassandra has been killed along with Agamemnon, as she herself had foreseen in her prophetic visions. Clytemnestra describes, with unseemly glee, how she used her husband's royal robes to immobilize him, as though trapping fish with a net—part of a pattern of net and cloth imagery that, in typically Aeschylean fashion, recurs throughout this play and also helps bind it to the two that will follow.

In a final scene, Aegisthus enters, heavily guarded, to remind the Chorus that this family murder has also been a coup d'état. Argos is now ruled by a new regime, and force will be used to control the populace. The city has descended from monarchy to tyranny, and the scornful way Aegisthus refers to the Chorus as those "down on the rowing bench"—meaning, in Athens, those without property—shows that it also now belongs to the rich. For an Athenian audience in 458 B.C., who had just seen their own city enact sweeping democratic reforms (see the introduction to *Eumenides*), this was a hateful turn of events.

As the drama ends, the Chorus unsheath their swords, and civil war is only narrowly avoided by the intervention of Clytemnestra. The Chorus's question— "But is Orestes living somewhere?"—haunts both the Argive people and their bloodstained rulers. The next play in the trilogy will see it answered.

The Oresteia

Agamemnon

Translated by Sarah Ruden

Throughout the translation, I have used the following Greek text of the play, indicating in footnotes where and why I have felt it necessary to depart from the text: West, Martin L., ed. *Aeschylus: Agamemnon* (Berlin and New York: Teubner, 2008). I owe profound thanks to the John Simon Guggenheim Foundation for its generous support of this work.

Cast of Characters (in order of appearance)

Watchman belonging to the royal house of Argos
Chorus of elderly male citizens of Argos
Clytemnestra, wife of Agamemnon
Herald belonging to the Greek army
Agamemnon, king of Argos
Cassandra, daughter of the Trojan king, Priam, and
    Agamemnon's war captive
Aegisthus, cousin of Agamemnon and lover of Clytemnestra

Setting: Before dawn, on the hill of Mycenae over the town of Argos; the scene opens on the roof of the palace.

WATCHMAN: I beg the gods to free me from this hardship.
  Doglike—my head laid on my arms—I've watched
  on the Atreides' rooftop through this long year.
  Now I'm familiar with the stars' assembly,
  potentates shining and distinct on high,
  heavenly bodies bringing, as they perish
  or in their risings, frost and heat to mortals.
  I'm still on lookout for that beacon's pledge,
  by fiery ray and oracle from Troy—
  news of its capture. This is her stern pleasure,   10
  her womanly hopeful-hearted man-strong purpose.
  My dew-soaked bed, my pacing—which is worse?
  Dreams never care for me, they never keep
  a vigil—fear, not sleep, is at my side,
  so steadfast slumber never shuts my lids.
  When I decide to sing, or chirr as birds do,
  agony, out of tune with rest, seeps in;
  I cry and groan then for this home's condition,
  with things not run—the best way—as before.
  Still—may my effort find a lucky end   20
  when the good news shines through in murky flame.
      (Rises up, looking off into the distance.)
  Oh, welcome, lamp as powerful as daylight,
  gleaming announcement! Think of all the dancing
  prompted in Argos by this joyful blessing!
      (Gives a high-pitched cry.)
  To Agamemnon's wife I give the clear sign
  to rise from bed, swift as a star appearing,
  and lift her voice in honor of the lamp

throughout her halls—if truly Ilium's city*
is taken: but the beacon's news is clear.   30
And on my own account, I'll dance a prelude.
My masters' luck is reckoned up as mine:
the signal fire has thrown me triple sixes.
For all that, let me feel, when he comes home,
the well-loved heft of my lord's hand in mine.
I have no more to say. A giant ox
stands on my tongue. But if the house weren't mute,
you'd hear, and no mistake. My choice is this, though:
if those who don't know ask, I'm empty-headed.

> CHORUS: (*entering*) A decade now, since the great plaintiffs, Lord
> Menelaus   40
> and Agamemnon, took their fleet against Priam.†
> By Zeus's will, two honored thrones and scepters,
> Atreus' sons, like a strong yoke of oxen,
> set out with Argives on a thousand ships
> as a relief force from this country.
> In their souls' rage, they shrieked for the great god Ares,
> shrieked in preposterous pain, like eagles   50
> high up over their children's bed, eddying, wheeling,
> sweeping fast on their oars of wings,
> since the work of guarding their chicks' pallet turned out worthless.
> Up above, somebody hears—maybe Apollo or Pan or Zeus—
> the bird-wail, howl, sharp shout of the settlers in his country,
> and he sends the violators their late penalty: a Fury.
> So the overlord, the guest-god Zeus   60
> inflicts the children of Atreus on Alexander‡—
> for the sake of a woman bound to many men. He lays on
> an overload of grappling holds, sinking the body.
> In the dust the knee is driven down, the spear-shaft
> shattered first off, inaugural
> sacrifice. This is his will, the same
> for Danäans§ and Trojans. Now it stands

---

* Troy.

† King of Troy.

‡ Alexander is another name for Paris, Helen of Troy's lover and kidnapper.

§ "Danäans" is one of the names used in the *Iliad* to designate the Greeks; it implies that they are descended from Danaus (a descendant of Io) who settled in Argos with his daughters (see *Prometheus Bound* 853-56).

where it has come, becomes what fate has set down.
Whatever's burned and poured and wept on altars
won't coax away the anger tightly fastened   70
to gifts no fire should touch.
We remain, our destitute, our ancient flesh
left behind, since that far time, by the voyage of rescue.
We must use these canes to shepherd childlike strength.
As in fresh years the life that spurts up in the heart
is elder-weak—no War God's posted there—
so beyond mere old age, when the leaves have withered   80
to nothing, three feet walk the path;*
and no more vigorous than a little boy
a dream goes wandering, strange sight in daytime.
You, though, Tyndareus' daughter, Queen Clytemnestra,
what's this that's happened, what's the news you've caught?
What message brings conviction and dispatches offerings
of perfume through the town? All the gods who govern the city
or live in the sky or the Underworld, in houses or the marketplace, 90
have altars blazing with your gifts.
There—and there—one torch, then another springs up, reaching
    heaven.
each flame is wheedled forth with holy unguent,
tender, plainspoken, persuasive,
compounded in the royal women's chambers.
Say what you can about all this,
and what the gods permit. Your story will heal this anguish,
my enemy, who was thriving until now;   100
but now, at your display of sacrifices,
hope comes—and hope beats back the fretting,
endless hunger, the heart's and mind's tormentor.

strophe 1

I have the right to make it known: the road with happy omens,
powerful men leading blossoming manhood. The great age time has
    reared in me
still breathes persuasion, strength from the gods for singing.
Twin-throned, the Achaean magnates at the head of Greek youth,
the marshals with one purpose,   110

---

* Because a walking staff is used.

were sent by the charging omen-bird to the Teucrians'* country
to collect the debt by force, at the point of a spear.
To the kings of ships the king of birds appeared:
a black one,
and a white one at its back;
verging on the palace they alighted, on the spear-hand side,
where everyone could see.
They were browsing on a hare's heroic womb, her fruitful brood,
after they'd cut off her final, losing race.   120
Tell the story of grief, of grief—but may what is good have the
    victory.

antistrophe 1

And the army's trusted prophet† saw. He recognized
Atreus' warrior sons, with their two different hearts,
in the guests served the hare: these were the sendoff
for the fleet's commanders. He voiced the omen's meaning:
"Time will see the travelers here lay their hands on Priam's city;
in front of its towers
Fate will drain off the people's flourishing herds
in violence.   130
Only look out for the gods' malice darkening
over you, though your army has been hammered out
into a giant bit for breaking Troy. Holy Artemis' pity seethes
at her father's winged hunting dogs‡
offering up a miserable, cringing thing, her unborn little ones with
    her;
she hates the eagles' banquet.
Tell the story of grief, of grief—but may what is good have the
    victory.

epode

The lovely lady,§ out of her great favor   140
toward the fresh, soft whelps of raging lions;
out of her gladness in all the clinging nurslings

---

of animals ranging through countryside,
demands fulfillment of the signs—
favorable, but still full of blame—from the towering birds.*
But I call on Paean the healer:†
don't let her craft ship-binding, voyage-banning
winds of lingering against the Danäans,
or chase a new sacrifice,   150
without law, without feasting,
a feud-builder born in the family, and not timid
toward men. The keeper of the house remains,
fearsome and unforgetting, looming, wily Nemesis for her child's
    sake."
These words rang out of Calchas,
and along with them greatly favorable things:
the fate of the king's house seen in the birds of the journey.
Blend your own voice in:
tell the story of grief, of grief—but may what is good have the
    victory.

strophe 2

Zeus, whoever he is—if he's pleased to hear   160
that name in invocations,
then I address it to him:
I hold the scales up and find
nothing that is can be like him—
no, not like Zeus, if I'm truly to throw off this weight
of emptiness from my mind.

antistrophe 2

Even the god who, long ago, was great,‡
swollen with champion gall—yes, he was there,
once, but no one now will even say so.   170
And the one born after him
was thrown to the mat three times, and was gone.
But the man zealous in shouting the victory of Zeus
will hit the level-headed bull's-eye.

---

* They are literally "ostriches," if the text is not corrupt—as its editor strongly suspects.

† Apollo.

‡ The original king of the gods, Uranus, who was overthrown by his son Cronus; Cronus was overthrown in turn by his son Zeus.

strophe 3

> Zeus puts us on the road
> to mindfulness, Zeus decrees
> we learn by suffering.
> In the heart is no sleep; there drips instead
> pain that remembers wounds. And to unwilling   180
> minds circumspection comes.
> But this is the gods' favor, I suppose,
> claiming by violence the place of awe, the helmsman's bench.

antistrophe 3

> Then the revered commander
> of the Achaean fleet,
> faulting no prophet,
> blended his spirit with the blasts of chance;
> when the Achaean army's jars were emptied
> in suffering weather when there was no sailing,
> on the shore facing Chalcis,*   190
> by the circling, roaring tides, in the country of Aulis;

strophe 4

> and winds that came out of Strymon
> meant evil leisure, hunger, painful anchorage,
> sent men off wandering, ate away at the cables,
> bent time back double:
> the precious Argive army
> was worn to fragments. For the punishing weather
> a different remedy, then,
> one that fell harder on the chieftains,   200
> rang from the prophet's mouth.
> Artemis was his warrant. The sons of Atreus
> beat on the ground with their staffs,
> tears escaping their eyes.

antistrophe 4

> The older of the two, the chieftain, spoke now—these were his
>   words:
> "It is grim Death not to obey—
> but the same if I cut my child down, jewel of my house—

---

* Chalcis, in Euboea, was the point from which the Greek army planned to sail against Troy, but contrary winds kept them pinned down there while their jars of provisions were emptied.

my hands stained—they're her father's hands—with runnels
of a slaughtered young girl's blood   210
by the altar. But which choice is safe for me?
How can I jump ship, fail
this allied expedition?
It swells with huge lust
for an offering of virgin blood to stop the winds—
but Righteousness forbids it.
May that guide me well."

strophe 5

But when he put on necessity's harness,
his spirit swerved—now, it was ungodly,
unclean, unhallowed; from then on   220
he turned against thinking anything outrageous.
Folly, sorry conniver of shame,
fills mortals with recklessness—it's her from the onset.
Bare-faced, he officiated
at his daughter's death, to move a relief force
toward punishing a woman,
and to anoint the ships with sacrifice.

antistrophe 5

Her pleading, her shrieking for her father,
the girl's short life—these were worth nothing
to the lovers of battle, her judges.   230
Her father prayed first, then he told the attendants
to lift her high up, over the altar, like a goat—
though, frantic, she clung to his legs in their robes—
to keep her facing the ground,
and to guard her exquisite mouth,
keeping in sounds
of a curse for his house,

strophe 6

With a bit forced in, a power that silenced her.
Now her robes—dyed with saffron—poured to the ground
and each man who offered her up
she pierced with a pitiful gaze—   240
she was like a painting's central figure—struggling
to speak to them, since often
in her father's generous banqueting hall

she'd sung a hymn full of blessing, in the chaste voice of a virgin,
when the father she loved poured out the third libation;
with loving reverence she sang.

antistrophe 6

The rest I didn't see; I have no tale to tell;
but Calchas' skills find proof in what's fulfilled.
Anyway, Justice tips the scales; some learn through pain.   250
You'll know the future when it's born;
you might as well rejoice
before its time, as mourn before its time.
With dawn, the truth is coming, in those rays.
But let what follows now be some good ending—that's the wish
of the Apian land's sole defense,
its bulwark that stands close beside me here.

(Clytemnestra has by this point entered from the palace.)

I've come, awed by your power, Clytemnestra.
I know respect is due the chieftain's wife
as long as there's a desolate, unmanned throne.   260
If you have some dear news or not—perhaps
these busy rites serve hope alone—I would
be pleased to hear—but silence won't offend me.

CLYTEMNESTRA: May Dawn arrive with good news—you must know
the saying—from the pleasant Night, her mother.
The joy for you is greater than your hopes:
the city of Priam's captured by the Argives.

CHORUS: What? That's beyond belief, beyond my grasp.

CLYTEMNESTRA: The Achaeans now hold Troy. Are those words plain?

CHORUS: Bliss, stealing over me, draws out a tear.   270

CLYTEMNESTRA: Your eye gives evidence of your firm favor.

CHORUS: But what convinced you? Is there any proof?

CLYTEMNESTRA: Of course there is—unless a god has tricked me.

CHORUS: Do signs in dreams have so much hold on you?

CLYTEMNESTRA: A dozing mind does not supply my views.

CHORUS: Perhaps, then, some raw rumor urged you on.

CLYTEMNESTRA: You sneer! My mind's not like a little girl's!

CHORUS: How long ago, then, did they sack the city?

CLYTEMNESTRA: During the night from which this day was born.

CHORUS: What messenger could reach his goal so quickly?   280

CLYTEMNESTRA: Hephaestus, who sent the blazing light from Ida;
    then beacon after beacon's courier flame:*
    from Ida first, to Hermes' crag at Lemnos.
    Third came the Athos summit, which belongs
    to Zeus: it, too, received the massive firebrand.
    Ascending now to shoot across the sea's back,
    the journeying torch in all its power and joy
    [...]†
    The pine wood, like a second sun, conveyed
    the gold-gleam to the watchtower on Macistus.
    Prompt and triumphant over feckless sleep,   290
    unslacking in its task as courier,
    passing Euripus' streams, the beacon's light
    signaled far off to watchmen on Messapion.
    They sent out light in turn, sent on the message,
    setting alight a rick of graying heather.
    Potent against the dimming murk, the light
    went leaping high across Asopus' plain
    like the beaming moon, and at Cithaeron's scarp
    roused missive fire for still another relay.
    The lookout there did not defy the light   300
    sent from far off; the new blaze shot up stronger.
    The glow shot past the lake called Gorgon's Face;
    arriving at the mountain where the goats roam,
    it urged the fire-ordnance on [...]
    With all their strength, men raised a giant flame,
    beard-shaped, to overshoot and pass beyond
    the headland fronting the Saronic strait—
    so bright the blaze. Darting again, it reached
    Arachne's lookout peak, this city's neighbor;
    then it fell here, on the Atreides' mansion.   310
    The light we see descends from Ida's fire.
    Torchbearers served me in this regimen,
    with every handoff perfectly performed.
    The runners who came first and last both win.

---

* The speech that follows describes seven stages of relay in the transmission of the fire beacons from Mount Ida, near Troy, to Argos. The distances of the stages range from about a hundred miles to less than fifteen. Some of the places named by Aeschylus cannot be identified with certainty.

† There is a short gap (known as a lacuna) in the manuscript text.

This is my proof, the pledge of what I tell you.
My husband passed the news to me from Troy.

CHORUS: Later, the gods will have my prayers of thanks.
Please, let me hear the story from the start,
clear through, and you will wear my wonder out.

CLYTEMNESTRA: Today—now—Troy belongs to the Achaeans.　　320
I think the shouts don't blend as they rise up.
Into one bowl pour vinegar and oil—
you'd say the two were factions and not friends.
So, in their separate fortunes, you would hear
two kinds of sounds, from conquering and conquered.
Some people sprawl on husbands', brothers' corpses,
or clutch the gray-haired dead—who in their lives
gave life to them. Already they have voices
of slaves to howl the end their loved ones found.
Others have worked all night in ranging battle.　　330
Famished, they're now arrayed to break their fast
on the town's goods, without order, without warrant,
but merely as each man drew Fortune's lot.
In the Trojan homes that they took prisoner
they live already. They've escaped the frost
and dew. Like favorites of the gods, they sleep
all night—there's no more watch for them to keep.
If they respect the gods who keep the city,
the seized land's gods, and holy habitations,
then victory won't fight back against the victors.　　340
But let no overreaching, plundering lust—
defeat by lucre—pitch into the army.
Homecoming is their rescue: they must round
the turning post and race back to the finish.
On course with gods, the army might return,
but if the torment of the dead should wake,
[...]
it may be, if no sudden evil strikes.
This is the woman's news you have from me.
May the good rule—and no one see it stagger.
I choose to profit by these many blessings.　　350

CHORUS: Woman, you show the sense of a discreet man.
And I, now that I've heard good evidence,
am ready to address the gods as due.

Their kindness now is worth my suffering!
Zeus our king, and dear Night,
with such great jewels in your possession!
Onto Troy's towers you threw a net not even water could slip through:
no one grown, no one young rose up beyond
that seine, huge and calamitous, of slavery.   360
Zeus, great god of guests, I revere, who has done these things,
from the start aiming his bow at Alexander;*
not short of the mark, and not beyond the stars
would the arrow fall down useless.

strophe 1

A blow of Zeus—they can cite that;
this at least is traceable.
He did as he decreed. It's been said
gods turn their backs on mortals   370
who trample the blessing of things set apart—
irreverent people.
A curse has dawned for the descendants
of the reckless†
who blast outrageous arrogance from their mouths
when their homes luxuriate, turn lavish,
run over the brim of what's best. Leave me content—
since this is safe—with my good understanding.   380
There is no bulwark
for the man wealth gluts—
not when he's kicked great Justice's
altar out of sight.

antistrophe 1

Now ruthless Persuasion storms in,
the overpowering child of Ruin counseling ruin from the start;
and every remedy is useless. She's not hidden—
she's right there, bright, a grim light, a visitation.
If bronze is shoddy, grinding or striking will   390
discolor it. This is
its punishment. A child
will chase a flying bird.

---

* Alexander is another name for Paris.
† An uncertain restoration of a difficult stretch of text.

A man like this will brand the city, break it.
No god will listen to his prayers.
Dealings like his must bring him
down. He is the enemy of justice.
Paris* was like this, guest of
Atreus' sons; seizing the wife,   400
he shamed the welcoming table.

strophe 2

She left her citizens the clanging
of shields, squadrons to muster, ships to rig out,
and brought a new kind of dowry to Ilium: its ruin.
She tripped through its gates,
daring what no one should dare. The palace prophets
groaned from their hearts in pronouncing:
"Pity the house, pity the house and the chieftains.   410
Pity the bed, still rumpled with her husband's love.
Look at him, silent, dishonored, but not berating,
Not entreating, after her desertion.
In his longing for the voyager over the sea,
like a ghost he'll rule the household.
Lovely the contours of statues,
charming—the man reviles them.
Before his helpless gaze, all
passion drains away.

antistrophe 2

The images of mournful dreams   420
are there instead, mere alluring suppositions.
They're empty, naturally; whatever pleasant sights
he thinks he sees go free
from his grasp, are gone, never again
to be his winged attendants on the roads of sleep."
These are the agonies in the house, at the hearth,
and agonies still beyond these.
And each of the mustered men who voyaged from Greece
has left on display at home a stoic wife,   430
who sets her face against mourning.
Plenty, plenty here to strike our hearts!

---

* See note to line 61.

How familiar were those men
everyone sent out.* Now, instead of men,
jars of ashes come back
home by home.

strophe 3

And Ares, money-changer of bodies,
is plying his scales in the battle's clash.
From Ilium he sends   440
the families heavy gold-shavings,
the pyres' leftovers soaked with bitter tears;
he neatly loads the crocks
full of men turned to ashes.
They say, as they grieve, that this one
was clever at fighting,
another fell splendidly
in the slaughter—
"For somebody else's wife."
Low-pitched, this is their snarl.
And rancorous grief steals into them   450
toward Atreus' sons, the counsel in this case—
while there, around the wall,
the lovely fighters hold their conquests,
their tombs in Trojan soil.
The enemy land they seized
has hidden them.

antistrophe 3

A heavy anger strains the citizens' talk.
He pays the debt of the curse they certified.
My brooding waits to hear
a thing the night roofs over—   460
since the gods aren't careless
of those who kill and kill;
in time, the black Furies
throw darkness on the man whose luck
lacks justice. Then his life wears out
in another kind of luck.
There is no strength for him

---

* I do not see a serious enough problem in the text here to decline any reading or translation, as M. L. West does.

among the dead beyond our sight.
Heavy, too, is the excess
of fame. Zeus sees it,
and lightning hits it.   470
I choose the wealth no one envies.
I wouldn't sack a city—
or be taken, either, and watch my life go on
under an alien power.

epode

The flame of good news gave the sign,
and through the city
the rumor sped—whether it's true,
who knows, or a falsehood sent from heaven?
Who's such a child, or so far off his head,
that he lets his heart light up   480
at the sudden, commanding message—
then suffers when it changes.
This is a woman in command, conceding
her thanks before she sees.
A woman's belief goes grazing over the boundaries,
quick on its way. But quick to die in turn
are facts made public by a woman crier.

CLYTEMNESTRA: We'll soon see, through the beacon-torches loaded
    with light, the fire passing hand to hand.   490
    Is their news real? Did their sweet brilliance come
    for nothing but to cheat our understanding?
    I see a herald from the shore, with bay twigs
    shading his brow. Thirsty dust on his clothes
    next door to mud, its kin, serves as my witness:
    he won't be speechless, won't just raise a flame
    from mountain wood. Bare smoke won't be the message.
    Either he'll voice the grounds for more rejoicing—
    the opposite is sickening to think of.
    May what we hear confirm what looks so cheerful!   500
    The man whose prayer is different for our city
    should reap his heart's depravity himself.
HERALD: Joy to our father's soil, the Argive land!
    This tenth year's daylight breaks as I return.

This one hope I've secured—the rest are shipwrecked.
I didn't ever boast that I would die
at home and have my tomb here—such a dear right.
But joy now to the land, and to the sun's light,
our local Zeus on high, and Pytho's lord,*
who's sending no more arrows out against us—   510
beside Scamander he was fierce enough.
Become again our savior and our healer,
ruler Apollo. And I call on you,
all the presiding gods, and my protector,
Hermes, sweet herald, whom all heralds worship;
and heroes who dispatched us, be propitious:
take back what enemy spears left of the army.
Hall of the kings, dear residence, their seats
of honor, and you gods who face the sun!
If long ago your bright eyes fittingly   520
greeted the king, greet him again at last.
To you lord Agamemnon comes and brings
a light in darkness—all these people share it.
Welcome him graciously, as this is right:
he tore Troy from the root with Zeus's harrow
of justice, and he worked the whole ground over.
Altars and settlements of gods have vanished;
all of that country's seed is dying out.
This yoke was put on Troy by Atreus' son,
the lord, our elder, favored fighter, now   530
arrived; no man alive deserves more honor,
since Paris and the city vouching for him
can't boast of profit from their enterprise.
Tried for that theft and pillage, he's convicted,
his plunder forfeit. He has cut the house
of his fathers, and the ground below, to ruin.
Priam's sons guilty, double damages!
CHORUS: Herald from the Achaean army: joy!
HERALD: I have it! And the gods can have my life now.
CHORUS: Love for your native land here overcomes you?   540
HERALD: Yes, from the power of bliss, tears fill my eyes.

---

* Apollo.

CHORUS: The sickness that has hold of you is pleasant!
HERALD: What? Teach me, and I'll master what you say.
CHORUS: The longing that afflicts you was returned.
HERALD: The army and the land yearned for each other?
CHORUS: My spirit often groaned aloud in darkness.
HERALD: What was the hateful gloom that weighed on you?
CHORUS: Silence has kept me healthy all this time.
HERALD: Were certain persons threatening—with your lords gone?
CHORUS: So much, death seemed a privilege—as for you.   550
HERALD: It's turned out well—though in the sweep of time
    you'd say some things were lucky, while for others
    you'd curse our luck. But who besides the gods
    is free, his whole life long, from suffering?
    The hardships that we had, the dismal housing
    […]*
    cramped gangways, scanty blankets—what was missing
    from our daily rationed reasons to complain?
    On dry land there was more, more hateful still.
    Our beds were up against the hostile walls.
    Out of the earth and sky, the meadow dew   560
    dripped over us, kept ruining our clothes
    and lodging tiny wildlife in our hair.
    And what about bird-killing winter, made
    an agony by snowfall off Mount Ida?
    Or the hot season, when the sea slept waveless
    and windless, fallen on its noontime bed?
    But why mourn now? Our hardships all are bygones,
    gone by for good. No longer would the dead,
    given a chance, care to rise up again.
    To us, the Argive soldiers still alive,
    our profit triumphs; pain won't tip the scale.
    Why must the living count those thrown away,   570
    or agonize at others' festering luck?
    Good riddance to bad fortune—that's what I think.
    […]
    to justify our bragging to this sun's light
    as we come soaring over land and sea

---

* A lacuna; see note to line 288.

[...]
"In its day, the Argive force that came by sea
Took Troy and nailed this splendor of the ages,
Spoils for the gods, in all of Greece's temples."
Everyone hearing ought to praise the city   580
and the generals. Zeus's favor, which has done this,
we'll honor, too. That's my report in full!

CHORUS: I now surrender freely to your words.
Old age that's quick to learn is always young.
The home and Clytemnestra have the most right
to pay attention, but I share their riches.

CLYTEMNESTRA: I gave a shriek of joy sometime ago
when the first envoy came, the nighttime fire
declaring Troy was sacked and overthrown.
They sneered at me: "So it's through beacon fires   590
that you're convinced? Troy's taken, in your view?
Just like a woman, carried clear away!"
That's what they made me out to be: unhinged.
I sacrificed, no matter. Women's custom
raised howls of happy omen everywhere
in the town—where the gods live, a lullaby*
to the sweet-scented flame that gulps the offerings.
What can you tell me that's more comprehensive?
From the king in person I'll hear everything.
But let me, when my honored spouse returns,   600
take him in swiftly, graciously. What day
is sweeter for a wife to see than this one?
Her husband's back from war, saved by a god,
and she unbars the gate. Relay him this:
the city's sweetheart needs to hurry here;
he'll find a steadfast woman in the house,
just as he left her, like a household dog,
good to her man, at war with any malice—
his match in everything, who broke no seal
in all this time, knew pleasure from no man   610
or spoke with one—not so that you could blame me.
I might as well know how to temper bronze.

---

* Text very uncertain.

This is my boast to you, which swells with truth.
A lady has no shame in saying this.
CHORUS: (*to Herald*) So that's her speech, and if plainspoken people
interpret it for you, it's plausible.
But Herald, let me know of Menelaus.
Did he survive, has he come home again
with you? The man's a power this land holds dear.
HERALD: How could I sow a pretty speech with lies?   620
My friends would harvest them long in the future.
CHORUS: I wish a truth we cherished hit the mark.
Clearly, the "truth" and "cherished" are divided.
HERALD: The man is gone from the Achaean forces,
his ship along with him. That's not a lie.
CHORUS: But did he sail from Ilium in plain sight?
Or did a storm weigh down the fleet and take him?
HERALD: An archer in peak form! You've hit the target.
That's our long suffering expressed succinctly.
CHORUS: But was he dead or living in the rumors   630
you heard from other people who were sailing?
HERALD: Nobody has a clear report to bring;
but the Sun, who nurtures earthly life, must know.
CHORUS: Tell us, how did the storm of heaven's anger
attack the fleet? Tell us, clear to the end.
HERALD: This blessed day is not for dismal news
to dirty. The gods' honor must be spared!
When a grim-faced messenger reports an army
toppled, pain that defies the city's prayers,
a common wound that strikes the commonwealth,   640
cursed men in thousands banished from their homes
by Ares' cherished double whip, two spear-points
of calamity, a yoke of blood-stained horses—
the man who's freighted with this agony
properly hymns the Furies in his speech.
But when I bring the news of danger past
to a city reveling in its salvation,
how could I blend the good with evil, saying
a storm, full of the gods' rage, struck the Greeks?
Two former enemies, fire and the sea,   650
plotted together, pledging their good faith

through the ruin of wretched Argive fleet.
Catastrophe rose from the nighttime waves.
Gales blasting out of Thrace hurtled the ships
together, forcing them to gore each other
in a blind surge of whirlwind, loud with rain.
A circling, careless shepherd let them vanish.*
But when the dazzling sun's light rose, we saw
Aegean waters blossoming with corpses
of Achaean manhood and their splintered ships.   660
Our hull was not corrupted. Some god stole us
and our ship away, or somehow begged us off—
no human hand was on the tiller handle.
Fortune, our kind deliverer, sat there.
We had no waves, no squall, where we found refuge;†
we didn't run ashore on jagged boulders.
Once we escaped this hell that was the sea,
then in white day, dazed by our own good luck,
we found new grief and worry in our flock:
our fleet was in a bad way, from its pounding.   670
If breath remains in any of those men,
they count us with the dead—of course they would.
And we assume that's how it went with them.
I hope it's for the best! But Menelaus
will come—you must expect him, absolutely.
Well—if some ray of sun discovers him
alive and well—as Zeus devised, unwilling
to bring that lineage to annihilation—
there is some hope that he'll come home again.
You can be sure these words you've heard are true.   *680*
    (The Herald exits.)‡

strophe 1

    CHORUS: Who named her so very aptly?
        Was it some invisible being
        seeing the future, who directed

---

* I have kept these three lines in their original order, though West adopts the order 656, 655, 657.

† Text of the line is very doubtful.

‡ It is rare in Greek drama for a character to remain onstage alone during a choral ode, but Clytemnestra seems to do so here, unless she exits and reenters as the ode concludes.

language that whirred to the mark,
calling her Helen—for Hell? She's the one
they fought for, the one the spear courted. How fitting:
ships destroyed, men destroyed, city destroyed when she sailed   690
out from among her dainty curtains,
on the breath of a monstrous zephyr;
and a mass of fighters, hunters carrying shields
hot on the disappearing trail of her oar-blades,
put in at Simois' verdant headland.
Wet with blood, Strife had brought them there.

antistrophe 1

That was the right word, too—"marriage" for "mar"—   700
for the way Anger drove home
her will to Ilium in the time that followed.
For the dishonor to the host's table,
to Zeus Hearth-Sharer, she levied the price
from the raucous singers
who paid the bride honor with the wedding song,
the hymn her new in-laws
found themselves chanting.
Now I suppose Priam's white-haired city   710
has learned a new tune, and it wails in mourning, groans,
calling on Paris the Bedder of Ruin.
Ransacked, howling in grief, the citizens must live on,
enduring a pitiful slaughter.

strophe 2

The offspring of a lion was nurtured
in a man's house, simply taken
from the teats and milk it loved.
In the opening strains of life   720
it was tame, and a darling to children,
and to the old people delightful.
Time after time in his arms he held it—
it was like a child at the breast;
its eyes gleamed as it licked his hand
so humbly—that's the way its belly drove it.

antistrophe 2

Then time worked on it, and it showed
what its parents had been. It gave

those who had brought it up
the thanks of carnage and ruin in their flocks: 730
to the feast it prepared no one was invited,
and the home was polluted with blood.
Helpless, the pain for the household,
a slaughtering curse in its power.
Through a god's will, the new child reared
in the house was Disaster's priest himself.

strophe 3

I think a spirit of windless calm arrived
in Ilium at the start—   740
jewel of wealth, soothing bad omens,
arrow shot soft from the eyes,
flower of love that gnawed at the heart.
Then she swerved off, then she made the marriage
bitter in its fulfillment.
What a sad house where she stayed, where she kept company.
There swept to Priam's sons
a Fury,* a bride who brought weeping,
under the escort of Zeus the guest-god.

antistrophe 3

This saying, now grown old, has lived among mortals forever: 750
When a man's great prosperity has reached its prime,
it will be fertile, it will not die childless.
Out of good fortune the shoot
rising is ravenous misery.
On my own here, apart, I think my own thoughts;
since an unholy act
gives birth to more in their turn,
and they have the look of their lineage.   760
But the destiny of houses true to justice
is a child of beauty, always.

strophe 4

An ancient arrogance begets its own
to grow in mortal misery; sooner or later
when the time comes that is ordained,

---

* The Furies or Erinyes are ancient, terrifying goddesses charged with certain kinds of punishment and vengeance. Furies make up the Chorus of the third play in the *Oresteia* trilogy.

this fresh rancor is born,
this spirit enduring all battles, all wars,
unholy insolence full of   770
Black Ruin for the palace—
the image of its parents.

antistrophe 4

In houses dim with cooking smoke, Justice shines,
honoring the life
of righteousness. Precincts that filthy hands have hung
with cloth of gold, she turns from
in disgust and moves along to holy places.
She doesn't honor money when its   780
power counterfeits praise.
No, she guides all things to their fitting end.

(Agamemnon enters on foot and slowly moves forward;
Cassandra, dressed as a priestess of Apollo, is brought into sight
on a chariot but remains silent and impassive throughout the
following scene.)

CHORUS: Tell me, my king, sacker of Troy, Atreus' offspring,
how shall I speak to you, how shall I revere you?—
not falling short of your favor, not going beyond it.
Much of mankind gives first honor to what
only appears to be—but this trespasses on justice.
Everyone's ready to groan along with misery.   790
But the teeth of the pain don't sink into their own hearts.
Oh, they tune their features perfectly to joy,
forcing a smile onto their dreary faces
[…]
Whoever, though, knows his flock well
can't be deceived by the eyes of a man
whose purpose is specious, who fawns,
though his affection's thin as water.
Well—in my eyes, when you sent your expedition
for Helen's sake—no, I won't hide it from you—   800
you hardly were acting a part that invited applause;
there was no skill in your hand as it steered your spirit.
[…] the willing courage
you tended for your men, even as they were dying.

Now, though, it's not at my mind's, not at arms' length
that I smile at you [...
...]* hardship to those who have reached a good ending.
In time you'll make your inquiries, and then you'll know
which of us citizens tending your city like a house
were just, and which ones were—unwarranted.

AGAMEMNON: Argos and this land's gods, accessories   810
  in my return, and in my punishment
of Priam's city, must be first accosted.
In the gods' court, the case stood on the facts.
Every vote went one way, into the blood-urn,
and told me, Kill the men and sack the city.
There were no chits to fill up the opposing
jar, and the Hope attending it was helpless.
The city's still conspicuous—from smoke.
The cyclones of destruction live, while ashes
in their sad dying breathe wealth's oily fragrance.   820
    For this we owe the gods our thanks, recalling
our vengeance on the riotousness of rape.
For a woman's sake, the sharp-toothed Argive beast
nesting inside the horse,† the shield-slung army,
roused itself, sprang, and smashed the town to dust
around the time the Pleiades set. A lion
in its raw hunger bounded past the tower
and licked up all the tyrant blood it wanted.
It is the gods my long preamble serves.

(*to the Chorus*) I've heard and bear in mind your thoughts as well;   830
I voice the same concerns, I take your case,
since few men have it in them to respect—
and not resent—one of their own who's lucky.
Malice lodged in the heart is a disease,
a blight that doubles pain in the infected:
they feel the weight of their own misery
and groan to see prosperity in others.
I know of what I speak, from long experience:

---

* A series of lacunae; see note to line 288.
† The so-called Trojan horse was used to sneak Greek soldiers inside the walls of Troy.

people are just a mirror. Those who've seemed
kindest were phantoms' shadows in the end—   840
except Odysseus: he was *forced* to sail,
but yoked beside my traces, he proved willing;
for that I give him—dead or living—credit.
Well, as to matters civic and religious,
we'll have our formal national assembly
and set our policy. What's going well
must hold, and we'll see how—as policy;
but as for what requires the healing arts—
cutting or cauterizing for its own good—
we'll try to drive back that disease's pain.   850
Now that I'm at my hall, my hearth and home,
I'll give the gods my hand in greeting first:
they brought me back from that far place they sent me.
May Victory—which did follow me—stand steady!

CLYTEMNESTRA: Gentlemen, citizens, honored Argive elders,
I'm not ashamed to tell you how attached
to a man I am, by nature. People's fear
withers with time. It's not from second hand
that I report a miserable life
endured the whole time this one was in Ilium.   860
It is a fearsome thing, first, that a wife
sits at home desolate, without her husband,
malignant noises rising all around her.
Messengers, screeching evil for her household,
keep coming, each with worse news than the last.
I must say, if my man caught all the wounds
news of which kept on sluicing to this house,
a net would have as many holes to count;
and if his deaths had tallied with the stories,
he'd be a second Geryon,* three-bodied,   870
boasting a cloak of earth allotted three times—
thick above, and beneath him, just imagine—
when all three versions of his body perished.
Time and again, after such awful rumors,

---

* Geryon was a giant, usually described as three-headed, whom Hercules killed in the course of his twelve labors.

they seized me forcibly and from my neck
wrenched the noose I had fastened to a roof-beam.
And so our son, that forceful guarantee
of our mutual bond, does not stand here beside me.
I know Orestes should, but don't be startled.
Your ally, Strophius of Phocis, meant well   880
in fostering the boy, as he foresaw
harm—and both places muttered it: for you
in Ilium; here, lawless civil uproar,
the council overthrown—it's in the blood
of humankind to kick at someone fallen.
Certainly, my excuse is hiding nothing.
Oh, but the roaring fountain of my sobbing
has been extinguished—not one drop remains.
My eyes are bad, so late at night I lay
weeping for you and piles of brush deprived always   890
of beacon fires. From my flimsy dreams
I used to startle wide awake at gnats' wings
in their shrilling onrush. I saw more disasters
for you than my companion, sleep, had time for.
I have endured all this; empty of grief now
I can address my man: the sheepfold's guard-dog,
strong rope that holds the mast, the stalwart pillar
of the high roof, a father's only child,
land to the eyes of sailors past all hope,
the glorious daylight following a storm,   900
a spring's gush for a thirsty traveler.
So pleasant is escaping all compulsion!
I think you worthy of such salutations—
and banish envy: all that we have suffered
already warrants this. Come on now, darling,
step from your vehicle—but keep your feet
from the ground, great ravager of Ilium.
Maids, hurry! Carry your commission out:
cover the earth he'll walk on with these fabrics;
spread purple on his passage—now! And Justice   910
will lead him to the home he scarcely hoped for.
As for the rest, let prudence, undefeated
by sleep, settle it justly, with the gods' help.

AGAMEMNON: Offspring of Leda, left to guard my house:
    The speech you've given suits my absence well,
    since both were quite extended. Proper praise
    is a tribute other people ought to give.
    Furthermore, don't indulge me—that's just like
    a woman. I am no barbarian
    for you to gape and squeal at as you grovel—   920
    and don't spread clothing in my path to lead me
    to resentment. Only gods should reap these honors,
    and I'm a mortal—I'd be terrified
    in setting foot on these embroidered splendors.
    Revere me merely as a man, I tell you.
    Word of me rises and resounds without
    foot-wiping tapestries. Lack of presumption
    is a god's greatest gift. Call a man happy
    who ends his life in sweet prosperity.
    If everything were like that, I'd be fearless.   930
CLYTEMNESTRA: But tell me this—and give me your sincere view.
AGAMEMNON: Count on it: I won't throw my view away.
CLYTEMNESTRA: Would you have vowed to do this, out of fear?
AGAMEMNON: Yes, as a rite an expert had prescribed.
CLYTEMNESTRA: Think: what would Priam, as the victor, do?
AGAMEMNON: Step on embroidery, I really think.
CLYTEMNESTRA: Don't be concerned, then, when the people blame you.
AGAMEMNON: But there's great power in the citizens' voice.
CLYTEMNESTRA: To be unenvied is—unenviable.
AGAMEMNON: Surely a woman shouldn't long for battle.   940
CLYTEMNESTRA: It's gracious for the fortunate to lose.
AGAMEMNON: You'd really value victory in this clash?
CLYTEMNESTRA: Listen and give in freely, and you win.
AGAMEMNON: If that's your judgment—someone, quick, untie
    these boots, the slaves beneath my feet. As I
    set foot on heaven's property, these dyed works,
    I hope no envious gaze strikes from a distance.
    I feel great shame in trampling on my household,
    wrecking its wealth, these weavings silver bought us.
    Well, be that as it may.
    (indicates Cassandra) Bring in this stranger   950
    with kindness. From far off a god's gaze falls

propitiously on gentle use of power.
No one would volunteer for slavery's yoke;
and she's the pick, the flower of great possessions,
my present from the army, as it happened.
I am subdued, however; as you order,
I step into my halls on purple cloth.

    (He steps down onto the tapestries.)

CLYTEMNESTRA: There is a sea—who'll scorch it dry?—that feeds
    a giant ooze of dye, renewed forever,*
    for purple clothing worth its weight in silver.   960
    By the gods' grace, this is on hand, my lord.
    Our household isn't trained in poverty.
    I would have vowed to trample endless clothing
    if orders came from any oracle's seat,
    and I could pay for this lost life's return.
    If the root lives, the house will come to leaf,
    a Shadow stretch to shield us from the Dog Star.†
    Back to the hearthside of your residence
    you've come; your coming signals warmth in winter;
    and Zeus is crafting wine from bitter grapes,   970
    the halls already have grown cool whenever
    the man of consequence walks through his home.

        (Agamemnon reaches the end of the purple walkway and exits
        into the palace.)

    Zeus, Zeus, Fulfiller, come fulfill my prayers,
    look after all these things you mean to do.

strophe 1

    CHORUS: Tell me, why is this terror
        fixed in its hovering
        here, before my prophetic heart, like a guard at a gate?
        Nobody called for, nobody paid for this song of divination.
        The boldness I would need to shove it away   980
        (like dreams that baffle me)
        is overthrown—it has lost my mind's kingdom.

---

* Clytemnestra refers obliquely to the murex snail, a marine creature that was crushed to produce the purple dye that colored royal robes.

† Sirius, the Dog Star, rose during the hottest, unhealthiest time of year.

Old age has come to the moment the ropes
were tossed to the sandy shore*
when the voyaging army
set off for Ilium.

antistrophe 1

I am the witness myself; my own eyes
take in his homecoming;
yet my heart learns on its own, here inside me,   990
a song that no lyre can play to: the dirge
of a Fury. The whole of my darling
courage is gone.
Instincts couldn't be gibberish.
Close to my righteous mind, my heart
wheels in the whirlpools that bring these things' fulfillment.
Still I pray: may what I forecast
turn out untrue, may it not come to pass.   1000

strophe 2

Flourishing vigor gorges
full on itself, <it strains>
[…] at the limits. But sickness
is living next door and pushes the shared
wall between them outward.
Though a man's fate holds a straight
course […]
<still he might>† strike on the hidden, sunken rock.
Dread may throw part
of his profit overboard to save the rest,
sling it out in prudence—   1010
then his whole house will not sink,
stashed full of overfullness;
the sea will not take his small boat.
Thick grows and wide spreads Zeus' gift, his cure,
from each year's furrows,
killing the plague of famine.‡

---

* Text uncertain.

† I have supplied the words "it strains" and "still he might" as an attempt to fill in part of a gap in the manuscripts.

‡ The text of this stasimon is uncertain. It contains a phrase at the beginning that the editor has despaired of emending, and several lacunae (see note to line 288), of which I have marked only those not plausibly filled in.

antistrophe 2

But once the black life-blood strikes
the ground in front of a man,
how can anyone's spells   1020
call it back to the body again?
Even the one with the mastery
to bring the dead up from Hades
did not win Zeus' assent. He was not spared.*
Gods deploy one fate to cut off
another—if not for that
I would pour out what I know—my heart would run
out of my tongue's control—
not mutter in the dark,
dismally, without hope of winding the skein   1030
clear to the end at the moment of the crisis—
but my mind leaps in a blaze.

CLYTEMNESTRA: Come, get yourself inside—that's you, Cassandra.
    Zeus makes you share our household rites—but not
    to punish you. You'll stand with many slaves
    by the altar where he's Guardian of Goods.
    Get off your vehicle—don't be too proud.
    They say Alcmene's child once went for sale   1040
    and had to tolerate the bread of slavery.†
    At any rate, though you've no choice in this,
    there's comfort in your owners' ancient wealth.
    Those who've reaped richly, when they never hoped to,
    are cruel to slaves [...
    ...] strictly by the book.
    I've told you—so you know—how things are done here.
CHORUS: (*to Cassandra*) She's finished, and she gave you clear instructions.
    Here you are, tangled in the net of fate.
    You might, perhaps, obey her. Or you might not.
CLYTEMNESTRA: Unless there's nothing in her head except   1050
    a strange barbarian language like a swallow's,
    the things I say to urge her should make sense.

---

* Apollo's son Asclepius was killed by Zeus for using his medicinal skill to bring the dead to life.
† Heracles, son of Zeus and Alcmene, had to live as a slave for a time.

CHORUS: (*to Cassandra*) Follow her. Your best choice is as she orders.
    Obey and leave your seat there in the carriage.
CLYTEMNESTRA: I don't have time to waste with her outdoors.
    Already, cattle stand beside the hearth
    for slaughter in our house's central shrine,
    [...]
    though we had lost all hope of such a blessing.
    You! Hurry, if you're planning to oblige me.
    You're feeble-minded? You don't understand?   1060
    Wave your outlandish hand, if you won't speak!
CHORUS: The foreigner must need someone to translate
    clearly. She's like a newly captured wild thing.
CLYTEMNESTRA: She's listening to her own demented thoughts;
    coming here from her freshly captured city,
    she doesn't know enough to take the bit
    until her strength bleeds from her foaming mouth.
    I won't waste further words on her contempt.
          (*Clytemnestra exits into the palace.*)
CHORUS: I only pity her; I'm not provoked.
    Come on, poor thing, and leave the cart behind you.   1070
    Give in, since there's no choice. Try on your new yoke.

strophe 1
    CASSANDRA: (*wails in grief and horror*): Apollo! Apollo!*
CHORUS: Why raise this wailing in the name of Loxias?
    What has he ever had to do with mourning?
antistrophe 1
    CASSANDRA: (*wails*) Apollo! Apollo!
CHORUS: Again, it's him she calls on—a bad omen:
    for those in grief, he's not the proper helper.
strophe 2
    CASSANDRA: Apollo, Apollo!   1080
        God of the Highway—leading to my death—
        destroying me once more—destroying me merely in passing.
CHORUS: Foresight about her own poor life is coming.
    Though she's a slave, the holy power remains.

---

* Cassandra's relationship to Apollo is a complicated one. Apollo conceived a passionate desire for Cassandra, a princess of Troy, and granted her the gift of prophecy. Cassandra accepted the god's advances but then, for some reason, pulled away at the last minute (see lines 1202–12 below). Apollo did not revoke his gift, but he added a codicil that Cassandra's prophecies would not be understood or believed.

antistrophe 2

CASSANDRA: Apollo, Apollo!

God of the Highway—leading to my death—

Where have you brought me, who does this house belong to?

CHORUS: The sons of Atreus. Don't you understand?

Take it from me, then, and rely on it.

strophe 3

CASSANDRA: (*shrieking*) A house that hates the gods, a house in   1090

on the wicked murder of its own, of itself, a house full of nooses;

a butchery men are driven into, to spatter its floor with their blood.*

CHORUS: The stranger's got a good nose, like a hound's.

She's on the track of victims—and she'll find them.

antistrophe 3

CASSANDRA: That's right, and here are the witnesses I trust:

the babies wailing over the sacrifice,

and the roasted meat on which their father was fed.†

CHORUS: We've heard about your gift. But we're not looking

for anyone to explicate the gods' will.

strophe 4

CASSANDRA: Horrible! What is she plotting?   1100

What's this fresh suffering? Terrible,

terrible, the evil schemed in the house,

beyond its friends' endurance, beyond healing, while help

stands to the side, far off.

CHORUS: These later prophecies are quite beyond me;

I know the rest, though; this whole city shouts them.

antistrophe 4

CASSANDRA: Monster, will you see it through?

This is your spouse, your mate you bedded with.

You wash him bright in the bath—and how can I speak of the

ending?

It rushes ahead. She stretches out one hand   1110

and then the other, reaching.

CHORUS: I still don't understand. These oracles

riddle, they cloud my eyes and leave me helpless.

---

* The text in the second half of both these lines is very doubtful.

† An oblique reference to the so-called banquet of Thyestes. Atreus, father of Agamemnon, in an effort to neutralize a perceived threat from his brother Thyestes, fed him a disguised meal of his own children's flesh. The savage crime took place in the same palace that Cassandra now stands before.

strophe 5

CASSANDRA: (*a prolonged shriek*) What's this in front of my eyes now?
Is it a hunting net out of the Underworld?
Yes, but a mantrap, too, that sleeps with him, helps plot
his murder. Let the mob endlessly gorging on this clan
raise a shriek over the sacrifice—on which stones will fall in their
turn.

CHORUS: Who is this Fury you summon to howl
over the house? This hardly leaves me cheerful!   1120
All the blood runs to my heart, I am left
the color of men who have fallen
in battle and lie in the rays of their life as it sets;
blood drips to its finish
that same moment—then, swiftly, ruin.

antistrophe 5

CASSANDRA: (*shrieks*) Look at this! Look! Keep the bull
away from the heifer! She's caught him
in her dress, her engine, on her black horn, striking.
Into the basin he falls, where the water lies.
He met his death in the bath, it lay in wait for him, I tell you.

CHORUS: Well, I can't boast perfect skill in making sense   1130
of oracles—but evidently something's wrong here.
What's the good news from prophecy that ever came
to humankind? Evil alone supplies
the profession that wordily chants
the gods' will, that brings us terror.

strophe 6

CASSANDRA: My torment! My torment, my calamity, this life!
It's my own pain I'm now keening, new poured onto the old.
Where do you bring me in my anguish today?
What is it for, but death along with his?

CHORUS: You're out of your mind, I think—a god has seized it.   1140
You wail for yourself
in a song without music like the trilling,
the insatiable crying from the poor, heart-piercing heart,
the moans of "Itys, Itys!" as the nightingale chants
a life overgrown with suffering.*

---

* There are several versions of this myth, but in the one Aeschylus probably alludes to, Queen Procne of Thrace, after her transformation into a nightingale, laments her son Itys, whom she herself has killed as revenge against her husband, Tereus, for the rape of her sister Philomela.

antistrophe 6

CASSANDRA: Out of my reach, the shrill nightingale's destiny!
The gods enclosed her in a body with wings,
and then her life was sweet—there were no tears.
But for me, the wide, the cleaving spearhead waits.

    CHORUS: Who sent you these surges of inspired anguish—   1150
    that are useless?
    With an unspeakable scream you beat
    fear's time, in a rending melody.
    Who marked out your prophetic road
    with these evil words?

strophe 7

    CASSANDRA: I mourn the marriage, Paris' marriage
    that doomed his own people—
    and Scamander, the river my fatherland drank from.
    On your waterside—to my grief—I was raised
    and came to womanhood.
    On the banks of Acheron, by Cocytus,   1160
    soon now, I think, I'll chant my second sight.

    CHORUS: Why have you given us this prophecy? Yes, it's clear—
    a newborn who heard it would understand.
    Like a bloody bite your miserable fate
    strikes me—you shriek it, whimper it;
    it crushes me to listen.

antistrophe 7

    CASSANDRA: The suffering, the suffering of my city
    in its annihilation!
    My father's sacrifices at the citadel's gates,
    the massacre of cattle from the field—the remedy wasn't
    half strong enough to spare   1170
    Troy its allotted agony; and I,
    my mind on fire, fall to steadfast Death.

    CHORUS: Now you're retracing your oracles.
    Some power fills your mind with its spite
    bearing you down, crushing you,
    setting you tunes of wailing, death-freighted torment—
    out of my hands, the ending.

CASSANDRA: I'll prophesy no longer like a new bride
timidly peering out beneath her veil;

my words will be a clear, bright wind, assailing 1180
the rising sun, surging against the rays
like a wave, which carries suffering far greater
than mine. It isn't riddles now that teach you.
You run with me, a witness as I track,
like a hound, the crimes committed long before.
A troupe of singers squats beneath this roof,
voices in jarring and ill-omened concert.
The human blood they've drunk has made their gall
stronger, for endless riot in the house.
You can't dislodge these Furies, who are family. 1190
Blockaders of the halls, they sing in praise
of primal Ruin, and they take turns spitting
on a brother's bed and loathe the bed's defiler.
Do I strike it like an archer? Am I wrong—
babbling, panhandling prophet of what can't be?
First swear an oath, then certify my knowledge
of this household's crimes, told in the ancient story!

CHORUS: How could an oath, though fixed in our pure hearts,
be healing? You amaze me, though: brought up
across the sea, you've struck this foreign city 1200
straight on the mark as if you were a witness.

CASSANDRA: The seer Apollo placed me in this office.

CHORUS: Though he's a god, his longing made him helpless?

CASSANDRA: I was ashamed to tell you this before.

CHORUS: That was conceit; it comes with doing well.

CASSANDRA: The wrestler breathed his heady grace on me.

CHORUS: It came—as usual—to what makes children?

CASSANDRA: No, I gave in, but then tricked Loxias.

CHORUS: The holy art had captured you already?

CASSANDRA: I was foretelling all my people's anguish. 1210

CHORUS: How could you be immune from his revenge?

CASSANDRA: Once I'd offended him, no one believed me.

CHORUS: We find, though, that we trust your prophecies.

CASSANDRA: No, no, the torment!
Once more, the hideous pain of a true seer
whirls me to chaos <with another> prelude.
You see these creatures seated near the house
in their first years, like forms inside a dream?

The children—as if enemies had killed them—
have filled their hands with food from their own bodies,   1220
pathetic weight of guts, the heavy entrails—
yes, I see clearly what their father tasted.*
I tell you, someone plans the punishment.
A feeble lion, rolling in the bed,
guards the house—no! no!—from its master's coming—
<my master: it's a slave's yoke that I carry;>†
the ships' premier and Ilium's destroyer
will meet misfortune, ruin skulking here.
Not seen for what she is, the hateful bitch
licks his hand, cheery ears prick—till she bites: 1230
as bold as that, a female who can murder
a male! What name would strike the traitorous monster
on target? She's a viper, she's a Scylla
housed on the cliffs to lash at ships, possessed
Mother of Hades, breathing war—with no truce—
on her own family. Oh, her endless daring!
Her triumph-screech, as when a battle turns,
was like rejoicing at his safe return!
Believe or don't believe me—it's no use,
since what will come, will come. Right here, right now,   1240
you'll say—in pity—I'm too true a prophet.
CHORUS: Thyestes' banquet of his children's flesh
 I recognize, and horror seizes me:
 I hear the truth, not some mere picture of it.
 And yet the rest—I'm running off the scent.
CASSANDRA: I tell you, you'll see Agamemnon's death.
CHORUS: Poor thing! Now sing your reckless mouth to sleep.
CASSANDRA: The Healer's‡ not presiding over these words.
CHORUS: If they're fulfilled, then no—but may they not be!
CASSANDRA: You're praying, but they're busy with their killing.   1250
CHORUS: But who's the man contriving this destruction?
CASSANDRA: My oracles have made a fool of you.
CHORUS: But I don't see what scheme will see it through.

---

* Another impressionistic vision of the banquet of Thyestes (see note to line 1097), described more explicitly below.

† The line in angle brackets was probably not written by Aeschylus but inserted later.

‡ Apollo.

CASSANDRA: I speak your language better than I'd like to.
CHORUS: As Pytho* does: its oracles are murky!
CASSANDRA: Oh! Such a fire is sweeping over me!

I'm finished, finished, Lycian Apollo!
A lioness with two feet made her bed here
with a wolf—the noble lion was away.
She'll kill me—I'll be helpless; there's a payback   1260
for me she pours in as she cooks her poison.
For a man she's sharpening her sword but boasting
lethal revenge on me for being brought here.
Why do I keep these jokes about myself,
the staff, the seer's ribbons on my neck?
I'll put an end to *you* before my own.

        (Throws the accouterments to the ground and stamps on them.)

Go to your ruin—where you fall I'll follow.
Somebody else can have your rich destruction.
Look, it's Apollo in the flesh who strips
my prophet's outfit. He was overseer   1270
as I was laughed at—even in this finery!—
by hostile friends, so stubbornly and wrongly:
[...]
I was a crazy vagabond, in their words,†
poor beggar, starving, half-dead—and I took it.
The prophet's now unmade the prophetess,
dispatched me to this deadly destiny.
No father's altar waits there, but a block—
scarlet and warm when I'm the sacrifice.
And yet the gods will send our deaths reprisal.
Someone will come, with vengeance in its turn,   1280
and kill his mother, vindicate his father.
Banished, estranged, a wandering refugee
come home will round out ruin for his family,
his father's sprawling corpse will bring him back.

Why do I keen this stricken, lost lament?
At the start, I saw the Trojan city going

---

* The oracle of Apollo at Delphi.
† I prefer the original manuscript reading over the conjecture adopted in West's text, which depicts
Cassandra as reduced to actual physical misery.

the way it went, but now the gods have judged
its sackers, and the end they have is this.
I'll go and take this hard death in my hands.
<There is a great oath that the gods have sworn.>   1290
Now I address the gates of hell themselves
and pray that this blow hits me where it should,
making my blood spurt out without a struggle,
so that an easy death will close my eyes.

CHORUS: Woman, your pain is great; so is your wisdom.
   You've spoken at some length. But with your own death
   clearly in mind, how can you step so bravely
   to the altar, like an ox the god is driving?

CASSANDRA: I can't evade it any longer, strangers.

CHORUS: Yet life's last hour sits in the place of honor.   1300

CASSANDRA: The day's come. I could run; it wouldn't help.

CHORUS: Your courage makes you steadfast—you must know that.

CASSANDRA: Compare that to what lucky people hear!

CHORUS: A famous death's a privilege for us mortals.

CASSANDRA: Poor father—you and your pure-blooded children!
   I'll go into the halls and keen my fate
   and Agamemnon's. But life's long enough.
   Oh—strangers!

CHORUS: What is it? Why this turning back in terror?

CASSANDRA: No, no!

CHORUS: Why "No!"? What's this repulsion in your mind?

CASSANDRA: The palace reeks of dripping blood and murder.

CHORUS: What? That's the smell of offerings at the hearth.   1310

CASSANDRA: No, it's the stench of tombs*—I can't mistake it—

CHORUS: No Syrian incense in the house, you're saying . . .

CASSANDRA: I'm not a bird, who panics at the breeze
   in empty scrub. Testify to my death's words
   when a woman dies to pay for me, a woman,
   and a man for one who's married to betrayal:
   so, as your guest, in death I call on you.   1320

CHORUS: I pity your sad fate, decreed by heaven.

CASSANDRA: Once more I want to make a speech, or sing
   my own dirge. To the sun of this last day

---

* I am following the original manuscript reading instead of West's conjecture.

I pray that the avengers of my master
exact my murder's price in this same way,
although a slave's death caused so little trouble.
Poor mortal life! Even when greatly blessed,
it scurries when a shadow falls. Bad fortune's
a dripping sponge slapping away what's written.
More than myself, by far, I pity them.*   1330

> CHORUS: Nobody mortal can eat himself too full of life's good things;
>> no one will keep them out, bar them from halls people point at in
>>> awe.
>> "Never again will you enter" will not be pronounced.
>> This man has sacked Priam's city, by the blessed gods' decree,
>> and the gods honor him as he comes home.
>> If he will now pay with blood of the bygone,
>> if for his own dead he dies, which will bring
>> the retribution for still other deaths—   1340
>> who among mortals, hearing about it, would boast
>> of having been born with a fate that cannot be broken?

AGAMEMNON: (*heard from offstage, inside the palace*)
> No! I've been hit! The wound is deep and deadly ...

CHORUS: Quiet! Who's shouting? What's this deadly wound?

AGAMEMNON: No! Stop! Again—a second blow has landed ...

AN INDIVIDUAL IN THE CHORUS: I think it's done—that's why the king is
> wailing.
> We must discuss what measures might be safe.

ANOTHER: Listen to me—here's what I recommend:
> call out a rescue force of citizens.

ANOTHER: We ought to break in right away—that's my view—   1350
> and seize the proof, the sword that drips fresh blood.

ANOTHER: I'm for a policy along those lines:
> I vote for action. Now's no time for dawdling.

ANOTHER: The truth is here to see: this is the prelude
> that signals despotism for the city.

ANOTHER: They're wide awake, they strike while we waste time.
> They're trampling the regard we had for waiting.

ANOTHER: I'm lost: I can't arrive at a suggestion.
> The one who does a thing should also plan it.

---

* A tentative translation of an unclear line, in which the pronoun ("them") has no clear referent.

ANOTHER: I'm just as lost as you. There is no way   1360
  to make a speech that resurrects the dead.

ANOTHER: How could we even stand to live, condoning
  leadership that defiles the royal house?

ANOTHER: No, it's unbearable, and death is better,
  a gentler destiny than tyranny.

ANOTHER: In point of fact, taking those groans as proof,
  can we divine the gentleman is dead?

ANOTHER: Clear knowledge must precede deliberation,
  since guessing is a thing distinct from knowing.

ANOTHER: Here I have broad majority support: 1370
  we should make sure how Atreus' son is doing.

> *(The palace doors open and Clytemnestra is revealed, standing
> over two bloody corpses.)*

CLYTEMNESTRA: Though all I said before was right for then,
  I'm not ashamed to state the opposite.
  How else would someone, paying evil back
  to those disguised as friends, raise suffering's net
  around them to a height they can't leap over?
  I gave my full attention to this struggle
  from far back. Victory came, though that took time.
  Right where I struck, I stand, on my achievement.
  I acted—I'm not going to deny it—   1380
  to trap him so he couldn't fight off death.
  As if he were a school of fish, I cast
  a rich robe in inextricable circles.*
  Twice I strike, and a double groan announces
  his legs' collapse. He's fallen, but I add
  a third, an extra blow, thank-offering
  to Zeus below ground, savior of cadavers.†
  He falls, convulsively gasps out his soul,
  and spouts a headlong slaughter-gush of blood,
  striking me with dark-scarlet showers of dew,   1390
  and I rejoice, as in wet, quickened sowings

---

* This entangling robe will be displayed onstage in the *Libation Bearers* and spoken of, in horror, in the *Eumenides*. Just how it immobilized Agamemnon is unclear.

† "Zeus below ground" is Hades, lord of the Underworld. Clytemnestra here perverts the Greek ritual by which someone drinking wine would pour three libations, the third in honor of "Zeus the Savior." Here the "libations" are knife thrusts, and the third goes to Hades the Savior—of corpses.

of Zeus's grace, when buds emerge from labor.
If a libation for a corpse is proper
and right—and more than right—then this is it.
He filled this cup of curses for the house,
and drank it up himself when he returned.
So there you have it, honored Argive elders.
Be glad, or don't—but triumph fills my heart.

CHORUS: We're stunned at this defiance in your mouth,
 this bragging speech above your husband's body.   1400

CLYTEMNESTRA: You think you're prodding at a female moron,
 but I don't shake inside, addressing those
 who understand. And you can praise or blame me—
 it doesn't matter. This is Agamemnon,
 my husband. He's a corpse now. My right hand,
 an honest builder, made this. Here we are.

strophe 1

 CHORUS: Woman, what evil thing—
  eatable, drinkable—that the ground or the flowing
  sea nourishes—passed through your lips?
  You've burned this sacrifice, earned the town's clamorous curses;
  you have cast us off, you have cut us off, you are exiled from the
   city;   1410
  to the citizens, you are abomination.

CLYTEMNESTRA: So now you sentence me to banishment,
 allot me hatred, rumbling civic curses.
 Back then you offered *him* no opposition
 when he, as casual as at one death
 among the crowding and luxuriant flocks,
 sacrificed his own child, my dearest birth-pangs,
 to conjure up some blasts of air from Thrace.
 Wasn't it that polluted criminal
 you should have driven out? You hear what I've done,   1420
 and you're a savage judge. But pay attention:
 threaten away, and know that I'm prepared
 to let the winner of a fair fight rule
 over me. But if god wills otherwise,
 you'll learn restraint, and well, however late.

antistrophe 1

 CHORUS: Monstrous your enterprise,
  haughty the words you spoke—and your mind, along with them,

reels in the passion of your bloody triumph;
and the smear of blood in your eye is unmistakable.
All those you love must be taken in revenge
and a wound pay back each wound that you have given.   1430
CLYTEMNESTRA: There's more to hear, an oath that's sanctified
by Justice—realized for my child—and Ruin,*
And the Fury, since I slaughtered him for these:
from now on, hope won't pace the house of fear,
as long as there's a flame lit on my hearth
by Aegisthus, who has been my champion
this whole time, and the shield that gives me courage.
            (Indicating the two corpses at her feet)
He lies here, after wronging me, his wife,
and soothing every Chryseis at Troy;†
and here's the seer of the signs, his captive,   1440
who shared his bed; rely on her for saying
sooth—and for other services: the whore
among the sailors' benches. Rightly honored,
the two of them: him, as I stated; her
like a swan, whose song and dance were rites of death—
his lover lying next to him. He brought
this side-dish in—but it was for *my* pleasure.
strophe 2
    CHORUS: Only, if only quickly, with no great torture,
        with no long nursing vigil,
        the end would come for us, bringing   1450
        sleep without end, for all time—now that the man who
            guarded us
        close to his heart is brought down.
        He endured so much for a woman;
        now a woman has obliterated him.
ephymnium 1
        You were out of your mind, Helen, Helen,
        annihilating great numbers, terrible numbers
        of lives beneath Troy's walls.
        Now you've won the consummate, the immortal prize:

---

* *Atē*, a Greek word that can be translated "ruin" or "rash blindness (leading to ruin)," is sometimes personified as a goddess.

† Chryseis, according to Homer's *Iliad*, was the daughter of a Trojan priest, taken as war booty by Agamemnon and enslaved for sexual purposes.

the blood that will not wash away. It was some spirit   1460
of unassailable discord in the house, a husband's anguish.

CLYTEMNESTRA: No, don't pray—in your distress—for your share
of death.

And do not turn your rage away toward Helen,
calling her the one murderer of many,
destroyer of the Danäan men's lives,
creator of a sorrow never to be made good.

antistrophe 2

CHORUS: Spirit who falls on the house, on the brace
of Tantalus' sons;* Power that grows out of women. It is a match for
my life,   1470
overpowers me, gnaws on my heart.
Over his body she stands
like an evil crow, singing a holy
song off-key, and gloating.

CLYTEMNESTRA: So now you've set your thoughts on the matter
straight:
you call on the spirit, gorged again and again, of this clan;
the blood-licking lust is from him, he feeds it in the belly.
Before the old agony stops, a new sore runs.   1480

strophe 3

CHORUS: Powerful, full of hard rage
is the spirit in your story toward this house—
terrible, terrible fable, glutted with blighting misfortune.
The hand of Zeus, the fearful hand
that causes, that does everything, lies on it.
What happens without Zeus in mortal lives?
In all this, what did heaven not accomplish?

ephymnium 2

My king! Tell me, how will I weep for you, my king?   1490
Is there anything that my loving heart can say
as you lie in the web this spider wove,
panting your life out in an ungodly death?
I grieve for your resting place—fit for no free man—
and the death by trickery that brought you down,
the stroke from the two-edged weapon in her hand.

---

* The Greek word here rendered as "sons" is a loose expression indicating descent; it refers to Agamemnon and Menelaus, who are Tantalus' great-grandsons.

CLYTEMNESTRA: You contend that this act is mine.
   But don't count me, then, as Agamemnon's consort.
   This corpse's wife is only the form you see—   1500
   an ancient, pitiless avenger has paid this man
   for Atreus and his brutal banquet.*
   He killed this man (*indicates Agamemnon*), a full-grown sacrifice to
      follow the young ones.

antistrophe 3

CHORUS: Guiltless you call yourself, in this
   murder—but who would be your witness?
   How could you do it, how? But maybe your accomplice in vengeance
   came from the father. Through channels of brothers' blood,
   the black War-God advances,   1510
   in his hands the judgment for the gore
   of little children, clotting as it was swallowed.

ephymnium 2

CHORUS: My king! Tell me, how will I weep for you, my king?
   Is there anything that my loving heart can say
   as you lie in the web this spider wove,
   panting your life out in an ungodly death?
   I grieve for your resting place—fit for no free man—
   and the death by trickery that brought you down,
   the stroke from the two-edged weapon in her hand.   1520

CLYTEMNESTRA: No, I don't think that his death was slavish, that
   […]
   Didn't he scheme catastrophe for his house?
   My little one whom he fathered, who was raised here,
   Iphigenia, bitterly mourned
   […]†
   What was due he rendered—and he suffered it also.
   He has got nothing to bluster about in Hades
   but his death on a sword—the price of his own doings.

strophe 4

CHORUS: Now lost, I stand outside of deft   1530
   and careful thinking.
   Where shall I turn, while the house falls?

---

* This refers to the slaughter of Thyestes' children (see note to line 1097).

† Another lacuna. The previous line presents good evidence of corruption but does not appear at all unsalvageable for a translator.

I am afraid of the rain that pounds, that shakes the home,
a bloody rain. But now it drizzles away.
Justice moves on, and Fate is whetting her knife
on another stone, for another job of havoc.

ephymnium 3

Earth, earth, I wish you'd taken me to yourself
before I saw this man sprawled over
his bath with its silver sides—pathetic bed.   1540
Who will bury him? Who will mourn for him?
You—would you dare? You have killed your own
husband. Will you mourn him loudly? Will you
perform for his ghost this favor that's no favor,
in return for all he's done? Will you wrong him this way?
Who will send out praise, with tears, at the grave for the man
who was like a god? Who will do this work
with the truth in his heart?

CLYTEMNESTRA: That's no concern of yours, nothing you need to do.
     By our hands.   1550
he fell and he died; we will bury him also—
and not to the sound of wailing from those in the house.
But Iphigenia will be delighted;
his daughter will do what's right and meet her father
face to face at the fast-skimming ferry of wailing,
throwing her hands around his neck to kiss him.

antistrophe 4

CHORUS: One insult meets another now—   1560
     who could decide?—it's a deadlock:
the plunderer plundered, the killer paying in full.
Still, while Zeus lasts on his throne, the law will last
that what a man does, he will endure. This is laid down.
Tell me, who'll drive this fertile curse from the house?
Disaster and this race are mortared together.

CLYTEMNESTRA: It's a truth, it's an oracle you've stumbled on.
     But I'd make a pact with the Pleisthenids" guardian spirit   1570
to be content with this—though it's unbearable—
granted he goes from this house and grinds another family
to dust with these deaths—no better than suicides.

---

* Pleisthenids is another name for Atreids.

Wholly enough for me, a tiny share of these possessions,
    if I do away with the frenzy of killing back and forth in this palace.
    (Enter Aegisthus, from the palace, surrounded by guards.)

AEGISTHUS: O genial sun that lights the day of justice!
  At last I think the gods above look down
  on the earth's pain and vindicate us mortals,
  now that I see the man who lies here wearing   1580
  the robe the Furies wove—heartwarming sight!—
  and paying for the trap set by his father
  who reigned here, Atreus. That man, in plain terms,
  banished Thyestes—my own father—though
  he was his brother, from his home and city,
  when the right to rule this country was disputed.
  On his return to Atreus' hearth for mercy,
  wretched Thyestes' life remained secure—
  which means he didn't bloody native ground
  with his own death. But this man's godless father   1590
  gave keen but unkind hospitality
  to mine. He made a show of sacrifice
  on the special day, but served up children's flesh—
  the digits of the feet, the serried fingers
  minced in a covered dish—and sat apart.
  His unsuspecting guest reached out at once[*]
  and ate, to this clan's ruin, as you see.
  Then, when he sensed the monstrous thing he'd done,
  he fell back, howling, retching out the slaughter,
  and called down harrowing doom on Pelops' sons.   1600
  The table he kicked over sealed the curse:
  annihilation for the race of Pleisthenes;
  so on these grounds, he's there to look at, fallen,
  and I'm the one who—justly—stitched this murder.
  Atreus drove out my poor father and me—
  the thirteenth born,[†] still in my baby clothes,
  and Justice brought me back when I was grown.
  I fastened this whole grim device together
  and caught him in my hand before I came here.

---

[*] This is a possible general meaning of two lines that are too corrupt to allow any precise reconstruction or translation.

[†] In most versions of the myth there were only three children.

Death itself would be sweet for me, since now   1610
   he lies before me in the net of Justice.
CHORUS: Aegisthus, I don't honor gloating gall—
   you, though, now say you killed this man on purpose?
   You schemed his pitiful murder on your own?
   Be sure of what I say: when Justice comes,
   your life won't dodge the people's stones and curses.
AEGISTHUS: So that's your tone, down on the rowing bench?*
   Those with the power are sitting at the rudder.
   You're not too old to learn how hard a lesson
   prudent obedience can be—at your age.   1620
   Chains and starvation are preeminent
   physicians for the mind; they even school
   elders. Why can't you see this? You're not blind.
   Kick back when goaded? You'll grow sore from beatings.
CHORUS: Woman, house-watcher, when they came from war,
   you joined your marriage bed's defiler, plotting
   this death for the commander of the army?
AEGISTHUS: These words will father pain to make you sob.
   You don't have Orpheus' eloquence†—far from it.
   All living creatures trailed him in their joy;   1630
   with idiotic yips you're rousing me
   to haul you off. Soon you'll be tamed by force.
CHORUS: So you're the Argives' tyrant, who consulted
   in this man's death, but didn't have the courage
   to stretch your own hand out and do the killing.
AEGISTHUS: Plainly, it was a woman's job to trick him,
   while I, the clan's old enemy, was suspect.
   Now I'll deploy his property to rule
   the citizens, and set a heavy yoke
   on those who won't obey. No barley-fattened   1640
   show-horses here! No, hateful hunger, rooming
   with darkness, will be jailers of their weakness.
CHORUS: Your heart was quaking—or why didn't you
   face the man down? A woman did it for you!
   That filthy outrage to our land and gods

---

* A nautical metaphor that the seafaring Athenians would easily appreciate. In their military, the lower classes, who owned neither horses nor metal armor, rowed the warships that made up the navy.

† Orpheus was a mythical musician whose lyre playing and singing were able to enchant even the gods.

killed him. But is Orestes living somewhere?
Fortune might favor him and bring him home
to be the champion killer of this pair.

AEGISTHUS: You choose to say and do this—soon you'll learn.

CHORUS: (*refusing to back down*)
Come on, then, fellow soldiers, here's our duty!   1650

AEGISTHUS: (*to his own bodyguard*)
You all, come on, get ready. Draw your swords.

CHORUS: I'm ready, too. I don't refuse to die.

AEGISTHUS: I'm glad to hear that—it will be our omen.

CLYTEMNESTRA: No, precious darling, let's not do more damage.
There's plenty here to reap, a mournful harvest
and good supply of pain—we don't need more.
Honored old men, move on toward home. Give way
to fate before you suffer [...
...] chance. What we did was necessary.
And if these troubles have a cure, it's welcome:
a spirit's heavy hoof—too bad!—has struck us: 1660
a woman's words, if someone cares to listen.

AEGISTHUS: These people talk as if they're picking flowers,
pelt me with silly words—and take their chance.
They've lost their minds, to flout the man in power.

CHORUS: We're Argives. We don't fawn on worthless men.

AEGISTHUS: I'll settle with you in the days ahead.

CHORUS: Not if good fortune steers Orestes home.

AEGISTHUS: I know myself that exiles feed on hope.

CHORUS: You eat! Get fat, soil justice—since you can.

AEGISTHUS: You're quite a fool. You'll pay for it, I promise.   1670

CHORUS: And you're a cock beside your hen. Keep crowing!

CLYTEMNESTRA: Ignore their empty barking. I will rule
over this house with you, and set it right.
            (*Aegisthus and Clytemnestra exit into the palace, leaving the
            corpses onstage as the Chorus look on in silence.*)

INTRODUCTION TO AESCHYLUS'
LIBATION BEARERS

Years have passed between the close of *Agamemnon* and the opening of *Libation Bearers*, the second play in the *Oresteia* trilogy. Word of Agamemnon's murder has long since reached Phocis, the mountainous region of northwest Greece ruled by Strophius, an ally of Argos. For years Strophius has played guardian to Orestes, the only son of Agamemnon and Clytemnestra, at the latter's request; evidently Clytemnestra wanted her son out of the way as she prepared her husband's murder. Orestes has grown to young manhood at Strophius' court, alongside Strophius' son Pylades, who has by now become Orestes' best friend.

By exiling her son, Clytemnestra also placed him beyond her own power; she cannot control him as she and Aegisthus now control his sister, Electra, isolating her from potential allies and keeping her under guard. How Clytemnestra ultimately expected to deal with the problem her son presented is unclear; perhaps she hoped to win him over by sending messages across the mountains. But other messages, from a much nearer source, have reached Orestes first. Phocis borders on Delphi, the Greek world's most important shrine and the seat from which Apollo delivers his oracles. That god, often referred to as Loxias in his role as prophet, has given Orestes a directive to kill Clytemnestra and a promise to protect him afterward, and has even threatened him with physical harm should he not carry out this deed (lines 1028–33). And so Orestes has come back to Argos, to the tomb of his murdered father, where we see him leaving offerings as this play opens, his best friend, Pylades, by his side.

Tombs often figure prominently in Greek tragedy, since they loom so large in Greek religion. The mythic figures portrayed in tragedy were imagined to exercise power even after death, to become semidivine beings the Greeks called *heroes* (the English derivative word has much weaker force). A kinsman or suppliant seeking the aid of a hero could bring ritual offerings to his or her tomb, pouring liquids such as wine, milk, or honey onto the ground so as to nourish the person below it. These drink-offerings to the dead are known in Greek as *choai*, a word usually translated as "libations" (though that word is also used to translate the Greek word *spondai*, drink-offerings made to the gods). Other gifts, too, were sometimes left at heroes' tombs, including locks of clipped hair—the gift that Orestes leaves on his father's grave in the opening lines of this play. No sooner has this been done than Orestes hears others approaching, and hides.

The Chorus that give the play its title, *Libation Bearers*, now enter: elderly slave women who have come to Agamemnon's tomb bearing drink-offerings on behalf of their mistress, Clytemnestra. (Sometimes the play is referred to instead by its Greek title, *Choephoroe*, which means "libation bearers" but makes more specific reference to the purpose of the libations.) Their dirgelike song and their cheeks torn by their own fingernails attest to the unease within the palace. Agamemnon's ghost has been haunting it, crying out in the night and bringing bad dreams to the queen. A particularly vivid nightmare has prompted her to send these propitiatory gifts: as we hear later, she has dreamed that a viper was suckling from her breast, drawing blood out together with milk. Accompanying these slaves is Electra, now virtually a slave herself, or a prisoner, forced to do the bidding of a bloodstained mother whom she loathes and fears.

The reunion of brother and sister, sole allies long parted from each other, was clearly a part of this story that offered great theatrical energy, and all three of the Electra dramas in this volume (this play plus the *Electra*s of Sophocles and Euripides) develop it into powerful recognition scenes. Aeschylus allows Electra to detect her brother's return, before meeting him, by the lock of hair and footprints he has left at the tomb. That artifice was later spoofed by Euripides, whose Electra protests, in a direct reference to this play, that no sibling could be identified by such clues (lines 524–38). The differing approaches reveal much about the techniques of the two playwrights and the distance that tragic drama had traveled from its middle to its late stage. For Aeschylus, composing the *Oresteia* in 458 B.C., the mythic world of tragedy did not admit such practical questions as whether footprints run in families. Euripides, by the time of his *Electra* in 413 B.C., had brought a new concern with realism and plausibility (or the lack of it) to the Athenian stage.

Once they have joined forces, Orestes and Electra, together with the Chorus, join in a long exchange of lyric invocations to the hero who lies beneath them, imploring his help in the fight ahead. As the incantations rise in fervor, we might well expect (given the precedent of the *Persians*) that Agamemnon himself will emerge from the earth, but this doesn't happen; it's a ghost-raising scene with no ghost. But even if they don't appear onstage, the supernatural powers that are here summoned can be felt near at hand, silently allying themselves with Electra and Orestes. It's a kind of alliance we never felt in the case of Clytemnestra in the *Agamemnon*, her preparations for murder, one imagines, did not include pious prayers of this kind.

Orestes contrives to play the role of a messenger in order to gain access to the palace, bearing a false report of his own death. The effect this report has on Clytemnestra is stunning. Though the news delivers her from fear, she feels only grief and dismay. She is, despite her history of tyranny and murder, a mother, and this will make it hard for Orestes to bring himself to kill her. Fortunately, as things play out, he takes on Aegisthus first, and he gets to deal with him alone, after the Chorus—taking an unusually active part in the plot—persuade the royal nurse, Cilissa, to omit an important message telling him to bring his bodyguard along.

The moment of truth arrives: the reunion of mother and son, very different in tone from the earlier reunion of brother and sister. Orestes, sword in hand, at first shrinks from the deed he has sworn to do, especially when Clytemnestra bares the breast that suckled him. But the viper she saw in her dream had drawn blood from that breast as well as milk. Orestes, reminded of Apollo's orders by Pylades—who now breaks his play-long silence, creating a theatrical effect as though Apollo himself had spoken—forces his mother into the palace and goes forward on the path of matricide. He knows the cost will be steep. His crime, under Greek religious sanctions, stains him with *miasma*, a pollution so toxic that none may touch or speak with him, and enrages the Erinyes, dread goddesses who torment kin-murderers. The claim these haglike creatures now have on Orestes will be the problem of the trilogy's third play, the *Eumenides*.

The palace doors open and two bloodied corpses are wheeled out, just as in the last scene of the *Agamemnon*. Orestes holds up the bloody robe with which his two victims, years earlier, had ensnared his father, binding him fast so as to butcher him more effectively. One more new cloth has been added to the dense weave of imagery Aeschylus develops in this trilogy, starting with the nets and snares referred to in its opening chorus, proceeding to the purple carpet on which Agamemnon is made to tread, continuing here with the entangling robe, and ending, in the *Eumenides*, with the red cloaks the Erinyes wear as they march in a festal procession—garments that, for Athenians, identified them as metics (*metoikoi*, coinhabitants), foreigners living in their city as welcome guests. Aeschylus typically builds up accretions of motifs in this way; in the *Persians* we see him doing likewise with shackles, bonds, and yokes. It's astonishing today, when we pore over his written works to unlock these patterns, to realize that he wrote his plays to be seen just once and never read or studied.

Exploiting the natural structure of the trilogy, Aeschylus has in the *Agamemnon* and *Libation Bearers* brought us to a point of homicidal balance. Stroke has been met by counterstroke; two rulers of Argos have died, in symmetrical fashion, with their consorts. The score has in some sense been evened, yet the fundamental questions surrounding the house of Atreus have not been resolved. As in a "best of three" wrestling match—an analogy evoked by the Chorus of *Agamemnon* in their great opening ode—it is up to the final play, the *Eumenides*, to break the tie.

The Oresteia

Libation Bearers

Translated by Sarah Ruden

Throughout the translation, I have used the Greek edition of D. L. Page (Oxford Classical Texts, 1972) as reproduced with commentary in A. F. Garvie, ed., *Aeschylus: Choephori* (Oxford: Clarendon Press, 1986). Wherever I have disagreed with both of these scholars on the reconstruction or interpretation of the text, I have indicated the variance in a footnote.

Cast of Characters (in order of appearance)

Orestes, son of the late king Agamemnon and his widow, Clytemnestra

Pylades, son of King Strophius of Phocis, with whom Orestes was sent to live by his mother, Clytemnestra, before her murder of Agamemnon

Chorus of elderly female slaves belonging to the Argive royal house

Electra, daughter of the late king Agamemnon and his widow, Clytemnestra

A male slave of the Argive royal house

Clytemnestra, widow of Agamemnon, present ruler of Argos along with her lover, Aegisthus

Cilissa, elderly nurse who helped raise Orestes and Electra

Aegisthus, cousin of Agamemnon, lover of Clytemnestra and present joint ruler of Argos

Setting: The play takes place at the grave of Agamemnon in the town of Argos. The palace with its gate is in the background. Enter Orestes and Pylades from outside the city.

ORESTES: Hermes Below,* you guard my father's power:
    fight with me, save me—I appeal to you.
    I've now returned from exile to my homeland.
    On my father's mounded grave I call on him
    to hear my need [... †
    ...] to Inachus,‡ for fostering me,
    a hank of hair, and one to you I mourn for.
    Father, I wasn't here lamenting, stretching
    my hand out as they carried you away.
           (Enter from the palace a Chorus of old women in black, carrying
           jars. Electra is with them, also in black.)
    What's this I see? What sort of gathering   10
    of women in those stark black shrouds is coming
    on the march? What does this tell me happened here?
    Did some fresh grief fall on the house? Does this
    procession pour libations for my father,
    the offerings that soothe the dead below?
    It must be! And that seems to be Electra,
    my sister, as she walks along in grief—
    just look. Zeus, grant me vengeance for the death
    of my father. Bless my fight and fight beside me.
    Pylades, let's stand back to get a clear   20
    idea of the women's supplication.

---

* Hermes, the divine messenger and guide, here addressed in his capacity as the intermediary between the living and the dead.

† The text of the prologue is uncertain, because the single extant manuscript through which the play comes to us from antiquity is missing these opening lines, and their reconstruction through citations in ancient authors remains incomplete. The bracketed periods indicate a lacuna, or gap in the known text, that cannot be filled in by a satisfactory editorial conjecture.

‡ The major river of a territory was traditionally personified as a god and offered a lock of hair by each young man as thanks for "nurturing" him. Inachus was the principal river of Argos.

strophe 1

    CHORUS: I have come, dispatched from the house,
      conducting these libations, battering, clawing my face.
      My cheeks glare with the gashes,
      my nails cut their fresh furrows.
      All my life, there is nowhere to graze
      my heart but here, in cries of mourning.
      These rents demolish the linen weave,
      a snarling sound rises from the pain.
      Even the robe that falls over my breasts is stricken   30
      by the calamity that kills all laughter.

antistrophe 1

      How our hair stood on end at the shrill, clear voice
      of the spirit who turns our household's dreams to prophecy!
      His rage panted out through sleep
      in the dead of night. His fearful war-cry
      rang at the heart of the house.
      Fierce, he fell on the women's quarters.
      And from the judges of dreams, whom heaven vouches for,
      the divine message rang, it echoed:
      those who went under the earth now lay their blame   40
      with a passion of fury. Their rancor stands against the killers.

strophe 2

      (*indicating libation jars*) Eagerly she has sent me, O Mother Earth,
      to try to turn evil away with this favor he cannot favor—
      the godless woman. But I am afraid
      to make my speech for her.
      What, after all, can ransom blood poured on the ground?
      Oh, the unending anguish at this hearth!
      This house might as well be razed to its foundations!   50
      Humankind loathes the sunless
      dusk that fell like a veil on the palace
      when its rulers died.

antistrophe 2

      The awe that no battle, no violence, no war could overcome
      before, as it shot through the ears and minds of the people,
      has drawn away. A person
      is afraid. Prosperity
      is a god, in human eyes, and more than a god—   60

but Justice, with her scale, loses sight of no one:
rushing to some in daylight, or letting
suffering wait for the loiterers
between the light and darkness;
or leaving them to sink in night's pure lightlessness.

strophe 3

The earth—that nurtures us—was given blood to guzzle,
but the gory vengeance never washed in, never vanished.
Ruin, limitless pain in her hands, puts the offender off
until the full power of his sickness bursts against him.

antistrophe 3

There is no cure for laying a hand on a bride   70
in her room. Just so, all earth's watercourses, rushing
together over the hand that murder dirtied
would be no use to clean it.

epode

And me—I was driven out from the house of my fathers
to a slave's share in life. It was the gods—they laid on me
what must be, whenever a siege chokes a city:
so "Yes!" and "Of course!"—in my mouth—are proper for both the
    just
and unjust acts of those who govern my existence.
My mind is in their fist; I should fight down   80
bitter revulsion.* Still, I weep behind my sleeve
for my masters' empty luck,
and my body is frozen hard with secret grief.

ELECTRA: Bond-slaves who keep the palace in good order,
since you attend me in this invocation,
help make my policy. What should I say
while pouring out these funeral offerings?
Is there a tender prayer I could address
to my father here? "I bring a cherished husband
a message from his cherished wife"—my mother?   90
Or else—since this is mortal people's custom—
"Make us a fair return for gifts of honor"?
These worthless gifts deserve what they deserve!

---

* I concur only in part with Garvie's reconstruction and interpretation of the stanza up to here.

What about silent shame? That's how my father
died. I could pour this out for earth to guzzle
and sling the jar away, not even looking,
and walk back home as if I'd thrown out garbage.
No, I don't dare. But what is there to say
while pouring grain and honey on his tomb?
Come in with me and help me plan it, friends: 100
the evil in this house is our shared usage.
Don't hide what's in your heart, in fear of someone.
The end that's fated waits for both the free
and those who live beneath a master's hand.
So tell me, is our thinking on one level?
CHORUS: Here, at your father's grave—to me an altar—
    I'll give my heart a voice, as you command.
ELECTRA: Speak, in your reverence for my father's tomb.
CHORUS: (*indicating libation*) Pour out, with that, the words goodwill must
    welcome.
ELECTRA: Who has good will, among those close to me?   110
CHORUS: Yourself! And then whoever hates Aegisthus.
ELECTRA: So only I—and you—should hear my prayer?
CHORUS: Work it out on your own, then you can tell us!
ELECTRA: Who else belongs in our association?
CHORUS: Orestes isn't here, but don't forget him.
ELECTRA: Yes, I agree. That's excellent advice.
CHORUS: And pray that those who're guilty in this murder—
ELECTRA: What? Tell me what you mean—I wouldn't know.
CHORUS: That someone—god or mortal—comes to them—
ELECTRA: Who would that be? A judge or an avenger?   120
CHORUS: Simply prescribe the rite—death for a death.
ELECTRA: Could I, in reverence, ask the gods for this?
CHORUS: Why not? It's paying back an enemy.
ELECTRA: Greatest of messengers to heaven and hell
    [...]* the deep earth's Hermes, call on
    the spirits underground to hear my prayers,
    call the protectors of my father's palace,
    and Earth herself, mother and nurturer
    of everything, whose young return to her.

---

* A lacuna; see note to line 5.

And I, who send the dead these holy streams,
call to my father: "Pity me and dear   130
Orestes. Strike a light inside the house.
The two of us have lost our home; we're sold
by our mother, and her 'husband' is our price—
Aegisthus, the accessory in your murder.
You couldn't tell me from a slave. Orestes
is driven from his property. They preen,
they gloat—they romp in what your suffering won.
I pray to you that blessed chance, somehow,
will bring Orestes here. And listen, Father:
give me a life more decent than my mother's   140
by far, and hands kept to their sacred duty.
These prayers are for ourselves; for our opponents,
Father, I pray that your avenger comes,
and Justice makes the killers pay with death—
I break off prayer for those good gifts to curse
these persons; but for us, come from below,
an escort for our blessings; and the gods,
and Earth, and Justice, who brings victory, help you!"
Over my prayers I pour my offerings.
(*to the Chorus*) Honor him with your customary wailing,   150
and raise your song in reverence for the dead.

> CHORUS: Let a tear sound aloud as it falls—since it goes to its
>   destruction
>   for our master who was destroyed.
>   Let it fall in this stream of loyal weeping that is filth
>   and a curse to wrongdoers, that keeps them away.
>   Weep, now that our jars of offerings are empty.*
>   Hear me, hear me, my honored master,
>   through your mind's darkness.
>   (*prolonged keening*) Let some powerful fighter come   160
>   to set the house free, and let Ares in combat threaten
>   with Scythian spears, let him work his broadsword at close quarters.

---

* I was so dissatisfied with *any* editorial or interpretive ingenuity displayed over these lines that I supplied my own version, based on two simple ideas: the slaves weep because it is the only offering they have left now; and whereas loyal people (the word *kednos* is rare except for persons and their personal attributes) weep, the guilty must regard weeping for the victim with disgust and fear. This seems especially fitting because *agos* is the pollution of guilt.

ELECTRA: My father has his gifts; the earth has drunk them—
      (noticing Orestes' offerings)
  but what does *that* mean? Look! Come here and look!
CHORUS: You tell me, please. Fear's making my heart dance.
ELECTRA: I see a severed curl laid on the tomb.
CHORUS: From whom? What man, what girl with her deep bosom?
ELECTRA: It signals clearly—anyone could guess!   170
CHORUS: Explain and school me, though I'm so much older.
ELECTRA: I must have cut it from my head—who else?
CHORUS: Others who owe him mourning gifts are hostile.
ELECTRA: Really, it looks like plumage from the same bird …
CHORUS: Plumage, mane, tresses—whose? I need to know!
ELECTRA: It looks extremely similar to mine.
CHORUS: You mean this was Orestes' smuggled gift?
ELECTRA: It gives me quite a striking sense of him.
CHORUS: But how could he have dared to make his way here?
ELECTRA: For his father's sake, he sent a hank of hair.   180
CHORUS: But what you say is nothing less to weep for—
  suppose he never sees this land again?*
ELECTRA: A wave of gall laps at my heart as well;
  an arrow strikes and drives clear through my body.
  Insatiable, thirsty for themselves,
  my tears run, like a flood beneath a storm,
  at this sight, this lock of hair. How could I picture
  anyone else from Argos as its owner?
  The killer didn't cut it off, that's certain;
  no, not my mother—not that "mother" suits   190
  the monstrous spite she's shown to us, her children.
  But how can I affirm that this thing crowning
  the tomb is from Orestes, whom I love
  most among humankind? Hope fawns on me.
  (cries in distress) I wish it were a messenger, whose mind
  and voice kept doubt from whipping me in circles,
  with clear advice: "No, turn your back on me:
  it's from an enemy's head that I've been cut"—
  or else, "I'm family; I can mourn with you,

---

* The Chorus think that he sent the lock from permanent exile, or that he is dead and this is his memorial (Garvie).

gracing the tomb and honoring our father."   200
The gods whose help we call on are aware
what heavy, storming blasts are whirling us
like sailors. If we're meant to find salvation,
a tiny seed could yield a massive trunk.
       (Looking more closely at the ground)
And here—more evidence is in these footprints:
they're just like mine, they really have the same look.
An outline drawn around our feet would match!
It's him!—and a companion in his journey.
The traces of the heels, the shaping muscles
tally with what my own tracks have to show.   210
The pangs for me, the chaos in my mind!

ORESTES: *(emerging with Pylades)* Announce your prayers' fulfillment to the gods,

and pray that what's to come will turn out well.

ELECTRA: *(not recognizing him)* But why? Tell me the blessing I have now.

ORESTES: Your long and earnest prayers have brought this sight.

ELECTRA: But who on earth do you suppose I called on?

ORESTES: Orestes—it's for him that you're tormented.

ELECTRA: And if that's true, what answer do my prayers find?

ORESTES: It's me. There's no one dearer you could look for.

ELECTRA: Stranger, is this a trick you twine around me?   220

ORESTES: Yes, if I ply the cord to trap myself!

ELECTRA: You find the horrors of my life amusing?

ORESTES: Well, if I do, I find my own the same.

ELECTRA: So can I speak to you as my Orestes?

ORESTES: You're slow to know me here before your eyes,
but when you saw the lock I cut in mourning,
and then when you observed my tracks, my footprints
you started like a bird—you thought you'd found me.
Hold the curl to the spot I cut it from:
your brother's hair, exactly matching yours!   230
Look at this cloth—you made it—and your loom
struck into place these pictured animals.
Keep yourself steady; don't go wild with joy:
I know the ruthlessness of our own family.

ELECTRA: You, dearest darling of our father's house,
my tearful hope of rescuing our line!

Confident, brave, you'll set the family upright.
Sweet presence, with four purposes for me:
I'm bound, first, to address you as my father.
Then, the affection that I owe my mother   240
falls to you—strictest justice makes me hate her.
You are the sister brutally cut down
and the faithful brother who has honored me.
If only Power and Justice take our part—
with one more, Zeus, the greatest of the gods.

ORESTES: Zeus, Zeus! Come witness what's been done to us.
Look at the father eagle's young, bereaved
after he died, caught in the wreathing writhing
of a hideous viper. Desolate, they're crushed
by famine, famished. Still unfledged, they can't   250
carry prey homeward, as their father did.
You have me here—and her as well, Electra—
before your eyes, a brood robbed of its father,
both of us banished, equally as homeless.
If you destroy the nestlings of a father
who gave you gifts and fervent worship, why
would someone like him honor you with feasting?
Destroy the eagle's offspring, and you'll never
again send mortals signs that they believe.
A royal branch you let dry out can't serve   260
your altars on the days for slaughtering oxen.
Save the house, lift it from the place it sprawls
to a great height—though we know how hard it fell.

CHORUS: Oh, children, saviors of your father's home,
quiet! Someone might hear you, little ones,
and bring your news, for the sheer joy of chatter,
to those in power—whom I long to see
dead, burning in the bubbly, oozing pitch.

ORESTES: Apollo's potent oracle will stay
faithful to its command to meet this danger.   270
A lingering, shrill shriek pronounced for me
curses that now lodge in my warm heart, naming
the cost, should I not chase the guilty down
and hand them back the death they gave my father.
He said my own dear life would make this good.

Otherwise, I would bellow with repulsive
suffering, and the forfeit of my goods—
then, the explicit tally of afflictions
appeasing hateful powers beneath the earth:
the fierce boils that assail, that gnash the skin,   280
the lichen growths devouring stem and root,
and the white down that blossoms on the damage.
He spoke of other raids the Furies make
in answer to the murder of a father,
<the shining glance that he directs through darkness>*
shadowy arrows from the powers below
when the fallen in a family plead for vengeance:
lunacy, terror in the night at nothing
prey on a man and hound him from the city,
his body mangled by a bronze-strung whip.   290
He may not share the drinking bowl or pour
glad offerings. Unseen, his father's rage
stands between him and altars like a wall.
No one can take him in or stay with him.
Friendless, held in contempt, in time he'll die,
pitifully shriveled, wasted from existence.
So shouldn't prophecies like these convince me?
If not, I still must undertake this one
relief of many needs that run together:
the god's commands, my great grief for my father,   300
besides the destitution hounding me;
that way, the people of the greatest city
on earth, who gloriously conquered Troy,
won't be two women's henchmen—the male's female
inside, or if he's not, he'll prove it soon.†

> *(During the ode that follows, Orestes and Electra pour libations
> on the tomb and address their words to it.)*

CHORUS: Powerful Fates, bring this to the end
    that Zeus has sanctioned!

---

* The line is difficult to understand in the context and may be an interpolation, or addition to the text, by someone other than the author. But a lacuna (see note to line 5) or other textual corruption may simply mean that the line is out of place.

† There is serious corruption here. I translate somewhat along the lines of Garvie's proposed emendation, which he expands in English as "I have called him a woman; whether or not I am right in doing so he will soon find out."

Come the way Justice's steps turn.
Justice the goddess shouts: "Let an evil word
pay for an evil word!"—and she   310
exacts the debt herself;
"For a bloody stroke let a bloody
stroke be the penalty! Let the wrongdoer suffer wrong!"
So goes the saying; again and again it has grown old among us.

strophe 1

ORESTES: Father, father of misery, what can I say,
what can I do to give you a good wind
for the voyage from that far place*
and the bed of death that is your home?
The light is counter to the darkness,
but all the same, a lament recalling glory   320
brings joy, they say, to the sons
of Atreus in their palace courtyard.

strophe 2

CHORUS: My child, the fire's greedy jaws†
don't tame a dead man's pride;
long afterward, his rage shows.
Wailing comes at his death—
but the light falls on the guilty, too.
The righteous groaning of fathers,
of parents, their uproar is the way   330
to the hiding-place of vengeance.

antistrophe 1

ELECTRA: So listen, Father! This is our rightful share
of tear-soaked mourning.
Over your grave the loud song of your loss
rises from your brace of children.
We are suppliants and refugees alike
at your tomb; it must take us in.
What trace of good is here outside it? What is only free from evil?
Is ruin not left wholly undefeated?
CHORUS: Even so, the god, if he wishes,   340
could make this a happier clamor:

---

* West retains a word that means "on the bent elbows" or "from above," which does not make sense to
me, so I have accepted the alternate manuscript reading.
† Cremation.

not dirges at a grave,
but the triumph song in the royal halls
ushering in the cherished cup of celebration.

strophe 3

ORESTES: If only, Father, under Ilium's walls
some Lycian warrior with a slashing spear
had made a quick, clean end of you.
Your fame would linger in your house;
all through our lives, the streets would turn
their gaze at us, your children.   350
A generous heap of earth would be your home
in that country across the sea,
and your house here could have endured it.

antistrophe 2

CHORUS: Others you loved, who had their own fine deaths at Troy,
would have looked, with love and awe and honor,
to their illustrious lord beneath the ground,
who marshaled the processions
of the greatest rulers in the Underworld—
yes, since as long as you lived, you were king,   360
and held in your hands the appointed, the doomed,
the dooming scepter other mortals must obey.*

antistrophe 3

ELECTRA: No, Father, not that—I wouldn't have
you dead beneath Troy's walls and buried
by Scamander's path of water
with the mass of men the spear took.
Instead, I wish your murderers
had been brought down so viciously
[…]† that their destiny in death
came to the ears of everyone, no matter how far off,   370
no matter that our sufferings had never touched him.

CHORUS: This is worth more than gold, child;
greater than great good fortune; better than earthly
paradise is what you speak of—since you can have it.
Two voices, like a double whip as it lands,

---

* These two lines are corrupt and the possibilities for emending them uncertain. I translate with some of the ambiguity or irony I see traces of.

† A lacuna (see note to line 5) not persuasively filled in by any of several conjectures.

have thudded through: under the earth they rally
to this side already, but the powers here—
how we loathe them—have defiled their hands.
The children are gaining ground!*

strophe 4

ORESTES: Your words have shot clear through   380
my hearing, like an arrow.
Zeus, Zeus, send up from below
the penalty that takes its time, send ruin
to mortals in their gall, their limitless
violence. Parents, come what may, will be paid out.

strophe 5

CHORUS: May my song of triumph
be a piercing shriek over the man
struck to the ground, and the woman
lying lifeless. Why should I hide this?
Though I might try, it hovers
out in front of my mind. And at my heart's prow   390
blasts this keen rage,
this malignant hatred.

antistrophe 4

ELECTRA: When will Zeus in his flourishing strength
move his hand against them
and cleave—oh—and cleave their skulls?
Let the land have a pledge of this!
I demand justice from the destroyers of justice!
Listen, Earth, and the powers below that we honor!

CHORUS: Yes, because this is the law, that the trickles of blood   400
let onto the ground demand more,
more blood. Havoc shouts for a Fury,†
who follows ruin with new ruin
once someone has fallen.

strophe 6

ORESTES: I cry to those who rule below, unchallenged!
You overpowering Curses of the fallen, look!

---

* These are a very corrupt couple of lines, and my translation is only one rough consensus about them.
† The Furies, or Erinyes, are female goddesses of the Underworld who avenge the murder of blood relatives. The killing of Clytemnestra will turn their attention to Orestes at the end of this play and in the next, the *Eumenides* (*Kindly Goddesses*), which takes its title from another name by which the Furies were known in the Greek world.

See what is left of Atreus' line: defenseless,
despised and robbed of its home!
Zeus, where can we turn?

antistrophe 5

CHORUS: I am shaken deep, to the heart,   410
to hear your pitiful wailing.
Now my hope fails;
darkness fills my body
as your words reach my ear—
but once again stout defiance
[…] overthrows the pangs;
its beauty comes before my eyes.*

antistrophe 6

ELECTRA: What can we tell of to hit the mark? The grief
we have suffered—at the hands of our own parent?
What if she tries to fawn on him? There is no charming the pain
    away.   420
Inconsolable, a raw-minded wolf
is the soul our mother gave him.

strophe 7

CHORUS: I pummeled out the beat of an Arian dirge, like a Kissian
woman with her wailing music.†
Picture my blood-spattered hands, clenched hard for pounding,
and my arms stretched high to fall in steep blows
running almost together—and the echoing thudding
as they land, the torture of my skull.

strophe 8

ELECTRA: Oh, you are monstrous,
Mother, endlessly reckless! Monstrous the burial   430
you gave him, a ruler without his people
to wail for him. Brazenly, you put
your husband in the ground unmourned.

strophe 9

ORESTES: No outrage, no outrage was missing in what you did,
but for degrading my father you will pay
at the hands of the spirits,

---

* Three seriously corrupt lines, not only left incomplete by the editor but containing two phrases marked with the symbol for "hopeless."

† Cf. the Kissian women's intense lamentation in *Persians* 121–22. The musical reference is uncertain in meaning.

at my own hands;
    then I can die, when I've cut the life from you.

antistrophe 9

CHORUS: His arms and legs, hacked off—you ought to know it—
    were buried hanging from his neck.* The one who did it   440
    was keen to make his death a weight
    your life would buckle under.
    Your father's shameful agony is yours to hear.

antistrophe 7

ELECTRA: You can say how my father died; I was shoved aside,
    despised, degraded,
    locked in a hole like a vicious dog.
    Was I laughing there, where I was stashed,
    or more inclined to wailing, to gushing rivers of tears?
        (addressing the grave)
    Listen to what I tell you [...];† write it in your mind!   450

antistrophe 8

CHORUS: Write it, and let your mind stand fast and calm
    as our story, like a spike, runs through your ears.
    All of these things are true,
    and more wait for your zealous grasp.
    You are bound to face this battle; face it with unbending rage.

strophe 10

ORESTES: Father, I call on you: stand with your own.
ELECTRA: My voice falls in with his—I'm choking on my tears.
CHORUS: All of our company seconds them in a single shout.
    Hear us and come to the light!
    Stand with us against our enemies!   460

antistrophe 10

ORESTES: War god will clash against war god, Justice against Justice.
ELECTRA: Gods, bring the ending we beg you for—it is a just one.
CHORUS: A tremor creeps over me as I hear their pleading.
    From long before, what is destined waits—
    let it come! We are praying for it!

strophe 11

    Suffering bred in this race!
    Hideous sound

---

* A special form of mutilation called *maschalismos*, evidently designed to prevent the spirit of the dead person from taking vengeance.

† The meter makes clear that there is a word missing, but it is impossible to be sure how to fill it in.

of ruin's bloody stroke!
Troubles no one could endure, heartsickness,
anguish we cannot lay to rest!   470

antistrophe II

The house must keep its wounds open;
the people inside it—not strangers,
not outsiders—must draw out the poisons and cure it
through this raw and bleeding rift.
It is the gods below the earth we call on, singing.

You, the blessed in the Underworld,
have mercy, send the aid we beg
for the children and their victory.

ORESTES: Father, you met your death as no king should!
Grant what I claim from you, to rule your household.   480

ELECTRA: Father, I beg for what I need as well:
to settle with Aegisthus, and escape [...]*

ORESTES: Do this to earn the ritual feasts that mortals
offer, or let earth's rich and redolent gifts
burn here while you sit by, unfed, unhonored.

ELECTRA: And I will bring libations for my wedding
from my restored inheritance, your house.
Your tomb will have the first rank in my worship.

ORESTES: Earth, send my father up to view this battle.

ELECTRA: Persephone,† give me triumph in its beauty.   490

ORESTES: Think of the bath where you were murdered, Father.

ELECTRA: Think of the strange new net that wrapped you there.

ORESTES: Woven, not forged, your snaring shackles, Father!

ELECTRA: The shameful plot that veiled and netted you!

ORESTES: The insult in our words won't wake you, Father?

ELECTRA: Won't you unbend the head we love so much?

ORESTES: Send Justice as our ally, since you love us,
or let them feel the headlock that you felt.
You're beaten—will you pay them back with victory?

ELECTRA: Now, Father, hear this final, straggling cry: 500
see how your nestlings huddle by your tomb,
the male, the female keening—pity both!

---

* This is just one possible way to deal with this apparently mutilated line.
† Queen of the Underworld and consort of Hades.

ORESTES: Don't cut the stock of Pelops from the earth:
    it is through us you live, though you are dead.
ELECTRA: Children are saviors, heralds of a man
    who's died. They're corks that lift the net and rescue
    the cord he wove from sinking to the bottom.
ORESTES: Listen! Our grief and grievance is for you.
    Honor our words, and you will save yourself.
CHORUS: So many words, but faultless: you have given   510
    this unlamented tomb its compensation.
    Now, since your plans are driving toward success,
    see them clear through and see what fortune brings you.
ORESTES: I will. But I can't be off track in asking
    why, on what rationale, she sent these offerings,
    her late redress for pain that can't be cured.
    For a dead man unaware of it, the favor
    is a petty one—I can't work out the meaning
    of the gift—which isn't worth the wrong she did.
    To pour out all you own to pay for one life   520
    is wasted effort, as the saying goes.
    But if you can explain, I want to hear.
CHORUS: I know it at first hand, my child. Her nightmares,
    that labyrinth of fears, have jolted her
    to send drink-offerings—the godless woman.
ORESTES: What was the dream? Can you precisely tell me?
CHORUS: She dreamed a snake was born from her—her own words.
ORESTES: With what result? How did the story end?
CHORUS: She nested it on blankets, like a baby.
ORESTES: What was the food the newborn monster craved?   530
CHORUS: She offered it her own breast, in the dream.
ORESTES: How could the hateful thing not wound a breast?
CHORUS: It sucked a clot of blood out with the milk.
ORESTES: That's not a vision granted for no reason!
CHORUS: She started from her sleep, shrieking in terror,
    and many lamps that had sat blind in darkness
    blazed in the palace for the lady's sake,
    and then she sent libations for the dead—
    she hopes this surgery will ease her pangs.
ORESTES: I pray to Earth, then, and my father's tomb   540
    to see this dream accomplished in my favor.

It fits without a single gap, I think.
Given the snake came out from where I came,
and then was wrapped, like me, in baby blankets,
and sucked, wide-mouthed, the breast that fed me, too,
and mixed a clot of blood with that kind milk,
and she howled out her horror as it happened,
then—since she fed that ghastly visitation—
she must die violently. I am a snake now
in killing her—that's what the dream relates.   550
CHORUS: I choose you as the signs' interpreter.
    Let them unfold! Now tell your various friends
    the rest: what some should do, what others shouldn't.
ORESTES: It's simple. First, Electra will go in—
    and I entrust her to conceal our pact,
    so those who lured an honorable man
    to his death will be lured into that same snare
    and die, as Loxias, our lord Apollo,
    promised—who never was a lying prophet.
    In all my traveling gear, I'll play a stranger   560
    arriving at the gates here with Pylades,
    this foreign guest and ally of the house.
    We'll both speak the Parnassus dialect—
    I'll mimic how the Phocian language sounds.
    Granted no cheerful welcome from the keepers
    of the gates into this house possessed by wrong,
    we'll wait, and someone passing by the palace
    will judge from our appearance there and speak:
    "A suppliant's at the gates. Why does Aegisthus—
    if he's at home to know this—lock him out?"   570
    And if that gets me past the courtyard threshold
    to find that person on my father's throne—
    or surely, if he comes back home, he'll summon
    me to his presence. Then, before he asks,
    "Where is the stranger from?" I'll make a corpse
    of him, a skewer of my quick bronze weapon,
    and the Fury, so well entertained with slaughter,
    will raise a toast—the third—of blood at full strength.
    (*to Electra*) You, now, keep your eyes open in the house,
    so all this comes together, piece by piece.   580

(*to the Chorus*) And I rely on you, too: think how much
silence can help, and careless words can hurt us.
(*indicating the tomb*) In what remains, I ask for him to guard me
and guide me in this contest of the sword.

      (*Orestes, Pylades, and Electra exit in the direction of the palace.*)

strophe 1

> CHORUS: The earth fosters many afflictions,
>   monstrous things, engines of terror;
>   and the arms of the sea are teeming
>   with creatures who are enemies
>   of humankind. High in the air, between
>   the armies of earth and heaven, flaming wraiths   590
>   prey on the winged and the striding races; we hear as well
>   of hurricanes' roaring anger.

antistrophe 1

>   But a man's reckless pride—
>   who can describe it?
>   Or women's scheming arrogance,
>   their passions at the pitch of recklessness—
>   a herd cropping itself full [...] of human folly?*
>   The loathsome love that is a female's power
>   perverts the yoked pair, the stable-mates—   600
>   beasts, and ourselves no less.

strophe 2

>   Who, with a mind on solid ground,
>   would deny the evidence of legend?
>   Of Thestius' wretched daughter†—plotting her own child's
>   destruction that was forecast—
>   incendiary woman, who turned
>   her son's blood-glowing log to ashes?
>   It was his same age, born with the howl he gave
>   in coming from his mother; its life's hours were his   610
>   till the day his destiny found its fulfillment.

antistrophe 2

>   We must revile the blood-stained

---

* My attempt to deal with a highly problematic pair of lines with a clear lacuna (see note to line 5).

† Althaea, the mother of the hero Meleager, murdered him, in her rage during a feud, by burning a magic log that controlled his life span.

girl in the stories, too,[*]
who for those she hated killed a man she loved. She was
    enticed—
the crafty bitch—by the Cretan gold-work
of the necklace, Minos' gift,
to do away with the lock that lent unending life
to Nisus in his deep   620
and unpremeditating breath of sleep,
where Hermes overtook him.

strophe 3

It is time, then, since I have cited these sufferings
nothing can soothe, to speak of the enemy marriage
defying the prayers of the house,
the woman's planning, the cunning in her mind,
against her husband in battle gear—
you made war on him, you marched against your husband!
I honor a house where the flame is low in the hearth,
and a woman whose only exploit is shrinking back.   630

antistrophe 3

But the crime of Lemnos[†] has first rank
in legend—the people bemoan it, spit on it,
measure each new disaster
by what the Lemnians suffered.
In a defilement the gods hate,
in human dishonor, the race is gone.
Nobody honors what the gods revile.
Which of these stories am I wrong to bring together?

strophe 4

Grazing the lungs, the sharp,
the piercing sword rams through—   640
for Justice trampled
in contempt of heaven's law;
for the trespass from all sides
on the majesty of Zeus.

---

[*] Scylla took a necklace as a bribe from King Minos of Crete to cut off her father's, Nisus', purple lock of hair, which gave him immortality. His kingdom of Megara was defeated and he was killed, and Scylla was turned into a sea monster as a punishment.

[†] Having murdered their husbands, who had been consorting with female captives, the women of Lemnos were afflicted with a disgusting smell.

antistrophe 4

> Justice is an anvil, planted steady,
> and Fate the swordsmith pounds out the bronze
> to be ready long before. A son follows
> into the house, to settle its debt at last for the defiling
> blood let over and over from ancient times—   650
> the deep-brooding Fury we know so well has brought him.

(Orestes knocks at the outer door, stands waiting impatiently,
then knocks again.)

ORESTES: Boy! Can't you hear me knocking at the gate?
Answer me! Who's inside? Who's in the house?
Someone come out—I'm calling one more time,
in case Aegisthus lets you welcome guests.
SLAVE: (*opening the gate*) Very good. And the stranger's home, his country?
ORESTES: Announce me to the people at the head
of this household; I have come to them with news—
and hurry, since night's chariot of shadows   660
is rushing on. It's time for travelers
to find their mooring in receptive houses.
Bring someone out who makes decisions here,
the mistress—but a man would be more fitting.
Embarrassment makes any conversation
with a woman quite constrained. One man's at ease
with another, clearly signaling his meaning.
CLYTEMNESTRA: (*appearing at the gate*) Strangers, if there is anything you
need,
tell me. We have what such a household should:
hot baths, and beds made up to heal exhaustion   670
like magic, and our honest faces near you.
But if there's something to consult and act on—
men's business—we will tell that to the men.
ORESTES: I am a Daulian, traveling from Phocis,
walking with my own knapsack on my back
to Argos—here my journey finds its rest.
I met a man I didn't know, who queried
my journey's purpose and made clear his own.
I learned his name was Strophius of Phocis.
"Stranger," he said, "you're on your way to Argos: 680

be sure—it's only right—to tell Orestes'
parents that he is dead—do not forget.
Convey his friends' decision back as well,
to bring him home for burial or make him
an alien and foreigner forever.
For now, the belly of a bronze urn hides
his ashes, and we've mourned as he deserved."
That's what I heard. I don't know whether chance
brings me to the authorities, who are
concerned with this; his father, though, should know it.   690

CLYTEMNESTRA: I cry our devastation in its fullness.
You Curse, our family writhes against your hold.
You watch so widely, and your dead aim finds
what's laid by—safe, out of your reach, we thought.
I'm piteously stripped of those I love.
Orestes now, so steady in his shrewdness,
who kept his feet out of destruction's mire,
[...]*
Give up—since it's betrayed us—hope of healing
afflictions that run riot in the house.

ORESTES: As for me, visiting a home so wealthy,   700
I'd rather the acquaintance and your welcome
resulted from good news—since who can feel
more warmly than a stranger toward his hosts?
I knew, though, that I'd go against the gods
unless I saw this through and told his family
since I had promised, and I was their guest.

CLYTEMNESTRA: Don't worry, you'll get all that you deserve,
and have as good a friendship with the household.
Someone else might have brought the news—no matter.
It's time for travelers, whose road was long   710
and took all day, to have the proper care.
(*to a servant*) Show him—and the attendant in his travels—
into our quarters set aside for male guests,
and make them comfortable, as suits our house.
I'll follow up my orders, to the letter.
(*to Orestes and Pylades*) Let me go share what you have said with those

---

* A lacuna of at least one line; see note to line 5.

who rule this house. A good supply of friends
will then confer with us about this trouble.
> CHORUS: So it goes, then, dear women who serve in the house!
> Tell me, when will we show our voices' strength   720
> to congratulate Orestes?
> Goddess Earth, Goddess of the looming
> barrow, you who stretch over
> the king's, the admiral's body,
> listen now, come to the rescue now.
> Now is the crisis: let cunning Persuasion come
> into the ring on his side, and let Hermes
> of Earth and of Night be the umpire
> of this bout that brings death by the sword.

The man, it seems, is crafting some misfortune.   730
But here's Orestes' nurse, sodden with tears.
Why are you going out the gate, Cilissa?
The grief you bring with you seems far from welcome.
CILISSA: Our ruler orders me to call Aegisthus
quickly: he must be here to learn the details,
face to face with the messenger, of news
that's just come. For the servants' benefit,
she wept through scowling eyes and hid a smirk
over events that turned out very well
for her—though for the house they're catastrophic: 740
that's where the foreigners' clear message leaves us.
For sure, he'll be delighted when he hears,
and learns the story. But for me, what anguish!
The ancient interlocking sufferings
in Atreus' house could hardly be endured.
The pain of them has pierced my heart, but never
before was there such agony to bear.
I shouldered all those evil things with patience,
but now Orestes, reared from birth by me,
my darling, into whom I poured my life,   750
stumbling from bed at his commanding shrieks
[…]*

---

* Ibid.

through many other quite unpleasant tasks
I toiled. A young thing's mindless, to be reared
like an animal, of course. The nurse must mind him.*
A child who's still in baby clothes can't say
he's hungry, thirsty, or he needs to go.
A law unto itself, the newborn's stomach!
My prophecies about it often proved
false enough, and I scoured baby linen,
on double duty as a nurse and laundress: 760
one woman with two skilled trades, I was given
Orestes, for his father's benefit.
But now I'm grieving, since I hear he's dead.
I'm going to the man who overthrew
this house, and he'll be keen to hear the story.
CHORUS: How did she tell him to approach the stranger?
CILISSA: What do you mean? Say more, and make it clearer.
CHORUS: Is he to go alone, or with attendants?
CILISSA: With bodyguards, his followers with their spears.
CHORUS: Don't give that message to our hated master.   770
      Tell him to hurry here alone—he won't
      be frightened, then. Tell him, with secret joy.
      A messenger can straighten crooked words.
CILISSA: What? Are you happy at the news today?
CHORUS: Zeus might at last turn back this storm of troubles.
CILISSA: How, since Orestes took this clan's hope with him?
CHORUS: Not yet. That's what a bungling seer would say.
CILISSA: What do you mean? Have you heard otherwise?
CHORUS: Go take the message, do as you were ordered.
      What the gods care about, they care about.   780
CILISSA: All right, I'm listening and on my way.
      May the gods grant that this is for the best.

strophe 1

      CHORUS: Now grant me the favor I beg, Zeus,
            father of the Olympian gods:
            let the house thrive in the appointed
            light of salvation—

---

* I've adopted Thomson's conjecture *trophou phreni* ("by the mind of the nurse"), commended by Garvie.

how we long to see it!*
Justice composed my whole litany—
Zeus, watch over Justice!

mesode 1

Set, oh, set the man down in the palace   790
in front of his enemies, Zeus. If you raise him to greatness,
doubly and triply and joyfully
he will repay you.

antistrophe 1

Mind that the son of a man you loved is bereaved,
he is yoked like a colt to disaster's
chariot—you, lay his course out,
keep him in bounds and steady
his pace, let us see him stretch his strides
over the ground clear to the finish.

strophe 2

You, the gods throned deep in the house,   800
where the inner shrine revels in its riches,
hear us and have compassion,
come […]†
Blood was let over and over,
from long ago—let your fresh verdict redeem it.
Murder, the old man in the house, has got enough children!

mesode 2

And you, the god whose home is that majestic hollow,‡
let the warrior's household lift its eyes.
May the glowing light of freedom
turn a kind face   810
on him, lifting her dim veil.

antistrophe 2

May Maia's son,§ too, rightfully
take the man's part—with this god comes a powerful
and following wind, that drives to fulfillment.
If he's willing, he uncovers much from blind places.
He has the look of—what we cannot see—

---

* The text is thought to be badly damaged. I credit Garvie for help in translation.
† A lacuna; see note to line 5.
‡ Apollo in his cave at Delphi.
§ Hermes.

he carries night's shadow, holds it before his face;
but the day brings no more evidence of him.

strophe 3

Then instantly we will send out
a glorious female song,   820
like a steady and prosperous
wind. Our cry will ring
to the heights: "Our city is safe!"
My profit, my profit in what has happened swells,
and ruin rebuffs my friends.

mesode 3

(*to Orestes*) And you, in hardiness, when action has its turn,
and she screeches, "My child!"—
shout, "It is my father who does this!"
and finish it—the reckless, blameless act.   830

antistrophe 3

Borrow the heart
of Perseus, [...]* keep it in you,
and exact what will please the ones you love
below earth and above it,
when, like a grisly Gorgon, you lay
bloody destruction on the ones indoors—
but you, look at your victim in his guilt.

AEGISTHUS: (*entering*) I didn't come unasked; a message brought me.
I've learned that certain foreigners were here
with news for which I hardly could be eager: 840
Orestes' death, since this would give the house—
which is already gouged and festering
from murder—one more horror-dripping wound.
Is this truth's living self? How will I tell?
Maybe it's only women's terrors, sparking
into the air, then dead and leaving nothing.
(*to the Chorus*) How can you give it clarity and sense?
CHORUS: We've heard it, but go in and ask the strangers
yourself. Listening to go-betweens is worthless
compared to asking questions face to face.   850

---

* A lacuna; see note to line 5.

AEGISTHUS: I'll go interrogate the man in person.
    Was he on hand there when the other died,
    or did he only hear a murky rumor?
    My reason isn't blind—no, he won't cheat me.
         (Exits.)
       CHORUS: Zeus, Zeus, what must I say, where must I start
         in praying, in calling on the gods for vengeance?
         How can my goodwill
         equal the need as I end my prayer?
         Now the murderous, blood-filthy
         blades and bludgeons are poised   860
         to destroy the house of Agamemnon,
         all of it, for all time.
         Or Orestes will kindle a glaring torch
         in freedom's cause, and rule a lawful city,
         with his father's great wealth back in his possession.
         In this match the young man the gods sent
         alone against two (with no one to step up in his place
         for a second round) will grapple—let him find the victory there!

AEGISTHUS: *(screams in agony)* ototototoi!
       CHORUS: What? What's that?   870
         What's happening? What does it mean for the house?
    Let's stand aside and see how it turns out:
    in this sad business we should show we're not
    to blame, since now the battle has a winner.

SLAVE: Horror on top of horror—it's the master
    cut down. I scream deep horror, on and on:
    Aegisthus—dead. But hurry, hurry, bring
    crowbars and pry apart the gates that lead
    to the women's quarters, someone young and strong!
    But not for him—he's finished—what's the use?   880
    (shouts repeatedly) They're deaf, they're sleeping while I call—it's futile,
    no good. Where's Clytemnestra? What's she doing?
    Her neck must now be on the butcher's block—
    justice will strike it, and her head will fall.

CLYTEMNESTRA: *(rushing onstage)* What's this alarm you're raising in the
    house?

SLAVE: The dead—the living—kill, I'm telling you.

CLYTEMNESTRA: Then pity me. I understand the riddle.
    We'll die the way we killed, by trickery.

Somebody, quick, give me a cutthroat ax.
Winners or losers, which are we? We'll see—   890
that's what I've come to now, in all these troubles.
ORESTES: *(entering with Pylades)* Good! You're the one I want. I'm done with
    him.
CLYTEMNESTRA: The champion I love, Aegisthus, dead!
ORESTES: You love the man? You'll lie, then, in a tomb
    with him. You'll never leave him, though he's dead.
CLYTEMNESTRA: Hold back, my child, my son: this breast demands it:
    often you dozed here, as you gummed my nipple
    and sucked from me the milk that nourished you.
ORESTES: *(to Pylades)* What should I do? Shrink back, or kill my mother?
PYLADES: Would you have Loxias' oracles at Pytho,   900
    and the oaths you swore sincerely, lose their force?
    Turn against all mankind, but not the gods.
ORESTES: I choose you, for your good advice, the winner.
    (to Clytemnestra) Come on, I want to slaughter you beside him.
    While he lived, you favored him above my father:
    now sleep with him in death, because you love
    this man, and hate the one you should have loved.
CLYTEMNESTRA: I brought you up—let me grow old with you.
ORESTES: You kill my father, and you'll live with me?
CLYTEMNESTRA: Fate shares the blame, my child, for what has
    happened.   910
ORESTES: Then Fate has made your bed now, which is death.
CLYTEMNESTRA: Child, you don't fear a parent cursing you?
ORESTES: No—you're my mother, but you threw me out.
CLYTEMNESTRA: —to an ally's home! That isn't throwing out.
ORESTES: You sold a free man's son, which is a crime.
CLYTEMNESTRA: You say so! Where's the price I got for you?
ORESTES: I'm too ashamed to taunt you with the words.
CLYTEMNESTRA: Your father played around—don't leave that out.
ORESTES: You sat at home: don't blame him in his hardships!
CLYTEMNESTRA: A wife kept from her husband grieves, my child.   920
ORESTES: A husband's hard work feeds the sheltered women.
CLYTEMNESTRA: My son, I think you're going to kill your mother.
ORESTES: No, your own hand will cut you down, not mine.
CLYTEMNESTRA: Watch out! A mother's raging demon-hounds*—

---

* The reference is to the Furies, often imagined as monstrous dogs.

ORESTES: And my father's, if I leave this thing undone?

CLYTEMNESTRA: You're like a grave that cannot hear my wailing.

ORESTES: My father's fate now gusts you to your ending.

CLYTEMNESTRA: My grief! I gave this viper birth and food.
   My nightmare really was a prophecy.

ORESTES: (*forcing her indoors*) Suffer in turn the wrong you did in
      killing.   930

CHORUS: Even for these two, I make my lament—
   but seeing poor Orestes reach the summit
   of murders, I would rather have it this way
   than for the house, its eyes put out, to fall.

strophe 1

      In time, Justice arrived for the sons of Priam,*
      with a heavy sentence.
      Into the house of Agamemnon came someone
      who was a lion twice over, a war god twice over.
      The exile, sent by the oracle at Pytho,
      raced to the finish line   940
      with the god's warnings to goad him.

mesode 1

      Shriek for the victory, for the escape
      of our masters' house from poverty and ruin
      under two criminal infections—
      a dirge of a destiny.

antistrophe 1

      Now an expert in the sneak attack has come,
      insidious Vengeance.
      And the true daughter of Zeus was there, guiding
      his hand in the fight. We mortals
      call on her by the name
      of Justice—   950
      and our arrow hits the mark.
      She breathes the rage of death on the enemy lines.

strophe 2

      Apollo, living in Parnassus,†
      in the hollow of the land,

---

* The royal family of Troy.

† Parnassus is a mountain near Delphi.

proclaimed no riddle when he called
Justice baffled and outraged.
Late, late is her onslaught—
but may sanctity prevail, and release me
from serving the wrongdoers.
Awe for those who rule heaven is our duty.   960

mesode 2

The light is here, you can see it. In the household
the spiked bit leaves our mouths.
Stand now, poor house. Long, too long
you lay groveling on the earth.

antistrophe 2

Soon now, Time, who finishes everything,
will leave by the courtyard gate,
once the rites for washing ruin away drive out
from the hearth whatever is defiled.
Luck will turn back to our gaze a lovely face,
a face altogether gentle   970
toward the sojourners in the house.*

*(Enter Orestes; the corpses are brought out and displayed, and a
robe stained with old, discolored blood is set next to them.)*

ORESTES: (*to the Chorus*) You see this country's double share of tyrants,
my father's killers, sackers of the house.
Haughtily, once, they sat here on their thrones.
They love each other even now: you see it
in what they suffered for their covenant,
bound by their oaths to murder my poor father
and die together: and the oaths have held.
(indicating the robe) Hearing this wretched story, you can also   980
see this device, which chained my helpless father,
like manacles, like shackles for his feet.
Spread it out, stand around it, show my father
what she put on her spouse. No, not my father,
but the Sun, who watches this whole world, should see
the shameless, godless workings of my mother
and be my witness, if I'm ever tried,
that it was right to seek the penalty

---

* An approximate translation of some corrupted lines.

of death for her. (Aegisthus' death is simply
the law, since he debauched somebody's wife.)   990
She plotted hatefully against her husband,
whose children grew beneath her belt—a dear weight
briefly, but one she came to loathe, that's clear.
What your view? Born a monster in the sea,
wouldn't she—lawless, reckless, insolent—
putrify victims with the slightest touch?
(*indicates robe*) And this—is there a decent term to give it?
A hunter's snare? A bathrobe tripping him
and turned into a shroud? No, wait, a net
for fish, for birds—a hobbling robe of state.   1000
This thing is the equipment of a bandit,
who lies in wait for travelers, whose living
is rifling money. With this crafty tool,
he'd murder on and on delightedly.
Before I have a housemate like this woman,
the gods can send me childless to my death.

CHORUS: (*keening*) The anguish of these doings!
　　With a hateful death, you come to the end.
　　But he is left, for pain in its full flower.

ORESTES: Was it her act or not? I call as witness   1010
　　this cloak, dyed scarlet by Aegisthus' sword.
　　The blood sprayed here has worked with time to ruin
　　the many dyes in the embroidery.
　　I'm here at last to eulogize and mourn
　　with words aimed at the cloth that killed my father.
　　All that's been done and suffered, all my bloodline
　　grieves me, in my defiled, unenvied victory.

CHORUS: No one of humankind can spend
　　his life unharmed, and in perfect honor.
　　(*keening*) One trouble's here, another's coming.   1020

ORESTES: You need to know—since I can't see the ending—
　　I'm like a charioteer who's left the track
　　far to the side. My mind runs wild and drags me—
　　I've lost the fight. The terror in my heart
　　is poised to sing and dance to fury's music.
　　While I'm still sane, though, I affirm to friends
　　in public that I justly killed my mother—

filth the gods hate, assassin of my father.
The chief authority who braced and nerved me
is Pytho's prophet Loxias,* who declared   1030
that I could do this blamelessly, but if
I shirked—it's not a punishment to speak of:
arrows of words can't reach the agony.
But witness now the bough and wreath that arm me
to be a suppliant at Loxias' shrine,†
at the world's midpoint, where the flame they call
undying lights his sacred ground. I'm exiled
for shedding blood I share and can't take refuge
at any hearth but his—so he commands.
I charge the Argives all to vouch for me,   1040
from now on, in accounting for these troubles.‡

CHORUS: No, you did right. Don't let such noxious words
escape your mouth; don't take yourself to task.
You gave the Argives back their city's freedom
by deftly cutting off two serpents' heads.

ORESTES: (*shrieks*) Here they are! Hideous women!§ They're like
    Gorgons,
black-robed, with teeming, twining snakes instead
of hair—no, I can't stay here any longer.   1050

CHORUS: What's in your mind—so loyal to your father—
to trouble you? Be brave, stand fast, great victor!

ORESTES: This torment is no vision. Hunting dogs—
roused by my mother's rage—I can't mistake them!

CHORUS: You think so, with the fresh blood on your hands;
no wonder that this fit attacks your senses.

ORESTES: Look, there are even more now, Lord Apollo!
The blood of hatred oozes from their eyes.

CHORUS: A single thing can cleanse you: Loxias'¶ hand
laid on to liberate you from this torture.   1060

---

* Apollo at Delphi.

† Orestes carries the ritual bough and wreath used when supplicating a god.

‡ The line transmitted as 1041, which mentions Menelaus, seems hopelessly corrupt, and I opt for Blomfield's simplified emendation.

§ I reluctantly accept Lobel's conjecture for a word meaning "hideous," though the actual word is not attested. The beings appearing to Orestes are the Furies, or Erinyes.

¶ Apollo at Delphi.

ORESTES: You tell me you can't see them—*I* can see!
　　They drive me like a horse, and I can't stay.
　　　　　(Rushes off.)
CHORUS: Then take our blessing. May the god, in kindness,
　　watch over you and protect you, come what may.
　　　　　Now the clan's third storm has breathed
　　　　　its blasts on the royal halls,
　　　　　now it has ended.
　　　　　First was the food—the children—
　　　　　a pitiful affliction;
　　　　　second, the violence against the king, the husband,　　　　1070
　　　　　in the bath the rending, the death of the Achaeans'
　　　　　strong leader in war;
　　　　　third now, a rescuer—or should I speak of a fatality?—
　　　　　has come—from somewhere.
　　　　　Where at last will this fierce havoc find something
　　　　　to lull it to sleep, to end it?

INTRODUCTION TO AESCHYLUS' *EUMENIDES*

The title of the third play in the *Oresteia* trilogy, *Eumenides*, means Kindly Ones and refers to the Chorus of ancient female deities that dominate the drama. These goddesses, however, are not called Eumenides anywhere in the play, and for most of its length they are anything but kindly. Their more familiar Greek name is Erinyes, sometimes translated (via Latin) to Furies, and their costumes, in Aeschylus' original production, attested to their power to harm: hair in the form of snakes, funereal black robes, and ugly, angry masks. Among the audience that beheld them that day, according to one ancient source, men fainted and women miscarried (though it's unclear whether in fact women attended the Athenian tragic festival). The title *Eumenides*—not one that Aeschylus himself gave the play, but something imposed on it later—anticipates the transformation these hags will undergo before the play's end.

The Erinyes were given different origins in different mythic accounts, but they were always considered primeval beings, linked to the earth—the place where the dead are buried, but also the source of growth and fertility—and the Underworld. They oversaw obligations of various kinds, oaths in particular, and had the power to torment those who broke them. Any mortal who had incurred blood-guilt by killing a family member—thus shattering the most essential social obligation—became their prey. Thus in the *Libation Bearers*, the play that precedes this one, Orestes, having just emerged from the palace where he slew his mother, Clytemnestra, thinks he sees the Erinyes pursuing him and runs in terror off the stage. That flight began an arduous exile, perhaps months long by the time the *Eumenides* begins, during which Orestes, always pursued by the Erinyes, sought purification—the ritual cleansing of his blood-guilt—at shrines throughout Greece, and finally at the most sacred shrine of all, the temple of Apollo at Delphi.

Delphi has a complicated history, as the priestess of Apollo, the Pythia, describes in her opening speech. The goddess Earth once used it as her prophetic seat, and after Earth, her daughter Themis; then her sister Phoebe took over the shrine and gave it to Apollo as a birthday present. The happy tale of peaceful transfer contrasts markedly with a myth found elsewhere in which Apollo seized the site by force, using his bow and arrows to kill a dragon who dwelled there. Both versions construct Delphi as a token of cosmic rule, passing from Earth and her offspring to the Olympians, who stand for enlightened governance and lawful power. But by putting a new, harmonious spin on the story, Aeschylus prefigures the surprising twists of his tragedy, by which he will arrive at an ending that, tonally, is anything but "tragic" in modern terms.

The opening scene at Delphi takes us into a drama dominated by gods and primal forces. Thus far in the *Oresteia*, the will of the gods has been the subject of confused debate, or has been relayed by intermediaries; Pylades, for instance, reminds Orestes, at the critical moment in the *Libation Bearers* when he shrinks from killing his mother, that Apollo's oracles have commanded him to do so. Now Apollo appears in person to uphold that command and stand by Orestes' side; ranged against him are the Erinyes, visible to all, and the ghost of Clytemnestra, practically an Erinys herself in her demand for blood vengeance. Soon Athena, too, will take her place onstage, as the scene shifts, after line 234, to the city of Athens (a unique break, among surviving plays, in unity of time and place). Orestes' personal crisis has become a battleground on which immense supernatural forces are ranged.

The killing of Clytemnestra has brought two generations of gods into a direct clash. Apollo claims to represent the will of Zeus, his father, who decreed that Clytemnestra should die as the just penalty for her murder of Agamemnon. The Erinyes align themselves with an older order—Earth and the primal forces linked to her—that pays no heed to such abstractions as divine justice. They refer contemptuously to the Olympians as "younger gods" and invoke the ancient principle that "blood will have blood"—the slaying of kin must be punished by death. Theirs is a clan-based view of the world, in which crimes against *homaimous*, those who share your bloodlines, must be deterred by the severest punishment or chaos will ensue. Apollo will try to counter them by claiming, as we shall see in a moment, that Orestes and Clytemnestra were not *homaimoi*, so the rule does not apply.

Athena, appointed to adjudicate the cosmic showdown, feels the task is too daunting, and too dangerous, for her alone. She might have called on other gods for help, but instead she empanels a board of Athenian citizens, nameless, mute characters who file onto the stage at around line 570. This is the first time any such jury has been convened, and Athena proclaims it to be a template for the future: we are witnessing the foundation of the jury trial system, with its faith in the power of ordinary mortals to determine facts and distinguish right from wrong. Significantly, Aeschylus situates this event at Athens, and he gives credit for it to that city's patron goddess. Athens, by 458 B.C., had gone further than any other Greek city toward radical (for its time) democratic government, in part by creating a vast jury system employing thousands of citizens. Athenians who watched this play in the Theater of Dionysus beheld, among other things, an elevation to mythic dimensions of their own political evolution.

That evolution, however, had not been easily achieved and was not universally supported. Many in Athens disliked diffusion of power, especially the aristocratic families who had traditionally held it. Just before this play was produced, the city had gone through a turbulent series of constitutional changes, greatly strengthening the hand of the people but angering the nobles. The governing body dominated by the latter, named the Areopagus for the "Hill of Ares" on which it met, had been stripped of much of its role so that larger, more representative bodies could expand theirs. The changes were so controversial that Ephialtes, a democratic leader who spearheaded them, had been assassinated by reactionary foes. But one important function was kept in the hands of the Areopagites: the right to try cases of deliberate homicide.

This of course is exactly the privilege that Athena accords to the nameless jurors of the *Eumenides*, who are sometimes identified by scholars not just as any trial jury but as the court of the Areopagus in mythic guise. The play thus cannot be read as a simple, univocal endorsement of democratic reforms at Athens; the old order, too, gets its share of the glory. It's also crucial to note that the new jury system, though clearly celebrated by the playwright as a triumph of social progress, is not seen operating smoothly or autonomously. The jurors reach an impasse when their votes are tied, and the goddess Athena leads the way out of the dilemma by breaking the tie (or, in some interpretations, by casting the tying vote, which under her own trial rules secures an acquittal).

Was the decision a fair one? Aeschylus does not make it easy to answer yes. The Erinyes score major debate points by equating Orestes' murder of his mother with Clytemnestra's killing of her husband. Apollo's rebuttal is one that many of Aeschylus' contemporaries would have found specious (as do all modern readers): the mother is not *homaimos*, blood-related, to her child, since she only supplies the vessel in which the father's seed can grow. Though some Greek thinkers did endorse this theory, it was hardly a consensus view, and Apollo's deployment of it here can only be seen as a legalistic maneuver. Likewise, Athena's autobiographical reason for voting to acquit Orestes—"There is no mother who gave birth to me. / With all my heart, I hold with what is male" (lines 736–37)—smacks of favoritism and bias rather than, as we would hope for from a modern judge, universal principles.

The Olympians are allowed to win the case, but not to lay claim to the moral high ground. The Erinyes are, understandably, enraged, and they threaten to use their ancient power to make barren the soil of Athens and the wombs of

Athenian women. Athena, for her part, hints that she can call down the thunderbolt of Zeus, the ultimate weapon of destruction, should she choose to do so (lines 826–29). The threat of an all-out war, and a return to cosmic chaos, is very real. But then Aeschylus' play takes a surprising turn. Persuasion—*peitho* in Greek—rather than the thunderbolt is invoked to soothe the outraged Erinyes; new honors are offered up to replace, and more, those they have lost. Their war dance turns into a ballet of joy. Torchbearers arrive with animals for a sacrificial feast. Suddenly the whole city has turned out for a festal procession and a celebration of the Eumenides—the Kindly Ones, fulfilling their titular role at last.

How did it happen so quickly? The sudden transformation seems almost miraculous. But, Aeschylus might say, all compacts and compromises partake of the miraculous, in a city whose political passions might at any moment erupt into civil war. Those passions had been at fever pitch just before this play was put on, but they had begun to cool; disaster had been averted. The city's relief can be felt throughout the final scene, in which curses are turned to blessings and hatred to love.

The Oresteia

Eumenides

Translated by Sarah Ruden

Throughout the translation, I have used the Greek edition of Alan H. Sommerstein, *Aeschylus Eumenides* (Cambridge: Cambridge Greek and Latin Classics, 1989.) Wherever I have disagreed on his reconstruction or interpretation of the text, I have indicated the variance in a footnote.

Cast of Characters (in order of appearance)

The Pythia, head priestess of Apollo's oracular shrine at Delphi

Orestes, son of Agamemnon and Clytemnestra, murdered rulers of Argos

Apollo

Ghost of Clytemnestra

Chorus of Furies (Erinyes), also known as Eumenides (Kindly Ones)

Athena

A group of Athenian jurymen

Escort, a procession of women bearing torches and offerings

Setting: Early morning, at Delphi, in front of the entrance to the oracular shrine of Apollo.

PYTHIA: Earth I address, the primal seer, giving
  her precedence; then Themis,* the successor
  to her mother in the seat of prophecy—
  tradition says. The third who got this place—
  willingly, by no violent overthrow†—
  was also Earth's child and a female Titan,
  Phoebe.‡ And as a birthday gift, she gave it
  to Phoebus,§ adding that name to his others.
  He left the lake and rocky spine of Delos¶
  and sailed the busy route to Pallas' shrine   10
  and reached Parnassus,** which would be his homeland.
  Hephaestus' sons, the artisans of roads,††
  honored his journey here by rendering
  untempered country tame beneath their hands.
  He came to find great honor from the people,
  and the ruler Delphus at the region's helm.
  Zeus sent this art to seize the young god's mind
  and placed him on the throne as its fourth prophet,
  as Loxias, who speaks for Zeus, his father.‡‡

---

* A deity who personifies the idea of divine law or moral sanction. Themis was one of the six children of Earth and Sky (Gaea and Uranus).

† Aeschylus stresses that the shrine of Delphi changed hands peacefully, in contrast to other sources that portray Apollo seizing it violently from a monstrous serpent, Pytho.

‡ Phoebe, a goddess sometimes identified with the moon, belonged to the first generation of gods, the Titans. Aeschylus alone associates her with the early history of Delphi.

§ Apollo, an Olympian god, Phoebe's grandson.

¶ The small Aegean island said to be Apollo's birthplace.

** A sacred mountain in north central Greece.

†† The Athenians (who traced their descent from a mythical king Erichthonius, one of Hephaestus' off-spring) are referred to here. Athens was connected to Delphi by an important road, said to have been the route Apollo first used to reach the shrine.

‡‡ That is, Zeus, the king of the gods gave his son Apollo the gift of prophecy. Loxias is Apollo's name in his capacity as prophet.

These gods are in the prelude of my prayers. 20
Pallas Before the Temple* has her tribute
now, too. The nymphs of the Corycian grotto—
the birds' delight, the gods' resort[†]—I honor.
Bromius[‡] lives here also, as I'm mindful,
ever since he led phalanxes of Bacchants
and twined death around Pentheus, like a hare.[§]
Pleistus' source[¶] and Poseidon's power I call on,
and Zeus Fulfiller, highest of the gods;
and now I take the seat of prophecy.
May they all grant, as I go in, the very 30
best fortune yet. And let the Greeks who're here
come in turn and draw numbers;[**] it's the custom.
However god commands, I prophesy.

> *(She exits into the temple, leaving the stage momentarily empty.*
> *Then she returns, on all fours, in distress.)*

A horror on my tongue and in my eyes!
It threw me backward, out of Loxias' house—
no sinew's left in me—I can't stand upright—
my *hands* run—hardly agile: an old woman
is useless in a panic, like an infant.
I came into the wreath-hung shrine, and there
a man was seated on the navel stone[††] 40
in godless filth, a suppliant for cleansing:
hands dripping blood, sword pulled from some fresh wound.
He held an olive branch, grown straight and high,
wreathed with a mass of wool, the proper way—
a silvery fleece, as I can best describe it.[‡‡]
In front of this man was a shocking band

---

* Athena. Her title at Delphi probably indicated the position of her temple at the approach to Apollo's larger one.

† A sacred place near the summit of Mount Parnassus.

‡ The Noisy One, a title of Dionysus the wine god.

§ As punishment for rejecting the new god Dionysus, Pentheus, a king of Thebes, was torn to pieces by Bacchants, the god's ecstatic worshippers.

¶ Pleistus is a river near Delphi.

** That is, draw lots to determine the order in which visitors could consult the oracle.

†† A stone situated in the center of the oracular shrine was said to represent the midpoint of all lands on earth, literally "the navel."

‡‡ The suppliant's ritual objects.

of women, sleeping upright on their chairs—
not women, though: I want to call them Gorgons*—
but no, and they're not like the creatures, either,
I saw once in a painting as they robbed   50
Phineus of his supper.† These were wingless—
and black, and absolutely nauseating.
Out of their mouths repellent snores were blasting,
and from their eyes disgusting matter streamed.
It isn't right to bring in clothes like theirs
to the gods' images or human homes.
I never saw the tribe this cohort came from;
no land I know could boast of nurturing
this breed without a deep groan for its trouble.
I leave what follows this to Loxias   60
himself, the potent master of this house;
Seer and healer, he can read the omens
in others' homes and be the purifier.

> (*The Pythia runs offstage. The temple door opens to reveal
> Apollo, Orestes, and the sleeping Furies, monstrous creatures
> dressed in black with snakelike hair. Orestes clings to the navel
> stone at the center.*)

ORESTES: Ruler Apollo, you know how to act   85
righteously. Add attention to this skill!
Your power soundly pledges what I need.   87

APOLLO: I won't betray you. Till the end, I'll stand   64
guard over you, close by or from a distance—
I'm no soft rind your enemies can bite through.
You see these lunatics now, in a trap,
tripped into sleep—girls ripe for spitting on,
decrepit husks of children, whom no god
or man or animal would ever touch.   70
For evil's sake they came to be: their portion
is evil darkness, Tartarus underground,
which men and the Olympian gods both loathe.
Run and don't weaken, even though they're sleeping.
They're going to stride across paths wanderers

---

* Female monsters with snakes for hair.

† Phineus, the king of Thrace, was tormented by the Harpies ("Snatchers"), hideous winged women who stole his food.

wear down, they'll drive you over sprawling mainland
and sea, and through the cities skimmed by water.
Don't tire too soon; be like a careful shepherd
of this labor. When you come to Pallas' city,
sit and embrace the ancient wooden image.[*]   80
With judges of this matter there, with speeches
that work like spells, we'll find the right devices
to free you wholly from these trials—since I
urged you to kill the body you had come from.   84
Watch out, or fear will win, outwitting you.   88
But brother, and my father's other true son,
Hermes, take charge of him, escort him, prove   90
your epithet's the right one;[†] guard this lamb,
my suppliant—Zeus *has* regard for exiles—
your lucky guidance speeds back to the world.

> (*The ghost of Clytemnestra rises up as if from below the ground
> and speaks to the Furies.*)

GHOST OF CLYTEMNESTRA: Sleep on, then ... No! What good are you
    asleep?
Look at me! Thanks to you, I'm stripped of honor
among the dead, since there the noise of blame
for killings that I carried out won't cease.
Look at my abject wandering, and listen:
this is a fearful charge they lay against me.
My closest kindred made me suffer all this,   100
but no god takes my part with his resentment,
though I was slaughtered by my own son's hands.[‡]
Look, with your mind's eye, at the wounds he gave me.
<The sleeping mind has eyes, it's bright and sharp;
mortals by day can't see their fate ahead.>[§]
Often you licked my gifts up—never wine,
but the appeasements of sobriety.
I offered solemn banquets by the hearth's flame
at night, a time no god can share with you.
But now I see you trampling all of this!   110

---

[*] Referring to a prominent statue of Athena housed on the Acropolis.

[†] "Guide" or "escort."

[‡] The murder of one family member by another, in Greek religious thought, was a violation of natural order and therefore fell to the Furies for punishment.

[§] Very likely, these two lines are interpolated (added by a hand later than the author's).

He's gone, a hunted fawn slipped from the nets
strung high around him—no, he *gamboled* out,
jumped free, but turned to make a face at you.
You've heard, and for my soul's sheer sake I spoke.
Take it to heart, goddesses from below.
This vision, Clytemnestra, calls on you!

CHORUS: (*whimpers*)

GHOST OF CLYTEMNESTRA: Whine away, but the man's run off, he's
    vanished.
    [Suppliants don't lack friends, though I have none.]*

CHORUS: (*whimpers*)   120

GHOST OF CLYTEMNESTRA: Plenty of dozing, but for me no pity!
    His mother's murderer, Orestes, gone!

CHORUS: (*groans*)

GHOST OF CLYTEMNESTRA: You groan, you doze. Wake up, and wake up
    now!
    What work, what skill was granted you but evil?

CHORUS: (*groans*)

GHOST OF CLYTEMNESTRA: Fatigue and sleep have powerfully conspired
    to drain the ghastly serpent of his spirit.
        CHORUS: (*giving two sharp yelps*) Catch him, catch him, catch him, catch
        him! Look there!   130

GHOST OF CLYTEMNESTRA: You dream you're on the creature's trail.
    You're baying
    like a dog. The urge for slaughter never leaves you.
    What's this? Don't slack, don't soften, don't surrender
    to weary mindlessness of what I suffer.
    I'm right to taunt you. Let it stab your entrails.
    Send your breath after him, a storm of gore!
    Blast, shrivel him with fire from your womb!
    Wither him as you hound him once again!

CHORUS LEADER: Wake up, and now that you're awake, wake her!   140
    Sleep's got you still? Kick it aside, get up!
    Does our dream open to the truth? We'll see!

        (The Chorus arise and begin an agitated dance. In the first
        strophe, after the first line, the song is passed from one member to
        another.)

---

* The line is corrupt and controversial, and my translation is speculative and tentative.

strophe 1

    Chorus: (*together*) No! No! The outrage! The suffering for us, my
        darlings!
    (*severally*)—The torment, and nothing to show for it!
    —The anguish, the agony fallen on us, I shriek it, it's
        affliction I can't endure.
    —The beast has leaped over our nets, he is gone.
    —Sleep pulled me down—I lost my quarry.

antistrophe 1

    (*together*) I storm at you, Zeus's son—you're a bandit,
    a boy who's ridden us down—though we're gray-haired
        goddesses—   150
    you've honored the suppliant, the godless man,
    his parents' enemy.
    You—a god!—stole him away, when he'd struck his mother dead.
    What justice could anyone name in this?

strophe 2

    The taunts let loose in my dreams!
    The charioteer got a firm grip
    on the goad and thrust it
    into my heart, my liver.
    The appointed torturer steps up, with his scourge   160
    inflicting the pain beyond pain, the searing chill.

antistrophe 2

    This is the work of the young gods*
    in their power that overflows justice.
    We can see the holy throne
    dripping blood from its feet to its headrest,
    and the navel of this round earth† now endowed
    with a bristling pelt of blood-defilement.

strophe 3

    What a prophet,‡ to smear his own hearth, his own shrine
    with this filth! He brought it on, invited it,   170

---

* Throughout the play the Furies taunt the Olympians as "younger gods." The origin of the Furies was explained in two different ways by the Greeks, but both versions make them much older than the Olympians. Either they were children of the primordial deity Nyx (Night), or they emerged from the drops of blood that were scattered when Cronus castrated his father, Uranus.

† See note to line 40.

‡ Referring to Apollo, god of prophecy.

when he granted human privilege that divine law
forbids. He destroyed our portion,* born with the world!

antistrophe 3

He flies in my face—but he won't untangle this man,
even below the ground there will be no refuge, no freedom for him.
He begs to be rid of his defilement, but as far as he goes he will find
no one but his own murderer to take it on.

APOLLO: (*addressing the Furies*) *Get out!* Do what I tell you! Leave this
    house,
now! It's a prophet's shrine—remove yourselves,   180
unless you'd like a glistening, winged snake
sped out of my gold bowstring into you.
The pain would bring up cannibal black froth—
you'd spew back gobs of blood sucked from your killings.
It's a disgrace that you come near my temple;
here we don't have beheadings, gouged-out eyes
from guilty verdicts, massacres, uprooting
of manhood as it sprouts in boys, hacked limbs,
stoning, and pitiful loud moans from those
impaled beneath their spines. Can't you believe   190
how much the gods abhor the celebrations
you're so attached to?—as your bodies show
in every feature. You should share a cave
with a blood-guzzling lion, and not wipe
your dirt on others at this oracle.
You strays, you feral goats, move off! No god
has any fondness for a herd like yours.
CHORUS: Give us our turn and listen, Lord Apollo!
It isn't only that you share his guilt:
you took on all of it, from the beginning.   200
APOLLO: What? Draw your speech out, make me understand.
CHORUS: The stranger killed his mother, at your word.
APOLLO: Certainly, since I said, "Avenge your father."
CHORUS: You promised refuge, though he dripped with blood?
APOLLO: Commanding his atonement in my house.
CHORUS: But we're his escorts here! How can you taunt us?

---

* See note to line 102.

APOLLO: You're not the visitors this house deserves.

CHORUS: You're wrong; this is the charge that we were given.

APOLLO: What's this high office? What's this great distinction?

CHORUS: We drive from home whoever kills his mother.   210

APOLLO: And if a wife disposes of her husband?

CHORUS: She doesn't raise her hand to draw shared blood.

APOLLO: Then you degrade—annihilate—the bonds
of Hera the Fulfiller,* and of Zeus.
What you urge throws the Cyprian,† who brings
the dearest mortal gifts, into the dirt.
A husband and wife's bed, their destiny
that Justice guards, is stronger than an oath,
now that one's killed the other‡ and you looked
away from anger and revenge, I tell you   220
you've wronged Orestes, whom you made an outcast.
You seem to me to take his crime to heart,
yet clearly in *her* case you're not so troubled.
At the trial, the goddess Pallas will preside.

CHORUS: I'm never going to leave this man in peace.

APOLLO: Then after him! Keep up your useless struggle.

CHORUS: Don't speak with such contempt about my birthright.

APOLLO: Birthright? I wouldn't take it as a gift.

CHORUS: You stand on high by Zeus's throne, we hear.
But then there's me. A mother's blood trail guides me   230
on this man's heels to punishment, to justice.

APOLLO: I'll help the suppliant and rescue him.
For mortals and gods, too, a suppliant's anger
is ghastly, if he's willingly betrayed.

> *(Apollo, Orestes, and the Chorus exit, leaving the stage and orchestra empty. The scene shifts to the city of Athens, many months later.§ Onstage is a wooden statue of Athena. Orestes enters and addresses this image as he puts his arms around it.)*

---

* The wife of Zeus in her capacity to bless marriages.

† Aphrodite, the goddess of sexual love.

‡ Referring to Clytemnestra's murder of Agamemnon. Since such a murder does not involve the violation of blood ties, the Furies took no role in punishing it.

§ This shift of scene, with a corresponding gap in the time frame, is very unusual for Greek drama, and there's no evidence as to how it was accomplished. The new setting would have been signaled to the audience by the presence onstage of a cult statue of Athena, an imitation of the famous one on the Acropolis, and by the reference at lines 239–41 to Orestes' long wanderings after leaving Delphi.

ORESTES: Athena in your majesty, I come here
at Loxias'* command. Look gently on me,
outcast but clean now, as I prayed to be.
My guilt is blunt, its edge has worn away
on houses where I stayed, on peopled roads.
I crossed dry land, the sea as well, to follow   240
what Loxias' oracle ordained for me.
Now as your guest I hold your image, goddess,
safe in this place, and wait for my trial's end.
        (The Chorus of Furies enter, as though tracking Orestes.)
CHORUS: Good! Here is it. The man has left clear traces!
Follow the mute informer's evidence.
Like dogs that run behind a wounded hare,
we sniff his dribbled blood, we're going to find him.
I pant clear from my belly; men would flag
from the effort. We have flocked to every place
on earth, and winglessly soared over water   250
pursuing him, no slower than a ship.
And now he's here—here somewhere—cowering.
The scent of mortal blood is smiling at me!
        (They break into a short song.)
    Look, and keep looking!
    Search everywhere, keep the matricide
    from making off, from slipping away scot free.
    There he is! He's found sanctuary, wrapping
    himself around the immortal goddess's image.
    He wants his day in court for his murderous doings—   260
    not for him! A mother's pitiful blood
    is hard to draw up from the earth again.
    It runs down into the ground at your feet, it is gone.
    You must atone: from your living body
    let me slobber up the red gruel offering. From you
    I will plunder my fodder, drink what makes mortals gag.
    Why would I kill you? I'll make you a husk and drag you
    below for your retribution, the woeful price of your mother's death.
    And there you'll see them, other impious mortals
    who have outraged a god, or a stranger,   270

---

* See note for line 19.

or their own parents—
and each kind of torment will settle in full with Justice.
Hades, who chastises humankind, is mighty
below the earth.
His mind surveys the world; what he sees he writes in his mind.

ORESTES: Through hardship's tutelage, I sense what's right
at various times—especially when to open
my mouth or not. But here in this proceeding
a shrewd instructor ordered me to speak.
The blood is weak, unconscious on my hand,   280
the matricidal stain washed off, expelled
while still fresh, at the hearth of holy Phoebus
by pigs who died in purifying rites.*
How long I'd take, reciting the full tally
of those my company has left unharmed!†
[Time cleanses all things, growing old beside them.]‡
It is a guiltless mouth that reverently
calls on Athena, ruler of this country:
"Come to my aid and win, without a spear-thrust,
myself, the people, and the land of Argos   290
as true, unfailing allies for all time."
On Libyan terrain, perhaps, her birthplace
near Triton's banks beside the pouring channel,§
she's fighting forward or repels an onslaught
to help her friends; or eyes the plain of Phlegra¶
like a bold man, commander of the ranks.
No matter—from far off, a god can hear.
Let her arrive to be my rescuer!

CHORUS: There's no release, not even with Apollo's
or strong Athena's help. They'll shrug, and you   300
will fall beyond a trace or hint of joy,

---

* Greek priests performed ritual purification by slitting the throat of a young pig above the head of a suppliant.

† Orestes' point is that he must now be ritually cleansed of his crime, or else his presence would have brought harm to those who have taken him in.

‡ The line is probably not genuine but inserted later, an interpolation.

§ Athena was thought to have been "born" (that is, released from Zeus' head) near a river or lake called Triton, in Libya (the Greek term for North Africa).

¶ In the Chalcidice, in northern Greece, reputedly the site of the battle between the Olympian gods and the giants, in which Athena took part.

where spirits feed on you, a bloodless shadow.
You have no answer? You spit back my words—
you, fattened, consecrated as my victim?
A living feast, no slaughter at the altar!
So listen to this song, and it will bind you.

> *(They begin to dance, in an attempt to enchant Orestes and make him powerless.)*

> Come and join hands in the dance.
> We have decided to flaunt
> our talent—though you loathe it.
> We'll tell you how our troupe deals   310
> mankind its destinies.
> We're sure of our integrity;
> no rage of ours will stalk
> anyone holding out clean hands.
> Unharmed, he will pass through his life.
> But if anyone sins, like this man,
> and tugs a cloak close to hide his bloody fingers, then we
> are the upright witnesses for the dead,
> we second them, we exact what is owed their blood.
> There is no appeal from us, as we confront him.   320

strophe 1

> Mother who brought me to the world,
> Mother Night, as vengeance
> for those in the daylight,
> and those it was taken from! Listen to me!
> Leto's son* has outraged me,
> wrenching away my cowering
> prey, the sanctioned
> sacrifice to pay for his mother's murder.

ephymnium 1

> Here, over our sacrifice,
> our music sounds. There is madness,
> frenzy, the mind is broken   330
> by the Furies' hymn. This tune
> that will never ring from the joyful lyre

---

* Apollo.

chains up the senses,
turns mortals into dry stalks.

antistrophe 1

I was allotted this, it is mine forever,
spun out for me by Fate with her piercing spindle:
when someone in the race of mortals happens,
Stupidly, to kill one of his own,
with his own hand, I become
his—companion—until he goes
beneath the earth. And even in death
my grip is on him, tight enough.   340

ephymnium 1

Here, over our sacrifice,
our music sounds. There is madness,
frenzy, the mind is broken
by the Furies' hymn. This tune
that will never ring from the joyful lyre
chains up the senses,
turns mortals into dry stalks.

strophe 2

This was our allotment, decreed when we were born.
But we must hold our hand back from immortals, and no one   350
sits at a feast in company with us both;
and pure white robes are not my fated portion.*
[...]†

ephymnium 2

I have, you see, elected
to uproot households. When Ares‡
is brought up in the house and strikes his own down,
his agent, yes, we make after.
Strong he may be, but we put him
in darkness, while the blood he shed is fresh.

antistrophe 2

I am at eager pains not to share this trouble!   360
I am careful to exempt the gods—they do not even have

---

* The Greeks wore white robes at joyous or celebratory events.
† A lacuna, or gap, in the surviving manuscript text.
‡ The god of war, here standing for violence generally.

an inquiry to attend.*
Hatred alone stoops to our blood-dripping race, and Zeus
never saw fit to speak to us.

strophe 3

All of men's greatness, all that is grandiose beneath the sky's heights,
shrivels beneath the earth, shrinks away unregarded
under our black-robed inroads and the dancing   370
of our malignant feet.

ephymnium 3

With a great force I leap,
I soar down with a great weight.
I strike with the point of my foot.
They run at full stretch but I trip them:
Ruin unbearable brings them down.

antistrophe 3

The man falls, but he does not know it—his wits are maimed,
and a huge, a filthy darkness hovers above him.
And a voice tells, with loud groans, of the murky mist
above his house.   380

strophe 4

What must be is set in the ground. We are contrivers.
We bring our work to its end,
unforgetting, fearsome,
inexorable to mortals.
What is appointed for us has no honor
but a place apart from the gods, in sunless mire.
We lay a rocky path for those who see the daylight
and the blinded dead alike.

antistrophe 1

Who among mortals lacks
awe, lacks terror at all this,   390
hearing me speak of the law laid down
by destiny—and its fulfillment that the gods concede?
The ancient prerogative is mine,
and I meet no insults in it,
though I stand at my post underground
in sunless murk.

---

* The text and interpretation of these three lines are in vast dispute.

(The goddess Athena enters, dressed in armor and carrying her
aegis, a magically powerful goatskin shield.)

ATHENA: Far off, at the Scamander's banks, I caught
   your summoning clamor, while I took possession
   of land that the Achaeans' marshaling chieftains
   granted to me, an ample share of plunder   400
   in victory, as my freehold for all time—
   the choicest gift for Theseus' descendants.*
   From there, I raced my own untiring feet;
   the aegis flapped against my wingless body.†
   Seeing this troop the land has never seen,
   I'm not afraid, but wonder fills my eyes.
   Who are you? That's one question for you all
   to share: the stranger crouching by my image,
   and you—since nothing like you springs from nature.   410
   You are no goddesses the gods have seen,
   yet don't resemble mortals in your *forms*.
   But hateful words addressed to harmlessness
   are far from just, and Righteousness disdains them.

CHORUS: No lengthy speech is needed, Zeus' daughter.
   We are Night's children, and we live forever.
   At home beneath the earth, they call us Curses.

ATHENA: I know your clan, its titles, and their meanings.

CHORUS: Now you must learn about my post of honor.

ATHENA: I'll try; a clear account of it would help me.   420

CHORUS: We're charged with driving murderers from home.

ATHENA: Where is the endpoint of the killer's exile?

CHORUS: A place beyond experience of joy.

ATHENA: That's where he's being routed by your shrieking?

CHORUS: He took it on himself to kill his mother.

ATHENA: Through sheer necessity—or fear of someone?

CHORUS: What goad is sharp enough to drive this crime?

ATHENA: There are two parties here—but half a case.

---

* Theseus was a mythical early king of Athens, so his "descendants" are the Athenian people. The idea that the goddess Athena had secured for the Athenians sovereignty over a region near the river Scamander—that is, near Troy, in Asia Minor—seems to refer to political events close to the time of the *Oresteia*'s original production. Athens had been expanding its imperial reach into Asia Minor during the first half of the fifth century and had taken control of Sigeum, a city near the site of Troy, only a few years before this play was written.

† A line that follows this one has been excised, since it seems to have been added by a later hand.

CHORUS: (*pointing to Apollo*) *He* won't accept our oath or give his own.

ATHENA: You want the justice that's a mere display.　　　430

CHORUS: What's that? Explain! Your mind has power enough.

ATHENA: I mean that oaths can't make the wrong cause win.

CHORUS: Then question him and give an honest verdict.

ATHENA: You trust the outcome of this trial to me?

CHORUS: Naturally, with the full respect I owe you.

ATHENA: (*to Orestes*) Stranger, how will you answer in your turn,
　　naming your clan and country, telling us
　　your story, and then making your defense?
　　If you rely on justice as you sit
　　clutching this wooden image by my hearth,　　　440
　　a sacred suppliant, like Ixion,*
　　respond and let me understand all this.

ORESTES: Sovereign Athena, first I will remove
　　the last—and critical—concern you speak of:
　　I'm not a suppliant, I haven't sat here
　　beside your image with my hands defiled.
　　The evidence I give must carry weight:
　　ritual law will keep a felon speechless
　　until a purifier spatters him
　　with a suckling's blood to drive away the blood guilt.†　　　450
　　Long ago, strangers cleansed me in their houses
　　with slaughtered animals and running water:
　　so take my word for this and ease your mind.
　　Now I'll inform you briefly where I come from:
　　it's Argos; naturally, you know my father,
　　the marshal of the war fleet, Agamemnon.
　　Alongside you, he rendered Ilium
　　a town no longer, but died shamefully
　　when he came home: my mother, with her black heart,
　　struck him down cunningly. Embroidered snares‡　　　460
　　affirmed that he was murdered in his bath.
　　And I returned, after a time of exile,

---

* The mythic hero Ixion murdered his father-in-law and then became a suppliant, appealing to Zeus for mercy. He was purified by Zeus and freed of guilt, but later he attempted to rape Hera and was condemned to eternal torment in the underworld.

† See note to line 283.

‡ The robe with which Clytemnestra immobilized her husband before killing him.

and killed—I did—the woman I was born from,
striking back for the sake of my dear father.
Loxias also is accountable:
he warned of piercing, killing agony
should I not act against the guilty parties.
You must decide the case. Did I do right?
I won't dispute the fate your words assign me.

ATHENA: This is a weightier matter than a mortal   470
could hope to judge, but even I'm not sanctioned
to give a verdict on enraging murder.
Besides this, you are tamed now, as a pure
and harmless suppliant come to my house.

        (indicates the Furies)

But *their* prerogative should not be slighted.
If they don't find themselves victorious,
their rancor's venom will infect the ground
it falls on with a never-ending ruin.
So, a dilemma! Would it bring less anger   480
and trouble if I let you stay or not?*
But since the controversy falls to me,
I'll select men beyond reproach, to honor
their oaths as they preside at trials for murder,
and what I institute will last forever.†

        (to Orestes and the Chorus)

Now both, bring in the evidence to prove
your cases, props to hold them safely upright.
I'll go and choose the best men in my city,
and bring them to decide this matter justly,
keeping within their oaths, in strictest conscience.

        (Athena exits.)

strophe 1

    CHORUS: Now the ordained ways   490
        are overthrown
        if this matricide's menacing

---

* A hopelessly corrupt line, but a meaning in this direction is likely.

† Athena has in effect invented the system of trial by jury, an institution very much in use in Athens in Aeschylus' day. See introduction for further discussion.

plea wins out—
an event that will bind all mortals
together, give them all dexterous free hands:
no mere nightmare, the wounds after wounds awaiting
parents, the children's weapons sinking in
relentlessly in the future.

antistrophe 1

Not even from us, the raving
sentinels over humankind, will anger   500
find its way to felons like this man:
I will let every species of death off its leash.*
People will turn to each other, telling
of their neighbors' disaster and asking how
their troubles could find some ending, some remission.
And some poor fool will mouth
useless, flimsy prescriptions.

strophe 2

No use then, for anyone
battered by calamity
to shout an appeal   510
of "Justice!
You Furies on your thrones!"
But with these words, maybe, some father or
some birthgiver with a fresh wound
will lament the fate of lamenting
when the house of Justice falls.

antistrophe 2

There is a fitting place for terror:
the overseer of the mind
must sit there constantly.
It is good to gain   520
discretion from distress.
What man, what city
on earth, without fear
to train the heart,† would honor
Justice as in the past?

---

* That is, the Furies will refuse to punish murderers in the future if Orestes is let go.

† A hopelessly corrupt pair of lines, translated with the help of Sommerstein's comments.

strophe 3

> Neither a lawless life
> nor an oppressed one merits
> your praise.* Everything in the midway prevails, as god grants—
> but he sends one life here, one there, under his watch.   530
> To fasten onto this saying, I shape another:
> outrage is blasphemy's child, in a true bloodline.
> But with a wholesome
> mind you prosper in that dear way
> all mankind prays for.

antistrophe 3

> In everything, I tell you,
> revere the altar of Justice.
> Don't give it a godless kick   540
> into the dust, at a glimpse of profit,
> as a penalty must follow.
> The ending waits that is ordained.
> Let a man mind this, above all honoring his parents, as is right,
> and welcoming strangers
> to the freehold of his hospitality
> with constant reverence.

strophe 4

> This conduct, unaided by force, will keep him just,   550
> and prospering in good measure.
> The utmost ruin will never take him.
> I say the arrogant, mutinous criminal—
> with his freight, the cluttered plunder
> he got by violence—will lower his sail
> in time, trouble will seize him
> beneath his shattered yardarm.

antistrophe 4

> He calls, but no one hears a sound. Caught in the center
> of a whirlpool, he cannot wrestle free.
> The god laughs at hotheadedness, seeing the man—   560
> who bragged it was impossible—helpless in these straits,
> exhausted as he fights, as he fails to reach the wave's crest.
> He has wrecked prosperity, lifelong until this moment,

---

* The "you" here is generic.

on the submerged rock, which belongs to Justice,
and is destroyed, yes, every trace of him—and no one weeps.

*(While Apollo, Orestes, and the Chorus remain onstage, the scene
shifts slightly; we are still in Athens, but now on the Areopagus
or "Hill of Ares." A bench is now onstage and a table with two
urns upon it, to be used for casting ballots. Athena enters
accompanied by eleven jurymen, who take their seats upon the
bench.)*

ATHENA: *(to a herald)* Make your announcement, call this group to order,
let the Tyrrhenian trumpet stab the heavens,
once human breath has filled it, and display
its voice at full pitch for this body coming
to crowd the courtroom and deliberate.   *570*
To learn my laws in silence is a fitting
observance for all time, for the whole city
and these men: that is how just judgment happens.
Now, lord Apollo, take in hand what's yours.
What is your interest in this matter? Tell us!
APOLLO: I am a witness; it was I who cleansed
this man of blood-pollution when he sat,
a lawful suppliant, beside my hearth.
And I'm his advocate: the matricide
is my responsibility. *(to Athena)* Present   *580*
the case, and be a skillful arbitrator.
ATHENA: *(to Apollo)* Yes, I'll present the case, *(to Chorus)* but *you* must speak
first, as the prosecution, and set out
accurately what happened, from the start.
CHORUS: We're no small group, but we can be succinct.
(to Orestes) Counter our words by answering in turn.
First, tell us, did you strike your mother down?
ORESTES: I killed her. There's no way I could deny it.
CHORUS: I've pinned you once—twice more, and I'm the winner.*
ORESTES: You're bragging, but I'm not yet on the ground.   *590*
CHORUS: We'll see. *(indicates jury)* You need to tell them how you killed her.
ORESTES: I will. I drew my sword and cut her throat.
CHORUS: But who persuaded you? Who planned the crime?

---

* Invoking the rules of a Greek wrestling match.

ORESTES: (*indicating Apollo*) His holy words did that—and he's my witness.
CHORUS: The prophet guided you to matricide?
ORESTES: Yes, and I never faulted what occurred.
CHORUS: Once in the verdict's grip, you won't say that.
ORESTES: I trust him—and the help the grave will send me.
CHORUS: Yes, trust a corpse, good—though you killed your mother.
ORESTES: I did, because her hands were soiled twice over.   600
CHORUS: What do you mean? Explain it to the judges!
ORESTES: She butchered both her husband and my father.
CHORUS: So? You're alive, she's murdered—that absolves her.
ORESTES: Why didn't you hound *her*, while *she* was living?
CHORUS: Because she didn't kill a blood-relation!
ORESTES: But do I share my mother's blood myself?
CHORUS: How else could you have grown beneath her belt,
    you monster? You disown your mother's own blood?
ORESTES: Now you, Apollo, testify and tell me
    what the law dictates: Was I right to kill her?   610
    Those are the facts—I don't deny I did it.
    But give your reasoned judgment of this bloodshed
    as just or not, and I'll inform the men here.
APOLLO: (*to jurymen*) To you, Athena's lofty institution,
    I pronounce this act just. I am a prophet
    of truth, who never from my seer's throne
    spoke of a man, a woman, or a city
    except as Zeus, the Olympians' father, ordered.
    I ask you all to understand this plea's force,
    and fall in with my father's plan, since over   620
    the will of Zeus your oath cannot prevail.
CHORUS: You say Zeus sent this oracle, which told
    Orestes to avenge his father's murder
    with no regard whatever for his mother?
APOLLO: Yes—it is different when a nobleman,
    who's honored with the scepter Zeus bestows,
    dies, and a woman kills him—not the rushing
    arrows a far-off Amazon might launch,
    but an event you, Pallas, and those sitting
    with you will hear about and vote to judge.   630
    Back from his expedition (for the most part
    a profitable venture), sweetly welcomed

[...]*
He underwent a bath, but at the end
she wrapped her husband in a cloak, a tent,
a shroud, an endless hobbling maze, and struck him.
This sets the man's death out for you. The marshal
of the ships was a sublime, majestic man.
[...]†
I end a speech that's meant to sting the people,
stationed here to decide the case, to rage.

CHORUS: Zeus privileges a father's fate, you tell us.   640
But Zeus chained up his own old father, Cronus.‡
What can this do but fight with what you say?
(*to the jurymen*) I call on you to hear this evidence.

APOLLO: Monsters! Loathed by the world, despised by gods!
Zeus could take off those chains, since there are cures
for bonds, expedients of every kind.
But once a man is dead, and dust has guzzled
his blood, he's never going to rise again.
For this, there are no healing spells my father
devised; other conditions he can turn   650
back and forth effortlessly, at his will.

CHORUS: Look how you plead for him to be acquitted!
He soaked the ground with blood he shared, and now
he'll live in Argos, in his father's house?
Which of the public altars can he stand at?
What phratry will admit him to its rites?§

APOLLO: I'll say still more—you'll see how sensibly.
The person called the mother's not the parent.
She only nourishes the embryo
planted by mounting her, and for a stranger   660
she keeps the shoot alive—if no god blights it.¶
And I can prove my claim: without a mother

---

* A single line is missing from our manuscripts.

† A longer gap in the text, perhaps several lines.

‡ After overthrowing Cronus by force, Zeus had him, and his siblings, bound in chains in Tartarus.

§ A *phratry*, or brotherhood, was an association based on clan relationship.

¶ This theory of reproduction, which (in modern terms) would mean that all the child's genetic inheritance comes from the father, was advanced by certain radical thinkers in fifth-century Athens but was not widely held.

there can be fatherhood. For this we have
proof here (*points to Athena*), the offspring of Olympian Zeus,
not nurtured in the darkness of the womb.*
No goddess could give birth to such a child.
Athena, I will use all my skill to make
your city and its people great. This man
is part of that; I sent him to your hearth,
which will ensure eternal faithfulness,   690
securing both himself and his descendants
to fight beside you, goddess, for all time.†
These judges' sons will not regret the pact.

ATHENA: Shall I now order them to cast their votes
as they think right? Is what they've heard enough?

APOLLO: Yes, we've shot every arrow in the quiver.
I'll wait to hear their judgment of the case.

ATHENA: (*to the Chorus*) How to proceed, then—blamelessly, in your
eyes?

CHORUS: What we have heard, we've heard, so cast your ballots,
strangers—but keep your sacred oaths in mind!   680

ATHENA: People of Athens, hear what I decree
as you decide in this first trial for bloodshed.
Into the future, too, Aegeus' cohort‡
will never lack this council and tribunal
at Ares' Crag,§ the Amazons' encampment
when they had marched here on campaign, in rancor
at Theseus.¶ They built a stronghold facing
our own:** the two high towers went head to head.
They sacrificed to Ares—hence the name
the rocky hill is known by. Reverent fear,   690
inborn in people of the town, will keep them

---

* According to mythic traditions, Athena was born from the head of Zeus, not from a mother's womb.

† Orestes will have the status of "hero," a city's immortal protector even after death. Recent events stand behind this claim that Orestes will "fight beside" Athens forever: the Athenians had, not long before this play was produced, become military allies of Argos, the city to which Orestes belonged.

‡ Aegeus was a mythical early king of Athens.

§ The Areopagus (Hill of Ares), the place where a high council of the Athenian state met and where murder trials were held.

¶ The legendary campaign of the Amazons, a nation of warrior women from Asia Minor, against Athens was vengeance for Hercules' and Theseus' theft of the Amazon queen Hippolyta's girdle.

** The Athenian stronghold during the Amazon invasion was the Acropolis.

from all wrongdoing here, in light or darkness—
if citizens themselves don't change the laws.
Once you've run noxious mire into the spring,
then what you find to drink will never glitter.
I urge this polity: esteem and guard
what's neither lawlessness nor tyranny.
And leave some fear: don't banish all of it.
What man on earth can be both just and fearless?
So if the thought of justice terrifies you,   700
you'll have salvation for your land and city.
There's no such fortress elsewhere for mankind—
no, not in Scythia or Pelops' country.*
Greed won't lay dirty fingers on this council
that I ordain: it's upright, quick to anger,
a wakeful sentry in a sleeping country.
I've taken time admonishing the people
of my town about the future. You must rise now
and cast your ballots to decide the case,
keeping your oaths. My speech is at an end.   710

> *(During the next exchanges, jurors come forward one by one and*
> *place their ballots in one of the two urns at center stage, one a*
> *receptacle for votes to convict, the other for those to acquit.)*

CHORUS: I urge you to give visitors like us—
a hazard to your land—no kind of slight.
APOLLO: I tell you, hold my oracles—and Zeus's—
in proper awe, and let them bear their fruit.
CHORUS: *You* have no right to be concerned with bloodshed.
The shrine you live and speak in will be sullied.
APOLLO: That means my father erred when he approved
Ixion's plea and cleansed mankind's first murder.†
CHORUS: You say so! If the verdict disappoints me,
from now on I'll deal harshly with this land.   720
APOLLO: All the same, both the young and older gods
have no regard for you, and I will win.

---

* Two places that were on opposing extremes from Athens, both geographically and culturally. The Scythians to the north were considered quintessential "barbarians," tribal and nomadic; the Peloponnese to the south were associated with the authoritarian Spartans, who dominated that peninsula.
† See note to line 441.

CHORUS: You overstepped in Pheres' house, persuading
　　the Fates to stop the wilt of mortal lives.*

APOLLO: Is kindness not a just return for reverence
　　always, but most of all when it's most needed?

CHORUS: You did away with primal dispensations,
　　gulling the ancient goddesses with wine.

APOLLO: Soon, when the verdict fails you, you'll spew venom
　　that gives your enemies no pain at all.　　　　　　　　　　　　730

CHORUS: A high young horse, to ride your elders down with!
　　Waiting to hear the verdict, I suspend
　　the anger I might level at the city.

　　　　　(The last juror has cast his ballot, and Athena now comes
　　　　　forward to do so.)

ATHENA: The final judgment lies in my hands now:
　　I mean to give it in Orestes' favor.
　　There is no mother who gave birth to me.
　　With all my heart, I hold with what is male—
　　except through marriage. I am all my father's,
　　no partisan of any woman killed
　　for murdering her husband, her home's watchman.　　　　　740
　　Even with equal votes, Orestes wins.
　　Whichever judges were assigned this task,
　　empty the urns as quickly as you can.

　　　　　(Two jurymen come forward and move toward the urns. During
　　　　　the next eight lines, they empty the contents of the urns onto the
　　　　　table in two rows, so that their numbers are visible to those
　　　　　onstage.)

ORESTES: Phoebus Apollo, what will be the verdict?

CHORUS: Black mother, Night, do you look on, this moment?

ORESTES: I'll die now by the noose, or live in daylight.

CHORUS: We'll go to ruin, or go on in honor.

APOLLO: The votes are poured out. Strangers, count them right,
　　in awe of justice as you do the sorting.
　　Without good sense, great damage can be done;　　　　　750
　　a whole house can stand upright on one pebble!†

---

* "Pheres' house" is the palace of King Admetus, in Thessaly. While Apollo was staying there incognito, the day of Admetus' death arrived, but Apollo, who had grown fond of his host, tricked the Fates (by getting them drunk; see p. 445) into allowing another to die in his place. Alcestis, Admetus' wife, agreed to die in her husband's stead (with consequences that form the plot of Euripides' *Alcestis*, in this volume).

† Pebbles were used as ballots in many kinds of Greek voting.

ATHENA: This man's acquitted from the charge of bloodshed.
  The ballots have been reckoned up as equal.*
ORESTES: You, Pallas, are the savior of my house,
  settling me in the fatherland they stole.
  The Greeks will say, "This man's once more an Argive
  and living on his father's property,
  and this he owes to Pallas, Loxias,
  and the all-fulfilling Savior we invoke
  with the third cup."† He faced my mother's patrons,   760
  taking my father's death to heart, and saved me.
  And now as I depart for home, I swear
  to this country and the people living in it:
  for all of time, into an endless future,
  no chieftain from my land will ever bring
  an army, with its deadly gear, against you;‡
  when I am in my grave, I will make certain
  that anyone who violates my oath
  will find frustration in that enterprise.
  I'll place him on dispiriting roads, ill-omened   770
  passages, so that he regrets his trouble.
  But if what's right prevails and Pallas' city
  always finds honor in the allied spear,
  I'll look more kindly on my citizens.§
  (*to Athena*) Farewell to you, then, and the city's people!
  May your opponents feel the iron headlock
  that brings you victory in war and saves you.

> (*He exits. The Furies, who have been silent since the counting of
> the votes, begin to chant in angry rhythms that recall their first
> song. Athena, more restrained, responds to them in iambic
> trimeters.*)

strophe 1

  CHORUS: Younger gods, tearing ancient laws
    from my hands, riding them down and trampling them!
    I am miserable, so miserable in this land's contempt   780
    and my deep rage.

---

* Under Athenian law, a tie vote went in favor of the defendant.

† Zeus. He was invoked with libations at a fixed point during a banquet.

‡ The recent Athenian treaty of alliance with Argos is once more being referenced by Aeschylus (see line 672 and note).

§ The extant text of this line makes little sense; I translate what was probably the general sense.

Poison, the poison of revenge for grief,
I will let loose from my heart,
I will drip the excruciating
liquid on this land.
No leaf, no child will survive my blight—oh, Justice, Justice,
skim over the ground,
hurl your miasmas, your massacres through the country.
What can I do but groan?
They laugh at me. The town's tribunal
wounded me unendurably.   790
Pity us, Night's stricken daughters,
stripped of our honor.

ATHENA: Don't groan so heavily—let me persuade you.
You're not defeated, since the verdict was
truly divided, which is no disgrace.
The evidence of Zeus was merely plain;
the oracle's own source has testified
about the act: Orestes is absolved.
I ask you not to bring your heavy rancor,   800
your rage, down on this land and spoil its harvests,
dripping infections from another world
that froth up, running wild, devouring seeds.
I make a promise unreservedly
to settle you in hollows of this just land.
You'll sit on glistening thrones beside those hearths,
receiving homage from these citizens.

antistrophe 1

CHORUS: Younger gods, tearing ancient laws
from my hands, riding them down and trampling them!
I am miserable, so miserable in this land's contempt   810
and my deep rage.
Poison, the poison of revenge for grief
I will let loose from my heart,
I will drip the excruciating
liquid on this land.
No leaf, no child will survive my blight—oh, Justice, Justice,
skim over the ground,
hurl your miasmas, your massacres through the country.
What can I do but groan?
They laugh at me. The town's tribunal

wounded me unendurably.   820
Pity us, Night's stricken daughters,
stripped of our honor.

ATHENA: You have your honor—and you're gods; don't rage
beyond all bounds and cripple human land.
I place my trust in Zeus. Why must I mention
that I, alone among the gods, know where
the key is to the storeroom for the lightning
under his seal? But there's no need for that!
Listen, relent, and don't rain senseless words   830
on the land to rob its yield of all success.
Lull the dark breaking wave of bitter passion,
and be my neighbor, held in awe and honor.
This land, in all its wealth, will always grant you
the choicest gifts for marriages' fulfillment
in children—making you commend my words.

strophe 2

CHORUS: For me to endure this!
   (moans)
For me, with my ancient wisdom, to live beneath this land,
disgraced, defiled!
   (moans)
Absolute is my rage, my fury.   840
   (a prolonged moan, rising in pitch)
What is this agony, creeping into my body?—
Oh, Mother Night!
The gods, who win every match, have wrenched me away
from my venerable post. I am nothing now.

ATHENA: I bear with your bad temper, since you're older,
and—owing to your age—much shrewder, too.
But it's no worthless mind Zeus gave me, either.   850
Once in a strange tribe's land, you're going to pine
for this one: this I solemnly affirm.
Time will move forward on the path of honor
for this land's citizens. Your settled home
beside Erechtheus' house will be revered.*
You'll get more from processing men and women

---

* The Erechtheum was a hero's shrine on the Acropolis, dedicated to a mythical Athenian king, Erechtheus.

than other mortals ever could provide.
But don't afflict my country, raining on it
whetstones for bloodshed, to incite young men.
Their furor ought to come from wine alone!   860
These are no fighting cocks—don't make their hearts seethe;
don't plant a civil war among my townsmen
that turns their courage back against each other.
Let there be foreign wars, though, plenty of them,*
for anyone who grimly lusts for glory—
but not a rooster feuding in his yard.
These things are in my gift, for you to choose:
kindness returned, great honor, and a share
of a country that the gods love best of all.

antistrophe 2

CHORUS: For me to endure this!
    (moans)   870
For me, with my ancient wisdom, to live beneath this country,
disgraced, defiled!
    (moans)
Absolute is my rage, my fury.
    (a prolonged moan, rising in pitch)
What is this agony, creeping into my body?—
Oh, Mother Night!
The gods, who win every match, have wrenched me away
from my venerable post. I am nothing now.   880

ATHENA: But I won't flag in telling you good news:
You'll never say that I, a younger god,
and men who hold this town affronted you,
alienated, drove you from this land.
If you accept Persuasion's holy power,
the soothing, the enchantments of my tongue,
you ought to stay. If you choose otherwise,
it is not right to bring down rage or rancor
on the city, or to persecute its people:
You might be a proprietor, with full rights   890
and every kind of honor in this land.

CHORUS: Sovereign Athena—what's the home I'll have?

---

* A rather shocking prayer to modern ears. Athenian militarism was at a peak at the time the *Oresteia* was written, a time when Athens' empire was at its greatest extent and conflict with Sparta was beginning.

ATHENA: A home that's safe from all distress. Accept it!
CHORUS: Grant that I do—what honor waits for me?
ATHENA: No household here could thrive apart from you.
CHORUS: You'd do this, making me so powerful?
ATHENA: I'll lead your worshippers to every good thing.
CHORUS: You give your pledge to me, for all of time?
ATHENA: I'm free to make no promise I won't keep.
CHORUS: You may well charm me out of my resentment.   900
ATHENA: Good—then the land will grant you loving friends.
CHORUS: What blessings must I sing it, on your orders?
ATHENA: Nothing to do with victory for evil!

From earth and limpid waters of the sea,
from the sky blessings come, from puffs of wind—
those sun-warmed breathings that draw near this country.
Rich yields will come from animals and furrows
for the citizens, unfailing as time passes,
so human seed will find its safety, too.
But prove yourself more fertile for the pious;   910
I cherish, like a man who tends a garden,
the righteous breed and will not let it grieve.
All this belongs to you; and I won't spare
the city honor in the splendid contests
of war, in victory all mankind can see.

> *(The meter changes as the Furies, now the Eumenides or "Kindly*
> *Ones," begin to dance in joy rather than anger. Athena breaks*
> *out of her iambic trimeter and into half-sung marching*
> *anapests.)*

strophe 1

CHORUS: I'll accept a lodging with Pallas,
and not turn my back on a city
that all-powerful Zeus, that Ares
keeps as a garrison of the gods,
protector of Greece's altars,   920
and the delight of heaven.
This is the city I pray for
with tender prophecies:
may blessings rush on, may they help its life on
as they teem from the earth
beneath the sun's lighthearted brightness.

ATHENA: All this I do in kindness
for these citizens. Great, haughty, and exacting
are the deities I settle in this place.
They are allotted the right to dispose of   930
everything touching mortals.
Stumble into their anger,
and something you can't see will jar your life's course,
since the sins in your blood, from your ancestors, drag you
before this female tribunal, and doom comes silently,
loud as he might boast:
their spiteful fury pulls him down to the dust.

antistrophe 1

CHORUS: May hurt, may destruction for the trees never blow—
this will be a gift from me.
May no scorching flames, robbers of buds,   940
pass over this land's boundaries.
May no ghastly sickness creep in
and ruin the harvests.
May Pan raise flocks whose twinning
at the appointed season
shows how they thrive. May the people's descendants
always find wealth in the soil, and repay
its troves with gifts to the gods.

ATHENA: (*to the jurymen*) You, the city's bulwark, do you hear
what this will bring to pass?
A Fury is queenly, she has great power   950
among the immortals and the dead beneath the earth.
And for mankind they do their will
with plain finality: some, at the goddesses' hands,
will sing with joy; others will spend
their lives in the blindness of tears.

strophe 2

CHORUS: Even so, I forbid anything to happen
that brings men down before their time.
And you goddesses, the Fates, our sisters from a single mother,
in your domain,* keep charming girls   960

---

* Lines 963–64 are extremely difficult, and probably corrupt; my translation represents a probable general meaning.

from going husbandless their whole lives.
You are divinities righteous
in sharing out blessings.
You share in every household;
your will weighs on every hour.
Justly you come as a guest,
the most honored, everywhere, of the gods.

ATHENA: Now that they graciously bring all this
    to pass for my country,
    my heart is bright. I am content with Persuasion,   970
    sharp-eyed guard of my tongue, my mouth,
    in the face of their fierceness, when they would not yield.
    But Zeus the Orator triumphed:
    our strife is for the good,
    it has victory for all time.

CHORUS: But I pray that civil strife
    with its endless greed for evil
    never takes a loud stand in this city.
    May the dust never guzzle the citizens' black blood.   980
    May lust for revenge never seize
    in its arms disaster for the city
    of murdering back and forth.
    May the people trade joy for joy
    in concord, in communion,
    and hate with one spirit—
    which is good against all sorts of human ailments.

ATHENA: Are the goddesses shrewd enough to find
    the path of merciful words for the people?
    From their fearsome faces I see   990
    a great advantage for my citizens here.
    If you will honor their kindness kindly,
    generously, continuously, you will keep
    your land and city
    on the straight, righteous road, in every kind of glory.

CHORUS: (*to the jurymen*) Joy to you, joy, in the wealth of destiny!
    Joy to you, people of the city
    sitting at Zeus' side,
    darlings of the darling virgin.
    Of you, who are more temperate with time,   1000

who are under Pallas' wing,
her father stands in awe.

ATHENA: *(to the Chorus)* Joy to you also! But I must walk
ahead, and show your rooms
by the sacred light your escort carries.

> *(The Escort, a group of Athenian women in purple robes*
> *carrying torches and sacrificial animals with which to honor*
> *the Furies, have been entering as she speaks.)*

Now, as the holy sacrifices fall to you,
hurry beneath the earth, and keep all mischief
far from the land. Send up
profit, send victory for the city.

(to the jurymen) Lead us, you with the city in your hands,   1010
children of Cranaus,* lead those who'll settle among you,
and be noble-minded, all you citizens,
toward their noble gifts.

CHORUS: Joy, joy again—my redoubled greeting
to all the gods across the city
and all the mortals!
If you care for Pallas' town,
if you revere me, your neighbor,
you will find no fault
in the fortunes of your lives.   1020

ATHENA: I give you thanks for such well-spoken prayers
and send you, by these torches' flaming brightness,
into the place below this territory
with the attendants who protect my image.
These are just dealings. To the very heart
of Theseus' land you'll come; a glorious post
[...]†
Children, wives, and old women on this mission
[...]‡
to honor them, put on your best, that's dyed
with purple. Let the splendor of the flame rise,
and they'll keep cheerful company with this land   1030
forever, blessing it with manly glory.

---

* A mythic Athenian king.
† Probably a lacuna, a gap in the surviving text.
‡ Another lacuna, this one possibly quite long.

(A grand procession, led by torchbearers, forms and begins marching offstage, still dancing. It includes Athena and the Furies, the jurymen, and the members of the Escort, who sing the play's final song, in dactylic meter.)

strophe 1

> ESCORT: Come our way,* powerful goddesses, lovers of honor!
>> Children of Night, childless but children no longer, cheerfully
>>> guided!
>> Words of good omen alone must you speak, people of this country.

antistrophe 1

>> Under the earth's primordial secret places,
>> may you find honors and offerings reverent beyond all reckoning.
>> Words of good omen alone must you speak, with one voice, all you
>>> people.

strophe 2

>> Bless the land, show it your righteous heart.   1040
>> Come this way, Dread Goddesses, in the light of the flame
>> that feasts on the torch. Rejoice along our road,
>> shout with the joy of our rites, to crown our song.

antistrophe 2

>> A pact for peace: you will live for all time†
>> with the citizens of Pallas. All-seeing Zeus
>> and Fate have come to our aid in the fight.
>> Shout with the joy of our rites, to crown our song.

---

* The text appears to be quite corrupt, but Headlam's plausible reconstruction is the basis for my translation.

† Garvie's reconstruction is the basis for my translation.

Introduction to *Prometheus Bound*
(possibly by Aeschylus)

Prometheus Bound is both the most stationary and the most wide-ranging of Greek dramas. Its protagonist lies immobile from the first scene to the last, chained to an outcropping of rock in remotest Scythia, the Siberia of the Greek world. But from that fixed point, the play surveys the entire universe. In two great speeches, Prometheus describes the future wanderings of Io, the young girl horribly transformed into a hybrid of human and cow, across the most alien and distant stretches of geographic space. In other speeches he looks back across all of time, describing his own role in bringing Zeus to power and in leading humankind out of a bestial condition. Though Prometheus' body is bound by iron chains, his all-seeing mind carries us to realms far beyond the reach of other dramas, even to Olympus and its cadre of impetuous young gods.

The phrase "young gods" strikes the modern ear strangely. Most religions of our day center around a God who transcends time, indeed who precedes time and the physical universe. But in the more temporal scheme of Greek mythic cosmology, the universe had been ruled by three generations in turn, first grandfather Uranus, then father Cronus, then Zeus. The early Greek poet Hesiod, in the *Theogony*, cast this evolution as a story of progress, in which the triumph of Zeus over the older Titans brings in a new era of justice and stability. Aeschylus—perhaps the author of *Prometheus Bound* but perhaps not—developed that idea in his *Oresteia*. In the final play of that trilogy, the *Eumenides*, a set of older divinities, the Furies, bow to a youthful Olympian regime represented by wise, sound-minded Athena. But newer rulers, as the Greeks had often learned from harsh experience, were not always better ones. The play before us inverts the evolutionary scheme of the *Eumenides*, taking its stand with an older Titan order against the upstart Olympians.

Prometheus Bound and *Eumenides* are the two surviving Greek dramas in which gods dominate the stage and human beings have mere supporting roles. In both plays, everything is at stake: in *Eumenides*, the fertility or sterility of the earth; in *Prometheus Bound*, the stability of Zeus' rule and therefore of the very universe. Like the *Eumenides*, moreover, *Prometheus Bound* seems to have belonged to a connected trilogy—a triptych of plays presented together, the format Aeschylus used to trace a single myth over long stretches of time. But while the *Eumenides* concludes the *Oresteia*, *Prometheus Bound* came either first or second in a trilogy that ended, as seems clear from surviving traces, with a *Prometheus Unbound*. In the original production, the play's bleak, apocalyptic ending was only prelude to a reconciliation of Zeus and Prometheus, aided, as is here foretold (lines 772–74), by the arrival of a figure, Heracles, who somehow breaks the stalemate.

Modern readers of *Prometheus Bound* find it hard to imagine how this reconciliation was achieved. It is the absolutism of Prometheus, the stoniness of his defiance, that thrills us, and that has made this play an inspiration for romantics and rebels through the ages. But the circumstance by which this one play out of three has survived, detached from its larger context, has undoubtedly distorted its meaning. In the end, intransigence is unacceptable; the rift between the gods must be healed, or the whole cosmos is threatened. Somehow the way forward will require compromise and a letting go of old hatreds.

The roots of those hatreds are explored in the play's opening scenes, as Prometheus gets shackled to his rock and is lamented over by the airborne Chorus, the daughters of Ocean. Prometheus has given "all-crafting fire," the source of progress, to humans, in defiance of Zeus, who (as we learn at lines 231–32) wanted to keep them weak in order to destroy them. The punishment Zeus has decreed—imprisonment plus exposure—is stern, but also ungrateful, given that Prometheus had played a crucial role in putting him in power. In the war between Olympians and Titans, here seen as a fairly recent event, Prometheus and his mother had switched sides. Though Titans themselves, they had shared their strategic wisdom with Zeus, enabling him to subdue their own nearest kin (including Atlas, identified in lines 347–50 as Prometheus' brother).

Traditional Greek stories about Prometheus, known from Hesiod's poems, have here been radically reworked. The idea that Prometheus is son of a goddess called both Themis and Gaea (line 209) is totally new. This unique genealogy makes Prometheus far older than in Hesiod and also gives him greater moral weight, since *themis* in Greek signifies a code of justice sanctioned by the gods. And since Gaea, or Earth, has prophetic powers, Prometheus, her son, is here given knowledge of the future, including one very powerful secret: a goddess whom Zeus will one day marry—her name, Thetis, is never spoken in this play—will bear him a son who will overthrow him. This secret gives Prometheus a bargaining chip in his showdown with Zeus, and Zeus' need to extract it prompts him to devise new torments for his adversary, including the famous liver-eating eagle (first mentioned at lines 1021–25).

From knowledge comes power, and Prometheus' theft of fire is reimagined, in two crucial speeches at this play's center, as a gift of knowledge. Here we learn that "all arts that mortals use come from Prometheus" (line 506)—not only the kindling of fire but agriculture, medicine, letters and numbers, and even Prometheus' own great skill, prophecy. Thanks to these teachings, humankind has risen out of its original state of darkness and misery: "Like crawling ants they hid themselves in holes" (line 452). This unique conception of Prometheus as a hero of enlightenment, who dispels fear and ignorance with technology, has made him a compelling figure in a modern world constantly reshaped by science. Mary Shelley gave her novel *Frankenstein*, the story of a man who uses technology to conquer death, the subtitle *The Modern Prometheus*; nuclear scientists who created a new element in an atomic laboratory in 1945 named it promethium.

Prometheus never explains why he made himself the civilizer of early mortals, or why he saved them from destruction. As a victim of Zeus' power he seems to feel a deep bond with other victims, including even the monster Typho, a serpentlike creature blasted by thunderbolts (lines 351–72). Prometheus' strongest connection, however, is to a mortal woman. When Io, a beautiful maiden turned part cow, makes her grotesque entrance at line 561, singing in frenzied meters as a stinging fly goads her onward, the *Prometheus Bound* moves in a surprising new direction. We see Zeus now portrayed not only as tyrant but as sexual predator. The sufferings of Io—her exile, metamorphosis, and phantasmagoric future wanderings—attest to the cruelty of an Olympian regime that can treat human beings as mere instruments of gratification.

Zeus never appeared onstage in any known Greek drama, but in no play is he more at issue than in the *Prometheus Bound*, and in none is he more harshly indicted. His projections of power, through brutal henchmen, lackeys, and implements of torture, anticipate those of the modern fascist dictator; there are even hints of a secret police or an ability to spy on his subjects. Defiance of such a ruler seems the only sane alternative, and the final scene, in a departure from normal conventions for Chorus behavior, shows even the daughters of Ocean declaring themselves in revolt. How such a despot could have been rehabilitated by the end of the *Prometheus* trilogy, such that an audience could celebrate his reconciliation with Prometheus, is very hard to imagine.

More so than other plays in this volume, *Prometheus Bound* presents scholars with grave uncertainties as to date and even authorship. Though manuscripts include it among the plays of Aeschylus, that attribution has been questioned—with good reason, in the eyes of the present editors. Since Aeschylean authorship cannot be disproved, and the play cannot be assigned to any other known playwright, we have followed convention in listing it among the plays of Aeschylus. But that should not be taken as assurance that it was written prior to 456 B.C., the presumed date of Aeschylus' death. Indeed, the play's interest in the connection between scientific knowledge and political power seems more at home in the cultural milieu of the late fifth century B.C., and some experts would even place it in the early fourth.

Prometheus Bound

Translated by James Romm

This translation is based on the text of Mark Griffith's edition for the Cambridge Greek and Latin Classics series, with variants noted in footnotes.

Cast of Characters (in order of appearance)

Power and Might, two servants of Zeus
Hephaestus, an Olympian god and son of Zeus
Prometheus, a Titan (one of the gods who preceded the
  Olympians)
Chorus of the daughters of Ocean, sisters-in-law to Prometheus
Ocean, a Titan, father-in-law to Prometheus
Io, a mortal woman
Hermes, son of Zeus and messenger of the gods

Setting: A desolate scene dominated by a huge rock outcropping. Power and Might, servants of Zeus, walk onstage, with Hephaestus following behind, dragging a chained prisoner, Prometheus.

POWER: We have come to the most far-flung tract of the earth,
 to the Scythian road, a wasteland without men.*
 You, Hephaestus, must execute the orders
 your father has laid on you: to pin this villain
 to these bare rocks with their steep, rocky faces;
 to wrap him in firm fetters of steely chain.
 Just think, he stole *your* glory—all-crafting fire—
 and gave it to mortals. For this grave misstep
 he must pay compensation to the gods.
 Thus he will learn to love the rule† of Zeus   10
 And cease his fondness for the human race.
HEPHAESTUS: Power and Might, the jobs Zeus gave to *you*
 are done already; nothing stands in your way.
 But *I*—I cannot find it in myself
 to bind a kindred god to this wintry cliff.
 Yet I am forced to find the strength to do it;
 it's no light thing to flout my father's words.
 (*turning to Prometheus*) High-minded son of wise-planning Themis,
 Though neither of us wishes it, I shall stake you
 to this deserted waste with tight-knit bonds.   20
 Here you shall hear no voice, see no man's form,
 but scorched beneath the bright blaze of the sun
 your skin will lose its youth. Your only joys
 will be when starry night conceals the daylight,
 or when the sun returns to scatter frost;

---

* Scythia was variously defined by the Greeks but generally meant the northeast quadrant of the known world, starting from today's Ukraine and Armenia. Later traditions situated the scene of Prometheus' punishment in the Caucasus mountains (but these, too, were variously located).

† The Greek word translated here as "rule" is *tyrannis*, meaning sovereignty seized by force or without constitutional legitimacy. Our English derivative, "tyranny," has harsher connotations.

each pain in turn will wear you down with burdens,
for there's no one yet born who can release you.*
Such are your rewards for loving humans.
You did not fear the gods' wrath; though a god,
you gave to mortals honors beyond limit.   30
For *that* you will stand guard on this grim rock,
sleepless, unable to sit or bend your knee,
your many wails and moans uttered in vain,
for the mind of Zeus cannot be turned by pleas.
Harsh is the ruler when rule is new-begun.†

POWER: That's enough. Why delay, indulge in pity?
You should hate the god whom all the gods hate most,
the one who gave *your* prize away to mortals.

HEPHAESTUS: But to harm my kin is dreadful, or my comrade.

POWER: This I admit. But to shirk your father's words—   40
How can you do it? Don't you fear this more?

HEPHAESTUS: Pitiless as ever, I see—and over-bold.

POWER: Your whimpering for *him* won't cure his ills.
Don't trouble over what will do no good.

HEPHAESTUS: Hateful skill of my hands—I curse it now!

POWER: Why so? I tell you, and it's no long tale,
Your craft is not the cause of his hard labors.

HEPHAESTUS: Still, I wish some other had my calling.

POWER: No job is light, except to rule the gods.
No one except for Zeus is truly free.   50

HEPHAESTUS: (*indicating the chains and tools he has brought*)
I can't deny it; these things give me proof.

POWER: Then go ahead and put the fetters on him,
lest father look and see you loafing here.

HEPHAESTUS: He'll see a bridle—ready to be used.

POWER: Put it around his hands, use all your strength.
Strike with the hammer. Pin him to the rocks.

HEPHAESTUS: It's done. You see the work did not take long.

POWER: Hit harder. Bind him tightly, don't leave slack.
He can devise impossible escapes.

---

* Hephaestus appears to speak with unconscious irony. He means that no one can possibly help Prometheus, but his words allude to the birth of Heracles, who will do so, many generations from now.

† It has not been long since Zeus overcame his father, Cronus, and the generation of the Titans to take control of the cosmos.

HEPHAESTUS: One arm is bound and will not soon come free.   60
POWER: The other now—strap firmly. Let him learn
   that all his cleverness* cannot outsmart Zeus.
HEPHAESTUS: No one could fault my work, except its victim.
POWER: Now drive the keen edge of this steely spike
   right through his chest. Put strength behind the blow.
HEPHAESTUS: *aiai* Prometheus! Now I groan for your pains.
POWER: What, shirking again, and groaning for Zeus' foes?
   Watch out, you'll soon be pitying yourself.
HEPHAESTUS: You see a sight that pains the eyes to look on.
POWER: I see somebody getting what he deserves.   70
   Now fasten the restraints around his sides.
HEPHAESTUS: I do what I must do. Don't heap on orders.
POWER: I *will* push you. I'll shout it in your ears.
   Go lower now—use force to bind his legs.
HEPHAESTUS: The job is done. It didn't need much effort.
POWER: Now strike with all your force to lock the shackles.
   The great Inspector† won't be trifled with.
HEPHAESTUS: Such ugly words—they match your ugly form.
POWER: Better to speak more gently. It's not your place
   to cast insults if I'm strong-willed and tough.   80
HEPHAESTUS: I'm going now. His limbs are tightly bound.
   (Exits.)
POWER: (*to Prometheus*) *Now* go and do your worst—steal from the
    gods
   and give their prize to mortals! Your human friends—
   how can *they* help you drain this sea of troubles?
   The gods who called you Foresight‡ named you wrong.
   It's foresight that you lack. You need it now—
   to tell you how you can get out of *this.*
   (Power and Might exit, leaving Prometheus alone onstage.)
PROMETHEUS: You, sacred air, and you, swift-soaring winds,
   you, springs of rivers, you, endless sparkling sheen
   of ocean waves, and you, all-mothering earth,   90

---

* Power here labels Prometheus a *sophistēs*, using a Greek word that can mean simply "wise man" but also, in a negative sense, "sophist." In the late fifth century, this word evoked a particularly controversial kind of sage, a teacher of rhetoric who taught morally dubious ways of winning arguments.
† Zeus.
‡ In Greek, the name Prometheus translates roughly to Foresight.

all-seeing circuit of sun—I call on you.
See what I suffer, a god, at the hands of gods.*
    Worn down, outraged—See how!—
    I shall drag out ten thousand years
    of weary time.
    Such is the outrageous penalty
    the new prince of the gods has found.
    (*moaning*) *pheu! pheu!* I groan at every pain,
    the one that's here, the one to come,
    wondering where the end of burdens lies.   100
But what am I saying? I knew what lay ahead,
knew everything beforehand. Nothing strange
will ever come to pain me. I must endure
my destined lot, certain that the power
of Necessity is too strong to be broken.
I cannot keep my evil fortunes silent,
yet cannot voice them, either. Such are the bonds
by which I'm yoked, for giving fire to men.
Yes, I did give it—hunted it, sealed it in fennel—
the wellspring of flame, teacher of every craft,   110
a help for every need in mortal life.
That's the crime for which I now must pay,
beneath the open sky, spitted to the rocks.
    (*listening*) *Ah! Ah!*
    What sound? What noiseless smell is this?
    Is it divine, or mortal, or mixed,
    This thing that has reached me at earth's end?
    What does it want—To watch me suffer?
    You there! Look at me, a god in chains,
    foe of great Zeus, the target of hate   120
    for all the gods, those courtiers
    who come and go in Zeus' halls—
    because I loved mankind too much.
    pheu! pheu! Is that rustle I hear
    the sound of nearby birds? The air
    is whistling with the strokes of wings!
    Whatever nears me brings me dread.

---

* The meter shifts in the next line from iambic trimeters to anapests, a marching rhythm, then back to iambic trimeters at line 101, then to anapests again at line 114. Such rapid shifts of meter in an opening speech are highly unusual for Greek drama.

(The Chorus of young women, the daughters of Ocean, appear, seeming to hover in an airborne vehicle.)

strophe 1

CHORUS: Don't be afraid. We are your friends,
we who now vie on fleets of wings
to reach this place, with hard-won leave   130
from Ocean, our father.
We found swift winds to bring us here,
for a dreadful din of hammered steel
shot through our cave, shaking away
all grave-faced shame. No time for shoes;
we sped here in our winged car.

PROMETHEUS: *(cries in surprise) aiai! aiai!*
Children of Tethys—she who bore many—
and of the one who twists around
the whole of the earth with unceasing flow,
father Ocean—look here, see here   140
how I am pinned with chain, and hold
on the upper crag of this jagged cliff
a guard-post none would want.

antistrophe 1

CHORUS: We see, Prometheus. A fearsome mist
of tears has clouded our eyes, as we look
at your body stretched out here,
baked and withered on this rock,
outraged by chains of hardest steel.
New are the steersmen who hold Olympus;
new are the laws by which Zeus rules,   150
laws that do not deserve the name.
He has locked away the gargantuans of old.*

PROMETHEUS: Would he had buried me with them, deep down,
bound me *there* with unbending chains,
in Tartarus' endless pit, and the halls
of Hades, trader in corpses. Then no one,
no god, no mortal, would laugh over *this*.
But no—I suffer in open air,
tossed by the winds, a joy to my foes.

---

* Referring to the imprisonment of the Titans in Tartarus.

strophe 2

> CHORUS: Who takes such joy? What god   160
>> has such a flinty heart? Who wouldn't
>> mourn instead for your pains? Only Zeus—
>> the one who has set his mind forever
>> against the race of Uranus,*
>> the one who will not cease from spite
>> until he is sated, or until
>> some trickster seizes his hard-won crown.
>
> PROMETHEUS: Yes, that's so. Even though I'm now disgraced,
>> bound hand and foot,
>> yet the head man of the blessed   170
>> will one day need *me* to reveal
>> the new design by which his staff
>> of power will be snatched away.
>> When that day comes I will not yield
>> to the spell of his honeyed, coaxing words,
>> nor bend before his iron threats;
>> nothing will make me tell what I know,
>> until he undoes these pitiless bonds
>> and pays me back the ways that he's outraged me.

antistrophe 2

> CHORUS: That's brave. You don't give in   180
>> to the gnawing pain.
>> But you speak too freely.
>> A piercing fear stirs up my mind,
>> a dread of where your path might lead,
>> where you might find
>> an end of strife
>> and reach safe harbor. For Cronus' son
>> has an iron heart that can't be swayed.
>
> PROMETHEUS: He's tough, I know, and gives no ground
>> when he makes his verdicts. Even so,   190
>> his heart will soften in the end,
>> when he's destroyed by what's to come.
>> *Then* his temper will be soothed,
>> and he'll look to me as ally and friend.
>> He'll *rush* toward me—and I toward him.

---

* Uranus, or Sky, was Zeus' grandfather, and father of the Titans.

CHORUS: Uncover all and tell us everything.
    On what charge did Zeus make you prisoner,
    heaping such shame and outrages upon you?
    Teach us your tale—unless it might bring you harm.
PROMETHEUS: It's painful even to speak these things, but also
    pain *not* to speak them. Ill fate either way.   200

When the gods began their rage at one another
and civil strife was stirred up in their ranks,
some wanting to pitch Cronus off his throne
so that their precious Zeus might reign, the rest
striving to guarantee Zeus *wouldn't* rule,
then I brought forth my strategies, and urged them
on Titan gods—offspring of Earth and Sky—
but couldn't win their trust. Minds set on force,
they spurned my tricks and subtleties, and thought
that they'd use strength to stay in power, no trouble.   210
And yet my mother—Themis, call her, or Gaea,
she's the same under all her names—had often
foretold to me just what the future held,
that force and strength of arm would not be needed,
but those with greater craft and wiles would rule.
Though I explained these matters to the Titans
they didn't care to even look them over.
Of all my options then, this seemed the best:
to take my mother with me, and join sides
with Zeus, as both he wanted and I wanted;   220
it was by *my* schemes that the deep, dark pit
of Tartarus now hides the ancient Cronus,
him and his allies. But getting all this from me,
the tyrant of the gods has paid me back
with foul rewards—these chains you see me in.
An illness somehow sickens all usurpers:
the inability to trust their friends.

But I'll now answer what you asked: the charge
on which he visits outrages upon me.

Newly seated on his father's throne,   230
he set out to divide up spoils and put

his reign in order. But he had no regard
for the long-suffering race of men. He planned
to make them vanish, and create a new race.
No one opposed this plan, except for me.
I had the courage. *I* spared humankind
from going, broken, to the depths of Hades.
Thus comes it that I'm bent under these scourges—
painful to suffer, grievous to look upon.   240
I put men first in pity, and then found
there was none left for me. Without mercy
I'm forced into line—a sight to bring Zeus shame.

CHORUS: Iron-hearted or made of stone are they
    who would not grieve, Prometheus, for your troubles.
    As for me, I wish I'd never seen them.
    But having seen, I'm pierced straight through the heart.

PROMETHEUS: To friends I am indeed a sight to pity.

CHORUS: Did you perhaps do more than what you've told us?

PROMETHEUS: I allowed mankind to stop foreseeing doom.   250

CHORUS: What medicine did you find for that disease?

PROMETHEUS: I planted in them hopes that would obscure it.

CHORUS: That was a worthy gift you gave to mortals.

PROMETHEUS: There's more. I gave them fire as their companion.

CHORUS: So now the mortal race owns blazing fire?

PROMETHEUS: Yes, and they'll learn many arts from it.

CHORUS: Then it's for crimes like these that Zeus decided—

PROMETHEUS: —to wreak atrocities and not relent.

CHORUS: Is there no appointed limit for your struggle?

PROMETHEUS: None, except whatever day *he* chooses.   260

CHORUS: Choose—why would he? What hope in that? Don't you see
    that you've gone wrong? No joy for me to say
    how wrong you've gone—and pain for you to hear.
    Let's leave that. Seek some respite from your toils.

PROMETHEUS: An easy thing, when standing clear of troubles,
    to counsel and advise with thoughtful words
    those laboring on the rack. I *know* all this.
    I *chose* to go wrong, and I won't deny it.
    I helped mankind, and brought pains on myself.
    But I never thought he'd give me pains like these—   270
    hung out to parch upon this spire of rock,
    exiled to a desert, neighborless, alone.

But don't, I pray you, grieve for present evils.
Step down onto the ground, and hear what's coming—
learn how my story runs, and how it ends.
Do this, I beg you! Share the heavy burden
of him who toils before you. For you know
that pain's a wanderer—it roams now here, now there.

> CHORUS:* What you ask, Prometheus,
> is what I want. With nimble foot   280
> I now desert this speedy perch
> and the air, the holy path for birds,
> to join you on your jagged rock;
> for I want to hear straight to the end
> your tale of troubles.

> *(The Chorus step from their conveyance onto the stage. At that
> moment Ocean, their father, enters, mounted on a monstrous
> bird, perhaps a griffin.)*

> OCEAN:† I have come to you, Prometheus,
> at the end of a very long road,
> steering this swift-winged bird
> by my thoughts, without need of reins.
> Know this: that I grieve your misfortunes.   290
> Kinship‡ alone decrees this, I think,
> but also, beyond our ties of blood,
> there is no one whom I favor more
> than I do you.
> You will soon know how true I speak;
> I use no empty, wheedling words.
> Just say what I can do to help.
> You'll never claim a surer friend
> than I who stand before you—Ocean.

PROMETHEUS: Ha! What's this? Are you here, too, arriving   300
    to gawk at pains? How did you find the nerve
    to leave the river that bears your name, your caves,

---

* The Chorus here speak in anapestic meter, as does Ocean, who enters below. At line 298 the dialogue returns to iambic trimeter.

† Ocean (*Okeanos* in Greek) was often personified by the Greeks as a god, the form in which he must have appeared in this play; but the name also signifies the ring of seawater thought to surround the landmass formed by Europe, Asia, and Africa.

‡ Since they are both sons of Earth, Ocean and Prometheus are brothers—to the extent that such familial labels can be applied to the earliest generation of gods. Ocean is also the father of Prometheus' wife, as we learn later.

those rock-roofed caves that nature carved, to come here—
to a land that's iron's mother?* Come to see
my misfortunes, as you say, and share my pain?
Behold the sight. See how the friend of Zeus,
the one who helped establish him in rule,
is crippled by him under pains like these.

OCEAN: I see them, Prometheus, and I bring advice,
    what's best for you—though I know you're always scheming.   310
Learn to know yourself, and learn new ways.
For new, too, is the ruler of the gods.
If you throw down these harsh and whetted words,
perhaps, though throned on high and far removed,
Zeus may hear you, and make this host of toils
you suffer now seem only children's games.
You must, poor wretch, give up this mood of yours
and seek a way to free yourself from troubles.
Perhaps my words will seem old-fashioned to you.
But the wages of a too-proud tongue, Prometheus,   320
are the kinds of things you're undergoing now.
You're not yet humbled; you don't yield to troubles,
but always seek to add to those you have.
Adopt my teachings, and you will no longer
kick out against the goads that sting; you'll see
that cruel monarchs can't be audited.†

Yet I shall go to him. I'll do what I can
to free you from the pains that now beset you.
Just hold your peace. Don't give your tongue free rein.
With all your wisdom, you find it hard to see   330
that useless ranting brings on punishment.

PROMETHEUS: Congratulations. You've stayed free of blame,
    although you dared to share my lot with me.‡

---

* Scythia was famous as a source of ore.

† See note to *Persians* line 213. The Greek word used here, *hupeuthunos*, is borrowed from Athenian political vocabulary, where it referred to an annual review of the financial dealings of officeholders.

‡ Prometheus seems here to refer to some previous episode when Ocean took his side, but it is not clear what this is. According to his own earlier account, Prometheus was the only Titan who switched sides and supported Zeus in the war between the gods. Ocean apparently stayed on the sidelines during that war and thus was spared the banishment to Hades that the other Titans suffered.

I tell you, let this be. Don't let it vex you.
You won't persuade him anyway; he's past that.
Look to your safety. Going there might harm you.

OCEAN: You're better at looking out for those near to you
than for yourself. I judge by deeds, not words.
But don't stand in the way of what I've started.
I tell you this: Zeus *will* give what I ask;   340
as a gift to me, he'll free you from these labors.

PROMETHEUS: I praise this in you, and I'll go on praising:
You have no lack of zeal. But save your effort.
Your troubles will be in vain and will not help me,
if indeed you're willing to go so far—to act.
Remain at peace, don't get yourself involved;
Just because *I'm* suffering, I don't want
my sufferings to spread to each and all.
No way. My brother's fate already grieves me,
Atlas, who stands in the western tracts of the world,   350
propping upright the pillar of earth and heaven
with his two shoulders, a weight beyond all bearing.*
I've seen as well the earth-born one—grim monster—
as he crouched in Cilician caves, and pitied him;
he of the hundred heads, brought low by might,
the raging Typho.† He fought all gods at once,
hissing out terror from his fearsome jaws,
ferocious lightnings shooting from his eyes,
as if to take down Zeus' rule by force.
But at him came the unsleeping bolt of Zeus,   360
the sky-dropped thunderclap all wreathed in flame,
and knocked him down from his high-hearted boasts.
The blow went deep into his heart and mind;
his strength was lightning-seared, reduced to ash;
and now he lies, a useless, sprawling mass,

---

* Atlas, a Titan (and thus a brother of Prometheus), fought in the war against Zeus and the Olympians. After being defeated, Atlas was given the task of keeping the sky and earth apart, so that the deities Uranus and Gaea would produce no more offspring.

† Typho (also called Typhon or Typhoeus), a hundred-headed monster born from Earth, posed the last, and most serious, challenge to the rule of Zeus, according to Hesiod (*Theogony* 821ff.). The thunderbolting of Typho firmly established Zeus' power, even more than did the defeat of the Titans in the cosmic war.

crushed beneath the base of mighty Aetna,*
beside the straits of the Messinian sea.
Hephaestus sits there, on the highest ridges,
and smites hot iron. Streams of fire will burst forth,†
devouring with the jaws of savage beasts   370
the spreading fields of Sicily fair in fruit—
such is the bile that Typho will set boiling,
with hot blasts of a deadly fire-storm—
despite the bolts of Zeus that cindered him.

But you know this, no need to have me teach you.
So save yourself the best way you know how.
As for me, I'll plumb the depths of troubles
until such time as Zeus relents from wrath.
OCEAN: But you must know, Prometheus, that words are healers.
They cure the temper of a mind that's sick.   380
PROMETHEUS: True—if the time is ripe for hearts to soften.
When the tumor of pride still swells, don't use the lance.
OCEAN: What cost do you discern in eagerness
and trying something bold? Teach me your thoughts.
PROMETHEUS: I see a useless toil and empty folly.
OCEAN: Then let me suffer this disease. It's better
to think right thoughts, though others deem them wrong.
PROMETHEUS: But *your* misstep will seem to come from *me*.
OCEAN: Clearly your words would have me travel homeward.
PROMETHEUS: Yes, lest your dirge for me make *you* a target.   390
OCEAN: For the one new-seated on the throne of might?
PROMETHEUS: It's *his* heart you must take care not to anger.
OCEAN: Your ruin is my teacher, Prometheus.
PROMETHEUS: Get going then. Keep to the course you're on.
OCEAN: You speak to one already under way.
My four-foot bird is skimming with his wings
the level paths of air. He will be glad
to bend his knee, I think, in his own stall.
(*Ocean exits as he had entered, flying on his winged beast.*)

---

* An active volcano in Sicily. The playwright imagines that the fire of Typho's breath survived as the lava that spewed forth from the mountain, furnishing Hephaestus with the heat for his smithy. Pindar in *Pythian* 1 makes a similar connection between Typho and Aetna.

† Prometheus suddenly breaks into prophecy, foreseeing a great eruption that in fact destroyed much of the country around Aetna in the 470's B.C.

strophe a

> CHORUS: I grieve for your fate, Prometheus.
> A tear-dropping stream from my delicate eyes   400
> runs down my cheek;
> wet fountains bedew me.
> This is the baneful rule of Zeus,
> the self-made laws, the arrogant might
> he brandishes over
> the gods who once were.

antistrophe a

> Every land groans in lament for you.
> The [...]* cry for your honor,
> so grand and age-renowned,
> and that of your kindred gods, too.
> All those who inhabit the settled land   410
> of holy Asia, mortal men,
> suffer along with
> the sufferings you groan for.

strophe b

> Those in the Colchian land—
> maidens fearless in battle†—
> and the Scythian race that inhabits
> the uttermost region of earth
> around Lake Maeotis,‡

antistrophe b

> the warrior chiefs of Arabia,   420
> who dwell in the high-walled city
> near to the Caucasus mountains,
> their terrible host battle-roaring
> with sharp-pointed spears.

epode§

> The waves of the sea shout their grief   431
> by splashing together; the depths moan,
> the black cave of Hades groans below ground,

---

* The name of a tribe or people is missing here from the manuscripts.

† Colchis (approximately modern Armenia) was thought by some to be the home of the Amazons, female warriors who disdained marriage and childrearing.

‡ The modern Sea of Azov.

§ As the line numbers indicate, a passage of six lines, found in the manuscripts but in a form almost impossible to interpret, has been omitted here.

the springs of sacred rivers lament
for a pain deserving of pity.

PROMETHEUS: Don't imagine that pride or self-regard
keps me from speaking. It's rather the agony
of seeing myself misused; I'm bit to the heart.
Who else but I gave out, from first to last,
rewards and honors to these younger gods?   440
But I'll not speak of that. You know already.
Instead, hear now the pains of humankind.

They were like children in their wits before,
until I taught them how to use their minds.
I speak as one who has no blame for humans.
I only mean to show what good I did them.
Though they had power of sight, they did not see,
hearing, they did not hear; like shapes of dreams
they spent their whole lives shuffling things together
in random patterns. They knew no brick-built houses   450
to shield them from the sun, nor works of wood;
like crawling ants they hid themselves in holes,
in dark and sunless caverns underground.
No signposts did they have of winter's coming,
nor that of flowery spring, nor fecund summer;
no certainties, haphazard all year long,
until I showed the risings of the stars
to them, and settings, too, both hard to read.
There's more. The ways of numbers, wisdom's crown,
I found for them, and letters forming words,   460
from which come memory's power and every art.
I was the first to tie their beasts in teams,
enslaving these to yokes and saddle-bags,
that they might take men's burdens on their backs;
I put their horses under reins and tamed them,
to be the badge of wealth and luxury.
And none but I discovered carriages
that cross the seas on wings of woven flax.*

---

* A fanciful description of ships traveling under sail.

All these things I devised for mortal men.
But now I'm lost myself. There's no contrivance   470
to get me free from all this suffering.
CHORUS: Disgraceful pain indeed: your wits have failed you.
You're like a doctor who has fallen ill,
no courage left and no way to discover
what medicine to take to get you well.
PROMETHEUS: But hear the rest, you'll marvel even more—
the arts that I devised, the smart solutions.
This was the greatest: whenever men got sick,
there was no remedy, no drink nor salve
nor healing food; and lacking medicines   480
they simply wasted away—until I showed them
how to mix up the gentle curatives
with which they now ward off every disease.
I showed them, too, the ways of prophecy,
how to divine from dreams what was to come,
and how to find the meanings in odd sounds
or chance encounters on the paths and ways.
I marked out patterns in the flights of birds—
the lucky from the right, the left unlucky—
and habits of each kind—which birds they favor,   490
which they avoid, or which they prey upon.*
I taught them to read entrails: which are smooth,
what color gives most pleasure to the gods,
what spotting is most lovely in a liver.
I showed the mantic arts of sacrifice:
the burning of the thighbones wrapped in fat
and great backbone, and how to read the signs
they give when burnt, which used to be obscure.†
So much for that. The things below the earth,   500
the hidden benefits for humans, namely
iron, bronze, and gold and silver—who

---

* The habits of birds are important to the art of augury, since the diviner needs to know which bird activities are normal and which constitute signs.

† The manner in which the sacrifice burned, and the direction of the smoke, were assigned various meanings by diviners. Despite having said here that the sacrificial portion consists of bones wrapped in fat—the meat being consumed by the worshippers gathered at the sacrifice—Prometheus here omits mention of the legend told by Hesiod and others, that he tricked Zeus into choosing bones and fat as the gods' portion of the sacrificial animal, leaving the meat for humankind.

could say he found them earlier than I?
No one, except a braggart blowing smoke.

To sum it all up in the briefest words:
All arts that mortals use come from Prometheus.
CHORUS: But don't give mortals too much benefit
   while you neglect your own unhappy lot.
   I'm hopeful that you'll one day be set free
   from these harsh bonds, and be as strong as Zeus.   510
PROMETHEUS: Not yet does Fate, which brings all things to pass,
   allow this outcome: that I flee these bonds,
   though broken by a thousand pains and woes.
   All art is weaker than necessity.
CHORUS: Who charts the course of this "necessity"?
PROMETHEUS: The threefold Fates, and unforgetting Furies.
CHORUS: Does even Zeus lack power over these?
PROMETHEUS: He can't escape from things that are ordained.
CHORUS: And what's ordained for Zeus, except his rule?
PROMETHEUS: You won't learn that from me. Don't ask again.   520
CHORUS: I see. You have some holy secret—so?
PROMETHEUS: Let's talk of something else. It's not yet time
   that *this* be spoken of. It must stay hid,
   as much as is in my power. If I hide it,
   someday I'll flee these shameful bonds and pains.

strophe 1

   CHORUS: This be my prayer: May Zeus,
         ruler of all, never set his power
         against my mind. May I not be slow
         when I make for the gods holy slaughters of oxen   530
         by the ceaseless stream of my father, Ocean.
         May I never give offense with my words.
         May these prayers abide and not melt away.

antistrophe 2

         Sweet it is to stretch out life
         amid confident hopes, and to feed
         one's heart on bright and cheery things.
         But looking at *you*, your countless wounds
         and lacerations, I shudder.   540
         You have too little fear of Zeus
         and too much reverence for mortals, Prometheus.

strophe 2

> What help is there for the help you gave?
> Where is your rescue? Tell me, friend.
> What can mere mortals do to save you?
> Didn't you see the weakness, the trance,
> that fetters all of their blind race?   550
> Their plans can never evade the orchestration of Zeus.

antistrophe 2

> So I discovered as I beheld
> your fate, Prometheus.
> How different the song—I hear it now!—
> that I sang around your bath and your bed
> on your wedding day, when you married my sister,
> Hesione, and brought her home as your wife.   560

Io: (*entering in wild confusion, her form partly that of a cow*) What place?
> What people? Whom do I see here?
> He's chained to the rocks and beaten by storms!
> You there—what crime are you paying for? Tell me,
> what land have my miseries brought me to?
> (*Struck by sudden pain*) ai! ai! aiee! aiee!
> That stinger—it sticks me again, again!
> It's Argus' ghost—the earth-born monster.*
> *Get him off!* Help me! It's horrible,
> the sight of the hundred-eyed shepherd!
> He walks about with his magical eyes,
> he's dead—but he won't stay underground.   570
> He comes from below and hunts poor me,
> won't let me eat, drives me about
> across the sands by the barren shore.

strophe

> *Wait!* I hear the wax-joined pipes
> answering me with sleep-bringing song.†
> Oh, the pain! Where have my far-roving wanderings brought me?

---

* Argus, a giant herdsman with a hundred eyes, had been posted by Hera to guard Io and keep Zeus from arranging a tryst with her. Argus had by this time been killed by Hermes, but Io still feels tormented by his ghost.

† According to one version of the myth, Hermes put Argus to sleep by playing a soporific tune on a reed pipe before killing him with a stone.

Why, son of Cronus, why? What wrong did I do
that you yoke me to torments like these—
(*cries again*) *aiee!*—and drive a wretched girl to madness   580
in fear of the gadfly's sting?
Scorch me with flame, bury me alive, feed me to monsters of the
    deep;
only grant my prayer, O king. My travels have traveled far enough.
They've done me in. I cannot see
a way to flee from this torment.
Do you hear? It's the voice of the cow-horned girl.

PROMETHEUS: Hear? Yes of course. It's the daughter of Inachus speaking,
the one driven on by the gadfly. She heats Zeus' heart   590
with passion, and so, the target of Hera's hate,
she is driven perforce to run her unending races.

antistrophe

IO: How did you learn my father's name?
Who are you? Tell me, wretch though I am.
One wretch to another, who are you to speak so much truth—
putting a name to my god-sent disease,
whose touches destroy me with far-roaming stings?
(*she is stung again*) *aiee!*
Here I come, leaping and jerking,
unable to eat, an outrageous fate,   600
a victim of Hera's spite and schemes. Tell me, who else
among the unlucky have suffered as I?
Or else show me clearly, what troubles await me?
Is there a help or a cure for my illness?
If you know this, then tell me.
Speak out, for the sake of the maid of hard travels.

PROMETHEUS: I'll tell you clearly all you want to know.
I won't use riddles, only simple speech,   610
the right way for a friend to talk to friends.
I am Prometheus, who gave fire to mortals.

IO: Alas, Prometheus, boon to humankind!
For what, then, do you pay this penalty?

PROMETHEUS: I've just now reached the end of telling those troubles.

IO: Well, would you offer this small boon, to me?

PROMETHEUS: Ask what you will, I'll answer anything.

IO: Then tell me who has bound you to this cliff.

PROMETHEUS: Zeus made the plan; Hephaestus did the deed.

Io: What sort of errors do you thus atone for?   620
PROMETHEUS: I've made this clear already. That's enough.
Io: Then let me ask about my end of wandering.
    How much time yet remains for my misfortunes?
PROMETHEUS: It's better not to know this than to know.
Io: Whatever lies ahead, don't hide it from me.
PROMETHEUS: I don't withhold it simply out of spite.
Io: Why, then, will you not utter everything?
PROMETHEUS: I grudge you not, but fear to shake your wits.
Io: Don't take more care for me than I would want.
PROMETHEUS: It seems you're firm, and I must speak. So hear.   630
CHORUS: Not yet! Give me a portion, too, of pleasure.
    Allow us first to learn of her disease,
    and let her tell the perils in her past;
    then you can add the sequel of her sufferings.
PROMETHEUS: It's up to you, Io, to grant this favor,
    especially since they are your father's sisters.*
    To make lament and to bewail one's troubles
    before an audience that will be moved
    to weep for them, is hardly wasted time.
Io: (*to Chorus*) I don't see why I shouldn't trust you all.   640
    You'll learn in clear words everything you ask,
    though telling it brings grief—the god-sent storm
    that wrought this transformation of my body,
    from where it came to strike a wretched girl.

    Dream visions used to come and visit me
    within my maidens' chambers; they spoke to me
    with cloying words: "You lucky, lucky girl!
    Why stay so long a virgin, when you can
    contract a royal marriage? Zeus himself
    has felt the heat of passion's dart, for you;   650
    he yearns for Aphrodite's rites. Don't spurn him!
    Go from your home, to Lerna's deepest meadow,
    There where your father has his flocks and cow-stalls,
    So that the eye of Zeus may cease from longing."
    Such dreams held me in thrall, night after night,

---

* A strangely literal statement, based on the idea that Inachus, Io's father, is a river god and hence (according to Hesiod's *Theogony*) a son of Ocean.

until, downcast, I dared to tell my father
about what I was seeing in the dark.
He sent off swarms of messengers to ask
at Delphi and Dodona* what to do,
or what to say, to satisfy the gods.   660
They came back bearing slippery replies,
obscure and hard to read, until one day
a clear instruction came to Inachus,
enjoining him to thrust me from my home
and from my native land, and set me roving
like some untethered beast in furthest realms,
saying that if he did not, Zeus would send
a fiery bolt to blot out all his kin.
He trusted in these oracles of Apollo;†
he drove me out, and locked the doors against me,   670
a heartache to us both, but forced upon him,
for Zeus' reins were driving all he did.

My shape and mind now both became contorted.
My gait became mad leaping, as I went
toward Lerna's spring and the sweet stream of Cerchne,
and I had horns—you see them;‡ a stinging fly
now grazed on me. And the earth-born herdsman, Argus,
implacable, now walked beside me, watching
with all his many eyes my every step.
But suddenly, against all expectations,   680
Fate robbed him of his life. Meanwhile, fly-bitten,
I ranged from land to land, the gods my goaders.
(*to Prometheus*) You've heard what's happened. If you know anything
about the toils ahead, speak out; don't give me
the comfort of false tales. For I proclaim
invented words to be the basest illness.
    CHORUS: (*with cries of dismay*)
        Keep her away! Keep her away!
        Never did I think I'd hear

---

* The two principal oracular shrines of the Greek world.
† The god who was thought to prophesy at Delphi.
‡ Io's mask in the original production must have had horns.

such alien words. I never thought
my soul would ever be stung like this   690
by sufferings, outrages, terrors,
hard to see and hard to bear.
Alas for Fate!
The sight of Io fills me with fear.

PROMETHEUS: Your groans and fearfulness have come too soon.
Hold back a while, until you learn the rest.

CHORUS: Speak on and teach it. It's always best,
when one is ill, to know the pains ahead.

PROMETHEUS: (*to the Chorus*) The first of your requests has now been
      granted   700
with help from me; you asked to hear the story
of this girl's suffering from her own lips.
Now hear the sequel: what must be endured
by this young woman, at the hands of Hera.
(*turning to Io*) Daughter of Inachus, now heed these words,
that you may know the limits of your journey.
When you leave here, head east toward the sun's risings.*
Seek out the fields that have not known a plow.
You'll reach the nomad Scythians, whose straw homes
stand off the ground, up high, on well-wheeled carts,   710
whose weapons are the arrow and twanging bow.
Do not approach them. Stay right by the shore,
your feet in briny sand, as you pass by them.
On your left hand you'll find the Chalybes,†
workers of iron; these you must watch out for.
They're brutal men and do not take to strangers.
You'll reach the Hybristes river, aptly named;
don't cross it; this is not a stream to ford.
You'll follow it to Caucasus,‡ highest of mountains;
from its steep sides the river gushes out   720
in torrents. You must cross sky-grazing peaks
and take a southern path, toward the noon sun,
to reach the Amazon host, haters of men,

---

* Io's journey describes a rough circle, moving counterclockwise through the whole known world, but both the route and stopping points are very uncertain.

† A tribe usually situated by the Greeks on the Black Sea, in modern Turkey.

‡ Not the same mountain chain as the modern Caucasus.

who one day will remove to Themiscyra
and dwell around the river Thermodon,*
where Salmydessus juts like a jaw in the sea,
hazard to sailors, stepmother to ships.†
These Amazons will gladly be your guides.
You'll reach an isthmus, by the narrow gates of the Marsh;
it's called Cimmerian. You must steel yourself   730
to leave it and to swim the Maeotic straits.
Mortals will tell the legend of this crossing
forevermore, and the place will get its name:
the Cow-ford, Bosporus. This takes you out of Europe.
You'll come to Asia now.‡
      (*to the Chorus*) So now you see
the tyrant of the gods is even-handed
in cruelty. He set these wanderings
because he, a god, lusted for her, a mortal.
(*to Io*) How harsh a suitor came to seek your hand,
dear girl. For all the words I've said so far   740
are but a prologue to your tale of woe.

IO: (*cries in pain as though stung*) No! aiee! aiee!

PROMETHEUS: Again, you cry and moan. What will you do
    when you have learned your full forecast of evils?

CHORUS: Can there be still more trials left to tell?

PROMETHEUS: Yes—a storm-tossed sea of woe and ruin.

IO: Then what's the use of living? Why not jump
    this moment from the rock on which I stand?
    Smashed on the ground below, I would be free
    of all my troubles. Better to die once   750
    than live out all one's days in suffering.

PROMETHEUS: How would *my* toils defeat you, then—since I
    am fated to endure them and *not* die?

---

* Themiscyra and the river Thermodon are in modern Turkey. The playwright seems concerned to reconcile two different traditions about where the Amazons lived by forecasting that they will relocate from one to the other. The promontory of Salmydessus is far west of these places, but the playwright's sense of space is very blurry.

† Stepmothers in ancient myth were universally cruel.

‡ "Bosporus" comes from the Greek words for "cow-ford." The name was applied in antiquity to several different straits. Here it designates the waterway formed by the eastern tip of the Crimean peninsula and the mainland, the Maeotic Straits (so called because Lake Maeotis is the ancient term for the present-day Sea of Azov, also referred to above as "the Marsh"). These straits are not a major landmark in the modern world, but in the eyes of many Greeks they formed the boundary between Europe and Asia.

Death would be my release from pain, but no.
No endpoint lies ahead for my long labors,
except the fall of Zeus from off his throne.

IO: The fall of Zeus—but can that ever be?

PROMETHEUS: You would rejoice to see that fall, I think.

IO: How could I not? I'm ruined, thanks to Zeus.

PROMETHEUS: Rejoice then, for this will indeed take place.   760

IO: But who will take away the tyrant's scepter?

PROMETHEUS: By foolish plans he'll strip it from himself.

IO: What do you mean? Say more, if there's no danger.

PROMETHEUS: He'll make a marriage that will bring him grief.

IO: With god or mortal? If this can be spoken.

PROMETHEUS: Don't ask me for a name. That *can't* be spoken.[*]

IO: Then will his *wife* remove him from his throne?

PROMETHEUS: She'll bear a child who can defeat its father.

IO: There's no escaping from this destiny?

PROMETHEUS: There isn't, until I am freed from prison.   770

IO: But who will free you, if Zeus stands against it?

PROMETHEUS: One of your offspring[†]—so it needs must be.

IO: *What?* A son of *mine* will end your troubles?

PROMETHEUS: The grandson of your tenth-removed descendant.

IO: The prophecies surpass my understanding.

PROMETHEUS: Then don't seek out the secret of *your* future.

IO: Don't offer me this boon and then refuse it!

PROMETHEUS: I'll give you only one of two accounts.

IO: Which ones? Say what they are, then let me choose.

PROMETHEUS: Choose then. I'll either say what lies ahead   780
in your tale of woe, or else tell who will free me.

CHORUS: Give one to her, the other tale to us.
Don't disregard the ones who crave your story.
Tell *her* what still remains of wandering;
tell *us* of your deliverer. That's my wish.

PROMETHEUS: (*to Chorus*)
Since you're so eager, I will not refuse
to tell you everything you want to hear.

---

[*] The name that can't be spoken is that of Thetis, a sea nymph. According to the knowledge Prometheus possesses, the son born to Zeus and Thetis would have grown to be mightier than his father. As things turned out, Thetis had a son by a mortal, Peleus, instead—the hero Achilles.

[†] Heracles, as Prometheus explains in his next speech.

(*to Io*) First you—the tale of the road on which you're driven.
Inscribe my words on the tablets of your mind.

When you have crossed the stream between the continents,[*]   790
head toward the fiery risings of the sun.
You'll cross a billowing sea,† and finally come
to Cisthene‡ and the Plain of Gorgons. There
the daughters of Phorcys dwell: three ancient virgins,
like swans in form, sharing a single eye,
each with one tooth.§ Neither the sun's bright rays
nor nightly moonshine ever reach these three.
Near them are their three sisters, winged creatures,
the Gorgons, snaky-haired, reviled by mortals;
no one who looks upon them still draws breath.   800
Guard against these as you would a hostile army.
Now hear your next unfriendly spectacle:
watch out for sharp-beaked, barkless hounds of Zeus,
the griffins, and the Arimaspian host,¶
the one-eyed horsemen who inhabit there,
beside the gold-flecked stream of river Pluto.**
Avoid these men. You'll reach a distant land
and a dark-skinned race that dwells by springs of the Sun,
there where the river flows called Aethiops.††
Follow along its banks until you come   810
to a cataract, where from the Byblian mountains‡‡
the Nile pours forth its sweet and sacred waters.

---

* The Cimmerian Bosporus, the point Io's route had reached in the previous speech of Prometheus.

† I follow the reading of most manuscripts; a few have "non-billowing sea" instead, the reading adopted by Griffith. In either case it is unclear what sea is meant (possibly the Caspian).

‡ An obscure place name, associated with the far East.

§ These mythic hags are generally known as the Graeae, three white-haired women who took turns using a single eye and tooth. It is unclear why the playwright calls them "like swans in form."

¶ Griffins were generally depicted as giant birds with lion's claws and sharp beaks. The Arimaspians, a mythic one-eyed tribe living in the far north, were thought to rob the griffin nests of heaped-up gold and then escape on horseback from the enraged griffins.

** Pluto in Greek means "wealthy" and thus is usually used as an alternate name for Hades, who was thought to own all mineral wealth underground.

†† The name, signifying "burnt-face," shows that Io has by this point entered Africa; the Greeks were very vague as to how Asia and Africa were attached. Aethiops is perhaps here used as another name for the Nile, or else it is a purely mythical river.

‡‡ Unknown, but the name associates these mountains with the papyrus plant and therefore with Egypt.

This river leads you to a three-sided land,
the Delta, where you, Io, and your children
are fated to found a thriving settlement.

If any of what I've told you seems obscure,
just ask again, and I'll repeat more clearly.
I have more leisure than I want just now.
CHORUS: If you've skipped anything, or if there's more
 to tell about her ruinous wanderings,   820
 then tell it. But if that's all, then grant us
 the favor we requested. You recall it?
PROMETHEUS: She's heard it all, the endpoint of her journey.
 But lest she think she's listened uselessly,
 I'll tell what she endured before she came here.
 I offer this as pledge my words are truth.
 (*to Io*) I'll leave aside the bulk of storytelling
 and go to the last leg of your past journey.

When first you reached the Molossian plains
that lie about the steep site of Dodona,*   830
the seat of prophecy of Thesprotian Zeus,
the speaking oaks†—a wonder past belief—
hailed you distinctly, in no riddling words,
as the illustrious wife-to-be of Zeus.
Does any of this story bring you pleasure?
Then, gadfly-stung, you took the seaside path
and reached the great bay named for a goddess, Rhea.‡
Storms drove you off from there, with backward steps.
But for the rest of time this gulf of sea
will have the name Ionian—know this well—   840
a signpost to all men that once you came there.

So there's a token of my powers of mind,
which see things far beyond the reach of sight.

---

* Dodona was situated in the far northern reaches of the Greek world, in what is today Albania. Io's own tale of her journey from Argos (lines 669–83) took her only a short way from home before the pursuit of the gadfly sent her bounding madly northward; Prometheus now picks up that thread.

† Zeus supposedly gave prophecies at Dodona by way of the rustling leaves of a sacred oak.

‡ The Adriatic.

(*to Io and to Chorus*) I'll tell the rest to both of you at once.
I here resume the track of my former tale.*

A city, Canobus, lies by the Nile,
on the very tip of silt at the river's mouth.
It's here Zeus will restore you to your wits,
by merely touching you with a harmless hand.
You'll bear a dark-skinned child named Epaphus   850
in memory of how Zeus sired him.† He will reap
the fruits of all the land the broad Nile waters.
But his great-great-grandchildren, a clan of fifty,‡
all women, will return to Argos, your homeland,
unwillingly, to avoid an incestuous marriage
with cousins. These men, quivering with impatience,
hawks in pursuit of doves, and catching up,
will chase them, hunting marriages they should not.
The god won't let them have the women's bodies.
Pelasgian land will drip with female slaughter;   860
the men will be crushed by a boldness that lurks in the night;
for each of the women will take the life of her husband,
dipping two-bladed swords in streams of gore.
Thus may the Cyprian§ visit all *my* foes!
But passion will bewitch one of these women,
stop her from slaying her bed-mate, blunt her purpose;
she will prefer to hear herself called coward
rather than blood-stained murderess. She's the one
who'll bear a royal race to rule in Argos.

It would require long words to tell it clearly.   870
From her descendants there will come a bold one,¶

---

* After a digression on Io's past wanderings, Prometheus here resumes the thread he left at line 815, following Io's future arrival in Egypt.

† The Greek word for "touching" in line 849 is *epaphon*. Epaphus, the son of Io by Zeus, was identified by the Greeks with an Egyptian deity, the Apis, who had the form of a calf.

‡ The Danaids, or daughters of Danaus, whose flight from Egypt is portrayed in Aeschylus' play *Suppliants* (not in this volume). They fled back to Argos to avoid a forced marriage to their fifty first cousins, but the cousins pursued them there and the marriages went forward. Still struggling to avoid incest, all fifty Danaids plotted to kill their husbands on their wedding night, but one of the fifty did not go through with the murder, and thus it was through her that Io's line was carried on.

§ Aphrodite.

¶ Heracles, whose rescue of Prometheus from imprisonment was portrayed in *Prometheus Unbound,* a lost play that probably concluded the trilogy of which *Prometheus Bound* was a part.

a famous archer, who will set me free
from these travails. Such was the prophecy
my ancient mother, Titan Themis, told me.
The how and why would need long explanation,
and learning it would be no use to you.

    IO: (*stung again, crying wildly*) *alalai! alalai!*[*]
    Again the seizure, the mind-shaking madness!
    It sets me ablaze. The gadfly, the barb
    not forged by fire—it punctures me.   880
    In fear my heart kicks against my chest,
    my eyes whirl round in spiral orbits,
    I'm off the track, beyond what's sane,
    blown by a raging wind, my tongue babbling.
    A torrent of words dashes disordered
    into the waves of my hateful folly.

       (*She runs offstage.*)

strophe

    CHORUS: Wise, wise indeed was he
    who first weighed this in his mind and proclaimed it with his tongue:
    marriage on equal terms is much the best lot.   890
    A poor farm-hand ought not yearn for a spouse
    whose life has been made soft by wealth
    or whose lineage contains exalted names.

antistrophe

    Never, O Fates,
    may you see me becoming the sharer of Zeus' bed.
    Never may I wed one of the sky-dwellers.
    I'm afraid as I look upon Io,
    her maidenhood, which lacked man's love, destroyed
    by Hera, with wanderings and hard travels.[†]   900

epode

    But if my marriage is on equal terms,
    I've nothing to fear.
    Let not the passion of powerful gods
    cast inescapable eyes on me.
    That's a war that can't be fought,
    contriving things beyond contrivance.

---

[*] This cry is usually given by warriors advancing in battle. Like the rest of Io's speech, it is in the anapestic meter, suggesting a vigorous, agitated dance movement.

[†] The Greek text of this line is uncertain. I have adopted Page's emendation.

Who would I be? For I can't see a way
to flee from the guile of Zeus.

PROMETHEUS: Zeus! However insolent his thoughts,
Zeus will be humbled. He's headed toward a marriage
that will eject him from his tyrant's throne
and make him nothing. Thus his father's curse,   910
the curse of Cronus, uttered as *he* fell
from the throne he long had held, will be fulfilled.*
No one among the gods can show him clearly
how to avert these toils, except for me.
I know what's coming, and how it'll come. Let Zeus
sit there, unfearing, trusting in thunderclaps,
holding aloft the fiery lightning bolt;
these weapons will do nothing to protect him
from falling a shameful fall, a fall past bearing.
He himself is preparing to beget   920
his own opponent: a dangerous foe to fight,
who will discover a fire greater than lightning
and mighty crashing louder than any thunder;
he'll splinter, too, the trident, spear of Poseidon,†
that sickly staff he wields to shake the seas.
Once broken by this evil, Zeus will learn
how far apart is rule from slavery.

CHORUS: This prophecy is merely what you wish for.

PROMETHEUS: It's what will come to pass, *and* what I want.

CHORUS: Zeus will be conquered—this is what awaits us?   930

PROMETHEUS: He'll suffer pains more arduous than mine.

CHORUS: Why are you not afraid to make such boasts?

PROMETHEUS: Why should I fear, since death is not my fate?

CHORUS: Zeus might send trouble even worse than this.

PROMETHEUS: Well, let him do so. I've foreseen it all.

CHORUS: It's wise to bow before Necessity.

PROMETHEUS: Go fawn upon the ruler of the hour.
This Zeus is less than nothing in my eyes.

---

* This is the only reference in any of our sources to a curse spoken by Cronus.

† It is unclear why Poseidon, too, should be attacked, except that he is Zeus' brother and a natural ally. In a story related by Pindar, Poseidon competed with Zeus to marry Thetis, the fateful bride, but both in the end chose not to do so when they learned that the son she would bear would be stronger than themselves.

Let him rule on for his short time, and do
what pleases him; his reign will not be long.   940
    (seeing Hermes, son of Zeus, approaching his rock)
But look! The errand-boy of Zeus is coming,
the lackey of the tyrant's new regime.
No doubt we are to have some fresh decree.

HERMES: You there—the clever one,* the rebels' rebel,
the one who wronged the gods and gave their honors
to lowly humans—the famous thief of fire—
My father orders you: Reveal this marriage
you boast about, the one that brings his downfall.
And tell it all in detail, don't use riddles.
Don't give me cause to come back here again,   950
Prometheus. You see that Father Zeus
will never yield to idle threats like yours.

PROMETHEUS: A lofty speech, and full of self-regard—
how fitting for the boot-lick of the gods.
You young gods, new in rule—you think you dwell
in towers that never topple. Have I not
seen tyrants twice already hurled from them?†
And I shall see a third, the one now reigning,
fall shamefully and soon. *Now* do I tremble?
Or do I seem to fear these greenhorn gods?   960
Not much; no, not at all. But as for you:
Trot back along the road on which you came.
You'll get no answers to your questions here.

HERMES: More insolence—the same kind as before
that got you anchored in this misery.

PROMETHEUS: Perhaps, but I choose punishment like mine
over servitude like yours. Go think on that.

HERMES: *(with sarcasm)* Oh, sure—to be a servant to a *rock*
is better than trusted messenger of Zeus.

PROMETHEUS: [...]‡
—an insult that insulters well deserve.   970

HERMES: You seem to revel in imprisonment.

---

* See note to line 62.

† Referring to the downfalls of Uranus and Cronus.

‡ It seems that a line has been lost here, containing a barbed rejoinder of Prometheus.

PROMETHEUS: Revel, do I? Then may I see my foes
 reveling just like me. And you among them.

HERMES: Do you hold *me* to blame for your misfortune?

PROMETHEUS: I'll make this easy: I hate *all* the gods
 who hurt me so unjustly, and still prosper.

HERMES: Your words are proof: You're mad. Your mind's diseased.

PROMETHEUS: If hating the gods is sick, then I'll be sick.

HERMES: If you were well, you'd be unbearable.

PROMETHEUS: (*groans in mock distress*) ōmoi!

HERMES: What was that cry of pain? Zeus doesn't know it.   980

PROMETHEUS: Just wait. Great lengths of time teach every lesson.

HERMES: Yet here you are, not learning to be wise.

PROMETHEUS: True—or I wouldn't be talking to *you*, chore-boy.

HERMES: Clearly you'll give my father no information.

PROMETHEUS: I'd happily pay him back what he's got coming.

HERMES: You taunt me just as though I were a child.

PROMETHEUS: But aren't you one, or something even simpler,
 if you think you'll learn anything from *me*?
 There's no invention, no new form of torture,
 that Zeus could use to make me tell him this
 before he loosens these disgraceful shackles.   990
 Rain down the scorching fire on my head,
 whirl everything into chaos, let the air
 be filled with blizzards and the ground with thunder;
 nothing of this will make me bend, or tell
 at whose hands he must fall from off his throne.

HERMES: You'd best consider: will this help your cause?

PROMETHEUS: It's been considered and planned out, long ago.

HERMES: You are misguided. Look at your present woes
 and bring yourself, one day, to change your mind.   1000

PROMETHEUS: You swamp me with a useless wave of words.
 Don't ever let this thought enter your head:
 that I'll fear Zeus' judgment, turn soft-minded,
 and kneel to supplicate the one I loathe—
 my hands held up to him in women's fashion—
 to free me from these bonds. I'll never do it.

HERMES: If I say more, I *will* be wasting words,
 since my entreaties have not softened you.
 Rather you bite, like an unbroken colt,

the bridle with your teeth and fight the reins. 1010
But it's an unsound plan that fuels your rage.
Mere stubbornness, without the help of wisdom,
is weaker, by itself, than everything.

Consider, if you don't obey my orders,
what storm of evils, what gigantic wave
will break on you, with no escape. My father
will smash this rocky cliff with thunderclaps
and fiery lightning-bolts; he'll bury you,
entomb you in an envelope of rock.
After an endless stretch of time goes by, 1020
you'll come back to the daylight. Now the eagle,
that murderous bird, the winged hound of Zeus,
will savagely slash tatters from your body,
a daily banqueter who comes unbidden;
he'll feast upon your mangled, blackened liver.
And don't expect these sufferings to end,
until some god agrees to take your place
and volunteers to go down into Hades,
the sunless realm, and Tartarus' gloomy depths.

Take stock of this. It's not a boast or fiction. 1030
The future I've described is all too real.
The mouth of Zeus does not know how to lie.
Whatever he says, will be. Just look around you.
Consider then. Don't count on stubbornness,
or ever think it better than good counsel.

CHORUS: It seems to us that Hermes speaks in season,
bidding you let go your willfulness
and choose instead good counsel, a wiser course.
Do as he says. The wise should not do wrong.

PROMETHEUS:* All that he said, I knew he would say. 1040
What's more, there's no shame if a foe
will get mistreatment from his foes.
So let the two-edged swirl of flame
be hurled at me, and let the air

---

* The meter changes to anapests, bringing a quicker, more urgent pace to the final speeches of the play.

be roiled with thunder and with winds
in wild convulsion, let the earth
be shaken to its very roots,
let waves of sea foam up and flood
the paths of stars as they cross the skies,
let *him* throw down my body   1050
into Tartarus' black pit
with harsh tornadoes of force;
there's no way he can kill me.

HERMES: One hears such words and schemes
often, from raving madmen.
Such boasts are clearly striking wide
of the mark, close to insanity.
(*to the Chorus*) You there, who showed
some sympathy for this one's pains:
Leave this place, and leave it fast,   1060
or else the cruel thunder's roar
may stun you into witlessness.

CHORUS: Give us some other kind of command
and we might obey. The words you dragged in
we cannot tolerate.
How can you bid us be base?
(*pointing to Prometheus*) We'll share with *him* that which we must.
We've learned to hate those who turn traitor.
There's no disease
I spit on more than treachery.   1070

HERMES: Well, then, remember what I've said.
And when you're caught in folly's snares,
don't blame bad luck. Don't ever say
that Zeus hurled ruin down on you
without forewarning. Don't, I tell you.
You did this to yourselves. You knew.
Not suddenly or stealthily
or in ignorance will you be coiled
inside blind folly's endless net.

> (*Hermes exits. Roaring and thunder are heard as Zeus begins to
> unleash his cataclysm.*)

PROMETHEUS: So! In truth, not just in threats,   1080
the earth begins to quake.

The crash of thunder rumbles back
from the depths below; bright curls of flame
flash forth, and whirlwinds spin the dust.
The clashing winds leap madly about,
vying as if in civil war,
all against all. The upper air
is mingled with the sea below.
Such is the fearsome stroke of Zeus,
leveled at me, in sight of all.   1090
Majesty of my mother Earth,
bright sky that lets the common light whirl round,
you see me here, and see my lot: *injustice.*

SOPHOCLES

Sophocles (496/5–406/5) was the most prolific of all the tragic poets, but he also found time to serve as a public official in Athens. A genial person who was popular with his fellow citizens, he was state treasurer in 443, elected a general in 441 in the war between Athens and the island of Samos. In 411 (when he was in his eighties) he was elected one of the commissioners who arranged for Athens to be governed as an oligarchy. He won his first victory in the tragic competitions in 469/8, defeating Aeschylus. In the course of his life he won some twenty victories in the tragic competitions, and second prizes in others, but he never came in last.

According to his ancient biographers, Sophocles learned about tragedy from Aeschylus, but his style is markedly different, more compressed and less metaphorical than that of his predecessor—in his own words, "sharp and artificial"—with unusual word choice and complex structures that make his writing thought-provoking. He increased the size of the Chorus and introduced innovations in music and costuming. His seven surviving dramas all feature characters who are remarkable for their determination and inflexibility, and who (although deserving of respect and even sympathy) isolate themselves from the other characters in the dramas. Like the historian Herodotus (whom he seems to have known), he recognizes the role played by the gods in human life but prefers to concentrate on the actions of human beings, most especially on their consistent inability to recognize the limitations of their knowledge. After his death he was worshipped as a hero.

Introduction to Sophocles'
Oedipus the King

The essence of the Oedipus story is laid out in four crisp lines of Homer's *Odyssey*. Oedipus' mother, there called Epicaste (rather than, as in Sophocles' version, Jocasta), married her son, unknowingly, after he had killed her husband, his father. "In time," this brief sketch goes on to say, "the gods made matters known to men" (11.274). That sentence focuses our attention on the questions of ignorance and knowledge, secrecy and discovery, that must have been central to the Oedipus myth as Homer knew it. Those questions also loomed large for Sophocles as he composed the drama that, ever since Aristotle's *Poetics* (written about a century after the play itself), has been anointed as the summit of perfection in the craft of Greek tragedy.

Homer's account describes an epiphany, sudden and terrifying, in which the gods revealed to Thebes the truth of Oedipus' condition. But Sophocles keeps the gods off the stage of his *Oedipus*, representing them only by indirections and implications: remembered oracles, extreme coincidences, and the dark pronouncements—fiercely rejected by Oedipus, who is not yet ready to understand—of the blind seer Tiresias. Instead, Sophocles arranges for truth to emerge slowly, piece by agonizing piece, in the way that mortals must endure when no divine revelations come to their aid. And he leaves it to a lowly shepherd, a nameless slave, to unveil the final clues to the terrible puzzle. At the start of the play, this shepherd is far from Thebes, in the high hills of Mount Cithaeron, where he tends his flocks and hides his secrets. By the end, he will have been brought to the royal palace and, as Oedipus prepares to torture the truth out of him, will speak what he knows.

Many years before, it was Oedipus himself who had been the victim of a cruel interrogation. The monstrous Sphinx was at that time terrorizing the Theban countryside, demanding of all passersby that they answer her riddle or die. (Later Greek sources specified the riddle, which was, "What creature has a single voice but goes on four legs, then two, then three?" The required answer is "man"—the animal that crawls as a baby, then walks upright, and finally uses a cane in old age.) Sophocles does not mention the riddle; its content does not seem to matter to him. Oedipus, en route from his native Corinth (at least, he *thinks* it is native) to Thebes, answered the riddle and saved the city, gaining its empty throne as his reward and, for his mate, the widow of Laius, the previous ruler. Thus he became Oedipus Rex, or Oedipus the King, a Latin translation of the more accurate Greek title *Oedipus Tyrannos,* "Oedipus who wielded sole power without the sanction of a monarchic line." (Both titles were contrived to distinguish this play from another of Sophocles' tragedies, *Oedipus at Colonus*; Sophocles himself, if he even thought of the play as having a title, would have called it simply *Oedipus.*)

The distinction between *rex* and *tyrannos* is an important one, even if it gets lost in translation from Greek to Latin (and sometimes, as at line 128, is ignored by Oedipus himself). Kings have scepters, thrones, and ancient lineages to prop up their power; the line of Laius, for example, goes straight back to Cadmus, the legendary founder of Thebes. Tyrants—the English derivative is our best equivalent for the Greek *tyrannoi,* if we strip away some of the modern word's connotations of abusive, cruel behavior—must work harder to maintain sovereignty, either by public works and benefices in the best instances, or by use of military force in the worst. The former case defines Oedipus in this play, a man who has already saved Thebes from the Sphinx and now vows to save it from a devastating plague; the latter, interestingly, defines Creon, who will succeed Oedipus as tyrant of Thebes and use exemplary punishment to firm up his rule, as portrayed by Sophocles in *Antigone.*

The parallels between the central figures of the two plays are close and revealing, even though the original productions are separated by a decade or more. (The three surviving "Theban plays" of Sophocles, *Oedipus Rex, Antigone,* and *Oedipus at Colonus,* are sometimes discussed, or packaged by modern publishers, as though they formed a connected trilogy, but in fact they were written for three separate dramatic festivals over a period of thirty-five years.) Both Oedipus in this play and Creon in the next preside over crises that threaten to destroy the city of Thebes; yet neither has the heroic stature or natural authority that such crises demand. Their zealous efforts to save their cities lead to unforeseen consequences. Both men confront the prophet Tiresias, and both respond vituperatively to his dark warnings, accusing the seer, in remarkably similar terms, of corruption and conspiracy. Both are quick to perceive threats in any obstacles that thwart their will.

Oedipus and Creon, the tyrant who saves and the tyrant who punishes, are twin Sophoclean studies in the toll that political power takes on the human spirit. It's instructive to read the confrontation between the two men in the *Oedipus Rex* (lines 532–678) in light of the role Creon had played in the *Antigone,* a play probably written earlier but taking place, according to mythic chronology, a few years later. Creon protests to Oedipus that he has no designs on rule, for, as Oedipus' brother-in-law, he enjoys the prerogatives of power without any of the responsibility:

> *Consider first, whether you think anyone*
> *would choose to rule in fear rather than sleep*
> *safe in his bed at night, yet have the same power...*
> *Now, I gain all this from you, without the fear,*
> *but if I were in charge, there'd be plenty to do*
> *not to my liking.* (584–86, 590–1)

These are sane, reasonable thoughts, spoken by a reasonable man. But that same man, as seen in the *Antigone*, will soon go down the very path he here abjures.

The supreme irony of the *Oedipus Rex* lies in the fact that Oedipus is, after all, the rightful monarch of Thebes: eldest son of Laius and Jocasta, though cast off at birth, and heir to the throne. The truth of his origins, the last of the truths revealed in the play and the one that makes sense of all the others, bears out the legitimacy of his rule at the same time that it utterly destroys him. Indeed, Homer's brief synopsis in the *Odyssey* has Oedipus retaining sovereignty over Thebes even after this truth was revealed, rather than, as Sophocles depicts, casting himself out of power by self-blinding and self-exile.

The slow steps by which Sophocles takes Oedipus, and the audience, to this revelation make this play a masterwork of dramatic construction. Signs, oracles, rumors, and remembrances come trickling out, harmonizing at one moment, contradicting the next. At several points, especially when news arrives of the death of Polybus, Oedipus' putative father, the emerging picture brings relief and puts all fears to flight; then, as that picture gets clearer, they return with redoubled force. The urgency of the inquest intensifies as it draws nearer to its goal. When at last the one man who can reveal all, the herdsman, is brought onstage, tension rises to a fever pitch. Oedipus by this point has guessed the truth, and Tiresias had largely revealed it well before, but the herdsman's testimony is nonetheless among the most gripping moments in theater. "I'm close to saying what I dread to say," the herdsman warns, to which Oedipus replies, with grim determination, "And I to hearing it, but hear I must."

It is difficult today to read *Oedipus*, or watch it onstage, without an awareness of Sigmund Freud, who not only named one of his central psychic complexes after its main character but also regarded the play generally, with its quest to recover origins and earliest experience, as an analogue for the type of therapy he championed: psychoanalysis. Whatever one thinks of Freud's reading, there can be little dispute that myth and psychology, always intertwined in Greek drama, stand in a particularly close embrace in this play. Jocasta, for example, points out that the incest Oedipus fears is a common theme of dreams (lines 981–82), and both forms of mutilation Oedipus undergoes—the piercing of his ankles at birth, and the gouging of his eyes at this play's end—have symbolic connections to castration. Part of the drama's power comes from the fact that its unveiling of the past is also a journey into the deepest, most universal levels of psychic experience.

Aristotle, in his *Poetics*, selected the *Oedipus* as the most exemplary of Greek tragedies for its capacity to produce pity and fear, and many subsequent ages have concurred. It is startling therefore to learn that Sophocles took second prize in the dramatic competition at which the play was staged, losing to Philocles, the nephew of Aeschylus. One would give a great deal to read the play that in its day was judged superior to the *Oedipus*, but the works of Philocles are entirely lost.

Oedipus the King

Translated by Frank Nisetich

Aristotle refers to the play simply as *Oedipus*, which was probably its original title. I have based this translation on the Greek text of the play edited by Hugh Lloyd-Jones and N. G. Wilson, *Sophoclis Fabulae* (Oxford: Oxford University Press, 1990, 1992). Occasionally, I refer to the same two authors' *Sophoclea: Studies on the Text of Sophocles* (Oxford: Oxford University Press, 1990); to R. C. Jebb, *Oedipus Tyrannus* (Cambridge: Cambridge University Press, 1893); and to R. D. Dawe, *Sophocles: Oedipus Rex* (Cambridge: Cambridge University Press, 2006). In a few instances, I have preferred readings by other scholars, noted where they occur. Passages considered as interpolations by Lloyd-Jones and Wilson are omitted from the text of the translation but are included in the notes.

Cast of Characters (in order of appearance)

Oedipus, son of Laius and Jocasta; king of Thebes
Priest of Zeus
Chorus of Theban elders, with their Leader
Creon, brother of Jocasta
Tiresias, a blind Theban prophet
Jocasta, wife and mother of Oedipus
Messenger from Corinth
Shepherd
Messenger from within the palace
Antigone and Ismene, young daughters of Oedipus and Jocasta
    (nonspeaking parts)
Guards and Attendants of the main characters (nonspeaking
    parts)

Setting: The play takes place in front of the royal palace of Thebes. The palace has a central door and two doors, one on either side. There is an altar in front of the central door and two smaller altars, one in front of each side door. A group of citizens of all ages led by an elderly priest is seated on the steps of the altars in the garb and attitude of suppliants. The central door of the palace opens and Oedipus emerges.

OEDIPUS: Children, latest in the line of ancient Cadmus,[*]
    what is the meaning of your sitting here?
    Why these suppliant branches, why these garlands?
    The city is full of the smoke of incense, prayers
    to the healing god,[†] lamentations, all at once.
    I didn't think it right, children, to hear of it
    at second hand, from messengers, but came myself—
    I, Oedipus, renowned in the eyes of all.
    (*to the priest*) Speak up, then, you whose age makes you
    the one to speak for these: Why are you here—   10
    is it something you're afraid of, something you want?
    I'll do all I can, for I'd be hard of heart
    if this appeal did not move me to pity.
PRIEST: Oedipus, ruler of my country,
    you see us, and you see our different ages
    as we take our seats at your altars—some not yet
    strong enough to fly far, others heavy with years.
    I am priest of Zeus, and these are the flower
    of our unmarried young; the rest of the people
    sit in the market places, garlanded, some at the twin   20
    temples of Pallas,[‡] others near Ismenus' mantic ash.[§]

---

[*] Cadmus was the son of Agenor and the legendary founder of Thebes. "Children" is a term of endearment here and in line 6.

[†] Apollo.

[‡] Athena, often called Pallas Athena or, as here, simply Pallas.

[§] Ismenus is a river at Thebes, on the banks of which stood a temple of the oracular god Apollo. The phrase "mantic ash" refers to an altar in the temple holding the ashes of sacrificial animals. Seers could foretell the future by observing the sacrifices conducted there.

For the city, as you see yourself, is pitched
and tossed beyond endurance. It can no longer
lift its head from the depths, the surge of blood.
There's death in the fruit-enfolding buds of earth,
death among the pasturing flocks, death in the barren
pangs of our women. A fiery god swoops down
and drives the city headlong—the hateful plague*
by which the house of Cadmus is emptied
and black Hades made rich with cries and groans.   30

    I wouldn't liken you to a god, Oedipus,
nor would these children sitting here as suppliants.
No, we consider you foremost among men
in the hazards of life, and when we have to deal
with powers more than human. It was you that came
to the town of Cadmus and freed us of the tax
we paid the cruel Sphinx.† No one taught you to do that,
we did not help you. Guided by a god—
they say and we believe—you lifted up our lives!

    But now, Oedipus, mightiest in the eyes of all,   40
we turn to you, in prayer: Find us help
in any way you can—from a god's utterance,
or a man's, anything you've heard and know.‡
Advice from men tested, like you, in action,
will not miss the mark. Come, then, best of mortals,
restore our city. Come, think of yourself.
We call you savior now because you sped
to our defense before. May we never
look back on your reign as the time
we stood up, only to fall down again later!   50
No—raise this city on a sure foundation.
The auspices§ were good back then, when you secured

---

* The plague afflicting the city is personified as the god who sends it.

† The Sphinx was sent by Hera to afflict the Thebans for neglecting to punish their king, Laius, for the rape of Chrysippus, son of Pelops. As a result of that sexual crime, Laius was warned by Apollo that if he had a son, that son would kill him. The Sphinx devoured any Theban who could not solve the riddle she posed. When Oedipus succeeded in solving it, she leaped to her death.

‡ Line 43 of the Greek text ends with the two words *oistha pou* ("you somehow know"), evoking Oedipus' name, Oidipous. One popular etymology of the name derives its first syllable from *oida*, meaning "I know."

§ Metaphorical: Oedipus' success in dealing with the Sphinx boded well for the future of his rule in Thebes.

our luck for us; be the same once more!
For if you mean to go on ruling the land,
better to rule it full of men than empty.
For what are city walls or ships without
men alive in them? Nothing, nothing at all.

OEDIPUS: Children, you have my sympathy. Known
and not unknown to me are the needs
that brought you here, for well I know   60
you are all sick, yet none so sick as I.
The pain *you* feel comes to each of you
alone, apart from others, but *my* heart
groans for city and self and you alike.
You haven't roused me, then, as if from sleep.
No, often—I tell you—I have wept
and traveled many a road, wandered in thought.
I've looked long and hard, and found
a single remedy: I've sent Creon,
my brother-in-law, to the Pythian* house,   70
the oracle of Phoebus† at Delphi, to learn
what I must do or say to guard this city.
And now, when I reckon the time he's been away,
I worry how he is, for he's been gone
too long, well beyond what you'd expect.
When he returns, I'd be of no account
if I didn't do everything the god prescribes.

PRIEST: Your words are well timed—just now these men
signal to me that Creon is approaching.

OEDIPUS: O lord Apollo! May his coming be a stroke   80
of luck, salvation shining like a light!

PRIEST: My guess is, he brings good news. Otherwise
he wouldn't be coming crowned in radiant laurel.

OEDIPUS: We'll know soon. He's within hearing now.
(*calling offstage*) Lord, son of Menoeceus, my kinsman,‡
what news do you bring us from the god?

---

* A constant epithet of Apollo and of his oracle at Delphi, which was also known as Pytho, from the serpent Python, slain by Apollo when he took possession of the site.

† The most familiar epithet of Apollo, often standing for the god himself. It means "radiant" or "bright."

‡ The Greek word here translated "kinsman" (*kēdeuma*) denotes relation by marriage only, not by blood. But the audience knows that the relation between Oedipus and Creon is closer than that.

(Enter Creon.)

CREON: The news is good, on the whole, for even
    hardships, if they come out right, are fortunate.

OEDIPUS: But what did the god say? What you've hinted so far
    leaves me neither encouraged nor alarmed.   90

CREON: I'm prepared to speak, if you want to hear while these
    are present *(indicating the Chorus)*, or would you rather go inside?

OEDIPUS: Speak out for all to hear. The suffering
    of these, my people, means more than my own life.

CREON: Well, then, what I heard from the god was this:
    Phoebus orders us, my lord, to expel
    a pollution nurtured in this land of ours
    and not still nurture it till it's past cure.

OEDIPUS: How rid ourselves of it? What's the remedy?

CREON: Exile, or killing in return for killing   100
    since it is blood that engulfs the city now.

OEDIPUS: Whose blood? Who met this fate? Does the god say?

CREON: We had a leader,* my lord—Laius, who ruled
    this land before you took the city's helm.

OEDIPUS: I know of him, by hearsay—never saw him.

CREON: Well, he died, and the god commands us now
    to punish his murderers, whoever they are.

OEDIPUS: But *where* are they? The track of this old crime,
    so faded now—where will it be found?

CREON: Here, he said, in this land. "The thing pursued   110
    is catchable; the thing ignored escapes."

OEDIPUS: Did Laius meet his death in Thebes,
    at home or out of doors, or was he traveling?

CREON: He went to consult the oracle, as he said
    at the time. He never came home again.

OEDIPUS: Was there no one to report, no fellow traveler
    who saw, whose testimony might have helped?

CREON: They all died, all but one who fled in terror
    and couldn't say what he saw, but for one thing.

OEDIPUS: What was it? Knowing one thing, you may learn many,   120
    if you are eager, and start searching right away.†

---

* Perhaps in deference to Oedipus, Creon does not call Laius what he was, and Oedipus (as far as he knows) is not the hereditary king of Thebes.

† I render the emendation suggested in *Sophoclea* (82–83) and printed by Lloyd-Jones in his Loeb edition.

CREON: Bandits, he said, met and killed him. The strength
of many, not just one, brought him down.
OEDIPUS: How could this "bandit"* dare go so far, unless
he acted with support—money from here?
CREON: We thought so, too. But once Laius was killed
no one emerged to help us in our troubles.
OEDIPUS: The tyranny† brought down the way it was, what
"troubles" could keep you from looking into it?
CREON: The riddle-chanting Sphinx kept our eyes   130
on things at hand. Those out of sight we left alone.
OEDIPUS: I'll bring them back to light, from the beginning!
Phoebus is right, and so are you, Creon,
to show concern for the man who was killed.
And now you'll see me also take his side,
as I should, supporting land and god together.
It's not for the sake of a distant friend
that I'll dispel this pollution, but for my own.
For the man who killed *him* may well want
to turn on *me* with the same violence.‡   140
By taking up his cause, I help myself.
        Rise up now, children, from these steps. Hurry,
and take your suppliant branches with you.
Let someone else gather the people here,
and leave the rest to me. For either
we fare well with the god's help, or we fall.
        (Oedipus exits into the palace; Creon exits offstage.)
PRIEST: Let us rise, children. What we came to hear
we have heard proclaimed just now.
And may Phoebus, who sent these prophecies,
come, save, and deliver us from plague!   150

---

* Oedipus already suspects that more than banditry was involved. The switch from plural to singular is also significant: Laius was in fact killed by a lone individual, Oedipus himself, not by a band of robbers.

† Oedipus uses the Greek word *tyrannis*, whose English equivalent "tyranny" has a pejorative sense not always felt in Greek and felt here, if at all, in a way very different from the way it is felt in English. Laius was a legitimate king who had inherited his power; Oedipus is a "tyrant" who has won his. His reference to the rule of Laius as a "tyranny" does not imply that there was anything "tyrannical" (in our sense of the word) about his reign; it is a way of putting himself on a par with his predecessor, a hint at his own insecurity. See the preface to this play.

‡ Athenian law required that a murdered man's closest kin prosecute his killer. Oedipus, unaware of his relationship to Laius, gives other reasons for his involvement in the case.

*(Priest and suppliants leave. The Chorus of elders, representing
"the people of Cadmus" referred to by Oedipus in line 144, enter
the orchestra, singing the* parodos *or entry song.)*

strophe 1

Oracle of Zeus, coming from Pytho* steeped in gold
to radiant Thebes, what, what do you mean
by this welcome message? I am prostrate with dread,
my fearful heart beating—O Delian Paean!†—
in awe of you. What is the debt you will exact of me?
Is it new, or come back again
with the seasons coming round?
Answer me, O child of golden Hope, immortal Voice!

antistrophe 1

Calling first on you, immortal Athena,
daughter of Zeus, and on your sister   160
Artemis, our land's guardian,
throned in glory in the market place,
and on Apollo who strikes from afar:
appear to me now, O triple averters of doom!
If ever before, when ruin towered above our city,
you put the flame of pain to flight, come to us now!

strophe 2

Ah, numberless are the pains
I bear—my people sick, sick
to the core, and in my mind
I find no sword to ward it off.   170
The glorious earth
puts forth no fruit, the pangs
of women do not end in birth.
You may see now one,
now another, like a bird
on the wing, faster than resistless fire, speed
to the shore of the western god.‡

---

* Delphi. See note to line 70.

† A healing god, often identified, as here, with Apollo, called "Delian" because he was born on the island of Delos.

‡ Hades. The darkness of the west, into which the sun disappears at evening, is conflated with the darkness of the Underworld.

antistrophe 2

> The city, perishing, loses count
> of her dead—her sons, unpitied,
> no one to lament them,   180
> strew the ground
> to breed yet still more death. Here
> and there young wives and gray-haired
> mothers huddle at the altars,
> groaning, crying to be freed of pain.
> The paean* blazes to the sound of voices
> keening. O against all this, golden
> daughter of Zeus, send us protection!

strophe 3

> And may savage Ares†
> armed in no armor but with cries   190
> clashing around him, charging,
> scorching me—turn in retreat and run
> far from my country, sped
> on the breeze, off to the great
> chamber of Amphitrite‡
> or the waves of Thrace
> that brook no anchorings,§
> for what the night fails to kill
> falls by his hand next day.
> Him, O father Zeus, master   200
> of fiery lightning, destroy
> with your thunderbolt!

antistrophe 3

> How gladly would I see shot
> from your bow strung with gold,
> Lycian lord,¶ arrows invincible
> in our defense, and the fiery
> torches of Artemis with which she scours

---

* Not, as often, a joyful hymn, but here an appeal to the healing god Paean.
† God of war, personifying the plague afflicting Thebes.
‡ A sea nymph, wife of Poseidon, god of the sea. The epithet "great" indicates that the Atlantic is meant.
§ The "waves of Thrace" are the Black Sea, known for its storminess and the savagery of the peoples living near it.
¶ Apollo. His weapon is the bow.

the mountains of Lycia,
and I call on the god who binds
his hair in gold and gives his name to our land,* 210
Bacchus, to whom they cry *euoi*†
when, wreathed in clusters, he leads
the maenads:‡ come, ablaze
with torches of pine, against
the god who has no honor among the gods!§

(Enter Oedipus from the palace.)

OEDIPUS: You've made your prayer, and what you pray for,
protection, relief from these ills, you will obtain
if you listen to me and so give the disease
the care it requires. I speak to you as stranger
to the tale and stranger to the deed. For I 220
could not get far on the track of it without
a clue. But as it is, and since I became
your fellow citizen after the crime, I say
to all the people of Cadmus: whoever knows
by whose hand Laius, Labdacus' son, was killed,
I order him to tell me everything.
And if he is afraid that, by freeing <others>¶ 227
of the charge, <he will bring his own death
down>on himself, he needn't fear; he'll suffer 228
no worse than exile, and go away unhurt.
But if anyone knows that some other Theban 230
or foreigner is the killer, let him speak;
I'll make it worth his while, and show thanks, too.
But if you hold back, and any of you, afraid
for a friend or himself, spurns this command,
hear from me now what I'll do next: I forbid
anyone in this land—the land whose power

---

* Dionysus, also known as Bacchus, was born in Thebes. The city, in consequence of the god's birth there, is called Bacchic Thebes.

† A cry of joy, linguistically meaningless, uttered by the worshippers of Bacchus.

‡ Frenzied female attendants of Dionysus, also called Bacchae or Bacchants.

§ Ares.

¶ A line seems to be missing between lines 227 and 228. The words between angle brackets translate the supplement proposed by Lloyd-Jones. The phrase "by freeing <others> of the charge" is a euphemism for "by admitting that *he* is the killer."

and throne I possess—either to welcome
or talk to him, whoever he is, or join him
in prayers to the gods, or share with him
in sacrifice, or in the lustral water.* No,   240
but all must drive him from their houses—he's
our pollution, as the oracle of the god
in Delphi has just now disclosed to me.
This, then, is the role I take upon myself—
ally of the god and the man who died.†   245
      All this I charge you to accomplish,   252
for my sake and Apollo's, and this land
so blighted—barren and hated by the gods.
For even if the god weren't forcing this on you
you shouldn't leave it festering so, and this
the case of a noble man, your murdered king.‡
No, you'd have to search it out! But now,
since I enjoy the power that was his, and have
his bed and the woman he embraced in it,   260
who would have borne him children, siblings
to my own, had not his hopes of offspring
foundered and bad luck swooped upon him—
for all these reasons, I will fight for him
as for my own father, go to every length
in my determination to catch the killer
of the son of Labdacus, son of Polydorus,
son of Cadmus before and of ancient Agenor.
      For those who do not do as I command, I pray
the gods send them no harvest from the earth,   270
no children from their wives. Let them be destroyed

---

* Water played an important part in sacrificial ritual. All sacrifices began with the washing of hands by priest and participants. To be denied access to this "holy water" was to be denied membership in the community.

† Lines 246–51 are interpolated. They read:
    And I pray that he who did it, whether he's
    escaped detection alone or with others,
    wear out his life in doom, evil in evil.
    I pray, too, that if I shelter him
    in my own house, and do it knowingly,
    I feel the curses I have just pronounced.

‡ Oedipus here calls Laius by his legitimate title, that of king, though he had referred to his rule as a "tyranny" before (line 128). He reverts to calling him a "tyrant" at lines 799 and 1043.

by the very fate upon us now, and by one
worse still. But all you other Thebans, to whom
my commands are welcome, may Justice fight
for you, and the gods favor you forever!

CHORUS LEADER: Since you've put me on oath, so, lord, I'll speak:
I did not kill, nor can I reveal the killer.
It lies with Phoebus, who launched this search,
to say who did the deed, so long ago.

OEDIPUS: Right, but to compel the gods to act   280
against their will—that no one can do.

CHORUS LEADER: May I suggest, then, what seems second best?

OEDIPUS: And third best, too: leave nothing out.

CHORUS LEADER: The lord Tiresias, I know, sees with the eyes
of Phoebus, his lord: from him, my lord, would a man
tracking all this learn of it most clearly.

OEDIPUS: Here, too, I haven't been remiss. I've sent, twice now,
at Creon's suggestion, escorts to bring him here.
I've long been wondering why he hasn't come yet.

CHORUS LEADER: Apart from him, all we have is ancient gossip.   290

OEDIPUS: Gossip? What sort? I'll leave no stone unturned.

CHORUS LEADER: They say it was some highwaymen that killed him.

OEDIPUS: I've heard that, too, but no one sees the doer.*

CHORUS LEADER: If he has a trace of dread in him, he won't
stay hidden—such are the curses you have uttered.

OEDIPUS: A man not afraid to strike won't fear a threat.

CHORUS LEADER: (*glancing offstage*) No matter; here's the one who will
convict him.
For here I see them, bringing the godlike prophet;
in him, alone among men, truth is inborn.

> (*Enter Tiresias, a blind prophet, accompanied by Oedipus'
> attendants. A boy guides his steps.*)

OEDIPUS: Tiresias, master of all that can or can't   300
be taught or said, in heaven, or treading the earth—
you know, though you don't see, what sort of disease

---

* Again, as at line 124, Oedipus answers his interlocutor's plural ("highwaymen") with a singular ("the doer"). The manuscripts have "the one who saw" (*ton d'idont'*) as object of the verb here. I've translated the text of Lloyd-Jones and Wilson, which prints the anonymous eighteenth-century emendation *ton de dront'*, "the one doing," i.e. the killer. The three lines immediately following this one, especially 296, make it certain that the reference here is to the killer, not the witness.

feeds on our city; against it, lord, we find
no champion, no savior but you alone!
For Phoebus—if you haven't heard already—
has given us an answer to our question:
deliverance from this plague will come to us
only if we kill the killers of Laius
or banish them, once we know who they are.
Do not, then, begrudge us what you know   310
by augury, or other mantic means.
Save yourself, save the city, and save me—
drive out all taint that comes from that dead man!
We are in your hands. To help, with all you have
and all you can do, is the noblest task.

TIRESIAS: There's nothing to be said for understanding
if you have it and gain nothing. I knew that well,
and forgot it. Else I wouldn't be here now.

OEDIPUS: What's wrong? You've just arrived, and yet so downcast!

TIRESIAS: Send me home. You'll bear your part most easily   320
and I will mine, if you take my advice.

OEDIPUS: What you say is surprising, without regard for the city
that reared you. Don't deny us this response.*

TIRESIAS: I see that what you say is off the mark.
That's why, so as not to err like you—

OEDIPUS: By the gods! If you know, don't turn away.
We beg you, all of us, as suppliants.

TIRESIAS: Yes, for all of you don't know! But I will never
reveal *my* troubles—not to speak of yours.

OEDIPUS: What are you saying? You know, and will not speak?   · 330
Will you betray us, and destroy the city?

TIRESIAS: I'll vex neither myself nor you. Why probe
these things in vain? You won't find out from me.

OEDIPUS: No? *You traitor!* Or worse: you'd move
a stone to rage! So you'll *never* speak out,
just stay stubborn, and avoid the point?

TIRESIAS: You fault my temper but refuse to see
the temper in yourself. No, you blame *me*.

---

* The word has a formal, religious meaning here: what Tiresias says in answer to the question asked indirectly at lines 308–10 would have the authority of an oracle.

OEDIPUS: Who wouldn't be enraged when he hears words
    like yours, that show this city no respect?   340

TIRESIAS: Things will out, whether I speak or not.

OEDIPUS: Shouldn't you tell me, then, just *what* will out?

TIRESIAS: I'll say no more. Rage at *that*, if you want to,
    with all the anger, all the savagery you can.

OEDIPUS: Anger, you say? Yes, I'll let fly, I'll lay out
    all I see going on here. It's plain to me
    you hatched the scheme and did the deed, just short
    of killing him yourself, with your own hands. And if
    you weren't blind I'd say you did that, too, unaided!

TIRESIAS: Is that so? Then I insist that you abide   350
    by your own proclamation, and from this day
    speak neither to these men here nor to me.
    For *you* are the unholy polluter of our land.

OEDIPUS: So shameless, to stir up a tale like that?
    Where can you run to, where find an escape?

TIRESIAS: I *have* escaped. The truth within me is my strength.

OEDIPUS: Who taught this "truth" to you? Not your art!

TIRESIAS: It came from you—you made me speak.

OEDIPUS: Made you speak *what*? Repeat it, make it clearer.

TIRESIAS: You didn't understand it the first time? […]*   360

OEDIPUS: Not so as to be sure. Say it again.

TIRESIAS: *You* are the killer you are looking for.

OEDIPUS: You'll live to regret saying that—twice now.

TIRESIAS: Shall I say more, to make you even madder?

OEDIPUS: Yes, all you like. Your words will come to nothing.

TIRESIAS: You don't know that you live in deepest shame with those
    most near to you†—you're sunk in evils you don't see.

OEDIPUS: You think you'll go on like this, and get away?

TIRESIAS: Yes, if there's any power in the truth.

OEDIPUS: There is, but not in your case. For you it fails,   370
    because you're blind—in ears and mind and eyes.

---

* The end of this line is corrupt. It is clear from the remains of it that Tiresias asks a second question, but what it was cannot be made out. Oedipus, in response, answers only the first one.

† The Greek word here rendered "live … with" may also have the meaning "live in intimacy with," "be married to." Likewise, "those most near to you" may refer simply to the members of the family but is more likely to be an allusive plural, a euphemism for Jocasta alone.

TIRESIAS: What a sad case you are, taunting me
    as all these here will soon be taunting you!
OEDIPUS: Wrapped as you are in endless dark, you can't
    hurt me or anyone who sees the light.
TIRESIAS: True—I'm not the one to cause your fall.
    Apollo, who wants to see it, will suffice.
OEDIPUS: Whose revelations are these? Creon's?
TIRESIAS: Creon's not your problem. It's you yourself.
OEDIPUS: O wealth and tyranny* and skill   380
    surpassing skill in the ambitious life!
    How great is the envy you have in store
    if, for this power, that the city handed to me—
    a gift, a thing I never asked to have—
    Creon, my confidant, my friend from the start,
    sneaks up on me and wants to cast me out;
    he bribes this fortune-teller, this conniver,
    a slick impostor with an eye for gain
    but blind when it comes to prophecy!
    (*to Tiresias*) So, tell us now: what makes you a real prophet?   390
    Why, when that rhapsodic hound† was here,
    did you say nothing to save these people?
    Yet hers was a riddle‡ not just anyone
    might solve. It required skill in mantic art,
    skill you didn't seem to have, from birds
    or from the gods. And then *I* came along,
    Oedipus the know-nothing.§ I stopped her,
    using my brains, not what the birds told me—
    and *I'm* the one you're forcing out? You think
    one day you'll stand by Creon's throne. Well, I think   400

---

* See note to line 128. The word, again, is not pejorative. Oedipus is thinking of supreme power in the city as a prize to be gained by ambition. He has that power, but he goes on to insist that he didn't aim to achieve it.

† Alluding to the Sphinx, called "rhapsodic" because her riddle was posed in dactylic hexameter, the meter of the Homeric poems, which were recited by professional "rhapsodes."

‡ The first of two direct references to the riddle in the play (the other occurs at line 1525). It is preserved in its most complete form as follows: "There is upon earth a thing two-footed and four-footed and three-footed, which has one voice, and which, alone of things that make their way on earth or up in the sky or down in the sea, changes its nature, and when it goes supported on most feet, then is the speed of its limbs most feeble." The answer is "man," who crawls on all fours in infancy, walks on two feet in maturity, and needs the support of a staff, a third foot, in old age.

§ Alluding again (see note to line 43) to the popular etymology of Oedipus' name.

that you and he will rue the day you plotted
to purify this land! If you didn't look so old,
you'd know by now what plans like yours deserve.

CHORUS LEADER: It seems to me, Oedipus, his words before
and yours just now have been said in anger.
We don't need that, but rather to consider
how best to unravel the god's prophecies.

TIRESIAS: Though you are tyrant here, others still have
the right to answer you at equal length.
I claim it, too, for I'm no slave of yours   410
but of Loxias*—*he's* my sponsor here, not Creon.
And since you mock my blindness, I say
you see all right, but not the evil you're in,
or where you live, or whom you live with. Do you know
your origins? You don't even know that you
are loathsome to your kin, both those beneath
and those upon the earth. Your mother's and father's
double curse will hound† you from this land
one day, in terror—sighted now, but seeing
darkness then. What refuge for your cries?   420
What Cithaeron‡ will not echo them,
when you've seen it for what it was—that wedding
in the palace, that port no port at all, into which
you sailed so smoothly! Nor do you see
what evils will make you equal to yourself
and to your children.§ Go on, then, trample Creon
and my predictions in the mud. No mortal man
will ever be crushed more cruelly than you!

OEDIPUS: (*to the Chorus*) Must I hear all this from *him*?
(*rounding on Tiresias*) To hell with you! Show us your back—   430
hurry, leave this house, be *gone*!

---

* An epithet of Apollo, from *loxos,* "slanted, crooked," presumably because his oracles were obscure, indirect.

† Curses uttered by parents against children who have offended or harmed them were carried out by the Erinyes, or Furies, often imagined as hounds in pursuit of prey.

‡ Mount Cithaeron, south of Thebes, where the infant Oedipus was put out to die. Here Tiresias makes it stand for any mountain that will echo to the cries of the man Oedipus as Cithaeron had echoed to those of the baby. Oedipus knows nothing of this as yet.

§ I retain the reading of the manuscripts and take the line as Jebb takes it: "you" is Oedipus as he sees himself now; "yourself" is Oedipus as he really is. He will be "equal to" his children when he realizes that he is their brother as well as their father.

TIRESIAS: I wouldn't have come if you hadn't called me.

OEDIPUS: Had I any idea you'd utter such drivel,
  I'd never have summoned you to my house.

TIRESIAS: A driveller I seem to you, but your parents,
  the ones who gave you life, thought I made sense.

OEDIPUS: What parents? Wait! Who brought me forth?

TIRESIAS: This day will bring you forth, and will destroy you.

OEDIPUS: More of the same—words too puzzling, too dark.

TIRESIAS: Aren't you our champion riddle solver?   440

OEDIPUS: That's right—revile me where you'll find me great.

TIRESIAS: And yet success in this has been your ruin.

OEDIPUS: I don't care, if I've saved this city by it.

TIRESIAS: I'm going now. Boy, help me on my way.

OEDIPUS: Yes, go, get out! You're nothing here
  but trouble: leave, and cease to cause me pain.

TIRESIAS: I'll go. I've said what I came here to say,
  no fear of you—for you cannot destroy me.
  And I tell you: this man, the one you've long
  been looking for, with threats and proclamations   450
  about the death of Laius—he's *here*, a guest
  from abroad, so they say, but soon to emerge
  a native Theban, though he'll take no pleasure
  in *that* discovery! Blind instead of seeing,
  beggar instead of rich, he'll make his way
  to a foreign land, feeling the ground with a stick.
  And he'll be found to be both brother and father
  to his children, son and husband to
  his mother—breeding where his father bred,
  having spilled his father's blood! Now go inside   460
  and think that over. If you catch me lying,
  then say I have no skill in prophecy!

  *(Tiresias exits to the side. Oedipus watches him leave for a
  moment, then turns abruptly and goes back into the palace.)*

strophe 1

  CHORUS: Who is the man the oracle-echoing rock of Delphi
    sings of, who did unspeakable deeds with bloody hands?
    Time for him to set his foot
    in flight faster than horses

with storm in their hooves!
For the son of Zeus,* armed
with fiery lightning leaps upon him   470
and the dread avenging Spirits of Death†
join in pursuit and will not lose the trail.

antistrophe 1

Just now flamed the command from snow-capped
Parnassus:‡ all must hunt him down, the man unseen.
For under the wild wood,
in caves, among rocks
he roams, like the bull bereft
of his herd, hampered, with hampered foot§
trying to outrun the prophecies   480
from earth's center,¶ that hover
around him, ever on target, ever alive.

strophe 2

Terribly, terribly now the wise
prophet has shaken me—
I neither agree nor deny—
I don't know what to say,
I flutter with hopes, unable to see
here, or into the future.
Not now or before have I ever heard
that in the past there was strife   490
between the Labdacids**
and the son of Polybus,††
nothing <I could rely on>‡‡
to put to the test, or cause me

---

* Apollo, speaking through his oracle at Delphi.

† *Keres*, often identified with the Erinyes, or Furies.

‡ A mountain of the Pindus range, north of the Corinthian Gulf. The oracle of Delphi is located on its southern slope.

§ A hint, perhaps, at Oedipus' lameness, referred to later in the play (lines 1031–36).

¶ Delphi, seat of Apollo's oracle, here, as often, thought to be the center of the earth.

** Descendants of Labdacus, who was father of Laius and (unbeknownst to the Chorus) grandfather of Oedipus.

†† Polybus was king of Corinth and supposed father of Oedipus, having reared him after Laius had put him out to die.

‡‡ The meter indicates that a word is missing from line 494. The words enclosed in angle brackets translate the supplement of G. Wolff as reported by Lloyd-Jones.

to doubt the glory of Oedipus
and come to the aid*
of the Labdacids, for a murder sunk in darkness.

antistrophe 2

Zeus and Apollo are wise, and know
the ways of men. But whether among men
a seer counts more than I do,   500
there is no way of knowing,
for one man's wisdom
may surpass another's. But I would not,
before I've seen what's said is true,
add my consent
to those who condemn Oedipus.
For once, in sight of all, the winged girl†
swept against him
and he showed himself wise
in the contest, a joy to my city.   510
So in my thoughts
he could not be guilty of a crime.

(Enter Creon.)

CREON: Citizens, I'm here because I've heard
news that I can't bear to hear—
that Oedipus the tyrant‡ is accusing me!
For if in times like these he thinks that he's
been hurt by me, by what I've said or done—
if *that's* what he says, I tell you I don't want
to go on living. It's no little thing,
the damage done to me by such a charge.   520
It's huge, to be called a traitor by my city—
a traitor, by you and by my friends!

CHORUS LEADER: The charge *did* pass his lips, but it could be
that anger more than judgment forced it out.

---

* The prosecutor of a murderer acted in defense of the victim.

† The Greek Sphinx, unlike the Egyptian, had wings.

‡ Perhaps the phrase (repeated at line 925) that suggested the title given to the play in the manuscript tradition, *Oedipus the Tyrant*, the Latin translation of which, *Oedipus Rex*, gives us *Oedipus the King*. Creon uses the word as if it is the normal way of referring to Oedipus, but the latter's suspicion of his closest associate is typical of a tyrant. The nuance may have been picked up by the audience, if not by the characters onstage.

CREON: But didn't he say that it was *my* idea
 to make the prophet utter falsehoods?

CHORUS LEADER: He did, but I know he didn't think it through.

CREON: Was he seeing straight, was he thinking straight
 when he made this accusation?

CHORUS LEADER: I don't know. Power acts beyond my ken.*   530
     (Enter Oedipus, from the palace.)

OEDIPUS: You! What are *you* doing here? Where do you get   532
 the nerve, the gall to come to my house—you,
 my killer plain as day, the thief with clear
 designs upon my throne? Speak up, by the gods!
 Was it cowardice or feeble-mindedness
 you saw in me, that you could hatch this scheme?
 Or did you think I wouldn't see who set
 the plot in motion, and not defend myself?
 Isn't it foolish, this attempt of yours,   540
 to seek a tyranny,† without wealth and friends?
 For that you need popular support and money.‡

CREON: You know what's called for now? Quit talking,
 listen, and then judge, when you've heard me out.

OEDIPUS: You speak well, but I won't learn well
 for I have found a deadly enemy in you.

CREON: First listen to what I have to say.

OEDIPUS: Just don't "say" that you're not treacherous!

CREON: If you think stubbornness, without knowledge,
 worth having, you aren't thinking straight.   550

OEDIPUS: If you think you won't pay for abusing
 a kinsman,§ you haven't thought it through.

CREON: I agree. There's justice in what you say.
 But what is it, this "abuse" you've suffered?

OEDIPUS: Did you, or did you not, persuade me
 that I should send for that pompous seer?

---

* The next line (531) is probably interpolated:
 But here he is, come from the house just now.

† See note to line 380.

‡ Historical tyrants (Pisistratus in Athens, for example) seized and maintained power by using their wealth to curry favor with the people.

§ The word used here (*suggenēs*) may mean "of the same blood" as well as "of the same family" (e.g. an in-law). Oedipus has the latter in mind, but the audience, knowing that Creon is in fact his uncle, may think of the former, too.

CREON: I did, and I'd advise the same again.
OEDIPUS: How long is it now since Laius—
CREON: Did what? I don't know what you're driving at.
OEDIPUS: —vanished, a victim of deadly violence? 560
CREON: It would be years now—a long time ago.
OEDIPUS: At that time, then, was this seer in practice?
CREON: He was—wise then as now, and just as honored.
OEDIPUS: Did he say anything about me then?
CREON: Not when I was around. I'm sure of that.
OEDIPUS: And didn't you try to find the killer?
CREON: We did—how could we not?—but we heard nothing.
OEDIPUS: What kept our wise man from speaking up?
CREON: I don't know. When I don't know, I don't speak.
OEDIPUS: This much you know and, if you're wise, you'll say— 570
CREON: What? If I can, I won't refuse to answer.
OEDIPUS: —that if he hadn't been suborned by you
  he'd never have said that *I* killed Laius.
CREON: *You* know if he said that. But *I've* the right
  to ask as much from you as you from me.
OEDIPUS: Ask on. You won't convict *me* of the murder.
CREON: To begin, then: you're husband to my sister?
OEDIPUS: Indeed I am—there's no need to deny it.
CREON: And rule the land, hand in hand with her?
OEDIPUS: She gets, from me, everything she wants. 580
CREON: And am I not third, equal to you two?
OEDIPUS: Yes, and a bad friend, for that very reason!
CREON: No, not if you can look at it my way.
  Consider first, whether you think anyone
  would choose to rule in fear rather than sleep
  safe in his bed at night, yet have the same power.
  Just so, I would not prefer to be
  tyrant myself, but to do what a tyrant does,
  and so would anyone who had any sense.
  Now, I gain all this from you, without the fear, 590
  but if *I* were in charge, there'd be plenty to do
  not to my liking. How then would tyranny
  look better to me than power without pain?
  I'm not so deluded that I crave
  anything that isn't noble *and* enjoyable.

As it is, all greet me, all welcome me,
and those in need of *you* confide in me;
that way they get everything they wish for.
Why give up all of that, just for this?*   599
I've never hankered after thoughts like those   601
nor would I work with anyone who did.
For proof, go to Pytho, check the oracle,
see if it tallies with the one I brought;
and then, if you find that I've conspired
with the seer, seize and kill me, not by a single
but a double vote, mine and yours together—
but don't accuse me at a whim, a guess!
For, without evidence, it is unjust
to think bad men are good or good men bad.†   610
But you'll know all of this for sure, in time,   613
for time alone reveals the man who's just
while you can know a bad one in a day.

CHORUS LEADER: (*to Oedipus*) A careful man would say he argues well.
A choice too quickly made is soon regretted.

OEDIPUS: When anyone who plots in secret against me
moves fast, I must be fast to counter him.
If I let down my guard and bide my time,   620
he will achieve his aims, mine come to nothing.

CREON: What, then, do you want? To send me into exile?

OEDIPUS: Not at all. I want you dead, not banished.
Let the whole world know what envy comes to.‡

CREON: You mean you won't relent, you won't believe me?   625

OEDIPUS: <No. I'm not sure you ought to be believed.>§

CREON: Nor am I, that you make sense!   **OED.:** I do—in *my* eyes.   626

CREON: You should, in *mine*, too.   **OED.:** Not when you're a traitor.

CREON: And if you're wrong?   **OED.:** I still must rule this land.

CREON: Not when you rule it badly.   **OED.:** O city, city!

---

* I.e. to supplant Oedipus as "tyrant" in Thebes. Lines 587–99 refute the charge made at 540–42. The next line (600) is interpolated:
    A man of sense won't make a bad choice.

† The next 2 lines (611–12) are interpolated:
    And a good friend, the man whom one loves most,
    just like one's life, must not be thrown away.

‡ I follow Jebb here, assigning this line, as slightly emended by Jebb, to Oedipus.

§ Something has dropped out between lines 625 and 626. I translate Jebb's supplement, which bridges the gap.

CREON: This is my city, too, not yours alone.   630

CHORUS LEADER: Enough, my lords! I see Jocasta coming
    from the palace, just in time. With her help,
    you need to bring this quarrel to an end.
        (Enter Jocasta.)

JOCASTA: Why this senseless storm of words?
    Is this the time to stir up private ills,
    when the country's sick? Aren't you ashamed?
    (to Oedipus) You, go inside! And you to your house, Creon;
    don't make so much of nothing!

CREON: Sister, Oedipus your husband has just passed
    a dire sentence. He's weighing only whether   640
    to banish me, or seize and have me killed.

OEDIPUS: Just so—for I have caught him plotting
    against my person with his evil wiles.

CREON: May I not prosper, but die accursed
    if I did anything you say I've done!

JOCASTA: By the gods, Oedipus, believe his words!
    Respect, above all else, the oath he's sworn;
    respect me, too, and these men here before you.
        (The Chorus and Oedipus now sing together.)*

strophe

    CHORUS: Be persuaded, lord,
        in mind and heart, I pray.   650
    OEDIPUS: Persuaded of what? What do you want from me?
    CHORUS: That you respect one who's been no fool before
        and stands strong now by the oath he's sworn.
    OEDIPUS: Do you know what you're asking?
    CHORUS: Yes.
    OEDIPUS: Say it, then!†
    CHORUS: Don't cast aside, without clear proof,
        a friend bound by oath. Don't scorn his plea.

---

* A lyrical passage shared between actor and Chorus is called a *kommos* (literally, "a striking, beating of the head and breast in lamentation"; hence, "a dirge, a lament"). This is the first such passage in the play (lines 649–97); another occurs later (1313–66). Here Sophocles varies the *kommos* in several ways, first by having different voices in the strophe (Oedipus and Chorus) and antistrophe (Jocasta joins in), then by inserting spoken dialogue (Oedipus and Creon) between the two sung portions (669–77).

† This one line, broken into three parts, is in iambic trimeter, the regular meter of spoken verse, suggesting that it was either spoken rather than sung, or delivered in a kind of recitative. The same thing happens in the corresponding line of the antistrophe (683).

OEDIPUS: Make no mistake: in asking this, you're asking
    death for me, or exile from this land.

CHORUS: No, by the Sun, god at the head   660
    of all the gods! May I perish
    in the worst way, godless, friendless,
    if I have such thoughts!
    It is the land withering away
    that tears my heart, ill-fated
    as I am, if the two of you
    add your own
    troubles to the ones we have.

OEDIPUS: All right then, let him go, even if it means
    that I must die or be driven out of here   670
    in violence and disgrace! Your words, not his,
    have moved me. Wherever he is, he'll still be hated.

CREON: You cling to hate even in yielding, so
    far gone are you in wrath. People like you
    deserve to be their own worst enemies.

OEDIPUS: Will you not leave me, and be gone?   CRE.: I'm on my way,
    no thanks to you. (*indicating the Chorus*) It's *their* good sense that saves me.
        (*Exit Creon.*)

antistrophe

CHORUS: (*to Jocasta*) Woman, what are you waiting for?
    Take him into the house!

JOCASTA: I will, when I've learned what the matter is.   680

CHORUS: A difference of opinion—it lacks proof,
    but unfair suggestions also have a sting.

JOCASTA: Did it come from both men?

CHORUS: Yes.   JOCASTA: And what was it?

CHORUS: Enough! It seems to me, for the city's sake,
    that it should stop right there, where it left off.

OEDIPUS: See what it comes to! You and your good judgment
    end by scanting my cause and blunting my resolve.

CHORUS: My lord, I've said not only once
    and I assure you again, that I would seem   690
    out of my mind, unable to think,
    if ever I turn my back on you.
    It was you who set my beloved country,
    distracted with pain, on her way again.
    Now be her guide once more!

JOCASTA: By the gods, my lord, let me, too, know
    why such anger has come over you.
OEDIPUS: I shall; you mean more to me than they do.   700
    It's Creon—and the plots he made against me.
JOCASTA: Go on, if you can clearly place the blame.
OEDIPUS: He says that I'm the one who murdered Laius.
JOCASTA: Does he know this himself, or from another?
OEDIPUS: He's had a prophet do the dirty work—
    to guard himself, to keep his own lips clean.
JOCASTA: In that case, you can call yourself acquitted!
    Listen to me and know no mortal man
    has any share in arts of prophecy.
    I'll prove it to you, and at no great length.   710
        An oracle came to Laius once—I won't say
    from Phoebus himself, but from his underlings—
    that his fate was to be killed by his own child,
    the son that would be born to him and me.*
    Now as for Laius, the rumor is that strangers,
    bandits, killed him one day where three roads meet.
    As for the child, not three days past his birth
    Laius bound his feet together and had him
    thrown out onto a pathless mountainside.
    And so Apollo *didn't* cause the child   720
    to be his father's killer or make Laius
    meet the fate he feared at that child's hand.
        Such were the prophecies, all laid down clearly.
    None need trouble you, for what a god
    desires, he'll easily reveal to us.
OEDIPUS: My wife, when you spoke just now,
    my spirit wandered, my mind was in turmoil!
JOCASTA: What's the matter? Why this sudden, anxious turn?
OEDIPUS: I thought I heard you say that Laius
    was murdered near where three roads meet.   730
JOCASTA: That's what was said, and has always been said.
OEDIPUS: Where is the place, where did it happen?
JOCASTA: The land's called Phocis, and the road splits there—
    one branch to Delphi, the other to Daulis.
OEDIPUS: And how much time has gone by since then?

---

* See note to line 37.

JOCASTA: The message reached the city just before
 you emerged as the ruler of this land.

OEDIPUS: O Zeus, what have you planned to do with me?

JOCASTA: What *is* it, Oedipus, that so troubles you?

OEDIPUS: Don't ask me yet. But tell me about Laius—   740
 what did he look like, how old was he?

JOCASTA: His hair was dark, just breaking into gray;
 in looks, he didn't differ much from you.

OEDIPUS: (*cries in distress*) *oimoi!* It seems I didn't know
 I cast *myself* under a deadly curse just now.

JOCASTA: What is it? I fear to look at you, my lord.

OEDIPUS: I'm full of dread. Maybe the seer *did* see!
 But shed more light, tell me one thing more.

JOCASTA: Though I'm afraid, I'll answer if I can.

OEDIPUS: Was Laius travelling light, or with many guards, 750
 as you'd expect of one who is a king?

JOCASTA: They were five in all, counting the herald,
 and a single wagon. Laius rode in that.

OEDIPUS: *aiai!* It's coming clear now! Who was it—
 who was the man who told you this story?

JOCASTA: A slave, the one who came back, sole survivor.

OEDIPUS: Does this man happen to be in the house?

JOCASTA: No. The moment he returned and saw
 that you were on the throne and Laius dead,
 he touched my hand and begged that I send him off 760
 to the fields, to pasture flocks and be as far
 from sight of the city as he could.
 And I sent him. He was a good man, for a slave,
 and worthy of more recompense than that.

OEDIPUS: Can we get him to come back here, right now?

JOCASTA: We can. But why do you insist on this?

OEDIPUS: I'm afraid, for myself, wife: I may have said
 too much; that is why I wish to see him.

JOCASTA: Well, he'll come. But I, too, have a right
 to know, my lord, the cause of your distress. 770

OEDIPUS: I won't keep it from you, I've gone so far
 in my forebodings! In whom if not in you
 may I confide when fate takes such a turn?
  My father was Polybus of Corinth, my mother

Merope, a Dorian. Among the people there
I was held in most esteem, until
something happened, remarkable enough
though not enough, you'd think, to worry me.

     A man who'd had his fill of wine at dinner
baited me, saying I was not my father's son. 780
I was troubled, but held it in that day.
On the next day I went to my parents
and questioned them. They were annoyed
both at the insult and the man who'd made it.
I was pleased on their account, but all the same
it kept bothering me, for word of it got out.
I went then, unbeknownst to my parents,
to Pytho, and Phoebus sent me away
without what I'd come for, but to my sorrow
he gave me terrifying, miserable prophecies: 790
that I'd lie with my mother, and bring to light
a brood intolerable for men to see,
and be the killer of the father who sired me!

     When I heard this, I shunned the land of Corinth,
determined, from now on, to let the stars
guide me away, to where I'd never see
the disgrace of my evil oracles fulfilled.
And on my way I reached the very place
where you have said this tyrant* met his death.
To you, my wife, I'll tell the truth. 800
On my way to the crossing, I met a herald
and another man riding in a wagon
drawn by colts; he was just as you describe.
The man in front, and the older man as well,
both tried to force me off the road.
The driver, who was pushing me, I struck
in anger; the older man, when he saw that,
watched till I was passing, then came down
on my head with his double-pointed goad.
But he paid the price for that, and more: 810
I hit him with my staff and sent him tumbling,

---

* See note to line 257.

head first, straight from the middle of the wagon.
I killed them all. But if there's some connection
between that stranger on the road and Laius,*
who now would be more wretched than I,
what man could be more hated by the gods?
No foreigner or citizen could bring him
into his home, no one could talk to him:
they'd drive him from their houses. And I'm the one
who placed these curses on myself!   820
And with the very hands by which he perished
I have defiled his bed. Am I not vile?
Unholy to the core?—if I must be exiled
and in my exile never see my own,
never set foot on native land, or else
lie with my mother and kill my father,
Polybus, who gave me life and brought me up?
Whoever took all this to be the work
of a savage god would speak the truth!
May I never, never, pure and holy gods,   830
see that day! Let me vanish instead
from the sight of men before I see
the stain of such disaster come upon me!

CHORUS LEADER: All this, my lord, is alarming, but until
    you've heard from the one who saw, be hopeful.

OEDIPUS: Yes, that's what my hopes amount to now—
    nothing to do but wait for him, the shepherd!

JOCASTA: And when he has appeared, what then?

OEDIPUS: I'll tell you "what then." If he turns out to say
    the same as you, then I escape, I'm free.   840

JOCASTA: What did I say that meant so much?

OEDIPUS: You said that he reported it was bandits
    who cut him down. If then he still says
    the same number, I am not the killer,
    for one cannot be the same as many;
    but if he speaks of one traveler alone,
    then the balance turns against me.

JOCASTA: Well, rest assured he said it that way then
    and can't unsay it now, for the whole city

---

* Oedipus is speaking euphemistically: "some connection between" means "identical with."

heard him, not just I alone. And even if   850
he tells it somewhat differently now,
he'll never make the murder of Laius
square with Loxias' prediction, which said
the son he had by me must kill him.
And yet that poor creature never
killed him, but died himself before.
As for prophecy, then, I wouldn't look
to the right or to the left,* not after this!

OEDIPUS: Your point's well taken, but all the same, send
someone to fetch the slave, and make sure you do it.   860

JOCASTA: I will, at once. Meanwhile, let's go inside—
I'll do as you desire, and nothing else.

> *(Exit Oedipus and Jocasta into the palace. The Chorus now
> sing their second ode.)*

strophe 1

May it be my lot to go on throughout my life
with holy reverence in all my words
and deeds, reverence whose laws are made
to stride on high, sired
in the heavenly ether, Olympus
alone their father—the mortal
nature of men had no share
in their birth, nor shall oblivion ever   870
put them to sleep.
Great is the god in them, and he grows not old.

antistrophe 1

Arrogance† breeds the tyrant—arrogance, when
it is fed, glutted on a plenty
neither right nor fitting,

---

* An apparent allusion to the augural practice of judging the meaning of a bird's appearance—propitious, if on the right; unpropitious, if on the left. Jocasta is saying she will not pay any attention to such omens.

† The Greek here is *hybris* (in English, "hubris"), a word notoriously difficult to translate. "Arrogance" is but one of its several meanings. "Violence," "insolence," "outrage," even "rape" are others. The Chorus itself, not yet knowing who killed Laius, would not have "violence" in mind at this point, but it is in fact through an act of violence that "Oedipus the tyrant" has made his way to the throne. The audience, along with Sophocles, knows that, and they might take the word in that sense as well as the one meant by the Chorus, for whom the *hybris* or "arrogance" of Oedipus has shown itself so far in his attacks on Tiresias and Creon.

clambers up to the topmost cornice
and rushes to the edge
of the abyss, where its feet
have no use. But I beseech the god
never to abolish the strife   880
that benefits the city,
the god I will never cease to hold as my protector.

strophe 2

But if a man goes his way with disdain
in his hands or on his lips, having no
fear of justice, no
reverence for the shrines of the gods,
may an evil fate lay hold of him
for his recklessness, doomed to misery
if he reaps his gains unjustly
or does not run from the unholy,   890
or if in folly he touches the untouchable.
How can a man so steeped in crimes still find
strength to guard his life from the gods' bolts?*
If deeds like his meet with honor,
why celebrate the gods in dance?†

antistrophe 2

No longer will I go in reverence
to the untouchable navel of earth,‡
or to the temple at Abai,§
or to Olympia,¶   900
if these prophecies do not come true
for all men to recognize.
But O god of power, Zeus, lord
of all—if that is what you are—let none of this
escape you and your rule, deathless forever.
For they are wiping them out,

---

* I translate line 892 as emended by Hermann ("gods") and 893 as emended by Enger ("find strength").

† Almost all Greek choruses, dramatic and otherwise, sang and danced in honor of the gods. The literal Greek here ("Why should I dance?") implies "Why should I worship the gods?" The antistrophe ends on a similar note of religious uneasiness.

‡ The oracle of Apollo at Delphi.

§ A town in Phocis, where there was another oracle of Apollo, less famous than the one at Delphi.

¶ Site of the ancient Olympic Games, held in honor of Zeus, who had an oracle there.

the oracles of Laius wither away
and nowhere does Apollo shine in honor.
Religion has perished.   910

*(Enter, from the palace, Jocasta, carrying garlands and incense
to offer at Apollo's statue. She is attended by one or two maid-
servants.)*

JOCASTA: Lords of the land, my thought is now to go
to the temples of the gods, bringing in my arms
offerings of wreaths and incense. For Oedipus
is in the grip of feelings running too high, whipped
by pains of every sort; he does not read
new in light of old, and judge sensibly,
but whoever speaks of terror has his ear.
Since, then, I've made no progress with advice,
to you, Apollo—for you are nearest*—
I've come with these offerings, to seek   920
deliverance from our impurity.
For now we all shudder to see him,
the pilot of our ship, hurled overboard.

(Enter a messenger.)†

MESSENGER: Can any of you strangers tell me where
Oedipus the tyrant‡ lives? Is it here?
Or better yet, is he himself here?§

CHORUS LEADER: This is his house, and he himself's inside;
and here's his wife and mother of his children.

MESSENGER: Well, blessed and ever with the blessed
may she live, as she's a perfect¶ wife to him.   930

---

* Apollo's altar is situated in front of the royal palace.

† According to Dawe, with "the possible exception of some scenes from Homer, the next three hundred lines constitute the finest achievement in Greek poetic technique to have survived to our era."

‡ See note to line 515.

§ The first three lines spoken by the Messenger all end with the same syllable, *-pou*, bringing into play again (as at 43 and 397) the untranslatable pun on the name of Oedipus. The first and third line endings contain forms of the Greek verb meaning "to know," the root of which is embedded in the name at the end of the second line: *mathoim' hopou ... Oidipou ... katoisth' hopou* ("may I *learn* where ... Oedipus ... do you *know* where?"). The triple repetition of *-pou* would also have brought to mind the Greek word for "foot" (*pous*), preparing the way for the introduction of a different popular etymology of the hero's name, which comes in the course of the ensuing dialogue (lines 1032–36).

¶ The marriage is complete, or perfect, when the wife bears children to the husband.

JOCASTA: Blessings on you, stranger, in return for these
    compliments. But tell me why you've come.
    What do you seek? What do you want to tell us?
MESSENGER: Blessings, my lady, to house and husband both.
JOCASTA: What blessings? And from where have you arrived?
MESSENGER: From Corinth. And the news I have, perhaps
    you'll be gladdened—or maybe saddened—by it.
JOCASTA: What is it? How might it cut both ways?
MESSENGER: The people who live in the Isthmian land*
    will make him tyrant†—that was the talk there.   940
JOCASTA: But why? Is old Polybus no longer in power?
MESSENGER: No, for Death has him in his house.
JOCASTA: What did you say? Is Oedipus' father dead?
MESSENGER: If I don't speak the truth, I deserve to die.
JOCASTA: (*to a servant*) You! Quick, take this message
    to your master!
           (*Exit servant into the palace, to fetch Oedipus.*)
       O, oracles of the gods,
    where are you? This is the man Oedipus avoided
    for so long, dreading to kill him; now he's died
    by chance, and Oedipus has had no hand in it!
       (*Enter Oedipus.*)
OEDIPUS: Jocasta, dearest, my beloved wife,   950
    why have you had me summoned from the house?
JOCASTA: Listen to this man, and when you've heard him
    see what the god's dread oracles have come to!
OEDIPUS: Who is he, and what has he to tell me?
JOCASTA: He's from Corinth, and he says your father
    Polybus is no more. No, he is dead!
OEDIPUS: What do *you* say, stranger? Tell me yourself!
MESSENGER: If that's what you insist I tell you first,
    you can be sure of it: he's dead and gone.

---

* I.e. Corinth, located on the Isthmus, a narrow neck of land connecting the Peloponnese with the rest of Greece.

† Two interpretations are possible. One, that the Messenger uses the word "tyrant" as if it were the equivalent of "king" or "ruler." The other, that he uses it more precisely. He knows that Oedipus was not the son of the late king of Corinth (1016–18) and so would not be called "king" there. He would be "tyrant" instead, as he has been at Thebes until now. In the latter case, the implication—that "the people" of Corinth know more about Oedipus' paternity than he does—would be an example of Sophoclean irony.

OEDIPUS: Was it through treachery, or falling ill? 960

MESSENGER: A slight tilt puts an old body to sleep.

OEDIPUS: The poor man perished, then, from illness.

MESSENGER: That, and the length of time he'd measured out.

OEDIPUS: Ah, there it is, my wife! Why should one look
 to Pytho's prophetic hearth, or the birds
 shrieking above, on whose showing I
 would one day kill my father? But he's dead
 and lies beneath the earth, and I am here
 and never touched a weapon, unless he died
 from missing me; then one could say I dealt 970
 the blow. But these oracles—Polybus packed them up
 and lies with them in his grave. They mean nothing!

JOCASTA: And did I not say so all along?

OEDIPUS: You did, but I was led astray by fear.

JOCASTA: Take none of it to heart any longer now.

OEDIPUS: *None* of it? Not fear my mother's bed?

JOCASTA: Why should a human being live in fear?
 Chance rules his life, and nothing is foreknown.
 It's best to live at random, as one can.
 You, too—why dread marrying your mother? 980
 Many before, in dreams as well,* have lain
 with their mothers. It's the man to whom all this
 means nothing who gets along most easily.

OEDIPUS: I wouldn't fault anything you've said
 if my mother weren't alive. As it is,
 no matter what you say, I am afraid.

JOCASTA: Still, your father's death is a bright light.

OEDIPUS: Bright, yes, but while she lives, the fear is there.

MESSENGER: What woman is the cause of all this dread?

OEDIPUS: Merope, old man—the wife of Polybus. 990

MESSENGER: What is there about her that makes you afraid?

OEDIPUS: A fearful oracle, sent by the god.

MESSENGER: Can it be spoken? May others hear it?

OEDIPUS: Yes, it can. Loxias once declared it was
 my fate, to lie with my mother and take
 the blood of my own father on my hands.

---

* Jocasta means "in dreams as well as in such prophecies as the ones given to you."

That's why I've lived far from Corinth
all these years—a good thing, too, although
the eyes of parents are the sweetest sight.

MESSENGER: *That's* what kept you far from Corinth?　　　　　　　1000

OEDIPUS: Yes. I didn't want to kill my father.

MESSENGER: Why don't I free you of this fear, my lord,
since I have come here with kind intentions?

OEDIPUS: You'd have the thanks from me that you deserve.

MESSENGER: The very reason why I came! I hoped
to earn a favor, when you came back home.

OEDIPUS: But I'll never go near where my parents are!

MESSENGER: Son, you clearly don't know what you're doing—

OEDIPUS: How, old man? By the gods, instruct me.

MESSENGER: —if those are your reasons for not going home.　　　1010

OEDIPUS: They are—I feared that Phoebus would keep his word.

MESSENGER: And that you'd be defiled* through your parents?

OEDIPUS: That very fear, old man. I feel it, always.

MESSENGER: But don't you know your fear's not justified?

OEDIPUS: How so, if I'm the child of these parents?

MESSENGER: Because Polybus was no kin of yours.

OEDIPUS: What do you mean? Wasn't he my father?

MESSENGER: No more than I am, but only just as much.

OEDIPUS: As much as one who's nothing to me? How?

MESSENGER: Since neither he nor I produced you.　　　　　　　1020

OEDIPUS: Why, then, did he call me his son?

MESSENGER: You were a gift—he took you from my hands.

OEDIPUS: And loved so much what came from another?

MESSENGER: He was childless up till then—that's what moved him.

OEDIPUS: Had I been bought or found, when you gave me?

MESSENGER: Found, in the wilds of Mount Cithaeron.†

OEDIPUS: What were you doing, going to those regions?

MESSENGER: I was in charge there, of mountain flocks.

OEDIPUS: A shepherd, then, a wanderer for hire?

MESSENGER: Your savior, too, my child, at that time.　　　　　　1030

OEDIPUS: What pain was I in, when you took me up?

MESSENGER: Your ankles ought to testify to that.

---

* Literally, "that you'd acquire *miasma*"—the taint of guilt, often of homicide but here for the commission of unnatural crimes, parricide and incest.

† See note to line 421.

OEDIPUS: *oimoi,* why have you brought up that old wound?

MESSENGER: I freed you, undid the pins piercing your feet.

OEDIPUS: Horrible disgrace, mine from the cradle!

MESSENGER: From it you got your name,* who you are today.

OEDIPUS: Was it my mother's or my father's doing? Tell me!

MESSENGER: I don't know. The one who gave you to me knows more.

OEDIPUS: You didn't find, but got me from another?

MESSENGER: Yes. Another shepherd gave you to me.   1040

OEDIPUS: Who was he? Do you know him? Can you tell me?

MESSENGER: I think he was called one of Laius' men.

OEDIPUS: The tyrant of this land once, long ago?

MESSENGER: Yes, the very same. He was his shepherd.

OEDIPUS: Is he still alive, so I may see him?

MESSENGER: You people, who live here, would know that best.

OEDIPUS: Does any of you who are standing here
  know of the shepherd whom he mentions?
  Have you seen him in the fields, or here?
  Speak up! It's time these matters were found out.   1050

CHORUS LEADER: I think he is no other than the one
  you were seeking before, from the fields. But
  Jocasta here might best tell us that.

OEDIPUS: My wife, you know the man we sent for
  a moment ago: is he the one he means?

JOCASTA: What if he is? Ignore it. All this talk,
  all to no purpose, don't even think of it!

OEDIPUS: No, it will never happen, that I—
  with clues like these—not discover my birth!

JOCASTA: By the gods, if you care for your own life,   1060
  don't look into this. My sorrows are enough.

OEDIPUS: Don't worry; even if *I*'m found out a slave
  three generations back, *you*'ll not be found low-born.

JOCASTA: Still, listen to me, I beg you: don't do this!

OEDIPUS: You won't dissuade me from finding out!

JOCASTA: I'm saying what's best for you. I'm on your side.

OEDIPUS: That "best for you" is getting on my nerves.

JOCASTA: Doomed man! May you never know who you are!

---

* A second popular etymology (for the first, see note to line 43) of the name Oidipous derived it from *oidos,* "swelling," and *pous,* "foot." Hence Shelley's coinage, *Swellfoot the Tyrant.*

OEDIPUS: Will someone bring that shepherd here to me?

As for *her*—let her rejoice in her royal blood!*   1070

JOCASTA: *iou, iou!* Unhappy: that's all you'll hear

from me—no other word in time to come.

> *(Exit Jocasta into the palace.)*

CHORUS LEADER: Oedipus, why has your wife rushed off

in a fit of savage sorrow? I fear

evils will break out of this silence.

OEDIPUS: Break out what will! I'll still insist

on seeing my origin, even if it's low.

As for her (*he gestures toward the palace*), maybe she'd be ashamed of that.

She's a woman, she has a woman's pride.

But I will not be dishonored. I'm the child   1080

of Chance, Giver of Good. *She's*

my mother, and the months, my brothers,

have marked me out, now small, now great.

Being what I am, I will never prove to be

other than myself, and not learn my birth!

> *(Oedipus remains onstage† while the Chorus sing their third ode.)*

strophe

CHORUS: If I am a prophet

and keen in judgment,

by Olympus you shall not fail,

O Cithaeron, to see tomorrow's full moon‡

exalt you as home of Oedipus,   1090

his nurse, his mother,

celebrated in our dancing

---

* As in lines 1062–63, Oedipus assumes Jocasta is troubled only because she fears he will discover that he came from humble roots.

† The Chorus address him at line 1098, which suggests he's still onstage. While the Chorus in a Greek tragedy may address an absent person, that is not likely to be the case here. Until now, Oedipus has been either onstage or in the palace. If he exits now, it can only be into the palace, and he is unlikely to go in so soon after Jocasta, whose actions, described by the Messenger at 1241–50, occur immediately after she leaves the stage. She could hardly do what the Messenger says she does with Oedipus only a few steps behind her.

‡ The meaning is "the next full moon." The Athenian festival of the Pandia, celebrated at full moon in April, followed immediately upon the Great Dionysia, at which the tragedies were produced. According to Jebb, the Chorus are saying that they will visit the temples at the next full moon in an all-night festival celebrating the discovery that Oedipus is of Theban birth, and that Mount Cithaeron will be a theme of their song.

for the favors you have bestowed
on my lord.
Phoebus, invoked in our cries,
may you find this pleasing!

antistrophe

Who, child,* was your mother?
One of the long-lived nymphs
embraced by mountain-pacing Pan—   1100
who'd be your father, then? Or a bed-mate
of Loxias, lover of all the pasturing plains?
Or maybe Cyllene's Lord†
or the Bacchic god‡
who haunts the mountain summits took you,
a foundling, from one
of the dark-eyed Nymphs with whom
he loves to dally.

OEDIPUS: (*to the Chorus*) If I, too, may guess, though I've never   1110
had any dealings with him, I think I see
the shepherd we're expecting. He's advanced
in years—as many as the man you've mentioned.
I recognize, too, as my own servants
the ones who bring him here. But you would know
better than I, having seen the man before.

CHORUS LEADER: Yes, it's him. He was a man whom Laius
trusted as much as any, though a shepherd.

(*Enter the shepherd, accompanied by Oedipus' servants.*)

OEDIPUS: I ask you first, Corinthian stranger: is this
the man you mean?   MESS.: Yes, him, the one you're looking at.   1120

OEDIPUS: You there, old man, look here and tell me
what I ask. Were you once Laius' man?

SHEPHERD: I was, a slave not bought but reared in the house.

OEDIPUS: What task, what way of life, did you work at?

SHEPHERD: I tended flocks for almost all my life.

OEDIPUS: What places would you frequent, most of all?

SHEPHERD: It was Cithaeron, and the lands around it.

---

* Oedipus, still onstage; "child," again (as in line 1), is a term of endearment.

† Hermes, born on Mount Cyllene in Arcadia.

‡ Dionysus.

OEDIPUS: Do you recall, then, meeting this man there?

SHEPHERD: Doing what? And what man do you mean?

OEDIPUS: This one. Have you had anything to do with him?   1130

SHEPHERD: Not that I can say offhand, from memory.

MESSENGER: And that's no wonder, master! But I'll remind him
    though he does not know me now. He'll know
    that when <the two of us were in>* the region
    of Cithaeron, he with two herds and I with one,
    I kept him company for three stretches lasting
    six months each—from spring until Arcturus† rose;
    and then, when winter came, I drove my flocks
    to their barns, and he drove his to those of Laius.
    Does this ring true, or did it never happen?   1140

SHEPHERD: You speak the truth, though a long time has passed.

MESSENGER: Come, then, tell me whether you remember
    that you gave me a child, to raise as my own?

SHEPHERD: What's this? What are you getting at?

MESSENGER: Here he is, my friend: the man who was that child!

SHEPHERD: A curse on you! Will you not hold your tongue?

OEDIPUS: Don't chastise him, old man. It's *your* words,
    not his, that stand in need of chastisement!

SHEPHERD: But how, O best of masters, am I at fault?

OEDIPUS: You won't discuss the child he asks about.   1150

SHEPHERD: He doesn't know what he says, and wastes his breath.

OEDIPUS: If you won't talk to please me, you'll talk in pain!

SHEPHERD: No! By the gods, don't torture an old man.

OEDIPUS: Someone tie his hands behind his back!

SHEPHERD: No, no—for what? What more do you want to know?

OEDIPUS: Did you give this man the child in question?

SHEPHERD: I did. Would I had perished when I did!

OEDIPUS: You'll come to that, if you don't tell the truth.

SHEPHERD: But if I do I'll perish all the more.

OEDIPUS: (*to his attendants*) This man, it seems, is bent on wasting time.   1160

SHEPHERD: I'm not! I've just told you I gave the child.

OEDIPUS: Whose child? Was it your own, or someone else's?

---

* Lloyd-Jones and others notice that a line is missing between 1135 and 1136. The words between angle brackets translate Lloyd-Jones's Greek, offered as an example of what Sophocles may have written here.

† Arcturus rises in the autumn.

SHEPHERD: No, not my own. I got it … from someone.

OEDIPUS: From which of these citizens here? Which house?

SHEPHERD: By the gods, master, look no further!

OEDIPUS: You're a dead man, if I ask this again.

SHEPHERD: He was … somebody from the house of Laius.

OEDIPUS: A slave, or born into his family?

SHEPHERD: I'm close to saying what I dread to say!

OEDIPUS: And I to hearing it, but hear I must!   1170

SHEPHERD: His, yes, the child was his. But she within,
    your wife, would best speak of it, how it was.

OED.: Was she the one who gave him?   SHEPHERD: Yes, my lord.

OED.: For what purpose?   SHEPHERD: To do away with him.

OED.: Her own child?   SHEPHERD: Yes, in fear of evil prophecies.

OED.: What prophecies?   SHEPHERD: That he would kill his parents.

OED.: Why, then, did you give him to this old man?

SHEPHERD: Out of pity, master. I thought he'd take him
    away, where he himself was from. But he
    has saved him for the worst of fates. For if   1180
    you're who he says you are, you were born doomed.

OEDIPUS: *iou, iou!* It's all come out too clear. Light,
    may I never look on you again! I'm the one
    born to those I shouldn't have come from, living with those
    I shouldn't live with, killing those* I ought not have killed.

> *(Exit Oedipus into the palace. The Messenger and the Shepherd
> exit to the side.)*

strophe 1

    CHORUS: *iō,* generations of mortals,
        how I reckon your lives
        equal to nothing!
        For what, what man
        wins more of happiness   1190
        than to seem and, having seemed,
        to seem no more?
        With your fortune, yours

---

* The three occurrences of "those" in as many lines are meant to evoke the horror of the situation. The first one refers to Laius and Jocasta, the second to Jocasta alone, the third to Laius alone. In the second one, the phrase "living with" recalls 366–67. See note to line 367.

in mind, yours,
unhappy Oedipus, I can call
no mortal blest.

antistrophe 1

You aimed your shaft
beyond all others, and hit
success not happy
in every way, when (O Zeus!)
you killed the hook-taloned,
oracle-chanting maiden,* and stood   1200
a bulwark against my city's dying.
Since then you are called
my king† and have met
with highest honors,
ruling in mighty Thebes.

strophe 2

But now whose tale is more painful to hear?
Who dwells with disasters, with pangs
more savage than yours in a shifting life?
iō, glorious Oedipus!
For you the same wide
harbor lay open
as son *and* husband   1210
fathering children—how,
how could the furrow
sown by your father‡
bear you in silence so long?

antistrophe 2

All-seeing Time has found you out against your will,
long ago condemned the unlawful marriage,
the marriage that bred children
for you and offspring

---

* The Sphinx. The conflation of her riddle with an oracle is due to its being posed in dactylic hexameter, as were the oracles of Apollo, and to its enigmatic character: Apollo's oracles were also enigmatic and hard to interpret.

† The Chorus speak as if Oedipus has been called king all along, but in fact this is the first and only time in the play that the actual word is used of him. Until this moment he has been "tyrant," "lord," or "master," never "king." Whatever the Chorus mean, Sophocles himself has delayed the bestowal of the title "king" upon him until now, timing it to coincide with his fall and not reverting to it later.

‡ A man's wife is, metaphorically, the furrow he sows; later, at lines 1256–57, the field he plows.

of its own.* *iō*, son of Laius,
if only, if only I
had never known you!
How I grieve for you above all, the dirge
pouring from my lips! In truth,   1220
you gave me the breath of life,
then closed my eyes in death.

(Enter a messenger from the palace.)

MESSENGER: Men most honored in this land of ours,
what deeds you'll hear of, what deeds you'll look upon,
what pain you'll feel, if you are still nobly
devoted to the house of Labdacus!
For neither the river Ister† nor the Phasis‡
could wash away the stain upon these walls,
the evils that hide within, and those that soon
will burst into the light—willed, not unwilled,   1230
self-chosen pains, which hurt the most to see.
CHORUS LEADER: What we knew before was cruel enough.
What sorrows can you add to these?
MESSENGER: The swiftest word to say and understand:
she's dead, Jocasta's dead, who was our queen.
CHORUS LEADER: The queen, dead! But how? How did she die?
MESSENGER: By her own hand. But the worst part of it
is missing, for you can't *see* what happened.
All the same, to the extent I can describe it,
you'll learn what that unhappy woman suffered.   1240
        When in a frenzy she had passed inside,
straight to her bridal bed she hurled herself,
tearing at her hair with both her hands.
Once there, she shut the doors and called
on Laius long since dead, reminding him
of the seed sown so long ago, the son
who killed him, and then begot with her
children cursed in their begetting. And then

---

* Lloyd-Jones and Wilson interpret this as a vague reference to "evil things, disasters" (*Sophoclea*, 108).

† Now called the Danube.

‡ Now called the Rioni, a river in Colchis, east of the Black Sea, into which it empties.

she mourned her bed, on which she bore a husband
from her husband, children from her child.   1250
But how she died I can't say, for Oedipus
broke in with a cry, preventing us from seeing
her agony to the end. Our eyes were fixed
on him instead, as he rushed here and there,
calling for a sword, asking where she was,
that wife no wife but a field
that had brought forth two harvests—
him and his children. And as he raved, some god—
for it was none of us close by—showed him the way.
As if guided to them, with a fearful scream,   1260
he sprang at the double doors, burst them
inward from their jambs, and fell into the room.
And there we saw the woman hanging, swinging
in the air, entangled in a twisted noose.
And when he saw her, in his grief he cried out
a dreadful groan, then loosed the hanging halter.
And when the poor woman lay upon the ground,
it was dreadful to see, what happened next. He tore from her
the golden brooches that pinned her clothes, raised them up
and dashed them against his eyes, crying out   1270
that from now on those eyes would not see him
or the evils he had done and suffered, but see
in darkness those whom he should not have seen,
and not know those he had wanted to know.
With such imprecations, again and again he raised
the brooches and struck his eyes. The bleeding
eyeballs soaked his cheeks and did not cease
to shed not oozy drops of gore, but all at once
a hail-like rain of black blood streaming down.*

      These evils broke forth not from one, but both,   1280
not separate† but mixed together, man
and wife. The happiness of old was truly
happiness back then, but now, and on this day
lamentation, disaster, death, shame—of all
the evils with a name, not one is missing.

---

* Lloyd-Jones and Wilson, following West, bracket lines 1278–79 as an interpolation.
† I render the text as emended by Wilamowitz and printed by Dawe.

CHORUS LEADER: Has the poor man any respite, now, from pain?

MESSENGER: He shouts for them to open the doors and show
all the Cadmeans the killer of his father,
his mother's—unholy words, I can't repeat them.
He says he'd hurl himself from the land,   1290
not remain at home, cursed by his own curses.
All the same, he needs help, a hand to guide him—
his sickness is too strong to bear. But you
shall see as well, for just now the doors
are opening, and soon you'll look upon
a sight even one who hated him would pity.

> *(Oedipus emerges from the palace, blinded.)*

CHORUS:* O suffering terrible for men to see,
    O most terrible of all that I
    have yet encountered! What was the madness
    came upon you? What divinity† is it   1300
    that leaped beyond all leaps
    upon your unhappy fate?
    pheu, pheu, unfortunate! I can't look at you,
    I want to ask so many questions,
    so much to hear about, so much to see.
    Such is the horror you arouse in me.

OEDIPUS: *aiai, aiai!* Where on earth
    am I swept in sorrow? Where
    is my voice flying, borne on the wind?   1310
    iō, my destiny, where, where have you sprung!

CHORUS LEADER: Into dread—not to be heard or looked on.‡

> *(Oedipus and the Chorus now engage in a second* kommos.*)*

strophe 1

OEDIPUS: *iō,* cloud
    of darkness, mine—repulsive, unspeakable, invincible
    onset, blown on an evil wind!
    oimoi!
    There it is, again! The sting,

---

* The Chorus now speak in regular anapestic measures for ten lines, answered by Oedipus in lyric anapests for four more.

† The Greek word here is *daimon*, repeated by Oedipus himself in line 1311. It can also mean "god" or "fate."

‡ This line is in iambic trimeter, the regular meter for spoken verse, suggesting it was spoken not by the whole Chorus but by its leader alone.

the goad piercing through me
with the memory of these evils.

CHORUS: No wonder if, in the midst of pain like this,
   your grief is doubled, and doubled your laments!   1320

antistrophe 1

OEDIPUS: *iō*, my friend—
   you alone are still beside me,
   still you remain and care for me, the blind.
   pheu, pheu,
   I am not mistaken but know it well,
   though I'm in darkness—I know your voice.

CHORUS: What horrors you have done! How could you bring yourself
   to quench your sight like this? What god drove you?

strophe 2

OEDIPUS: This was Apollo, my friends; Apollo
   brought these evils to pass, my evils,   1330
   these my sufferings.
   But no hand struck my eyes, none
   but mine, mine alone!
   For why should I go on seeing, I
   who had, when seeing, nothing sweet to see?

CHORUS: All this was, just as you say.

OEDIPUS: And what now is left for me to see
   or to love, what greeting
   to hear with any joy, my friends?
   Take me away, out of the country   1340
   at once—away, my friends,
   with the ruin of me, cursed
   three times over, and more—
   the mortal man most hated by the gods.

CHORUS: O ruined, ruined in mind and fortunes equally—
   how I wish I had never known you!

antistrophe 2

OEDIPUS: Perish the man, whoever he was, the shepherd
   who freed me from the cruel fetters on my feet,   1350
   rescued me from death
   and saved me, and did
   me no favor!
   For had I died then, I would not have been
   so great a sorrow to my friends or to myself.

CHORUS: I, too, would have wished it so.

OEDIPUS: I would not have come as my father's killer
    or be called by men
    husband to those that gave me birth.*
    But as it is, I am   1360
    god-forsaken, son
    of those I defiled†
    and father of children
    with those from whom I sprang.‡
    And if there is an evil yet more than evil,
    it is mine, the lot of Oedipus.§

CHORUS: I don't see how I'd say you've chosen well,
    for you'd be better off dead than living blind.

OEDIPUS: Don't lecture me that any of this is not
    for the best, or give me any more advice.   1370
    For I do not know with what sort of eyes
    I'd see my father when I came to Hades,¶
    or my wretched mother—against them both
    I have committed crimes too huge for hanging.

        Or do you think the sight of my children
    would be a joy to look at, born as they were?
    No, never, not to these eyes of mine!
    Nor would the city, nor its towers and statues
    and temples. I've deprived myself of these,
    I, the all-daring, the one raised best in Thebes   1380
    for I commanded all to drive away
    the sacrilege, the man the gods have now
    shown to be unholy *and* the son of Laius.

        Once I brought to light such a stain as mine,
    could I look with steady eyes on all of this?
    No! And if there were a way to plug my ears
    and clog the springs of hearing, I'd not refrain
    from sealing up this wretched corpse of mine,

---

* The plural, again, is allusive. Jocasta is meant.

† Jocasta, defiled by her incestuous union with him.

‡ Laius, whom he joins as the father of children by the same woman.

§ The *kommos* ends here. Dialogue resumes.

¶ In the fifth-century imagination, the dead in Hades remained as they were when last alive. Oedipus will take his blindness with him into the Underworld.

blind and deaf to everything. It would be sweet
for thought to dwell where evils have no entry. 1390
   O Cithaeron, why take me in, and then
not kill me outright, so I could not have shown
myself to men? Such was my origin!
O Polybus and Corinth, home I called
my native land, what a fine thing you nurtured,
lovely, with evils festering beneath its skin!
For now I'm found out—evil, and born of evil.
O threefold road and hidden glen and thicket
and narrow pathway where the three roads met—
from these hands of mine you drank my own, 1400
my father's blood. Do you still remember me,
remember what I did for you, what I went on
to do when I came here? O marriage, marriage
that brought me forth and having brought me forth
sent the same seed up again, and showed the world
fathers who were brothers, sons their fathers' killers,
brides who were wives and mothers, and whatever
else would bring most shame to humankind!
   But since what's best not done is best not said,
by the gods I beg you, quick as you can 1410
hide me somewhere, or kill me, or hurl me
into the sea, never to be seen again.
Come, do not hesitate to touch me, in my sorrow.
Trust me, and have no fear; these ills of mine
no mortal man, none but I alone, can bear.
   (Enter Creon from the side.)

CHORUS LEADER: Here, now, is Creon, coming just in time
  to act on your requests, or weigh them, for he
  alone is left in charge, as you once were.

OEDIPUS: Creon! *oimoi*, what shall I say to him?
  What trust can I expect, when it's been proved 1420
  I was wrong to him in every way before?

CREON: I haven't come to mock you, Oedipus,
  nor scold you for the wrongs you've done.
  (to the Chorus) But you here, if you aren't ashamed
  in the sight of men, be ashamed, at least, before
  the sun that nurtures all—ashamed to display, like this,
  unhidden, such pollution, which neither earth

nor sacred rain nor light of day will bear.
But quickly as you can, bring him inside.
Only one's kin can decently look on   1430
or listen to the evils done by kin.
OEDIPUS: By the gods, since you've put my fears to flight,
  coming as best of men to me, the worst,
  grant me a wish, not for my sake, but yours.
CREON: What do you have in mind, to ask me like this?
OEDIPUS: Hurl me from the land, right now. Send me
  where no man will ever speak to me.
CREON: I would have done so, but first it was my wish
  to ask the god what action must be taken.
OEDIPUS: But what he has declared is clear enough: 1440
  away with me, the father-killer, the unholy one!
CREON: So it was said, but in this crisis,
  it's better to inquire what must be done.
OEDIPUS: So you'll ask the god about a wreck like me?
CREON: Maybe this time even you will heed his answer.
OEDIPUS: But it's you I am entreating now, you
  I ask to bury the woman who's in there
  as *you* see fit—take care, rightly, of your own kin.
  As for me, may this, my father's city,
  never be forced to shelter me in life   1450
  but let me roam the mountains, the one they call
  my own, Cithaeron, which my parents made
  a living tomb for me,* so I may finally
  die at the hands of those who meant to kill me.
      And yet this much I know: sickness couldn't
  have killed me then, or anything. I wouldn't have been saved
  from dying except to meet with some great evil.†
  But let fate proceed wherever it will take me.
  As for my children,‡ Creon, you needn't worry

---

* By sending him there as an infant to be exposed to the elements to die.

† Namely, to grow up and become his father's killer, his mother's husband.

‡ Oedipus and Jocasta had four children, two sons (Eteocles and Polynices) and two daughters (Antigone and Ismene). The two daughters are still children in this play; the two sons, though Oedipus here calls them "men," are evidently not yet of age, as neither lays claim to the throne of Thebes. Instead, Creon seems to have become the ruler, at least for the time being (lines 1417–18 suggest a kind of regency). Later, the sons will attempt to share sovereignty and end by killing each other in the struggle for power. Sophocles had dealt with these developments in the earlier play *Antigone* and will deal with them again in his final work, *Oedipus at Colonus*.

about my sons. They're men, they'll never lack   1460
the means of life, wherever they may be;
but my pair of girls, unhappy, pitiful,
who never dined at a table set
apart from mine, but had
their share of everything I touched*—
them you must care for and, most of all,
let me touch them, let me lament my sorrows.
Come, my lord,†
come, as you are nobly born. If I held them
I'd seem to have them, as when I could see.   1470

> (*Enter, from the palace, Antigone and Ismene, daughters of Oedipus.*)

What am I saying?
Surely, by the gods, it isn't my two daughters
that I hear weeping? Has Creon, out of pity,
sent for the dearest of my children?
Am I right?

CREON: Yes, I'm the one who arranged for this, knowing
the pleasure they'd give you now, and gave you then.

OEDIPUS: May you prosper, then, and have the luck to find,
in return, a better god‡ than mine to guard you.
Children, where are you? Come here, here   1480
to these hands of mine, your brother's hands
that have made your father's eyes see as they see—
your father's eyes that once were bright;
your father, children, who, without seeing or knowing
fathered you where I myself was sown.§

　　　And I weep—I can't see, but I can weep
for you—the bitterness of the days ahead,
how people will treat you from now on.
What public gatherings will you go to,

---

* The phrasing in lines 1463–64 is strange, and the emphasis on eating at the same table with his daughters is puzzling at this point. There may be an allusion, by contrast, to the epic tradition, according to which he had cursed his sons because they had placed before him, at table, the wine cups used by Laius.

† A single bacchiac metron, here and again at lines 1471 and 1475, interrupts the iambic trimeters of spoken verse, a sign of intense emotion.

‡ *Daimōn* here has the sense of a divine power that oversees a man's life, for good or ill.

§ See note to line 1213.

what festivals from which you won't 1490
come home in tears, unable to take part?
And when you've come to the threshold of marriage,
who will he be, who will dare, my children,
to take upon himself such taunts, disgraces
heaped on your parents and on you as well?*
What horrors do we lack? "Your father killed
his father, plowed the same mother from whom
he himself was spawned, and from the same
womb whence he himself was born, got you."
That's what they'll say. And then, who'll marry you? 1500
No one, my children, but clearly you
are bound to perish barren and unmarried.

     Son of Menoeceus, since you alone are left
a father to these girls—for we, their parents,
are both in ruins—do not just look on†
while they wander, beggared, husbandless—your kin!
Don't let their sorrows be as great as mine.
Take pity on them, seeing them, so young,
bereft of all, unless you take their part.
Show that you agree, with a touch of your hand!‡ 1510
And to you, my children, if you could understand,
I'd offer much advice. But pray for this:
to live where opportunity allows, and have
a better life than the father who begot you.

CREON: Enough of tears for now! Inside with you.§

OED.: I must obey, however little I like it.   CRE.: All's well when its
                                          time has come.

OED.: Do you know my terms for going?   CRE.: I'll know them when I've
                                          heard them.

OED.: Send me away, into exile.   CRE.: You ask of me what is the god's to
                                        give.

---

* The transmitted text ("for *my* parents and for you") makes no sense here. I render Herwerden's conjecture, said by Dawe to give "the expected sense" (199) and described in *Sophoclea* as "the most plausible suggestion so far" (113).

† I render the text as emended by Dawes in 1781.

‡ Unable to see a nod of assent to his appeal, Oedipus asks Creon to touch his hand instead.

§ Creon switches from iambic trimeter to trochaic tetrameter, in which the dialogue continues to the end. The switch is indicative, perhaps, of a quickening in pace.

OED.: But the gods despise me!   CRE.: Then you won't have long to wait.

OED.: So you agree?   CRE.: I don't waste time saying what I don't
mean.   1520

OED.: Lead me away, now. It's time.   CRE.: Proceed, then, and let the
children go.

OED.: No, don't take them from me!   CRE.: Cease to desire power in
everything;

the power you had in life has not stayed with you to the end.

> *(The children are escorted away from Oedipus, joining Creon*
> *and his attendants. Exit Oedipus, led by attendants, into the*
> *palace. Creon and the children exit to the side. While all these*
> *are leaving, the Chorus Leader addresses the citizens of Thebes,*
> *represented by the rest of the Chorus.)*

CHORUS LEADER: Dwellers in our native Thebes, behold! Here is Oedipus,
who solved the famous riddle and rose to power
(what citizen did not look upon his life with envy?)—
see what he's come to, what a wave of grim disaster
washed over him, a warning to us all: bide the coming
of that final day, counting no man happy
till he has crossed life's boundary free of pain.   1530

Introduction to Sophocles' *Antigone*

The issue that propels this drama toward its violent end is the obligation of the living to bury the dead. The ancient Greeks believed that everyone, friend or foe, free or slave, was entitled to funeral rites and burial. In the course of this drama, Sophocles shows how in antiquity this obligation had deep moral and religious significance, pitting individual against state, natural law against political decree, women against men, piety against impiety. No wonder, then, that the play has been frequently performed in modern times, particularly in times of war; a famous production by Jean Anouilh, in 1944, covertly rallied French resistance to the Nazis.

The drama takes place on the day after the Thebans had defended their city from an attack by an army of Argives, led by seven captains (one for each gate of Thebes). The Argives were led by Oedipus' son Polynices, who sought to regain the throne he shared with his brother, Eteocles. But after Polynices and Eteocles killed each other in the course of the battle, their uncle Creon (formerly chief minister to their father, Oedipus) assumed the throne. Normally the victors would allow a defeated army to bury its dead, but in the traditional myth (as depicted in Euripides' *Suppliants*, not in this volume) the Thebans refused to do so. Sophocles appears to have departed from tradition by having Polynices be the focus of the drama; Creon's ban on burial, with a penalty of stoning to death for any who violate it, affects only him.

Antigone, as the elder of Oedipus and Jocasta's two daughters, commits herself to seeing that her brother receives burial, following the Greek pattern in which women were responsible for burial and for mourning rites. Her sister, Ismene, tries to stop her, arguing that women should not oppose what men have decided. But Antigone insists that Eteocles and Polynices were both her brothers, and as she explains later in the drama, after she dies she will join the rest of her family in the Underworld, where they will be together for all eternity. She resembles other Sophoclean heroes in her determination to do what she thinks right, no matter the cost to herself or others.

Creon's determination to leave Polynices' body to rot in the sun derives from his political insecurity: he has no royal lineage and no natural authority (as is seen also in *Oedipus*), yet circumstances have thrust him into power, and he fears opposition. He is so bent on his course that he does not perceive that the Chorus, Theban elders, hesitate to support him, and that his own guards—represented by the comically timid soldier who is sent to report to him—follow him out of fear more than loyalty. He is furious when the guard tells him that Polynices' body has been buried, and supposes that the guards had been bribed. His quickness to see conspiracies against him is the hallmark of the Sophoclean tyrant, a figure explored also (in a different register) in the *Oedipus*.

When the guard returns with Antigone, who had tried to bury the body again after the guards had uncovered it, Antigone claims that she would rather die than leave her brother unburied. In her view, the laws of Zeus and Justice are eternal and take precedence over any mortal decree. In fact, the gods seem to be on Antigone's side: a sudden whirlwind, as described by the guard, covered with dust everything on the field where the corpse was lying after the guards had exhumed Polynices' decaying body.

Creon is angry not only because Antigone did not abide by the "laws that were laid down," but also because he cannot stand being disobeyed by a woman. He condemns both sisters to death, even though Ismene took no part in the plot and Antigone, as Ismene reminds him, is engaged to marry his son, Haemon. But family relationships are less important to Creon than preserving civic order. His son can marry someone else: "He'll find other women, other fields to plow," he says, revealing again his misogynistic streak. When Haemon tries to persuade his father to relent, suggesting that order is best preserved by compromise and that the people of Thebes feel Antigone deserves to be honored, Creon refuses to listen to a person younger than himself and lets Haemon depart in anger. He does, however, back down to some extent. He allows the Chorus to persuade him not to execute Ismene, and he spares Antigone the penalty of stoning to death; instead, she will be placed in a cave and allowed to starve, so that the city will not be directly guilty of her death.

As she is being led off to the cave, Antigone, no model of emotional fortitude, laments her fate and complains that no one, not even the Chorus, seems prepared to weep for her. But she draws strength from the idea of being able to join her family in the Underworld. In her view—an argument based on the primacy of blood ties—a brother must be honored because, unlike a husband, she cannot get another, now that her parents are dead.

No one in the audience could have known what would happen next. No sooner has Antigone left the stage than the blind seer Tiresias, also seen in the *Oedipus* and *Oedipus at Colonus*, is led in. He knows from the terrible omens reported to him that the city is in danger because Polynices' body is unburied, and he predicts that the Erinyes and the gods will cause lamentations in Creon's household. Creon at first refuses to believe Tiresias, but then—remarkably for a ruler in a tragedy—vacillates and changes his mind. But his reversal comes too late.

No god has intervened to save Antigone, even though she clearly did what was right. Is Sophocles suggesting that, as the Greeks sometimes claimed, an early death, at a moment of heroic action, is a kind of reward? No answer is given to the problem of Antigone's fate, but Creon's is clear enough. The play's devastating ending makes clear that disobeying the laws of the gods brings suffering even worse than death.

The choral odes of this play deserve special comment because they are among the most beautiful and far-reaching of any in extant tragedy. After Creon makes his proclamation, the Chorus—departing entirely from onstage action to survey all of mortal existence—celebrate the great accomplishments of humankind, the race that has overcome all difficulties except death. This hymn to human intellect forms a strange counterpoint to Creon's increasing folly, but it is beautifully expressed, in Sophocles' most sublime verses. After Creon condemns Antigone and Ismene to death, by contrast, the Chorus take a darker tone, singing about the destruction of Thebes's ruling family (of which Creon himself is a part). As the old men of Thebes see it, the gods are slowly destroying the house of Laius, Oedipus' father, much as the sea's waves erode the shore; Zeus' power cannot be restricted. Wealth and power lead men to disaster, but it is the fate of humankind to be deluded, and no one sees what is coming until it is too late.

In its final ode, sung after Creon rushes off to save Antigone, the old men call on Dionysus, the powerful god who was engendered in Thebes. Like Creon, they seem to have only a partial understanding of the great moral issues that have been raised by Antigone, Haemon, and Tiresias. All they can convey is a sense of powerlessness, never more so than when they address the last lines of the play to Creon: "Have done with prayers. Mortals can have no release from ruin sent by fate"—a grim assessment indeed. But as Sophocles has suggested in his portrait of Antigone's courage, there were other, and much better, possibilities.

We cannot be certain when the *Antigone* was first performed. One of Sophocles' ancient biographers supposed that he wrote it after he served as general in the Athenian war against Samos in 441/0 B.C., and this date is accepted by many; but another source said that he died after straining his voice reciting the part of Antigone, which suggests that he wrote the drama toward the end of his life (406/5 B.C.). In either case, *Antigone* was not staged in conjunction with either *Oedipus* or *Oedipus at Colonus*, though the three plays are sometimes arranged as a trilogy in modern published editions. The action of *Antigone* comes last in that sequence, but the play may have been written well before the other two.

In modern times, *Antigone* has been among the most widely read and staged of Greek plays, and it has recently been adapted into new verse dramas by two great modern poets, Seamus Heaney (*The Burial at Thebes*, 2004) and Anne Carson (*Antigonick*, 2012).

ANTIGONE

Translated by Frank Nisetich

This is a translation of the Greek text of the play edited by Hugh Lloyd-Jones and N. G. Wilson, *Sophoclis Fabulae* (Oxford: Oxford University Press, 1990, 1992). From time to time in the notes I have referred to discussions of the text by the same two authors in *Sophoclea: Studies on the Text of Sophocles* (Oxford: Oxford University Press, 1992) and by Mark Griffith in *Sophocles: Antigone* (Cambridge: Cambridge University Press, 1999, 2007). I have also consulted Hugh Lloyd-Jones's Loeb edition, *Sophocles,* vol. 2 (Cambridge, MA: Harvard University Press, 1994, 1998). Occasionally, I have preferred readings by other scholars, noted where they occur. Passages considered as interpolations by Lloyd-Jones and Wilson are omitted from the text of the translation but included in the notes.

CAST OF CHARACTERS (IN ORDER OF APPEARANCE)

ANTIGONE, daughter of Oedipus and Jocasta
ISMENE, her sister
CHORUS of Theban elders, with their Leader
CREON, Jocasta's brother; uncle of Antigone and Ismene; the new
    ruler of Thebes
GUARD
HAEMON, son of Creon and cousin of Antigone; betrothed to
    Antigone
TIRESIAS, blind Theban prophet
MESSENGER
EURYDICE, wife of Creon and mother of Haemon
GUARDS and RETAINERS in Creon's service (nonspeaking parts)

Setting: The play opens in the hours before dawn, in front of the royal palace of Thebes. On the previous day, the army led by Antigone's brother Polynices against her other brother, Eteocles, king of Thebes, has been defeated. Antigone is alone onstage for a few moments, after which her sister, Ismene, emerges from the palace.

ANTIGONE: Ismene, my sister, my own dear sister,
    what evil left behind by Oedipus
    will Zeus not bring to pass while we still live?*
    There's nothing painful—no disaster,
    no shame, no dishonor—that I do not see
    among the troubles that beset us now.
    And what of this decree they say the commander†
    has laid upon the whole community?
    Have you heard of it? Or does it escape you
    that evils meant for foes are coming for our friends?   10
ISMENE: Not a word, Antigone, of our friends,
    neither good nor bad, has come to me
    since we two lost both our brothers‡
    on a single day, killed, each by the other;
    but since the Argive army§ vanished
    this very night, I know nothing further—
    if I'm better off, or worse than before.
ANTIGONE: I know that, and that's why I've called you
    outside, to speak with you, and you alone.
ISMENE: What's the matter? Clearly, something's troubling you.   20

---

* Antigone is thinking of the curse that has dogged her family for generations. As she and Ismene are the last surviving members of that family, the curse upon it may well come to an end with their deaths.

† Creon, whose personal name means "ruler," "lord," "master." His title here, *stratēgos*, designates him as leader of the army.

‡ Eteocles and Polynices, sons of Oedipus and Jocasta. They agreed to rule the city of Thebes alternately, Eteocles the first year, Polynices the following year, and so on, but Eteocles refused to step down when the time came, precipitating a civil war.

§ Polynices married Argeia, daughter of Adrastos, king of Argos, and led an army of Argives and others against Thebes. He and his six companions in arms were known as the "Seven against Thebes."

ANTIGONE: Don't you know that Creon has decided
  to honor one of our brothers with burial
  but not the other? They say that he has hidden*
  Eteocles beneath the earth, to have
  his share of honor with the dead below;
  but Polynices' corpse, fallen in disgrace—
  they say Creon's proclaimed to all that none
  may hide him in the earth or mourn for him,
  but he must lie unwept, untombed, a heap
  of treasure to entice the hungry birds.   30
  Such orders they say our noble Creon
  lays on you and me—yes, he means me, too!—
  and that he's on his way to make it clear
  to those who haven't heard. Nor does he take
  the matter lightly; he who disobeys
  will die, stoned by the people—so it's fixed.
  You have it now, the way things are, and soon we'll see
  if you're as noble as your birth, or not.
ISMENE: But if things are as you say they are, poor sister,
  will it make any difference, what I do?   40
ANTIGONE: The question is, will you work and act with me?
ISMENE: Do something dangerous? What can you be thinking?
ANTIGONE: Will you lend me a hand, and lift the corpse?
ISMENE: In spite of the ban on the whole city?
ANTIGONE: Yes, for he's my brother—and yours, too, even if
  you wish he weren't.† I'll not betray him.
ISMENE: So stubborn, though Creon has forbidden it?
ANTIGONE: He has no right to keep me from my own.
ISMENE: (*dismayed*) *oimoi!* Think, Sister, how our father
  came to ruin and died, hated and disgraced   50
  for crimes he himself detected, and then battered
  his own two eyes with self-assailing hands;‡
  and how his mother and wife—she was both to him—
  destroyed her life in the twisted noose;
  and how our two brothers, in a single day,

---

* It's clear from lines 192–97 that the burial has not yet occurred.

† I render Dawe's emendation.

‡ When he realized that he had killed his father and married his mother, Oedipus blinded himself.
Sophocles dramatized these events in *Oedipus the King*, written sometime after *Antigone*.

shed each other's blood, and wrought in misery
the doom they shared, hands raised against each other.
Now think: we two are left alone; we'll die
so cruelly, if we dare to break the law
or scant the tyrant's vote and spurn his power.   60
We must also bear in mind that we are women,
not meant to wage war with men; and then,
that we're compelled by those stronger than we are
to acquiesce in this, and things more painful still.
I'll ask those beneath the earth to understand
that I am acting, as I am, under compulsion.
And I'll obey the authorities. Trying to do
more than we can makes no sense at all.

ANTIGONE: I will not plead with you and, if you change
your mind, I won't welcome your assistance later.   70
No—be what seems best to you, and I
will bury him myself, and so die nobly.
I'll lie beside him in love, guilty
of devotion! For I must please the dead
a longer time than I must please the living.
With *them* I'll lie forever. But *you*—go on,
dishonor what's honored by the gods.

ISMENE: I'm not dishonoring them! I simply can't
act against the wishes of the citizens.

ANTIGONE: *You* can make these excuses. *I* will go   80
heap up a tomb for my beloved brother.

ISMENE: *oimoi!* How I fear for you, for all your daring!

ANTIGONE: Don't fear for me. Take the straight path, and prosper.

ISMENE: Then reveal this act to no one—keep it
hidden, in secret, and I will do the same.

ANTIGONE: No! Speak out. I'll hate you all the more
for keeping silent, not proclaiming it to all.

ISMENE: You burn to do what chills the hearts of others.

ANTIGONE: I know I'll please those I should please the most.

ISMENE: I wish you could! You crave what cannot be.   90

ANTIGONE: *Then* I'll stop, and only then—when my strength fails.

ISMENE: It's failed already, aimed at the impossible!

ANTIGONE: If that's all you have to say, you'll earn
my hatred, and *his*, too, as you deserve.

But leave me to endure this folly of mine
and suffer what you find so dreadful. In my view,
to die in shame would be much worse.

ISMENE: Go, then, if you must, but know that you are
foolish to go, though right to love your own.

> *(Exit the two sisters, Ismene back into the palace, Antigone by the side entrance leading to the battlefield. The stage is empty for a moment or two before the Chorus enter from the other side, singing the* parodos *or entry song, after each stanza of which the Chorus Leader speaks seven lines in anapestic meter.)*

strophe 1

CHORUS: Beam of the sun, most beautiful   100
    radiance that has ever shone
    on seven-gated Thebes—
    at last you have appeared, eye
    of golden day, dawning
    over the streams of Dirce,*
    driving the man of Argos†
    to flee with his white shield
    headlong in full array, his mouth
    bloodied by your piercing bit.‡

CHORUS LEADER: Polynices, true to the strife   110
    in his name,§ had loosed him on our land, and he
    with shrill cry flew
    like an eagle to the attack,
    covering the land with his snow-white wing,
    weapons aplenty and helmets
    plumed in horsehair.

antistrophe 1

CHORUS: Hovering above our houses, gaping with blood-thirsty spears
    around our seven gates,
    he left, before he had ever sated   120
    his jaws in the streams of our blood

---

* The famous river at Thebes, west of the city.

† Individual for collective: the famous army of the "Seven against Thebes." See note to line 15.

‡ The rising sun is pictured as a horseman; the hostile army is the steed whose ardor he curbs, forcing it to fly in defeat. The ancient Greek bit was equipped with spikes and could, when harshly applied, bloody a horse's mouth.

§ "Polynices" means something like "man of many quarrels," "man of strife."

and set the crown of our walls
ablaze with torches of pine.
Such was the din of Ares*
at his back, too much
for the dragon's† foe to overcome.

CHORUS LEADER: For Zeus, loathing the boasts of a big tongue
and looking down on them all
attacking in a great stream,
the arrogance of the clang of gold,   130
brandished his bolt and let fly at the one‡
already atop the battlements,
on the point of crying *alalai* in victory.

strophe 2

CHORUS: Hurled to the clattering earth, he fell
torch in hand,§ who in his mad onset
had snorted in rage, blasting
the winds of hate against us then. But now
it's otherwise for him, and mighty Ares
struck on, dealing death to the others,
each in his turn, and drove our chariot to victory.   140

CHORUS LEADER: For the seven captains, stationed
at the seven gates, equal against equal, left behind
to Zeus Turner of Battle their tributes of bronze¶—
all but the doomed pair,** born of one father
and one mother, who planted their doubly
victorious spears in each other, and have
their lot together, a death between them.

---

* The god of war.

† The Theban army is called a dragon or serpent (the Greek *drakon* can mean either) because the original Thebans sprang from the dragon's teeth sown by Cadmus.

‡ Capaneus, not named here but easily identified from his description, was one of the famed "Seven against Thebes" (see note to line 15). Overconfident to the point of blasphemy, he vowed to sack Thebes even against the will of Zeus and the other gods.

§ The device of Capaneus' shield was a naked man carrying a torch, and under it was written "I shall burn the city."

¶ The victorious Thebans are imagined mounting the armor stripped from the dead of their enemies on wooden frames erected at the place where they fell or turned and ran from battle; these were called *tropaia* (whence our word "trophies") in honor of Zeus Tropaios, Zeus who causes the enemy to *turn* (i.e. flee) from battle. The practice, familiar in Sophocles' own times, is an anachronism in the Heroic Age, in which the play is set.

** Polynices and Eteocles. See notes to lines 13 and 15.

antistrophe 2

> **CHORUS:** But since glorious Victory has come
>> bringing joy to Thebes rich in chariots
>> after the wars just past, let us   150
>> forget the rest and go to all
>> the temples of the gods in dances
>> lasting through the night, and may
>> earth-shaking Bacchus of Thebes* lead the way!

> **CHORUS LEADER:** But enough, for here he is, the king of the land,
>> Menoeceus' son,† the new \<leader\>‡
>> coming to meet the new
>> crisis the gods have sent us.
>> With what plan in mind
>> has he proposed this council of elders,   160
>> summoned by a proclamation that touches us all?

(Enter Creon by the side entrance, attended by armed men.)

CREON: Men, the gods who pitched and tossed our city
in the mighty waves of war have set it right again.
I sent messengers to summon you, apart from the rest,
because, in the first place, I'm well aware that you
always honored the power of the throne of Laius;§
and when Oedipus led the city, you were
loyal to him no less and, when he had died,
you remained steadfast in loyalty to his sons.
Now that they have perished by a double fate   170
on a single day, both striking and stricken
and polluting each other with kindred blood,
all the powers of the throne have fallen
to me as next of kin to the dead.

     And yet it is impossible to know the soul
and thought and judgment of any man before
you've seen him rule and make his laws.
I say this because a man who steers

---

* The god Dionysus, son of Zeus and Semele, the daughter of Cadmus, was born in Thebes. He is often called simply Bacchus.

† I translate the emendation of Hermann, followed by West. Creon is meant.

‡ Two or three syllables are missing here. "Leader" is offered by Griffith.

§ Father of Oedipus and ruler of Thebes before him.

the city and does not take the best advice
but keeps his tongue in check, afraid of someone,   180
now and always seems to me worst of all.
And whoever counts a friend of greater worth
than his own country—I say he's nowhere!
Let Zeus, who sees all things always, take note.
And I would not hold my tongue when I see
disaster instead of safety stalking the city,
nor would I count a man who's hostile to the land
a friend of mine, for this I know: it is the land
that saves us, and only if her ship stays upright
can we who sail on her make our friends.   190
       With thoughts like these, I'll build this city's strength.
And here as brother to these principles
is my decree, concerning the sons of Oedipus:
Eteocles, who fell fighting for this city,
in every way her champion with his spear—
him we shall hide in a tomb and honor with all
the offerings that go to the heroic dead;
but his blood-brother—I mean Polynices,
who came home from exile eager to burn
to the ground the country of his birth   200
and the gods* of his race, eager to drink
his brother's blood and enslave† the rest of us—
it has been proclaimed to this city that no one
honor him with burial or mourn for him,
but let his corpse lie, unwept, unburied, eaten
by birds and dogs, a hideous sight for all.
Such are my thoughts on the matter, and never
will bad men outdo the just in *my* esteem.
But whoever means this city well will enjoy
honor from me in death and life alike.   210
CHORUS LEADER: It's your decision, Creon, to treat
this city's enemies and friends this way.
You can make any law. Yours is the power
over the dead and those of us who live.

---

* I.e. the images of the gods in their temples.

† The sacking of a city was followed by the slaughter of its men and the enslavement of its women and children.

CREON: See that my orders, then, are carried out.[*]
CHORUS LEADER: You should ask younger men to do that.[†]
CREON: I have—they're at their post, watching the corpse.
CHORUS LEADER: What other task, then, do you have in mind?
CREON: Not to support those who disobey these orders.
CHORUS LEADER: No one's so foolish as to fall in love with death.   220
CREON: Death, indeed, is the payment, but often
    men have been destroyed by hopes of gain.
              (Enter Guard by the side entrance that leads to the battlefield.)
GUARD: King, I won't say that I've come in haste,
    out of breath, on light feet. No, to tell the truth
    I stopped often, to think it over,
    wheeling round on the way, turning back.
    For I had many a quarrel with myself:
    "Out of your mind, going where you'll be punished?"
    "What, delaying again? If Creon hears of this
    from someone else, *you'll* suffer for it."   230
    With thoughts like these, I took my time
    and so a short trip became a long one.
    In the end, though, it seemed best to come
    here, to you. And if what I have to say amounts
    to nothing, I'll say it anyway, for I'm sure
    I won't suffer more than what I'm fated to.
CREON: Why are you so dismayed?
GUARD: Let me speak for myself first. I wasn't
    the one who did it, I didn't see who did it,
    nor would I rightly come to any harm.   240
CREON: Clever, the way you feel me out and fence
    the matter round. Clearly, you have some news.
GUARD: Yes, but as they say, danger means delay.
CREON: Will you ever say your piece and then be gone?
GUARD: All right, then: someone pulled it off and got
    away just now—sprinkled, that is, the thirsty dust
    on the corpse and performed the rites required.
CREON: *What?* Who is the man who dared to do this?

---

[*] Literally, "Be guards of my commands."

[†] "Be guards" in the previous line is taken to mean "Be guards of the corpse"—i.e. see to it that no one buries it.

GUARD: I don't know. We found neither stroke
    of pick nor mattock-scoop of dirt—the ground   250
    was hard and dry, unbroken, no trace, anywhere,
    of a wagon's wheels. The doer left no clue.
    But when the first watcher of the day
    showed it to us, we were all amazed, perplexed.
    For the corpse was covered, not entombed—the light
    dust lay upon it, as if put there by someone
    afraid of pollution.* No signs appeared of beast
    or dog approaching or rending the corpse.
    And then a babble of evil words arose,
    guard accusing guard, and we'd have come   260
    to blows in the end, with no one to prevent it.
    For each seemed the culprit to the others,
    and none was clearly so, but each denied he knew.
    We were ready to take molten iron in our hands,
    walk through fire, call the gods to witness
    we neither did the deed nor joined with anyone
    in the planning or the doing of it.
        In the end, when nothing came of our searching,
    one of us spoke up, and made us all bow
    our heads to the ground in fear, for we had no way   270
    to argue with him or follow his advice
    with much enthusiasm. This deed, he said,
    must be reported to you, not hidden away.
    The motion carried, and I was the lucky one
    chosen by lot to get the prize. I'm here, no doubt,
    as unwelcome as I am unhappy,
    for no one loves the bearer of bad news.

CHORUS LEADER: For what it's worth, my lord, the thought has long
    been on my mind: the gods have had a hand in this.

CREON: (*to Chorus Leader*) Stop, before your prattle fills me with anger   280
    and you look every bit the fool—an *old* fool!
    What you're saying—that the gods took an interest
    in this corpse—is not to be endured.
    Did they cover it out of respect, as if he was

---

* The Greek word here is *agos*, "any matter of religious awe; pollution, guilt." An ancient annotator commented on this line: "Those who see an unburied corpse and do not pile dust upon it were thought to be *enageis* [in *agos*, i.e. guilty of an offense against the gods]."

their benefactor, the man who came to burn
their temples, their shrines ringed with columns,
and to tear their land and laws to pieces?
Or do you see gods honoring the wicked?
Impossible! The truth is that, right from the start,
men of this city, resenting my edicts,
took to muttering in secret against me,   290
shaking their heads, and wouldn't lay their necks
under the yoke and learn to like me as they should.
Led astray by them, I know it for a fact,
these men* have done these things—for pay.
For there is no human institution as evil
as money. This puts cities to the sword,
this uproots men from their homes;
this inures and perverts the minds
of good men to tend to evil deeds;
it's this that taught mankind to do anything   300
and grow familiar with every impious act.
Those hirelings who have done these things
have guaranteed their punishment in time to come.
(speaking to the Guard) But as I'm still a worshipper of Zeus,
know this well, and I say it on oath: if you
don't find the perpetrator of this burial
and bring him out here, before my eyes,
death alone won't be enough for you, not until,
hung up alive, you confess to this outrage.
That's how you'll learn, when seeking future profit,   310
where profit *should* be sought, and that you ought not
to make a habit of seeking it just anywhere.
For you would see that shameful gains
destroy more men than they preserve.
GUARD: May I speak, or am I just to turn and go?
CREON: Don't you know your voice alone annoys me?
GUARD: Does it sting you in your ears or in your mind?
CREON: Why trace the pain to *where* I feel it?
GUARD: The doer irks your mind; I, your ears.
CREON: A born prattler, that's what you are, for certain!   320

---

* The Guard and the other men posted to watch the corpse (217).

GUARD: Maybe, but not the man who did this deed.

CREON: You did it, though, and threw your life away—for cash.

GUARD: (*with a sigh*) *pheu!*

How terrible, to judge by false appearance!

CREON: Play with words all you want, but if you don't
reveal the doers of these deeds to me, you'll find
that there's a price to pay for evil gains.

(*Exit Creon, into the palace.*)

GUARD: Well, by all means! I hope he's caught.
But if he is or not—chance will determine that—
you won't see me coming back here. No way.
I'm safe now, beyond my wildest hope   330
or thought—and thanks to the gods for that!

(*Exit Guard the way he had entered. The Chorus now sing their
first ode.*)

strophe 1

CHORUS: Many are the wonders, the terrors,˚ and none
is more wonderful, more terrible than man.
He makes his way, this prodigy, over
the dim gray sea, riding the blast
of the south wind, the swells
of the deep cleaving before him;
he wears away the Earth, mightiest
of gods, imperishable, unwearied—
his plows turn her over and over, year
after year his mules plod on and on.   340

antistrophe 1

And he has cast his nets about
the race of lighthearted birds
and the tribes of wild beasts
and the swarms bred in the depths of the sea—
gathers them all in his woven coils,
over-clever man! And his inventions

˚ The Greek has a single word here, the neuter plural of the adjective *deinos* used as a noun. The range
of possible meanings is wide ("wonderful, terrible, strange, extraordinary," according to Griffith; "clever"
and "skillful" are frequent senses also), but since human daring is depicted throughout the ode as both
admirable and frightening, it seemed better to translate the word twice than to privilege one connotation
over the other.

master the beast of field
and crag—the shaggy-maned 350
horse and weariless mountain bull
bow beneath his yoke.

strophe 2

And now he's taught himself language
and thought swift as the wind, and how
to live in cities, shunning
exposure on the open hills,
the rain spearing down from heaven; he's ready
for anything—nothing 360
finds him unready. Death
alone he will not escape.
And yet he has contrived
ways to defeat intractable disease.

antistrophe 2

With his ingenious art, clever
beyond hope, he presses on
now to evil, now to good.
Allowing the laws of the land and the sworn
justice of the gods their place in the scheme
of things, he is high in his city. But he 370
whose daring moves him to evil
has no city at all. May he never
share my hearth, never share
my thoughts, a man who acts this way!

(*Enter Antigone, led by the Guard. The Chorus Leader, speaking
again in anapestic measures, reacts to the sight.*)

CHORUS LEADER: I am at a loss, what is this astonishing
sight? I know it is she; how could I
deny this is Antigone?
O sorrowful child
of sorrowful Oedipus, why? 380
Can it be you they are leading away,
you who have broken the king's law, you
they have caught in this folly?

GUARD: Here she is, the one who did the deed;
we caught her burying him. But where is Creon?

CHORUS LEADER: He's coming from the palace, just in time.
    (Enter Creon.)
CREON: What is it? What makes me "just in time"?
GUARD: King, a man should never swear what he won't do.
    Afterthoughts will prove him wrong. Me, for instance:
    I swore I'd never rush to get back here,   390
    thanks to your threats, that rattled me back then.
    But since a longed-for and unexpected joy
    is greater than any other, I've come—
    although I swore on oath that I would not—
    bringing this girl, who was caught tending
    to the burial. No drawing of lots this time,
    no, sir—she's my lucky find, all mine, right here.
    And now, lord, *you* take charge of her, as you wish.
    Question her, convict her. As for me, I'm free
    of these troubles, off the hook, and rightly so.   400
CREON: The girl you're bringing—how did you catch her?
GUARD: She was burying him herself: there you have it.
CREON: Do you know what you're saying, what it means?
GUARD: Yes. I saw her burying the corpse you forbade
    anyone to bury. Am I speaking plain and clear?
CREON: And how was she seen and caught in the act?
GUARD: It went like this. When we returned—
    those dreadful threats of yours ringing in our ears—
    we brushed all the dust from off the corpse
    and bared the damp flesh as best we could,   410
    then sat down on a hilltop, the wind at our backs,
    to escape the smell, keep it from hitting us,
    each man goading his neighbor with taunts flung
    back and forth, if anyone shirked his duty.
    It went on this way until the time when
    the sun's beaming disk stood in mid heaven
    and it was getting hot. And then, suddenly,
    a whirlwind raised a pillar of dust, trouble high
    as heaven—it filled the plain, it blasted all the leaves
    upon the trees, and the vast sky was engulfed.   420
    We shut our eyes and bore the gods' affliction.
    And when, after a long while, it had blown over,
    the girl was spotted. She let out a bitter wail

like the shrill cry of a bird when she sees
her nestlings stolen from their bed.
Just like that, when she saw the naked corpse,
she cried out in sorrow, and called down
evil curses on the men who did the deed.
Right away she brought in her hands the thirsty dust,
and from a well-wrought bronze jug, lifted high,   430
she tipped out three libations, honoring the corpse.
And we, seeing that, sprang into action
and caught her on the spot. She remained calm;
we charged her with what had been done
and done just now; she denied nothing.
That brought me joy and sorrow, both at once.
How sweet for me, to have escaped from evil
but painful, to bring my friends* to grief.
But to me, all of those matters
count far less than my own safety.   440

CREON: (*to Antigone*) You there, you with your gaze fixed on the ground,
do you admit or deny you did this?

ANTIGONE: I admit, and don't deny, that I did.

CREON: (*to the Guard*) Off with you now, wherever you want;
you're free, acquitted of a heavy charge.
(*Exit Guard.*)

CREON: (*to Antigone*) You now, answer me, not at length but briefly:
Did you know about my proclamation?

ANTIGONE: I knew. How could I not? It was public knowledge.

CREON: And yet you dared transgress these laws?

ANTIGONE: Yes, because, to me, it wasn't Zeus at all   450
who proclaimed them, nor did Justice who lives
with the gods below make laws like these for men,
nor did I think your decrees so formidable
that you, mere mortal as you are, could override
the laws of the gods, unwritten and unshakable.
They are not for now and yesterday, but live
forever; no one knows when they appeared.
No dread of what some *man* might think would ever

---

* The Guard and Antigone could hardly be "friends" in our sense of the word. Perhaps he is a slave of
the royal household and feels close to it.

make me break *them* and be guilty before the gods.
That I shall die, I knew well enough, even 460
without your proclamation—how could I not?
And if I die before my time, I call it a gain;
for how would one who lives, like me, beset
by evils, not gain by dying? And so
I say that meeting with this death will bring
no pain at all to me. But if I let my brother,
born of my mother, lie dead and unburied, *that*
would cause me pain, but this does not.
And if you think I've acted foolishly,
maybe I'm being charged with folly by a fool. 470

CHORUS LEADER: How clear it is: the girl's breed is savage
from her savage father. She knows not how to yield.

CREON: Well, I tell you, minds that are rigid
are most prone to fall, and it's the stiffest iron
tempered in the fire until it's adamant
that you'll most often see splintered and shattered.
I've seen spirited horses tamed by a small bit,
for all their bucking. Just so, we don't
tolerate big talk from someone else's slave.
She knew full well how to be outrageous then, 480
when she trampled on the laws that were laid down;
and here's a second outrage, now she's done it—
to exult and laugh because she did it.
For sure, I'm not a man now—she's the man
if she gains the upper hand and gets away.
But whether she's my sister's daughter, or closer
in blood than our courtyard Zeus and all my house,*
she—*and* her sister—shall not escape the worst
of deaths. Yes, I blame *her*, too, just as much
for this burial, the planning of it. 490
(*to his attendants*) So, call her out. Just now, when I was in
the house, I saw her raving, out of her mind.
        (*Exit attendants into the palace, to fetch Ismene.*)
Just like that, a heart plotting mischief

---

* Zeus of the Courtyard (Zeus Herkeios) was the presiding deity of a Greek household, whose altar in the center of the house was also the center of family worship. The phrase means "my entire family."

in darkness is often found out before it acts.
But what I hate most is when someone
caught in the act puts a pretty face on it.

ANTIGONE: Now I'm caught, you want more than my death?

CREON: Nothing more; having that, I have it all.

ANTIGONE: What are you waiting for, then? I don't like—
and never will like!—anything you say. Just so   500
nothing I say is to your liking, either.
And yet, how could I acquire fame more glorious
than by conferring the honor of burial
on my own brother? All these men (*indicating the Chorus*) would
    agree
with me, if fear hadn't locked down their tongues.
But tyranny enjoys many blessings, not least
the power to do and say what it pleases.

CREON: You alone among Thebans see it that way.

ANTIGONE: They also see it, but shut their mouths—for you.

CREON: You're not ashamed, to think so differently?   510

ANTIGONE: No, it's no shame to honor flesh and blood.

CREON: Wasn't he who killed him your brother, too?

ANTIGONE: He was, from one mother, and the same father.

CREON: Then why offer tribute impious in his sight?

ANTIGONE: His corpse won't testify to that.

CREON: It will, if you give the impious the same honors.

ANTIGONE: I do. It was no slave who died, but my brother.

CREON: He tried to destroy this land! His foe, to save it.

ANTIGONE: All the same, Hades insists upon these rites.

CREON: But good and bad do not deserve an equal share.   520

ANTIGONE: Who knows what rules apply in the world below?

CREON: An enemy, even in death, can't be a friend!

ANTIGONE: And I can't join in hate, but only in love.

CREON: Go down there, then, and love them, if love
you must—while I live, a woman will not rule!

> *(The palace doors open and Ismene appears, escorted by Creon's
> attendants. The Chorus Leader, speaking in anapestic measures,
> announces her entry.)*

CHORUS LEADER: Look now: here is Ismene, before the gates,
shedding tears of love for her sister;
the cloud above her brows mars

her blushing face,
bedewing her lovely cheeks.   530

CREON: You there, lurking in the house like a viper
sucking my life's blood in secret—all unawares,
I reared the two of you, pests, to overthrow my throne—
come, tell me: will you admit you, too, had a share
in this burial, or swear you knew nothing of it?

ISMENE: I did the deed, if *she* will allow it—
I share in the guilt and bear my part in it.

ANTIGONE: No! Justice will not grant you this, for you
refused, and I acted alone, without a partner.

ISMENE: But now that you're in trouble, I am not   540
ashamed to be a shipmate in your suffering.

ANTIGONE: Hades and the dead know whose deed it was.
I feel no love for a friend who loves with words.

ISMENE: Sister, don't deprive me of the honor
of dying and honoring the dead with you!

ANTIGONE: Don't die together with me, or make your own
what you had no hand in; my death is enough.

ISMENE: And what have I to live for, without you?

ANTIGONE: Ask Creon. He's the one you care about.

ISMENE: Why hurt me? It won't help you at all.   550

ANTIGONE: No, it won't. It hurts to jeer at you.

ISMENE: What help can I still be to you, now at least?

ANTIGONE: Save yourself. I don't begrudge you that.

ISMENE: *oimoi!* Then must I miss sharing your fate?

ANTIGONE: Yes, for you chose to live, and I to die.

ISMENE: But not because I chose not to speak!

ANTIGONE: Your thoughts appealed to some, mine to others.

ISMENE: And yet we're both found guilty, both alike.

ANTIGONE: Take heart; you are alive, but my life
died long ago, so I could help the dead.   560

CREON: Of these two girls, I say this one (*pointing at Ismene*) just now
proved herself mad; (*pointing at Antigone*) *she's* been mad from birth.

ISMENE: Yes, my lord. The mind we're born with doesn't
abide when troubles sink our lives; it vanishes.

CREON: As yours did, when you chose to side with evil.

ISMENE: Yes, for how could I live alone, without her?

CREON: "Her"—don't mention "her," for she no longer is.

ISMENE: But will you kill your own son's bride-to-be?
CREON: He'll find other women, other fields to plow.*
ISMENE: But not a marriage so well matched as theirs.   570
CREON: An evil wife for a son fills me with loathing.
ISMENE: Beloved Haemon, how your father wrongs you!†
CREON: You and your talk of marriage make me sick.
ISMENE: So you'll deprive him of her—your own son?‡
CREON: Hades will do it for me—stop this wedding.
ISMENE: The decision is made, then, that she's to die.§
CREON: You and I agree on that, at least!¶ But enough:
   servants, take them inside. From now on these two
   must be women, and not range where they please.
   For even those who are bold try to escape   580
   when they see death coming near their lives.

     (Exit Antigone and Ismene, led by attendants, into the palace.
     Creon remains onstage** while the Chorus sing their second ode.)

strophe 1

   CHORUS: Happy are they whose lives have no taste of sorrows!
     When the gods shake a house, no form of ruin††
     fails to come upon the whole family,
     like the swell of the salt sea
     when it runs, driven by stormy
     winds from Thrace over
     the darkness of the deep,

---

* In the Athenian marriage contract, the husband takes the wife "for the tillage of legitimate children." Metaphorically, the wife is the field the husband plows.

† Lines 572, 574, and 576 are assigned to different speakers by different modern editors: 572 to Antigone, 574 to the Chorus Leader; Dawe would give all three to Antigone. The manuscripts assign all three, as here, to Ismene (with one exception: see on 576).

‡ Boeckh gave this line to the Chorus Leader. There is no reason, however, why the Chorus Leader should suddenly take up the issue of Haemon, raised by Ismene at line 568.

§ In one group of manuscripts this line is assigned to the Chorus Leader, in another to Ismene. But, as Griffith points out, the Chorus Leader would not use the singular pronoun she (the same as in line 574) "when *both* sisters are under Creon's sentence of death" (Griffith, p. 218).

¶ Ismene, in the previous line, meant to say "it has been decreed that Antigone die." Creon answers as if her meaning were "it has seemed good that Antigone die" (the one phrase can mean either in Greek). The irony would lose its meanness if this line were addressed to the Chorus Leader (see previous note).

** It is untypical of Greek tragedy to have a character remain onstage during a choral ode, but some interpreters think that Creon does so during as many as three odes in this play.

†† *Ata*, the keynote of the ode, occurring four times within it. Here it is rendered "ruin," but it also designates the state of mind, the "delusion" (lines 614, 625) or "infatuation" that leads to "ruin," "destruction" (624) or "disaster."

churning black sand
up from the bottom   590
and cliffs battered
head on by hostile blasts groan in the din.

antistrophe 1

I see how of old the pains of the Labdacid˙ house
pile upon the pains of the dead, nor does one generation
let the next one go, but some god topples it, too,
and there is no deliverance.
For just now
over the last root†
in the house of Oedipus
the light of salvation was spreading.‡   600
The bloody knife of the gods below—
folly of words and Fury in the mind—
reaps it away in its turn.

strophe 2

Zeus, what is the step men might take
to curb your power?
Sleep that overtakes all else
touches it not, nor the months of the years§
that never tire, but time leaves your rule
ageless, and the radiant
gleam of Olympus is yours.   610
For now, for what will be
and what has been,
this is the law: to no mortal man
comes great prosperity free of delusion.

antistrophe 2

For hope roams abroad, bringing
profit to many a man, deception
of light-hearted longings to many another.
It comes to a man who knows nothing; he learns

---

* The adjective means "descended from Labdacus." Laius, Oedipus, Eteocles, Polynices, Antigone, and Ismene are all members of the Labdacid dynasty.

† Antigone and Ismene, the last surviving children of Oedipus.

‡ Antigone's prospective marriage to Haemon offered hope for the continuance of the family. Now that she and her unmarried sister have been sentenced to death, that hope has disappeared.

§ I render Schneidewin's emendation. The manuscripts have "the months of the gods."

when he burns his foot in the fire.
Someone wise it was who brought   620
to light this famous
utterance: soon or late
evil looks good to him
whose wits a god steers to destruction.
The man of modest means lives free of delusion.*

(Enter Haemon by the side road that leads to the city.)

CHORUS LEADER: Here now is Haemon, last and youngest
   of your children. Has he come
   in anger at the fate
   of Antigone, feeling
   stung to be cheated of his marriage?   630
CREON: We'll soon know, more than seers could tell us.
   Son, have you come furious at me
   because the vote was cast against your bride?
   Or whatever I may do, will you still love me?
HAEMON: Father, I'm yours. It's your good judgments
   that set me on the right path, and that I follow.
   No marriage will ever be a greater prize
   for me to win than your good guidance.
CREON: Yes, son, so you ought to feel at heart;
   a father's judgment is supreme in everything.   640
   It's for this reason that men pray to have
   sired obedient children in their house—
   to pay their father's enemy with evil
   and honor his friend just as he honors him.
   But the man who produces worthless children—
   wouldn't you say he's sired only sorrows
   for himself and a good laugh for his foes?
   Never toss away your good sense, son,
   for pleasure, for a woman; you know
   her embrace will grow cold within your arms—   650
   an evil woman in your bed, your house.
   What wound is greater than an evil love?

---

* Exactly the same phrase in the same position at the end of the strophe reinforces the contrast between the man of "great prosperity" there and the man of "modest means" here (*Sophoclea*, p. 131).

This girl, then—spit her out, I say, and let her
marry someone in Hades! For now that I've
caught her, plain as day, rebelling, alone
in all the city, I won't make myself
a liar in the city's eyes. No, I'll kill her.
With that ahead, let her go on invoking
Zeus of Kindred Blood!* For if I encourage mischief
in my own kin, I'm sure to meet with it elsewhere.   660
A man who tends to his own household
will show himself just in the city, too.†
He's the man I would have confidence in,
to rule well, and be glad to obey well, too,
and when he's stationed in the storm of war,   670
to stand his ground, a just and brave comrade in arms.‡
But there is no greater evil than anarchy.
Anarchy destroys cities, tears up houses
by the roots, turns to flight the spears
of allies; it's discipline that preserves
the greater part of us when we succeed.
We must defend good order, then, and in no way,
I tell you, let a woman lord it over us!
If we must lose, better to lose to a man
and not be called weaker than a woman.   680
CHORUS LEADER: If old age hasn't tricked me, I think
you speak well and know what you're talking about.
HAEMON: Father, the gods give men intelligence,
the best of all their possessions, and I
could never say—and may I never learn to say—
that you are wrong in speaking as you do.§   686

---

* Zeus in his capacity as god of the household. See note to line 487.

† In his Loeb edition, Lloyd-Jones, following Blaydes, brackets lines 663–67:
  But whoever transgresses or does violence
  to the laws, or thinks he can tell rulers
  what to do, won't meet with praise from me.
  The man the city has appointed—him we heed,
  in matters small and just and in their opposites!
Others follow Seidler, retaining the lines but transposing them, so that they fall between 671 and 672.

‡ An Athenian ephebe, on being admitted to service in the hoplite ranks, swore not to abandon the man fighting beside him. This is another anachronism, transferring to the Heroic Age a practice familiar in Sophocles' day (see note to line 143).

§ Line 687 is interpolated:
  Yet all might turn out well another way.

And yet it's not for you to notice everything   688
people say or do or can complain of;
your glance alone makes ordinary men   690
afraid to say what you don't want to hear.
But I can hear them, muttering in the shadows
how the city is grieving that this girl
must die in the worst way, of all women
most undeservedly, for deeds most glorious;
she refused to leave her own brother unburied
after he'd fallen in blood, to be torn
to shreds by some savage dog or bird:
does she not deserve a golden honor?
So run the rumors whispered in the dark.   700
For me, Father, nothing's to be valued more
than your good fortune. For what greater honor
is there for sons than their father's good repute,
or for a father than that of his sons?
Don't cleave, then, to a single frame of mind—
that what *you* say, and nothing else, is right.
For he who thinks that he alone has sense,
or eloquence that others lack, or character,
when opened up, shows an empty page.*
But for a man, even one who's wise, to learn   710
often, and be flexible, is no cause of shame.
So trees beside a swollen river, bending
in the storm, preserve their twigs, while those
that resist and stiffen go down, trunks and all.
So, too, the captain of a ship, who pulls
the rigging tight and won't let up, ends
upside down, the rowing benches under.
Let your anger go, then, and give yourself
a change. For if, at my young age, even I
can offer some advice, it's best to be   720
born wise in everything; but, barring that—
it's not the way things usually turn out—
it's best to learn from others' good advice.

---

* The metaphor is from a writing tablet: two slabs of wood, one of which, smeared with wax, has words inscribed on it; the other serves as a protective cover. Haemon imagines opening such a tablet, only to find it blank.

CHORUS LEADER: (*to Creon*) King, you should learn from him, when he speaks

  to the point; (*to Haemon*) and you, from him. You've both argued well.

CREON: Am I, at my age, now about to be

  taught how to think by a man his age?

HAEMON: Only in what's right! And if I'm young,

  you should consider my actions, not my age!

CREON: Is it one of your "actions" to approve rebellion?   730

HAEMON: I wouldn't advise you to honor criminals.

CREON: *She* hasn't fallen sick with that disease?

HAEMON: This whole city of Thebes says she has not.

CREON: So now *the city* will give *me* my orders?

HAEMON: You see now who's talking like a child?

CREON: I'm to rule this land for others, not myself?

HAEMON: No city belongs to just one man.

CREON: Rulers own their cities—isn't that the saying?

HAEMON: A fine ruler you'd make, alone, in a desert.

CREON: (*to the Chorus*) This fellow, it seems, is on the woman's side.   740

HAEMON: If *you're* a woman: it's you I care for.

CREON: And show it (you disgrace!) by accusing me?

HAEMON: Yes, when I see you doing what is wrong.

CREON: Am I wrong to revere my position?

HAEMON: You don't revere it when you trample the gods' honors.

CREON: You're despicable, yielding to a woman!

HAEMON: But you won't find me yielding to disgrace.

CREON: This whole argument of yours is all for her.

HAEMON: Yes—and for you and me and the nether gods.*

CREON: You can't marry her, ever—not while she's alive.   750

HAEMON: She'll die, then, and, in dying, destroy another.

CREON: Insolent now, even to the point of threats?

HAEMON: Is it a threat, to tell you what I think?

CREON: You'll regret these thoughts; there's nothing in them.

HAEMON: If you weren't my father, I'd say you've lost your mind.

CREON: A woman's slave! Don't waste your wiles on me!

HAEMON: Do you want to talk and talk and never listen?

---

* The gods of the Underworld, whose claims Antigone has honored. To punish her for that will anger them.

CREON: *That's* what you think? By Olympus,* be sure
    you won't get away with abusing me like this!
    (*to his attendants*) Bring out the loathsome thing. Let her die right now,   760
    before his eyes, at her bridegroom's side!
          (*Exit attendants into the palace, to fetch Antigone.*)
HAEMON: No, she won't die at my side—never
    imagine that! Nor will you ever see
    my face again. Go on raving, then, among
    your friends,† if any still care to listen!
          (*Exit Haemon.*)
CHORUS LEADER: The man rushed off, my lord, in anger;
    the mind of one his age, when hurt, is dangerous.
CREON: Let him go, act, forget he's just a man!
    He won't save these two girls from death.
CHORUS LEADER: You mean, then, actually to kill them both?   770
CREON: No, you're right—not the one who didn't do it.
CHORUS LEADER: What kind of death‡ have you in mind for her?
CREON: I'll bring her by a path no mortals tread
    and hide her, living, in a cave hewn from rock,
    with just enough food to avoid defilement,
    so the whole city may escape pollution.§
    And there, she can pray to Hades,
    the only god she reveres, to win a reprieve
    from death, or she'll learn at last that it's a waste
    to honor what belongs to the Underworld.   780

        (*Exit Creon. The Chorus now sing their third ode.*)

strophe 1

    CHORUS: Love, invincible in battle,
        Love, plunderer of wealth,
        keeping watch nightlong in the soft
        cheeks of a girl
        and roaming over the gray sea
        and into the lairs of the wild—

---

* Creon is swearing an oath. "Olympus" here means the Olympian gods, Zeus in particular, who punishes oath breakers.

† The word is used in the broadest sense, to include family as well as friends.

‡ The sentence proclaimed in Creon's edict was death by public stoning (line 36).

§ The small offering of food will make possible the claim that nature, not the king, is responsible for the death of the victim. Were Creon to shed the blood of Antigone, his niece, he would bring pollution on the city by committing familial murder.

you even the immortal
gods cannot escape, nor anyone
among men who live but a day: he
who catches you is driven mad.   790

antistrophe 1

You wrench the wits of the just
aside to injustice, to their own disgrace
and it is you who have roused
this quarrel of men, kin against kin.
Shining in the eyes
of a bride lovely
to lie with, desire
is victorious, seated in power beside
the great laws,* for the goddess
Aphrodite is here at play, irresistible.   800

> (*Enter Antigone under guard, from the palace. Here begins the
> first* kommos† *of the play, a lyrical passage shared between
> actor and chorus. In the first part, the Chorus Leader speaks or
> chants in anapests, Antigone sings in lyric meters [lines 801–38].
> The pattern changes in the second part.*)

CHORUS LEADER:‡ Now I, too, waver and swerve
from the laws§ at this sight—no longer
can I hold back the springs of my tears
when I see her, Antigone, on her way
now to the chamber where all things sleep.

strophe 2

ANTIGONE: Citizens of my native land, behold me
setting out on my last journey, casting
a last glance
at the sun's radiance,
then never again, but Hades who puts   810
all things to sleep brings me
alive to the banks

---

* These are the laws that make Aphrodite's power the formidable thing it is in the experience of all living beings (as in lines 781–90). She has her place among the powers that rule the world.

† Literally, "a striking, beating of the head and breast in lamentation"; hence, "a dirge, a lament." A second *kommos* concludes the play (lines 1257–1353).

‡ The entire Chorus sing the last four verses of the two stanzas begun by Antigone (839–70). Antigone then sings alone again, bringing the lyrical dialogue to an end with an epode (876–82).

§ Creon's orders, forbidding anyone to mourn for Polynices (line 28) or "support those who disobey" (219).

of Acheron,* denied my share
of wedding rites, and without a bridal
song for my marriage,
I shall be the bride of Acheron.

CHORUS LEADER: Yes, but in glory and with praise
you depart for the deep vault of the dead.
Not stricken by wasting disease,
not paying the sword's wages, but as a law   820
unto yourself, alive and alone among mortals,
you will go down to Hades.

antistrophe 2

ANTIGONE: I have heard of one who died
most piteously—our guest from Phrygia,
the daughter of Tantalus,† whom
the living stone, like tenacious ivy,
embraced on the steep slopes of Sipylus,‡
where rain—the story goes—
and snow never abandon her
as she melts away,   830
showering the mountain sides
from ever-streaming brows. Most like her
am I—a god brings me to bed.

CHORUS LEADER: Well, she was a god and a god's descendant§
but we are mortal and of mortals born.
Still, when you have died
you'll be renowned, you'll share the fate
of the gods' equals—in life, in death.

strophe 3

ANTIGONE: *oimoi!* To be laughed at now!
Why, by the gods of our fathers,
why do you insult me, not yet gone   840
but here, in plain view?

---

* A river in Hades, "the river of pain" (*achos*). In line 816 this river is personified as Antigone's bridegroom.

† Niobe, who came from Phrygia to Thebes (hence her description as "our guest") and married Amphion, by whom she had fourteen children (twelve, according to Homer). Her pride in their number led
her to taunt the goddess Leto with having only two, Apollo and Artemis, who retaliated for the insult to
their mother by slaying all of Niobe's brood. Niobe then returned to her native land, where, weeping
inconsolably for her dead children, she turned gradually to stone.

‡ A mountain of the Tmolus range, south of Sardis.

§ Niobe's father, Tantalus, was a son of Zeus, making her Zeus' granddaughter.

O city, O men of my city,
men of wealth!
iō! Springs of Dirce, sacred
plain of Thebes glorying in chariots—you,
at least, take my side, bear me witness
how I go, unwept by friends, what sort
of laws bring me to the piled stone
of my strange tomb. *iō*, unhappy
alien,* neither mortal   850
with mortals nor shade with shades, at home
not with the living, not with the dead.

CHORUS: You drove to the limit of rashness
and dashed your foot against the lofty
pedestal of Justice, my child. It is some debt
of your fathers that you pay now, in suffering.

antistrophe 3

ANTIGONE: There you touch on it—
my most painful thought,
my father's thrice-turned fate†
and the entire   860
destiny that is ours,
we the renowned Labdacids.‡
iō, disasters of a mother's
bed, a mother's incestuous
embraces that ruined my father!
From such as them was I born to sorrow;
to them I go now—an alien§
in their midst, unmarried and accursed.
iō, brother married
to misfortune!¶ With your death   870
you have killed me, though I breathe still.

---

* The Greek word here, *metoikos*, expresses Antigone's indeterminate status. The technical meaning is "resident alien," one living in a city but not a citizen of it; here, it refers to Antigone's inhabiting a tomb yet not being one of the dead.

† The metaphorical "turning" involved is that of the plow. "Thrice-turned" may be taken literally, alluding to the fate that has destroyed three generations (Laius, Oedipus, and now the last of the latter's children), or it may be taken idiomatically, "thrice" meaning "over and over."

‡ See note to line 593.

§ Antigone again calls herself a *metoikos* (see note to line 850).

¶ Antigone alludes to the marriage of Polynices and Argeia; it was unfortunate in that it enabled Polynices to attack Thebes. See note to line 15.

CHORUS: Your reverence to him is reverence of a kind;
    but power, in the eyes of him who has power to wield,
    must never be transgressed. The temper
    you chose for yourself has destroyed you.

epode

ANTIGONE: Unwept, unloved, unmarried
    I am led away in sorrow
    to the path that awaits me,
    no longer allowed to see
    that sacred eye of flame;*   880
    tearless is my doom, lamented
    by none of my friends.

      (Enter Creon. He speaks to the attendants escorting Antigone.)

CREON: Don't you know that no one sentenced to death
    would stop singing and wailing till they died?
    Take her away, right now, and seal her,
    clasped in her tomb of stone, as I've decreed!
    Leave her there alone, if she wants to die
    or live there, and go on staging funerals!†
    For I am pure as far as she's concerned;
    at any rate, she's lost her residence up here.‡   890
ANTIGONE: Tomb, my bridal chamber, my home, dug
    deep down, imprisonment forever, where I
    go to meet so many of my own, already dead,
    welcomed by Persephone among the shades.
    I'm the last of them and will go down by far
    the saddest of them, before my turn has come.
    And yet as I go I nurse the hope that I'll
    arrive dear to my father, dear to you, Mother,
    and to you, my brother, for it was I
    who bathed you when you'd died, it was I   900
    who dressed you for burial, who poured libations
    at your graves. But now, Polynices, this is what

---

* The sun, as at the beginning of her lament (lines 806–10).

† This line could also be rendered "or go on living entombed there."

‡ The noun *metoikia* ("residence") can mean a settlement in a foreign city; "up here" refers to the upper world, as opposed to Hades. Antigone's indeterminate status is highlighted: she has no place in the company of the living. See notes to lines 850 and 867.

I earn for tending to your body. And yet,
on reflection, I did well to honor you.*
For if I'd been a mother, or if it were my spouse
who lay there rotting, I would not for that reason
have acted in defiance of the citizens.
What law have I in mind in saying this?
My husband dead, another could take his place,
and a child by another man, if I lost   910
the one I had, but with both parents buried
in Hades, no brother could ever come to light.
This is the law I acted on, selecting you
to honor so, but Creon thought what I did
a crime, an act of awful daring, my brother.
And now he has me dragged away like this—
no bridal bed, no wedding song for me,
no share in marriage or in rearing children.
I go instead, stripped, as you see, of friends,
accursed, alive, into the pit of the dead.   920
Which of the laws of heaven have I broken?
Why still look, in sorrow, to the gods?
Which of them can I summon to my side—
I, whose piety has made me impious?
If, then, the gods approve all this, I'll learn
from experience that I've been wrong; but if
these men are the ones who're wrong, may they suffer
no worse than what they've done to me, unjustly!

> *(Creon's attendants begin to escort Antigone offstage.)*†

CHORUS LEADER: She's in the grip of them still—
the same storm-winds raging in her soul.   930

CREON: All the more reason why those who lead
her away will regret their reluctance!

ANTIGONE: *oimoi!* The meaning of that must be
death is very close.

CREON: I wouldn't advise confidence
that it's not so, and won't happen as decreed.

---

* The authenticity of Antigone's self-defense in lines 904–20 has been doubted. See the appendix to this play.

† From here to the end of the scene (lines 929–43), the Chorus Leader, Creon, and Antigone speak their lines in marching anapests.

ANTIGONE: Ancestral city of the land of Thebes,
    gods who guard my race,
    now at last I'm led away, and will be no more.
    Behold, masters of Thebes, the last   940
    of the royal line, all that's left of it—
    see what I suffer, and at whose hands,
    because I revered reverence!

> *(Exit Antigone, led by attendants. Creon evidently remains onstage while the Chorus sing their fourth ode, addressed to Antigone in her absence.)*

strophe 1

CHORUS: Danaë* in all her beauty also bore the loss
    of heaven's light—in a cell bolted
    with bronze, hidden in her bridal
    chamber, she was constrained, as in a tomb
    and yet she, too, was nobly born, child, my child,
    and Zeus' seed, the showered gold, was in her care.   950
    But the power of fate is an awesome thing.
    Neither wealth nor war
    nor walls can ward it off, nor will
    black ships churning the sea escape it.

antistrophe 1

    And the sharp-tempered son of Dryas,† king
    of the Edonians,‡ was brought to his senses,
    clapped in a prison of stone
    by Dionysus for his anger and his taunts.
    So the dread, frothing might
    of madness§ drains away. He came to know   960
    the god he'd grappled with
    in madness and in taunting speech.
    For he tried to suppress the women¶

---

* Daughter of Acrisius, king of Argos, who imprisoned her in a tower or a vault of bronze (called by Sophocles her "bridal chamber" because Zeus made love to her there), to keep her from becoming pregnant because it had been prophesied that if she had a son, that son would cause the king's death. Zeus came to her in the form of a golden rain (line 950).

† Lycurgus, whose persecution of Dionysus and his followers is cited in the *Iliad* (6.130–43) as an example of a mortal contending against a god.

‡ A Thracian people.

§ Madness is the punishment of those who resist Dionysus.

¶ The maenads, female attendants of Dionysus.

swept by the god, the Bacchic fire,* and he stung
to wrath the Muses who love the pipes.†

strophe 2

And hard by the strand
of the Bosporus,‡ between
the dark depths
of the doubled sea,§ is a place,
Salmydessus of the Thracians, where Ares,   970
not far from the city, saw the cursed
blinding of Phineus' two sons
by his savage wife,¶ the wounding
of eyeballs robbed of sight, calling
on vengeance for the blow
of bloody hands
and the stab of the shuttle's point.**

antistrophe 2

They wasted away in misery,
in misery bemoaning their pain, their birth
to a mother unhappily married.††   980
She was a princess, seed
of the Erechtheidae‡‡ born of old
and grew up in faraway caverns, amid her father's
storm-blasts, a Boread§§ running
wind-swift over the steep hills, a daughter
of gods. But even against *her*, my child,
the long-lived Fates launched their attack.

(Enter the blind prophet Tiresias, accompanied by a young boy, his guide.)

---

* Torches carried by the maenads.

† The musical instrument favored by Dionysus, as was the lyre by Apollo. The Muses, frequently depicted together with Dionysus, are imagined enjoying the ecstatic music that accompanied his worship.

‡ I follow the text as emended here in the Loeb edition of Lloyd-Jones. "Hard by" is vague. Salmydessus, the site of the atrocity about to be described, was sixty miles northwest of the Bosporus.

§ The Hellespont and the Black Sea, on either side of the Bosporus.

¶ Phineus was son of Agenor and king of Salmydessus. It is not clear in this passage why his "savage wife" (possibly named Idaia) blinded his two sons, her stepsons.

** The loom's shuttle, the instrument employed to blind the boys, "has an extremely sharp point, like a large knitting needle" (Griffith).

†† The mother of the blinded boys was Cleopatra, daughter of Boreas (god of the north wind), Phineus' first wife (not to be confused with the famous Egyptian queen of the same name).

‡‡ Descendants of Erechtheus, a mythical, semidivine king of Athens.

§§ A daughter of Boreas (see note to line 980).

TIRESIAS: Lords of Thebes, we've come together, two of us
    seeing with the eyes of one—that is the path
    the blind travel, led by their guide.   990
CREON: What is it, aged Tiresias? What news?
TIRESIAS: I will explain, and you—obey the prophet!
CREON: Well, in the past, I've followed your advice.
TIRESIAS: Yes, so you've steered the city straight.
CREON: You were helpful. I can testify to that.
TIRESIAS: Now think! Once more you're on the razor's edge.
CREON: What is it? How I shudder, when I hear you!
TIRESIAS: You'll know, when you hear the signs my art reveals.
    For when I'd sat upon the ancient seat
    of augury, where birds of every kind   1000
    come and go, I heard a sound they'd never
    made before—evil, incoherent, frenzied.
    I knew they were tearing one another
    with bloody claws, for the whirring of their wings
    was not without its sign. Straight away, in terror,
    I turned to sacrifice, kindling the fire all
    around the victim, but it wouldn't burn—instead
    an oozing juice slid down the flesh into the ash
    and smoked and sputtered, the gall sac burst, spewing
    its contents into the air, and the dripping   1010
    thigh-bones shed their envelope of fat.
    So my consultation came to nothing—the rites
    yielded no sign, as I learned from this boy.
    For he is guide to me, and I to others.
    And it's your thinking that's made the city sick.
    Our altars and hearths are all glutted
    with carrion ripped by birds and dogs
    from the ill-fated, fallen son of Oedipus.
    The gods no longer welcome prayers of sacrifice
    from us, nor the blaze of thigh-bones;   1020
    no bird shrieks out an omen good to hear,
    once gorged on the fat blood of manslaughter.
        Give some thought to this, my son. For to go astray
    is common to all men, but if you go astray,
    you won't stay senseless or helpless
    if you seek a remedy, and if you fall

into evil, you do not persist in it.
It's being stubborn that looks foolish.
Yield to the dead, and don't keep stabbing
one who's down. Is it brave, to kill the dead again? 1030
     I'm giving you good advice. It's best to learn
from one who speaks well and brings you profit.

CREON: Old man, all of you are taking shots at me
like archers at a target! Even *your* mantic skills
are deployed against me. I've been bought
and sold away long since by the tribe of seers.
Go on reaping profits, bargain for electrum*
from Sardis, if you like, or gold from India.
You won't hide that man in a tomb, not even
if Zeus' own eagles rip the meat from him 1040
and wing their way with it to Zeus' throne!
Not even then will I, scared of "pollution,"
let someone bury him. For well I know
no mere man has power to pollute the gods.†
     Many people, old Tiresias, even the shrewdest,
go down in shame when they make shameful
arguments sound good for the sake of gain.

TIRESIAS: *pheu!*
Does any man know, can he say, by how much—

CREON: What is it, what cliché will you utter now?

TIRESIAS: —good sense is the best thing one can have? 1050

CREON: Just as much, I think, as folly is the worst.

TIRESIAS: And yet that's the sickness you've come down with.

CREON: I'm in no mood for trading insults with a seer.

TIRESIAS: You do that when you call my prophecies false.

CREON: I do, for the whole tribe of seers is corrupt.

TIRESIAS: The tribe of tyrants also shames itself for gain.

CREON: Surely you know you're taunting those in power?

TIRESIAS: I know, it's through me you saved this city.

CREON: You're a clever seer, with a liking for crime.

TIRESIAS: You'll soon make me say what I'd rather not. 1060

CREON: Out with it, then—but don't speak for hire!

---

* A natural alloy of gold and silver.

† A shocking claim, within the context of traditional Greek religion.

TIRESIAS: Is that what you suppose I'm doing now?
CREON: Yes, but it won't work. Be sure of that!
TIRESIAS: And you be sure of *this*: that you won't live
    through many racing circuits of the sun, before
    you've paid up one corpse, born of your own loins,
    in return for these, for you have cast
    below one who belongs above—yes, buried
    in dishonor a living soul; and you keep up here
    a corpse belonging to the gods down there,   1070
    robbed of its due, its offerings, its rites.
    In none of that have you or the gods on high
    a share˙—but *you* bring them into it by force!
    And so the destroyers, the late-avenging Furies
    of Hades and the gods lie in wait for you,
    to trap you in evils you've unleashed yourself!

      And think again, whether I've been bribed
    to say all this. It won't be long before you'll see
    men and women wailing in your house.
    Meanwhile all the cities† are seething with hostility   1080
    <over their dead,>‡ whose scatterings the dogs
    have consecrated,§ or wild beasts, or winged birds
    wafting unholy stench on city and hearth.

      Such are the shafts I've launched at you
    for provoking me!—and I've aimed them like an archer
    straight at your heart. You won't dodge their sting!

      Lead me away, boy—take me home, so he
    may hurl his rage at younger men
    and learn to cultivate a milder tongue
    and better thoughts than those he's thinking now.   1090
        (Exit Tiresias and boy.)

---

* Creon, as Antigone said earlier (line 48), has no business coming between her and the burial of her brother, a duty that falls to her as next of kin. Compared with her, he has no "share" in these matters. The gods above, the Olympian gods, have no "share" in them in a different sense: they concern the chthonian powers of gods beneath the earth. Creon's interference has disturbed the natural order, the right balance between life and death, the gods above and the gods below.

† Presumably, the cities that joined Polynices in the expedition against Thebes (see note on line 15).

‡ The phrase enclosed in angle brackets is supplied following Lloyd-Jones and Wilson, who argue that a line in which the bodies of the dead were mentioned is missing at this point.

§ The consecration referred to is that of due burial. The bodies of the dead are imagined receiving burial not, as they should, in the earth, but in the bellies of scavenging animals.

CHORUS LEADER: He's left us, my lord, with dreadful prophecies.
   To my knowledge, ever since the time I draped
   this white hair about my head in place of black,
   he's never uttered falsehood to the city.
CREON: I realize that, too, and my mind is shaken.
   To back down is hard, harder still the thought
   that standing firm will steep me in delusion.*
CHORUS LEADER: You must take good advice, son of Menoeceus.
CREON: Well, what should I do? Speak, and I will listen.
CHORUS LEADER: Go, free the girl from her house underground,   1100
   then build a tomb for the one who lies unburied.
CREON: Is this your advice, and is it best to yield?
CHORUS LEADER: Yes, lord, and quickly, for the gods' Harms†
   move swiftly and cut off those whose minds delay.
CREON: *oimoi!* It's hard, but I give up, I won't press on.
   One must not fight in vain against necessity.
CHORUS LEADER: Go! Do it now, don't leave it to others.
CREON: I will go just as I am. Come, come, my men,
   all of you, wherever you are! Take up
   axes in your hands and hurry there with me.   1110
   It was I who bound her, and I myself
   will free her—so my judgment's been reversed.
   For I'm afraid it may be best to live
   to the end observing the established laws.
      (Exit Creon, with attendants. The Chorus sing their fifth ode.)

strophe 1

   CHORUS: God‡ of many names, the Cadmean
      bride's§ glory
      and son of deep-thundering
      Zeus; you who guard glorious
      Italy and hold sway in Eleusinian
      Demeter's folds, open   1120

---

* I render line 1097 as transmitted in the manuscripts, not as emended by Lloyd-Jones and Wilson. On "delusion," see note to line 583.

† A euphemism for the Furies.

‡ Dionysus. The ode, addressing Dionysus in second person throughout, is a hymn summoning the god to the aid of Thebes, his native city.

§ Semele, one of the four daughters of Cadmus. She was mother of Dionysus by Zeus.

to all*—Bacchus,
who haunt the mother-city
of the Bacchae,† Thebes beside
the running waters of Ismenus‡ and near
the savage dragon's sowing!§

antistrophe 1

The black glare of torchlight
above the twin cliffs
towering where Corycian nymphs
roam in ecstasy, and Castalia's
stream have caught sight of you.¶   1130
You leave behind
the ivy slopes of Nysaean** mountains
and the green cluster-laden cliffs
to gaze upon the streets
of Thebes, immortal cries
of joy attending your footsteps—

strophe 2

her, of all cities, you and your mother,
bride of the lightning, ††
honor the most. But now,
when she and all her people   1140
are in the grip of a violent plague,
come with purifying foot over
Parnassian peak or booming strait.‡‡

---

* The famous Mysteries of Demeter were held at Eleusis, not far from Athens and under Athenian supervision.

† Female worshippers of Bacchus.

‡ A river at Thebes, east of the city.

§ An extremely poetic expression, equivalent to "near [the place where] the savage dragon's [teeth] were sown." See note on line 126.

¶ Lines 1126–30 abound in references to the Dionysiac cult at Delphi. The famous Castalian spring was there, and a cave called Corycian.

** A reference, perhaps, to Nysa on the northwest coast of the island of Euboea, an island famed for its wines. The ivy (line 1132) and the grape (1133) were the god's favorite plants.

†† Semele, pregnant with Dionysus, asked her lover Zeus to show himself to her in his full divinity. Zeus obliged, destroying her in a lightning flash but rescuing his son, the unborn god. Semele was later restored to life and joined the gods on Olympus.

‡‡ The god is leaving either Delphi or Euboea on his way to Thebes. Leaving Delphi, he would pass over Mount Parnassus; leaving Euboea, he would cross the Euripus, the turbulent strait between Euboea and the mainland.

antistrophe 2

> *iō*, leader of the dance
> of fire-breathing stars, lord
> of the night's voices,*
> born of Zeus! Appear,
> master, with your Thyiads†   1150
> crowding about you, frenzied, dancing
> all through the night
> Iacchus giver of blessings!‡

(Enter a Messenger, from the direction Antigone had been taken.)

MESSENGER: Neighbors of the house of Cadmus and Amphion,§
the life of man is not the sort of thing
I'd ever praise or criticize: it's always changing.
Moment by moment, chance lifts up the lucky
and chance throws down the unlucky, and there's no
predicting what's ordained for men.   1160
For Creon, I would say, was enviable, once—
he saved this land of Cadmus from her foes,
and when he'd gained sole sovereignty over it,
he ruled, blest in the sowing of noble children;
now all is lost. Yes, all: for when a man's
pleasures give out, I don't consider him
alive, but see him as a breathing corpse.
Go on, make yourself hugely rich at home,
if that's your wish; live a king's life—but when
the joy runs out, I wouldn't give a shadow,   1170
a wisp of smoke for what's left, shorn of its pleasure!

CHORUS LEADER: What sorrow have you brought now, for our king?

MESSENGER: They're dead; the living are guilty of their death.

---

* The nocturnal, ecstatic cries of the god's worshippers, referred to at lines 1135–36.

† Another name for the maenads or ecstatic female worshippers of the god, derived from a verb meaning "rage, seethe." A *thyiad*, like a *maenad*, is a madwoman.

‡ Dionysus was identified with the Eleusinian deity Iacchus, apparently a personification of the ritual cry uttered by the initiates at Eleusis in nighttime celebrations (see note to line 1121). The blessing desiderated is evidently purification (1142).

§ Son of Zeus and Antiope, husband of Niobe (see note on line 825). Together with his brother Zethus, he built the walls of Thebes.

CHORUS LEADER: And who is the killer, who the killed? Speak!

MESSENGER: Haemon has fallen, bloodied* by no stranger's hand.

CHORUS LEADER: Whose hand? His father's, or his own?

MESSENGER: His own, driven by the death his father caused.

CHORUS LEADER: O seer, how truly you've spoken, after all!

MESSENGER: Such are the facts; now we must deal with them.

CHORUS LEADER: Look, now, I see poor Eurydice, Creon's wife   1180
   on her way here, out from the palace; has she
   heard about her son, or has she come by chance?
      (Enter Eurydice, from the palace.)

EURYDICE: Citizens, I overheard what you were saying
   on my way out of the house, to go address
   my prayers to Pallas Athena, the goddess.
   I was just opening the door, drawing
   the bolt back, when it struck my ears, the sound
   of evil tidings for my house. I fell back
   into my maids' arms, and fainted.
   Whatever you were saying, say it again.   1190
   I'll listen. Sorrow is no stranger to me.†

MESSENGER: I will speak, dear mistress, since I was there,
   and leave out nothing. For why should I say
   what will soothe you now, only to be caught lying
   later on? Truth is always what is right.
      I went with your husband, guiding the way
   to the high part of the plain, where Polynices'
   body still sprawled, unpitied, ripped by dogs.
   We beseeched the goddess of the crossroads
   and Pluto‡ to be kind, restrain their anger,   1200
   then washed him in pure water, and burned
   what was left of him, on branches newly torn;
   we heaped up a mound of his native earth,
   then started back to the girl's bridal room,
   Death's nook padded with stone, and made our way in.
   Someone, hearing a shrill sound, a wail
   from deep inside that unhallowed chamber,

---

* An untranslatable play on Haemon's name: *haima* is the Greek word for "blood."

† Alluding, perhaps, to the death of her son Megareus, mentioned later (line 1303).

‡ "The goddess of the crossroads" is Hecate, who had strong associations with death and the Under-world. "Pluto" is a euphemism for Hades (Death).

ran to tell our master Creon, who hurried
in now, closer and closer, a babble
of sad shouts pelting him about. He cried aloud,   1210
a groan terrible to hear: "O no, no!
Am I a prophet, then? Am I on the most
ill-fortuned journey I have ever made?
That voice I hear is my son's! Hurry, men!
Go in by the breech torn in the stone, go
deeper in, to the very mouth, to see
if it's the voice of Haemon
that I hear, or if the gods deceive me."
So charged by our despairing lord,
we looked inside; in the deepest part   1220
of the tomb we saw her hanging by the neck,
fastened in a noose of woven silk,
and him, his arms about her waist, pressing
her close, bewailing his bride lost to death,
and his father's deeds, and his unhappy love.
And when Creon saw it, with a dark groan
he kept on toward him, calling him, crying:
"What have you done? What came over you?
When, when were your senses stolen from you?
Come out, my child, I beg you, I implore you!"   1230
But his son, glancing at him with wild eyes,
spat in his face and, not answering a word, drew
his two-edged sword, but missed his father
who dodged the blow; and then, turning his rage
against himself, without a pause, he leaned
down hard and drove the blade into his side
halfway to the hilt. Still conscious, he took the girl
in a failing clasp and, gasping out his life,
sprinkled her white cheeks with drops of blood.

      He lies, a corpse embracing a corpse, his sad   1240
marriage ended—in Hades' halls, at least—
an example to mankind, that the worst evil
a man can own is lack of sense.

      (Eurydice goes back into the palace.)

CHORUS LEADER: What do you make of that? The lady
has left again, without a word, good or bad.

MESSENGER: I'm troubled, too, but I feed on the hope
    that now she knows of her son's sorrows, she won't stand
    to hear them wailed in public, but at home
    will trust her maids to lead the dirge within.
    For she has good sense, and won't go astray.   1250

CHORUS LEADER: I don't know; I think that too much silence
    and loud, useless crying are both worrisome.

MESSENGER: I'll find out, then, if she's not holding
    something in, concealed in her heart's rage.
    I'll go into the house. Yes, you have a point.
    Too much silence, as you say, seems ominous.

> *(Exit Messenger, into the palace. Creon now enters, from the
> side, escorted by attendants bearing the body of Haemon.)**

CHORUS: And now here comes the lord himself,
    bearing in his hands a glaring reminder,
    if I may say so, that no one else's
    but his own delusion is at fault.   1260

strophe 1

CREON: *iō*, blunders of a senseless mind,
    stubborn, deadly!
    (*to the Chorus*) You are looking on killers
    and victims, all blood relatives!
    The misery my plans have come to!
    My son, young, with a young death—
    aiai, aiai!—
    you died, you've lost your life
    for my mistakes, not your own!

CHORUS LEADER: *oimoi!* Justice! You've seen it, I think, too late.   1270

CREON: *oimoi!*
    I *have* learned, to my sorrow. It was a god
    on my head then, bearing down hard;
    he struck and hurled me into savage ways,
    uprooting joy, trampling it underfoot.
    O sorrows, harsh sorrows of mortal men!

---

* From here to the end, Creon, Chorus, and Messenger—who comes back out of the palace with news of what has happened inside—join in an elaborately structured lamentation, the second kommos, begun and concluded by the Chorus speaking or chanting in anapestic measures. All three voices speak at times in iambic trimeters arranged, with one exception, in corresponding sets of 1, 6, and 5 lines each, within and between the lyrical stanzas, all of which are sung by Creon.

(The Messenger emerges from the palace and addresses Creon.)

MESSENGER: Master, it looks as if you've come with these
   troubles in your hands only to find others
   waiting in the house, soon to be seen!   1280
CREON: What worse evil could follow after these?
MESSENGER: Your wife is dead, the mother of this corpse,
   in grief just now, of a stab wound still fresh.

antistrophe 1

   CREON: *iō,*

      iō, haven of Hades, too clogged to cleanse,
      why, then, is it me, why me you destroy?
      You there, with your bad news,
      your message of sorrow, what do you tell me?
      aiai! You've killed me again, a man already dead.
      What do you say, boy?* What is this new blood—
      aiai, aiai!—   1290
      death on top of death,
      my wife's, that you drape about me now?
      (The palace doors open and servants emerge, bearing the body of
      Eurydice, which they place at Creon's side.)

CHORUS LEADER: You can see it now; it is no longer within.
   CREON: *oimoi*—
      I see a second evil in my sorrow.
      What fate, then, what fate awaits me still?
      Just now I held my child in my arms
      in sorrow, and now I see
      her, face to face, a corpse.
      pheu, pheu! Unhappy mother! O my child!   1300
MESSENGER: Fallen upon the sharpened sword, beside the altar . . . †
   she closed her eyes in darkness, wailing
   a marriage bereft of Megareus,‡ who died before,
   and now of Haemon; and finally she invoked
   your evil deeds against you; you killed her children.

---

* The Messenger is a slave, and Creon here addresses him as such.

† Critics posit a gap in the text at this point, probably of a single line (only one is needed to match the six in the corresponding passage at lines 1278–83). I have rendered line 1301 as emended by Arendt.

‡ Son of Creon and Eurydice. When Thebes was in danger of being destroyed by Polynices, Tiresias prophesied that it would survive if one of Creon's sons were sacrificed. The implication is that Creon endorsed the sacrifice. Lines 993–96 and 1058 may allude to these events.

strophe 2

CREON: *aiai, aiai!*
 I shudder with dread. Why doesn't someone strike me
 in the chest with a sharpened sword?
 Miserable, *aiai!*   1310
 And miserable the anguish I dissolve in.

MESSENGER: Guilty of these deaths and those,*
 you were indicted by your dead wife here.

CREON: In what way did she shed her life's blood?

MESSENGER: She stabbed herself beneath her liver,† when she heard
 of her son's fate, and the house filled with wailing.

 CREON: *ōmoi moi!* Never upon another will these
  deeds of mine, this guilt of mine, be fastened.
  For I killed you, I killed you, I
  am the one, the guilty one, truly. *iō*, attendants!   1320
  take me, as quickly as you can,
  take me away from here,
  I who am not, I who am no more than no one.

CHORUS LEADER: I commend your wish, if any wish makes sense
 in evils. Quickest is best, when they beset us.‡

antistrophe 2

 CREON: Let it come, let it come,
  let it appear, the fate that is fairest,
  that brings me my final day—   1330
  the best fate. Let it come, let it come,
  that I not look again on another day.

CHORUS LEADER: These things are in the future. We must deal
 with what's at hand. That's where our concern must be.

CREON: I've made my prayer for all I want.

CHORUS LEADER: Have done with prayers. Mortals can have
 no release from ruin sent by fate.

 CREON: Lead away this empty shell of a man.
  I killed you, my son, unwillingly—and you,   1340
  lying here as well. *ōmoi*, unhappy! Nor do I know

---

* The references are vague. Perhaps "these" refers to the bodies of Haemon and Eurydice (the two onstage at the moment), "those" to the bodies of Antigone and Megareus (the two not onstage).

† Thought to be the seat of passion.

‡ These two lines of spoken verse, dividing strophe from antistrophe, are not answered by a corresponding pair.

which of you two to look upon, where to lean;
everything's crooked in my hands, and for the rest
a fate too hard to bear has leapt upon my head.

> *(Exit Creon, followed by attendants carrying the bodies, into the palace. As they are leaving, the Chorus speak the final words in anapests.)*

CHORUS:

Wisdom is laid down as the first part
of happiness, by far; and then, to be
irreverent in nothing
that concerns the gods.   1350
Resounding words
repaid with resounding blows
in old age teach wisdom to the proud.

> *(Exit Chorus, to the side.)*

APPENDIX

The authenticity of Antigone's self-defense in lines 904–20 has been doubted by a number of distinguished Sophoclean critics and defended by a number of others, and Goethe famously expressed the wish that some talented scholar might prove the passage spurious. Discussion of the question will probably continue, though the balance of opinion in recent criticism inclines in favor of authenticity. Those who doubt the passage raise two principal objections to it.

The first objection is that in these lines Antigone seems to contradict what she had said earlier. The "unwritten laws" she cites at lines 450–70 would demand that she tend to the bodies of her own kin, no matter who they might be, but here she says she wouldn't have done that for a husband or a child, but only for a brother, and only for a brother under certain circumstances.

However surprising this apparent correction might seem to us, there is strong external evidence that Sophocles himself put it into Antigone's mouth: Aristotle cites and discusses it in his *Rhetoric* (3.16.1417a32–33), quoting lines 911–12 with no hint of doubt as to their authenticity. Almost as important is the point he makes about the passage, which he cites as an example of inconsistency in character portrayal—precisely the point that troubles modern critics; Aristotle, however, *approves* of it, arguing that Sophocles gets away with the inconsistency because he has given adequate reasons for it.

The second objection is based on the fact that the argument made in lines 909–12 is also made by the wife of Intaphernes in Herodotus (3.119). In the Herodotean passage, King Darius has condemned Intaphernes and all male members of his household to death for conspiracy. Moved by the persistent appeals of Intaphernes' wife, Darius relents and grants her a choice: he will spare one of the condemned, the one she chooses. When she names her brother, the king is astonished and asks the reason for her choice. The one she gives is the one Antigone gives in lines 909–12: "O king, I may acquire another husband, if fate wills, and other children, if I should lose these. But with my father and mother no longer alive, in no way can I get another brother."

The objection made by those who dispute the authenticity of the passage is that this argument, which makes sense in Herodotus, does not make sense here. The choice made by the wife of Intaphernes saves the life of the one chosen; Antigone's choice does not save anyone's life—on the contrary, it puts an end to her own. The difference between the two situations is something that Sophocles, the supreme dramatic artist, would not have overlooked, and so the Herodotean adaptation must be the work of a clumsy interpolator.

Defenders of the passage have dealt with this problem in various ways. I would only remark here that the wife of Intaphernes herself has nothing to lose in making her choice. Antigone has everything to lose in making hers, nor will she know, while alive, whether the gods, in whose name she had acted, even approve of what she has done (lines 921–28). Or is she trying (not entirely convincingly) to justify her own actions to herself? There is nothing like this complexity in the Herodotean original, which has logical simplicity in its favor, but not emotional depth. Perhaps it is a mistake to make logic our own criterion at this particular moment, even though it is the criterion applied by the heroine herself.

Introduction to Sophocles' *Electra*

This drama, like Aeschylus' *Libation Bearers*, depicts how Orestes returns to Argos and avenges his father Agamemnon's murder. In the *Oresteia*, Aeschylus had portrayed Electra as reserved and hesitant. She asks the Chorus of old women what she should do with the offerings her mother, Clytemnestra, has asked her to leave at her father's tomb; she follows their advice and prays for Orestes' return. When she discovers that he has indeed returned, she follows her brother's lead in praying to Agamemnon's ghost, then leaves the stage and takes no part in the rest of the action. But Sophocles' Electra steps forward assertively, even aggressively. It was she (and not a nurse) who looked after the child Orestes; it was she who took him away from his mother and sent him off to Phocis to Pylades' family. When Orestes at last returns to reclaim his patrimony, it is Electra's passion and intensity that propel him to murder Clytemnestra without the slightest hesitation.

Sophocles makes it clear that Electra has reason to be angry. As she explains to a sympathetic Chorus of women from Argos, she has not been allowed to marry, but rather is treated like a slave by her mother and Aegisthus, forced to serve them in the palace that belonged to her father and rightfully now belongs to Orestes. Sophocles contrasts her with one of her sisters, a dramatic technique he also employs in the *Antigone*. Like Ismene in that drama, the pliant and cooperative Chrysothemis—known as Electra's sister from Homer's brief mention in the *Iliad*, though Aeschylus had ignored her in the *Oresteia*—here argues that it is not sensible to fight against superior power. She warns Electra that if she does not stop her endless lamentation she will end up an exile, confined to a sunless dwelling in another country. But Electra replies that she would prefer that existence to her present life. Electra stops her lamentations when Chrysothemis reveals that Clytemnestra has had a frightening dream and has asked her to pour libations on Agamemnon's tomb. The dream omen echoes Aeschylus' *Libation Bearers*, in which Clytemnestra dreamed of a snake suckling her breast; in this play, she sees Agamemnon's wooden scepter (symbolically, his royal line) sprouting a living branch. Electra is hopeful, and Chrysothemis agrees to throw away Clytemnestra's offerings and offer instead locks of her and her sister's hair.

The Argive women of the Chorus respond to the news about the dream with an excited song. Agamemnon, they vow, will hear their prayers and an Erinys (or avenging Fury) will come "with many feet and hands," a prediction that will come true in the form of Orestes and Pylades, who have already appeared on-stage in the prologue. The Chorus explain that the troubles in Agamemnon's family began when his grandfather Pelops won his bride by cheating in a chariot race, then threw the charioteer who knew about the plot into the sea. They understand the cause of all this trouble to be *aeikeia*, "uncivilized behavior" or savagery, which will manifest itself in the next generation as well, when Orestes and Pylades will ambush Clytemnestra, with Electra cheering them on, and then, without a pause for reflection or pity, lure Aegisthus to his death.

Clytemnestra now enters and confronts Electra, her harsh behavior making clear that everything Electra has said about her is true. Because of the frightening dream, Clytemnestra has come to offer sacrifice to Apollo, asking him to protect her household and the wealth that they enjoy. But the audience already knows that the god will not receive her prayer, because he has, through his oracle in Delphi, persuaded Orestes to return to Argos. Clytemnestra, however, believes that the god has answered her prayer when Orestes' old tutor arrives, pretending to be a messenger from a friend in Phocis, to announce that Orestes was killed in a chariot race. In a thrilling messenger speech, he describes the racing accident vividly and in horrific detail. Unlike Aeschylus' Clytemnestra, who was sad to learn of her son's death, this Clytemnestra is more relieved than sorry. Electra, however, believes she has lost her best hope for revenge; in her despair she refuses to believe Chrysothemis when she returns from Agamemnon's tomb and reports that she had seen there, among the offerings left by kin, a lock of Orestes' hair. Now she asks the passive Chrysothemis to help her kill Aegisthus, but she of course refuses. During a pause in the action, the Chorus wonder why, when birds care for their children, no parent has come to help Electra in her pious search for justice.

Just at this point, two "strangers" arrive with an urn that supposedly contains Orestes' ashes. Electra mourns her brother with the sorrow that Clytemnestra was unable to express for her own child. Once Orestes realizes that this grieving woman is his sister, and understands what she has suffered, he lets her know that he is alive and has returned. The excitement of the reunion of brother and sister (a high point also of Aeschylus' *Libation Bearers* and Euripides' *Electra*) is in this play made more tense by Orestes' need for secrecy, especially after Orestes' old slave comes out of the palace to remind the siblings of the danger they are in. As Orestes and Pylades enter the house, Electra prays to Apollo to help them execute their plan; she knows that without that god's help, the plot can never succeed. Apollo has imperceptibly made that success possible: Aegisthus is away from home, while Clytemnestra is taken off guard by the story of Orestes' death and does not hear Electra's cries of joy when she recognizes Orestes.

The Chorus see that Orestes is the promised "avenger of the dead … coming with devious feet into the house" and that the prediction of an Erinys arriving "with many feet and many hands" has been fulfilled. As the gruesome killing of Clytemnestra takes place offstage, Electra urges the killers on: "If you can, hit her twice as hard!" Her ardor has heroic models, both positive and negative: like Sophocles' Antigone, she never doubts that she is right to do as she does; but like the rage-blind Achilles in Homer's *Iliad*, she expresses no remorse and has no pity for her enemies. Her years of servitude to her father's murderers have, it seems, taken a toll on her humanity, but she nonetheless stands on the side of divine justice, as decreed by Apollo.

Orestes reenters from the palace, proclaiming "All's well inside the house. Apollo's prophecy was true!" and assuring his sister that her mother's pride will never again dishonor her. But no sooner has he spoken than Aegisthus appears, just too late to rescue Clytemnestra (another case in which perfect timing suggests divine aid). Electra now takes a more active part in the plot, deceiving Aegisthus into thinking that his wife is inside mourning over Orestes' ashes. Aegisthus is elated; at long last he will be able to rule Argos without fear of resentment or rebellion. Electra craftily concurs: "I've learned reason, and to serve the powerful." The doors of the palace open to reveal a covered body; Aegisthus supposes it to be Orestes, until he lifts the covering. Once he understands that Orestes has returned, he asks to say a few words, but Electra will not allow it. Aegisthus asks: "So it's inevitable; this house must see the woes of Pelops' family, now and to come?" The question is never answered.

There is no reference in the play to the Erinyes who will come to pursue Orestes, or to the long journey Orestes must take to Delphi and then to Athens before he can be acquitted (see Aeschylus' *Eumenides*). Perhaps Sophocles relied on a version of a story (mentioned in Homer's *Odyssey*) that ended here, with Orestes offering a feast of reconciliation for the Argives and assuming the throne. But it's more likely that his Athenian audience knew the version that had him pursued by Erinyes and put on trial, as recounted in Aeschylus' *Oresteia* and many other depictions of Orestes' visit to the oracle of Delphi. The Theater of Dionysus where they sat as they watched *Electra* was only a short distance from the Areopagus, the hill where Orestes was supposedly tried and acquitted, and where the Erinyes were worshipped as the Sacred Goddesses (Semnai Theai). So the original spectators could probably have mentally supplied this epilogue.

There is no evidence, either external or internal, for the date of Sophocles' *Electra*, and it is not clear whether it was performed before or after Euripides' play of the same name (also in this volume). In modern times, the play has been recast as an opera by Richard Strauss (1909).

ELECTRA

Translated by Mary Lefkowitz

Essentially this is a translation of the text in *Sophoclis Fabulae*, ed. Hugh Lloyd-Jones and N. G. Wilson (Oxford, Oxford University Press, 1990); I have also consulted Sophocles: *Electra*, ed. P. J. Finglass (Cambridge, Cambridge University Press, 2007).

CAST OF CHARACTERS (IN ORDER OF APPEARANCE)

OLD SLAVE
ORESTES, son of Agamemnon and Clytemnestra
ELECTRA, Orestes' sister
CHORUS of local young women
CHRYSOTHEMIS, sister of Electra and Orestes
CLYTEMNESTRA, mother of Electra and Orestes
AEGISTHUS, Clytemnestra's husband and Agamemnon's first cousin

Setting: The play takes place in front of the palace of Mycenae. Orestes enters, accompanied by his friend Pylades and an old slave; they stand before the palace and speak as if they could see from there the town of Argos.

OLD SLAVE: Son of Agamemnon, who once commanded
the army at Troy, here now before you
is the place you've always hoped to see.
This is the ancient Argos you have longed for:
the grove of Io, Inachus' daughter, gadfly-driven,
and this, Orestes, is the Lycian marketplace,
sacred to the wolf-killer god;* here on your left
is Hera's famous temple. We have reached the place
where you can say you see golden Mycenae;
here is the house of Pelops, home of many deaths.   10
Long ago I took you from here after your father's murder
from your closest kin, your sister's hands.
I carried you and saved you and raised you
till you became a man, to avenge your father's murder.
So now, Orestes, and Pylades, dearest friend,
we must plan quickly what we need to do.
Look: already the sun's dazzling brightness
arouses the birds' clear morning song;
the dark night of the stars has gone away.
Before any man sets foot outside the house,   20
we must make plans. We have reached the point,
where there is no time for delay; no, we must act.
ORESTES: My dearest servant, everyone can see
how faithful you have been to me.
You're like a noble horse who despite his age,
Never loses heart, not even in a crisis,
but pricks up his ears; that is how you

---

* Apollo; the Argives thought the title Lycian derived from the Greek word *lykos* (wolf), but the real origin of the term is not known.

urge us on and stand in the front lines.
So I shall tell you what I think, and you
pay keen attention to what I say,   30
and if I lose the track, then set me straight.
For when I went to the oracle at Delphi,
to learn by what means I could exact
justice from my father's murderers
Phoebus* told me what you shall now hear:
"Without weapons or soldiers, but with the treachery
Of a righteous hand, you'll steal your slaughter."
Now since this is the oracle I heard,
when the right moment comes, you go
into that palace, learn all that they are doing,   40
and then tell us exactly what you know.
They will not recognize or suspect you,
gray with old age and the long lapse of time.
Tell them a story, that you are a stranger,
sent by Phanoteus the Phocian, since he
is the most powerful of their allies.†
Tell them (and for the purpose take an oath)
that Orestes is dead because of an accident;
that he was rolled from his wheeling chariot
at the Pythian Games;‡ let that be your tale.   50
And we, as the god commanded, shall adorn
my father's tomb, first with libations,
with locks of hair; then we shall come here again
holding in our arms a bronze-plated urn,
which (as you know) is hidden in the bushes,
to deceive them with a story, and bring them
welcome news that my body is destroyed,
consumed by flame and turned to ashes.
Why should this worry me? I'm dead in words,
but in reality survive and may win glory!   60

---

* Apollo. The oracles were usually expressed in obscure or contradictory language, here "justice through treachery."

† The old slave would be welcomed as a servant of their friend. The lie contains elements of truth: Orestes came to Mycenae from Phocis, where he was living with Strophius, Pylades' father. Phanoteus was an enemy of Strophius.

‡ Contests held every two years at Apollo's oracle in Delphi.

No speech, I think, that brings reward is bad.
Indeed, I have often seen clever men who die
(falsely) in words and return home again,
are then more greatly honored than before.
And so I state that because of this story
I shall live and like a star shine on my enemies.
You, land of my fathers and you native gods,
welcome me with good fortune on this path.
You, my father's house, I come with justice
to cleanse you, on a mission from the gods.   70
No, do not cast me out, dishonored from this land;
let me regain my wealth and rescue my house.
Now I have said this, old man, you must see
to it that you go, and carefully pursue your task.
Pylades and I will now set off; opportunity
is man's chief control in every enterprise.

        (Electra's voice is heard coming from the palace.)

ELECTRA: Oh, I am so miserable!

OLD SLAVE: My son, from behind the door I think
I hear a slave inside the house.

ORESTES: No, that is Electra in her misery. Shall we   80
remain here and listen to her cries?

OLD SLAVE: No, we should not! We should only seek to do
what Apollo has ordained. Begin there;
pour out libations to your father. I believe
this will bring victory, and power to our deeds.

        (The Old Slave leaves the stage; Orestes and Pylades depart in
        the opposite direction. Electra begins to chant in anapests.)

  ELECTRA: O sacred light
    and air that together share the earth,
    how many dirges have you heard me sing;
    how many blows bloodying my breast,   90
    when the day has left the dark night behind.
    My wretched bed understands the cares
    of my nights in this house of sadness,
    how often I sing a dirge for my poor father.
    Brutal Ares did not slaughter him
    in a foreign land;
    no, my mother and her bed-sharer Aegisthus

split his head open with a bloody axe
like woodmen cutting down an oak.
And no one weeps for you, Father,   100
except for me, that you were killed
so shamefully and so sadly.
No, I shall not leave off
the dirges and miserable wailing,
as long as I see the shining banks
of the stars, and the light of day,
like the nightingale who killed her child,*
lamenting I proclaim my sorrow to all,
loud wailing at my father's doors.
House of Hades and Persephone,   110
Hermes of the Underworld, powerful Curse,
and Erinyes, the gods' reverend children,†
you see those who have died in injustice;
you see when marriage beds are stolen;
come, help me, avenge
the murder of my father,
and send my brother to me.
For alone I am no longer strong enough
to support the heavy burden of my grief.   120

> *(Electra remains onstage as the Chorus of Argive women enter the orchestra; they sing and Electra responds to them in song.)*

strophe 1

    CHORUS: My child, child of a mother hated by the gods,
Electra. What is this lamentation
that wears you away, unrelenting?
You mourn the man taken down long ago
without consent from the gods, by your treacherous mother,
Agamemnon, betrayed by deceit
and a coward's hand.‡ I say the man who planned this
should die, if it is right for me to speak these words.

---

* Procne punished her husband, Tereus, for seducing her sister Philomela by killing her son Itys and serving him to Tereus for dinner; she was then turned into a nightingale. The story was the subject of Sophocles' drama *Tereus* (now lost).

† The Erinyes (called the Furies in Latin) were deities who avenged blood crimes by pursuing the perpetrators.

‡ In this account of the myth, Aegisthus killed Agamemnon with Clytemnestra's help.

ELECTRA: Noble women,   130
   you have come to comfort me in my sorrows.
   I know and understand this, it does not escape me.
   But still I do not want to abandon my lamentation,
   and not keep on weeping for my poor father.
   Repay my steadfast friendship with kindness;
   let me drift along as I have done,
   aiai, I implore you.

antistrophe 1

CHORUS: But with lamentation and prayers
   you will never bring back your father
   from Hades' lake, where all must go.
   No, by turning from moderation to grief   140
   unremitting, you will destroy yourself in sorrows
   that bring no release from evil.
   Why cling to your misfortune, tell me?
ELECTRA: Only a fool could forget
   the terrible death of a parent.
   The lamenting bird grips my mind;
   she always mourns "Itys, Itys,"
   stunned by her sorrows, Zeus' messenger.*
   Niobe, for all your suffering, I think of you as a god   150
   since in your tomb of stone
   aiai, you weep eternally.†

strophe 2

CHORUS: My child, you are not the only mortal
   that has seen sorrow;
   yet you suffer more than others in your house;
   they have the same parents and connection in blood,
   Chrysothemis is living, and Iphianassa,‡
   and the son fortunate because he spent his childhood
   hidden from sorrows, and someday   160
   the famous land of Mycenae

---

* The nightingale was a harbinger of spring; on the myth of Itys, see note to line 107.

† All of Niobe's children were killed by the gods Apollo and Artemis because she boasted that she had more children than their mother, the goddess Leto; Niobe was turned into a stone with streams of water running down her face.

‡ Here Sophocles follows the (now lost) epic *Cypria* for the names and number of Agamemnon's children. A fourth daughter, Iphigenia, was sacrificed at Aulis.

will welcome when he returns to his homeland
a noble father's scion, guided by Zeus, Orestes.

ELECTRA: I wait for him, never tiring; I go on living
miserably, still without child or husband,
drenched in tears, clinging to an unending
fate of suffering. But he has forgotten
all he has lost, all he has learned. Every message
that comes to me has proved to be deceptive.   170
He always longs to come,
but though he longs, he chooses not to appear.

antistrophe 2

CHORUS: Courage, my child,
courage! Great Zeus is in heaven;
he observes and rules everything.
Trust him with your too painful anger.
Do not be too harsh to your enemies and do not forget:
Time is a gentle god.
For even though he stays
in the coastal pastures of Crisa,*   180
Agamemnon's son has not forgotten,
nor has the god who rules beside the river of Acheron.†

ELECTRA: But most of my life has left me
without any hope. I have no more strength.
I waste away, without children;
no kind husband protects me,
but like some base household slave
I serve in my father's palace, like this,   190
in disgraceful clothing,
and the tables I stand at are bare.‡

strophe 3

CHORUS: There was a terrible cry when your father returned,
terrible as he lay there,
when the blow of the bronze blade
came to meet him.
Deceit was the planner, passion the killer.
The brutal god or mortal who did this,
brought to birth a brutal scene.   200

---

* The valley below the sanctuary at Delphi.

† Hades.

‡ The servants get what is left after the family has eaten; Electra does not eat with the family.

ELECTRA: When it came, that day of all days
was the most hateful to me.
That night, the appalling anguish
of that unspeakable feast!
My father saw
the shameful death brought by two hands,
the hands that betrayed me,
that destroyed my life.
May the great god on Olympus
repay them with pain and punishment!   210
May the doers of this deed
never enjoy their luxury!

antistrophe 3

CHORUS: Take care not to say more!
Don't you understand that your present condition
dates from that day? So you are falling
into your own ruin, savagely.
You will come to own still more misery,
in your angry heart, giving birth
to conflicts. Don't fight with the powerful;
endure your hardship.   220

ELECTRA: To cruelty I must respond cruelly. I know,
my wrath does not escape me.
But in the midst of cruelty
I cannot restrain my madness,
as long as life sustains me.
Who could suppose, dear friends,
I might heed a kind word,
or timely advice.
Leave me alone, leave me, advisers.
This must be called insoluble.   230
I shall never cease from my sorrows,
nor reckon up my lamentations.

epode

CHORUS: But I offer you good advice,
like a mother you trust,
not to add madness to madness.

ELECTRA: What limit is there to my misery, tell me?
How can it be right to neglect the dead?
What person would find that natural?
I would not want to have their respect,

I could not enjoy any good thing 240
I might have, if I clipped the wings
of shrill dirges for my forebears.
If a dead man is earth or nothing at all
and will lie there in misery,
and they never pay back
the penalty for their crimes,
reverence would be doomed
and piety among all mortals. 250

CHORUS: My child, I have come both on your behalf
And on mine. If what I say is wrong,
I'll yield, and follow along with you.

ELECTRA: Friends, I am ashamed if I seem to you
to be overcome by my many sorrows.
But a compulsion forces me to do this;
forgive me. For how could any woman of noble birth
observe her father's pain and not do what I've done?
Every day and night I watch his pain
growing, and never withering away. 260
First, I hate what my mother has done,
though she gave birth to me. Then, I live
in the same house with my father's murderers.
They are my masters, and it is up to them
whether I receive or waste away without.
What kind of days do you think I spend
when I see Aegisthus seated
on my father's throne, I see him wearing
the same clothes as my father, pouring libations 270
on the same hearth where he murdered him,
and when I see the worst outrage of all
my father's murderer in his bed,
with my wretched mother, if I can call her
mother, since she sleeps beside that man.
She is so foul that she cohabits with a polluted
murderer, with no fear of the Erinys' vengeance.*
It's as if she is proud of what she has done,

_____

* See note to line 112.

and celebrates the day on which she killed
my father through her treachery; on that day
she puts on choral dances and sacrifices cattle   280
every single month to her Guardian gods.
I look on disconsolate within the house,
I weep, refuse to eat, and wail about
the wretched festival named for my father,
alone by myself, since I am not allowed,
to weep as much as my heart desires.
Supposedly she is noble, but that woman
shouts and taunts me with bad names,
"You filthy creature, hated by the gods,
are you the only person in the world   290
who's lost a father? I wish you dead and hope
the gods below compel you to weep forever."
So she insults me, but if she hears someone say
Orestes is coming, then she cries out in rage
and stands beside me screaming: "This is your fault,
this is your work! You are the one who stole
Orestes from my arms and hid him away.
I tell you, you'll be punished for this crime."
She barks like this, and her illustrious husband
stands at her side and gives her courage,   300
that feeble creature, who everyone despises,
a man who fights his battles with the help of women.
But I go on waiting for Orestes to come back
to put a stop to this; I'm dying miserably.
For by putting off his return he has destroyed
the hopes I had and the hopes I did not.
In times like this, my friends, there can be
no restraint or piety. No, the presence of evil
requires in response evil behavior.

CHORUS: Now tell us, can you speak like this,   310
    when Aegisthus is around? Is he away from home?

ELECTRA: Of course he is away, do you suppose if he were here
    I could be outside? He is now in the farmland.

CHORUS: If that is so, then I am more confident
    that I can have a conversation with you.

ELECTRA: He is away, so ask me what you please.

CHORUS: I shall ask you. What can you say about your brother?
    Has he come, or will he come? I wish to know.

ELECTRA: He says he is; says it, but does not do it.

CHORUS: Men often hesitate to take on a major task.   320

ELECTRA: When I rescued him I did not hesitate.

CHORUS: Have faith, he is well-born. He will help his friends.

ELECTRA: I trust him, or I would not have lived this long.

CHORUS: Now say nothing more. I see your sister Chrysothemis,
    coming from the house, child of the same father
    and the same mother, holding in her hands
    tomb-offerings for someone beneath the earth.

CHRYSOTHEMIS: What have you come out again to say
    before the entrance door, my sister?
    Not in all this time have you wished to learn   330
    not to indulge yourself in useless anger!
    I know myself well enough by now
    that I regret the way things are at present.
    If I had power, I'd show them how I feel.
    But in times of trouble I must furl my sails,
    seem to be inactive, not cause pain.
    I want you also to do the same.
    I know there's no justice in what I say,
    but in what you think right. But if I don't want to
    be treated like a slave, I must obey my rulers.   340

ELECTRA: It's dreadful that though you are his daughter,
    you forget your father, and care for your mother.
    It is from her that you learned all the advice
    you give to me. There's nothing there that's yours.
    You choose: either be a fool, or wise up
    and forget about your "friends."*
    You said yourself just now, that if you were strong
    You would demonstrate just how much you hate them.
    But when I do everything I can to avenge my father
    you won't help me, but sabotage my work.   350
    So add cowardice to your other faults!
    So tell me, or learn from me, what benefit
    might come to me if I stopped my lamentations?

---

* Clytemnestra and Aegisthus.

I'm living, miserably, I know, but that's enough for me.
I give pain to them, and in that way bring honor
to the dead, if in that place there is any consolation.
As I see it, you hate them, but only talk of hating.
In practice you go on living with your father's killers.
I could never do that, not even if someone brought
as gifts to me the luxuries you now enjoy,   360
could I go along with *them*. You can have
your rich table, and the easy flow of food.
All the nourishment I need is not to harm myself.
As for your wealth, I've no desire to share it,
nor would you, if you had sense. You could
be known as a child of a most noble father,
but instead you're called your mother's child.
So most people will regard you as a coward,
a traitor to your dead father and your friends.

CHORUS: (*to Electra*) By the gods, do not turn to anger. There is benefit
in what each of you has said, if you could learn   370
from what she says, and she in turn could learn from you.

CHRYSOTHEMIS: Friends, somehow I have adjusted to her ways
of speaking. But I would not have ever brought this up
if I had not learned that great trouble was coming
to her, that will put an end to her lamentations.

ELECTRA: So tell me about this horror. If you can tell me something
worse than what I have, I won't argue with you.

CHRYSOTHEMIS: Yes, I shall tell you everything I know.
If you do not stop your lamentations, they will send you
to a place where you shall never see the sunlight.   380
You shall be living in a shuttered dwelling
away from here, and sing your sorrows there.
Think about that, and don't blame me if in the future
you're imprisoned. Now's the time for good sense.

ELECTRA: And this is what they have planned for me?

CHRYSOTHEMIS: Yes, as soon as Aegisthus comes home!

ELECTRA: I hope he comes soon, if that's what they want.

CHRYSOTHEMIS: Why have you uttered this curse against yourself?

ELECTRA: So he will come, if he intends to carry out these plans.

CHRYSOTHEMIS: What do you want to happen? What are you thinking?   390

ELECTRA: I want to get as far from you as I can.

CHRYSOTHEMIS: Don't you recall what your present life is like?

ELECTRA: My life is wonderful, beyond amazement!

CHRYSOTHEMIS: It would be, if you knew how to think straight!

ELECTRA: Don't teach me to betray my friends.

CHRYSOTHEMIS: I don't teach that; just to respect authority.

ELECTRA: Go ahead and fawn on them. That's not what I do.

CHRYSOTHEMIS: Nothing good comes from dying from stupidity.

ELECTRA: If I must, I'll die, and bring honor to my father.

CHRYSOTHEMIS: Our father, I know, forgives our failure to act.　　　400

ELECTRA: Those are words cowards approve of!

CHRYSOTHEMIS: You won't listen and take my advice?

ELECTRA: No, never. May I never be so devoid of sense!

CHRYSOTHEMIS: Then I shall leave to go where I have been sent.

ELECTRA: You're heading where? Who'll get these burnt offerings?

CHRYSOTHEMIS: My mother sent me to pour libations at my father's tomb.

ELECTRA: What did you say? Offerings to her worst enemy?

CHRYSOTHEMIS: To the man she killed? That's what you mean to say.

ELECTRA: Did one of her friends advise her? Who wants this done?

CHRYSOTHEMIS: She was frightened by a nightmare, I believe.　　　410

ELECTRA: Gods of my fathers, now's the time to stand beside me.

CHRYSOTHEMIS: You're in some way encouraged by her fears?

ELECTRA: If you tell me what she saw, then I could tell you.

CHRYSOTHEMIS: I don't know much; I can only say a little.

ELECTRA: Then tell me that, for often it's the little stories
　　which sink mortals or set them straight.

CHRYSOTHEMIS: The story is that she saw in a dream
　　a second encounter with your father and mine,
　　who had come back to life. And then he took the staff
　　he used to carry, which Aegisthus carries now,　　　420
　　and planted it beside the hearth.* And from it
　　grew a bough with leaves that shaded
　　all the country of the Mycenaeans.
　　I heard this from someone who was there
　　when she told the Sun about her dream.†

---

* Since dead wood cannot grow again, the leaves are miraculous (see *Iliad* 1.234–37); that it takes root beside the hearth indicates that Agamemnon's descendants will rule again. Similarly, Astyages, king of the Medes, dreams that from his daughter's genitals a vine grew that covered all of Asia, and so he tries to have his grandson killed (Herodotus 1.108).

† In drama, characters who feel isolated or oppressed, because they have no one else to talk to, address the gods of the sun or air or earth.

More than this I do not know, except
it was her fear that made her send me out.*
ELECTRA: Then, dear sister, bring nothing to the tomb   431
that you hold in your hands. It is not right
or holy to set down burial offerings or libations
to our father from the woman who's his enemy.
Give them to the winds or hide them deep within
the dust, so that no part of them comes near
our father's grave. Then when she dies,
they'll be a keepsake for her down below.
Only the most shameless of all women,
would have placed her hostile libations   440
on the grave of the man she murdered.
Do you suppose that the dead man
in his grave would welcome such a gift
from the woman who mutilated his body,†
and used the blood from his wounds to rinse away
pollution?‡ Do you think these offerings
will bring her absolution from his murder?
Impossible! No, throw them out. Instead
cut locks of hair from your head
and from my sad head, too, a small gift,   450
but all I have. Give them to him, this dull hair
and my sash, though it has no rich ornament.
Kneel down and ask him to come to us,
a kindly helper from below against our enemies;
ask that his son, Orestes, with his strong arms
be living, on his way to trample on our enemies!
Then in future we can adorn his tomb
and bring him gifts with hands richer than these.
I believe, yes, I believe, that our father still cares
and sent her the dreams she could not bear to see.   460
So, my sister, take on this task both for yourself

---

* Lines 428–30 do not seem to belong here: "Now by our family gods I implore you, / take my advice and don't fail because of bad planning; / if you reject me, you will be living with evil again."

† A murdered man's hands and feet were cut off, strung together, and tied around his neck under his armpits in order to prevent him from avenging his death.

‡ The blood on the knife used to kill a sacrificial victim was wiped back onto the victim as if to indicate the victim's consent. Ordinarily water would be used to wash a corpse.

and me, to help us, and the dearest of all mortals,
the father whom we share, who lies in Hades.
CHORUS: Your sister speaks words of piety, my dear,
and if you are wise, you will do what she says.
CHRYSOTHEMIS: I shall, for justice does not provide an excuse
for two people to argue; it urges us to act.
But while I dare to carry out this deed,
friends, by the gods I ask that you keep silent,
since if our mother learns about this, I am sure   470
I will regret that I have dared to do this deed.

*(Chrysothemis leaves; Electra remains onstage while the Chorus
sing the first stasimon.)*

strophe

    CHORUS: If I am a prophet, not misguided
or lacking in good sense,
an earlier prophet, Justice, is coming,
bringing just power in her hands.
She is coming, my child, in a short time.
Courage supports me
now that I have heard   480
of her dream with its sweet message.
For your father has not forgotten,
the lord of the Greeks,
nor has the old bronze-forged
two-bladed axe
that killed him in shameful savagery.

antistrophe

She is coming, with many feet, many hands,
hidden in a cruel ambush,   490
the Erinys with feet of bronze.*
For the conflicts from their polluted union,
with its accursed bed, accursed marriage,
has attacked them† for their crimes.
Because of this I have courage;

---

* The Erinyes were sometimes portrayed with multiple feet. The phrase may also suggest how, later in the drama, Orestes and Pylades together ambush first Clytemnestra and then Aegisthus.

† Clytemnestra and Aegisthus.

never, never, I think
shall a favorable portent
come to the murderers and their accomplices.
Terrifying dreams or oracles
would have no value
as prophecy,   500
if this night apparition bodes well.

epode

Pelops' horse-race*
Long ago, cause of many sorrows,
you came and destroyed
this land:
Myrsilus, laid to rest,
thrown in the sea,
hurled headlong   510
from the gilded chariot,
in miserable savagery.
To this day never
has it left this house,
cause of many sorrows: savagery.

(Clytemnestra enters from the palace.)

CLYTEMNESTRA: I see that you are on the loose again, outside,†
because Aegisthus is not here. He always keeps you in,
so you won't run about and disgrace your family.
Now that he is away, you do have no respect for me.
You have said many things to many people,   520
that I am shameless and rule unjustly,
and treat you viciously, and your friends.
I am not vicious, but I must say harsh words
when I hear harsh words from you about me.
Your father, nothing else, is always your pretext,
because I caused his death. I did, I know that well.
I cannot deny that this is what I did.
Yet the goddess Justice killed him, not I alone,

---

* In order to win Hippodamia as his bride, Pelops, Agamemnon's grandfather, needed to beat her father, Oenomaus, in a chariot race; if Pelops lost, Oenomaus would kill him. Pelops bribed Oenomaus' charioteer to tamper with the wheel of Oenomaus' chariot, won the race, and threw Myrsilus into the sea.

† In fifth-century Athens, unmarried women from propertied families did not leave the house unescorted.

and you would have helped her, if you had sense.
Since this father of yours, the one you always mourn,   530
was the only Greek who dared to sacrifice your sister*
to the gods. He planted the seed, but did not endure
the same pain as I did, who gave birth to her.
So, explain this to me. For whose sake
did he sacrifice her? You say for the Argives?
It was not up to them to kill my child.
If he killed her to help his brother Menelaus,
by dying he should have compensated me!
In any case Menelaus had two children,
they should have died instead of her, if   540
for their parents' sake the ships had sailed.†
Did Hades have such a great desire to feast‡
upon a child of mine, instead of one of hers?
Or was there present in your killer father
Some need for my children, rather than Menelaus'?
Isn't that the thinking of a foolish and evil parent?
I believe it is, even if you do not share my opinion.
The dead girl would say so, if she had a voice.
So I am not disheartened by what happened.
If I seem to you to reason wrongly, reason rightly   550
yourself, before you blame your relatives.

ELECTRA: You cannot say that I was the first to say
    something painful, not after what you said.
    Now, if you will let me, I would like to speak
    the truth about the dead man and my sister, too.

CLYTEMNESTRA: Of course I'll let you. I would have listened to you,
    if you'd ever begun your speech like this.

ELECTRA: Now I'll tell you. You say you killed my father.
    What words could be more disgraceful than these,
    whether you were justified or not. I'll tell you,   560

---

* The goddess Artemis demanded that Iphigenia be sacrificed, because she was angry about the deaths that would result from the expedition to Troy. For a vivid description of the sacrifice, see Aeschylus, *Agamemnon* 205–46.

† The Greek fleet was sent to Troy to bring their mother, Helen, back to their father, Menelaus. Menelaus and Helen had two children, a daughter, Hermione, and a son, Pleisthenes (Homer also mentions Megapenthes, Menelaus' son by a slave woman).

‡ The gods participated in sacrifices offered to them by mortals, if only by smelling the smoke of the bones and skin offered to them.

You did not act justly. Persuasion drove you to it,
from an evil man, the man you live with now!
Ask the hunter goddess Artemis why in Aulis
she made him suffer before she stopped the winds.*
I'll explain, since we cannot ask her to tell us.
My father once, so I have been told,
in his leisure time, frightened with his step
a dappled horned stag, and when he killed him,
he happened to throw out some kind of boast.
Because of that Artemis, Leto's daughter   570
held back the fleet until my father sacrificed
his own daughter in compensation for the stag.
That's the reason for her sacrifice. There was no other way
to free the army to go home or on to Ilion.
So he was forced to do it, and though he fought it,
he sacrificed her, not for the sake of Menelaus.
But if he had, for I'll also take up your argument,
and he killed her to help him, because of this
you had to kill him? Under what law?
Watch: if you create this law for mortals   580
that law will bring you suffering and regrets.
For if we kill one person in requital for another
you'd be first to die, if justice was served.
No, watch out: you have invented an excuse!
If you wish, tell me the reason why you now
commit the most shameful of all deeds:
you are sleeping with the murderer
who in the past helped you kill my father.
You bear his children, you've cast out
your legal children, scions of a legal marriage.   590
How could I approve of this? Even if you say
you're owed in payment for your daughter?
So you insist, but it's still shameful. It is wrong
to marry enemies for your daughter's sake.
But there's no way I can advise you,
because you'll never miss a chance to say

---

* Artemis kept the Greek fleet from sailing out of the harbor at Aulis until Agamemnon sacrificed Iphigenia.

I'm badmouthing you. Indeed, I think of you
more as my master than my mother.
My life is hard, because I keep on living   600
with evils caused by you and your partner.
Elsewhere your other child, the one you almost killed,
poor Orestes, wears away his miserable life.
You're always accusing me of keeping him alive
to get revenge. You must understand
that if I had the power, I would have done so.
Go ahead, tell everyone, if you need to
that I badmouth you, that I'm so shameful.
If I've become an expert in this behavior,
I'd guess that I've been emulating you!

CHORUS: (*to Clytemnestra*)[...]*
I see you breathing rage, but I do not see   610
you asking if justice is on her side.

CLYTEMNESTRA: What sort of questions should I ask about her,
when she speaks to her mother with such insolence,
though she's a child. Surely you must realize
that she is without shame, capable of anything.

ELECTRA: You know quite well that I'm ashamed,
Though I don't act it. What I do is wrong
for someone my age and unlike myself.
But your enmity and your actions
have driven me to do these deeds.   620
Shamelessness inspires shameless action.

CLYTEMNESTRA: Shameless child! So it's me and my words
and my deeds that make you talk like that!

ELECTRA: You say that, I don't. But you do it,
and deeds find their own descriptions.

CLYTEMNESTRA: No, I swear by queen Artemis, you'll pay for
your insolence, when Aegisthus comes home.

ELECTRA: You see, you fall into a rage, after you said
I could speak. You don't know how to listen.

CLYTEMNESTRA: Won't you let me offer a sacrifice without   630
ill-omened shouting,† since I let you speak freely?

---

* The context indicates that a line is missing here in which the Chorus would have addressed Clytemnestra.

† Sacrifices needed to be conducted in an atmosphere of peace and decorum.

ELECTRA: Go ahead, please, make sacrifice, and don't blame
me for speaking, for I shall say nothing more.

> *(Electra remains near the door, while Clytemnestra and a slave*
> *approach the altar at the front of the stage.)*

CLYTEMNESTRA:
You, stand near me and bring me my offerings,
fruits that I may raise to this god to free
my sleep from the fears that I have now.
Phoebus our protector, I hope you listen
to my secret utterance. I am not speaking
among friends; it is not safe to unfold
the whole tale to the light when *she* is near me;[*]   640
with her hatred and endless talk
she'd scatter harmful rumors everywhere in town.
No, listen to me now: for I'll speak to her as well.
For during this past night I have seen visions
of ambiguous dreams; grant, my lord, that these
may come to pass, if they are favorable.
If they are hostile, send them against my enemies.
Let me know if some are planning now
by treachery to cast me from my present wealth.

    No, let me go on living thus, a life unharmed   650
in the house of the Atreidae,[†] wielding the scepter,
living with the friends I live with now,
happily and with the children who bear me
no ill will or give me bitter grief.
Hear me, Lycian Apollo, with kindness,
and grant me everything I ask.
Everything else I think you know,
because you are a god, despite my silence.
For surely Zeus' children can see everything.

> *(As Clytemnestra completes her prayer, the Old Slave enters and*
> *delivers the false message that Orestes is dead.)*

OLD SLAVE: Ladies of Mycenae, how might I come to know   660
if this is the home of king Aegisthus?

CHORUS: This is it, stranger. You have guessed correctly.

---

[*] Clytemnestra describes her message as if it were written in a book roll that she was not prepared to open.

[†] Atreus was Agamemnon's father.

OLD SLAVE: (*gesturing toward Clytemnestra*)
    And am I right in supposing that this lady
    is his wife? She has the appearance of a queen.
CHORUS: Yes, absolutely. She is standing beside you.
OLD SLAVE: Greetings, my lady. I have come bringing you,
    and Aegisthus, good news from a friend.
CLYTEMNESTRA: I welcome your news. But first I need to know
    who it is who has sent you.   670
OLD SLAVE: Phanoteus of Phocis, with a message of importance.
CLYTEMNESTRA: What is it, stranger? Tell me. I know that coming
    from a friend, you'll bring us welcome news.
OLD SLAVE: Orestes is dead. I have stated it concisely.
ELECTRA: Oh, no, take pity on me, I've died this day.
CLYTEMNESTRA: What can you tell me, stranger? Don't listen to her.
OLD SLAVE: I said it then; I say it now: Orestes is dead.
ELECTRA: I'm dead, poor me, I'm nothing now.
CLYTEMNESTRA: (*to Electra*) You, mind your own business! Stranger,
    tell me the truth. How did he die?
OLD SLAVE: I was sent here for this and shall tell all.*   680
    Orestes went to Greece's famous showplace,
    To win a prize at Delphi at the contest.†
    When he heard the loud proclamation of the herald
    announcing the footrace that comes first of all,
    he entered in glory, admired by everyone.
    His finish was as glorious as his start.
    He brought back the honor and reward of victory.
    To tell you all in a few words, I do not know
    any other man who has achieved so much.
    Understand this: whatever contest was announced,   690
    <races on the double track, the pentathlon>,‡
    in all of these he took the victor's prize.
    He was proclaimed as an Argive, called
    Orestes, the son of Agamemnon, who long ago
    assembled the famous army from Greece.§
    That is how it was. But when a god destroys,

---

* The wealth of detail in this narrative makes it credible, even though it is a complete fabrication.

† The Pythian Games, held every two years in honor of Apollo.

‡ This line was probably not in Sophocles' original text.

§ The language here echoes the opening line of the drama.

not even a strong man can escape.
So on another day, when at sunrise,
the swift-footed horse contest took place,
he came in with the other charioteers.   700
There was an Achaean and a Spartan.
Two were Libyans, masters of yoked chariots.
Orestes was fifth, with Thessalian horses.
The sixth contestant came from Aetolia
with chestnut colts. A Magnesian was seventh.
The eighth, a man from Aenia, had white horses.
A ninth came from Athens, founded by the gods,
then a Boeotian, filling the tenth chariot.
They took their stands after the official judges
sorted lots and assigned their places.   710
They raced away when the bronze trumpet sounded.
The drivers shouted at their horses, grasped and shook
their reins. The whole racecourse was filled
with noise and the rattling of chariots.
Dust flew up; all were clustered close together.
They laid on their goads; each sought to go
beyond the wheels and snorting of their horses.
The breath of horses fell on them; foam covered
the horses' backs and the turning wheels.
Orestes kept close to the far turning post,   720
grazed it with his wheel.* Slacking his right horse's rein
to block the path of the chariot next to him.
Before this all were standing in their chariots.
But then the Aenanian's unreined colts broke loose,
and carried him away. Sixth out of the turn,
they started on their seventh lap and struck
their foreheads against a Libyan chariot.
And after that, one after the other crashed and fell.
From this one mistake, the whole plain
of Crisa† was filled with the shipwrecks of chariots.   730
The clever charioteer from Athens saw this,
pulled his horses aside, held them back and avoided

* Antilochus wins the race in *Iliad* 23 by using the same tactic.
† Chariot races were held on the flat plain of Crisa below the hills where the sanctuary of Delphi is located.

the tidal wave of chariots in the middle of the course.
He drove on last, because his horses were inferior,
Orestes did, and trusted in the final outcome
of the race. He saw that only the Athenian was left,
and hurled a sharp command into the ears
of his swift horses and pursued him. The two charioteers
drew level and drove on, first one, then the other
pushed his horses and chariot into the lead.   740
And through all the other laps he remained safe,
poor man, standing straight in his upright chariot.
Then he let his left rein go slack, as his horse turned.
He didn't see he'd struck the tall turning post.
He broke the axle between the wheels,
slipped off the chariot rails, got twisted
in the reins. He hit the ground; the horses
dashed off to the middle of the track.
When the crowd saw that he'd fallen from the chariot,
they cried out in sorrow for the young man,   750
who did such deeds and then had such bad luck,
dragged on the ground, then on his back, his legs
toward the sky, until the charioteers
managed to rein in the rushing horses
and freed him, so bloody that no friend
could recognize his poor remains.
Men appointed by the Phocians*
burned him in pyre, and in a small bronze urn
are bringing his great body, now sad ashes,
so he can be buried in his ancestral land.   760
That is how it was. A sad tale to tell,
and for those of us who saw it, as did we,
the worst disaster that I've witnessed.

CHORUS: Oh, no! All my old master's family is gone,
    torn from its roots, or so it seems.

CLYTEMNESTRA: Zeus, what should I do? Shall I call it lucky
    or terrible or good? It is so cruel
    that my own misfortune has saved my life.

OLD SLAVE: Why does this story trouble you so much?

---

* Delphi was in the district of Phocis and was managed by its residents.

CLYTEMNESTRA: Giving birth is strange: one cannot hate   770
   a child even when he can do you wrong.
OLD SLAVE: It seems that we have come in vain.
CLYTEMNESTRA: No, not in vain! How could you say in vain,
   If you have come bringing certain proof
   that he is dead. Though I gave life to him,
   he turned away from my breast and nurture,
   became an exile, a stranger. Once he left
   this land, he didn't see me, but he blamed me
   for his father's death and swore to do me harm.
   So not by night nor day does sweet sleep   780
   shelter me, but time stands near me
   and keeps on telling me that I'll be killed.
   But now—for on this day I've been freed from fear,
   from her (*pointing to Electra*) and him. She's the worse pain
   because she lives with me, and sucks out the blood
   straight from my life—now we'll be secure,
   safe at least from that creature's threats.
ELECTRA: Oh, misery, now, Orestes, I can weep
   for your misfortune, because though you are dead
   this mother of ours insults you. Is my life good?   790
CLYTEMNESTRA: Yours is not, but his is good, as it is now.
ELECTRA: Hear her, Nemesis* of the man who has just died.
CLYTEMNESTRA: She's heard what she needs; she made the right
      decision.
ELECTRA: Insult me! For now you're fortunate in your good fortune.
CLYTEMNESTRA: Why can't you and Orestes stop mocking me?
ELECTRA: We've been stopped, but not so we can stop you.
CLYTEMNESTRA: Stranger, you would be a valued friend
   if you could stop her endless talk.
OLD SLAVE: May we now depart, if you are satisfied?
CLYTEMNESTRA: No indeed. That would be unworthy of me   800
   and of the friend who sent you. No,
   go inside, and let her keep up her loud lament
   for her misfortunes, and her friends' sorrows.
   (*Clytemnestra and the Old Slave go into the palace.*)

---

* Electra invokes the goddess Nemesis because she was believed to punish people who had no *aidōs*, or respect for righteous behavior.

ELECTRA: Don't you think that she should have been sad
 and sorrowful and wept and wailed
 in misery for the son who'd died like that?
 No, she laughed and left. And I am suffering.
 Dear Orestes, your death has destroyed me.
 You've gone and torn out of my mind
 the few hopes I had left, that you were alive   810
 and would return someday to avenge your father
 and mine. Poor me, now where can I go?
 I am alone, left without you and my father
 both. Now I must be a slave again
 in the home of the people I most hate,
 my father's murderers. Is my life good?
 No, I shall not live in the same house
 In future time, but here at this very gate
 without a friend I'll eke out my life.
 For that, anyone inside is free to kill me,   820
 if it troubles them. Killing me would be a favor;
 keeping me alive, a pain. I have no wish to live.

strophe 1

 CHORUS: Where then are Zeus' thunderbolts, and where
  is the blazing Sun-god. Can they look on this
  calmly and keep it dark?
 ELECTRA: *ē ē aiai.*
 CHORUS: Dear child, why are you weeping?
 ELECTRA: *pheu.*
 CHORUS: Do not cry so loudly!
 ELECTRA: You're destroying me.   830
 CHORUS: How?
 ELECTRA: If you hold any hope for those
  who have clearly gone to Hades, you are trampling
  me down in my suffering.

antistrophe 1

 CHORUS: I know that noble Amphiaraus
  was trapped by a woman's golden chains*
  and now beneath the earth—

---

* Amphiaraus was betrayed by his wife, Eriphyle, who was bribed with the gift of a golden necklace.

ELECTRA: *ē ē iō.*   840

CHORUS: he lives and rules.*

ELECTRA: *pheu.*

CHORUS: *pheu*, yes, his destroyer

ELECTRA: was killed,

CHORUS: she was.†

ELECTRA: I know, I know. An avenger came
   for him in his grief. But there is no one alive for me.
   There was once, but he is gone.

strophe 2

CHORUS: In your misery you have won misery.

ELECTRA: I know this, I know too well,   850
   in a life filled with hateful sorrows
   in full flow, never ending.

CHORUS: We have seen what you are saying.

ELECTRA: Never, never, persuade me to go where—

CHORUS: What are you saying?

ELECTRA: —I cannot find help from a noble sibling.

CHORUS: Death comes to all mortals.   860

antistrophe 2

ELECTRA: Indeed, but like that, in the contest
   of swift hooves, as that poor man died,
   caught and cut in the reins?

CHORUS: An infinite outrage!

ELECTRA: Indeed, as if he were a stranger,
   he lies there—

CHORUS: *papai.*

ELECTRA: —where I could not give him burial‡
   or lamentation.   870

   *(As the lyric lamentation ends, Chrysothemis returns from
   Agamemnon's grave.)*

CHRYSOTHEMIS: Dearest, I'm rushing to you in joy,
   I have put aside decorum and come swiftly.
   I bring you joy and release from the troubles
   you had in the past and are still lamenting.

---

* Like Tiresias, Amphiaraus retained his mental powers after death.

† Amphiaraus' son Alcmeon avenged his father by killing his mother.

‡ It was customary for female family members to prepare the bodies of their relatives for burial and to take part in formal lamentation; in Sophocles' drama, Antigone defies the king's orders in order to bury her brother Polynices.

ELECTRA: How could you have found me any help
    from troubles that clearly have no cure?

CHRYSOTHEMIS: Orestes is here for us. You've heard me say this
    as clearly as you see me standing here.

ELECTRA: You poor thing! Have you lost your mind,
    making a mockery of your troubles, and of mine?   880

CHRYSOTHEMIS: I swear by our father's hearth, I do not speak
    in mockery: Orestes is here for us!

ELECTRA: *oimoi*, I am so miserable! Who in the world
    told you a tale you're too ready to believe?

CHRYSOTHEMIS: No one told me. I believe it because
    I saw for myself clear evidence.

ELECTRA: What proof did you see? What did you behold
    that without fire warmed your heart and mind?

CHRYSOTHEMIS: By the gods, listen to me, so that you can learn
    the rest, and say if I'm a fool or sensible.   890

ELECTRA: Then tell me, if it will make you happy.

CHRYSOTHEMIS: Indeed, I'll tell you everything that I saw.
    When I came to our father's ancient tomb,
    I saw fresh streams of milk flowing
    from the column's top and all kinds of flowers
    wrapped around our father's tomb.* I saw it,
    wondered, and looked around to see
    if someone was standing somewhere near.
    I took my time and surveyed the whole place,
    and went close to the tomb. But then I saw   900
    at the pyre's edge a new-cut lock of hair.
    As soon as I saw it, a familiar image struck
    my mind: I was seeing evidence
    of the dearest of all men, Orestes.
    I took it in my hand and in pious reverence
    my eyes soon filled with tears of joy.
    I know now just as I knew then, that gift
    could only have been brought by him.
    Who else would do it, other than you and me?   910
    I did not do it, I am certain of that
    and you did not. How could you? You'll be punished,

---

* These are traditional gifts to the dead, here offered in unusual abundance.

even if you go from home to the gods' temples.
No, certainly our mother's not inclined to do this,
and if she did, we would know about it.
No, these tomb-offerings come from Orestes.
So, take heart, my dear. The same misfortune
does not always hover over the same people.
Our old fortune was hateful, but perhaps today
will bring an encounter with great good.

ELECTRA: Oh, I have been pitying you for your folly. 920

CHRYSOTHEMIS: Why? Doesn't my message make you happy?

ELECTRA: You don't know where you are or think you are.

CHRYSOTHEMIS: How can I not know what I have plainly seen?

ELECTRA: Orestes is dead, poor thing, no help can come
  to you from him. Look to him for nothing.

CHRYSOTHEMIS: *oimoi*, poor me, who on earth told you that?

ELECTRA: A man who was near him when he died.

CHRYSOTHEMIS: And where is he? It's astonishing!

ELECTRA: In the house, welcomed, not rejected by our mother.

CHRYSOTHEMIS: *oimoi*, poor me. But who on earth was it 930
  who left the grave-offerings on Father's tomb?

ELECTRA: I believe that someone placed them there
  as offerings in memory of Orestes.

CHRYSOTHEMIS: Poor me, and I had hurried here in joy
  to bring you the news, and didn't know
  how foolish I was being. But now I'm here,
  I find old troubles and new ones besides.

ELECTRA: That's how things are. But if you listen to me
  you'll lift the burden of our present sorrow.

CHRYSOTHEMIS: How will I ever bring the dead to life? 940

ELECTRA: I didn't say that. I am not that foolish.

CHRYSOTHEMIS: What do you tell me to take part in?

ELECTRA: To let me do what I shall recommend.

CHRYSOTHEMIS: If I can be of any help, I won't refuse.

ELECTRA: You know nothing goes well without a struggle.

CHRYSOTHEMIS: I know. I'll lift any weight that I can carry.

ELECTRA: Now listen: here's what I've planned to do.
  You and I both know that we have no friends
  here to help us. No, Hades has taken them
  away from us and we two are left alone. 950

So long as I had word that my brother
was still alive and well, I had hope
that he'd come to avenge our father's murder.
Now since he's dead, I must look to you,
not to be afraid along with me your sister
to kill our father's murderer, Aegisthus.
I must no longer hide anything from you.
How can you stay passive, if you can see
one hope still standing? You can lament
that you've been cheated of your father's wealth.   960
You can complain that during all this time
you've been growing old, unwed, unmarried.
And all of this you can never hope to have,
not ever. Aegisthus is not such a fool,
he won't allow offspring to grow from you
or me; clearly they would bring him grief.*
But if you go along with what I plan,
first you'll win the rewards of piety
from both our father and our brother.
And then in the future you'll be free,   970
as you were born to be, and win the marriage
you deserve. Every man admires the best!
Don't you see how much glory we'd amass
both you and I, if you listen to me,
natives and foreigners would look at us
and welcome us with praise like this:
"My friends, look at this pair of sisters.
Those two rescued their ancestral home.
Their enemies were prospering, but those two
risked their lives and avenged a murder.   980
We must love them; all must revere them.
All must honor them for their courage
in feasts and in public gatherings."
Everyone will speak of us like that while we're alive,
and fame won't leave us when we're dead.
No, my dear, listen, work for your father,
fight for your brother, save me from suffering,

---

* As head of the family, Aegisthus would pick husbands for his stepdaughters.

save yourself, and realize this: living in disgrace
disgraces anyone who's nobly born.
CHORUS: In such matters forethought's an ally   990
for a speaker and a listener both.
CHRYSOTHEMIS: My friends, before she spoke, if she'd had
good judgment, she'd have used
restraint, but she did not use it.
(*to Electra*) What do you seek when you arm yourself
With rashness and ask me to join you?
Don't you see? You are a woman, not a man.
You have less power than your enemies.
Day by day they have good fortune;
ours drains away and comes to nothing.   1000
Who could plan to kill a man like that
and get away untouched by pain or harm?
Look out: things are bad, but we'll take on
more troubles for ourselves, if anyone hears us talking.
It won't stop our suffering or help us at all
if we win renown by dying miserably.
<For dying is not the issue, but to seek to die,
and then not to be able to do that.>*
I beg you, before we all are destroyed
totally, and our family obliterated,   1010
restrain your rage. And I shall regard
your words as unsaid and unfulfilled.
Be sensible, at least as time goes on,
and yield to rulers when you have no power.
CHORUS: Listen to her. It's best for humans to take
advantage of forethought and wise counsel.
ELECTRA: Nothing you've said surprises me. I realized
that you'd reject whatever I proposed.
No, with my own hand alone I must do
this deed. I won't leave it unattempted.   1020
CHRYSOTHEMIS: Oh!
I wish you'd the same determination
when our father died. You'd have won out.
ELECTRA: I'm the same person now; then I didn't understand.

---

* These lines do not seem to fit the context and were probably added by an ancient actor or editor.

CHRYSOTHEMIS: Try not to understand throughout your life!

ELECTRA: So you advise, because you will not work with me.

CHRYSOTHEMIS: No, because if we try, we shall also fail.

ELECTRA: I admire your sense, but I despise your cowardice.

CHRYSOTHEMIS: I can endure your blame, as well as your kind words.

ELECTRA: Kind words are what you'll never hear from me.

CHRYSOTHEMIS: The long time to come will determine that.   1030

ELECTRA: Go away! You cannot be of help to me.

CHRYSOTHEMIS: I can, but you cannot learn from me.

ELECTRA: Go and tell all this to your mother.

CHRYSOTHEMIS: I do not hate you quite enough for that.

ELECTRA: You don't understand that I'm now dishonored.

CHRYSOTHEMIS: I don't seek to dishonor, but to care for you.

ELECTRA: Must I go along with your idea of justice?

CHRYSOTHEMIS: Yes, if you're sensible; then you can lead us.

ELECTRA: It's dreadful that you speak well and are wrong.

CHRYSOTHEMIS: That describes the trouble you are in!   1040

ELECTRA: What? Don't you think I say what is right?

CHRYSOTHEMIS: There is a point when being right does harm.

ELECTRA: I do not wish to live under such laws.

CHRYSOTHEMIS: If you do this, you'll applaud my advice.

ELECTRA: Indeed, I'll do it, and not be scared by you.

CHRYSOTHEMIS: So it's true! You won't think again?

ELECTRA: Nothing's more hateful than bad thinking.

CHRYSOTHEMIS: You seem not to understand anything I say.

ELECTRA: I thought of this long ago; nothing is new.

<CHRYSOTHEMIS: Then I am leaving. You won't appreciate   1050
    my words; I won't appreciate your ways.

ELECTRA: Yes, go away. I shall never follow you,
    not even if you eagerly desire it.
    A hunt for nothing is great foolishness.>*

CHRYSOTHEMIS: Yes, if you suppose you make some sense,
    you do that! But then when you land
    in trouble, you'll appreciate my words.

      (*Chrysothemis goes into the palace. Electra remains onstage*
      while the Chorus sing the second stasimon.)

---

* These repetitious lines appear to have been added to Sophocles' original text by a later actor or editor.

strophe 1

> CHORUS: We see that the wise birds above
> think and care and feed
> their parents, in return   1060
> for the support they gave them.*
> Why don't we do the same?
> No, by Zeus' lightning
> and Themis† above,
> we shall soon be punished!
> Word that goes beneath the earth
> tell this sad tale to the Atreidae,‡
> bring my joyless message of disgrace.

antistrophe 1

> Tell them their house is sick   1070
> between their children strife is
> two-faced, still not balanced
> in a loving existence.
> One daughter betrayed, alone,
> is sea-tossed, poor thing
> always mourning her father's fate.
> Like the nightingale, always grieving.
> She does not care about death.
> She is ready to leave the light,
> and bring the two Erinyes.§   1080
> Who else has been so loyal to her father?

strophe 2

> No noble person seeks to soil
> his reputation by a wretched life
> without glory, my dear, dear friend.
> So you, too, have chosen
> a glorious life, lamentable,
> arming a sharp remedy,¶
> and win double praise in a single speech
> a daughter both wise and best.

---

* The stork and other species were believed to look after older birds.

† Zeus' second wife, the goddess of justice among the gods.

‡ Descendants of Atreus, Agamemnon's father.

§ Aegisthus and Clytemnestra, acting as avengers (see note to line 112) for the murders of Aegisthus' siblings and of Iphigenia.

¶ The meaning of the transmitted text is unclear.

antistrophe 2

> May you live as high above   1090
> your enemies in might and wealth
> as you now dwell below them.
> Since I have found you
> enduring an evil fate,
> but winning top prize
> in the highest duty,
> in your piety to Zeus.
>
> *(Orestes enters, carrying an urn, accompanied by Pylades and*
> *their attendants, pretending to be the Phocians sent by the*
> *magistrates of Delphi to bring Orestes' ashes to Argos.)*

ORESTES: Ladies, have we heard the right information,
  and made our journey to the land we seek?

CHORUS: What are you looking for? What do you want here?   1100

ORESTES: For some time I've been asking where Aegisthus lives.

CHORUS: This is the right place and your informant accurate.

ORESTES: Could one of you inform those inside the house
  of the welcome presence of our two pairs of feet.*

CHORUS: She can, if the nearest person must announce it.

ORESTES: Come, lady, go inside and inform them
  that some men of Phocis seek Aegisthus.

ELECTRA: *oimoi*, misery. We have heard the story.
  Have you come to bring the evidence?

ORESTES: I don't know what you heard. But the old man   1110
  Strophius† told me to tell you about Orestes.

ELECTRA: What is it, stranger? Now fear comes over me.

ORESTES: We have come to bring the few remains
  of the dead man, as you see, in a small urn.

ELECTRA: Oh, me, misery, it's clear that this is it,
  I see, it seems, a burden for my hands.

ORESTES: If your tears are for what Orestes suffered,
  know that this urn covers his body.

ELECTRA: Stranger, by the gods, place it in my hands,
  if it is true that this urn holds him,   1120
  so that I can weep and start the lamentation
  for myself and all my family with these ashes.

---

* This unusual phrasing echoes the dramatic prediction given by the Chorus in lines 489–91: "She is coming, with many feet, many hands, hidden in a cruel ambush, the Erinys with feet of bronze."

† Electra had the Old Slave take the child Orestes to Strophius to protect him from Aegisthus.

ORESTES: (*to his attendants*) Bring it here and give it to her, whoever she is,
    since she asks for it not in enmity,
    but as one of his friends, or blood relations.

ELECTRA: Last memorial of the man dearest to me,
    Orestes, I welcome you home, but without
    the hopes with which I sent you forth.
    Now I hold you in my hands and you are nothing,
    yet I sent you off in glory from your home.   1130
    I wish that I had left this life before I sent you
    with these hands forth to a foreign land,
    stole you away and rescued you from death,
    you could have died then on that day
    and been buried, to share your father's grave.
    Now far from home, an exile in another land,
    you perished cruelly, without your sister.
    So sad that with my loving hands I did not wash
    your body and place it in the blazing fire
    as I should have done, a painful burden.   1140
    No, you were cared for by foreign hands
    and come here, a little weight in a little urn.
    Oh, I weep for the care I gave you long ago,
    now wasted, a labor of love. For you were not
    so dear to your mother as you were to me.
    It was not the servants, it was I,
    your sister that you called your nurse.
    Now everything is lost in a single day,
    dead along with you. You've swept everything away,   1150
    like a whirlwind, and gone. Our father's dead.
    I've died with you. You've died and gone away.
    Our enemies mock us; she's mad with joy,
    our mother who is no mother. You often told me
    in secret messages that you would come
    and get revenge. But now your unlucky fate
    and mine have taken everything away,
    the fate that instead of your dearest self
    sent these ashes and a useless shadow.
        (*chanting*) oimoi moi.   1160
        Your pitiful body. *Pheu pheu.*
        You were sent, *oimoi moi*
    on a cruel path, my dearest. You have killed me,

you have killed me, yes, my own brother.
So now take me into this your house,
my nothing to your nothing, so that with you
I'll live below forever. For when you were above,
I shared everything with you. And now I wish
to die and to be with you in your tomb.
For I see that the dead do not feel pain.   1170

CHORUS: Remember, Electra, your father was a mortal.
Orestes was a mortal. So do not grieve too much.
Every one of us must pay this debt.

ORESTES: *pheu pheu.* What can I say? Words fail me.
I've lost the power to control my speech.

ELECTRA: What pains you? Why are you saying this?

ORESTES: Yours is Electra's renowned beauty, this?

ELECTRA: This is what it is, and a most wretched thing.

ORESTES: *oimoi,* for this miserable disaster!

ELECTRA: Stranger, surely you're not mourning over me?   1180

ORESTES: Your body wasted dishonorably, impiously!

ELECTRA: Your cruel words suit no one else but me, stranger.

ORESTES: *pheu,* your condition, unmarried, miserable—

ELECTRA: Stranger, why do you stare at me and lament?

ORESTES: I did not know the measure of my sorrows.

ELECTRA: What did I say that made you understand?

ORESTES: I saw that you were singled out for suffering.

ELECTRA: But you have only seen some of my troubles.

ORESTES: Could there be troubles worse to see than these?

ELECTRA: Yes, because I'm living with the murderers.   1190

ORESTES: Whose murderers? What killing do you mean?

ELECTRA: My father's. And I'm forced to be their slave!

ORESTES: Who on earth torments you with this task?

ELECTRA: My mother in name, but nothing like a mother.

ORESTES: What does she do? Attack you; wreck your life?

ELECTRA: Attack and wreck and every other crime.

ORESTES: And no one comes to help you or hinder them?

ELECTRA: No. There was, but you've brought me his ashes.

ORESTES: Poor thing. Since I first saw you I have pitied you.

ELECTRA: You're the only man on earth who's pitied me.   1200

ORESTES: The only one to come and suffer for your misery.

ELECTRA: You can't be a relative of mine from somewhere!

ORESTES: I could say I am, if these women are your friends.

ELECTRA: They are, and can be trusted when you speak.

ORESTES: Put down that urn, so you can learn everything.

ELECTRA: No, please, by the gods, don't ask that, stranger.

ORESTES: Listen to what I say, you won't go wrong.

ELECTRA: No, by your beard,* don't take my beloved away.

ORESTES: I won't let you keep it.   ELEC.: Oh, misery, Orestes,
   your tomb has been taken from me.   1210

ORESTES: Watch your tongue. There's no reason to mourn.

ELECTRA: No reason for me to weep for my dead brother?

ORESTES: It's not appropriate to speak of death.

ELECTRA: So I'm kept from my rights over the dead?

ORESTES: You're being kept from nothing. This isn't yours.

ELECTRA: I do, if this is Orestes' body that I hold.

ORESTES: It's not Orestes', except as dressed in words.

ELECTRA: But where is that poor man's tomb?

ORESTES: There isn't one. The living have no tombs.

ELECTRA: Friend, what are you saying?   ORE.: Nothing I've said is
                              false.   1220

ELECTRA: Then Orestes is alive.   ORE.: Yes, if I draw breath.

ELECTRA: And are you he?   ORE.: Look at my father's seal ring! See if I
                              speak the truth.

ELECTRA: Oh, dearest light!   ORE.: Dearest, I, too, can swear.

ELECTRA: Voice, have you come?   ORE.: Don't ask for any other.

ELECTRA: Do I hold you in my arms?   ORE.: As you may hold me from
                              now on!

ELECTRA: Dearest friends, women of my city,
   Look, this is Orestes, dead through deception
   now through deception saved from death.

CHORUS: We see, my dear, and for your good fortune   1230
   a tear of joy comes from my eyes.

    ELECTRA: (*singing, while Orestes continues speaking in recitative meter*)
strophe

      iō son, son
      of those dearest to me
      now you have arrived!
      You have found and come and seen those you have longed for.

---

* A suppliant asking for mercy touched the chin of the person who could help him or her.

ORESTES: Here I am! But keep quiet and wait!

    ELECTRA: What's wrong?

ORESTES: Best to keep quiet, so no one inside hears us.

    ELECTRA: No by the virgin goddess Artemis,

        I do not think it right to fear

        the women who live in there,   1240

        a vain burden on the earth.

ORESTES: Look, even women can wage war.

  You know that well. You've tried it.

    ELECTRA: (*weeping*) *ottotoi ottotoi*

        You have brought up evil too great

        to cover up or escape

        and that I can never forget.   1250

ORESTES: I know that well. But when we have them

  with us, then we can recall their deeds!

antistrophe

    ELECTRA: The whole,

        the whole of time should be here

        to speak with justice,

        for only now are my lips free.

ORESTES: I agree, and so protect that freedom.

    ELECTRA: By doing what?

ORESTES: Wait till the right time to speak at length.

    ELECTRA: Who could opt for silence   1260

        once you appeared,

        and I saw you

        beyond thought, beyond hope.

ORESTES: You saw me, when the gods urged me to come

  [...]*

    ELECTRA: The grace you speak of

        is higher than past graces, if the god

        sent you to our halls. I call it

        an act of god.   1270

ORESTES: I'm reluctant to restrain your joy,

  but I fear it's carried you too far.

epode

    ELECTRA: *iō*, after a long time

        you made the journey that I longed for

---

* A line appears to be missing here.

and so came to me. Do not
—you see me and my many sorrows—
ORESTES: What should I not do?   ELEC.: Don't rob me, do not take away
my joy in seeing you.
ORESTES: If I saw another do this, I'd be angry.
ELECTRA: Will you let me?   ORE.: Yes, of course.   1280
ELECTRA: My dear, I've heard
a voice I never hoped to hear!
and yet I held my excitement silent
and listened in misery without a sound.
Now I have you, you're here,
I see your dearest face
I could not forget it, even in my troubles.
ORESTES: Leave out what isn't needed in the narrative.
Don't tell me that our mother's evil,
that Aegisthus drains, pours out, throws away   1290
and wastes the wealth of our ancestral home;
the speech would keep you from taking action.
Now tell me what will fit the present time.
Where should we go, where should we hide
to stop our enemies' mockery by our presence?
Make sure our mother doesn't find you out
from your happy face, when we two go into the house.
No, lament the disaster that was falsely told you,
And then, when we have triumphed
We can rejoice and laugh in freedom!   1300
ELECTRA: Yes, Brother, your wishes shall be mine
as well, since you have brought me
joy, and without you I had none.
I would not cause you pain just to win
a little pleasure for myself, for that
would not assist the god who's with us.
You know what waits inside. How not?
You know why Aegisthus is not at home,
and our mother's in the house. Don't be afraid:
she will not see my face radiant with smiles.   1310
Long-standing hatred for her fills my mind.
and now I've seen you, I shall never stop
weeping with joy, how could I stop,
when just today I've seen you die

and come to life? You've worked a miracle!
Now, if my father came to life, I wouldn't think
it strange; I would believe I saw him.
Since you have come to us on this day,
tell me what you desire. If I were alone,
I'd have had two choices: to rescue myself   1320
with honor or to perish with honor.

ORESTES: My advice is to keep quiet, since at the door
    I hear someone inside coming.

ELECTRA: (*to Orestes, Pylades, and their servants*) Strangers, go inside,
    since you are bringing them a gift that they
    won't thrust aside, but will not like to have.
          (*The Old Slave comes out of the house.*)

OLD SLAVE: You total fools, you have no sense at all!
    Do you place no value on your lives?
    Don't you have any inborn sense?
    Don't you know that you're not just near,
    but on the brink of great disaster?   1330
    If I had not long since been standing by
    these doorposts, we would have had your doings
    inside the house sooner than your bodies.
    But now I made myself look out for you.
    And now say farewell to your long speeches,
    and your unceasing cries of joy,
    and go inside. Delay on such occasions
    brings danger. It's time; tell delay farewell.

ORESTES: When I go in—what is it like inside?

OLD SLAVE: It's fine. It helps that no one knows me.   1340

ORESTES: You've told them, I suppose, that I am dead.

OLD SLAVE: Know that there you're a man in Hades.

ORESTES: Are they pleased by that? What do they say?

OLD SLAVE: When they're done, I can tell you. As it stands,
    for them all's good, even what isn't good.

ELECTRA: Brother, who is this man? By the gods, tell me.

ORESTES: Don't you know?   ELEC.: No, I've never seen him.

ORESTES: You don't know that you once placed me in his arms?

ELECTRA: Who is it? What do you mean?   ORE.: In his arms
    through your plans, I was brought to the plain of Phocis.   1350

ELECTRA: Is this the man that long ago I found faithful,
    the only one of many, when father was murdered?

ORESTES: This is he. Do not keep asking me more questions.

ELECTRA: Dearest light! You alone are the savior of the house
 of Agamemnon. How did you come here? Are you the one
 who saved him and me from our many sorrows?
 Dearest hands, and the dearest feet
 that serve you, how could you be here
 so long, not let me know, but destroy me
 with your stories, while bringing me great joy?   1360
 Welcome, Father. For I think I see a father!
 Welcome. Know that in one single day
 I hated and loved you more than any man.

OLD SLAVE: Enough, I think. The story of the time between,
 many nights and also days shall tell you
 as they roll on, in detail, Electra.
    (He turns to Orestes and Pylades.)
 I say now to the pair of you who stand here,
 now's the time to act. Now Clytemnestra is alone.
 Now there's no man in the house. If you delay,
 remember that you'll be fighting with these men   1370
 and others, more of them and more skilled.

ORESTES: This our task no longer needs long speeches,
 Pylades. As soon as we can, we must go inside,
 after we salute the seats of my ancestral gods,
 all those who dwell before the palace gates.
    (Orestes, Pylades, and the Old Slave enter the palace.)

ELECTRA: Lord Apollo, listen to these two with favor,
 and to me as well. I have often stood before you
 to offer what I had with an imploring hand.
 Now, Lycian Apollo, with what I have
 I ask, I fall before you, I implore, show favor   1380
 to us and help us with our plans.
 And show to humankind the price the gods
 will make them pay for their impiety!

strophe

 CHORUS: See where Ares sets forth breathing
  the blood of bitter strife.
  Now they have come beneath the palace roof,
  hounds in pursuit,
  tracking down evil wrongdoing.

My heart's dream will not be delayed
or left hanging in the air.   1390

antistrophe

The avenger of the dead is coming
with devious feet into the house,
the stores of his father's ancient wealth,
holding in his hands blood new-sharpened!
Hermes leads him, he hides the plot
in darkness to the end, no more delay.

(*Electra comes out of the palace.*)

strophe

(*sung in excited, syncopated iambics*)

ELECTRA: Dear friends, the men are now finishing
their work. Wait for them in silence.
CHORUS: How? What are they doing?
ELECTRA: She is adorning   1400
the urn for burial; those two are standing near her.
CHORUS: Then why have you come out?
ELECTRA: To keep watch
so we'll know when Aegisthus goes inside.

(*Clytemnestra's voice is heard from within the house.*)

CLYTEMNESTRA: *aiai*, oh, my friends
have left; the house is full of killers.
ELECTRA: A cry from someone inside! My friends, do you hear?
CHORUS: I heard the dreadful cry
of a victim, terrifying.
CLYTEMNESTRA: Oh, misery! Aegisthus where could you be?
ELECTRA: Yes, someone is crying out again.   1410
CLYTEMNESTRA: My son, my son,
take pity on your mother!
ELECTRA: But you never
took pity on him or on his father!
CHORUS: Oh, city, oh, family, in misery
this house's fate is dying, day by day!
CLYTEMNESTRA: *ōmoi*, I am struck!*
ELECTRA: If you can, hit her twice as hard!

---

* Clytemnestra here repeats the words spoken by Agamemnon when Clytemnestra murders him in
Aeschylus *Agamemnon* 1343–45.

CLYTEMNESTRA: *ōmoi*, again!

ELECTRA: And for Aegisthus, too!

CHORUS: The curses of the dead are working.
Beneath the ground they are alive,
for those who died long ago drink   1420
their killers' blood, as it flows back!

antistrophe

And here they are! From your bloody hand
drips an offering to Ares, but we cannot think it wrong!

ELECTRA: Orestes, how did it go?

ORESTES: All's well inside
the house. Apollo's prophecy was true!

ELECTRA: Is the poor woman dead?

ORESTES: Don't be afraid
that your mother's pride will again dishonor you!
[...
   ...
   ...]

CHORUS: Stop! For I can clearly see
Aegisthus.
[...]

ELECTRA: (*to Orestes and Pylades*) You two, go back inside!

ORESTES: Where do you see the man?   ELEC.: He is coming toward
us from the city outskirts,
smiling. [...]*   1430

CHORUS: Go back through the door as fast as you can,
now! What you did so well before, now again—

ORESTES: Never fear; we'll do it.   ELEC.: Go now where you intend
to go!

ORESTES: I've gone!   ELEC.: I'll take care of matters here.

CHORUS: Say a few words
in his ear, gently
that's the best idea, hide that he's heading   1440
for a contest with Justice.
(*Aegisthus enters.*)

AEGISTHUS: Which of you knows where to find the Phocian strangers,
the men, they say, who've come to tell us that Orestes

---

* The rest of the line is missing.

lost his life in the shipwreck of the chariots?
(*turning to Electra*) You there, I mean you, yes, you! In the past
you were so fierce. I think you're the one
who cares most, knows most, and will tell me.

ELECTRA: I know. How could I not? I can't be set apart
from the fortune of those dearest to me.

AEGISTHUS: Where would the strangers be? Tell me!　　　　　　1450

ELECTRA: Inside. They met with a kind hostess.

AEGISTHUS: And did they inform her that he was dead?

ELECTRA: Yes, they both said and proved it.

AEGISTHUS: Can I then learn what she has seen?

ELECTRA: You can, and it's a not a pretty sight.

AEGISTHUS: For once, what you say makes me happy.

ELECTRA: You might be happy, if this is what you find.

AEGISTHUS: Open the doors, I say, and show
for all Mycenaeans and Argives to see,
if in the past vain hopes for this man to come　　　　　　1460
held anyone aloft, they can see his corpse,
accept my bridle and learn sense
and avoid harsh punishment from me.

ELECTRA: I've done what you asked. For over time
I've learned reason, to serve the powerful.*

AEGISTHUS: Zeus, I see a sign sent by divine envy.†
If divine anger is present also, I do not say.
Turn back the covering from his face,
So I, too, can mourn my kinsman.

ORESTES: You do it yourself; it is your task, not mine,　　　　　　1470
to look at this and to speak kind words.

AEGISTHUS: Your advice is good, and I shall take it.
Now summon Clytemnestra, if she's at home.

ORESTES: She is near you. Don't look elsewhere.

AEGISTHUS: Oh, no! What do I see?　　ORE.: Are you afraid? Someone you
　　　　　　　　　　　　　　　don't recognize?

AEGISTHUS: Who has laid the trap I've fallen into,
miserably?　　ORE.: Don't you see that
though alive, you've been talking with the dead?

---

* Thrasymachus uses the same phrasing to define justice in Plato's *Republic* 338b.

† Envy from the gods was thought to follow such great success, such as Orestes' supposed string of
victories in the Pythian Games.

AEGISTHUS: Oh, no, I see what you're saying. This must be
    Orestes with whom I have been speaking.   1480
ORESTES: Such a great prophet! Why were you deceived so long?
AEGISTHUS: I am afraid, all is lost. But let me speak,
      even if briefly.   **ELEC.:** Don't let him say more,
    by the gods, my brother, no long speeches.
    <When mortals are caught up in troubles,
    what does a man gain by delaying death?>
    Kill him as soon as you can; kill him and put him
    out for those who will soon come upon him,*
    out of our sight. For me that would be
    the only recompense for my past troubles.   1490
ORESTES: You should go inside now. We are not talking
    about speeches, but about your life!
AEGISTHUS: Why take me into the house. Why, if the deed is good,
    must it be done in darkness? Why don't you kill me here?
ORESTES: Don't give me orders! Go inside where you killed
    our father, so you can die in the same place.
AEGISTHUS: So it's inevitable that this house must see
    the present and future woes of Pelops' family?
ORESTES: It shall see yours. Of that I'm a true prophet.
AEGISTHUS: You possess a skill your father didn't have.   1500
ORESTES: You respond at length and travel slowly.
    Get going!   **AEG.:** Lead the way.   **ORE.:** You must go first.
AEGISTHUS: So I can't get away?   **ORE.:** So you can't die where you please.
    I must take care to make this hard for you.
    <Swift death must be the punishment for all
    who wish to do what is outside the law.
    Then there would not be so much criminality.
        CHORUS: (*chanting*) Scion of Atreus, you have suffered much
            but through struggle have come to freedom,
            empowered by this attack.>†   1510

---

* Without saying so directly, Electra suggests that Aegisthus' body should be left for birds and animals of prey to dispose of.

† It is possible that the rather trite generalizations in these anapestic were added to the text by a later writer.

INTRODUCTION TO SOPHOCLES'
OEDIPUS AT COLONUS

Only two plays in this volume, Aeschylus' *Eumenides* (the third play of the *Oresteia* trilogy) and Sophocles' *Oedipus at Colonus*, are set in the city of Athens, and they configure that setting in similar ways. In both, Athens represents a humane place of refuge, where those shunned by other cities—Orestes in the former play, Oedipus here, men contaminated by violations of primal law—can find sanctuary. The arrival of these wanderers, in both cases, forces Athens to choose: Will it lend support to the exile and uphold its traditions of liberality and rule of law, even at the risk of offending great powers? Their decision to do so, both times, brings the blessing of divine protection. For the Athenians who watched these dramas, the exaltation of their city, and the promise that the gods themselves would preserve it, must have been exhilarating.

Yet much had changed for Athens between the productions of the *Oresteia* and *Oedipus at Colonus*. In 458 B.C. the city had been riding high on a wave of imperial expansion, mercantile wealth, and populist political reform. By 401 B.C., the date at which *Oedipus at Colonus* was staged by Sophocles' grandson—the playwright himself had died five years earlier at the age of (perhaps) ninety, leaving this play behind among his last compositions—Athens had undergone plague, revolution, and a humiliating defeat at the hands of Sparta in a war that had drained its treasury. Sophocles wrote the play before that defeat became certain, but he must have guessed it was coming, and in any case he knew that no matter what the war's outcome, Athens had suffered mightily. The blessings showered on the city in *Oedipus at Colonus* were not, in the end, enough to save it.

Oedipus at Colonus shares with the *Oresteia* a special interest in the ancient goddesses who guard oaths and punish those polluted by blood-guilt, whose dual nature is attested by dual names—Erinyes, often translated as "Furies," and Eumenides, "Kindly Ones." Aeschylus' trilogy ended with the founding at Athens of a shrine, a kind of home, for these creatures, part of a pact by which the city gained their benevolence. *Oedipus at Colonus* opens when Oedipus, blind after his self-mutilation (depicted at the end of *Oedipus the King*) and weary from years of wandering, arrives at a similar shrine, a grove sacred to the Erinyes in the Attic district of Colonus. His feet have been directed by destiny to this grove—the place where he is fated to die—and he seats himself inside it, much to the horror of the inhabitants. He will remain on this forbidden ground, defying its taboos, during most of what follows. It represents the nodal point linking the earth, the gods, and the city of Athens, and Oedipus needs to stay connected to all three.

Oedipus has a dual nature, too, the legacy of his incestuous and parricidal past. His violation of the most fundamental human codes have made him a *miasma*, a danger to anyone who comes in contact with him. But his polluted body also has a benign power, as we learn from reports of oracles and prophecies throughout the play. Oedipus can confer victory to any army he accompanies in life (lines 1331–32), or to any city that buries him after death (lines 411–15). In Greek terms he has become *hagios*, a word that—illogically from a modern Judeo-Christian perspective—can translate both as "holy" and as "accursed." His crimes have put him beyond the human condition; transcending that condition does not render him simply good or evil, but numinous, awesome, unapproachable.

But merely to call his deeds "crimes" is misleading, for the play rejects that characterization. Oedipus has already claimed, at the end of *Oedipus the King*, that Apollo, overseer of fate and prophecy, had brought his sufferings to pass (lines 1329–31), not he himself. In *Oedipus at Colonus*, Sophocles develops this idea, especially in the play's great central scene, a confrontation between Oedipus and his former chief minister, Creon. Oedipus here speaks like a defendant at the bar, arguing that ignorance acquits him of the charges both of incest and parricide, while self-defense acquits him of murder. Nothing he did was intentional, and nothing could have been avoided; all was predestined, as proved by the foreknowledge of the oracles. The larger question, of *why* Oedipus was thus singled out, goes unanswered; "so it pleased the gods, who held, / it seems, some ancient grudge against my family," is all the explanation we are offered (lines 963–64). A profound mystery lies at the core of Oedipus' life, but not a profound guilt. His self-blinding was too great a punishment, he now realizes (line 439), as were his exile from Thebes and his loss of rule, both forced on him by his power-hungry sons.

Those sons are now at war with each other, and civic order at Thebes is teetering. Creon, who attempted to take control at the end of *Oedipus the King*, is now serving as aide to Oedipus' younger son, Eteocles; together they are preparing for an invasion by the older son, Polynices, who has recruited an army (the "Seven against Thebes" dramatized by Aeschylus, in a play not in this volume) in Argos. Both sides in the conflict see Oedipus as the safeguard of victory, and so Creon and Polynices both arrive in Colonus, separately, in an effort to get hold of him. Caught in the middle is Theseus, the famously just and moderate king of Athens, who stands with Oedipus against these onslaughts, especially against the violent coercions of Creon. (Creon's violent methods will, in a later stage of the "Theban cycle," lead to the central crisis of *Antigone*, a play that takes place after this one though it was written long before. Between the two plays, Polynices and Eteocles are both killed in the Argive attack on Thebes, leaving Creon in control of the city; to intimidate his opponents, he decrees that Polynices must lie unburied for all to see.)

By taking up arms to stop Creon, Theseus risks provoking war with Thebes, but, Oedipus promises, Athens is bound to win such a war—thanks to his presence on Attic soil. There was important resonance here with the political backdrop against which the play was composed. Thebes had allied with Sparta during the long war between Sparta and Athens, known today as the Peloponnesian War. Athenian prospects in that war had sunk to a very low ebb by 406 B.C., and a Spartan fortress stood on Attic soil, practically putting Athens under a state of siege. Yet Athens could hold out as long as its ships controlled the Aegean, as they did until 405, just after Sophocles' death. In Theseus' defiant stand against Creon, and Oedipus' promise that "your city shall not be destroyed / by men sprung from the dragon's teeth," that is, by Thebans (lines 1533–34), we hear the expression of a hope that was fading even as Sophocles set it down and would soon disappear altogether.

The play's final sequence deals with the solemn mystery of Oedipus' death and burial. Oedipus knows his time has come, and the thunder of Zeus confirms it. Attended by his daughters and Theseus, Oedipus bathes and says his farewells, then, with Theseus alone, he makes his way to a predestined place. There, the gods themselves seem to call him to join their company: "You there, Oedipus! Why are we not yet / on our way?" calls a disembodied voice (lines 1637–38). That plural speaks volumes. Having endured more than a mere mortal could, Oedipus has finally become a kind of god, or at least what the Greeks called a *hero*, an immortal being whose tomb becomes a focal point of divine power. Usually a hero's tomb receives cult worship, but in this case it must be kept hidden; only Theseus is allowed to know where it lies, lest some enemy of Athens steal the remains. Antigone and Ismene, in the play's beautiful closing lyrics, mourn a crypt they cannot ever visit, and make their uncertain way into a world rendered bleak by their brothers' looming war.

The miraculous disappearance of Oedipus, and the awestruck reaction of Theseus, might for modern readers evoke the story pattern of the Christian ascension; indeed, an acclaimed 1980s musical, *The Gospel at Colonus*, played on those associations, using gospel hymns to turn this play into a parable of sin and salvation. The Greeks did not have a doctrine of redemption from sin, nor does Oedipus regard his transgressions as sins, but the musical at least helped modern audiences to experience Greek tragedy as religious drama. *Oedipus at Colonus* is indeed a profoundly religious play, written by a man nearing the end of a long and pious life. If Sophocles meant it to be his farewell to Athens, after nearly sixty-five years of writing for its stage, he could hardly have composed a more meaningful one.

Oedipus at Colonus

Translated by Frank Nisetich

This is a translation of the Greek text of the play edited by Hugh Lloyd-Jones and N. G. Wilson, *Sophoclis Fabulae* (Oxford: Oxford University Press, 1990, 1992). Passages considered as interpolations by Lloyd-Jones and Wilson are omitted from the text of this translation but included in the notes.

Cast of Characters (in order of appearance)

Oedipus, son of Laius and Jocasta; formerly king of Thebes
Antigone, daughter of Oedipus by his mother, Jocasta
Stranger, from Colonus
Chorus of elderly men of Colonus, with their Leader
Ismene, daughter of Oedipus and Jocasta; sister of Antigone
Theseus, king of Athens
Creon, brother of Jocasta, Oedipus' wife and mother
Polynices, son of Oedipus and Jocasta
Messenger
Guards and Attendants of Theseus and Creon (nonspeaking parts)

Setting: The play takes place at Colonus, a rural village about a mile and a half northwest of the Acropolis of Athens. In the background is a grove, sacred to the Furies (also called the Eumenides, or Kindly Ones). Just inside the sacred area but not within the grove itself is a rock large enough to sit on. To the right and outside the sacred area is an equestrian statue of the hero Colonus. The entry on the spectators' left is for characters arriving from the direction of Thebes; that on the right, for those arriving from the direction of Athens.

(Oedipus enters on the left. He is old, blind, dressed in rags, holding a staff and a beggar's pouch. His daughter Antigone guides his steps.)

OEDIPUS: Antigone, daughter of the blind old man,
what country have we come to, or whose city?
Who will receive the wanderer, Oedipus,
with a meager offering today? I ask
for little, receive still less than a little,
and make do with that. Suffering,
and the company of long years,
and nobility, third in line, teach me patience.
But, child, if you see a place to sit,
on common ground or near a temple grove,   10
put me there, sit me down, so we may learn
where we are. As strangers here, we need
to inquire, and do what the locals tell us.

ANTIGONE: Father, unhappy Oedipus, to my eyes
those are towers in the distance, crowning a city;
and this place, it's easy to guess, is sacred, thick
with laurel, olive, vine, and deep inside
fluttering nightingales fill it with song.
Here, sit on this rough stone, sit, relax, since you
have walked a long way, for an old man.   20
    (She leads him to the stone.)

OEDIPUS: Help me sit, then, and stay by me, blind as I am.

ANTIGONE: As if, at this late stage, I need instructing!

(She helps him sit.)

OEDIPUS: Can you tell me, now, where we've come?

ANTIGONE: I know it's Athens, but I don't know this place.

OEDIPUS: Athens, yes—every traveler told us that.

ANTIGONE: Should I go find out where we are now?

OEDIPUS: Yes, child, if in fact people live here.

(Enter Stranger, on the right.)

ANTIGONE: Well, there are people here! No need
    to ask about that. I see a man nearby.

OEDIPUS: On his way here—is this his destination? 30

(The Stranger arrives at center stage.)

ANTIGONE: Actually, he *is* here. Whatever you think
    it's right to say, say it now. Here he is.

OEDIPUS: Stranger, hearing from this girl, who sees
    for the two of us, that you've come looking,
    just in time to tell us what we need to know, I—

STRANGER: *(interrupting)* Before you say anything more, leave that seat!
    The place you're in is holy, not to be trodden.

OEDIPUS: What place is it? Which god does it belong to?

STRANGER: No one may enter or live there. The dread goddesses,*
    daughters of Earth and Darkness, possess it. 40

OEDIPUS: What sacred name would I use to pray to them?

STRANGER: The people here call them Eumenides,†
    who see all things—but others use other names.

OEDIPUS: Well, may they be kind, and may they welcome
    their suppliant, for I will never leave this place.

STRANGER: What does that mean?   OED.: My destiny. The signs are clear.

STRANGER: Well, I dare not move you, without approval
    from the city, not before I report your actions.

OEDIPUS: By the gods, stranger, don't scorn my request,
    wanderer though I am, but answer my questions. 50

STRANGER: Speak up, and you'll not meet with scorn from me.

OEDIPUS: What is this place in which we find ourselves?

STRANGER: Listen, and you'll know as much as I do.
    This whole region is sacred. It belongs

---

* The Erinyes or Furies.

† "Kindly Ones," the most familiar euphemism for the Furies.

to dread Poseidon;* the fire-bearing god,
Titan Prometheus,† is also here. The ground
you walk upon is called the bronze-stepped
threshold of this land, bulwark of Athens,
and the local people boast that this horseman (*pointing to the statue*),
Colonus,‡ settled them here, and claim they share　　　　　　60
that name in common with him, and are known by it.
So it is, stranger—honored not in song
but in the hearts of those who live here.

OEDIPUS: There are people living in this place, then?

STRANGER: Yes, certainly, those named for this god.§

OEDIPUS: Does someone rule them, or do they have a voice?

STRANGER: They're ruled by the king, from the city.

OEDIPUS: Who is this king, who rules by word and might?

STRANGER: Theseus, son of Aegeus, who ruled before him.

OEDIPUS: Can a messenger be sent from you to him?　　　　　　70

STRANGER: Why? To say or to ask something for you?

OEDIPUS: To tell him "Small help may reap a big reward."

STRANGER: And what could he gain from one who can't see?

OEDIPUS: There will be sight in every word I say.

STRANGER: Listen, stranger, for your own good.
I see you are noble, though unlucky. Stay, then,
right here, till I've gone and told all this
to those who live here—not those in the city,
for it's the people here who will decide
if you're to stay, or be on your way again.　　　　　　80
　　　　(Exit Stranger, to the right.)

OEDIPUS: Has he gone, child, and left us to ourselves?

ANTIGONE: He has, Father. Now you may say anything,
and rest assured that only I will hear.

OEDIPUS: (*addressing the shrine of the Furies*)
　　　O queens, dreadful to see, as yours

---

* God of the sea and of horses. He had a temple at Colonus.

† The Titans belonged to the generation of gods preceding the Olympians. Prometheus, son of Iapetus, is most familiar as the god who gave fire to mankind. His statues show him holding a torch. The Athenian festival of the Prometheia included a torch race that began at his altar in the Academy, just south of Colonus, and ended at the Acropolis.

‡ The hero is named for the hill (*kolonos*) after which the village of Colonus was also named. The equestrian association is owing to the proximity of the sanctuary of Poseidon, creator and tamer of the horse.

§ The hero Colonus appears to receive divine honors.

is the place I've come to first in all this land,
be not without feeling for me and Apollo
who, when he gave me all those dread oracles,*
said this would be my respite in far time to come,
when I would reach my destination, and find
the seat of the Awesome Goddesses,† and a haven,   90
and bring my life of sorrows to an end.
He said I'd be a blessing to those who welcomed me,
a curse on those who drove me off;
and signs would come, he said, confirming
all of this—earthquake, or thunder, or Zeus' lightning.
I know now that no false omen from you
brought me along this path, into this grove,
for never, in my wandering, would I
have met you first, I who drink no wine
and you who shun it;‡ I would not have sat   100
upon this holy seat, that no tool has wrought.
But, goddesses, fulfill Apollo's words, grant me
a passage now, an end to life, unless
I seem beneath your notice, ever a slave
to the worst labors mortals have to bear.
Come, sweet daughters of ancient Darkness!
Come, Athens, most honored of all cities,
belonging, so they say, to mighty Pallas,§
pity this wretched shadow of the man
Oedipus—for *this* is not what I once was!   110

ANTIGONE: Silence! Someone's coming—men, advanced
in years—to check on where you've taken refuge.

OEDIPUS: I'll be silent, and you, be sure to hide me
in the grove, away from the road, until I've heard
what they will say. Once we've learned that,
we'll have the means to act with caution.

> (*Oedipus, led by Antigone, retires into the grove, out of sight.
> The Chorus enter from the right, chanting the* parodos *or entry
> song in lyric meters.*)

---

* That he would kill his father and marry his mother.
† Another euphemism for the Furies.
‡ Libations to the Furies consisted of water, milk, or honey; wine was not allowed.
§ Athena, often called Pallas Athena or, as here, simply Pallas.

strophe 1

CHORUS: Look! Who was he? Where is he now?
    Where has he run, out of this place, most
    insolent of men—of *all* men!   120
    Go on, look, ask,
    inquire everywhere! A wanderer,
    the old man is a wanderer, not
    one of us, else he'd never
    have barged into this inviolable grove,
    sacred to these fearsome maidens.
    We tremble to name them,
    we pass them by without a look,   130
    without a sound, moving our lips
    in silent prayer, without a word—
    but now we're told someone has come
    who has no reverence at all!
    I'm scanning round about
    the sacred grove, but cannot
    find him: where is he?
      (Oedipus, led by Antigone, emerges from the grove and addresses
      *the Chorus.)**

OEDIPUS: Here I am. I am he. I see by sound,
    as the saying goes.

CHORUS: *iō, iō!*—   140
    dreadful to see, dreadful to hear!

OEDIPUS: Do not, I beg you, think me a criminal!

CHORUS: Zeus, Protector, who *is* this old man?

OEDIPUS: Not one with the choicest fate, not one
    that you'd call blest, O guardians of this place.
    You may see for yourselves: why else
    would I grope my way, and use
    another's eyes, a full-grown man
    tied to so slight an anchor!

antistrophe 1

CHORUS: Ah! Were your eyes blind   150
    even at birth? You've had a hard life
    and a long one, I reckon.

---

* The Greek text is in anapestic meter from here through line 149, and again at lines 170–75 and 188–91.

But all the same, you shall not bring
down these curses* on me! For you're
trespassing, trespassing!
But now—before you stumble
on the hushed, grassy
grove where water swirls
with streams of honey†
in its mixing bowl—   160
be careful! Step back,
withdraw, there must be
a great distance
between you and there!
Do you hear me, man of toils, wanderer?
If you have something to tell me,
leave that holy ground
and speak where all are allowed
to speak—but, till then, refrain!

OEDIPUS: Daughter, what should we think of doing?   170

ANTIGONE: We must take care, Father, to do
    what *they* do, and yield and listen to them.

OEDIPUS: Take my hand, now.   ANTIG.: Here, I'm holding it.

OEDIPUS: Strangers, may I not suffer wrong
    for trusting you, and leaving this grove behind.

strophe 2

CHORUS: No one will ever lead you, old man,
    against your will, away from this refuge.

OEDIPUS: Is this far enough, then?   CHOR.: Farther, come farther
                                        toward me.

OEDIPUS: Farther still?   CHOR.: Lead him, girl, farther, toward me.
                        I know you understand.   180

ANTIGONE: Follow me, Father, this way,
    with blind steps, where I lead you
    [... ‡
    ...
    ...
    ...]

---

* The Chorus are evidently thinking of the wrath of the Furies, who would punish not only the perpetrator but also the local population for tolerating a violation of their sacred place.

† Libations to the Furies. See note to line 100.

‡ Four lines of the Greek text are missing here.

CHORUS: O sorrowful stranger in a strange land,
 have the heart to hate whatever
 the city hates, and to revere
 what she reveres.
OEDIPUS: Bring me now, child, where
 we may step without sacrilege,
 and speak and listen   190
 and not battle with necessity.

antistrophe 2

CHORUS: There! Turn your step no further
 than that ridge of native rock.
OEDIPUS: Here? CHOR.: That's enough, as I've said.
OEDIPUS: May I sit? CHOR.: Yes, move to the side, on the edge of
         the stone, crouch down low.
ANTIGONE: Father, this task is mine. Fit
 step to step—gently.
OEDIPUS: *iō moi moi!*
ANTIGONE: Lean your aged body   200
 on my loving arm.
OEDIPUS: *ōmoi*, the ruin, the madness!
 (Oedipus sits down.)
CHORUS: Poor man, now that you're at ease,
 tell us who you are—*who*,
 driven, laden with toil? What
 country would you say is yours?*

epode

OEDIPUS: Strangers, I'm an exile. But don't—
CHORUS: What don't you want to say, old man?
OEDIPUS: —don't, don't ask me who   210
 I am. Go no further with inquiries!
CHORUS: But why? OED.: It's terrible, my origin.
CHORUS: Speak out!
OEDIPUS: *ōmoi*, my child, what should I say?
CHORUS: Of whose seed are you?
 Tell us, stranger: who is your father?
OEDIPUS: *ōmoi*, what will become of me now, my child?
CHORUS: Speak! You're only a step away from it!

---

* These questions (who he is, where he's from) are two of the three standard questions asked of a stranger. The third (who his father is) occurs at 215.

OEDIPUS: Well, I shall. I have no means of hiding.

CHORUS: Delaying again! Speak up, and quickly.

OEDIPUS: Do you know of a son of Laius?   CHOR.: *ō!*   220

OEDIPUS: Know of the Labdacid* family?   CHOR.: *ō, Zeus!*

OEDIPUS: Of miserable Oedipus?   CHOR.: What? Are you *he*?

OEDIPUS: Don't take fright at what I say.

CHORUS: *iō! ō, ō!*   OED.: My evil fate!   CHOR.: *ō, ō!*

OEDIPUS: Daughter, what, what will happen now?

CHORUS: Out of this land, out this moment!

OEDIPUS: What of your promise? How will you keep it?

CHORUS: There is no punishment for hurting

    in return for hurt; deceit   230

  set against deceit

  repays with pain, not gratitude.

  But *you*—back, away from this refuge,

  on your way again, leave my land at once,

  lest you bring down on us

  some further calamity!†

ANTIGONE: O strangers, men of compassion,

  since you could not accept

  my aged father here, knowing

  the tale of what he did without willing it,   240

  have pity on me at least, in my misery—

  I am your suppliant, strangers, I appeal

  to you on my suffering father's behalf,

  appeal with eyes not blind, eyes

  fixed on yours, like one

  of your own flesh and blood: let the poor man

  meet with compassion! We the suffering

  are in your hands, as in a god's. Come, say yes

  to a favor beyond our hopes!‡ Please, by all

  that you hold dear at home—a child, a wife,   250

  a precious thing, a god.§ Look everywhere

---

* Descended from Labdacus, often named as the ancestor of the Theban royal family. The line of descent runs from Cadmus to Polydorus, Labdacus, Laius, and Oedipus. Jocasta and Creon, Oedipus' mother and uncle, descend from Agave, one of the four daughters of Cadmus.

† The Chorus fear that Oedipus has already offended the Furies, whose wrath might punish not only him but also them if they do not drive him away immediately.

‡ They have just ordered her and her father out of the country (lines 226, 234).

§ I.e. the statue of a god, kept in the house. The distinction is often ignored.

but you will not find a mortal man
who can escape when a god leads him on.
(The parodos *ends, and the meter returns to iambic trimeter.)*

CHORUS LEADER: You should know, child of Oedipus, we pity
you as much as him, for his misfortune,
but, since we fear the gods, we wouldn't dare
say more to you than we have said just now.

OEDIPUS: What help, then, is there in glory
or in a good name, if it's just a name?
Athens, they say, is most reverent   260
toward the gods, alone able to save,
alone to aid the stranger in trouble—but what
is that to me? Just now you lured me
from my seat, and now you drive me away,
afraid of my name, nothing more—not, for sure,
of my person or my deeds. For you should know
those deeds were suffered more than done by me.
My parents (if I must bring them up)—*they're*
the reason you dread me so. That's clear! And yet,
how am I myself evil, if I was *repaying*   270
what was done to me? I wouldn't be
judged evil even if I'd acted knowingly!*
But I went where I went in ignorance, while those
who tried to kill me knew what they were doing.†

   And so, strangers, I beseech you, by the gods:
as you've uprooted me, so must you save me
and not, even in honoring the gods, act
as if they're blind! No; believe that they
see those who are pious among men
and see those who are not, and that no   280
impious man has ever yet escaped them.
Accept their aid;‡ don't shroud your blessed Athens
by covering its glory in unholiness!

---

* His father, Laius, had struck him on the head when the two met at the crossroads. Oedipus, not know-ing who he was, retaliated. In traditional Greek morality, retaliation in kind was justified. See lines 229–32.

† A reference to the attempt by his parents to kill him in his infancy.

‡ The gods, by leading Oedipus to Athens, have given that city an opportunity to enhance its reputation for piety.

Just as you've taken the suppliant
under your pledge, save and protect me. Do not
look on me with disdain, hard though I am
to look at. For I come, sacred and reverent
and as a boon for the people here.
But when your lord, your leader, has arrived,
then will you hear and know all. But between   290
now and then, do not do me any harm!

CHORUS LEADER: We've many a reason, old man, to honor
these arguments of yours. They've been put
in words by no means unimpressive. All the same,
I'll let the lords of this land decide this matter.

OEDIPUS: And where, friends, is the country's ruler?

CHORUS LEADER: In the land's ancestral city. A messenger—
the one who brought me here—has gone for him.

OEDIPUS: Do you really think he'll feel some interest
in a blind man, or care enough to come himself?   300

CHORUS LEADER: Yes, surely, the moment he hears your name.

OEDIPUS: And who will bring him word of that?

CHORUS LEADER: It's a long way, and the talk of travelers
tends to circulate. Once he hears, he'll come,
you can be sure. Your name, old man, is huge,
is everywhere, so even if he's resting, tired,
when he hears it's you, he'll come at once.

OEDIPUS: Well, may he come with luck, for his city
and for me. A good man is his own friend.*

ANTIGONE: (*looking offstage*) Zeus! What shall I say? What does this mean,
    Father?   310

OEDIPUS: What is it, my child?   ANTIG.: I see a woman coming this way,
                         riding an Aetnean colt†
and, on her head, a Thessalian hat‡
with sun-shading brim circles her face.
What am I saying?§

---

* Proverbial: a good man helps others, thereby winning friends for himself. The implication is that
Theseus has something to gain from helping Oedipus, as hinted in line 288.

† The horse was most likely not seen by the audience and is not mentioned again. Ismene's arrival on a
horse imported from Sicily is in stark contrast with the impoverished condition in which she finds her
father and sister.

‡ Worn especially by travelers. Ismene has come from Thebes in search of her father and sister.

§ The short line here (and again three lines farther on), in the midst of a passage where all the other
lines are full iambic trimeters, is a sign of intense emotion.

Is it she, or not? Are my wits still with me?
I say yes, and no, and don't know what to say.
Poor fool,
    it's no one else! Yes, the brightness in her eyes
as she approaches signals that   320
she is no other than our dear Ismene!

OEDIPUS: What do you mean?   **ANTIG.:** I see your daughter,
my sister! Her voice makes it certain.

        (Ismene enters from the left, accompanied by a servant.)

ISMENE: Father, sister—two names sweeter to me
than any! How hard it's been to find you,
how hard to see you now, the pain it causes!

OEDIPUS: Child, you've come?   **ISM.:** Father, to see you like this!

OEDIPUS: Child, you're here?   **ISM.:** Yes—exhausted, but here at last!

OEDIPUS: Come, touch me, my daughter!   **ISM.:** You and her together.

OEDIPUS: Children, sisters!   **ISM.:** Misery, to live like this!   330

OEDIPUS: She and I?   **ISM.:** And I—the three of us.

OEDIPUS: Child, why have you come?   **ISM.:** For your sake, Father.

OEDIPUS: Eager to see me?   **ISM.:** Yes, and to report the news in person,
with the one servant I could trust.

OEDIPUS: Where are your brothers? No help from them?

ISMENE: They are—where they are. Things are bad between them now.

OEDIPUS: Those two! How like Egyptians
they've become, down to their bones, the very
lives they live. For in Egypt the men sit
at home, working the loom while the women   340
toil for a living outside the house.* So they,
who should be shouldering these burdens,
are keeping house instead, like girls,
while you, my daughters, in their place,
take my sorrows on yourselves. She (*gesturing toward Antigone*),
from the time she outgrew a child's nurture
and had the strength, has roamed, poor thing,
ever at my side, guiding me in my old age.
Wandering the wild woods, hungry, barefoot,
struggling, often, in the rain, in the sun's heat,   350
she thought life at home worth less

---

* The idea that Egyptian customs are the inverse of Greek derives from Herodotus (2.35); for another passage in which the influence of Herodotus is evident, see *Antigone* 904–12 and the appendix to that play.

than seeing that her father's needs were met.

(*turning toward Ismene*) And you, my child, came to my aid and brought me,
unknown to the Thebans, all the oracles
decreed about me, and loyally kept watch
when I was driven from the land.
But now, Ismene, what news have you brought
your father? What mission rouses you from home?
You've come for some purpose—of that
I'm sure. It's not, I hope, some cause of dread?   360

ISMENE: I'll pass over and leave aside the ordeals
I've endured myself, searching for where
you might be living. Why suffer twice, telling
over now the pains I went through then?
I've come to tell you of the evils that are
just now besetting your two sons.
They had agreed to leave the throne to Creon*
and spare the city more pollution—so wary
were they of the family's doom of old
that plagued your wretched house.†   370
But now foul dissension, sent by some god
and an evil mind, has set the two of them
against each other in a struggle for power,
for kingship. The younger, hot-headed one,‡
has stripped his older brother, Polynices,
of his throne and exiled him from his land.
And *he*, according to the rumor now abroad,
has fled in exile to Argos and got himself
a new marriage and new allies, intending
to occupy the Theban plain forthwith   380
and gain honor there, or else storm the heavens.§
All this is not mere talk, Father; no,
it's all too real. But in what way the gods
will take pity on *your* labors, I can't say.

---

* At the end of *Oedipus the King*, Creon takes charge of Thebes, whether as king or as regent is unclear. He is king in *Antigone*, which opens after the sons of Oedipus have both died in the struggle for power whose onset Ismene is describing here.

† Alluding to the Erinys or Fury persecuting the House of Labdacus.

‡ Eteocles.

§ The exact meaning of Polynices' boast is unclear. Perhaps he vowed either to earn a hero's burial ("occupy the Theban plain") or to achieve undying fame ("storm the heavens") as conqueror of Thebes.

OEDIPUS: What? Can you still have hope, that the gods
    will care for me, and I'll be saved one day?

ISMENE: Yes, I can, because of the latest oracles.

OEDIPUS: What are they? What do they predict, my child?

ISMENE: The day will come when you will be a prize
    to the Thebans—salvation, in death and life alike.   390

OEDIPUS: But who could benefit from such as I?

ISMENE: The power of Thebes, it's said, resides in you.

OEDIPUS: So *then* I'm a man, when I'm no more?

ISMENE: The gods, who cast you down, now raise you up.

OEDIPUS: Some favor, to crush the young man, lift up the old!

ISMENE: And yet you may be sure that just for this
    Creon's on his way, and won't be long in coming.

OEDIPUS: Coming to do what, daughter? Tell me all.

ISMENE: To settle you near Thebes, so they may have you
    in their power, though not within their borders.   400

OEDIPUS: What do they gain if I lie outside their walls?

ISMENE: Your tomb's misfortune would be theirs as well.

OEDIPUS: They need no oracle to tell them that.

ISMENE: It's for the sake of this they want to keep you
    nearby, and not where you'd be your own master.

OEDIPUS: They'll cover my body, then, with Theban dust?*

ISMENE: The spilling of kindred blood prohibits that.†

OEDIPUS: Then they'll never have me in their power!

ISMENE: That will mean disaster for them one day.

OEDIPUS: At what collision of events, my child?   410

ISMENE: They'll feel your anger when they confront your tomb.‡

OEDIPUS: From whom, child, have you heard all this?

ISMENE: From those sent to consult the oracle.

OEDIPUS: And this is what Phoebus§ said about me?

ISMENE: So they reported, when they returned to Thebes.

OEDIPUS: Has either of my sons heard any of this?

ISMENE: Yes, both of them, and they know what it means.

---

* I.e. "They'll bury me at Thebes?"

† Because Oedipus is guilty of his father's murder, his corpse will be a source of pollution if it is buried inside Thebes.

‡ Someday the Thebans will invade Attica and be defeated in the vicinity of Oedipus' tomb. The prophecy may allude to an actual encounter that took place at or near Colonus in 407 B.C.

§ Apollo, the god who speaks through his oracle at Delphi.

OEDIPUS: So, then, when those two traitors heard all this,
    they chose kingship rather than get me back?

ISMENE: It hurts to hear it said, but hear it I must.   420

OEDIPUS: Well, may the gods not quench the strife
    those two are in for now! May the end they come to
    be mine to determine, in this battle to which
    they've set their hands, for which they've raised the spear.
    May he who now holds scepter and throne
    not hold them long, and may he who's gone abroad
    not come home again—they who let me, their father,
    be driven out so shamefully, and didn't
    come to my defense when I, for all they cared,
    was sent away, cast out, declared an exile!   430
    Perhaps you'll say the city gave me what
    I wished for, with good reason, at the time?
    Not so! That day,* I tell you, when my heart
    was seething, and dying was what
    I wanted most, and even death by stoning,
    no one came forward to help me in that wish.
    But later, when my anguish was abating
    and I saw that passion had run away with me
    and punished, too severely, the wrongs I'd done,
    that's when the city chose to force me out   440
    after so long a time, and those sons of mine,
    who could have helped their father, didn't care
    to act, but for lack of one small word from them
    I fled, cast out, a beggar ever since!
            (gesturing toward Antigone and Ismene)
    These two saw to it, the best they could
    (since they're but girls), that I've had the means of life,
    a safe place, and family to fall back on
    while the other two, in preference to their father,
    chose thrones and scepters and rule over the land!
    Well, they will not have me for an ally.   450
    They will never profit from this Theban
    power of theirs; so much I know from hearing

---

* Oedipus looks back to the events following the revelation of his crimes, the immediate sequel to the end of Sophocles' earlier play, *Oedipus the King*.

these new prophecies, and from contemplating
the oracles that Phoebus once revealed.
        So let them send Creon to root me out—
or anyone else with power in that city!
(*turning to the Chorus*) For if you strangers choose to stand by me
together with these awesome, guardian goddesses,*
and help me, you'll win a mighty savior
for your city, and troubles for my enemies.   460
CHORUS LEADER: You're worthy, Oedipus, of compassion,
    you and your daughters here. And since, just now,
    you count yourself a savior of this land,
    I'd like to offer you some good advice.
OEDIPUS: Protect me now, friend; I'll do all you say.†
CHORUS LEADER: Perform a purification to appease
    these goddesses, whose ground you've trespassed on.
OEDIPUS: Appease them in what way? Teach me, strangers!
CHORUS LEADER: First bring libations from the sacred
    ever-flowing spring, and hold them in pure hands.   470
OEDIPUS: And when I've brought this stream of taintless water?
CHORUS LEADER: There are bowls, the work of a skilled craftsman—
    wreathe their rims and handles on both sides.
OEDIPUS: With olive shoots or wool, or in what way?
CHORUS LEADER: With the newly shorn fleece of a young lamb.
OEDIPUS: What must I do next, to complete the rite?
CHORUS LEADER: Pour the libations, looking toward the east.
OEDIPUS: Pour them from the bowls that you describe?
CHORUS LEADER: Yes, three streams from each, the last one all the way.
OEDIPUS: Having filled it with what? Tell me that, too.   480
CHORUS LEADER: With water and with honey, but add no wine!‡
OEDIPUS: And when the dark-leaved earth has drunk it down?
CHORUS LEADER: With both hands, lay three times nine shoots of olive
    upon the ground, and pray; make this appeal—
OEDIPUS: I'm eager to hear it, for it matters most.
CHORUS LEADER: —that they, the ones we call Eumenides,

---

* The Furies within the sacred grove.

† Oedipus is appealing to the Chorus to act as his host, to be his *proxenos*. In return, he will follow their advice.

‡ See note to line 100.

will take you and protect you with kind* hearts.
Beseech them, you yourself or one who acts
in your behalf, in silent prayer, not in a loud voice.
And then depart; do not turn back. Do all this   490
and I'll stand by you in full confidence;
if you do not, I'd be afraid on your account.

OEDIPUS: Children, do you hear these men, who live nearby?

ISMENE: We've heard. Now bid us do what must be done.

OEDIPUS: I can't go myself, for lack of strength
and lack of sight—my two afflictions.
Let one of you two go tend to these matters.
A single soul will be as good as many
to pay down this debt, with pure intentions.
See that it's done, both of you, quickly. And yet,   500
don't leave me by myself, for this body of mine,
alone, without a guide, couldn't take a step.

ISMENE: I'll see this done—but first I need to know
the place where I'm to perform these duties.

CHORUS LEADER: The other side of this grove. And if you need
something, the man who lives there† will show you.

ISMENE: I'm off now, to perform the rite. Antigone,
keep watch on our father here. Trouble taken
on behalf of parents shouldn't count as trouble.

> *(Exit Ismene into the grove.)*

strophe 1

CHORUS: A terrible thing it is, to awaken, stranger, an evil put   510
to sleep long ago,
and yet I yearn to inquire—

OEDIPUS: What is it now?

CHORUS: —into your suffering, intractable the moment
it appeared—the misery you grappled with.

OEDIPUS: By the hospitality you have shown me, do not
cruelly lay bare what I've endured!

CHORUS: The great, the never-fading tale
that is yours—as it was, I long to hear it told.

OEDIPUS: *ōmoi!*

---

* See note to line 42.
† A sacred grove would have a custodian who lived nearby.

CHORUS: Do as I ask—I implore you.

OEDIPUS: *pheu, pheu!*

CHORUS: Be persuaded: grant my wish, as I have yours.   520

antistrophe 1

OEDIPUS: I endured evil,* endured it willingly—
    the god† be my witness!—
    but none of *that* was of my own choosing.

CHORUS: Meaning what?

OEDIPUS: That I knew nothing when the city bound me
    in an evil union, to a marriage accursed.

CHORUS: With your mother, as I hear,
    you filled your bed, and made it infamous?

OEDIPUS: *ōmoi*, it is death, stranger, to hear
    these things; and then, from me, these two—   530

CHORUS: What are you saying now?

OEDIPUS: —my daughters, a pair of curses—

CHORUS: O Zeus!

OEDIPUS: —bloomed from the pangs of our shared mother!

strophe 2

CHORUS: So, they are both your daughters *and*—

OEDIPUS: my *sisters*, yes, the pair of them!

CHORUS: *iō!* OED.: *iō*, yes! Evils beyond count wheel around, and
          strike again!

CHORUS: You suffered— OED.: sufferings insufferable!

CHORUS: You committed— OED.: No, not committed!

    CHOR.: Well, *what*, then?

OEDIPUS: I was *given*
    a gift I never should have accepted—I,   540
    unhappy I, who came to the city's aid.‡

antistrophe 2

CHORUS: And then, ill-starred man? Did you kill—

OEDIPUS: What now? What do you want to know?

CHORUS: —your father? OED.: Ah, there's a second blow you've
          struck, affliction after affliction!

CHORUS: You slew— OED.: Yes, but not without—

---

* His self-blinding, for which, as in *Oedipus the King* 1328–33, he accepts responsibility.

† Most likely Apollo.

‡ Oedipus had solved the riddle of the Sphinx, thus saving the city. In return, he was offered the hand of Jocasta, the widowed queen.

CHORUS: Not without *what?* **OED.:** —a measure of justice.
      CHOR.: How so?

OEDIPUS: I'll tell you:

Gripped by a curse, I killed him, and destroyed him—
but did not break the law. *I did not know.*

CHORUS LEADER: Here now is our lord, Aegeus' son
Theseus, summoned at your behest. 550

      (Enter Theseus, from the right.)

THESEUS: I knew it was you, son of Laius. I'd heard
from many, in the past, of the bloody
destruction of your eyes. And now that I've come
and seen for myself, I'm all the more sure of it.
Your clothes and the look of sorrow on your face
show me who you are, and out of pity
I want to ask, poor Oedipus, with what appeal
to my city and to me you've taken your stand
here—you and she (*indicating Antigone*), your companion in misfortune.
Tell me. Your request would need to be 560
fearful indeed, if I refused to grant it.
I know that I myself, like you, grew up
a foreigner,* risked my life as no man has,
enduring dangers in a foreign land.
I wouldn't walk away, refuse to help
a stranger such as you are now, for I
know well that I'm a man, and that my claim
upon tomorrow is no more than yours.

OEDIPUS: Theseus, your nobility has, in few words,
permitted me to use but few in answer. 570
For who I am and who my father was
and from what land I've come—all that
you've told, leaving me no more to say
than what I need, and then my speech is done.

THESEUS: Tell me that now, so I may know it all.

OEDIPUS: I'm here to give to you my wretched body—
not a gift to delight the eye, but the profit
to come of it is greater than good looks.

---

* Theseus was the son of the Athenian king, Aegeus, and Aethra, daughter of Pittheus, king of Troezen. He grew up in Troezen and traveled to Athens as a young man to claim his rightful position there. Oedipus was born in Thebes but raised in Corinth, and he returned to Thebes as a stranger.

THESEUS: What sort of profit do you claim for it?

OEDIPUS: You'll learn in time—but not, I think, just now.   580

THESEUS: When, then, will your gift see the light of day?

OEDIPUS: When I die, and you have buried me.

THESEUS: Your thoughts look to life's end. What lies between
   now and then you forget, or count as nothing.

OEDIPUS: I do, for *then* the rest falls into place.

THESEUS: But it's a small favor you ask of me.

OEDIPUS: Take care. It isn't small, no—not this conflict.

THESEUS: Are you referring to your sons, or what?

OEDIPUS: They will compel me to go back there.

THESEUS: You don't *want* to go? You prefer exile?   590

OEDIPUS: When *I* wanted to stay there, *they* refused!

THESEUS: Foolish man, in troubles anger is no help.

OEDIPUS: Advise me when you've heard me, not before!

THESEUS: Tell me, then; I won't blame before I know.

OEDIPUS: I've suffered cruelly—evils heaped on evils.

THESEUS: You mean the ruin of your family long ago?

OEDIPUS: No—everyone in Greece talks about *that.*

THESEUS: How, then, did you suffer more than a man could bear?

OEDIPUS: The gist of it is, that I was driven out
   of my country by my own seed, forbidden   600
   ever to return—*father-killer*, they call me.

THESEUS: And yet they'll summon you to live *apart* from them?

OEDIPUS: The god's utterance will bring them to it.

THESEUS: For fear of what—what does the oracle threaten?

OEDIPUS: They're doomed to be defeated, here, in this land.

THESEUS: And how will they become *my* enemies?

OEDIPUS: O beloved son of Aegeus, for the gods alone
   there is no growing old, no dying ever.
   Everything else all-powerful Time destroys.
   Earth's strength fails, the body's strength fails,   610
   trust dies, distrust blooms in its place
   and the same spirit of friendliness never stays
   between one man and another, or city and city.
   For some men now, for others later, sweet
   turns bitter, and then affection
   comes round again. And if, right now, the sun shines
   between you and Thebes, endless time coursing on

brings forth endless days and nights, in which
they'll scatter with their spears the harmony
reigning now, all for a trivial reason, 620
and then, one day, my corpse, lying cold and hidden,
will drink their warm blood—if Zeus
is still Zeus and Phoebus, his son, speaks true!

But since there is no joy in uttering words
not to be uttered, leave me where I began.
Stay true to what you've promised, and you'll never
say that you made Oedipus a useless tenant
of this ground—unless the gods play me false.

CHORUS LEADER: My lord, for a long while now this man has shown
he means these and like blessings on this land. 630

THESEUS: Who would reject this man's good will?
He is, in the first instance, an ally of our spear,*
and as such always welcome at our hearth.
And then, he is a suppliant, and pays
this land and me no mean recompense.
Moved by all this, I'll never reject his favor
but welcome him, a fellow citizen.

(*to the Chorus*) If he, our guest, prefers to stay right here,
protect him; or he may choose to go with me.
Oedipus, I leave the choice to you. 640
Whatever you decide, I will support.

OEDIPUS: O Zeus, hear the prayers of men like this!

THESEUS: What do you want? To come home with me?

OEDIPUS: I would, if it were right; but this is the place—

THESEUS: Where you'll do what? I'll not stand in the way.

OEDIPUS: —where I will conquer those who cast me out.

THESEUS: Great, then, is the benefit, of staying here.

OEDIPUS: Yes, if you stand by what you say, and do it.

THESEUS: You may be sure I will. I won't betray you.

OEDIPUS: And I won't make you swear, as if I couldn't trust you. 650

THESEUS: You'd gain no more than by my word alone.

OEDIPUS: How, then, will you act?   THES.: What do you fear most?

OEDIPUS: Men will come—   THES.: These men here will tend to that.

---

* Referring, evidently, to an ancient bond of friendship or hospitality between the royal houses of Thebes and Athens.

OEDIPUS: Take care, when you leave—   **THES.:** Don't tell me my duty!

OEDIPUS: A man afraid must—   **THES.:** *My* heart is not afraid.

OEDIPUS: You don't know the threats—   **THES.:** I know that no one

    will lead you away from here against my will.* 657

    And if they've had the nerve to make dire threats 661

    to dislodge you, they'll find, I suspect, the sea

    between us wide, and not to be crossed.†

    Be confident, then, I tell you, even apart

    from my guarantee, since Phoebus has sent you here;

    and likewise, even if I'm not at your side,

    I know my name will keep you safe from harm.

        (Exit Theseus. The Chorus now sing their first ode.)

strophe 1

    CHORUS: You have come, stranger, to a land

        rich in horses, to the best

        haven on earth, radiant Colonus, where 670

        the nightingale's shrill warbling

        is most at home, in the green

        shade of the glens, the wine-dark

        of the ivy, the god's impenetrable

        foliage bursting in berries, shielded

        from sun, untouched ever by the breath

        of storm, where Dionysus

        steps in ecstasy amid

        the throng of his immortal nurses.‡ 680

antistrophe 1

      And here under the dew

      of heaven blooms anew each day

      the clustering narcissus, long ago

      the garland of the Great Goddesses§—and the crocus

---

* Lines 658–60 are interpolated:
    And as for threats, many a time they threaten
    in anger and in vain—but when the mind
    recovers, gone are all the threatenings.

† The sea meant is metaphorical, a sea of troubles.

‡ The original maenads, or female worshippers of Dionysus, were nymphs to whom he was entrusted as an infant after being rescued from the lightning bolt that destroyed his mother, Semele, when she was pregnant with him.

§ Demeter and Persephone.

beams with gold, and never sleep,
never wane the springs
of Cephisus,* whose streams day
by day wander over the breast
of the land, quickening the earth
with taintless moisture,   690
and the Muses' choruses have not
disdained this place, nor has
Aphrodite of the golden reins.†

strophe 2

And there's a plant whose like I never heard of
in Asia's land; it has not sprung in the great Dorian
isle of Pelops—
invincible, self-sown,‡ the dread
of enemy spears,§ that flowers
here in all its strength: the gray-leaved   700
olive tree, nurse of children.
No man, young or old,
will blot it out with might of hand
for the ever-seeing eye
of Zeus of the Olive keeps watch
and gray-eyed Athena gazes on it.

antistrophe 2

And I have yet more awesome praise to bestow
on her, my native city, a great god's gift, earth's
proudest boast—   710
her glory in horses, in colts, and on the sea!
Son of Cronus, lord Poseidon, it was you
who built this boast for her, who
fashioned the bit and curbed the horse¶
for the first time here, upon her roads.
And thanks to you the skillful oar
wafts her ships, marvelous

---

* A river just to the west of Colonus.

† Aphrodite rides in a chariot drawn by sparrows in Sappho (Fragment 1), by doves or swans in other sources.

‡ According to Herodotus (VIII.55), the sacred olive tree on the Acropolis, burned by the Persians in 480 B.C., flowered again the next day.

§ The Spartan king Archidamus II, invading Attica in 431, 430, and 428 B.C., spared the olive trees sacred to Athena.

¶ See the note to line 60.

to see as they skim along, flying beside
the Nereids dancing on a hundred feet!*

ANTIGONE: O land, praised beyond all others,   720
    now prove these glowing praises true!
OEDIPUS: What's happening, my child?   **ANTIG.:** He's coming, Father—
    Creon, heading for us. He's not alone.
OEDIPUS: (*to the Chorus*) Old men, my friends, now I look to you
    for safety. My life's end is in your hands.
CHORUS LEADER: Take heart, you will be safe: for even if
    I'm old, my country's strength has not grown old.
        (*Enter Creon from the left, with an armed escort.*)
CREON: (*to the Chorus*) Men, noble inhabitants of this land,
    the look in your eyes tells me that you've taken
    sudden fright at my arrival here. You shouldn't   730
    feel that way, or let drop a hostile word.
    I haven't come to *do* something. I'm too old†
    for that and, what's more, I know yours is a city
    great in power, as great as any in Hellas.
    I've been sent, old as I am, to persuade this man
    to come with me to the land of the Cadmeans.‡
    I've been told to fetch him, by one and all
    the Thebans, since it falls to me, as family,
    to feel for his sufferings as no others can.
        So, long-enduring Oedipus, listen to me: 740
    come home. All the people in the town of Cadmus
    rightly summon you, and I most of all—
    I would be deemed the worst man living
    not to feel pain at the sight of your afflictions.§
    I see that you, old man, are a sad exile,
    a tramp roaming about, stripped of the means of life
    and leaning on this girl for support, whom I—
    it breaks my heart to say it—would never have thought
    could sink so low in degradation as she
    has sunk, tending to you, in *your* condition,   750
    begging a pittance to live on—still, at her age,

---

* The Nereids, the daughters of the sea god Nereus, were traditionally fifty in number.
† Creon is a generation older than his nephew Oedipus, so he is often called "old" in this play.
‡ The Cadmeans are the Thebans, descendants of Cadmus and Harmonia.
§ Lines 743–44 are rendered as they are printed by Jebb and Lloyd-Jones in his Loeb edition.

unmarried, ripe for anyone to pluck!
  Is it cruel, what I've just said, feeling the pain,
the slur on you and me and all our family?
Well, cruel or not, what's out cannot be hidden.
Listen, then, to me, Oedipus. By the gods
of your ancestors, I beseech you! Return
to your city and your ancestral house; wish
Athens farewell, as she deserves, for even more
your native city claims your love, your nurse of old.   760

OEDIPUS: Brazen without limit! Ready to make
a cunning snare out of every just argument—
why come to get me now, why seek
to keep me again, where I would suffer most?
Back then, when I was sick with ills at home
and exile from the land was my desire,
you refused to grant the favor that I sought.
But when I'd had my fill of rage
and life at home looked sweet to me, *then*
you cast me off, drove me away. You had   770
no thought for "family" then, none at all!
And now, seeing this city take my side
and all her people warm to me, you try
to drag me off with soft words and hard designs.
Do you enjoy being kind when it's unwanted?
Suppose that someone, when you asked for something,
gave you nothing and refused to help, but when
you had what you wanted, only then
he gave it—then, when favor wins no favor!
Wouldn't your gratitude be empty then?   780
Yet such are the favors you offer me, wrapped
in fine words, but rotten underneath.
(*indicating the Chorus*) I'll show these men, too, just what sort you are!
You've come to *get* me, not to take me home—
to stow me nearby, so your city may escape
defeat one day, in this land, and go unhurt.
That's not what's in store for you. No, it's this:
my avenging spirit, there, in your land, never
to be cast out; as for my sons, they'll inherit
only this: enough dirt to be dead in!   790
  Don't I know more than you about affairs

in Thebes? Yes, because I've learned from better sources—
Phoebus and his father, Zeus himself.
Now comes that tongue of yours, forged
and sharpened to deceive, which all the same
won't do you any good, still less protect you.
I know you don't believe me. Go, then!
Leave us here, to live. We won't live badly,
even as we are, provided we're content.

CREON: Who do you think suffers more—I   800
from what you do or you from what you say?

OEDIPUS: Nothing makes me happier than to see
your arguments fall on deaf ears, mine and theirs!

CREON: Ill-fated man! Will you never show any sense
but go on living, a stain upon old age?

OEDIPUS: You have a clever tongue, but I believe
no just man speaks well on *all* sides of a case.

CREON: Saying much does not mean speaking to the point.

OEDIPUS: As if *you* speak concisely, and to the point!

CREON: I don't, to anyone who thinks like you.   810

OEDIPUS: Out of here! I speak for *them*, too: don't
hem me in, don't block my destined harbor!

CREON: I call on them, not you, to witness how
you answer us. But if I ever get my hands—

OEDIPUS: You'd dare lay hands on me, despite these allies?

CREON: No need for that: you'll suffer soon enough.

OEDIPUS: What have you done, that you make such a threat?

CREON: I've seized and sent away, just now, one*
of your two daughters, and soon I'll take the other.†

OEDIPUS: *oimoi!*   CRE.: You'll soon have yet more cause to cry.   820

OEDIPUS: You have my child?   CRE.: And this one, too, in a moment.

OEDIPUS: (*to the Chorus*) *iō*, friends! What will you do? Betray me?
Why don't you drive this godless man away?

CHORUS LEADER: (*to Creon*) Off with you, stranger, out, get out!
What you're doing isn't right, not then, not now!

CREON: (*to one of his men, indicating Antigone*) Now would be the time to take
her off—
against her will, if she doesn't want to go.

---

* Ismene, who left the stage at line 509 to perform the rites of the Furies.

† Antigone, still onstage.

ANTIGONE: *oimoi!* Where am I to turn? Who will help?
What god? What man?   CH. LEAD.: What are you doing, stranger?
CREON: Him I won't seize, but her, my own,* I will!   830
OEDIPUS: Lords of the land!   CH. LEAD.: Stranger, that's a crime!
CREON: No, it's *right!*   CH. LEAD.: *How* is it right?   CRE.: I claim my own.
>   *(Chorus and characters now engage in lyrical dialogue in*
>   *dochmiac and iambic meters, a sign of high emotion.)*

strophe

> OEDIPUS: *iō*, city!
> CHORUS: What are you doing, stranger? So—you won't let her go?
>   Soon enough you'll come to the test of blows!
> CREON: Back off!   CHOR.: No, not while you're attempting this.
> CREON: It means war with my city, if you hurt me.
> OEDIPUS: Did I not foretell this?   CHOR.: Take your hands off
>   that girl, right now!   CRE.: Don't give orders you can't enforce.
> CHORUS: Let her go, I tell you!   CRE.: And I tell you, leave!   840
> CHORUS: Men of Colonus, come, come here, to our aid!
>   The city, my city, is being destroyed, by force of arms!
>   Come, come here, bring help!
> ANTIGONE: O friends, my friends, they're dragging me away!
> OEDIPUS: Where are you, my child?   ANTIG.: I'm being forced to go!
> OEDIPUS: *(groping for her)* Stretch out your hands, my child!
>   ANTIG.: But I can't!
> CRE.: Won't you take her away?   OED.: Lost, I'm lost!
>   *(Exit Antigone, led by Creon's men.)*

CREON *(to Oedipus)*: You'll never ply your way again, leaning
on these two props. But since you wish to triumph
over your country and your family—whose wishes   850
I myself obey, though I'm a king†—go on,
triumph! For in time, I know, you'll understand
you do yourself no good, not now
and not before, when, despite your friends,
you gave way to your temper—ever your ruin.
CHORUS LEADER: Stop right there, stranger!   CRE.: I'm warning you, don't
                                                         touch me!
CHORUS LEADER: I won't let you go, until I have them back!

---

* Creon is Antigone's maternal uncle.

† Creon, descended from Cadmus (see note to line 221), is emphasizing his membership in the royal family. The actual king at the moment is Eteocles, son of Oedipus.

CREON: You'll make your city pay still more, then,
for I won't take just these two.
CHORUS LEADER: Who, then, is next?   CRE.: Him: he goes with me.   860
CHORUS LEADER: An awful threat!   CRE.: And I'll make good on it,
unless the ruler of this land prevents me.
OEDIPUS: You have the nerve to say that! You'll lay hands on me?
CREON: Be quiet, you!   OED.: No, I won't! May the dread
powers of this place no longer keep it back—
my curse on you, traitor, who tore away
my precious eye,* lost like those I had before!
For that, may Helios, the Sun
who sees all things, give you and yours
a life, an old age, one day, like mine!   870
CREON: Do you see this, people of this land?
OEDIPUS: They see the two of us, and know that I
have only words to ward off your attacks.
CREON: Though on my own and slow with age, I won't
restrain my anger. I'll take this man by force!

antistrophe

> OEDIPUS: *iō*, misery!
> CHORUS: What insolence you've come with, stranger,
> to think you'll get away with this!
> CREON: I *will*.   CHOR.: If you do, this is no city anymore.
> CREON: With justice on their side, the few defeat the many.   880
> OEDIPUS: Do you hear what he says?   CHOR.: Yes, what he won't do,
> <Zeus be my witness!>†   CRE.: Zeus will know, not you!
> CHORUS: This is an outrage!   CRE.: Outrage? Well, you must endure it!
> CHORUS: (*crying aloud*) You people, all of you! Chief men of the land!
> Come with speed, come, these men
> are going beyond all bounds!
>
> *(Theseus enters from the right. His first four lines are in trochaic
> tetrameter, reflecting his haste and the excitement of the moment.)*

THESEUS: Why all this shouting? What has happened? What fear
made you stop me, when I was sacrificing to the god
who guards Colonus? Speak up! I need to know it all—
what brings me here, faster than my feet could wish?   890

---

* Antigone (as at lines 33–34).

† There's a gap in the text here. The supplement is Jebb's.

OEDIPUS: O best of friends! It's you—I know your voice.
　　I've suffered outrage, just now, at this man's hands.
THESEUS: What outrage? Who has hurt you? Tell me!
OEDIPUS: Creon, the man you see here. He's gone
　　and torn from me my only pair of children!
THESEUS: What do you mean?　**OED.:** You've heard what I've suffered!
THESEUS: Then one of my attendants needs to go
　　at once, back to the altar, and give orders
　　that all the host, infantry and cavalry, must leave
　　the rites and rush with loosened reins* to where　　　　　900
　　the roads to Thebes converge, so that the girls
　　will not pass that point and I become a joke,
　　worsted by the high-handedness of this stranger!
　　Go, as I've ordered, with haste! And as for him,
　　if I were as angry at him as I ought to be,
　　I wouldn't let him escape my grasp unhurt.
　　But as it is, I'll treat him in accordance
　　with the laws he brought with him—no others!
　　　　　(turning to Creon)
　　No, you won't leave this country, not until
　　you've brought those girls back here, before my eyes.　　　910
　　What you've done disgraces me and your own
　　ancestors and the land you come from!
　　You entered a country that lives by justice
　　and rules by law; still, you ignored all that,
　　the customs here, and barged right in,
　　grabbed what you pleased, made it yours by force!
　　You thought my city had no men in it—to you
　　she† seemed a slave, and I a nobody!
　　　　　Yet Thebes didn't raise you to be a criminal.
　　It's not her way to nurture unjust men　　　　　920
　　nor would she approve, if she knew you were
　　plundering what belongs to me and to the gods,
　　rounding up helpless suppliants. I wouldn't
　　act that way in your country, even if I had
　　as just a cause as any; I wouldn't seize

---

* I.e. riding at full speed.

† Athens, personified here; so, too, with Thebes, in the next couple of lines.

and carry off at will, without consulting
the ruler of the land, whoever he was—no, I'd know
how a stranger should behave among citizens.
But you bring shame on your city, shame
she doesn't deserve; and time in its fullness, 930
at a single blow, has made you old and senseless.

      Well, then, I've said before, and say again,
have someone bring those children here at once,
unless you'd like to be a guest of this land
under constraint, against your will. I'm telling you
exactly what I mean—no more, no less.

CHORUS LEADER: You see where you are, stranger? You seem just,
    being from Thebes, but we've caught you doing wrong.

CREON: I don't say this city has no men, Theseus.
    And my actions were not, as you say, senseless. 940
I did what I did in the understanding that
your people wouldn't care so much for kin of mine
as to take them in against my will.
I knew that Athens wouldn't open her arms
to a father-killer, a man defiled, who'd been found
living in a marriage most unholy.
Such wisdom, I was sure, dwells in your land,
in the Areopagus,* which won't let vagrants
like these settle here, together with its own.
Confident of that, I seized them as my prey. 950
I wouldn't have done it, if *he* hadn't called
down bitter curses on me and mine. That's
what I endured, that's how I've retaliated!† 953

      Go ahead, then, do as you please, since 956
the fact that I'm alone makes me count for little,
however just my claims. Make your move.
Old as I am, I'll try to retaliate.

OEDIPUS: Insolence, unrestrained! Whose old age 960
    do you think you're insulting—mine or yours?

---

* The Hill of Ares, site of an ancient Athenian court named after it. In Sophocles' day, it had jurisdiction mostly in religious matters.

† Lines 954–55 are interpolated:
  For anger has no other way of passing on
  than death itself; no resentment stings the dead.

What a stream tumbles from your lips—murders,
marriages, catastrophes, all borne by me
against my will! For so it pleased the gods, who held,
it seems, some ancient grudge against my family.
As for me, you couldn't find a single crime
to blame me for, whose recompense I then
paid with all these crimes against myself and mine.
Come, tell me: if an oracle came from the gods
to my father, saying that he would perish   970
at his son's hands, how could you fairly put
the blame for that on me? Not yet begotten,
not yet conceived, I was as yet unborn!
And if, again, born, as I was, unhappily,
I came to blows with my father, and killed him,
not knowing what I did or who I did it to,
how can you blame me for what I didn't mean?
And now you feel no shame, forcing me to mention
my mother's marriage, though she was your sister
and it—I'll say it, I won't hold back   980
now that your unholy lips have led the way.*
She was my mother, my *mother*!
I didn't *know*, she didn't know. She bore me
and had children by me, to her disgrace.
But this one thing I know for sure: you mean
to drag my name and hers in the dirt, but I didn't
want to marry her, and don't want to speak of it now.
But neither my marriage nor my father's killing,
which you are always bringing up, bitterly
reviling me for it, will earn me the name of evil.   990
Care to know why? Answer, then, just this:
if, right here, right now a man appeared
and tried to kill you, would you wonder whether
he was your father, or deal with him at once?
If, as I presume, you want to live, you'd pay him back
in kind, and not look around for permission.
Yet such were the evils into which I fell,
the gods leading the way—I think even

---

* Creon, at lines 945–46, had only alluded to the incestuous marriage.

my father, if he were alive, would take my side.
But you, unfair as you are, think it's fine   1000
to say anything, even what should not be said,
and heap abuse on me, for these men to hear.

     You're fond of flattering Theseus to his face
and saying that Athens is well governed,
and then, in the midst of all this praise, you forget
that if any land knows how to pay respect
and give honors to the gods, it is this land
from which you tried to kidnap me, a suppliant,
old as I am—and made off with my daughters!
In return, I now call upon these goddesses,*   1010
I beseech, I importune them with my prayers—
may they come, my helpers, my allies,
and teach you what sort of men safeguard this city!

CHORUS LEADER: Our guest, lord, is a good man, and his
    afflictions, so ruinous, win him our support.

THESEUS: Enough of words! Those who've seized their prey
    rush off while we, the ones aggrieved, stand still.

CREON: What do you want from me, helpless as I am?

THESEUS: You lead the way there, and I'll escort you,   1019
    I and no other, to make sure, for I know that you†   1028
    would not have tried such blatant violence   1029
    if you'd been unarmed and unprepared—no,   1030
    there was someone you trusted when you did this.   1031
    I need to keep an eye on that, so this city   1032
    will not prove weaker than a single man. On, then,   1033
    and show me, yourself, where those girls are—   1020
    if you're holding them here, in this land; but if
    their captors have fled with them, we needn't bother—
    others will pursue them. They'll never get out,
    never thank the gods for their escape.
    Lead the way, now, and know the catcher's caught,
    the hunter's in the snare of Chance! The gains
    of guile and treachery are not secure.   1027
    Do you understand, or do my words, like those you heard   1034
    before you hatched this scheme, mean nothing to you?

---

* The Furies in the sacred grove.

† Lloyd-Jones and Wilson (following Housman) transpose lines 1028–33 from their position in the transmitted text, so that now they come between 1019 and 1020.

CREON: I can't argue with anything you say here;
    once home, though, I, too, will know what to do.

THESEUS: Threaten, if you must, but go, right now. And you,
    Oedipus, stay here and rest assured
    that, unless I die first, I shall not relax   1040
    until I've made your children yours again.

OEDIPUS: May fortune smile on you, Theseus, for your
    nobility and for your just concern toward us!

        (Exit Theseus, with Creon and attendants, to the left. The
        Chorus now sing their second ode.)

strophe 1

    CHORUS: I wish I were there,
        where the enemy's forces
        will spin round into battle
        with a brazen cry, near
        Apollo's shore* or the shore
        lit by torches† in solemn
        rites fostered by the Great Goddesses‡   1050
        for those whose lips are hushed
        under the golden seal put upon them
        by the priestly Eumolpidae.§
        It is there, I imagine, Theseus
        will arrive, urging his men
        to battle, sure of his power
        to save the two maiden sisters
        here, within this land.

antistrophe 1

        Yes! The enemy presses on
        west of the snowy rock,¶   1060
        I'd say—out of the pastures
        of Oea,** racing
        on horseback or on

---

* On the Bay of Eleusis, where there was a temple to Apollo.

† Also on the Bay of Eleusis, about five miles north of the temple of Apollo just alluded to. A nocturnal torchlit procession from Athens to Eleusis took place every year during the Eleusinian Mysteries.

‡ Demeter and Persephone, whose reunion was celebrated in the Mysteries at Eleusis.

§ Initiates in the Eleusinian Mysteries took a sacred oath of secrecy administered by the Eumolpidae ("Descendants of Eumolpus"), hereditary priests of the cult.

¶ Usually assumed to be Mount Aigaleos, east of Oea (see next note).

** A rural district in Attica, west of Mount Aigaleos, between Eleusis and Colonus.

chariots darting in flight. He will
be caught! Dread Ares rides
with our countrymen, and dread
is the might of Theseus' sons. Every
bridle flashes fire, all the riders, reins
loose on the wind, rush
in pursuit—those worshippers of Athena,   1070
goddess of horses, and of the earth—
embracing god of the sea,
Rhea's beloved son.*

strophe 2

Are they engaged, or on the point of it? For
a premonition comes to me—
that the dread sorrows
of these girls, who've been treated
dreadfully by their kin, will soon abate.
Zeus will bring victory, victory today.
I am a prophet of success!   1080
I wish I were a dove, riding the storm,
swift and strong, to perch on a cloud
in heaven, and from that height
gaze down on the battle!

antistrophe 2

Zeus, all-ruling, all-seeing lord
of the gods, may you grant
the guardians of this land
strength to win, and good
hunting in this ambush—you
and your daughter, awesome Pallas Athena,   1090
and I pray that Apollo
the hunter, and his sister,† harrower
of dappled, swift-footed deer, come,
twin allies bringing
aid to our land and citizens!

(*Enter, from the left, Theseus with Antigone, Ismene, and
attendants.*)

---

* Poseidon, son of Cronus and Rhea.
† Artemis, goddess of hunting.

CHORUS LEADER: My wandering friend, you will not call me
    a false prophet, for I see them coming now, close
    and closer—your daughters, on their way back here.
OEDIPUS: Where, where? What are you saying?   **ANTIG.:** Father, Father!
    O that a god would grant you sight, to see   1100
    this best of men, the one who's brought us here!
OEDIPUS: Child, are you here, both of you?   **ANTIG.:** Yes, saved by the
                           hands of Theseus and his
                           loyal men.
OEDIPUS: Come now, children, to your father, and let me
    touch those of whose return I had no hope!
ANTIGONE: You'll have your wish, for we desire it, too.
OEDIPUS: Where, then, where are you?   **ANTIG.:** Here, we're here,
                         together.
OEDIPUS: At last!   **ANTIG.:** Every father, every child, feels such love.
OEDIPUS: The staves I lean on!   **ANTIG.:** Your weight of sadness, ours, too!
OEDIPUS: I have what I love most, and I would never   1110
    die unhappy, with you two in my arms!
    Stand close to me, children, one on each side,
    clinging to your father; relieve the loneliness
    I felt when you went away so sadly.
    Tell me what happened—as briefly as you can.
    Girls your age have no need of long speeches.
ANTIGONE: The one who saved us is here, Father. Ask *him*
    how he did it. That's as brief as I can be.
OEDIPUS: (*to Theseus*) Friend, don't be surprised if I go on at length
    talking with my children. They've returned   1120
    beyond all hope. I know the joy I feel
    on their account comes from you:
    you saved them, you, and no one else.
    May the gods favor you as I would wish,
    you yourself and this land of yours, for here
    alone on earth have I found piety
    and fairness and love of truth! All this
    I know and now repay, with these words of mine.
    For I owe what I have to you, and none but you.
    And now, lord, give me your right hand to touch   1130
    and let me kiss, if I may, your cheek.
        But what am I saying? How could *I*, born

for misery, ask *you* to touch a man in whom
no evil has not left its stain? No, I won't ask
and wouldn't allow it! Only those who've felt
sorrows like mine may share the grief of them.
Accept my greeting, then, from where you are
and be my just protector, as you've been till now!

THESEUS: I'm not amazed that you have spoken
at some length, rejoicing in these children here,　　　　1140
or even that you preferred words with them
to words with me. That causes me no pain.
For it's not through words that I am eager
to make my life illustrious, but through deeds.
And so, in nothing that I swore to do have I
been remiss, old man. I've brought these girls of yours
alive, unscathed by all that threatened them.
As for how I did it—why should I boast of what
you'll hear from them yourself, when you're together?
But a report did come to me just now,　　　　1150
on my way here—tell me what you think.
It's brief, yet worthy of attention. No mortal man
should take any matter lightly.

OEDIPUS: What is it, son of Aegeus? Tell me! So far
I have no idea of what you're getting at.

THESEUS: They say that a man, not a fellow citizen
of yours, but a relative, has flung himself in prayer
at Poseidon's altar, and is sitting there now,*
where I'd been sacrificing before I rushed here.†

OEDIPUS: Where's he from? What does he pray for?　　　　1160

THESEUS: I know only one thing: they say he wants
to talk with you, briefly, no great matter.

OEDIPUS: What about, then? These appeals are serious.

THESEUS: They say he asks only to speak with you
and then to leave, safely, from his journey here.

OEDIPUS: Who could he be—this suppliant, with this prayer?

---

* The language used here (and again at lines 1160, 1163, and 1166) strongly suggests the ritual of supplication. A stranger, lacking the rights of a citizen, appeals to the gods for protection and aid, and through them to the king or other authority in the land. He makes his prayer at the god's altar and sits there until his request is granted.

† Theseus had interrupted his sacrifice to Poseidon in order to come to the aid of Oedipus, who was being threatened by Creon. See lines 887–90.

THESEUS: Consider: do you have a kinsman in Argos,*
   who might want to ask this of you?
OEDIPUS: Dear friend, stop right there!   THES.: What's the matter?
OEDIPUS: Don't ask of me—   THES.: *What?* Tell me!   1170
OEDIPUS: I know from what you say who the suppliant is.
THESEUS: And *who* is he, that I should disapprove of him?
OEDIPUS: My hated son. His words would cause
   me greater pain than those of any man.
THESEUS: Why? Can't you listen and then reject
   what he says? Why not hear him out?
OEDIPUS: I, his father, can't stand to hear his voice!
   You—don't force me to give way in this!
THESEUS: But think: his supplication may compel you—
   you should consider what the god may want.   1180
ANTIGONE: Father, take my advice, young though I am.
   Let this man please his own mind and please
   the god, as he wishes to; and for my sake
   and my sister's, let our brother come here.
   If what he says is bad for you, it won't—
   you may be sure—rob you of your judgment.
   What harm is there in listening to him? Deeds
   conceived in evil are revealed in speech.
   You're his father, so that not even if he were
   guilty of the most impious crime against you   1190
   would it be right to pay him evil in return.
   Take pity on him! Others have evil children
   and quick tempers, but the good advice
   of friends charms them out of their nature.
   Look not to the present but the past, the pains
   you suffered from your parents; and with your gaze
   fixed on those, you'll recognize, I know,
   what comes of a bad temper, the evil in its wake.
   Not slight is the cost you have to reckon up—
   the loss of your eyes, their blindness now.   1200
   Yield, then, to us. It's not right that we should beg
   when we seek justice, or that a man
   who's treated well should not respond in kind.

---

* See lines 374–81.

OEDIPUS: Child, you've won your case—a joy to you
but hard on me. All the same, let it be as you wish.
Only you, my friend, if he does come here,
let no one lay their hands on me!
THESEUS: Such prayers, old man, I need to hear once,
not twice. I wouldn't boast, but be assured
that you are safe if the gods also keep me safe!   1210
(Exit Theseus, to the right. The Chorus now sing their third ode.)

strophe

CHORUS: Someone who wishes to live too long,
who spurns a moderate share
in life, clings, all too clearly,
in my view, to delusion.
For the long days pile up
many things so much like pain
you'd look and not find
where pleasure's gone
once one has sunk too
deeply into life. But the Deliverer   1220
levels all endings, when Hades' doom
shows up—no wedding song,
no music, no dance, only
Death at the end.

antistrophe

Not to be born is best, by any
measure, and next best, by far, once born,
go back where you came from
as soon as you can.
For when one has let go
of youth's airy thoughtlessness,   1230
what painful blow is missing?
What misery is not at hand?
Murders, factions, strife, battles,
and envy. And then, last of all,
reviled old age is our lot—
strengthless, friendless,
loveless—where all the worst
evils make their home.

epode

This poor man is there now—not I alone—:
like a coast facing north, battered by waves   1240
in winter, assailed on every side,
so is he assailed, dread disasters
breaking over his head
in waves that never end—
some from where the sun sets,
some from where it rises,
some from the mid-day beam,*
some from the Rhipae† draped in night.

ANTIGONE: Here, it seems, is our stranger—alone,
no men at his side, and from his eyes,   1250
as he comes, the tears fall in streams, not drops.

OEDIPUS: Who is he? ANTIG.: The very one we've had in mind for some
time now. Yes, Polynices is here.

(*Enter Polynices, from the left. He speaks first to Antigone and
Ismene.*)

POLYNICES: *oimoi!* What am I to do? Bewail my own
afflictions first, or my old father's,
now that I see them? In a strange land
I've found him, cast out here along with you
and dressed in such rags! Their repulsive, aged
filth has settled in and aged on him; it eats
into his ribs, and from his eyeless head   1260
his wild hair waves in the wind.
Kin to all this, it seems, he carries a pouch
stuffed with food for his wretched belly.
Too late I learn of it—too late, and all to blame.
I've been worthless in your support—I admit it,
father: you needn't hear it said by others.
All the same, Compassion sits on Zeus' throne,
at Zeus' side, whatever he does; and father,
may she also stand by you! For mistakes
there's a cure, though mine could not be worse ...   1270

* That is, from the south.
† A mythical range of mountains in the far north, called by Alcman "the breast of black night." *Rhipai*
means "blasts" (of the north wind).

Why are you silent?*
Say something, Father! Don't turn away from me!
Have you no answer? None? Will you send me off
in disgrace? No word, no explanation, even,
of your anger? Children of this man, my sisters!
You at least, try to move our father, make him speak.
He's so hard to get near, so hard to talk to.
Don't let him cast me off like this, disgraced,
the god's suppliant, without saying a word to me!

ANTIGONE: Tell him yourself, unhappy brother, why   1280
you're here. Speak up! A plea spun out at length—
delighting, angering, or full, somehow, of pity—
may stir the voice in those who hold it back.

POLYNICES: That's good advice. I'll take it, starting
with the fact that the god himself is on my side,
from whose altar the ruler of this land
raised me up, sent me here, and granted the right
to speak and listen and depart unharmed.
From you, too, strangers, I hope to win all this,
and from my sisters here, and from my father.   1290

      I want to tell you now, Father, why I've come.
I've been driven from my native land, an exile
because I thought I had the right, being the older,
to sit with full power upon your throne.
But Eteocles, though younger, drove me out.
He didn't get his way by argument, or
by putting strength and merit to the test—
no, he bought the city.† I'm all but certain
your Fury‡ was the cause behind all this.§   1299
And so I went to Dorian Argos, and took   1301
Adrastus as my father-in-law, joined hands,
on oath, with all who call themselves chiefs

---

* Again (as at lines 315 and 318), the short line signals intense emotion.

† Literally, "he *persuaded* the city." The verb often has the connotation "bribe," even when, as here, the means of persuasion (money or the like) is not mentioned. The connotation is suggested by the prior assertion that Eteocles did not prevail "by argument"; that is, it wasn't speech but something else that proved decisive. Using money to gain power is typical of tyrants.

‡ The Erinys alluded to at line 370.

§ The next line, 1300, is interpolated:
    and this, too, is how the soothsayers see it.

of the Apian land,* their champions in battle.
I raised this host of seven spears against Thebes
either to die fighting with them in a just cause
or drive the evildoers from my land.

      What, then, brings me before you now?
I come to ask you for your blessing, Father,
for my own sake and that of my allies,   1310
who now in seven cohorts under seven spears
ring the entire plain of Thebes—men like
Amphiaraus, brandishing his lance, foremost
in might of war, foremost in prophecy;
second is Tydeus, from Aeolia, offspring
of Oeneus; third, Eteoclus,† Argive born;
Hippomedon is fourth, sent by his father
Talaus; the fifth, Capaneus, swears that he
will soon burn the city of Thebes to the ground.
Sixth is an Arcadian, Parthenopaeus,   1320
named to recall his mother's maidenhood.‡   1321
And I, your son—or if not yours, then   1323
some evil Fate's, yet *known*, at least, as yours—
now launch this fearless Argive host at Thebes.

      By these children here, by your life, Father,
we call on you, all of us together: let
your dire anger at me subside as I set out
to take vengeance on my brother, who has
thrust me from my country, stolen it from me!   1330
If oracles are to be believed, they've said
the side you're on will win this war.
By our sacred springs, by our family gods,
hear my plea and yield, I implore you—I,
a beggar and an alien, just like you.
The two of us live by pleasing others;

---

* The Peloponnesus.

† Not to be confused with Eteocles.

‡ Son of Atalanta and Milanion. Atalanta would marry only the suitor who could defeat her in a foot race. Many failed in the attempt until Milanion, diverting her with a golden apple, managed to win. Parthenopaeus, the son born of their union, owes his name to the fact that his mother stayed a virgin—a *parthenos*—until she lost that race. The next line, 1322, is interpolated, apparently to flesh out these allusions:

    Atalanta, who bore her loyal child at last.

we have a common lot, we share the same fate.
Meanwhile—how it hurts to say it!—that tyrant*
struts in our halls, laughing at the two of us.
If you'll make common cause with me, I'll   1340
dispose of him, with little trouble or effort.
And so I'll bring you home and settle you
in your palace, you and me, once he's thrown out.
I can claim all this, if you want what I want.
Without you, I lack strength even to survive.

CHORUS LEADER: Oedipus, for the sake of him who sent him here,
say what will help, and send him on his way.

OEDIPUS: Well, guardians of the people of this land,
if Theseus hadn't sent him here, and thought
that he deserved a hearing, he would never   1350
have known what I would say in response.
But now that he's judged fit to hear, he'll leave
with words of mine he'll wish he never heard!

When you, traitor that you are, had the scepter
and the throne your brother has today in Thebes,
you cast me out, me, your own father—yes, you!
You made me an exile, you dressed me in these clothes
that now you weep to see, now that you've come
into the maelstrom of evils where I am, too!
There's no point in crying over that, though I   1360
must live with it, and regard you as my killer.
For you put me in the arms of misery;
you drove me out; because of you I wander,
begging others for my food day by day.
And if I hadn't had these two daughters, my nurses,
I wouldn't even be alive, for all you care!
They keep me safe, they are my nurses, they
are men, not women, standing at my side.
But you two!† You're someone else's sons, not mine!

And so the god‡ watches you now, though not   1370
as soon he will, once those troops of yours

---

* See note to line 1298.

† Oedipus uses the second person dual pronoun, as if both his sons were present. He reverts, in the next line, to the singular, addressing Polynices alone.

‡ The Greek here is *daimōn*, which can mean "fate" as well as "divine power, god."

are on the way to Thebes. For you will never
tear that city down. You'll fall yourself first, defiled
in blood, you and your brother with you. Such curses
I've cast on you and him before, and now
I call on them to fight for me, so you
may learn to reverence and not despise
your parents—if, blind father that I am, I sowed
the two of you: my daughters didn't act that way!
So my curses overrule your supplication   1380
and your thrones—if Justice born of old
still sits by Zeus, and ancient law prevails.

      Go now, spat out, disowned, of all
bad men the worst, and take these curses
with you! I call them down now: you'll never raise
a conquering spear over your country, never
return to valleyed Argos; instead you'll die
by your brother's hand and kill the man who threw you out.
Such are my curses, and I call on Tartarus,*
father of loathsome darkness, to take you home.   1390
I call on these goddesses,† I call on Ares
who flung deadly hate between the two of you.
Go, with this in your ears, and on your way
announce to all the Theban people, together
with all your trusty comrades in arms, that such
are the blessings Oedipus bequeaths his sons!

CHORUS LEADER: Polynices, your coming hasn't brought me
    any joy; go back now, as quickly as you can.

POLYNICES: *oimoi*—my journey here, my bad luck!
    oimoi, my comrades! Such, then, is the end   1400
of our Argive invasion—unbearable!—
such an end, I can't breathe a word of it
to any of them, or lead them back again,
but I must go to meet this doom in silence.
My sisters, daughters of this man, you at least—
for you hear what he says, the implacable
curses of a father—by the gods, I beg you:
if these father's curses come to pass and you

---

* In Hesiod, the darkness beneath the earth; in mythology, the deepest part of Hades, here personified.
† The primeval goddesses in the grove, invoked in their capacity as Furies fulfilling a parental curse.

somehow make it home again, don't dishonor me
but lay me in the grave, perform the rites.* 1410
And the praise you've won for taking pains
in my father's behalf will bring you other
praises greater still, for services to me.

ANTIGONE: Polynices, please: listen to me now.

POLYNICES: What is it, dearest Antigone?† Go on, tell me.

ANTIGONE: Lead the army back to Argos! Don't delay,
don't destroy your city or yourself.

POLYNICES: Impossible! How could I take the lead
of my army once again, once I've shown fear?

ANTIGONE: But why, Brother,‡ why be angry once again? 1420
Why tear your city to the ground? For what?

POLYNICES: It's shameful to be an exile, shameful, too,
that I, the older, be laughed at by my brother.

ANTIGONE: Do you see, then, how you fulfill, to the letter,
his prophecy, his demand—that you kill each other?

POLYNICES: Yes, he wants it that way. Shouldn't we oblige?

ANTIGONE: *oimoi!* And who, who will dare to follow
once your father's prophecies are known?

POLYNICES: I won't announce what serves no purpose. A good
commander talks up his strengths, not weaknesses. 1430

ANTIGONE: So then, my brother, this is your decision?

POLYNICES: Yes, and don't hold me back. This is the path
I care to take, ill-fated and disastrous, thanks
to father there, and his Furies. (*addressing Ismene too*) But may Zeus
favor you both, if you do this for me.§ 1435
And now, let me go. Bid me goodbye, since you'll 1437
never see me alive again.   ANTIG.: I—I can't bear it!

POLYNICES: Don't mourn for me.   ANTIG.: And who would not mourn for
you, Brother, on your way to certain
death? 1440

---

* Polynices' request anticipates the action of Sophocles' earlier play, *Antigone.*

† That brother and sister address each other by name in lines 1414–15 is a sign of their intimacy and, as such, another of the links Sophocles has forged between this play and *Antigone* (see previous note). A similar if less intense affection is felt in line 1, where Oedipus addresses Antigone by name, and in line 357, where he does the same for Ismene. His loathing of his sons keeps him from uttering their names, even in the third person.

‡ Literally, "child," a term of endearment, repeated at 1431. See previous note.

§ Line 1436 is interpolated:
   when I'm dead, since you can't help me in life.

POLYNICES: I will die, if I must.   ANTIG.: No! No! Listen to me!

POLYNICES: Don't try! You must not!   ANTIG.: No, I can't go on, if I lose
    you.   POLY.: It's in the hands

of fate, to end like this, or not. And so I beg

the gods, may you two never come to any harm!

You don't deserve it. That, at least, is clear.

> *(Exit Polynices to the left. The Chorus now sing another*
> kommos, *two pairs of matching stanzas interrupted by spoken*
> *dialogue.)*

strophe 1

> New are these evils, new and newly revealed
> blows of disaster, our blind guest's doing
> or maybe it's Fate closing in.   1450
> For I cannot say that any
> decision of the gods is in vain.
> Time sees, he sees all things always,
> overturning some today,
> lifting others up again tomorrow.
> > *(A peal of thunder is heard.)*
> The sky thundered! O Zeus!

OEDIPUS: Children, children! Is someone at hand
    who could bring Theseus, the best of all men, here?

ANTIGONE: What is it, Father? Why summon him?

OEDIPUS: This winged thunderbolt of Zeus will bring me   1460
    soon to Hades.* Send for him, quickly!

> > *(More thunder is heard.)*

antistrophe 1

> CHORUS: Look, listen! That sound—I can't describe it—
> that peal of thunder crashing down, flung by Zeus!
> My hair stands on end,
> my heart cowers—lightning
> makes the heavens blaze again.
> What, then? Will he hurl his bolt?
> I am afraid, for never does it strike
> to no purpose, some dire result,   1470
> O mighty heavens, O Zeus!

OEDIPUS: Daughters of mine, the god-appointed end
    has come for me—there is no turning from it now.

---

* Oedipus is remembering the signs that would immediately precede his end. See lines 94–95.

ANTIGONE: How do you know? Why come to this conclusion?

OEDIPUS: I know it well. Someone must go at once
  to bring the lord of this land here to me!
      (Thunder again.)

strophe 2

CHORUS: *ea, ea!* There it is again, look: again
      that ear-piercing din, all around us!
      Gracious, O god, be gracious, if you come   1480
      bringing darkness to the land,
      our mother. May I find favor with you
      and not reap my reward in pain
      because I laid eyes on a man accursed!*
      Lord Zeus, to you I pray.

OEDIPUS: Is the man near, then? Will he find me, children,
  still alive, still in my right mind?

ANTIGONE: Why worry about that now?

OEDIPUS: Because I must fulfill the promise I made
  to pay him for the favor he showed me.   1490

antistrophe 2

CHORUS: *iō, iō* my son!†
      If you are still at the edge‡
      of the grove, sanctifying
      Poseidon's altar
      with the blood of oxen—come!
      Our guest believes he must repay
      you and your city and friends
      for kindness shown to him.
      Hasten, hurry, my lord!
          (Enter Theseus, with attendants.)

THESEUS: Why this commotion, once again, from all of you—   1500
      (to the Chorus) clearly from you, and also from our guest?
      Is a roaring bolt of Zeus the cause, or torrents
      of hail bursting upon you? For when a god
      storms like that, it may mean anything.

---

* Evidently the Chorus still fear divine retribution for helping a man who has his father's blood on his hands. See lines 220–36.

† Theseus, not yet arrived but on the way. "My son" ("child" in the Greek) is, again, a term of endearment. See note to line 1420.

‡ The Greek text of line 1492 is corrupt. I translate the second of the two possible emendations suggested by Lloyd-Jones and Wilson.

OEDIPUS: My lord, here you are, at last! And one of the gods
   has brought your journey here good fortune.
THESEUS: What is it, son of Laius? What new event?
OEDIPUS: My life's end looms, and I want to die true
   to my promises, to you and to your city.
THESEUS: What sign makes you sure the time has come? 1510
OEDIPUS: The gods, acting as their own heralds, tell me so,
   and keep their word: all the signs foretold are there.
THESEUS: What do you mean? How are they given?
OEDIPUS: In Zeus' constant thunder and the hail
   of bolts flashing from his invincible hand.
THESEUS: I believe it, for I've often seen you prophesy,
   none of it false. Tell me, then, what must be done.
OEDIPUS: I will lay out, son of Aegeus, what awaits
   this city of yours, safe from the wounds of time.
   In a moment, on my own, I'll lead you, without 1520
   a guide's touch, to the place where I must die.
   This you must not reveal to any man, ever—
   not where it's hidden, nor in what region it lies.
   So may it be a source of strength, mightier
   than hosts of shields and spears brought by allies.
   But what is sacred and not to be profaned
   by speech, you'll learn by going there, alone.
   I will not speak of it to any townsman here,
   nor to my own children, though I love them—
   no, keep it always to yourself, and when you've come 1530
   to life's end, reveal it to your heir alone,
   and he to his, and so on, forever.
   And in this way your city shall not be destroyed
   by men sprung from the dragon's teeth.* Countless cities,
   even those well-governed, easily turn violent.
   For the gods mark well, but late, when a man
   turns from them and swerves to madness.
   May you, son of Aegeus, never choose that path!
      Such are my lessons, taught to one who knows.
   But now—for I feel the prompting of a god— 1540
   let us go to the place, and hesitate no longer.

---

* The Thebans.

This way, children, follow me—look: now, strangely,
I've become your guide, as you were mine.
Come along, and do not touch me; no,
let me find, myself, the sacred tomb
where I'm fated to lie hidden in this land.
This way, here, come this way—this is the way
Hermes, escort of souls, and the goddess* below
are leading me. O light, darkness now! I saw you once
and now my body feels your touch   1550
for the last time. For now I go to hide my life's end
in Hades. So (*turning toward Theseus*), dearest of friends,
be blessed—you and this land and your attendants
and in your prosperity remember me
when I am dead, and so be fortunate forever!

> (*Oedipus exits to the right, followed by Theseus, Antigone, and
> Ismene. The Chorus now sing their fourth ode.*)

strophe

CHORUS: If it's right to honor in prayers
the goddess† unseen and you,
lord of those deep in night, Aidoneus,‡
Aidoneus, I beseech you: 1560
may our guest make his way free
of pain and fate's heavy grief, to the plains§
of the dead below, where all are hidden,
and their Stygian¶ home.
For though many sorrows
came to him undeservedly,
a just god may lift him up again.

antistrophe

O goddesses of earth!** O beast†† invincible
crouching at the gates

---

* Persephone.

† Persephone, queen of the dead.

‡ A lengthened form of the name Hades, husband of Persephone and lord of the dead.

§ The Underworld is imagined as a plain here and again at lines 1577 and 1681 (both times in the plural).

¶ A reference to the Underworld river Styx, which must be crossed on the way to the abode of the dead.

** Persephone and her mother, Demeter. The Furies may also be meant.

†† Cerberus, the three-headed hound who guards the entry to Hades.

crowded with guests* and baying   1570
from within the cavern,
Hades' untamable watchdog
as legend ever tells us:
let him slink—I pray you, son of Earth
and Tartarus†—out of the way
of our guest now passing
down to the plains of the dead;
on you I call, god of eternal sleep!

(Enter a messenger, from the right.)

MESSENGER: Citizens, the briefest way to tell the news
    would be for me to say that Oedipus is dead.   1580
    But what was done and what was said there
    wasn't brief, and can't be briefly told.
CHORUS LEADER: The poor man has perished, then?   MESS.: You may rest
                                                assured: he's left
                                              behind the life we
                                              know.

CHORUS LEADER: How? Blest by the gods, and without pain?
MESSENGER: That's the very thing that moves our wonder now.
    For when he left this place—as you no doubt recall,
    being there at the time—no friend guided his steps,
    but he himself showed all of us the way;
    and when he came to the sheer threshold rooted   1590
    to the ground in steps of bronze, he stopped,
    on one of many branching paths
    near the hollow basin where the ever-trusty
    pledges of Theseus and Perithous‡ are enshrined;
    midway between there and the Thorician§ stone,
    by the hollowed pear tree and the tomb of rock
    he sat down and undid his filthy clothes.
    And then, he called his daughters, bade them bring
    bath water and libations from a flowing stream.
    They went off to the hill nearby, sacred   1600

---

* The souls of the recently dead.

† Evidently Death is meant, though elsewhere his parentage is different.

‡ King of the Lapithae in Thessaly. He was the bosom friend of Theseus, with whom he ventured into the Underworld. The exact nature of the pact between the two friends is unknown.

§ Thoricus was a town and deme of Attica. The stone so called must have been familiar to the audience.

to Demeter,* and quickly they were back, bringing
all their father had commanded, and then they bathed
and arrayed him in the customary garb.†
And when he'd taken pleasure in the doing
of all this, and nothing he wanted was undone,
Zeus‡ thundered underground, and the maidens
shuddered when they heard it. They fell
at their father's knees, burst into wailing and wouldn't stop
beating their breasts, lamenting, and crying aloud.
And he, struck by the note of bitterness   1610
in their voices, gathered them in his arms and said:
"Children, as of today your father is no more.
For all that is mine has perished, and no longer
will you bear the pain of caring for me.
It was hard, I know, my daughters, but one
word alone puts all those toils to flight:
there is no love from any man greater than
the love you've had from me. And now you'll live
the rest of your lives bereft of me."
So they cried, all of them, sobbing, their arms   1620
around each other. And when they'd reached
the end of their laments, and wailed no more,
there was silence. Then suddenly someone's voice
called him, and the hair on all our heads
stood up in terror. The god called him
over and over again, from many places:
"You there, you, Oedipus! Why are we not yet
on our way? You're taking too much time!"
And when he knew that a god was calling him,
he asked for Theseus, lord of the land, to come.   1630
And when he came, Oedipus said to him: "Dear friend,
give my children the ancient pledge of your hand
and you, children, give him yours; swear, Theseus,
never to betray them, but always
wish them well and act in their behalf."
And Theseus, being noble, kept his own grief

* The Hill of Demeter, Guardian of Tender Shoots, lay about a quarter of a mile north of the hill that gave Colonus its name (see note to line 60).

† Preparing a corpse for burial included bathing it and clothing it in white.

‡ Hades, as the Zeus of the Underworld.

in check, and swore to all his friend desired.
When he'd done that, Oedipus at once
with blind hands grasped his daughters and said
"Children, now you must be brave and go   1640
nobly from this place, and not claim the right
to see what's not to be seen, or hear what we say.
Go as quickly as you can. Theseus alone
may stay, to learn what is done. He is master here."
Such were his words, heard by all of us together.
And now we left, in tears, escorting the girls.
And when we'd gone some distance away,
we turned for a moment, and saw from afar
that he had vanished utterly from sight,
and lord Theseus, alone, was holding his hands   1650
before his eyes, as if some terror
had appeared, that he couldn't bear to look at.
But then we saw him, briefly and without
a word, kiss his hand* to earth and heavenly
Olympus together, at the same time.
But by what fate Oedipus has perished, no
mortal man could say—none but Theseus.
For it was no burning thunderbolt of a god
that put an end to him, no whirlwind whipped up
that moment on the sea, but perhaps some god   1660
came to guide him, or the dark depth of earth,
home of the dead, opened to him in welcome.
The manner of his end was not full of groans, not
pained by illness, but worthy of wonder, if any
man's ever was. And if I seem to talk nonsense,
I won't persuade those who think I make no sense.

CHORUS LEADER: But where are the children, and their escorts?
MESSENGER: Not far off now. Those sounds of lamentation
    mean that they're on their way, and coming here.

> (*Enter Antigone and Ismene, from the right. A long lyrical
> dialogue—the third* kommos *of the play—now ensues between
> them and the Chorus.*)

---

* Theseus performs a *proskynesis*, literally a "kissing to." It could involve prostrating oneself to kiss the earth, but that seems unlikely here, since the gesture salutes the gods above and the gods below simultaneously.

strophe 1

    ANTIGONE: *aiai, pheu!* It falls to us—ours   1670
        to lament in every way the curse
        in our blood, our father's
        blood, for whom we've suffered
        much already, constant pain
        and now, at the end, we must tell what
        we saw and felt, beyond our understanding.
    CHORUS: What happened?   ANTIG.: We can only guess, my friends.
    CHORUS: Has he gone?   ANTIG.: Just as you would wish—
        for neither Ares
        nor the sea came against him   1680
        but the viewless plains* took him away,
        swept by a death invisible.
        But for us—deadly
        night has settled on our eyes,
        for how, wandering
        in a distant land or on the swell
        of the sea, shall we secure
        the hard-won means of life?
    ISMENE: I don't know. Down,
        down to death with my aged father   1690
        I wish cruel Hades would take me—
        miserable, for the life
        ahead is not worth living.
    CHORUS: O noble sisters, bear what comes from the gods
        nobly, and do not keep on
        whipping yourselves aflame. Till now
        your lives have been beyond reproach.

antistrophe 1

    ANTIGONE: There is such a thing, then, as pain
        that we miss, for what was never dear
        was dear after all, when I had him
        in my arms. O father, beloved father   1700
        cloaked in darkness under the earth,
        not even there will you ever
        be unloved by me and my sister here.

---

* See note to line 1562. The Underworld fields are almost personified here.

CHORUS: He did— ANTIG.: Did as he wished.

CHORUS: How so? ANTIG.: He died where he wanted to,
    on foreign ground. He has his bed
    in the welcome dark below, forever,
    and left behind a sorrow not unwept.
    For these eyes of mine, O father,
    shed tears of grief for you, nor do I know   1710
    how, in my sorrow, I shall get beyond
    the pangs I feel, they are so deep.
    ōmoi! You wanted
    to die on foreign ground, but in so doing
    died far away from me!

ISMENE: Unhappy! What fate
    awaits me and you, beloved sister,
    now, away from our father?*
    [...
    ...]

CHORUS: Well, since he brought his life   1720
    to its end happily, have done, dear children,
    with these laments, for there is no man
    whom grief may not easily overtake.

strophe 2

ANTIGONE: Back, dear sister, let's hurry back! ISM.: To do what?

ANTIGONE: A longing has come over me— ISM.: A longing for
                                    what?

ANTIGONE: To look upon his home in the earth.

ISMENE: Whose home? ANTIG.: Father's. O my sorrow!

ISMENE: But how can that be right for us?
    Don't you see? ANTIG.: Why scold me in this way?   1730

ISMENE: And there's this, too— ANTIG.: What? Still more?

ISMENE: He fell without a tomb, he lies utterly out of reach.

ANTIGONE: Take me there, and slay me, too!†
    [...]

ISMENE: *aiai!* My miserable fate!

---

* Ismene should speak five lines here, as at the corresponding place in the strophe. Two lines of Greek text are missing.

† The next line is missing. It would have been shared between the two speakers, as in 1747, the corresponding line of the antistrophe.

Where, where in the future, alone* and helpless,
will I live this life of hardship?

antistrophe 2

CHORUS: Beloved children, have no fear!   ANTIG.: But where am I to
flee?

CHORUS: Once before, too, you avoided—   ANTIG.: Avoided what?

CHORUS: —seeing your plight turn out badly.†   1740

ANTIGONE: I'm thinking—   CHOR.: What *is* it? What's on your
mind?

ANTIGONE: —how we shall make
our way home.   CHOR.: Don't even attempt it!

ANTIGONE: Things are hard for us here.   CHOR.: And were before,
too.

ANTIGONE: Helpless then, and worse off now.

CHORUS: A vast sea of sorrows is your heritage.

ANTIGONE: Yes, it is.   CHOR.: We, too, see it that way.

ANTIGONE: *pheu, pheu!* Where are we to go,
O Zeus? On to what last hope
is fate driving us now?   1750

(*Enter Theseus, with attendants, from the right. The* kommos
has ended. The rest of the play is in the anapestic meter.)

THESEUS: Cease your lament, children: those on whom
night beneath the earth lies as a blessing
must not be mourned: the gods will resent it.

ANTIGONE: O son of Aegeus, we implore you.

THESEUS: To obtain what wish, children?

ANTIGONE: We want to see
our father's tomb with our own eyes.

THESEUS: But it's not right for you to go there.

ANTIGONE: What do you mean, lord, ruler of Athens?

THESEUS: Children, he told me   1760
not to go near the place,
not to inform any mortal man
of the sacred tomb that holds him.
And he told me that if I did as he said
I would possess this land forever free of troubles.

---

* The phrasing suggests that in the missing line, Antigone had expressed again her determination to die
now, leaving Ismene alone.

† The Chorus are reminding them of their rescue by Theseus.

These promises, then, the divinity* heard me make
and Zeus' Oath,† who hears all things.
ANTIGONE: Yes, if this is what he wanted,
there is no more to say. But send us
to ancient Thebes, to see if somehow   1770
we can prevent the bloodshed
moving upon our brothers now.
THESEUS: This I will do, and I shall
do all I can to help you and to please
the one beneath the earth, who left us just now.
I must not be found wanting.
CHORUS: Cease, then, your weeping, and do not
rouse yet more lamentation, for
in all ways these things are as they must be.

    (Exit to the right Theseus, Antigone, Ismene, and the Chorus.)

---

* Theseus is referring to the mysterious "god" whose voice was heard summoning Oedipus to his end (lines 1623–29).

† Oath (Horkos) is a divine power, personified here and elsewhere as the servant of Zeus, the ultimate guarantor of the sanctity of oaths. Oath breakers were punished in the Underworld by the Furies.

EURIPIDES

As his name ("son of the Euripus") suggests, Euripides was said to have been born in 480, after Athens had been attacked by the Persians, and many Athenians fled across the Euripus strait onto the island of Euboea. After the Greeks defeated the Persians at the battle of Salamis, his family returned to Athens. He began to compete in the dramatic competitions in 455, and he eventually wrote ninety-two dramas, of which eighteen are extant. He died in 405, a year before Athens was defeated by Sparta and her allies in the Peloponnesian War.

Unfortunately, most of the other information that has come down to us about Euripides' life appears to have been reconstructed imaginatively from comedy and from his own poetry. His ancient biographers inferred that he had studied with philosophers such as Anaxagoras and Socrates because characters in his dramas occasionally allude to their theories. Because Aristophanes, in his comedy the *Frogs*, portrayed Euripides praying to newfangled gods, his biographers claimed that he had been torn to shreds by hunting dogs (a death suitable for atheists, modeled on the death of Pentheus in Euripides' own drama the *Bacchae*). Ancient speculation of this kind has led modern critics to suppose that in his dramas, Euripides sought to challenge traditional religion. But the gods in his dramas behave no differently from the gods in dramas by Aeschylus and Sophocles. Euripides does, however, manage to portray with great vividness the gods' cruelty and lust for honors. His characterizations of mortals also are more realistic than those of the other surviving dramatic poets. In the *Poetics*, Aristotle quotes Sophocles as having said, "I wrote about men as they ought to be, but Euripides wrote about them as they are."

In spite of what his ancient biographers said, in reality Euripides was highly regarded by audiences in his lifetime and for centuries afterward. Athenian prisoners in Sicily were said to have won their release because they could recite his poetry to their captors. Ten of his dramas were selected for reading in schools of rhetoric, as opposed to seven each for Aeschylus and Sophocles. The clarity of Euripides' style contributed to his popularity, and his exciting plots appear to have been the inspiration for the complex narrative structures for Greek-language plays in the fourth century B.C. and the adventure novels that were popular in later antiquity.

Introduction to Euripides' *Alcestis*

Athens in the second half of the fifth century B.C. was home to innovations of all kinds, and the *Alcestis* is one of its greatest innovations. It was staged by Euripides in the fourth position of the tragic tetralogy, the spot usually occupied by a bawdy, carnivalesque satyr play; yet it is a serious, emotionally intense drama that would not be out of place in one of the three earlier spots. Already at this early stage of his career—for the *Alcestis*, dating to 438 B.C., is probably his earliest surviving work—Euripides was bending the rules. It's hard to find the right term to characterize his hybrid creation. Some call it a tragedy, others a tragicomedy; still others highlight its strangeness by calling it "pro-satyric" ("taking the place of a satyr play"), a category to which no other surviving Greek drama belongs.

Euripides chose a minor myth and an obscure royal house as the focus of his theatrical experiment. Admetus of Pherae and his wife, Alcestis, were hardly names to conjure with for ancient Athenians; Homer, the great treasury of plots from which the tragedians drew, mentions them only once (as the parents of a Greek warrior named Eumelus), and neither Aeschylus nor Sophocles explored their strange story (though an early playwright named Phrynichus apparently produced an *Alcestis*, now lost). A drinking song known to Euripides' contemporaries spoke of the "story of Admetus" and the lesson it taught: be a friend to the brave and good, and avoid the company of cowards, for from cowards no benefit can be gained. That lesson is reassuringly straightforward, but Euripides' version of the story yields no such simple insights. Indeed, it's hard to say just who is good and who is cowardly in this most morally convoluted of surviving Greek dramas.

At the center of those convolutions stands the awful bargain that sets the plot in motion, the swap of one person's life for that of another. Such a swap might seem unexceptional in the world of folklore (the world from which the story of Alcestis originally sprang), but Euripides here takes a long, hard look at what it would actually entail. Anyone seeking to make this swap would have to ask the unaskable; friends and family would, to that person, become mere pawns, tokens to be exchanged in the ultimate zero-sum game. Euripides refers only briefly, but pointedly, to the exhaustive search Admetus went through to find a surrogate, when even his father and mother declined his terrible request. Miraculously, his wife, the only member of his family bound to him by marital rather than blood ties, finally agreed to take his place, and thus our story begins.

Unlike earlier tragedians, Euripides was deeply interested in the marital bond. Most Greeks of his day looked upon marriage as a practical institution, a way to secure a family's property or elevate its political position and, of course, produce heirs. But Euripides, in this play as well as in the *Medea, Hippolytus, Helen,* and other plays no longer extant, dealt with marriage (and other kinds of pair-bonding) in a way more familiar to modern readers, examining the complexities of intimacy and interdependence and, especially, the pain arising from betrayal. Moreover, Euripides took women seriously as partners in marriage, whose lives were in effect held hostage to their husbands, and his contemporary, the comic playwright Aristophanes, mocked him for it; such themes were felt to be beneath the high dignity of tragic drama. But it is this very shift in elevation, this interest in a domestic and personal realm far removed from the gods of Olympus, that made Euripidean theater immensely popular in its own time and enduringly compelling in ours.

Those gods are still present in the *Alcestis*, of course, but their distance from the stage action has increased as compared with the plays of Aeschylus and Sophocles. Here Euripides makes use of a structure he would often use elsewhere, in which an Olympian deity delivers a prologue speech, setting the scene and forecasting what is about to happen, but then departs the stage. Apollo plays this framing role in the *Alcestis*, in a scene delightfully enlivened by a snappy exchange with the allegorical figure of Death; but once action commences on the human plane, Apollo is never seen again, and Euripides offers us few clues as to what Apollo, or his father, Zeus, are contriving. Instead it is Heracles, seen here in human form before his transformation into a god, who takes part in events and brings about a resolution of the crisis. This portrayal of Heracles, as a deeply carnal being interested in food, wine, and sex, might be seen as Euripides' playful nod to the bawdy conventions of the satyr play—conventions he had otherwise demolished by putting on *Alcestis* in the fourth production slot.

Following this prologue scene, Euripides takes us into the bedroom of the royal palace of Pherae, where Alcestis, surrounded by husband, children, and worshipful servants, is breathing her last. The long scene shared between Alcestis and Admetus is unique in classical Greek theater, and not only because it depicts the only unambiguous onstage death in the surviving plays (in the *Hippolytus*, the title character could be alive, barely, at the close, and Sophocles' Ajax might well have gone out of sight to commit suicide in the play named for him). The complexities of the couple's unique situation are left implicit yet handled with great psychological insight, another hallmark of Euripidean technique. Alcestis bursts into lyric song as she enters, addressing the sun and sky; Admetus lamely tries to engage with her while speaking in more pedestrian iambic trimeters. Then Alcestis descends into trimeters, too, and addresses her husband in coldly pragmatic tones. Her aloofness contrasts sharply with his fervent, almost desperate efforts to hold on to her in her last moments, and with the extravagance of his vows of fidelity to her memory—vows that attest to the deep guilt he must feel at having requisitioned her death.

How is Admetus to be judged? Many of the interpretive problems surrounding the play hinge on this crucial question. Euripides allows us to see Admetus first through Apollo's eyes, as a pious man whose virtues merit rescue from death, but later through the eyes of Pheres, his father, to whom he appears a selfish coward and wife-killer. The disparity is not easy to resolve. The verbal battle between Admetus and Pheres is one of Euripides' masterpieces: a scorching confrontation between two opposed perspectives, partaking of both the ethical complexities of a philosophic dialogue and the visceral energy of all-out intergenerational war. In few other literary works—Shakespeare's *King Lear* is another—have the competing claims of the old and the young, and the hatreds that can fester between father and son, been explored with such merciless candor. For the audience, Admetus' limitations, carefully kept out of view in his farewell to Alcestis and in the choral ode that follows, have become suddenly, and brutally, exposed, even if the man who exposes them, Pheres, is himself deeply flawed (indeed, Euripides seems to have constructed this scene partly to show that the apple hasn't fallen far from the tree).

We know, from Apollo's forecast, that redemption is coming for Admetus, and Euripides brings his *xenia* to the fore to allow him to earn that redemption. *Xenia* is a strict social code that, for the Greeks, mandated the kind treatment of strangers and travelers. Admetus has already shown this social virtue in his humane treatment of his "slave" Apollo, for which he was rewarded by the chance to swap lives. Now *xenia* prompts Admetus to insist on hosting Heracles and enabling his drunken revel, even while he manages his household's rites of mourning over Alcestis. For this he will be rewarded a second time, more richly than before, when Heracles negates the swap and cheats Death of his prey.

Alcestis did not attract much attention in the ancient world. Later Greco-Roman writers largely ignored it, even those, such as Ovid and Seneca, who adapted other Euripidean stories to their own poetic purposes. Yet this short, untragic, anomalous play has generated a vast array of modern interpretations and adaptations. Critics disagree widely about its meanings, though all are impressed by its radical novelty. It is produced often for the modern stage, often to great acclaim, and has inspired operas by Handel and Gluck, a ballet by Martha Graham, and T. S. Eliot's play *The Cocktail Party*, among other works. Even Shakespeare appears to have been influenced by it, judging by how *The Winter's Tale*, with its closing restoration of a wife thought dead, parallels the return of Alcestis to Admetus at the end of Euripides' play. Both playwrights, moreover, leave their heroines eerily silent as the curtain descends. But perhaps the apparent parallel is only the result of the impossibility of expressing, in both cases, all that the woman in question would have wanted to say.

ALCESTIS

Translated by Rachel Kitzinger

The translation follows the text in *Euripides: "Alcestis,"* edited by L.P.E. Parker (Oxford: Oxford University Press, 2007). I have also consulted her commentary.

CAST OF CHARACTERS (IN ORDER OF APPEARANCE)

APOLLO

DEATH

CHORUS of men of Pherae who are friends of King Admetus

SLAVE WOMAN serving Alcestis

ADMETUS, king of Pherae; son of Pheres

ALCESTIS, Admetus' wife

CHILDREN of Admetus and Alcestis, son and (nonspeaking) daughter

HERACLES, son of Zeus and the mortal woman Alcmene

PHERES, father of Admetus

ATTENDANT, slave assigned to look after Heracles

Setting: The play takes place in front of the royal house of Admetus and Alcestis in Pherae, in Thessaly. The exit from the stage to the left leads to the north edges of Pherae and beyond to Thrace. This direction is also associated in the play with the trip to the Underworld. The right exit leads to the rest of the town and places to the south.

(*Apollo enters from the* skēnē, *Admetus' house. He carries a bow and arrows.*)

APOLLO: House of Admetus! Here I patiently agreed
  to sit at table with hired hands, though I'm
  a god! Zeus was to blame: he killed my son
  Asclepius by striking him with lightning.*
  I was enraged and killed the Cyclopes,
  who forge my father's bolts of fire. So he
  forced me to serve a mortal, in payment
  for their death. I came here and worked
  as herdsman for my host. I've protected his house
  until now: since I, a god, found that Admetus,   10
  son of Pheres, was a pious man, I saved him
  from death. I tricked the Fates,† to let him
  escape impending doom, if he could find
  someone to take his place among the dead.
  He went to all those he held dear and put them
  to the test—his aging father, the mother who bore him.
  He found that none but his wife was willing
  to die for him, to see the light no more.
  And now in this house he holds her up,
  supports her as she breathes her last.   20
  This is the day allotted for her death.‡

---

* Apollo's son Asclepius was a healer; Zeus killed him for violating divine law by restoring the dead to life.

† According to the story as told by Aeschylus in his play *Eumenides*, Apollo made the Fates drunk to extract from them the deal he describes here.

‡ In the play, the length of time that has elapsed between the deal that Apollo struck with the Furies and this day, when Alcestis must die, is not specified, but it is clear we should imagine that it is at least a year.

She will leave her life, but I leave
this dear house, to avoid the pollution*
I'd meet here. Already I see Death nearby.
He who consecrates the dead comes to lead her
down to the house of Hades. He's timed his coming
with care, to match the day she's due to die.

> (Death enters from the left, the direction of the Underworld,
> carrying a sword; he is chanting in anapests.)†

DEATH: (chanting) a, a!
Why are *you* here at the door, Phoebus? ‡
What are you doing hanging about?   30
Are you plotting another crime?
Usurping the rights of the gods below?
Wasn't it enough that you put a stop
to Admetus' death by tripping up the Fates
with your deceitful trick? Are you on guard again,
with bow in hand, to protect Pelias' child?§
She agreed to die in place of her husband.

APOLLO: Don't worry. I'm fair, my words trustworthy.

DEATH: Why the bow, then, if your intent is just?

APOLLO: It's my habit. I always carry it.   40

DEATH: It's your "habit" to help this house unjustly!

APOLLO: I feel sorry for the misfortune of a friend.

DEATH: And so you'll keep a second body from me?

APOLLO: But I didn't force the first away from you.

> (Death points to the house of Admetus.)

DEATH: Why then is *he* up here and not down there?

APOLLO: He gave his wife instead, the one you've come for.

DEATH: And I *will* take her down below the earth.

APOLLO: Go on, take her. I doubt I could persuade you—

DEATH: (sarcastically)—to kill the one I must? I have my orders.

---

* Gods do not permit themselves to come into contact with the dead or dying, who are considered unclean. Artemis, for example, also says she must leave before Hippolytus dies (*Hippolytus*, lines 1437–38).

† Anapests in tragedy can be chanted or sung. The rhythm (in its pure form, two short syllables followed by one long syllable) is associated with marching and is frequently used for the entrance of the Chorus.

‡ Phoebus is an epithet of Apollo; it is often used separately, as another name for the god.

§ Alcestis. Pelias, her father, usurped the throne of Iolcus from Jason and sent him to fetch the Golden Fleece from Colchis on the Black Sea, expecting that he would not return. But Jason was saved by Medea, the daughter of the king of Colchis, who returned to Iolcus with him. There she persuaded Pelias' daughters to kill their father (see Euripides' *Medea*). Alcestis, at least according to some versions of the story, did not participate in the killing of her father.

APOLLO: Not that, no. Can I ask you to delay her death? 50

DEATH: I see now what you mean, what you're after.

APOLLO: Is it possible for Alcestis to reach old age?

DEATH: No, it's not. Like you, I enjoy my rights.

APOLLO: You wouldn't get more than one life, then or now.

DEATH: When the young die my prestige grows.

APOLLO: But she'll be buried with riches if she dies in old age.

DEATH: Phoebus, you lay down a law that privileges the wealthy.

APOLLO: What?! Are you actually able to think?

DEATH: Those with means could buy a later death.

APOLLO: You're not inclined, then, to do me this favor? 60

DEATH: No, I'm not. You know my ways.

APOLLO: I do: hateful to mortals and hated by gods.

DEATH: You can't have *everything* you're not entitled to.

APOLLO: You'll give in, though, despite your savagery.
A man will come to the house of Pheres,
sent by Eurystheus to stormy Thrace
to bring back horses and a chariot.*
This man will be a guest in Admetus' house,
and he will force this woman from you.
I'll give you no thanks, only hatred, 70
when you do then what I ask for now.

DEATH: Say all you want, it'll get you nothing.
The woman will go now to the house of Hades.
I begin the rites as I approach her with my sword.
The person whose hair this sword sanctifies†
becomes an offering to the gods of the dead.

(*Death exits into the house; Apollo is raised up and off the stage
by the* mēchanē. *The Chorus of male citizens of Pherae enter
from the right, the direction of the town.*)

CHORUS: (*chanting; the first two lines are chanted by one section of the Chorus,
another section answers*)‡—Why this quiet outside the house?

---

* Apollo, the god of prophecy, foresees the arrival of Heracles. Heracles will arrive in the course of performing one of his labors for King Eurystheus: to bring back from Thrace the savage horses of Diomedes. His labors are payment for killing his family in a fit of madness sent by Hera, Zeus' wife.

† The priest performing a sacrificial ritual always begins with cutting off a lock of the victim's hair.

‡ Chanted lines are in an anapestic rhythm, often used for the entrance and exit of the Chorus. Division of the anapestic units into line lengths differs in different editions. Line numbers, however, follow standard numbering established in an early edition of the play and therefore don't always correspond to the actual number of lines in any particular edition.

Why has the house of Admetus fallen silent?
—There's no friend about
to say if we should mourn 80
the queen's death or if she's still alive.
Does Alcestis, daughter of Pelias, still see
the light of day? To us and to all
she seems the best of wives
to her husband.

strophe

CHORUS: (*singing*)* Does anyone hear moaning, or the beating
of breasts? Is there groaning in the house
that tells us it's over?
Not one slave
attends the doors. 90
Oh, Paian,† appear, we pray,
in this wave of disaster.

CHORUS: (*chanting; voices are again divided into two sections that respond to
each other*)—They wouldn't be silent if she were dead.
—At least it's certain the body hasn't left the house yet.‡
—How do you know? I'm not so sure. What gives you hope?
—How could Admetus have performed the burial
of his good wife all on his own?§

antistrophe

CHORUS: I see before the doors
no bowl of cleansing water, the custom
before the doors of the dead. 100
No lock of hair hangs
on the door, a sign we expect
of grief for the dead; no sound
of the beating of women's hands.

---

* After the Chorus's initial chanted anapests, they alternate anapests with four stanzas sung in unison. The line numbers in the songs of the Chorus also do not always correspond to the actual number of lines in this translation. Editors vary in how they divide lines into metrical units; however, standard line numbers are retained.

† Paian is the name given to Apollo in his role as healer. A "paean" is a hymn sung to invoke the healing god.

‡ This line has been emended to make it fit the metrical pattern. There are several emendations in the chanted sections, lines 93–97 and 105–11.

§ Traditionally a burial involves a procession to the tomb with mourners; a burial with only one person in attendance is unthinkable.

CHORUS: (*chanting*) —And yet this is the very day—
    —What are you saying?
    —when she must go beneath the earth.
    —You touch me, touch my heart.
    —When trouble plagues a noble house,
    anyone who's decent through and through   110
    must feel grief.

strophe

CHORUS: (*singing*) No voyage you could make—
    not to Lycia
    nor the dry sands where Ammon
    has his seat*—
    would save the life
    of this poor woman.
    Relentlessly her death draws near.
    I know no longer which god,
    which altar set for sacrifice I should approach.   120

antistrophe

    Only if Phoebus' son†
    still saw the light of day
    could she have come back,
    have left behind the gates of Hades,
    the dark places where Hades sits.
    He made the dead rise up,
    until a bolt of thunder-fire
    hurled by Zeus struck him.
    So now what hope of life can I expect?   130
CHORUS: (*chanting*) Already every rite's been tried
    by the royal pair and for the royal pair;
    the altars of every god
    run with the blood of sacrifice.
    There is no cure for this disaster.
        (*A slave woman enters from the house.*)
CHORUS: But look, here comes a slave from the house.

---

* The oracles in Lycia (an area on the southern coast of what is now Turkey) and northern Africa are the most remote the Chorus can think of. Ammon is the hellenized god Zeus Ammon, who corresponds to the Egyptian god Amon-Ra; his oracle was located in ancient Libya, at a site that is now on the Egyptian side of the border between Egypt and Libya.

† Asclepius. See note to line 4.

Her face is wet with tears. What news will I hear?
(*to the slave*) If something has happened to your master,
I understand your grief, but I'd like to know
if the lady is still alive, or has she died?   140
SLAVE WOMAN: You could say of her she's living *and* she's dead.
CHORUS: How could one person both die and live?
SLAVE WOMAN: She's collapsed and breathes her last breath.
CHORUS: Poor Admetus, to be who you are and lose such a wife!
SLAVE WOMAN: He doesn't know what he's losing until she's lost.
CHORUS: There's no more hope she can be saved?
SLAVE WOMAN: The fated day moves on; it won't be stopped.
CHORUS: So someone is making the preparations due her?
SLAVE: All is ready for him to adorn her dead body.
CHORUS: Let her know she's glorious in her death,   150
    the best wife of all there are under the sun.
SLAVE WOMAN: Who could deny she's the best? How could they?
    What name exists for a woman who surpasses her?
    How could any woman show more clearly
    she honors her husband? She's agreed to die for him!
    This much the whole city knows.
    But what she did inside the house will amaze you.
    When she knew the appointed day had come
    she washed her pale body in river-water
    and took clothing and jewelry from a cedar chest.   160
    She put them on and made herself beautiful.*
    And then she prayed at the altar of Hestia:†
    "Lady, now I go beneath the earth and so
    I kneel to you for the last time and ask:
    watch over my orphan children.‡ Find my son
    a loving wife, my daughter a noble husband.
    May they not, like me, their mother,
    die an early death. Let them prosper
    in their fatherland, live a long and happy life."
    She went to every altar in Admetus' house;   170

---

* In normal circumstances, women of the household would prepare a body for burial. Here Alcestis prepares her body herself, since she knows she is about to die.

† Hestia is the goddess of the hearth; she is worshipped as protector of the household.

‡ A child was considered orphaned if he or she lost one parent.

she placed on each a garland of myrtle,*
leaves she'd cut from the tree, and prayed.
She didn't weep. She didn't groan. The coming
of disaster made no change in the luster of her skin.
But then, in the bedroom, she fell on the bed
and burst into tears. And then she said:
"Oh, bed, farewell. Here I gave my husband
my virginity, and now I die for him.
I do not hate you: you have ruined me,
only me. I shrank from failing you   180
and him, my husband, and so I die. Another
will own you, luckier, perhaps, than me, but not
as wise." She kisses the bed, and all the covers
are damp with the tears that flow from her eyes.
When she exhausts her wealth of tears,
she stumbles weakly from the bed and starts to go,
but, many times, as she leaves the room, she turns
and hurls herself back again upon the bed.
Her children grasp their mother's dress
and weep. She takes them both in her arms and gives,   190
first one and then the other, a dying kiss.

All the household slaves wept out of pity
for their mistress. She reached out to each
with her right hand. Not one was too base
for her to address and hear an answer in return.
Such is the trouble in Admetus' house.
If he'd died, he'd be gone. But he lives,
and the pain he has he will never forget.
CHORUS: I'm sure he laments this misfortune,
to lose, as he must, his noble wife?   200
SLAVE WOMAN: He holds his dear wife in his arms and weeps.
He begs her not to abandon him; he seeks
what cannot be. Her body's wasted with illness,
she's fading and limp, a pitiful weight in his arms.
Still her breath is short and shallow,
and she wants to see the light of the sun

---

* Myrtle was used in a variety of ritual contexts, though it is particularly associated with Aphrodite.

once more—for the last time, she knows.*
I'll go now and announce you're here.
Not everyone wishes his rulers well   210
and stands kindly by them in their trouble.
But you are old supporters of my master.

(*The slave woman exits into the house. The Chorus sing and
dance as they appeal to the gods on Alcestis' behalf.*)†

strophe

CHORUS: Oh, Zeus, is there a way out?
          What release can there be
          from the troubles that surround our rulers?
          aiai
          Is relief near or should I cut a lock of hair
          and cloak myself now
          in a dark robe of mourning?
          It's all too clear, friends, but nevertheless
          let us pray to the gods. Their power
          is very great.   220
          Lord Paian,‡
          discover for Admetus some way out of his troubles.
          Deliver it, please deliver. You did
          before, so be now
          a savior from death.
          Put a stop to murderous Hades.

antistrophe

          papai [. . .]§
          Oh, son of Pheres, what you've suffered
          with the loss of your wife!
          aiai
          It calls for the sword
          or a noose raised high

---

* Line 208 has been omitted as an interpolation.

† The text of this song is problematic in several places. Some editors divide the Chorus into two groups because of the address to "friends" at line 218, which implies that one part of the Chorus is singing to the other. I prefer to think of the Chorus members addressing each other as a whole as "friends" and singing in unison.

‡ See note to line 91.

§ Some words have been lost from the text here.

or more, even, than that.
Your dear wife—no, your dearest wife,   230
you will see die
this day.
But look, look!
She comes from the house, and her husband, too.
Cry out, land of Pheres,
lament this best of wives,
as she wastes away with the sickness
that takes her down to Hades.

(*chanting*) I'll never say that marriage brings pleasure
more than pain. I have other proof
and now I see the suffering of the king
who's lost this woman, this best of wives.
He'll live hereafter   240
a life that's not a life.

> (*Alcestis and Admetus, with their son and daughter, enter from
> the house; Alcestis is carried on a bier; she sings in an exchange
> with Admetus, who is speaking.*)

ALCESTIS: Sun and light of the day
and sky that swirls
with scudding clouds!
ADMETUS: The sun, yes—it sees the two of us, our suffering,
but we've done nothing to the gods to warrant your death.
    ALCESTIS: Earth! Rooftops!
    Bridal chambers
    of my native Iolcus!*

> (*As Admetus speaks, slaves raise Alcestis to her feet and hold her
> up.*)

ADMETUS: Rise up, poor woman. Don't abandon me.   250
Beg the ruling gods to show you pity.
    ALCESTIS: I see two oars,† I see the boat
    on the lake. And the ferryman
    holds in his hand a pole: Charon

---

* Iolcus is a town in Thessaly near Pherae, at the head of the Gulf of Pagasae. It is Alcestis' birthplace.
† Alcestis sees the boat that carries the dead across the rivers of the Underworld. The ferryman is
Charon, whose name is mentioned here for the first time in extant Greek literature.

calls me, "Why do you delay?
Hurry, you're holding me back." Do you hear?
In his haste he urges me on.

ADMETUS: *oimoi!* This is a bitter tale you tell,
this voyage. How we suffer, unlucky one!

ALCESTIS: He's taking me, someone takes me, he takes me—
don't you see?—to the house of the dead.   260
Under dark brows dark eyes
stare: winged Hades!
What will you do? Let me go! Fear fills me:
what road, what journey lies ahead?

ADMETUS: A journey your friends pity, but most of all, I
and the children pity. Together we feel this grief.

ALCESTIS: Let me go, let me go now.
Lay me down, my legs lose their strength.
Hades is here,
dark night is covering
my eyes.
Children, children,   270
you have a mother
no more. May you live
and feel joy, my children.

ADMETUS:* *oimoi!* To hear her words
hurts me more than any death.
By the gods, don't dare abandon me!
For the children's sake, whom you will orphan,
get up, be strong!
If you die, I couldn't go on.
It's in your power whether we live or not.
We revere your love.

ALCESTIS: Admetus, you see the state I'm in.   280
Before I die, I want to tell you my wishes.
I placed you above all; I arranged for you
to live your life in exchange for mine.
I'm dying for you, although I had the option
not to die, to marry any man I wanted
in Thessaly and live richly in a king's house.

---

* Before this moment, Admetus has been speaking, while Alcestis sings. Now he chants in an anapestic rhythm, something between speech and song, and Alcestis then speaks.

I wasn't willing to live without you by my side,
with orphaned children. I did not spare
my youth, although I felt joy in it.
Your father, though, and your mother failed you.   290
The chance was there for them to die well,
nobly to save their child and win fame
in death. You're their only child; they had
no hope, with you dead, of having another.
And you and I would've lived out our lives,
and you would not be grieving now, without a wife,
raising orphaned children. But this is what
a god has brought about, that it be like this.
So be it, but remember what you owe me.
I won't ask you for a favor equal to mine—   300
there's nothing as valuable as a life—
but you'll agree it's fair. When you think straight,
you love these children no less than I.
Have the strength to raise them as masters of the house.
Don't marry again and give them a stepmother.
She'll be a worse woman than I, and out of envy
she'll do violence to your children and mine.
Do not do this, I beg of you.
A stepmother comes as an enemy to the children
of a previous wife; she's no kinder than a snake.   310
A male child has his father to protect him.*
(*addressing her daughter*) But how will *you*, child, safely reach the age
of marriage, when some other woman's your father's wife?
I fear, just as you're ready to marry, she'd start
a shameful rumor about you and ruin your chances.
Your mother won't be there when you marry,
won't give you courage when you're giving birth,
when a mother's kindness surpasses all, my child.
I have to die; I won't die tomorrow
or the next day but now, this moment,   320
they'll say that I am among the dead.
Goodbye! Be happy! And you, husband,
can boast you had the best of wives, and you,
my children, say you had the best of mothers.

---

* Line 312 has been omitted. It is identical to line 195.

CHORUS: Be certain he'll do this, if he has any sense.
    I don't hesitate to speak on his behalf.
ADMETUS: It will be as you ask. It will. Don't worry.
    You were my wife while you lived, and you alone
    will have that name even when you're dead.   330
    No bride in Thessaly will take your place,
    or call me husband: no woman is so well-born,
    her beauty so extraordinary as that.
    I have enough children. I pray to the gods
    that they provide for me as you will not.
    My grief for you will endure not just a year
    but for as long, dear wife, as I have life.
    And for *so* long I'll hate the woman who bore me
    and loathe my father, my kin in word but not
    in deed. *You* gave up all that's dearest to save   340
    my life; so it's up to *me* now, isn't it,
    to grieve the loss of my wife, a wife like you?
    I'll hold no parties, invite no dinner guests;
    there'll be no flowers or music, which used to fill
    my house. I'll never pluck the lyre's strings,
    nor raise my spirits by singing to the Libyan pipe.*
    For you have taken from me all joy in life.
    A sculptor's skillful hand will make your likeness,
    a statue that will stretch out on my bed.
    I'll fall beside it and take it in my arms.   350
    I'll call it by your name and think I hold
    my wife in my embrace, although I don't:
    a cold comfort, I know, but nonetheless
    it will lighten the weight that will be my life.
    Maybe you'll visit me in a dream, to delight me.
    It's sweet to see a dear one even in sleep,
    even for a moment. If I'd the voice and songs
    of Orpheus, to entrance Persephone or her husband†
    and win you back, I'd have gone to Hades.

---

* The description of a pipe as Libyan is unique to Euripides; it may be connected to the use of lotus wood to make pipes, since lotus grew abundantly in Libya and the word for pipe here is "lotus," also an unusual usage.

† Admetus refers here to the story of Orpheus and Eurydice. Orpheus was able to retrieve Eurydice from the Underworld through the power of his music, which bewitched even Persephone and Hades, the deities who ruled the dead.

Neither Pluto's hound* nor ferryman Charon   360
would've stopped me before I'd brought you
back into the light. But no. So wait for me;
I'll come when I'm dead. Prepare a house
to share with me. I'll order these children
to lay me out in the same cedar coffin,
with my side touching yours. I wish even
in death not to be apart from you,
for you alone have proved faithful to me.

CHORUS: I'll help you bear the grief and pain for her,
as a friend does for a friend. She's earned that right.   370

ALCESTIS: Oh, children, you have heard it yourselves:
your father's said he'll never take another
wife, to dishonor me and rule over you.

ADMETUS: This I say now and this I'll do.

ALCESTIS: With that promise, take from my hand the children.

ADMETUS: I take them, a dear gift from a hand as dear.

ALCESTIS: Now *you* are mother to these children in my place.

ADMETUS: Yes, I must be, since they've lost you.

ALCESTIS: Oh, children, I should live, but now I go below.

ADMETUS: *oimoi*, what will I do without you?   380

ALCESTIS: Time will ease your pain; the dead are nothing.

ADMETUS: Take me with you, take me below, I pray.

ALCESTIS: My death in place of yours is death enough.

ADMETUS: Oh, destiny, what a wife you take from me!

ALCESTIS: Yes, darkness fills my eyes now.

ADMETUS: I'm ruined if you'll really leave me.

ALCESTIS: You could say of me now I exist no more.

ADMETUS: Lift up your face: don't leave your children!

ALCESTIS: I don't do so willingly. Farewell, children.

ADM.: Look at them, look!   ALC.: I am no more.   390

ADM.: What are you doing? Leaving?   ALC.: Farewell.   ADM.: I'm ruined.

CHORUS: She's gone. The wife of Admetus is no more.

(*Alcestis' son falls on his knees at his mother's side and sings.*)

CHILD: *iō*, what's happened to me? My mamma
has gone below. She's here no more
in the sunlight, Father;

---

* The dog Cerberus. Pluto is another name for the god Hades.

her leaving has orphaned me.
Look, look at her eyes, her arms lifeless by her side.
Listen, listen, Mother!
I beg you.   400
It's me, Mother; I'm calling you.
It's me, your little one,
who falls on you with kisses.

ADMETUS: She neither sees nor hears. And so we're struck,
you two and I, by heavy misfortune.

CHILD: I'm young, Father, to be without
my mother, alone on life's journey.
What horrible things I've suffered,
and you also, my sister.   410
Oh, Father, Father,*
your marriage brought you nothing,
nothing—not even a companion
in old age. She died before you.
With you gone, Mother,
the house lies in ruins.

CHORUS: Admetus, you must endure your misfortune.
You're not the first, and won't be the last,
to lose a wife. You must learn this lesson:
all of us owe the debt of our death.

ADMETUS: I know that, and I've long known of this disaster   420
and felt distress. It hasn't come at me suddenly.
I'll prepare the body now for burial.
(*to Chorus*) You, stay here,
and while you wait, answer the god below
by singing a paean. Make no libation.†
To all Thessalians over whom I rule
I say: Share my grief for this woman.
Cut your hair and wear black robes.
You who drive yoked teams of horses or bridle

---

* The text of this line is corrupt.

† The text is slightly emended here. Admetus' request to the Chorus to sing a paean and not make a libation is unusual. Normally a paean is performed with a libation as a request for help in times of danger or in thanksgiving, when danger is averted. Parker (p. 140) suggests that Admetus asks for a paean in defiance of death. Perhaps the absence of a libation marks the unusual use of the paean here, or it may reflect the fact that the god of the dead never receives libations.

a single mount, cut short the hair of their manes.
Let no pipe* sound in the city, let no one   430
pluck a lyre for a full twelve months.
I'll never bury a dearer corpse than this one,
never a woman who's treated me better. She deserves
my reverence: she alone gave her life for mine.
              (Admetus and the children go into the house.)

strophe

> CHORUS: Oh, daughter of Pelias,
>   may you find a happy home
>   in the sunless house of Hades!
>   Let Hades, the dark-haired god, know
>   and let the old man know—
>   the one who sits at the tiller   440
>   and ferries the dead:†
>   this is the best woman, the very best,
>   he's carried across Acheron
>   in his two-oared pinewood boat.

antistrophe

> The servants of the Muses will sing
> your glory again and again
> to the music of the seven-stringed lyre
> and in songs no lyre joins in.
> They'll sing in Sparta when the seasons circle
> to the month of Carnea‡
> and the moon hangs high all night;   450
> they'll sing in brilliant, blooming Athens.
> Such is the story your death has left
> for the singers of songs.

strophe

> Would it were in my power
> to send you into the light
> from the house of Hades,

---

* The instrument translated here as "pipe" is an *aulos*. It was a double-reed wind instrument; there is no modern musical instrument exactly like it, but we speculate that the oboe is the closest in sound to it. The *aulos* is the instrument that accompanied the choral songs in tragedy.

† Charon. The river Acheron is one of the rivers of the Underworld.

‡ The month of Carnea was the time of a great musical festival in Sparta.

away from the streams of Cocytus,*
by plying an oar in the world below.
You alone—you, dear woman—   460
had the heart to free your husband
from Hades with your own life.
May the earth fall lightly
upon you, lady.
And if your husband should take another wife,
he'd earn your children's hatred and mine.

antistrophe

His mother and his aging father
would not give their bodies
to the earth instead of their child;
[…]†
didn't have the heart to save the life they gave.
Such white-haired fools!   470
But you in the bloom of your youth
die in a young man's place and are gone.
Would I, too, could find
the company of such a loving wife!
But in life that's rare.
In our time together she'd give me no pain.

> (*Heracles enters from the right, the direction of the town. He
> wears a cloak made of a lion's skin and carries a club.*)

HERACLES: Friends, natives of this land of Pheres,
　　will I find Admetus in his house?
CHORUS: The son of Pheres is at home, Heracles,
　　but tell us what brings you to Thessaly?
　　What do you need in the city of Pheres?   480
HERACLES: I'm performing a task for Eurystheus of Tiryns.‡
CHORUS: Where are you headed? How far must you go?
HERACLES: To Thrace, to get Diomedes' chariot and horses.§

---

* The Cocytus is another river in the Underworld. Its name is derived from the word for "lament."

† A line is missing here; we know this because the antistrophe must correspond in meter to the strophe, where there is an additional line.

‡ Eurystheus was Heracles' cousin and rival. Hera championed him in opposition to Zeus' championing Heracles. The imposition of the labors, whose immediate cause is Heracles' murder of his own family, is also part of this divine and human rivalry.

§ Diomedes, king of Thrace, was the son of Ares and Cyrene. Both he and his horses were known for their viciousness.

CHORUS: How can you? Don't you know the kind of host he is?

HERACLES: No, I've never been there, to Bistonia.*

CHORUS: You can't master his horses without a fight.

HERACLES: But I can't say "no" to these labors, either.

CHORUS: You'll come back a killer or stay there a corpse.

HERACLES: This wouldn't be the first contest I've entered!

CHORUS: If you beat Diomedes, what else must you do? 490

HERACLES: I'll bring the horses to the king of Tiryns.

CHORUS: It won't be easy to get a bit in those jaws!

HERACLES: I'll do it, unless their muzzles breathe fire.

CHORUS: No, their agile jaws tear men to bits.

HERACLES: That's food for wild beasts, not horses!

CHORUS: You'll see: their mangers stream with blood.

HERACLES: The man who raised them—who's his father?

CHORUS: Ares. He himself is lord of the golden shield.†

HERACLES: Ah, *that's* my destiny, the task you speak of:

it's an endless, rough and uphill journey, 500

if I must come to blows with every

son of the god Ares. First it was Lycaon,‡

then it was Cycnus, and now there's a third:

I'm going to fight Diomedes and his horses.

But no one will ever see Alcmene's son

tremble in fear at the hand of an enemy.

(Admetus enters from the house with an attendant slave.)

CHORUS: But look, I see the lord of this land;

Admetus himself is coming from his house.

ADMETUS: Joy to you, Zeus' son, descendent of Perseus.§

HERACLES: And joy to *you*, Admetus, lord of Thessaly. 510

ADMETUS: I wish—but I know you mean well.

HERACLES: What's this? Why is your hair cut in mourning?

ADMETUS: I'm about to bury someone who died today.

---

* Bistonia, a city in Thrace, was founded by another son of Ares, Biston.

† "Lord of the golden shield" is a poetic way of saying "lord of the Thracians," since the shield mentioned here is a small round shield frequently carried by Thracians, and Thrace was known for its gold mining.

‡ Lycaon is an obscure figure whom a late source identifies as a son of Ares, killed by Heracles on his trip to bring back the golden apples of the Hesperides. Cycnus, another Thessalian son of Ares, brutally murdered all travelers who passed by him until Heracles killed him.

§ Perseus was, in most mythical accounts, the great-grandfather of Heracles and grandfather of Heracles' human father, Amphitryon. Heracles does not become a divine figure until Zeus, his other father, takes him up to Olympus as he is about to die.

HERACLES: God keep your children free from harm!

ADMETUS: My children are alive, here in the house.

HERACLES: Well, your father was a good age, if he's gone.

ADMETUS: Both he and my mother are still here, Heracles.

HERACLES: But surely your wife, Alcestis, isn't dead?

ADMETUS: There are two stories for me to tell of her.

HERACLES: Are you saying she's alive or she's dead?   520

ADMETUS: She is and she isn't; she causes me sorrow.

HERACLES: I'm none the wiser. You speak in riddles.

ADMETUS: Don't you know the fate that awaits her?

HERACLES: Yes, that she consented to die for you.

ADMETUS: If she's agreed to *that*, how alive is she?

HERACLES: Ah, don't weep for her *now*! Wait until *then*.

ADMETUS: The one about to die is dead and gone—without dying.

HERACLES: Being and not being are thought to be different things.

ADMETUS: You judge it one way, I another, Heracles.

HERACLES: So why do you weep? Who in your house is dead?   530

ADMETUS: A woman. We were just speaking of a woman.

HERACLES: Someone born of your blood or not?*

ADMETUS: Not. Yet someone with close ties to the house.

HERACLES: Why was she in your house when she died?

ADMETUS: When her father died, she came here as an orphan.

HERACLES: *pheu!* I wish I hadn't found you in mourning, Admetus.

ADMETUS: Now you've said this, what do you mean to do?

HERACLES: I'll move on to another host's hearth.

ADMETUS: No, my lord! Save us from such disaster!

HERACLES: A stranger in the house disturbs the grieving.   540

ADMETUS: The dead are dead. Please come inside.

HERACLES: A guest feels shame to feast when others weep.

ADMETUS: The guest rooms where you'll be are far away.

HERACLES: I'd be most grateful if you'd let me leave.

ADMETUS: You must not go to another man's hearth.

(*to attendant*) Lead the way to guest rooms far from the house.

Open them up and tell those in charge

to prepare a meal. Then make sure the doors

---

* Since a wife is viewed as a kind of outsider, unrelated by blood to her husband's family, Admetus'
answers here could apply equally to Alcestis or to a woman with far looser ties to his house.

to the courtyard are shut. Guests must not
hear groaning or be upset as they feast.   550
     (Attendant goes into the house with Heracles.)
CHORUS: *What* are you doing? Burdened by such misfortune
    you can bear to play the host? Are you a fool?
ADMETUS: If I had driven from my house and city
    a man who's a friend and guest, would you approve?
    Surely not: my suffering would be no less
    but I would be more inhospitable.
    On top of the troubles I have, there'd be another:
    my house would gain a reputation for hating guests.
    He receives *me* with the finest hospitality
    when I'm at *his* house, in dusty Argos.   560
CHORUS: But why did you conceal your situation
    if, as you say, the man has come as a friend?
ADMETUS: He wouldn't have wanted to enter the house
    if he had any knowledge of my distress.
    To some, I know, my actions will seem unwise.
    They will not approve. But the doors of my house
    don't know how to be rude and shut out guests.
        (Admetus goes into the house.)
strophe
    CHORUS: House and master, friendly and generous to all,
        even Pythian Apollo, with his tuneful lyre,   570
        consented to make his home here,
        allowed himself to be a shepherd
        in these pastures.
        On the sloping hills
        he played his pipe for your flocks,
        played them marriage songs shepherds sing.
antistrophe
        Spotted lynxes joined the flocks, charmed
        by the shepherd's song. And a troop of tawny lions   580
        came from the valleys of Orthys.*
        And the spotted fawn pranced
        to the sound of your lyre, Phoebus.
        She came out from the tall fir trees

---

* A mountain of the Pindus range in Thessaly.

with a light step,
delighted by your sweet song.

strophe

And so Admetus dwells
in a house rich in flocks, by the lovely waters
of Lake Boibias.* He sets the boundaries   590
of his tilled fields and pasture lands
beyond the hills of Molossus†
to the west, where the sun stables his horses;
and to the east he's lord of Pelion
which offers no harbor from the Aegean sea.‡

antistrophe

And now, his eyes wet with tears,
he opens his doors to a guest,
while in the house he weeps
over the body of his dear wife, dead just now.   600
His high birth drives him to act with respect.
Among the noble everything is possible.
I marvel at his wisdom.
Deep in my being a sure feeling takes hold
that this pious man will prosper.

*(Admetus enters from the house attended by mourners who carry
Alcestis' bier.)*

ADMETUS: Men of Pherae, you're kind to be here.
Now my attendants raise and carry the body
with all it needs for the funeral and pyre.
Address the dead woman, as is the custom
as she departs on her final journey.   610

CHORUS: Wait now; I see your father coming,
bent with age. His servants carry in their arms
treasures for your wife, offerings for the dead.

(Pheres enters from the right, the direction of the town.)

---

* A lake in Thessaly near Mount Ossa, south of Pherae.

† The text here is corrupt but clearly refers to the land of the Molossians in Epirus, far to the west of Pherae.

‡ Mount Pelion borders the Aegean to the east of Pherae. The Chorus mention the lack of a harbor along the range of Mount Pelion presumably because it makes Admetus' kingdom invulnerable to attack by sea.

PHERES: I come to help you bear your troubles, child.
    You've lost a wife who no one will deny
    was noble and wise. But you must endure,
    although these things are hard to bear.
    So take this treasure; let it go with her
    beneath the earth. Her body must be honored.
    She died before her time to spare your life, child.   620
    She saved me from a childless old age
    wasting away in grief, bereft of you.
    She's burnished the reputation of every woman
    by steeling her heart to do this noble act.
    (*addressing the bier of Alcestis*) Savior of this man! You raised us up
    when we were falling! Farewell! Even in Hades
    may you prosper. I say that mortals gain
    from marriages like this. If not, why marry?
ADMETUS: I didn't ask you to be at her burial
    nor do I consider you one of my kin.   630
    She will never wear these treasures of yours.
    She needs nothing of yours in her tomb.
    The time for you to suffer with me was back then
    when I was dying. But you stayed away and let
    a young woman die, though you are old.
    And *you'll* mourn her? You're not my father
    after all, and the "mother" who claims
    she bore me didn't. Some slave gave me birth;
    I was smuggled in and placed at your wife's breast.
    Under pressure you've shown me who you are.   640
    I do not consider myself your son.
    You truly have earned the prize for cowardice:
    You were old, you'd come to the end of life,
    and you weren't willing to go. You hadn't the nerve
    to die for your son. You let this woman do it,
    an outsider whom I would justly call
    my only mother and father. And yet your struggle
    would have been a noble one, if you had
    died for your child. And in any case
    you had only a short time left to live.*   650

---

* Lines 651–52 have been omitted because they closely resemble lines 296–97 and fit better there.

You'd already experienced every happiness
a man can have. You were king in your youth;
you had me, a son, to inherit your wealth.
You weren't going to die without an heir
and leave the house empty for someone else to grab.
And you cannot say that you betrayed me
because *I* had shown *you* disrespect
in old age, you I always held in high regard.   660
In return *this* is the gratitude I get from you
and from my mother. Well, you'd better be quick
and have another child to tend you in old age
and prepare your body for burial when you're dead.
Because I will not lift a hand to bury you.
As far as you're concerned, I'm dead. If I live
because another saved me, that's the one I call
dear father, the one to care for in old age.
What empty prayers for death old people make
when they complain about a long life and old age: 670
when death is right there, no one wants
to die: old age no longer seems so bad.

CHORUS: Stop! The misfortune here before us is enough.
  Don't provoke your father's anger, Admetus.

PHERES: Son, whom do you think you're taunting?
  A Lydian or Phrygian you bought to serve you?*
  Don't you know I'm a free man, a Thessalian
  through and through, born of a Thessalian father?
  You go too far. You won't hurl insults
  like a child and then just walk away.   680
  I gave you life to be the master of this house.
  I raised you. I do not owe you my life.
  I didn't inherit a custom from my father
  that fathers die for sons. Greeks don't do that.
  Your good or bad luck is all your own.
  What we rightfully owe you, you possess.
  You rule many men, and I will leave you
  a large estate, exactly what I received

---

* People from Lydia and Phrygia, areas of Asia Minor, would have been brought to Greece through the slave trade, by which populations defeated in war were sold into slavery and traded among nations.

from my father. How have I wronged
or deprived you? Don't die for me, and I won't   690
die for you. You enjoy life; don't you think
your father does? I reckon the time below is long,
the time we live is short. But it is sweet.
You fought without shame not to die
and killed her to live past the time
allotted you. And yet you say that *I'm*
a coward? *You,* a wretch bested by a woman?
You, the brave young man she died to save?
You've invented a clever way never to die:
just persuade each wife in turn to die   700
for you. And still, though you're a coward,
you blame your kin who aren't willing to die?
Stop and think: if you love your life,
everyone else does, too. If you insult me,
your ears will fill with insults that are true.
CHORUS: More than enough insults have been spoken,
    before and now. Stop abusing your son, my lord.
ADMETUS: (*to his father*) Speak on! I've had my say. But if it hurts
    to hear the truth, you shouldn't have wronged me.
PHERES: Dying for you would be a greater wrong.   710
ADMETUS: The deaths of old and young men are the same?
PHERES: We're obliged to live one life, not two.
ADMETUS: Well, may *you* live longer than Zeus!
PHERES: You curse your parent without cause?
ADMETUS: I saw that you're in love with a long life.
PHERES: (*pointing to Alcestis' bier*) And aren't you burying this body in your
    place?
ADMETUS: A monument to your cowardice, you wretch!
PHERES: And yet you can't say *I* caused her death.
ADMETUS: *pheu!*
    May you be in need of me someday!
PHERES: Woo many wives, so many more may die!   720
ADMETUS: For that *you* are to blame, since you refused to.
PHERES: This heavenly light is dear, very dear.
ADMETUS: You're not a man; you've a cowardly heart.
PHERES: At least you're not mocking me at my funeral.
ADMETUS: But when you *do* die, you'll die dishonored.

PHERES: I don't care about abuse when I'm dead.

ADMETUS: *pheu, pheu!* The shamelessness of old age!

PHERES: *She* wasn't shameless, but she was without sense.

ADMETUS: Go now! Leave me to bury this body.

PHERES: I'm going. You, her killer, will bury her   730
    and later pay the penalty to her kin.
    For surely Acastus is no man
    if he doesn't avenge his sister's blood.

        (Pheres departs toward the town, with Admetus shouting after
        him.)

ADMETUS: Rot away in old age as you deserve,
    you and your wife! Your son lives,
    yet you are childless. You and I will never again
    meet under the same roof. If it were right for me
    to renounce publicly my paternal home,
    I would. *(to the slaves carrying the bier)* We must endure the pain before us.
    Let us go and place the body on the pyre.   740

    CHORUS:* *iō, iō!* You were steadfast and brave,
        noble and best of all women!
        Farewell. May Hermes† and Hades
        receive you with kindness. And if, even there,
        the good gain more, may you share their lot
        and sit beside Hades' bride.‡

        (Admetus and the slaves carrying the bier exit to the left, the
        direction associated with the Underworld. A slave enters from
        the house.)

ATTENDANT: I've served many men a meal before now,
    men from all over the world, who came
    as Admetus' guests. But I've never had to serve
    a worse guest than this one in this house.   750
    First, he saw my master was in mourning
    and came in anyway, dared to cross the threshold.
    Then he didn't show restraint by accepting
    whatever we put before him, knowing our misfortune.
    No. If something is missing, he demands we bring it.

---

* The Chorus chant in anapests here, a meter appropriate for the funeral procession.

† Hermes escorted the dead to the Underworld.

‡ Persephone.

He takes an ivy-wood goblet in his hands
and drinks the dark and potent wine unmixed*
until the wine's flame wraps him in its heat.
He crowns his head with myrtle branches
and bellows off-key. Two melodies were there 760
to be heard: *he* was singing without regard
for Admetus' suffering, and *we* were crying
for our mistress. But we didn't let the guest
see our tears. Those were Admetus' orders.
So now I'm here in this house entertaining
a villainous thief and bandit as a guest,
and she's gone from the house. I didn't attend
her going or extend a hand in grief to her,
my mistress who was mother to me and to all
the household slaves. She softened her husband's rage 770
and saved us so often from pain. Aren't I right
to hate this guest, intruder in our suffering?
> (Heracles lurches out of the house.)

HERACLES: You there! Why so haughty and serious?
An attendant shouldn't be grim with guests;
he should greet them with an open heart.
But *you* see your master's friend and guest
and welcome him with anger and a surly face.
And all this for a stranger's misfortune!†
Come here so you can learn and be wiser.
Do you know what it means to be a mortal? 780
I think not. How would you? Listen:
All mortals must die; no one can say
if he will live through another day,
the day that's yet to come. We have no way
to see where fortune will take us. It isn't
something we can learn or master with skill.
So, with this lesson of mine in mind,
cheer up and have a drink. Today

---

* Wine was usually mixed with water in the Greek world, the potency of the wine being regulated by the amount of water added. Only a man of enormous strength, like Heracles, would risk drinking unmixed wine.

† The Greek word translated "stranger" here means, literally, someone from outside the house. As at line 532, Euripides is playing ironically with the fact that wives were considered "outsiders."

belongs to you, the rest belongs to chance.
Pay homage to the goddess who gives us   790
the greatest pleasure: Cypris.* She wishes us well.
Ignore everything else and take my words
to heart, if you think I'm right. I'm sure
you do. So why not put aside grief—
your extravagant grief—and drink with me?†
I'm sure, when the drinking grips you,
it'll loosen your scowling, clotted mind.
Mortals must think like mortals.
Haughty people with frowning faces   800
are not, in my opinion, really living
a life at all: they're a living calamity.

ATTENDANT: Yes, we know. But our current state
  does not merit drinking and laughter.

HERACLES: The dead woman's a stranger. Don't grieve
  too much. The masters of the house still live.

ATTENDANT: They live? Don't you know what's happened?

HERACLES: Yes, if your master hasn't lied to me.

ATTENDANT: That man loves playing the host too much.

HERACLES: An outsider's death should've curbed my pleasure?   810

ATTENDANT: (*sarcastically*) An outsider alright! *That's* what she was!

HERACLES: Was he keeping some disaster from me?

ATTENDANT: Go enjoy yourself. His pain is *our* concern.

HERACLES: Your words suggest he's not in pain for a stranger.

ATTENDANT: *That* wouldn't cause distress at your carousing.

HERACLES: What terrible thing has my host done to me?

ATTENDANT: It wasn't a good time for you to be a guest.‡

HERACLES: It's not his child or father that's gone, is it?   820

ATTENDANT: No, my lord. It's Admetus' wife who died.

HERACLES: What? She died and then you entertained me?

ATTENDANT: Yes, because he felt ashamed to turn you away.

HERACLES: Poor Admetus, what a wife you've lost!

ATTENDANT: It's not just her, we all are lost.

---

* Cypris is another name for Aphrodite, goddess of erotic passion.

† Two half-lines have been deleted. A scribe copying the manuscript accidentally inserted parts of other lines here.

‡ Two lines, 818 and 819, have been omitted here as interpolations.

HERACLES: I noticed the tears in his eyes, his cropped hair,
   his sad face. But he said he was burying
   an outsider he cared for and persuaded me.
   Against my instinct I went through the doors,
   into the house of my welcoming host, and drank.   830
   He was in such a state and *I* was reveling
   with garlands on my head? But *you*! To say
   nothing when such ruin burdened the house!
   Where is he burying her? Where will I find him?
ATTENDANT: Beside the road that leads directly to Larisa.
   You'll see her sculpted tombstone, near the city.
HERACLES: You, my much-enduring heart and hands,
   show now what kind of son Alcmene,
   child of Electryon of Tiryns, bore to Zeus.
   For I must save the woman who just died;   840
   I must restore Alcestis to this house,
   returning Admetus' favor with this service.
   I'll go and watch for the lord of the dead,
   Death in his black robe. I'll find him, I expect,
   drinking the blood of offerings by the tomb.
   And if I ambush him and grab hold,
   clasping him in the circle of my arms
   and crushing his ribs, no one will release him
   until he gives up the woman to me.
   But if I lose my prey, if he doesn't come   850
   to drink the clotted blood, I'll go below,
   to the sunless house of the Lord and the Maiden,*
   and ask for her. I'm sure I'll bring Alcestis
   up here and put her in my host's arms.
   He welcomed me into his house, when he was struck
   with great misfortune. He didn't drive me away.
   He nobly hid his grief, out of respect for me.
   What Thessalian, what Greek honors the role of host
   more than he? And so this noble man won't
   have to say the man he treated well was bad.   860

        (Attendant goes back into the house. Heracles leaves by the left
        exit. After a pause Admetus and his attendants enter from the

---

* Hades and Persephone.

same direction. Admetus chants in an anapestic rhythm.)

ADMETUS: *iō*

Hateful return to this empty house,

a hateful sight!

iō moi moi, aiai aiai

Where can I go? Where should I stand? What can I say? What must I

not say? How can I die?

Truly my mother bore me for doom.

I envy the dead; I long for them;

their home is where I long to live.

I feel no joy in the light I see,

no joy in the earth my feet tread.

Such was the woman who took my place!

Death stole her and handed her to Hades.   870

strophe

CHORUS:[*] Move on, move on, into the dark house.

ADMETUS: *aiai*

CHORUS: Your suffering merits this cry *aiai*.

ADMETUS: *e, e*

CHORUS: You have felt pain, I know—

ADMETUS: *pheu, pheu*

CHORUS: but you're no help to the one below.

ADMETUS: *iō moi moi*

CHORUS: You'll never again see your dear wife

face to face: that's the pain.

ADMETUS: Your words tear me apart.

What greater calamity is there

than for a man to lose his faithful wife?   880

I wish I'd never married, never shared this house with her.

I envy mortals who never marry, have no children.

They have a single life to weep for,

a manageable pain.

Children's illnesses, a marriage bed

plundered by death:

---

[*] The Chorus start to sing and dance in a rhythm that includes some dochmiacs, the meter of intense emotion. Admetus' cries are a kind of accompaniment to this part of their song. After each stanza, Admetus chants in anapests. The second two stanzas are not accompanied by Admetus' cries, and their rhythm is less excited.

to see these is unbearable when life can be lived
unmarried and childless.
    CHORUS: Your fate is here, a fate hard to wrestle with—

antistrophe

    ADMETUS: *aiai*
    CHORUS: but you put no limit on your grief.   890
    ADMETUS: *e, e*
    CHORUS: Hard as it is to bear, yet—
    ADMETUS: *pheu, pheu*
    CHORUS: —bear it. You're not the first to lose—
    ADMETUS: *iō moi moi*
    CHORUS: —your wife. One misfortune weighs down a mortal,
        another comes then to crush someone else.
    ADMETUS: Endless the pain and the sorrow
        for dear ones below the earth.
        Why did you stop me from hurling myself
        into her empty grave, lying with her
        in death, she who was best of all?
        Hades would have gained not just one   900
        but two faithful lives together;
        together we would have crossed the lake below.

strophe

    CHORUS: I had a kinsman
        whose son died at home,
        an only child
        deserving lamentation. But steadfast
        and with restraint he bore his pain,
        his childlessness,
        bent with age, his hair going white,
        his life far gone.   910
    ADMETUS: Roof, walls, doors of my house,
        how can I go inside, live here
        with my life so changed, so different? *oimoi!*
        Back then, to the flare of pine torches from Pelion
        to the sounds of marriage hymns, I went inside
        with my dear bride, my hand on her wrist.*

---

* Part of the wedding ritual involved the groom's grasping the bride by her wrist and leading her into his house.

Behind us came a noisy crowd;
they called us happy, the dead woman and me:
we were a husband and wife
of noble ancestry, both   920
descended from the rich and powerful.
But now, groans instead of marriage songs
and black raiment instead of white
surround me as I go inside
to my empty marriage bed.

antistrophe

CHORUS: In the midst of a happy life
this pain has come upon you,
who aren't used to suffering.
But you spared *your* body; you saved *your* life.
Your wife died and left behind your love.   930
What's new in this? Death
has separated many before now
from their wives.

ADMETUS: I believe, my friends, her lot is happier
than mine, although it doesn't seem so.
No pain will ever reach her, and she gained
fame and put an end to many troubles.
But I, who shouldn't be alive, escaped
my death but will live out my life in pain.   940
Now I understand—for how will I bear
to go into this house? Whom will I speak to,
who will speak to me, to make my entry sweet?
Where can I turn? The loneliness inside
will drive me away: the sight of the empty bed,
and the chair where she sat, and the floors unswept
in every room. The children will clasp my knees
and cry "Mother!" and the slaves will weep
for the peerless mistress they have lost. That's how
it will be in the house. But outside, groups of women   950
and Thessalian weddings will drive me
back in. To see women my wife's age
will be unbearable. And someone, an enemy,
will say: "Look at him! He lives in shame!
He couldn't stomach dying, so, to escape it,
the coward gave Hades his wife instead.

After *that* he pretends to be a man? He hates
his parents, though he himself was unwilling
to die." That's the "fame" I'll have, to add
to my woes. So how can life profit me?   960
What they say and what I suffer is all bad.

strophe

> CHORUS: I've soared to the realm of the Muses
>> and the highest reaches of thought;
>> I've listened to many stories.
>> But I've found nothing more powerful
>> than Necessity,*
>> no cure in Thracian tablets†
>> engraved with words
>> Orpheus spoke
>> or in the remedies that Phoebus   970
>> gathered for mortals' troubles
>> and gave to the sons of Asclepius.

antistrophe

>> To Necessity, alone of gods, there are
>> no altars, no sacred statues to approach.
>> She pays no heed to sacrifice.
>> Lady, may you not bear down on me
>> with more force than before in my life.
>> For whatever Zeus nods his assent to
>> he completes with you at his side.
>> Your might is stronger   980
>> than Chalybian steel‡
>> and your relentless heart
>> knows no pity.

strophe

>> This goddess has seized you in her hands' relentless hold.
>> But be brave! You will never raise the dead
>> by weeping for them.

---

* The Chorus personify the force of necessity as a goddess the consequences of whose power cannot be averted or cured.

† Songs of Orpheus were supposed to have curative power; the Chorus also refer to herbal cures passed down to Asclepius and his sons by the god Apollo, Asclepius' father.

‡ The Chalybi were a people who lived on the coast of the Black Sea and were famous for their mining and treatment of iron to make a steel-like metal.

Even children of the gods
fade away and die.   990
She was loved when she was with us,
she'll be loved still in death.
The woman yoked to you in marriage
was the noblest of all wives.

antistrophe

Don't think of your wife's tomb
as a burial mound for a body dead and gone
but give it honor equal to a god's.*
Let it be revered by travelers on the road.   1000
One of them will climb the sloping path
and say: "This is the woman who died
in her husband's place. She's a blessed hero now.
Hail, Lady! May you be kind."
These are the words they'll speak to her.
    (*The Chorus point to Heracles entering from the left, leading a
    veiled woman.*)

CHORUS: But look, Admetus! I think this is
    the son of Alcmene approaching the house.

HERACLES: Admetus, one must speak freely to a friend
    and not keep blame pent up inside
    in silence. I feel it's right to prove myself   1010
    your friend and support you in your trouble.
    But you didn't tell me the body to be buried
    was your wife's. You entertained me in your house
    as if you dealt with the suffering of a stranger.
    And I put a garland on my head and poured
    libations to the gods in a house of grief.
    I blame you for this, I really do.
    But I don't want to hurt you in your pain.

    Now I'll tell you why I have come back.
    Take this woman and keep her safe for me   1020
    until I've killed the king of the Bistonians
    and come back with the Thracian mares.

---

* The Chorus are suggesting that Alcestis' tomb will become the site of a hero cult. As a hero, she will
have a godlike presence with the power to protect those who live in the area of her tomb.

But if something should happen—I hope not!
I want to return—I give her to you, a servant
in your house. I went through much to get her.
I came upon some men holding an open
competition, worthy of an athlete's sweat.
That's where I won her as a prize.
The victors in the minor events won horses;
those who won the wrestling and boxing,   1030
harder contests, took away cattle and also
a woman. Since I was there, I would have
disgraced myself if I'd passed up the chance
for gain and glory. But, as I said, you should
care for her. I didn't steal her; I won her
with effort. Perhaps even you will praise me, in time.

ADMETUS: It wasn't from disrespect or thinking you
an enemy that I concealed my wife's sad fate.
No, I would have added pain to my pain
if you'd set out for another host's hearth.   1040
Her loss was enough for me to weep about.
But, if at all possible, Heracles, I beg you,
ask another Thessalian, who hasn't suffered
as I have, one of your many friends in Pherae,
to keep this woman. Don't remind me
of my loss. I wouldn't be able to stop
my tears at the sight of her. I'm already sick;
don't make me worse. I'm burdened enough.
Where would a young woman stay in this house?
I can see she's young by the way she's dressed.   1050
So then will she live in the men's quarters?
How will she remain pure, moving around
among young men? It's not easy, Heracles,
to restrain a youth. I have your interest at heart.
Or should I put her in the dead woman's room?
And bring her into that woman's bed?
I fear blame from two sources: townspeople,
who'll say I've betrayed my wife, my savior,
by falling into bed with a young woman;
and my dead wife, who's owed my reverence.   1060
I have to think of her and take great care.

Woman, whoever you are, know you have
Alcestis' size and shape; you look just like her.
oimoi! Take her from my sight, I pray.
I'm already dead. Don't kill me again.
When I look at her, I think I'm seeing
my wife. My heart churns, and tears
spring from my eyes. What misery I feel!
Only now I taste the bitterness of this grief.

CHORUS: I couldn't call this good luck, but one must   1070
    tolerate a god's gift, whatever it is.

HERACLES: I wish that I were able to bring your wife
    into the light from the house of the dead,
    to do for you that act of gratitude.

ADMETUS: I know that's what you'd want, but what's the point?
    It isn't possible for the dead to rise to the light.

HERACLES: So then, don't overdo it; moderate your grief.

ADMETUS: That's easier to say than for the sufferer to do.

HERACLES: What would you achieve by mourning forever?

ADMETUS: Nothing, I know, but passion carries me away.   1080

HERACLES: Yes, loving a dead person leads to tears.

ADMETUS: My devastation is greater than I can say.

HERACLES: You've lost a noble wife; who would deny it?

ADMETUS: And so I can no longer enjoy life.

HERACLES: Time will ease the pain, which now is young.

ADMETUS: You'd be right about time, if time is death.

HERACLES: A new wife will cure your longing.

ADMETUS: Silence! Such words! Not what I'd expect from you!

HERACLES: Why? You won't marry? You'll stay a widow?

ADMETUS: There isn't a woman alive who'll lie with me.   1090

HERACLES: You can't think you're helping the dead woman?

ADMETUS: I must honor her, wherever she is.

HERACLES: Praiseworthy, yes, but you'll earn the name of "fool."*

ADMETUS: May I die if I betray her, even though she's gone.

HERACLES: Receive this woman with kindness into the house.

ADMETUS: Don't ask this, I beg you by your father Zeus.

HERACLES: You'll be making a mistake if you don't do this.

ADMETUS: And if I do, I'll wound my heart with grief.   1100

---

* Lines 1094–95 are omitted because they are repetitive and break the flow of the dialogue.

HERACLES: Trust me. Perhaps this favor is just what you need.

ADMETUS: *pheu!*

I wish you'd never taken her as your prize!

HERACLES: My victory, nonetheless, is also yours.

ADMETUS: All well and good, but let her go away!

HERACLES: If she must, she'll go. But first be sure she must.

ADMETUS: She must, unless you intend to make me angry.*

HERACLES: I know something. It makes me want this very much.

ADMETUS: Have your victory. But what you do doesn't please me.

HERACLES: A day will come when it will, but for now trust me.

ADMETUS: (*to attendant*) Take her in, since I must accept her into my
house.   1110

HERACLES: I'd rather not hand this woman over to attendants.

ADMETUS: Then take her in yourself, if that's what you want.

HERACLES: It is into *your* hands I will entrust her.

ADMETUS: I couldn't touch her. But she's free to go in.

HERACLES: I trust your right hand alone.

ADMETUS: My lord, you force me to do this against my will.

HERACLES: Courage! Reach out your hand and touch the stranger.

ADMETUS: I reach out my hand as if beheading a Gorgon.†

HERACLES: You have her?

ADMETUS: Yes.

HERACLES: Keep her safe,

and you will say the son of Zeus is a kind guest.   1120

(*Heracles pulls the veil away from Alcestis' face.*)

Look at her. Does she look like your wife?

With this good fortune stop your grieving.

ADMETUS: O gods! What should I say? I'm amazed!

I never hoped—Do I really see my wife,

or does a god send joy to mock and madden me?

HERACLES: Certainly not. The woman you see is your wife.‡

---

* This translation results from a slight emendation of the line, which would otherwise read "She must—as long as it won't make you angry with me." The line read in this way seems to make Admetus give in to Heracles out of fear of angering him, which would be consistent with his wish to spare Heracles any inconvenience as his guest but is also a very weak ending to this long debate.

† When Perseus beheaded the Gorgon he looked away from her, since looking directly at her would have turned him to stone. So here Admetus takes the hand of the veiled woman but faces away from her. The tableau of his holding the hand of a veiled woman evokes a wedding (see line 916 and note).

‡ The beginning of this line, here translated "certainly not," has been translated and emended in various ways. No translation, including this one, can claim with absolute confidence to capture the nature of Heracles' response.

ADMETUS: But look; this may be an apparition from the dead.

HERACLES: (*pointing to himself*) This friend of yours doesn't conjure with
    ghosts.

ADMETUS: The woman whom I buried, my wife—I see *her*?

HERACLES: I'm not surprised you don't believe your luck.   1130

ADMETUS: Can I touch and talk to her—my wife revived?

HERACLES: Speak to her. You have all you wished for.

ADMETUS: This face, this body of my dearest wife!
   I have you, though I never hoped to see you again.

HERACLES: You have. May the gods not begrudge you this!

ADMETUS: Noble son of greatest Zeus!
   May you prosper and may the father who gave
   you life protect you. You alone have restored me.
   How did you bring her from death to life?

HERACLES: I fought with the god who was in charge of her.   1140

ADMETUS: Where did you fight this battle with Death?

HERACLES: Beside her tomb. I ambushed him and grabbed him.

ADMETUS: But why does this woman stand here in silence?

HERACLES: You're not allowed to hear her greet you yet,
   not before the third day dawns, when she's
   released from her sacred bond to the gods below.
   But take her inside. Be just from now on,
   Admetus. Honor guests with reverence.
   Farewell. I go to perform the task the king,
   the son of Sthenelos,* assigned to me.   1150

ADMETUS: Stay here and be a guest at our hearth!

HERACLES: I will another time, but now I must move on.

ADMETUS: May you be fortunate and return with speed!
       (*Heracles exits to the left.*)
   To all citizens and the four cities I rule†
   I say: celebrate my good fortune with song
   and burn sacrifices on the altars in prayer!
   For the life I now adopt is better than
   the life before. I won't deny I'm lucky.
       (*Admetus exits into the house, leading Alcestis.*)

---

* Eurystheus.

† The best evidence for what Admetus refers to here with the word *tetrarchia* comes from Homer, who tells us that Eumelus, Admetus' son, ruled over four cities. *Tetrarchia* may also refer to the fact that Thessaly was divided in the sixth century into four regions, or *tetrades*; that reference would of course be anachronistic.

CHORUS: Divinity takes many forms;
 the gods accomplish many startling things.   1160
 What we expect does not take place,
 and the god makes way for the unexpected.
 And so it came about in this affair.

Introduction to Euripides' *Medea*

Medea was already a sorceress and a murderess by the time this play begins. Many years before, when Jason arrived in her native Colchis (part of modern Armenia) on his voyage to capture the Golden Fleece, a love-struck Medea—daughter of the reigning King Aeetes and granddaughter of the god Helios, from whom she inherited magical powers—used her potions to help the Greek stranger accomplish the task. Then she escaped with Jason in his ship the *Argo*, but first she killed her brother Apsyrtus to prevent him from pursuing. Her union with Jason, contracted by way of a pledge "of the right hand"—some ritual that Medea regards as binding, but Jason may not—thus came to birth amid betrayal and kindred bloodshed. Its death, as we will witness in *Medea*, will be similarly solemnized with blood.

The theft of the Golden Fleece was meant to establish Jason as ruler of Iolcus, a city in northeastern Greece. Jason's uncle Pelias, who had usurped the Iolcan throne, promised to restore it if Jason retrieved the fleece, never dreaming the boy could succeed. When Jason and Medea returned triumphant, Pelias plotted to destroy them, but Medea again sought safety in magic and treachery. She showed to Pelias' daughters how to use a witches' brew that could rejuvenate a dismembered sheep, turning it into a frisky young lamb. These daughters eagerly chopped up their father in an effort to rejuvenate *him*, but Medea this time prevented the charm from working. (Euripides dramatized the episode in his now-lost *Peliades*, staged as part of his very first tragic trilogy in 455 B.C.)

The killing of Pelias explains why Jason and Medea are now in Corinth, though Euripides remains vague about just how they got there. The bloodstained couple are exiles, cut off from the high rank and power to which their births would have entitled them. But Jason has glimpsed a route to regaining that high stature, this time in the Corinthian royal house. He has wedded a princess of Corinth, daughter of the reigning Creon (a different figure from Creon of Thebes, the ruler encountered in Sophocles' *Oedipus*, *Antigone*, and *Oedipus at Colonus*). He has cast off Medea, evidently regarding their pledges to each other, contracted in haste and in a foreign country, as falling short of a legitimate Greek marriage. Now, as we learn from the tutor to Medea's children, Creon has decreed that Medea must leave Corinth forever, with her sons, to remove any threat she might pose to the newly married princess.

Given Medea's history of witchcraft and crime, it would have been easy for Euripides to paint her in lurid colors (as did Seneca in a later, Roman version of this play), but he takes a different path. He domesticates Medea, allowing us to see her through the eyes of servants who pity more than fear her (a passage that tends otherwise, lines 37–45, is contested by some editors and may not be genuine). When Medea herself enters, she speaks in measured tones of how women, in the Greek world, suffer the burdens of marriage and pains of childbirth while men do as they please. She invokes the goddess Themis, guardian of oaths and social sanctions, rather than Hecate, the Erinyes, or other forces of darkness. We can hardly imagine this long-suffering housewife a murderess, yet she *has* killed, as she reminds us in lines 166–67. This disjuncture, between the very human woman Euripides creates and the monstrous deeds she will do, makes this play complex and compelling, an object of fascination to both the ancient and modern worlds.

Unlike Clytemnestra, who also takes revenge on a faithless husband, Medea has no well-laid ambushes and no allies. She has no plan in mind when we first meet her, and even when she wins a day's reprieve from Creon's exile decree, she is unsure how to use it. We watch her schemes take shape as circumstances change, becoming her confederates in that, like the Chorus, we are privy to her inmost thoughts. Perhaps we even rejoice with her as she gains from Aegeus, an Athenian king who passes through Corinth as he seeks a remedy for his childlessness, a promise of sanctuary in Athens. It's not clear when she forms the intention to murder her children—perhaps it was Aegeus' distress at his childlessness that suggested a terrible way to make Jason suffer—and Euripides' original audience may not have thought she would do so: an ancient commentator notes that in previous versions of the myth, the children died at the hands of vengeful Corinthians after Medea had fled. The filicide for which Medea has become notorious, the act depicted so stunningly in a superb Attic vase painting, may well have been invented by Euripides as this play's most wrenching plot twist. Medea herself may not have formed this intent before line 1007, where she cries out in pain as she receives her children; perhaps her murderous plan has spontaneously occurred to her at that moment (earlier hints and double meanings may reflect the playwright's foreknowledge, not her own).

Just as Euripides downplays Medea's ties to kindred bloodshed and black magic, so he also avoids typecasting her as a wild-eyed barbarian. She thinks and speaks like a Greek, and other characters treat her as one, at least until after her murders. The *Medea*, in other words, denies us the comfort we might have taken in the "otherness" of its title character. Her eastern extraction might have made her easy to hate—especially for Athenians whose city had been destroyed, only fifty years before this play was put on, by invaders from the East—but Euripides instead stresses the ways she is *like* us. Jason's cry in his final speech, "There isn't a woman in Greece, no Greek woman / who would have dared this," cannot be taken to represent Euripides' own view, given that Jason has in an earlier scene shown himself completely unable to "get it," for example when he attributes Medea's rage to mere frustration of female sexual desire (lines 568–72).

The play's final sequence builds toward a masterful coup de théâtre, a scene depicted on a number of memorable Greek vases. Medea, who has planned her crimes so cunningly, seems in the end to be trapped without means of escape; the forces of law and order, spearheaded by the hyperrational Jason, are fast closing in. But just when we expect that justice will be done, Medea appears in the sky above the house, riding in a chariot supplied by her grandfather Helios. She bears with her the slain children, denying Jason even the hope of mourning them and burying their bodies. The spectators of 431 B.C. had no hint of this, either from previous Medea tales or from Medea's confidences throughout the play. Or, indeed, from previous tragic productions, in which (as far as is known) the *mēchanē* used to lift actors into the air had carried only gods, not mortals, aloft.

Medea displays her superhuman powers with her final aerial ascent; she delivers the prophetic epilogue that in other Greek dramas issues only from a divine source. Where, then, are the traditional deities who might have appeared in this final scene, to comfort Jason or foretell that Medea, in the end, would pay the price? Their absence from this play is keenly felt, given the suffering Medea has inflicted and the outrage she provokes with her escape. "May the children's Fury destroy you," Jason prays, invoking the Erinys who punishes the spilling of kindred blood; but Euripides does not imply (as does Aeschylus at the end of the *Libation Bearers*, following Orestes' matricide) that such an avenging deity will in fact appear. Medea's reply—"What god, what spirit hears you, / breaker of oaths, deceiver of a stranger's trust?"—seems to be the play's last word on divine intervention, as well as its clearest, though still barely adequate, attempt to situate Jason's suffering in some scheme of cosmic justice.

Medea took only third place in the competition of 431 B.C. but loomed very large in the Greek mind, to judge by caustic jokes in the comedies of Aristophanes and by the above-mentioned vase paintings of the final scene (the artists were no doubt inspired by the original play or by a later revival; from their images we can infer that dragons or serpents were depicted drawing Medea's chariot in those productions). It deeply impressed the Romans as well: Ovid and Seneca both composed *Medea*s of their own for readers of the first century

A.D. (only Seneca's survives). In recent times, the Medea myth has perhaps attracted more comment, interpretation, and adaptation than any other Greek story, including film versions by the celebrated directors Pier Paolo Pasolini and Lars von Trier and a novelistic "retelling" by the German writer Christa Wolff. Euripides' play is lurking in the background of all such treatments, despite their modern twists.

MEDEA

Translated by Rachel Kitzinger

This translation is based on the text edited by David Kovacs for the Loeb Classical Library, *Euripides:* "Cyclops," "Alcestis," "Medea" (Cambridge, MA: Harvard University Press, 1994). I have also consulted Donald J. Mastronarde's text and commentary in the Cambridge Greek and Latin Classics series, *Euripides:* "Medea" (Cambridge: Cambridge University Press, 2002).

CAST OF CHARACTERS (IN ORDER OF APPEARANCE)

NURSE, Medea's personal attendant

TUTOR, teacher and minder of Medea and Jason's two sons

MEDEA, member of the royal family of Colchis, on the Black Sea; granddaughter of the Sun-god; wife of Jason

CHORUS of Corinthian women

CREON, king of Corinth

JASON, heir to the throne of Iolcus, living in exile in Corinth

AEGEUS, king of Athens

CHILDREN, Jason and Medea's two sons

MESSENGER, a slave in the royal house of Creon

Setting: The play takes place in front of Medea and Jason's house in Corinth. Of the two entrances to the stage, one is understood to come from the royal palace where Creon and his daughter live, the other from the town and surrounding countryside.

NURSE: I wish the ship, the *Argo*, had never flown
    to Colchis through the dark Symplegades;*
    that the timbered pines had never fallen
    in the vales of Pelion†; that hands of noble men
    hadn't rowed in search of the Golden Fleece
    for Pelias.‡ For then my mistress Medea
    would not have sailed to the towers of Iolcus,
    struck to the heart with passion for Jason.§
    She wouldn't have persuaded Pelias' daughters
    to kill their father;¶ she'd not be living now   10
    in Corinth with Jason and her children.** She came an exile
    to this land, but all the citizens welcome her,
    and for Jason she's turned all to the good.
    This provides the greatest security,
    when a wife doesn't oppose her husband.
    But now all is hate, the bonds of love are sick:

---

* The nurse refers to the story of Jason's voyage on the ship, the *Argo*, to retrieve the Golden Fleece from Medea's father, King Aeetes, in Colchis on the eastern shore of the Black Sea. In myth the entrance to the Black Sea is guarded by the Symplegades, the Clashing Rocks, which required skill and luck to sail through.

† Pelion, a wooded mountain in Thessaly, provided the wood to build the *Argo*, in mythology the first ship to venture to the east, beyond the Mediterranean.

‡ Pelias, Jason's uncle, had usurped Jason's father's throne in Iolcus in Thessaly, in northern Greece. It was Pelias who sent Jason in quest of the Golden Fleece, promising to return the throne to him if he fetched it.

§ Jason's success in gaining the fleece was largely the result of Medea's help; she aided him with her knowledge of potions (a characteristic of granddaughters of the Sun). Jason and Medea fled Colchis together in the *Argo*, pursued by Medea's father, Aeetes.

¶ When Jason and Medea returned to Iolcus with the fleece, Pelias reneged on his promise to return the throne. Medea persuaded Pelias' daughters to rejuvenate their father by cutting him up and cooking the pieces of his body in a cauldron, assuring them that at the end of the process, her magic spell would restore him to newly vigorous life. They did so, but Medea did not honor her pledge. Jason and Medea were forced to flee from Iolcus to Corinth.

** Kovacs inserts two lines here. I do not think they are necessary and have not translated them.

A traitor to his children and my mistress,
Jason spends his nights in a royal bed;
he's married the daughter of Creon, ruler here.
And Medea, wretched and dishonored, calls   20
on his promises, invokes the strong bond
of his right hand* and appeals to gods to witness
the kind of recompense she gets from him.
She lies without food, flattened by her pain,
melting into tears at every instant
since she discovered how her husband wrongs her.
She won't look up, won't raise her eyes
from the ground. She hears her friends' advice
no more than would a rock or ocean wave.
Only now and then she turns her white neck   30
and groans to herself, groans for her own dear father,
her land and house, which she betrayed to leave
with a man who dishonors and demeans her now.
In misfortune she has come to know, poor thing,
why she should not have left her native land.
She hates the children, gets no joy from them.
I fear her, fear she's planning something strange.†
Her mind is oppressed and dangerous. She won't put up
with abuse. I know her. And I fear her,
fear she might thrust a knife through her own liver,   40
or kill the king and the new bride and groom
and then take on even greater misfortune.
For she inspires dread. If you make her
your enemy, no victory song for you!
But here come the children. They're finished with
their game of ball. They have no thought for their
mother's trouble; young minds don't know pain.
TUTOR: Old woman, slave in my lady's household,
why do you stand alone outside the gates,   50
moaning to yourself about your troubles?
How is Medea willing to do without you?

---

* Jason took Medea from Colchis as his wife, although their marriage is not governed by the rituals of Greek wedlock. The "bond of the right hand" (or handshake) implies an arrangement between equals rather than the subordination of the woman (as would be the case in a true Greek marriage contract).

† Editors have edited lines 37–45 in various ways, including deletion of the whole passage. I follow Kovacs in deleting only one line (41).

NURSE: Old man, attendant to Jason's children,
    loyal slaves make their master's trouble
    their own; it touches their hearts.
    So for me: I'm so unsettled by my grief
    that longing came over me to escape out here
    and tell the earth and sky my mistress's sorrow.
TUTOR: She hasn't stopped her crying, then—wretched woman?
NURSE: I envy you your ignorance: Her pain
    has just begun; it's not yet in mid-course.   60
TUTOR: Poor fool, if I may address my mistress so.
    She knows nothing of more recent trouble.
NURSE: What is it, old man? Don't keep it to yourself.
TUTOR: Nothing. I regret what I've said already.
NURSE: I beg you not to hide it. I'm your fellow slave.
    If I must, I'll fold in silence what you say.
TUTOR: I heard a man talking as I drew near
    the gaming tables, the place where old men sit,
    near Pirene's spring.* I pretended not to hear,
    but he said that Creon intends to drive   70
    these children and their mother out,
    away from Corinth. I don't know if
    his story's right, but I hope it's not.†
NURSE: Will Jason allow his children to suffer so,
    even if he's quarreling with their mother?
TUTOR: Old ties make way for new. It seems
    he no longer feels a duty to this house.
NURSE: Then we're ruined if we must add new pain
    to the old, before we've drained it dry.
TUTOR: You must keep quiet, silence your tongue.
    It's not time yet for your mistress to know this.   80
NURSE: Children, do you hear what your father is?
    I don't wish his destruction: he's my master.
    But it turns out he's a torment to his dear ones.
TUTOR: What mortal isn't? Do you realize only now

---

* Remains of the fountain house in the center of Corinth, where the water of the stream Pirene collected, can still be seen. The water from the spring was used for ritual purposes, and the area around the fountain house functioned as a social space.

† Exile is the most extreme punishment in the Greek world short of death, although it is often considered worse than death, especially for women. The exclusion from community and family denies any settled existence or social status to the person in exile, who must often live as a nomad and beggar if no one is willing to take her in.

we care for ourselves more than for our neighbors?*

Their father, newly wed, now spurns these boys.

NURSE: (to the boys) Go into the house. All will be well, children.

(to the tutor) You: keep them on their own as best you can.   90

Do not allow them near their mother's rage.

I've seen her look at them with an eye as savage

as a bull's, as if she had something in mind.

She won't cease from her rage before she strikes.

May she harm foes at least, and not her dear ones!

> (In the following scene, Medea's lines are sung; the nurse
> responds in the same anapestic rhythm† but chanting, not
> singing.)

MEDEA: (heard crying aloud from inside the house) iō!

I'm so unfortunate, miserable, in pain—‡

iō moi moi! How can I end this?

NURSE: It's like this, children dear: your mother

roils her heart, whips up her rage.

Hurry inside, quick, into the house.   100

Don't go near her, don't enter her sight.

Beware of her savage mood

and the willful ways of her hateful mind.

Go now, get inside, quick as you can.

> (The tutor leads the children into the house.)

The cloud of her grief loomed large

from the start and will soon catch fire

with thunderous rage.§ What will she do

once her spirit, passionate and restless,

is bitten by her troubles?   110

MEDEA: (from inside) aiai!

My suffering, my misery! The world

should weep for what I've suffered! Curse you,

---

* A line here, "some with reason, others out of greed," appears to be a later addition to the text.

† The anapestic rhythm (in its pure form, two short syllables followed by one long syllable) can be chanted or sung. Chanted anapests are often used for the entrance of a Chorus, as they are associated with marching. Sung anapests can be associated with laments.

‡ Line divisions in sung and chanted sections of the play vary considerably from one edition to another. In the songs, editors differ in their sense of the metrical phrasing marked by line division; in the chanted sections, under some circumstances there can be disagreement about the number of anapests in a line. Therefore line numbers, which are retained from a very early edition of the play, do not always correspond to the actual number of lines in the songs in this translation.

§ The image here is of a thundercloud that will soon be accompanied by lightning.

sons of a despised mother! May you die!
Your father, too. May the whole household fall to ruin.

NURSE: (*speaking as though to Medea inside*) *iō moi moi, iō* my woe!
Why must your children share the blame
for their father's offence? Why hate them?
Children, my fear for you pains me so:
a terrible thing, the temper of the mighty.
They have great power and few command them,   120
and so their moods may make violent shifts.
It's better to learn to live
among equals. For myself, at least,
I'd wish to grow old securely,
without greatness. Moderation sounds best
on the tongue; its practice wins
the greatest gain. Excess can bring
no advantage to men; it delivers
even greater destruction to a house
already plagued by god's anger.   130
   (*A Chorus of Corinthian women enter from the direction of the
   town, singing.*)*

CHORUS: I keep hearing her voice, her cry,
the unhappy woman from Colchis.
Is she not calm yet?
Tell us, old woman. An attendant† said
she's been crying out loud,
inside the house. I feel no pleasure
at the pain there,
since friendship binds us.

NURSE: There is no house: that's gone now.
He has his marriage to the royal line;   140
she's in her room, her life wasting away;
my mistress takes no comfort
from the words of her friends.

MEDEA: (*heard from inside*) *aiai*,
Let lightning split my head

---

* Initially the rhythm of the Chorus's song is anapestic, the meter (in its chanted form) traditionally used for the choral entrance. Other rhythms then mingle with the anapests. Medea and the nurse continue in anapestic rhythms, singing and chanting respectively.

† This translation reflects an emendation of the text by Kovacs.

apart! What use to me to live?
pheu, pheu, let me die and be free.
Let me leave behind my hated life.

strophe

CHORUS: Do you hear, Zeus, Earth, and Light,
the song of pain she sings,
the wretched wife?   150
Why do you yearn for
that monstrous rest, fool?
Death will come soon enough;
don't pray for the end.
If your husband
devotes himself to a new wife,
don't upset yourself for him.
Zeus will be your avenger.
Don't go too far,
don't waste away lamenting your husband.

MEDEA: (*from inside*) O great Themis and lady Artemis,*   160
do you see what I suffer? I bound
my husband with great oaths, cursed man.
May I see him and his bride
ground to dust someday, with all the house,
since they dared, unprovoked, to wrong me.
Oh, Father, oh, city, to my shame
I killed my brother† and left you.

NURSE: (*to Chorus*) Do you hear how she invokes Themis,
receiver of prayers, daughter of Zeus,
whom we deem keeper of oaths?   170
It cannot be my mistress will bring
her rage to an end with a small act.

antistrophe

CHORUS: How I wish she'd come out here,
see us and hear
what we have to say!

---

* Themis is the goddess who is understood to enforce human law and custom, here specifically the keeping of oaths. Medea calls on Artemis perhaps because she is closely associated with women's lives, particularly moments of transition such as marriage or childbirth.

† To delay her father's pursuit, Medea, when fleeing Colchis with Jason in the *Argo*, cut up her brother and threw pieces of his body overboard. Aeetes stopped to pick up each piece, allowing Medea and Jason to escape.

Perhaps she might let go
her sullen anger and willful mind.
Let my efforts for my friends
never fall short.
But go to her now, 180
bring her here, outside
the house. Tell her we're her friends.
Hurry, before she does harm
to those within.
For her grief surges urgently on.

NURSE: I'll do that; but I doubt
I'll persuade my mistress. Still
I'll do you this favor and try,
though, like a lioness with young,
she casts a savage eye on her slaves,
if one comes near her and speaks.
You might call those men of old dim-witted, 190
not wise at all, and you'd not be wrong:
they thought up singing at a feast
or banquet or fair, a joy for the ear,
but they found no way to stop
the pain, the awful pain that brings
death and destruction and leads to
the fall of a house. And yet to cure
such pain with song, that would be
a gift to men. But why bother
at a feast to raise your voice in song? 200
There's pleasure enough in the lavish food;
no need for men to add more.

(The nurse exits into the house.)

CHORUS: *(singing)* I have heard resounding, wailing
cries as she shouts her shrill distress,
and names her bed's betrayer, her husband.
She declares the wrongs she suffers
to Themis, daughter of Zeus,
guardian of oaths that brought her to Greece* 210
from far away, across the dark water,

---

* The oaths that Jason swore to Medea persuaded her to go with him to Greece.

    beyond the salty straits few dare
    to cross, gateway to the Black Sea.*
       (Medea enters from the house and addresses the Chorus.)

MEDEA: Women of Corinth, I've come out of the house
    to avoid your blame: I know many people
    are arrogant, some in public view,
    some out of sight. And there are those who earn
    from quiet ways a bad name for indifference.
    If people hate someone at first sight,
    before they know what he's like deep down,   220
    though he's done no wrong, they're not just.
    For a stranger, there's a special need to meld
    into the city. I don't praise even a citizen
    whose self-will and bad manners distress others.

    As for me: this bolt from the blue has struck me down.
    It's wrecked my life. I'm finished. I've abandoned
    all life's joy. My dear friends, I long for death.
    The man who was everything to me (I know too well)
    turns out to be the worst of men: my husband.

    Of all creatures that live and understand,   230
    we women suffer most. In the first place
    we must, for a vast sum, buy a husband;†
    what's worse, with him our bodies get a master.‡
    And here's what's most at stake: Did we get
    a man who's good or bad? For women have
    no seemly escape; we can't deny our husbands.
    We've come to a household with new habits, new rules,§
    and must divine how best to manage our bedmates
    using skills we never learned at home.   240

---

* The gateway referred to is the Bosporus.

† Medea refers here to the necessity of the bride's family to provide a dowry (in the *Hippolytus*, lines 625ff., Hippolytus makes the same point, but in that case he's illustrating how much of a drain women are on a household's wealth); she also points out that most Greek women do not know their husbands when they marry because the marriage was arranged by their parents.

‡ Kovacs's text deletes line 234: "This disaster is worse than disaster."

§ When a girl married, she left her father's house and went to live with her husband and his family. Medea is describing Greek customs that she herself has not been subject to, in part to win the Chorus's trust.

If we do it right, our husband lives with us
and doesn't fight the yoke. Then life
is enviable. If we don't, it's better to die.
A man, when *he* is vexed by those at home,
goes out to ease the disquiet in his heart.*
But we have only one person to look to.
And they say of us that *we*'re never at risk,
sheltered at home, while *they* fight with spears.
How wrong they are: I'd rather three times over   250
stand behind a shield than give birth once.

The story's not the same, though, for you and me.
You have this city and your fathers' houses,
the joy of life and company of friends.
I'm on my own. I have no city. My husband
abuses me. I was brought as booty from far away
and have no mother, brother, or kin
to give me shelter from this storm of trouble.
So this I ask you, only this: keep
my secret, if a way is found, a scheme   260
to pay my husband back for what he's done.†
In other things a woman is full of fear,
without the courage to take up arms and fight.
But when she's wronged in marriage, no mind's
more deeply stained with blood than hers.

CHORUS: I'll keep quiet since it's just, Medea,
that you pay your husband back. Your grief
doesn't shock me. But I see Creon approach,
the land's ruler, coming to announce new plans.   270
    (Creon enters from the direction of the royal palace.)
CREON: You, Medea, who scowl and rage at your husband!
I've told the world that you must leave this land,
an exile, and take with you your two children.
There can be no delay. With this decree

---

* A line here, "in the company of a mate or someone close to him," is considered corrupt by many editors for metrical reasons.

† It is quite common for a character to ask the Chorus to keep quiet in order to "naturalize" the fact that although it is onstage for most of the play, the Chorus very rarely intervenes in the action. A line has been deleted here, in which Medea also mentions vengeance against Creon and his daughter.

I've made my judgment. I won't go back home
until I drive you beyond the limits of the land.
MEDEA: *aiai*, I'm destroyed! It's all over. Oh, misery!
My enemies attack at full sail, and I have
no haven from disaster in easy reach.
Yet I'll ask, even amidst calamity: Why   280
do you drive me from this land, Creon?
CREON: I fear you. No need to disguise my reasons.
I fear you might do my child fatal harm.
And there are many indications I am right:
you were born clever, you have dangerous skills,
and the loss of your marriage bed gives you pain.
I hear you're making threats. They tell me you say
you'll act against me, and the groom and bride I gave away.
So, before we suffer, I'll mount my defense.
I'm better off, woman, if I incur your hatred   290
now, rather than be soft and later lament.
MEDEA: *pheu, pheu!*
Not for the first time, Creon, but often
my reputation's hurt me, done me harm.
No man in his right mind should ever
overeducate his children, make them too smart.
Besides appearing idle, they will harvest
the envy and ill will of fellow citizens.
If you offer new and clever thoughts to fools
you'll seem to them both worthless and unwise.
Beyond this, if they think you better   300
than those they think know *something*, you'll seem
harmful to the city. I myself have shared this fate.
Because I'm clever, some men bear me a grudge,*
but *you* fear me, thinking you'll suffer—what?
something harsh? Don't fear, Creon. I'm not like that,
not one to cause offense to men in power.
What wrong have you done me? You gave your daughter
to the man you liked. It's my husband I hate.   310
But you, I think, acted with restraint.

---

* Kovacs deletes two lines here to keep the sharp contrast between "some men" and "you." The deleted lines read "others find me retiring; others the opposite; and others find me an obstacle; but I am not overly wise."

Even now I don't resent your prosperity.
Celebrate the marriage and be well. Only let me
live here, in this land. Believe me, even though
I'm wronged, I'll keep silent: I give in to my betters.
CREON: To my ears what you say is mild, but I fear
in your heart you are plotting something bad.
I trust you far less now than ever before.
A woman of fiery temper is easier to guard against
than one who's clever and quiet. A man's the same.   320
But no more talk—you must leave without delay.
I am set on this; you can't keep your place
among us when it's clear you wish me ill.
> (*Medea makes a supplicatory gesture toward Creon's knees and
> hand.*)*
MEDEA: By your daughter, newly wed, I beg you, don't do this.
CREON: You waste your words. You won't persuade me, ever.
MEDEA: You'll drive me out? No respect for a suppliant?
CREON: I don't love you more than my own home.
MEDEA: My country—how dear my memory of you!
CREON: I love mine, too, but my children are dearer.
MEDEA: *pheu, pheu,* how great the injuries of passion!   330
CREON: That depends, I think, on circumstances.
MEDEA: Zeus, remember who has caused these ills.
CREON: Get out! You're a waste of time. Free me from trouble.
MEDEA: Trouble's what I have. I don't need more.
CREON: Soon now my guards will seize and throw you out.
> (*Medea grasps Creon's knees and hand in full supplication.*)
MEDEA: Spare me that at least, Creon, I beg you.
CREON: Woman, you seem determined to harass me.
MEDEA: I'll leave, Creon. I wasn't pleading to stay.
CREON: Why, then, do you grip my hand? Let me go!
MEDEA: Let me stay just one more day.   340
Let me finish planning for our exile,
find refuge for my children; it's up to me
to work this out; their father doesn't care.
Pity them, since you, too, have children.

---

* The full act of supplication (see line 336 below) involves the suppliant's taking hold of the knees of the person he or she is supplicating and gesturing to the person's chin or grasping his or her hand. Medea's symbolic act here involves simply a gesture toward the knees and chin or hand.

It's only fitting you should wish them well.
I don't worry about myself when we're in exile;
I weep for *them*, for their misfortune.

CREON: I don't have the spirit of a tyrant:
I've often lost by showing others respect.
Even now I can see I'm making a mistake.   350
Still, I'll grant you this, woman. But hear me well:
if the coming dawn shines its light
on you and your children while still in this land,
you will die. I've said it and I mean it.
So stay now for one day, if stay you must.
In that time you won't do the harm I fear.

   (Creon exits toward the royal palace.)

  CHORUS: *(chanting)** *pheu, pheu*, your pain, your misery!
   wretched woman,
   where will you turn? what stranger's house,
   what land to shelter from disaster?   360
   Medea, a god has tossed you
   into a sea of calamity with no way out.

MEDEA: There's no good in this, who would deny it?
But don't think this is how it's going to end.
There's a challenge yet for the newlyweds,
and no small upset for the one who made the match.
Do you think I would have groveled as I did
before that man, except to help myself
and further my designs? I wouldn't have said a word
or deigned to touch his hand. But he's a fool.   370
He lost his chance to ruin my strategy
by casting me out of this land. Instead,
he gave me one more day—one day
in which to make corpses of three enemies:
the father, his daughter, and my husband.

So many roads might lead me to their deaths.
I don't know which to try first, friends.

---

* The Chorus usually responds to what has happened in a scene with a pair of spoken lines. The chanting of anapests is unusual and occurs again in this play at line 759, perhaps to contrast the Chorus's agitation with Medea's control. The opening lines have been transposed to have the Chorus begin with *pheu, pheu*. Kovacs deletes the line "wretched woman."

Should I put a torch to the newlyweds' house,
or quietly go in, where they've made their bed,
and thrust a sharp knife through their livers?* 380
But there's one problem: if they catch me
entering the house and carrying out my plan,
I'll die and give my enemies cause to mock me.
Best to follow a straight path, where I have
the greatest skill: use poisons to destroy them.
Now, say they're dead—what city will receive me?
Is there someone somewhere to shelter me,
give me asylum, a safe place to live?
No, there's not. So I must bide my time yet.
If a stronghold somewhere shows itself to me, 390
I'll work their deaths in silence and in stealth.
If there's no escape, and I'm forced into the open,
I'll take up my sword and kill them.
Even if it means my death, I'll dare it all.
May the goddess whom I revere most
be my witness—the one I've chosen as my aide
in the deepest reaches of my house—Hecate:†
not one of them will hurt me and rejoice.
I'll ruin their marriage, make bitter his royal
alliance, and my exile from this land. 400
Come now, Medea. Spare none of your skill
as you devise and execute your plan.
Go forward into danger; test your courage.
Hold their wrongs before your eyes. You mustn't
suffer the mockery of that Sisyphean marriage.‡
You have a noble father, descended from the Sun.
You have the skill. And, after all, we're women:
most helpless when it comes to noble deeds,
most skillful at constructing every evil.

---

* Kovacs has deleted this line, which is identical to line 40. I retain both lines, making the nurse at line 40 refer to Medea's possible suicide, while here Medea refers to the killing of Jason and his bride.

† Hecate is a goddess closely associated with magic, witchcraft, and the moon; it would be unusual to have a sanctuary of Hecate within the house, and the fact that Medea has one suggests her special connection to the practice of magic and the use of potions.

‡ Medea refers to Jason's new marriage as Sisyphean because Sisyphus was king of Corinth and therefore an ancestor of Creon's. Because Sisyphus was associated with terrible crime and punishment, the reference has a negative tone.

strophe

CHORUS: Uphill flow streams from sacred springs,   410
  the balance in all things is reversed;
  men's designs are deceitful; their oaths—
  sealed by the gods—dissolve.
  Common talk will change*
  and a woman's life will shine with glory.
  Honor comes to women:
  The harsh sound of ill repute   420
  will bind them no more.

antistrophe

  The muses will silence long-ago songs
  that sing of my treachery.
  Ours is not the gift of the lyre, the skill
  to join it with god-inspired song.
  Had Phoebus, lord of singing,† given us the gift, we would have
  sung in answer to men's voices.‡
  The long stretch of time has much to tell
  of my lot and of men's.   430

strophe

  You sailed from your father's house
  with madness in your heart, crossed between
  the two rocks that bound the Pontus;§ you're
  in a strange land: no husband
  in your bed, your marriage lost,
  in misery you're driven from here—
  an exile without honor.

antistrophe

  Gone the binding power of oaths; no more
  does shame abide in mighty Greece;   440
  it's flown into thin air. And you have no father,
  no home to give you shelter from your troubles.

---

* The Chorus refer to the prevalence of negative judgments about women in men's talk and in literary works.

† Phoebus is the god Apollo.

‡ The Chorus imagine that women's voices might be heard in response to men's in public celebrations involving songs that portray women in a negative light or that view a story from only a male perspective. Women do not sing in public.

§ The Pontus is the Black Sea, and the two rocks are the Symplegades, or Clashing Rocks (see note to line 2).

Another woman has taken her place
in that house, her royal bed
a stronger union than yours.

(Jason enters from the direction of the royal palace.)

JASON: *(to Medea)* This is not the first time; often I've seen
that a harsh temper's impossible to deal with.
You had the choice of living here, having a home,
calmly accepting your superiors' will.
But no, for the sake of useless talk, you'll leave.   450
For me it's not a problem. Go on and on
calling Jason the very worst of men.
But consider exile a small price to pay
for what you've said against the rulers here—
a profit really. I've tried to soothe their rage,
the king's angry spirit: I'd prefer for you to stay.
But you can't let your folly go. You keep on
slandering the king. And so you'll leave.

Even so, despite all this, I've not come here
to disown my loved ones. I'll look out for you: 460
you and the children won't leave without money;
you'll lack nothing. Exile brings with it
many hardships, and, in truth, I couldn't
wish you ill, even though you despise me.

MEDEA: Worst of the worst! I can say only this,
the greatest insult I can offer your cowardice.
You have come here, my bitterest enemy, *here.**
This is no sign of boldness or of courage,
to stand and face the family you've wronged.   470
It's the worst of all human diseases:
shamelessness. But you've done well
to come. I'll relieve myself by speaking
ill of you, and you will hear, and suffer.

I will begin the story at the beginning:
I saved you, as all those Greeks know
who sailed with you on your boat, the Argo.

---

* A line, identical to line 1324, "bitter to the gods and to me and the whole human race," is deleted here.

You were sent to harness bulls breathing fire,
to sow the fields that sprouted death.* I raised
the torch of safe return for you by killing   480
the sleepless serpent with his twisted coils
that guarded the Golden Fleece. Then I chose
to betray my father and home, and go
with you to Iolcus, home of Pelias—an act
more zealous than wise. I killed Pelias; he died
in the worst way, at his daughters' hands;†
I destroyed his house. And after all I'd done
for you, worst of men, you betrayed me.
We had children, but you took a new wife.
Had you been childless, I could forgive   490
lust for a new woman. Now your oaths
mean nothing. I can't know if you think
the gods in power then no longer rule,
or now new laws are laid down for men.
For you surely know you haven't honored
your oath to me. *pheu!* Right hand and knees
so often clasped by you, evil man—how empty
your supplication! And I'd placed my hopes in you.

Well, now. Let me consult you as a friend—
not that I expect any good from you;   500
still my questions will make you look worse.
Where should I turn now? To the house of the father
I betrayed—and my country—when I came with you?
Or to Pelias' wretched daughters? They would
receive me well, for sure, into the house
where I killed their father! So it is: I'm hated
by my own family, and to help you I've
made enemies of those I should not have.
No doubt for this you've made me happy
in return, as lots of Greek women suppose: 510
my husband is marvelous, loyal in my misery—
if, that is, I'll leave this land, an exile,

---

* These are two of the tasks that Medea's father, Aeetes, demanded of Jason before he would relinquish the Golden Fleece. The second task was to sow a field with dragon's teeth from which armed men sprang up whom Jason had to conquer.
† See note to lines 9–10.

without friends, alone, with only my children.
A beautiful tale about this brand-new groom:
his children and his savior, wandering in penury.
O Zeus, you gave a sure test for false gold:
why is there none for human baseness?
Why is there no mark stamped on a man's body
to make us know he isn't any good?

CHORUS: The anger when loved ones battle loved ones   520
is terrible; there is no easy cure.

JASON: It seems I mustn't be clumsy in my speech
but, like a skilled helmsman, outrun
with shortened sails the blasts of your empty talk.
Since you inflate your generosity,
I claim that Cypris was savior of my voyage:*
She, no other god or mortal, saved me.
You have a fine mind, it's true—but if I told
how Eros aimed unerring shafts and forced
you to rescue me, I would invite envy.   530
In fact, I won't keep that tally too carefully.
It wasn't too bad, the help you gave me then.†
But, even so, you got more than you gave
from my salvation, as I will now lay out.
In the first place you live now in Greece, and not
your savage homeland. You know justice and
the rule of law, that doesn't brook the use
of force. All Greeks know of your skill;
you're famous. If you were living at the ends
of the earth, no one would have heard of you.   540
I'd wish for the life of a distinguished man
over a house full of gold or the skill
to sing more sweetly than Orpheus.‡
I have spoken, briefly, about my trials

---

* Cypris is another name for Aphrodite, the goddess of sexual love; Eros (line 529) is her son, who carries a bow and arrows that cause whomever they strike to fall in love. Jason's point is that these gods made Medea fall in love with him, so it is they, not she, who deserve credit for his success in winning the Golden Fleece.

† Jason makes a claim to piety here by not boastfully recounting in detail the extent of Medea's love and by acknowledging the minor help that he can attribute to her skill rather than to Cypris.

‡ Jason evokes Orpheus, the great musician who was said to have been able to bewitch even the god of the dead with his song, because he is comparing different sources of power: money, fame, and, in Orpheus' case, artistic talent.

since you set up this contest of words.
As for your reproaches of my royal
marriage: I will show, first, that I was wise,
then that I was prudent, and finally that I acted
as a great friend to you and the children—No!
Calm down. When I moved here from Iolcus   550
I brought with me a mountain of misfortune.
What luckier escape could I find in exile
than to marry the daughter of the king?
I know it gnaws at you but I don't hate
the bed we share. I wasn't overcome with lust
for a new bride; I'm not competing for the most
children. Those I have are enough: I've no
complaints. No, my main concern was that
we would live well and wouldn't be in need.
I know that everyone runs from a poor friend.   560
I'd raise children worthy of my heritage,
beget brothers for the boys I had with you
and hold them in equal esteem: two families
in one. I would be happy, and you—what need
have you for children? But I profit when
my living children gain from those to come.
I've planned well, no? You would not deny it,
if jealousy didn't gnaw at you. But you women
are so far gone that you believe you have
everything, if things go well in bed.   570
If there's some failure there, you turn what's best
and loveliest into what's most despised.

Really, mortals should reproduce in some
other vessel. The female sex should not exist.
Then no more trouble would afflict mankind.*
CHORUS: Jason, you have framed your words well,
    but, in my opinion—I know you don't agree—
    the betrayal of your wife was not a just act.
MEDEA: I differ from many people in many ways:

---

* Jason's wish that children could be born without women is similar to that of Hippolytus', at lines
616–22 of the *Hippolytus*.

I think, for instance, the unjust person who makes   580
clever speeches deserves the harshest penalty.
He's so sure he can deck out wrongdoing
with pretty words that he'd do any crime.
But he's not so clever. Nor are you. Don't pretend
with smart talk that you're on my side. One word's
enough to flatten you: You should—if you were decent—
have made me understand your marriage, not kept it secret.

JASON: And *you*, I'm sure, would've cheered this plan on,
   if I had told you of it—you, who even now
   can't bear to drop the fury in your heart.   590

MEDEA: *That* wasn't your worry. You saw that in old age
   a foreign marriage wouldn't serve you well.

JASON: Get this into your head: it wasn't for the woman
   I made the royal marriage I now have.
   As I said before, I wanted to protect you,
   to father royal children from the same seed
   as my two sons, a safeguard for my house.

MEDEA: Not for me a prosperous life that causes
   pain, or wealth that gnaws away my heart.

JASON: State that differently and you'd seem wiser: 600
   "Let me not think what's good for me is painful,
   nor think that good luck is misfortune."

MEDEA: Go on! Abuse me—since you are safe and sound!
   But I'm alone and go alone into exile.

JASON: That's your choice. Don't blame anyone else.

MEDEA: You mean, no doubt, I married and betrayed you?

JASON: You laid blasphemous curses on the king.

MEDEA: And I suppose I'm a curse on your house, too.

JASON: I'm not going to debate you anymore.
   If you want to accept the help my money   610
   can give you and the children in your exile,
   say so. I'm prepared to give without stint.
   I'll send tokens to my friends; they'll treat you well.*
   You're a fool, woman, if you're not willing
   to take it. You'll profit more, if you end your anger.

---

* Jason refers here to the practice of guest-friendship by which a person could establish a network of supportive connections with different families in different parts of Greece. Without such a network, a woman in exile would have been particularly vulnerable.

MEDEA: I wouldn't make use of any friend of yours
    nor would I take anything from you: give me
    nothing. The gift of a bad man is no help.

JASON: Well, then, I call on gods to witness that I wanted
    to help you and the children in every way.   620
    But you're not pleased by what is for the best.
    You're stubborn and reject friends: you'll suffer more.

         (Jason exits in the direction of the royal palace.)

MEDEA: *(shouting after him)* Go! Why waste time here when you're
    seized with craving for the girl you've won.
    (more quietly) Enjoy your bride, for it may be your marriage
    will make you weep—the god will prove my words.*

strophe

    CHORUS:
        When passions rise too high in a man they bring
        no goodness, no good name. But if Aphrodite   630
        enters with measured step, no god rivals her grace.
        Lady, never release from your golden bow
        an arrow anointed with desire,
        unerring, at my heart.

antistrophe

        May self-control, the gods' greatest gift, abide by me.
        Plague me not, dread Aphrodite, with angry quarrels,
        endless discord, or yearning for another's bed;   640
        select with keen sight
        a woman's bedmate,
        honor the strifeless union.

strophe

        My fatherland, my home, may I
        never lose you, my city,
        never live a life of desperation,
        a life hard to plod through,
        most pitiable of afflictions.   650
        May death come first,
        death to end my days.

---

* Medea displays her confidence that the gods will support her plans to "make Jason weep" for his betrayal of her and their children.

No worse distress, nothing worse,
than to lose my homeland.

antistrophe

I'm a witness, I can speak
from what I've seen, not others' tales.
For no city, no friend
will pity you
your dreadful suffering.
May he die without grace
who cannot value his nearest, dearest,   660
nor unlock a pure heart. I myself
will never hold him dear.

(Aegeus, king of Athens, enters from the direction of the town.)

AEGEUS: Medea, joy to you! No one knows
a better way to greet a friend than this.
MEDEA: Aegeus, son of wise Pandion, joy to you, too.
Where have you come from that you visit here?
AEGEUS: I come from the ancient oracle of Phoebus.
MEDEA: Why go to the earth's navel, where the god speaks? *
AEGEUS: I asked how I might beget a child.
MEDEA: Truly, you've had no children in your long life?   670
AEGEUS: I am childless, by the whim of some deity.
MEDEA: Have you a wife, or have you been celibate?
AEGEUS: I'm not unbound by the ties of the marriage bed.
MEDEA: What did Phoebus say, then, about children?
AEGEUS: Words wiser than a man's understanding.
MEDEA: Is it right for me to know the god's oracle?
AEGEUS: Indeed, yes, since it requires a clever mind.
MEDEA: What does it say? Tell me, if I may know it.
AEGEUS: "Do not loose the wineskin's jutting foot …"†
MEDEA: Until you do what? or reach where?   680
AEGEUS: "… before returning to your ancestral hearth."
MEDEA: Why sail here, then? What do you seek?

---

* Delphi was the site of the oracle of Apollo (Phoebus); it was thought to stand at the very center, or navel, of the earth.

† A container made from the skin of a goat or sheep was used to carry wine. The skin of one of the animal's legs formed a spout out of which one could drink. The oracle seems to be a riddling reference to the sexual act.

AEGEUS: One Pittheus, king of the land of Troezen.*

MEDEA: Yes, the son of Pelops, they say; a righteous man.

AEGEUS: I want to share the god's oracle with him.

MEDEA: Because he's wise, has experience in such things?

AEGEUS: And because he's dearest of all my allies.

MEDEA: I'll wish you well, then. May you get what you want.

AEGEUS: But why is your face so drawn, your eye so dull?

MEDEA: Aegeus, my husband is the worst of men. 690

AEGEUS: What do you mean? Tell me your sadness plainly.

MEDEA: Jason wrongs me, though I've done him no wrong.

AEGEUS: What has he done to you? Explain more clearly.

MEDEA: He's put a wife above me, as head of the house.

AEGEUS: Surely he wouldn't risk an act so shameful?

MEDEA: He has. Though once his love, I'm nothing now.

AEGEUS: Was he overcome by lust? Or loathed your bed?

MEDEA: Powerful lust caused him to betray his family.

AEGEUS: Then let him go, if, as you say, he's no good.

MEDEA: He longed to marry the daughter of a king. 700

AEGEUS: Who gave him his bride? Explain this, too.

MEDEA: Creon, the man who rules this land of Corinth.

AEGEUS: In that case I can understand your grief, Medea.

MEDEA: I'm ruined, and what's more, I've been exiled.

AEGEUS: By whom? You name another, fresh disaster.

MEDEA: Creon drives me out of Corinth, into exile.

AEGEUS: And Jason lets this happen? I don't approve.

MEDEA: He won't say so, but he's quick to accept it.

(*falling on her knees*) Aegeus, I beg, I grasp your knees and beard,†

I make myself your suppliant: Pity me, 710

pity my misfortune, unhappy as I am.

Don't stand and watch as I'm exiled, all alone.

Receive me in your land and home, give shelter

at your hearth. So may your desire for children

be fulfilled, by the gods, and you die a happy man.

You have no idea what a windfall you've found.

---

* Troezen is on the northeast coast of the Peloponnese; Aegeus would have had to travel through Corinth to get there. Pittheus was Aegeus' father-in-law; his reputation for good counsel is derived in part from his tutoring of Aegeus' son, the famously wise Theseus.

† It is impossible to tell whether Medea performs an actual or a symbolic supplication here. If it is an actual supplication, she would probably remain kneeling and clutching Aegeus' knees until line 731.

I'll end your childlessness, see to it you sow
your seed and reap children. I know a cure for this.
AEGEUS: On many counts I'm eager to do you
this favor, woman: first, for the gods; then 720
for the children whose birth you promise me.
I'm beside myself, when I see that goal in view.
Here's what I propose: if you reach my land,
I will try in justice to offer you protection.*
But let me be clear, woman, on this point:
I'll not consent to bring you away from here.
If you reach my house on your own, you'll be safe there;
you can stay; I won't hand you over to anyone.
Just free yourself from here without my help:
That way my allies have no cause to blame me. 730
MEDEA: So be it. But if I might have a guarantee
of your promise, all would be good between us.
AEGEUS: Surely you trust me? What is it that worries you?
MEDEA: I trust you, yes. But the houses of Pelias and Creon
are my enemy. If the oath I ask for binds you,
you won't send me away, when they come for me.
But if you make a pact unsealed by oath,
you might protect your friendships, be persuaded
by their demands. My position is weak,
while they have wealth and power on their side. 740
AEGEUS: Your reasoning shows great forethought.
So, if it's what you want, I won't refuse.
Safer for me that I can show your foes
a pretext to refuse them, and more secure
for you. By which gods should I swear?
MEDEA: Swear by Earth and by Sun, father of my father,
and the whole race of gods, all in one.
AEGEUS: Swear to do—or not do—what? You say it.
MEDEA: Never yourself expel me from your land.
Never, if one of my enemies wants to take me, 750
willingly hand me over, while you live.

---

* Some editors delete the next two lines (725–26) because of the repetition of Aegeus' statement that he will not help Medea escape. However, his insistence on this point seems perfectly within character.

AEGEUS: I swear by Earth, the pure light of the Sun,
  and all the gods, to abide by what you've said.
MEDEA: Good. And what if you don't fulfill your oath?
AEGEUS: I'll suffer what men suffer who spurn the gods.
MEDEA: Go in peace: all is as it should be.
  I will come to your city as soon as I can, once
  I've done what I intend, got all I want.

> *(Aegeus exits in the direction of the town as the Chorus chant in*
> *anapests.)*

    CHORUS: I call on Hermes, son of Maia, to be your escort,*
  Aegeus, and bring you home. May you achieve   760
  the purpose you so eagerly intend,
  since you have in my eyes shown you are
  a good and noble man.
MEDEA: By Zeus, Justice of Zeus, light of the Sun,
  now will I celebrate victory over my foes.
  I have stepped onto the path, friends.
  Now I expect my enemies will be punished.
  I was in difficulty, and this man appeared,
  a harbor so that I may launch my plans:
  to him I will fasten my ship's cables   770
  when I reach his city, the home of Pallas.†

  I'll tell you all I plan. Accept my words,
  although they give no pleasure to speak or hear.
  I'll send a slave from my house to ask
  Jason to come and see me. I'll
  speak gentle words to him. I will say
  I see things as he does: he's married well.
  The royal marriage he betrayed ours for
  brings good fortune; he has judged well.
  And I will ask that my children remain here.   780
  My reason for this is not to leave my children
  in this hostile place, to be abused by foes,‡
  but so that I can use guile to kill the king's child.

---

* The god Hermes, born of the goddess Maia, is the protector of travelers.
† Pallas Athena.
‡ Some editors omit this line because of its similarity to line 1061.

I'll send my sons with gifts in their arms,*
a delicate robe and headband of beaten gold.
If she takes the ornaments, puts them on her skin,
she'll die—and all who touch her—a terrible death.
I'll anoint my gifts with a poison that can do this.

That's enough for this part of the story.   790
Now hear what follows: I weep
for what I must do; for then I'll kill
my children. No one will give relief.†
When I've annihilated Jason's house, I'll leave
this place, flee from the murder of my dear sons,
that unholy act I've steeled myself for, friends.
To be mocked by enemies is not to be endured.
So be it. What gain for me to stay alive?
I have‡ no fatherland, no home, no escape
from disaster. I made my mistake   800
when I left my family home, when I listened
to the words of a Greek—a man who'll now be punished,
god willing. The children I bore him
he'll never see alive again; he'll never have
a child with his new bride: the wretched woman
must die from my poison, a wretched death.

Let no one think me weak, worthless, or docile.
Let me be thought the opposite of these:
harsh with my enemies, gentle with my friends.
Such people live lives of great renown.   810
CHORUS: Since you have shared your reasoning with us,
   I want to help you and, at the same time,
   uphold humanity's laws: I forbid this act.
MEDEA: There's no other way. But I excuse you
   for saying this: you have not suffered as I have.

---

* The following line, "carrying them to the bride, to escape exile," has been deleted for stylistic and grammatical reasons.

† It is unclear in the Greek whether Medea means that no one will save the children from death or that no one will save her from killing them.

‡ This and the next line are omitted by some editors because they perceive problems with grammar and tone. The preceding assertion, typical of the male heroic determination that an enemy's mockery is not to be endured, seems at odds with the despair of these lines.

CHORUS: Will you steel yourself to kill your flesh and blood?

MEDEA: I must. It's the only way to wound my husband.

CHORUS: And *you* will be most desolate of women.

MEDEA: So be it. More words before the act are useless.

(Medea turns to an attendant slave and gives her order.)

Go now and bring Jason here.   820

In all things requiring trust I count on you.

Say nothing of what I've decided, if you wish

your mistress well. For you're a woman, too.

(The attendant exits in the direction of the royal palace.)

strophe

> CHORUS:
>
> Sons of Erechtheus, fortunate of old,
> children of gods, raised from ground sacred
> and unconquered,* you who feed
> on celebrated wisdom, who walk
> in brightest light with supple step on ground   830
> where the nine Pierian Muses,† so they say,
> created fair-haired Harmony:

antistrophe

> They say that Aphrodite drew
> water from the clear-flowing streams of Cephisus,‡
> breathed on the land the sweetness of the winds'
> gentle breath; she wreathed her hair   840
> with the scent of roses that bloom forever,
> and guided Love to sit with Wisdom
> and work together excellence of every sort.

strophe

> How then will this city and its sacred streams
> this land that gives gods escort§
> give a place to you,

---

* The Chorus address the Athenians as sons of Erechtheus, the mythological founder of Athens, and refer to the Athenians' belief that their race sprang from the earth of Athens rather than coming there from elsewhere.

† Pieria is the region in northern Greece where the Muses lived. Harmony in the following line is most likely a personification of aesthetic beauty, as in mythology Harmony is the daughter of Aphrodite (see Mastronarde, 309).

‡ The stream called Cephisus runs just to the west of Athens.

§ Kovacs has emended the text here to read "gods" instead of "friends," given the emphasis in the previous stanzas on divine presence in Athens.

child-murderer, stained and impure,
among her citizens? 850
Imagine the striking of your sons,
imagine the slaughter you undertake.
Do not—we are your suppliants, we beg you
in every way we can—*do not*
kill your children.

antistrophe

Where will you find the resolve
in your mind, the strength*
in your hand and heart
to summon dreadful daring?
How will you look at your children 860
and hold to their slaughter, unweeping?
When they fall at your feet
in supplication, you will not be able
to dip your hand in their blood
with steely spirit.

(*Jason enters from the direction of the royal palace.*)

JASON: I've been summoned and I've come. I suppose
I owe you this, in spite of your ill will.
What do you want from me now, Medea?

MEDEA: Jason, I ask your forgiveness for the words
I spoke. But it's fitting that you put up 870
with my anger, since a great love came before it.
I've thought it through and I've reproached myself
with these words: "Idiot, why do you rave?
why resent the ones whose plans are good?
why be hateful to the rulers of this land and make
myself my husband's enemy? He's trying to do
his best for us by marrying a princess
and getting children, brothers for my sons.
No end to my rage? What's wrong with me? The gods
will see me through. Don't I have sons? Isn't it true 880
that I'm an exile, and in need of friends?"
These were my thoughts, and I knew I'd indulged
in folly. All my raging served no purpose.

---

* Kovacs has emended the text, which is corrupt here; the general sense is clear despite the corruption.

So now I praise you. All you've done for us
seems prudent now, while I have been a fool.
I should be part of the planning, I should help
to make it happen, be there by the bed,
rejoice in my connection with your bride.*
But we are who we are, we women. I won't say
that's a bad thing, but you must not be like us;†   890
you must not answer our silliness with your own.
I ask forgiveness. I admit my mind wasn't
right then, but I'm determined to do better.

>   (*Medea calls into the house; the children come out with the
>   tutor.*)

Children! come out here; leave the house,
join me in greeting your father, welcome him.
Let go of your hatred as I do mine,
exchange it for friendship, as your mother does.
We've made our peace; our anger has subsided.
Take hold of his right hand—*oimoi!*
My thoughts turn now to hidden sorrows!‡   900
Oh, my sons, will you reach out your dear arms
like this through a long life—unhappy me,
how ready I am to weep, how full of fear.
I'm free, finally, of this quarrel with your father,
and my tender eyes are filling up with tears.

CHORUS: I, too, feel pale tears well up in my eyes.
The pain's gone far enough; let's have no more!

JASON: I approve of your words now, woman, but I didn't
blame you before. It's normal that women rage
if their husband smuggles in another marriage.§
But your feelings have changed for the better; you've   910
recognized the winning plan—in your own time.
This is how a prudent woman behaves.

---

* The text has been slightly emended to get this meaning. Without the emendation, the line would mean "and take pleasure in caring for your bride."

† Kovacs's text here reads "but you should not be like us," implying that Jason is in fact like women and shouldn't be. A variant of the text allows the translation I've given, which, as Mastronarde (315) says, is "more suited to Medea's tone here."

‡ These words reveal to the audience Medea's distress at her secret plan to kill the children but also allow Jason to imagine she is referring to his secret marriage.

§ The text is corrupt here. I follow Mastronarde's emendation and translation of this line.

As for you, sons, your clear-thinking father
has found a haven for you, with the gods' help.
For I believe, in the course of time, you'll rise
to the top, with your brothers, in the land of Corinth.
So, grow up; let your father tend to the rest,
with whoever of the gods is well-disposed. May I
lay eyes upon you when you've grown to manhood,   920
great strapping lads who tower over my foes.
(*gesturing to Medea*) You, why drown your eyes in pale tears?
Why turn your white cheek away?
Aren't you glad to hear the words I've spoken?
MEDEA: It's nothing. I was thinking of our sons.*
JASON: I'll make things right for them. Take heart!
MEDEA: I'll do that, I won't distrust your words. But women
    are by nature delicate and prone to tears.
JASON: But why so headstrong in your grief for them?
MEDEA: I gave them birth; when you prayed that they live,   930
    I felt pity, not knowing if it will be so.
But you came to talk about a number of things.
Some we've discussed; others I'll raise now.
Since the rulers of this land plan to exile me,
—and I know it is best for me not to live
where I'll be in your way and the king's way,
since I'm considered an enemy to this house—
I'll take myself away, go into exile.
But our children—ask Creon not to exile *them*,
so that they may grow up here, in your care.   940
JASON: I don't know if I'll persuade him, but I must try.
MEDEA: At least tell your wife to make an appeal
    to her father not to exile the children.
JASON: Certainly. I expect that *her* I will persuade.
MEDEA: I'm sure you will, if she's like other women.†
    I'll contribute my efforts as well. I'll send
some gifts to her, ones I'm sure are thought
most beautiful by far in all the world.‡
The children will carry them.

---

* I do not follow Kovacs's transposition of lines 929–31 to follow this line.

† Some editors attribute this line to Jason: "I'm sure I will if she's like other women."

‡ Line 949 is identical to line 786 and is more suited to the context there; it is therefore omitted here.

(*to an attendant slave*) Quick,   950
get one of my servants to bring the dress here.
Her blessings will be countless, not just one:
she gets the best of men as her bedmate,
and these beautiful treasures which the Sun,
father of my father, once gave to his descendants.

> (*The attendant slave goes to the door of the house and receives the gifts from a household slave inside.*)[*]

(*to the children*) Take this bridal gift in your arms, sons,
and give it to the happy bride, the daughter
of the king. The gift she'll get is no mean thing.

JASON: You're foolish to deprive yourself of these.
Do you imagine the king's house lacks clothing,   960
or has no gold? Keep them; don't give them away.
If my wife considers me of any value,
she'll put me before objects, I'm sure.

MEDEA: Don't stop me. Gifts persuade even the gods,
and gold has more power over men than words.
Some god it is who lifts this woman's fortunes;[†]
she comes to power young. I'd give my life,
not gold alone, to save my sons from exile.
But you, my sons, go to her prosperous house
and throw yourselves at the feet of your father's bride,   970
who now rules me; give her these gifts
and beg her not to exile you. Be sure she takes
this gift in her own hands. This is most important.
Go quickly and do well! Bring me good news
that I have achieved what I long for.

strophe

CHORUS:
Now I can hope no longer for the children's lives,
hope no longer. Now they go to their death.
The bride will take the golden band,
will take her doom, her misery.
She'll put on the diadem with her two hands,   980
put Death around her golden hair.

---

[*] See Mastronarde (39) for a discussion of whether the gifts are carried in a closed chest or on a tray so they may be seen.

[†] Kovacs deletes this line, unnecessarily I believe.

antistrophe

> Their grace, their heavenly glow will coax her
> to wrap the robe around her, put on the golden crown.
> The bride will adorn herself, already one of the dead.
> Into the trap she'll fall:
> her lot, her death, her misery;
> she won't elude this doom.

strophe

> You poor man, cursed bridegroom,   990
> suitor of kings,
> you do not know
> you lead your sons to destruction,
> bring awful death to your wife.
> Miserable man, how you mistake your destiny.

antistrophe

> I weep then for your pain,
> unhappy mother
> of children you will kill
> in the name of your marriage,
> the bed your husband unlawfully fled   1000
> to live with another bedmate.
>> *(The tutor enters with the children from the direction of the royal house.)*

TUTOR: Mistress, your sons are released from exile!
  The royal bride has received your gifts
  with pleasure: there's peace there for the children.
  What's this?* Why are you shocked by your good fortune?

MEDEA: *aiai!*

TUTOR: Your cry doesn't harmonize with the news I've brought.

MEDEA: *aiai, aiai!*

TUTOR: Surely I haven't unwittingly
  reported some misfortune? Isn't this good news?   1010

MEDEA: You've brought the news you've brought; I do not blame you.

TUTOR: But why cast your eyes to the ground? Why weep?

MEDEA: I must, old man. Because of what the gods,
  and I, in my folly, have designed.

---

* The tutor's surprise is expressed in the Greek by a cry, translated here into "What's this?" After the following line, two lines have been deleted: "Why have you turned your face away? / Why do you receive my news without pleasure?" on the assumption that they are an actor's interpolation to give the explicit physical cause of the tutor's surprise.

TUTOR: Take heart. In time your sons will turn your fortune.*
MEDEA: First I'll turn the fortunes of others, wretched me.
TUTOR: You're not alone in being parted from children.
 You're mortal; you must bear misfortune lightly.
MEDEA: This I will do. Now go into the house
 and look to the children's needs.   1020
> *(The tutor starts to exit with the children; Medea delays them
> by suddenly addressing the children.)†*

Oh, children, my two children, you have a city
and a home in which you'll live on, always,
without your mother, once you've left me in misery.
I, in exile, will travel to another land
before I have delight in seeing you happy,
before tending to your wedding bath, your bride,
your nuptial bed, or holding the marriage torches.
Oh, misery born of my stubborn will!
I've brought you up to no purpose then;
to no purpose I toiled, wore myself out,   1030
bore the harsh pains of childbirth.
I'm wretched now, but once was full of hope
that you would care for me in my old age,
lay me out on my death bed with your own hands.
Men would have envied me. But now this sweet
thought is shattered. Without the two of you
I will lead a life of pain and misery.
And your sweet eyes will see your mother
no longer. Your lives will take another course.
pheu, pheu, why do your eyes rest on me, children?   1040
Why smile one last smile when you see me?
(to the Chorus) aiai, what should I do? I'm losing heart

---

* In the Greek, the tutor clearly states that the sons will bring Medea back from exile. Medea in her response uses a verb that can be understood as either "bring back from exile" or "send to the Underworld." In order to capture Medea's play on the tutor's words, I have translated the tutor's line as "turn your fortune" instead of "bring you back from exile."

† Medea's monologue has been revised in many different ways, depending on how much uncertainty an editor feels is appropriate for Medea to express at this point in the play about the killing of the children. Various suggestions have also been made for the stage action that accompanies the speech. For two extensive discussions of the emendations and their strengths and weaknesses, see Mastronarde, lines 388–97, and Burnett, 273–87. I have deleted only two lines in my translation, as I think the repetitions, swerves of thinking, and uncertainty are a powerful representation of the difficulty Medea has in bringing herself to kill her children.

as I look on my children's bright faces.
I couldn't ... Let me say goodbye to plans
I made before! I'll take my sons from here.
Why must I hurt their father with their pain
and so give myself double their suffering?
I will not. Goodbye to those plans!

But no, what's happening to me? Do I want
to be mocked while my enemies go unpunished?   1050
I must steel myself. What cowardice even
to let melting words into my mind.
Go into the house, sons. If anyone thinks
it wrong to attend my sacrifices, let him
look out for himself. I will not stay my hand.

> (*Medea starts to exit with the children and the tutor. She stops
> suddenly while they continue slowly toward the house, out of
> earshot.*)

ah, ah!
Don't. Don't do this, you, my strong spirit.
Leave them be, miserable heart; spare these children.
They'll bring you joy, living there with you ...

By the spirits of vengeance who dwell in Hades,
I will not hand over my sons to my enemies   1060
to be abused. This will never be.*
It's done, all done, and she will not escape.
Already the golden band sits on her head;
the royal bride dies in her robes, I know.
So I will walk a road most pitiable;
more pitiable yet the road I send these on.

> (*Medea hurries toward the children as they are about to enter
> the house and stops them from entering.*)

(*to herself*) I want to talk to my children. (*to her children*) Give me,
my sons, give me your right hands to kiss.   1070
Dearest hand, dear mouth, body and shape
most dear to me, and fine, noble face!

---

* Two lines—"They must die. And since they must / I who gave them life will kill them"—have been
omitted, as they are identical to lines 1240–42 and seem more important to that passage than here.

May you both be happy—if not here, then there.
What's here your father takes for himself.
Oh, sweet to touch, soft skin, and sweetest breath
of my children. Go, go. I can no longer look at them;
I'm overcome by what we must suffer.
I understand the ruin I'm about to cause,*
and yet my spirit is stronger than my plans.
Here is the cause of mankind's greatest ills.

    (Medea stands at the door as the children go inside.)

  CHORUS: *(chanting)*

    Often before this I've engaged
    in talk more subtle and
    problems more difficult
    than a woman should explore.
    But we, too, have a Muse,
    and on wisdom's behalf she joins
    with us—not all of us—but a few,
    a small group, a woman here and there
    you'd find, women the Muse touches.
    And I claim that anyone—man   1090
    or woman—who has no experience,
    has never had a child, exceeds
    every parent in happiness.
    The childless are spared many troubles
    by their inexperience;
    they never find out if children
    are sweetness or distress.
    But those whose houses blossom
    sweetly with children
    are all the time worn down with care.   1100
    First they worry how to bring them up well
    and at their death leave behind enough to live.
    On top of this it isn't clear
    whether they labor for children
    who are worthless or good.
    And now I'll name the last horror,

---

* Modern critics have debated the meaning of these final three lines. Some see Medea reneging on her plan to murder her children; others see her finally resolving to carry it out. In my view, the final lines cannot be resolved in either of these directions; rather, they show that Medea is still in doubt.

worst of all for any mortal woman or man:
let's say you've found a good enough
livelihood and your child has come
to adulthood healthy and good.
Then, if this should be its destiny,
Death goes off to Hades   1110
with your child's body in his arms.
What profit then for mortals
that, for the sake of children,
they suffer this most dreadful pain
the gods pile on to all their other troubles?

MEDEA: Dear women, I've waited long for the outcome,
anxious to know how it will turn out there,
in the palace. Now I see a man approaching,
Jason's attendant. His jagged breathing tells me
he's going to announce some fresh disaster.   1120

(The messenger runs onto the stage from the direction of the royal palace.)

MESSENGER: Medea, take flight, go by land or by sea;*
use any boat or cart to get away.

MEDEA: What's happened that demands my flight?

MESSENGER: The young girl, royal bride, and Creon her father
are dead—killed just now, and by your poisons!

MEDEA: The story you've told couldn't be better. Hereafter
you'll be among my close allies and friends.

MESSENGER: What are you saying? Are you insane, woman?
You must be mad to rejoice at this, to feel   1130
no fear, when you've defiled the royal hearth.

MEDEA: I have my own tale to tell in response
to yours. But hold nothing back, friend.
Tell me all. How did they die? You'd give me
double the joy if their death was horrible.

MESSENGER: When your two sons arrived with their father
and entered the house of the newlyweds,
we were glad, we household slaves who felt
distress at your troubles. Word spread fast that you
and your husband had resolved your differences.   1140

---

* A line before this one has been deleted—"Woman, you who've acted terribly, unlawfully"—on the assumption that it is a later addition to introduce clear moral censure of Medea.

One slave kisses the children's hands, another
their golden heads. I myself in my pleasure
followed the children into the women's quarters.
My mistress—the one we honor now instead
of you—held Jason in her eager gaze,
until she saw the pair of children, your sons.
Then she covered her eyes with her veil
and turned away her white cheek: she felt
such disgust at their coming in there.
Your husband tried to soothe the young girl's anger: 1150
"Don't be unkind to people dear to us,
don't be angry. Won't you turn your face back
to me? Hold dear the ones dear to your husband?
Take their gifts, beg your father for my sake
to release these children from exile."
When she saw their gifts, she didn't resist;
she agreed to everything, and, before
your children and their father were far away,
she took the gorgeous robes and put them on.
She placed the golden band around her curls   1160
and looked in a bright mirror to arrange her hair,
laughing at the lifeless image she saw there.
Then she stood up from her chair and walked
around the room, her white feet stepping softly.
She loved the gifts; she kept looking behind
as she stretched her ankle out below the robe.
What happened then was terrible to see.
Her skin changed color. She lurched backward,
trembling in every limb; she barely reached
a chair to sit on, so she wouldn't fall.   1170
A slave, an old woman, gave a ritual cry, thinking
her frenzy had come from Pan or another god.*
Then she saw the white foam bubbling
from her mouth, her pupils turned back
in the sockets of her eyes, her bloodless skin.
The cry turned into a great wailing shriek,
and the old woman rushed straight away

---

* When a person fell into a fit or an inexplicable illness, the god Pan was often posited as the cause.

to the king's house. Another ran to the new groom
to inform him of his bride's misfortune.
The rafters echoed with the running of feet.   1180
It took the time a sprinter takes to fly
to the finish of a one-stade course*
for the wretched girl to rouse herself and cry out
in horror, her eyes and mouth no longer shut.
The pain was attacking her on a double front:
the band of gold she'd placed around her head
shot out an astounding stream of devouring fire;
the delicate robe, your children's gift, was gnawing
the white flesh of the doomed girl. On fire
she rises from the chair and runs about,   1190
shaking her head and hair in all directions.
She was trying to throw off the golden band,
but it stayed tightly bound as the fire flared out,
now twice as fierce when she shook her hair.
Overcome by suffering she falls to the floor.
No one could recognize her, only
her father could: her eyes and fine-boned face
no longer had a clear shape; blood and fire
mingled together, fell dripping from her head.
Her skin like the sap of a fir tree oozed off   1200
her bones, loosed by the jaws of the unseen poison.
An awful sight. Everyone feared to touch the corpse,
taking our instruction from what had happened.

Her wretched father knew nothing of the disaster.
In ignorance he entered the room and ran to the body.
At once he cried out and folded her in his arms;
kissing her, he moaned: "Oh, my poor child,
which of the gods has destroyed you without honor?
Who takes you from me, an old man as good
as dead? *oimoi*, let me die with you, child."   1210
When he'd finished wailing and groaning
we wanted to lift up his aged body,
but he was stuck to the delicate robe like ivy

---

* About 200 yards. See Mastronarde (356) for an explanation of the measurement.

to a laurel branch. His struggle was desperate.
He tried and tried to get up on his knees,
but the corpse kept pulling him back. If he moved
with force, he ripped his ageing flesh from the bone.
In time, he gave it up and breathed his last,
rising no longer above calamity.
The bodies of the child and aged father lie   1220
side by side, a misfortune calling for tears.*

Your situation I won't address. You'll know
yourself the penalty that answers this.†
Once again I'm led to think what's mortal
is but a shadow. I wouldn't hesitate to say
those who seem wise and use fine words
are the ones who earn the charge of idiocy.
No human being, not one, is happy.
If wealth flows in, one man might be luckier
than another—but he still would not be happy.   1230
CHORUS: Heaven, it seems, has fastened Jason
    to great suffering on this day—and justly.‡
MEDEA: Friends, my course is set: quick as I can
    I kill the children and leave this land.
    I mustn't delay or give over to some other
    harsher hand the killing of the children.
    They must die, they must. And, since they must,   1240
    I, who gave them birth, will kill them.

    Come then, my heart, and arm yourself. Why wait
    to do this terrible but necessary wrong?
    Take hold of the sword, you, my wretched hand,
    take it. Move to the start of a life of misery.
    Don't turn coward, don't think of the children.
    Don't remember that you bore them, that they're

---

* The text of this line is uncertain. Many editors, including Kovacs, omit it.

† This translation depends on an emendation of one word. Without the emendation, the lines would read "You'll know for yourself / an escape from punishment."

‡ Three lines have been deleted, on the grounds that conventionally the Chorus speak only two lines at the end of a long speech like the Messenger's. The lines are "Wretched girl, how we pity your misfortune, / daughter of Creon. You go to the house of Death / because of your marriage to Jason." It would seem out of place for the Chorus to comment on the death of the princess, whom they elsewhere are not concerned with.

most loved. Forget for this short day they are
your children, and *then* grieve. Though you'll kill them,
they're your dear flesh and blood. I'm a luckless woman.   1250

> *(Medea exits into the house.)*

strophe

CHORUS:* *iō,* Earth and Sun's radiant light
look down, look on this accursed
woman before she casts
her murderous hand on her own children.
They are flowers grown from your golden seed;
a fearful thing that a god's blood spill
to the ground through human hands.
You then, Zeus-born light, hold her back,
stop her, drive this vengeful Fury, bloody
and pitiless, from the house.†   1260

antistrophe

Your labor for your children gone in vain,
in vain you bore them, beloved offspring,
you who left behind the unwelcoming pass
between the dark rocks of the Symplegades.‡
Desperate woman, why does anger
that weighs upon the mind fall on you, and rabid murder
follow murder?
The stain of kin's blood is a hard thing for mortals;
sorrow follows on it, falling from the gods,
its song in harmony with murder of kin.   1270

> *(The children's voices are heard from within the house.)§*

FIRST CHILD: *iō moi!*

strophe

CHORUS: Do you hear? hear the cry of children? ¶
iō, wretched, doomed woman!

---

* The meter of this song is predominantly dochmiacs, a meter unique to tragedy and expressing intense emotion.

† The text here is corrupt. The Chorus describe Medea as a Fury, a spirit of vengeance, but as the text stands, they go on to say that she herself is being driven by avenging spirits.

‡ See note to line 2.

§ The order of the lines has been slightly altered from the manuscript tradition. The Chorus's song continues in the same rhythm as the previous two stanzas; the strophe is interspersed with lines spoken by the children from within the house.

¶ In the strophe, the Chorus are singing and the children are speaking. In the antistrophe, the Chorus by themselves maintain the same alternation between singing and speaking.

FIRST CHILD: *oimoi*, what should I do? Where can I flee mother's hand?

SECOND CHILD: I don't know, dear brother. We are lost.

    CHORUS: Should I go inside? I should stop their murder, I think.

FIRST CHILD: Please, by the gods, help! We need you now!

SECOND CHILD: The snare of swords—it's coming very near.

    CHORUS: Wretched woman, then you are made from iron or rock,   1280
        since the children you bore you'll kill, their fate in your hands.

antistrophe
        One woman I know of, one of all before,
          who struck her beloved children with her own hand:
Ino, maddened by gods, when the wife of Zeus
sent her wandering from her home.*
        Wretched, she falls in the sea at their impious death.
Her foot stepping beyond the edge, into the sea,
she dies as she destroys her own two children.
        What horrible thing now couldn't yet come to be?   1290
        O women's bed of sorrows, how great the harm you've done
          mankind.

      (Jason rushes in from the direction of the royal palace.)

JASON: You, women who've been standing by the house,
is Medea—a woman who's done dreadful things!—
inside? Or has she fled? Is she gone?
Either she must be hidden deep in the earth,
or rise into the lofty air on wings,
if she's not to pay what's due to the king's house.
Does she imagine she'll flee from here
unpunished, when, on her own, she's killed the king?   1300
But it's not her I care about. It's the children.
The ones that woman harmed will try to harm her,
but I'm here to save my children's lives: I fear
Creon's kinsmen will do something to *them*,
exact from *them* the price of their mother's crime.

---

* Ino's story parallels Medea's in a number of ways. She was a sister of Semele, the mother of Dionysus; after Semele's death, Ino raised Dionysus and earned Hera's enmity, since Dionysus was Zeus' son by Semele. In one version of the story, Hera maddens Ino, who kills at least one of her two sons by boiling him in a cauldron and then jumps into the sea with the cauldron. (The other son, in most versions of the story, was killed by Athamas, Ino's husband; here she is said to have killed both of them.) Zeus took pity on Ino and transformed her into the sea goddess Leucothea. She is also the stepmother of Phrixus and Helle, whom she hated and plotted to kill but who were saved by a golden ram whose fleece is the Golden Fleece that Jason recovers from Colchis.

CHORUS: You've no idea the ruin you've come to, Jason;
    if you had, you wouldn't have said these words.
JASON: What is it? I suppose she wants to kill me, too?
CHORUS: Your children are dead—by their mother's hand.
JASON: *oimoi*, what can you mean? You have destroyed me.   1310
CHORUS: You must believe your children live no longer.
JASON: Where did she kill them? Inside the house? Outside?
CHORUS: Open the doors. Look on your murdered children.
    *(Banging on the doors, Jason shouts to slaves inside the house.)**
JASON: Undo the locks, you there! Quick as you can,
    open the doors, show me the double horror:
    the bodies of my boys, and *her*... *she*'ll pay.
    (Medea appears on the roof of the skēnē, *in a chariot with the*
    bodies of her two sons.)†
MEDEA: Why rattle and force these doors in search
    of these corpses and me, the one who made them?
    Stop this labor: If you have need of me,
    say what you want; but you will never touch me.   1320
    The Sun-god, my father's father, gave me this,
    a chariot to ward off my enemies' hands.
JASON: Hateful thing! Woman! The greatest enemy
    to gods and me and the whole human race!
    You dared, you who bore them, to thrust a sword
    into the children; made me childless; ruined me!
    You've done this, and still you look upon the sun,
    upon the earth? After daring this unholy crime?
    I want you dead! I'm sane now—I wasn't then
    when I brought you from your home, your savage land,   1330
    to a Greek household: an utter disaster,
    betrayer of your father and your homeland.
    The gods have sent to *me* the avenging spirit
    that lurked for *you*. You killed your brother at the hearth
    and boarded *Argo* with its beautiful prow.
    That's how you started. But then you were married

---

* It is impossible to tell whether Jason is ordering slaves outside the house with him or inside the house to open the doors. I think it is preferable to have him enter the stage at this point unattended and therefore have him ordering slaves inside the house.

† The roof of the *skēnē* is used in Greek tragedy for the appearance of gods, in this case represented by the Sun-god's chariot.

to me, and you bore me children. And for the sake
of the marriage bed we shared you destroyed them.
There isn't a woman in Greece, no Greek woman,
who would have dared this. Yet I thought you   1340
worthy of marriage instead of one of them—
a marriage of ruin and hate—not to a woman,
no: to a lion, more savage than Tyrrhenian Scylla.*
But no amount of insults I might speak
could make their mark on you: you are that bold.
Away with you and your foul acts,† stained with your
children's blood! There's little left for me except to weep.
I'll get no profit from my new marriage;
I'll never speak to the sons I sowed and raised,
or see them living; they are lost to me.   1350

MEDEA: I would have made long answer to this speech
if father Zeus did not already know
what you have gained from me, and what you've done.
Once you'd dishonored my marriage bed,
you weren't going to mock me and enjoy your life,
nor was the princess. Nor was Creon going
to give you a bride and throw me out, scot-free.
Go on, call me lioness if you want, call me
a Scylla who makes the Tyrrhenian rock her home.
I've done what I had to do to wring your heart.   1360

JASON: And hurt yourself; you have your share of ruin.

MEDEA: No doubt. But it's worth the pain if *you*'re not laughing.

JASON: Oh, children, what a wicked mother you had!

MEDEA: Oh, sons, you were ruined by your father's disease!

JASON: It wasn't *my* right hand that murdered them.

MEDEA: No, it was your insolence, your new-forged marriage.

JASON: You judged it right to kill them for your bed?

MEDEA: You think *that* pain's a small thing for a woman?

JASON: For one who's balanced, yes. But you're all bad.

MEDEA: They are no more. *These* words will tear your flesh.   1370

---

* Scylla is a sea monster (depicted with several heads and feet by Homer and by vase painters) who grabs sailors as they pass by her cave. The Tyrrhenian sea, where Scylla is imagined to have her home, is the area of the Mediterranean off the western coast of Italy.

† Later use of the word translated here as "foul acts" (literally, "doer of ugly things") suggests a tone of almost sexual disgust in Jason's speech. The word is found nowhere else in surviving tragedy.

JASON: They live in the curse of vengeance on your head.
MEDEA: The gods know who began their suffering.
JASON: What they know is your noxious mind.
MEDEA: Loathe me. I hate the sound of your piercing voice.
JASON: And I yours. Easy to put an end to this.
MEDEA: Tell me how. I want that. What shall I do?
JASON: Hand me those bodies to bury and to mourn.
MEDEA: No, indeed. With this hand I'll bury them.

I'll carry them to the temple of Hera Akraia
so that my enemies may not violate them   1380
by smashing their tomb. In this land of Sisyphus*
we will install a sacred feast and rites
to expiate for all time their unholy murder.†
I will go to the land of Erechtheus‡ to live
in the house of Aegeus, son of Pandion. You,
a bad man, will die a bad death, as suits you:
struck on the head by a piece of *Argo*, after
you've seen the bitter end of marriage to me.

(Jason and Medea chant in anapests.)

JASON: May the children's Fury destroy you,
and bloody Justice.   1390
MEDEA: What god, what spirit hears you—
breaker of oaths, deceiver of a stranger's trust?
JASON: *pheu*, *pheu*, foul child-killer.§
MEDEA: Go to the palace, bury your wife.
JASON: I go, without my two sons.
MEDEA: Don't mourn yet; wait for old age.
JASON: Oh, children dearest—
MEDEA: —to their mother, yes. Not to you.
JASON: And so you killed them?
MEDEA: To cause you pain.

---

* See note to line 405.

† Euripides often ends his plays with a god, or occasionally a human, explaining how a rite known to his audience is connected to the events the play has enacted. The temple of Hera Akraia was in or near Corinth. Since another version of the Medea story has the Corinthians killing the children, there may have been a rite in Corinth established to atone for their death. Pausanias locates the tomb of Medea's sons in Corinth.

‡ Athens.

§ The Greek word translated here as "foul" describes Medea as a polluted being whom no one will approach or touch. All murderers were considered polluted and in need of a ritual of purification, but murderers of family members especially so.

JASON: *oimoi*, I need in my despair
    to kiss their dear mouths.   1400

MEDEA: You talk to them now, now embrace them;
    then you pushed them away.

JASON: By the gods, let me touch
    the children's soft skin.

MEDEA: It cannot be. You speak to no purpose.
    (As Jason speaks, Medea departs with the boys' bodies in the
    chariot sent by the Sun-god, raised by the mēchanē.)

JASON: Zeus, do you hear? how I'm driven away,
    what suffering comes from this
    foul, child-murdering lioness?
    As best I can, as much as I am able,
    I mourn, I summon the gods
    to bear witness that you   1410
    killed the children, and now you stop me
    touching them, burying their bodies.
    Would that I had never given them life
    to see them destroyed by you.
    (Jason remains alone onstage as the Chorus chant the coda to
    the drama.)

CHORUS: Zeus on Olympus keeps many things in store;*
    the gods accomplish many startling things.
    What we expect does not take place,
    and the god makes way for what we don't expect.
    And so it came about in this affair.

---

* The final lines spoken by the Chorus are a variant of a conventional ending that Euripides uses for several of his plays, including the *Alcestis*, the *Helen*, and the *Bacchae*.

Introduction to Euripides' *Hippolytus*

Hippolytus, written in 428 B.C., has much in common with Euripides' last surviving play, the *Bacchae*, composed perhaps twenty years later. Both plays concern the price paid by mortals who fail to honor particular gods: Aphrodite wreaks vengeance on Hippolytus in the earlier play, Dionysus on Pentheus in the later one. In both, Euripides stares straight into the face of the moral problems raised by traditional Greek religion, with its tales of jealous, proud, and vengeful deities who often do great harm. Gods who use punishment to extract devotion are no better than despots, yet their divine nature, rising far above the mortal plane (and, thanks to the *mēchanē*, above the stage trodden by ordinary mortals) demands that we worship them nonetheless.

Unlike Dionysus in the *Bacchae*, who oversees in person every step of his revenge, Aphrodite here merely discloses in a prologue speech the plan she has set in motion, then departs the scene. Her target is Hippolytus, son of the Athenian king Theseus by an Amazon queen (not named here, elsewhere called either Antiope or Hippolyta) who has since died. The young man is now in Troezen, across the Saronic Gulf from Athens; his father has been exiled here to expiate the crime of kin-murder, after killing some of his cousins in battle. Here he devotes himself to hunting and to the worship of Artemis, goddess of the hunt and, importantly for him, a committed virgin. For Hippolytus scorns Aphrodite, and the sexuality she represents, with a kind of puritanical disgust: "No god worshipped in the dark can please me," he tells a disapproving servant (line 106). To pay him back for his renunciation, Aphrodite has made Hippolytus the object of an illicit passion: the desperate love of Phaedra, Theseus' new wife, a princess of Crete. As the play opens, Hippolytus and Phaedra, stepson and stepmother, have been left in Troezen by Theseus, who has gone to consult the oracle at Delphi.

It's worth noting that Aphrodite's appearance for this prologue speech is not crucial to the play's development; neither Seneca nor Racine, in later reworkings of this play, included her among their cast. (It's also noteworthy that both Seneca and Racine titled their versions of this play *Phaedra* rather than *Hippolytus*, placing her sufferings rather than his at the center of the story.) Powerful sexual passion, like Phaedra's for Hippolytus, was understood by the Greeks, in and of itself, as a divine force; they gave the name *erōs* both to this feeling and to a deity, the son of Aphrodite. By having Aphrodite lay claim to the kindling of this passion, Euripides gave special stress to the role of the gods in engineering the downfall of his human characters. It's also likely, based on surviving evidence, that he wrote this prologue in response to Athenian displeasure with an earlier version of his play, in which the incestuous passion of Phaedra was portrayed, scandalously for that era, as arising purely from her own impulses.

Unaware of the trap that has been set, Hippolytus comes onstage with a band of fellow huntsmen, singing a pious hymn to Artemis. We see him lay a wreath of wildflowers before the statue of his patroness and describe how he, alone among mortals, is able to converse with her (though without seeing her). The bond between god and mortal is here portrayed, like that of Odysseus and Athena in Homer's *Odyssey*, as a pairing of kindred spirits. The love of hunting, a sport pursued in the Greek world with dogs, spears, and nets, is deeply ingrained in both their natures; it takes both of them outside the ordered space of the *polis* and into wild glens and mountain ridges. Their shared violations of gender norms also transcends the order of the *polis*: Artemis, who resembles a barbarian Amazon in dress and behavior, adopts a role normally reserved for Greek males, while Hippolytus, the son of an Amazon, preserves a virginal purity that Greeks associated with females.

With deft psychological insight, Euripides also gives to Phaedra, as she raves in the throes of her lovesickness, a longing for the mountains, the glades, and the hunt. The Amazon way of life, as constructed in Greek myth and legend, was linked to extremes of sexual passion and chastity at the same time; both are seen as escapes from the sanctions of licit pair-bonding and marriage. Incestuous longing has put Phaedra, too, outside the bounds of society and connected her to the primal forces of the wilderness. Parallels with Euripides' *Bacchae* are again illustrative. Mount Cithaeron is configured in that later play as the site of animal energies that include both sexual desire and the aggression of the hunt, and above all the frenzy of Bacchic dance. Such energies, in both plays, are set profoundly at odds with those on which the *polis* relies.

As Phaedra struggles between conflicting impulses and contemplates suicide, she is counseled by the Nurse, one of many Euripidean characters whose pragmatism and quotidian concerns stand in contrast to the tragic world around them—the kind of figure who, in Shakespeare's plays, typically speaks in prose rather than verse. Though the Nurse at first feels shock and outrage at Phaedra's forbidden passion, she ultimately abets it on the grounds that life, even a life lived in shame and disgrace, is better than self-destruction. The question posed by her actions—whether the benefit of being alive is worth any price—is one that Euripides frequently contemplated (the *Alcestis* is a prominent example in this volume, the *Heracles* is another outside it), and his audiences were troubled by his willingness to do so. Aristophanes, in the comedy the *Frogs*, made the depiction of Phaedra's passion here a focal point in a debate between Euripides and Aeschylus, prompting Aeschylus' famous assertion that the tragic poet is the moral instructor of the city and should show more inspiring models. Though Phaedra herself is the primary target of this attack—Aeschylus claims she teaches decent women to become whores—the Nurse, too, with her antiheroic doctrine that nothing in the end is worth dying for, lurks in the background.

The Nurse's intervention in Phaedra's plight leads to disaster. Though she tries to protect her mistress by swearing Hippolytus to secrecy, the young man's outrage overwhelms his fidelity to his oath: "My tongue swore, my mind did not," he proclaims (line 612), another inversion of popular morality for which Aristophanes bitterly lampooned Euripides. With her secret out, Phaedra refuses to go on living, but, with anachronistic use of a written message—reading and writing are usually absent from the mythic world—she blames Hippolytus for her downfall. Her motive is not, as might be supposed, to get back at the man who scorned her, but to protect her reputation and the rights of her own children by Theseus (mentioned briefly at line 717).

As Phaedra enters the palace to put her plan into effect, the Chorus of Troezenian women sing one of Euripides' loveliest odes, evoking the peaceful shores of the river Eridanus in western Europe and, beyond that, the balmy island, somewhere in the Atlantic perhaps, where grow the golden apples of the Hesperides. As often in Euripides, a wistful vision of escape, set to what was no doubt haunting music, provides a serene interlude before disaster strikes. While satirists like Aristophanes might carp over the moral dimensions of Euripides' plots, no one contested the beauty of his lyrics. After the Athenian defeat in Sicily in 413 B.C., prisoners of war reportedly earned lenient treatment by singing snatches of odes from Euripidean plays.

Theseus now returns from Delphi to find his wife dead; he reads the mendacious note as the Chorus members look on in silence, preserving with too-great fidelity their oath not to reveal Phaedra's sorrows. In an instant, Theseus, portrayed in other tragedies as the soul of self-restraint (see *Oedipus at Colonus* in this volume), becomes as enraged and vengeful as any Creon. He calls on Poseidon—here portrayed as his father, though other legends made Theseus the son of Aegeus, a mortal—to fulfill one of three promised wishes, and the fate of Hippolytus, later described in a harrowing messenger speech, is sealed.

A final scene, counterpart to the prologue, brings on the goddess Artemis *ex machina* to reveal the full horror of what has taken place. She gives comfort when she decrees that hereafter, ritual offerings will be left for Hippolytus by the maidens of Troezen, and she tries gamely to reconcile father and son. But when she leaves the stage before Hippolytus dies, lest the taint of mortality stain her, we are reminded that gods such as these cannot truly befriend human beings or even understand their suffering. Euripides also makes clear that Artemis goes off to wreak destruction on some other innocent victim, merely for the sake of getting even with Aphrodite. The gods do not kill us for their sport, but they also make no great effort to prevent us from becoming their collateral damage.

HIPPOLYTUS

Translated by Rachel Kitzinger

CAST OF CHARACTERS (IN ORDER OF APPEARANCE)

APHRODITE, goddess of sexual love; also known as Cypris

HIPPOLYTUS, son of Theseus, the king of Athens, by an Amazon queen

HIPPOLYTUS' FELLOW HUNTERS, a group of slaves from his household

OLD SLAVE, an attendant to Hippolytus

CHORUS of young married women of Troezen

NURSE, Phaedra's personal attendant

PHAEDRA, wife of Theseus; daughter of King Minos and Queen Pasiphae of Crete

THESEUS, king of Athens

MESSENGER, an attendant of Hippolytus

ARTEMIS, virgin goddess of the hunt, of wild things, and of childbirth

Setting: The play takes place in front of the palace of Theseus in Troezen, on the north coast of the Peloponnese, facing Athens to the north across the Saronic Gulf. Of the two entrances to the stage, one is understood to come from places far from Troezen, the other from the town and surrounding countryside. On one side of the stage area is a statue of Aphrodite, on the other a statue of Artemis.

(Aphrodite appears on the roof of the skēnē, *which represents the palace of Theseus.)**

APHRODITE: I am famous and powerful among mortals
   and gods. I am called the goddess Cypris.†
   Of people everywhere—all who see sunlight
   between the Atlantic Ocean and the Black Sea—
   I rank highest those who revere my power.
   I crush those who are proud before me.
   For this holds true even for the gods:
   they feel pleasure when men honor them.
   Soon I will show how true this is.
   Theseus has a son, Hippolytus. An Amazon‡   10
   bore him, and righteous Pittheus§ raised him.
   Of all the citizens of this land of Troezen,
   he alone says I am the worst of gods.
   He spurns sex, will have nothing to do with marriage.
   It's Artemis, sister to Phoebus, daughter of Zeus,
   he honors and believes the greatest god.
   He's always in the green wood with the virgin goddess,
   ridding the earth of wild beasts with his swift dogs.

---

* Gods traditionally appear on the roof of the *skēnē* in Greek tragedy.

† The name Cypris probably originates from Aphrodite's cult site on the island of Cyprus, in myth her place of birth. She is thus called "the Cyprian," but in this play the epithet is used as if it were her name, equivalent to Aphrodite.

‡ In the mythic tradition, Theseus' first wife, named Hippolyta or (in some versions) Antiope, had been an Amazon queen.

§ Theseus' grandfather.

They keep each other company, man and god,
but I bear them no ill will. Why should I?   20
But today I'll punish Hippolytus for the wrongs
he's done me. Most of my plan I put in motion
long ago. There's not much more to do:
Some time ago he left the house of Pittheus
to attend the celebration of the Mysteries
in the land of Pandion.* There his father's wife,
noble Phaedra, saw him and was seized
with dreadful lust, all by my design.
So, before she came here to Troezen,
she founded close by the rock of Pallas†   30
a temple to Cypris, overlooking this land,
because her love was here. For the rest of time
they'll say it's for Hippolytus my shrine was founded.‡
But then Theseus left the land of Cecrops
to escape pollution by Pallantid blood.§
He agreed to a year-long exile and sailed
with his wife to this country. From that moment,
the wretched woman has been dying quietly,
her groans spurred on by the goads of her lust.
No one in her household knows of her disease.   40
But it won't stay that way. I will reveal
her passion to Theseus; it will come to light.
And the father will kill his son, the young man
so hostile to me. He'll use the gift the sea god,
Poseidon, gave him:¶ that he could make
three prayers the god would answer without fail.

---

* Attica is here called the land of Pandion after one of its legendary kings. The Mysteries were celebrated at Eleusis, near Athens, to honor the goddess Demeter.

† The rock of Pallas is the Acropolis in Athens; there was, in Euripides' day, on the slope of the Acropolis, a cult site to Hippolytus with a temple to Aphrodite.

‡ The Greek here translated "for Hippolytus" can be understood in two ways: either Hippolytus was the
cause of the founding of the shrine, or the shrine is located "in the precinct of Hippolytus." See Barrett,
p. 160.

§ Cecrops is the name of another legendary king of Athens, so the land of Cecrops is Athens. The Pal-
lantids, sons of Pallas, were Theseus' cousins, who had challenged Theseus' right to rule Athens. Theseus and his forces killed them, and Theseus thus incurred the pollution of kin-murder, which forced
him into exile.

¶ In myth, both Aegeus and Poseidon are fathers of Theseus, both having slept with his mother, Aethra,
on the same night.

And she, Phaedra, will die. She'll keep
her good name, but she'll die. I will not pay
more heed to her suffering than the penalty
my enemies must pay so that I may prosper.   50

But now I'll leave this place,
for I see Hippolytus on his way here;
he's put an end to the labor of the hunt.
A great crowd of attendants follows close
behind him and shouts out hymns to honor
Artemis. He has no idea the gates of Hades
are gaping wide; he'll see the light no more.
> *(Aphrodite exits.)**
> *(Hippolytus and his band of followers enter from the countryside,*
> *where they have been hunting, and approach the statue of*
> *Artemis, singing.)*

HIPPOLYTUS: Follow me, follow, sing
   to the heavenly daughter of Zeus,
   Artemis. We are in her care.   60†

HIPPOLYTUS AND BAND OF FOLLOWERS: Lady most holy,
   lady, child of Zeus,
   hail! I greet you,
   daughter of Leto and Zeus,
   Artemis, most beautiful
   of all maidens.
   You live in great heaven
   in the hall of the noble father,
   the golden home of Zeus.
   Hail, most beautiful! I greet you,   70
   of all in Olympus most beautiful.‡
> *(Hippolytus offers a crown of flowers to the statue.)*

HIPPOLYTUS: My lady, I bring to you a woven crown
   of flowers I plucked from a pure meadow.
   Shepherds never graze their sheep there,

---

* It is impossible to say whether Aphrodite leaves the roof by a staircase or is carried off by the *mēchanē*, a cranelike device that was often used for the appearance and departure of divinities.

† Line divisions in songs vary from editor to editor, so the numbering of lines in the lyric sections, which is conventional, does not always correspond to the number of lines in this translation.

‡ A line ("of maidens, Artemis") has been omitted, largely for metrical reasons.

and the plow has never plied there.
But in the spring the bee passes through it,
and *Aidōs*[*] waters it with pure river streams
for men who need no teaching: by nature
they give virtue its place in all things   80
always. *They* may pick the flowers there,
evil men may not. But, dear lady, accept
from my reverent hand a binding
for your golden hair. I alone of mortals have
this badge of honor: to be and talk with you.
I hear your voice; I do not see your face.
May I reach the end of life as I began it.

        (One of Hippolytus' followers approaches him.)

OLD SLAVE: Sir—for gods alone should be called master—
   would you accept some good advice from me?
HIPPOLYTUS: Certainly. Otherwise I wouldn't seem wise.   90
OLD SLAVE: Well, you know that law that mortals have?
HIPPOLYTUS: No. What law are you asking me about?
OLD SLAVE: To hate the proud who keep themselves apart.
HIPPOLYTUS: As is right. What proud man isn't troublesome?
OLD SLAVE: And is there grace in an open nature?
HIPPOLYTUS: The greatest, yes. And profit, with little work.
OLD SLAVE: Do you expect the same is true among gods?
HIPPOLYTUS: Yes, if we mortals borrow divine laws.
OLD SLAVE: Why do you ignore a righteous god then?
HIPPOLYTUS: Which god? Be careful your tongue doesn't slip.   100

       (The Old Slave gestures to the statue of Aphrodite.)

OLD SLAVE: This one, who stands before your door: Cypris.
HIPPOLYTUS: I greet her from far off, in my purity.
OLD SLAVE: And yet she is revered and important to men.
HIPPOLYTUS: Each to his own, whether man or god.
OLD SLAVE: May you have sense enough to prosper!

      (The Old Slave starts to leave but holds back to respond to
      Hippolytus once more.)

---

* The concept of *aidōs* is central to the play. No English equivalent exists, so I will leave the Greek term untranslated where it is personified. *Aidōs* is a gauge of a person's moral strength. It can take the form of respect for society's conventions; a sense of shame about how others will see you if you act inappropriately or immorally; or modesty and restraint in one's interactions with others. It can be viewed as either a positive or an inhibiting force.

HIPPOLYTUS: No god worshipped in the dark can please me.

OLD SLAVE: Son, you must treat the gods with honor.

> *(Hippolytus addresses his band of followers.)*

HIPPOLYTUS: Go in to the house, my followers, prepare
the meal. After the hunt there's pleasure
in a full table. And rub down the horses   110
so they're ready. When I've eaten, I'll yoke them
to the chariot and exercise them properly.
(*to the Old Slave*) As for your Cypris, to her I'll say: Farewell.

> *(Hippolytus exits into the house with his followers. The Old
> Slave remains.)*

OLD SLAVE: I mustn't copy the young when they think
as he does. So *I'll* pray to your statue,
Cypris, with words fitting for a slave.
One must be forgiving. If someone
says silly things because he's young
and his spirit intense, seem not to hear.
For gods should be wiser than mortals.   120

> *(A Chorus of young married women enter from the town.)*

strophe 1

> **CHORUS:** (*singing and dancing*)
> There is a rock that drips, they say, with Ocean's water.*
> Pitchers catch the stream that pours from the craggy peak.
> There a friend of mine
> soaked purple robes
> in the streaming water
> and spread them on the spine
> of the warm rock in the bright sun.
> From her I first heard the lady's story:†   130

antistrophe 1

> She keeps herself inside the house, she wastes away
> in her sickbed, delicate covers shadow her blond head.
> For the third day, I hear,
> no food passes her lips,
> her body's untainted by Demeter's grain.

---

* Ocean's water is fresh, not salty, so the stream fed by it is suitable for washing clothes.
† "The lady" is Phaedra.

From a hidden grief she longs
to reach her end in death's harbor.   140

strophe 2

Is it possession by a god, dear one?*
Is your wandering mind bewitched by Pan,
or Hecate, the holy Corybants,
or the mountain mother?
Do you waste away for wrongs
done to Dictynna† the great hunter:
no offering of grain at her altar?
For she roams across the Marsh here
and over the sandbars
in the eddies of the salt sea.   150

antistrophe 2

Or is someone in the house
tending your husband, noble man,
ruler of the sons of Erechtheus,‡
in a bed hidden away from yours?
Or has a sailor set out
from Crete and sailed here
into this welcoming harbor,
to bring bad news to the queen?§
Is her spirit bound to the bed
by the pain of her suffering?   160

epode

In women there's a harmony hard to tune;
pernicious, harmful, and wretched helplessness,
from birth pangs and mad thoughts,
often finds a place there.
Through my womb this current coursed once,
and I cried out to heavenly Artemis,
goddess in charge of arrows, who eases labor pains.
She always comes to me,
by the gods' will, to the envy of all.

---

* The Chorus speculate about the source of Phaedra's illness. In the strophe they mention various gods who are often thought to cause mysterious illnesses; in the antistrophe they consider human causes, such as infidelity or bad news from her family in Crete. The text is uncertain in the first and fifth lines of the strophe.

† Another name for Artemis.

‡ Athenians. Erechtheus was, in myth, the first king of Athens.

§ Phaedra comes from Crete, where her family still lives.

(The Nurse comes from the house with slaves carrying Phaedra on a litter.)

CHORUS: *(chanting)*** Here's the old nurse before the door.   170
　She's bringing Phaedra out.†
　My spirit longs to learn
　why the body of the queen
　is wrecked, its color changed.

NURSE: The troubles mortals have, the hateful diseases!
　What am I to do for you? What am I not to do?
　Here's the light, the bright air you wanted.
　Your bed's outside now,
　your sickbed.   180
　But your brow darkens, clouded with gloom.   172
　Before you talked only of coming out here;   181
　any minute now you'll hurry back in.
　You're quickly thwarted, enjoy nothing.
　You take no pleasure in what's right here;
　you think you want what's far away more.
　It's better to be ill than tend illness.
　The one is simple; the other attacks the mind
　with pain, the hands with work.
　All human life is labor,
　there's no rest from work.   190
　Whatever else, dearer than living, there is,‡
　darkness hides and clouds envelop it.
　So we seem desperately in love
　with the thing that glitters on the earth,
　because we know no other life,
　have no proof of what's beneath the earth.
　Aimlessly we're carried along by stories.

PHAEDRA: Raise my body up, hold my head straight.
　My muscles have no strength in them.
　Attendants, hold my lovely arms.   200

---

* The rhythm from here until line 266 is anapestic.

† Line 172 has been transposed to the Nurse's speech, between lines 180 and 181. The line, which refers to Phaedra's changing moods, is more appropriately spoken by the Nurse.

‡ Many editors of the play consider the last seven lines of the Nurse's speech a later interpolation because of their sententiousness and seeming irrelevance. I would argue that they belong in Euripides' text as an elaboration of the Nurse's deeply pragmatic and pessimistic nature, which is important for understanding her later actions.

Oh, the weight of my headdress—
Take it off. Spread my hair across my shoulders.

NURSE: Courage, child. Don't keep tossing
your body violently about.
You'll bear the illness more easily
with a calm, a noble disposition.
Hardship is necessary for mortals.

PHAEDRA: *aiai*
How might I drink
pure water from a cool stream?
Or find rest, lying down   210
under poplar trees in a meadow run wild?

NURSE: Oh, child, what are you saying?*
In front of everyone? Won't you stop such talk?
Madness drives the words you utter!

PHAEDRA: Take me to the mountain! I will go to the forest
among pine trees, where hounds
that kill wild things race,
in pursuit of the spotted deer.
O gods! I long to call to the hounds,
hold in my hand a pointed spear   220
and let it fly, a Thessalian javelin †
skimming my golden hair!

NURSE: What mad thoughts are these, child?
How can the hunt possibly concern you?
Why do you long for flowing streams?
Right here, near the walls, there's a cool slope
where you can drink.

PHAEDRA: Artemis, lady of the salty Marsh
and training grounds ringing with hoofbeats,
would I were there, in those sacred grounds,   230
taming Venetian horses.‡

---

* Given the limitations on aristocratic women's movement outside the house and Phaedra's usual concern for her reputation, this desire of hers to run free in the wild, and to hunt and race horses, as Hippolytus does, is shocking to the nurse.

† The Thessalian javelin was a light spear that hunters threw at a boar or deer when they had encircled it.

‡ The Greeks imported horses from a people called the Enetoi (Venetoi) who lived on the north coast of the Adriatic and after whom Venice is named.

NURSE: What mad words erupt from you again?
    Just now you were heading to the mountain,
    in love with the hunt, but now you long for
    horses in sand no waves have washed.
    I'd have to be a great prophet
    to know which god has you under his sway
    and addles your mind, child.
        (*Phaedra comes to her senses and her agitation abates.*)

PHAEDRA: Oh, miserable me, what have I done?
    Where have I strayed, far from right thinking?   240
    I went mad, I fell: the god clouded my mind.
    pheu, pheu, I suffer.
    Nurse, cover my head again,
    I cringe in shame* at what I've said.
    Keep me hidden. Tears fall from my eyes,
    My faces takes on my shame.
    To think straight pains me,
    but madness is disaster. Now
    oblivion and death are best.

NURSE: I'm covering you, but what about me?   250
    When will death hide *my* body?
    My long life has taught me much.
    Mortals should balance carefully
    their love for each other,
    never let it reach the very marrow of life.
    The heart's affections must be loosely tied,
    easy to tighten or undo.
    For one life to feel pain for two
    is a harsh burden,
    as is my pain for her.   260
    To live life on the straight path and narrow,
    they say, courts disaster more than pleasure,
    lays greater siege to health.
    So I praise "nothing in excess"†
    more than I praise too much of anything,
    and the wise will agree with me.

---

* The verb here has *aidōs* as its root.

† This phrase was inscribed on the entranceway to the temple of Apollo at Delphi, the site of his temple and oracle.

CHORUS: (*speaking*) Old woman, trusted nurse of the queen,
    we can see Phaedra's wretched state,
    but it's not clear what her illness is.
    We'd like to ask and learn what it is from you.   270
NURSE: I've no idea. She won't say.*
CHORUS: Not even what caused her pain?
NURSE: It's the same thing: total silence.
CHORUS: Her body's so weak, so tattered.
NURSE: Of course. She hasn't eaten for three days.
CHORUS: Is she mad, or is she trying to die?
NURSE: I don't know, but starving will lead to death.
CHORUS: Amazing that her husband condones this.
NURSE: She hides her pain and denies she's ill.
CHORUS: Doesn't he see the signs when he looks at her?   280
NURSE: No. By chance he's out of the country.
CHORUS: Then aren't *you* pressing her to learn
    what sickens her, what drives her mad?
NURSE: I've tried everything and gotten nowhere.
    But I won't lessen my effort, even now,
    so you may witness the kind of care
    I give my mistress in her distress.
    (*addressing Phaedra*) Come, dear child, let's both forget
    what we said before. You be gentler,
    no gloomy frown; change the path your thoughts   290
    take, and I will find a better way
    to talk to you; I won't defy you so.
    If your illness mustn't be spoken aloud,
    (*indicates Chorus*) these are the women to set it right.
    But if a man can know your problem,†
    speak, so doctors can be consulted.
            (*Phaedra says nothing.*)
    Come now, why the silence? Don't
    be silent, child: challenge me, if I'm
    wrong, or agree with my good advice.
            (*The Nurse waits for a response.*)
    Say something! Look at me! (*to the Chorus*) Oh, misery,   300

---

* The text is uncertain here and at line 277, where it has been emended.

† The nurse seems to suggest that Phaedra's illness may have to do with pregnancy or another gyneco-logical problem, for which she would seek help from a midwife or experienced older woman rather than a male doctor.

women, there's no point to this effort.
We're no closer than before. No words
touched her then, and still she is unmoved.
(*to Phaedra*) You know, don't you—if you die, you betray
your sons?* To *that* be as indifferent as the sea!
They'll have no place in their father's house,
I swear by the Amazon queen, rider of stallions.†
She bore a master for your sons, a bastard
who thinks he's legitimate. You know him well,
Hippolytus **PHAEDRA:** *oimoi!*— **NURSE:** This touches you?   310
PHAEDRA: You've ruined me, nurse. By the gods,
    I beg you, be silent about that man.
NURSE: See? You're perfectly sane but, even so,
    unwilling to help your sons and save your life.
PHAEDRA: I love my sons, but I'm racked by another storm.
NURSE: Surely your hands aren't stained with blood?
PHAEDRA: My hands, no, but my mind's—polluted.
NURSE: You don't mean by an enemy's curse?
PHAEDRA: Someone dear destroys me, against his will and mine.
NURSE: Has Theseus done you some wrong?   320
PHAEDRA: May *I* not be seen to do *him* wrong!
NURSE: What awful thing drives you to death?
PHAEDRA: I'm not wronging *you*, so let *me* go wrong.
NURSE: Not willingly. It's you who'll make me fail.
        (The nurse falls at Phaedra's feet and grasps her knees and
        hands in supplication.)‡
PHAEDRA: What are you doing? You force me by grasping my hand?
NURSE: Yes, and your knees. I won't let go.
PHAEDRA: Terrible for you, terrible if you learn—
NURSE: What could be worse than failing to reach you?
PHAEDRA: Your ruin. As it is, I'm gaining honor.
NURSE: *That's* why you *hide* it, when I beg?   330

---

* According to Apollodorus, Phaedra's sons by Theseus are named Acamas and Demophon (3.16.18). The nurse's point here is that without Phaedra's support, her sons may be displaced in Theseus' favor by Hippolytus, who is his first child, though illegitimate because his mother is a foreigner. In the mythic tradition, Demophon does eventually become king of Athens, although the tradition is not consistent in making Phaedra his mother.

† Hippolytus is the child of Theseus and an Amazon, either Hippolyta or Antiope.

‡ In the act of supplication, the suppliant kneels and takes hold of the knees and hand, or chin, of the person who has the power to grant him or her what he or she needs. The person thus supplicated is bound by the ritual act of supplication to respond to the request.

PHAEDRA: Yes, I'm making an ugly thing noble.
NURSE: Then by telling you'll appear more noble!
PHAEDRA: By the gods, let go my right hand.
NURSE: No, for you don't give me what you should.
PHAEDRA: I will, for I revere your suppliant hand.
NURSE: Now I'll be silent and you can speak.
PHAEDRA: Oh, Mother, miserable, what passion you felt—*
NURSE: For the bull, child? What do you mean?
PHAEDRA: And you, wretched sister, bride of Dionysus—
NURSE: Child, what's wrong? Why insult your family?   340
PHAEDRA: And I'm the third to die in misery.
NURSE: I'm at sea—where will this story end?
PHAEDRA: My misfortune started then, not just now.
NURSE: I'm no wiser about the thing I want to hear.
PHAEDRA: *pheu!*
    Could you somehow say for me what I must say?
NURSE: I'm no prophet, able to see what's invisible.
PHAEDRA: What is it they call "being in love"?
NURSE: The sweetest thing, child, but full of pain.
PHAEDRA: Yes, mine would be the painful kind.
NURSE: What do you mean? You're in love? With whom?   350
PHAEDRA: Whoever he is, the son of the Amazon—
NURSE: Hippolytus?
PHAEDRA: You spoke his name, not I.
NURSE: *oimoi*, child, what can you mean? You've ruined me.
   (*to the Chorus*) Women, I can't bear it, I won't endure it
   and live. Hateful day, light hateful to my eyes!
   I'll jump, hurl my body down, be released
   from this life. Farewell! I am no more.
   Not when the chaste are in love with evil—
   against their will but still—Cypris is no god,
   she's something more than a god, if she brings   360
   destruction to this house, this woman and me.
      (*The Nurse has fallen to the ground and remains there while
      Phaedra addresses the Chorus. The Chorus sing in the excited
      dochmiac rhythm.*)†

---

* Phaedra points to the illicit love of her mother, Pasiphae, for the Minotaur and (two lines farther on) that of her sister, Ariadne, for Dionysus, as a way of approaching the subject of her illicit love for Hippolytus, her stepson.

† The dochmiac rhythm was created to express the intense emotions of tragedy.

CHORUS: Do you see, oh,
    do you hear
    the queen weep
    for calamity woeful beyond words?
    I would die, dear one, before
    I thought your thoughts, *iō moi pheu pheu*,
    wretched as you are in your pain!
    What agonies attend a mortal life!
    Your ruin: you revealed your trouble to the light.
    What waits for you in the hours of this day?
    Something new will find its end here.   370
    Now there are signs where it will finish,
    this calamity Cypris made, oh, wretched child of Crete.

(Phaedra gets up from her bed, uncovers her head, and addresses the Chorus. The Nurse remains huddled on the ground but slowly, during Phaedra's speech, regains her composure, gets up, and listens.)

PHAEDRA: Women of Troezen, you make your home
    here at the edge of the land of Pelops.
    Here in different times, during the long stretch
    of the night, I've considered how a human life
    goes wrong. It's not, I think, their minds
    that make men blunder. Most are capable
    of sound thinking. But look at it this way:
    we know what's right, we recognize it,   380
    but we don't do it. Some from laziness,
    others from putting another pleasure
    before the good. And there are many:
    long, lazy talks, empty time (a dangerous joy),
    and *aidōs.** Of this there are two kinds:
    one good, the other a plague. If it were clear
    in each situation what's apt and right,
    one word wouldn't stand for two different things.†

---

* Phaedra calls *aidōs* (see note to line 78) a pleasure because it is the quality that allows a person to have a reputation for goodness.

† The "good" *aidōs* allows a person to restrain herself when to act would hurt her reputation. The "bad" *aidōs* makes a person unable to act to preserve her honor, out of fear of putting herself forward, or of condemnation, or of misplaced respect. As Phaedra says, it is never entirely clear whether restraint or action is the right thing in any given situation. If it were clear, she argues, there would be a different word for the two different reactions. *Aidōs* can be a bad pleasure because it can preserve a good reputation while stopping someone from doing what is right, since reputation is not necessarily based on what is actually good.

This is what I think; there's no magic charm
to change my mind or alter my point of view.   390

I'll tell you, too, the path my purpose took.
When Eros* wounded me, I sought the best way
to bear it bravely. And so I began with this:
I kept silent. I hid my disease.
One cannot trust the tongue: it knows
how to give advice to others but gets
only the greatest disaster for itself.
And then I planned to bear my insanity
nobly, by overcoming it with restraint.
But when I didn't succeed in controlling   400
Cypris this way, I made up my mind to die—
my best plan, no one will deny it.
For it is my wish my good deeds never go
unnoticed, but no one ever witness the base ones.
I knew the disease—let alone the act—was
a disgrace. I also knew, because I'm a woman,
I am an object of everyone's hatred. I curse
the first woman who shamed her marriage bed
with strangers. This evil had its beginning
with women from noble households;   410
when ugliness is beautiful to the well-born,
how much more so will it seem to others!
I despise, too, women chaste by reputation
but possessed in secret by lustful daring.
O Cypris, lady and mistress, how do wives
like that look their husbands in the eye?
Why don't they dread the darkness, their accomplice,
and fear the very walls will learn to speak?
I'll die, friends, before I'm caught
ever bringing shame to my husband   420
or my children. May they flourish
in famous Athens, free to speak their minds,

---

* Phaedra several times uses the Greek word *erōs* to describe the passion she feels for Hippolytus. The word can represent the feeling of lust itself or that feeling personified as the god Eros, whose bow and arrows instill desire in those they strike. The verb "wound" here seems suited to the personification.

with the fine reputation their mother gave them.*
A man, even one with true grit, turns slavish
when a parent's wrongdoing is on his mind.
One thing alone gives advantage in life:
the presence of a just and good mind.
Sooner or later evil men are revealed,
when time holds up his mirror to them
as to a young girl. May I never be one of them.   430
CHORUS: *pheu, pheu.* Everywhere a sound mind reaps
     goodness and a fine reputation among men.
NURSE: Lady, it's true, your misfortune struck me
     at first with a sudden, terrible fear.
     But now I realize I was a fool; somehow
     mortals' second thoughts are wiser.
     There's nothing untoward, nothing strange
     in your feelings; a goddess has visited her rage
     on you. You're in love—why the amazement?
     Many of us are. For *this* you'll ruin your life?   440
     It's not good news for lovers, alive now
     or in the future, if they must die for love.
     When Cypris rushes at you, you can't withstand her.
     She goes gently after the one who yields,
     but the one who's fanatic and stubbornly proud
     she attacks with a violence you can't imagine.
     She travels through the air, and she's there
     in the sea waves; all things come from her.
     She's the one who sows desire; it's *her* gift,
     and all of us on this earth descend from it.   450
     Whoever has read the old stories,
     or whoever does the Muses' work,
     knows that Zeus once loved Semele,
     and Dawn in all her light's beauty
     took Cephalus away to be with the gods
     out of passion.† But Zeus and Dawn live on

---

* A citizen's persuasiveness in the law courts or assembly of Athens depended on the strength and quality of his reputation. This reference to contemporary Athenian politics is anachronistic.

† The Nurse gives two examples of gods who fell in love with mortals. Their passion for an inappropriate object did not, the Nurse argues, cause them to feel shame before other gods and hide themselves away.

in heaven; *they* don't run away from other gods.
They accept, I think, that they're the victims
of misfortune. But *you* won't tolerate it?
Your father should've brokered special rules for you,   460
arranged for different gods to reign, if you won't
accept these laws. How many men of good sense
see proof of their wives' infidelity
and pretend not to? How many fathers pander
to a son's escapades with Cypris? It shows
a person's wisdom to keep wrongdoing hidden.
Men shouldn't strain to perfect their lives,
no more than a carpenter can fit a roof
to cover a house exactly. When you plunge deep
into ruin, as you have, how can you swim out?   470
But if you salvage more good than bad,
you're doing very well, by human standards.
Dear child, let go your wrong thinking,
put a stop to your arrogance. It's nothing else
but arrogance to want to defeat a god.
Endure your passion. It is god's will.
When you're ill, seek a cure that works.
There are incantations and soothing words;
some cure for your illness will come to light.
We'd wait forever for *men* to find the means,   480
if we women didn't discover them ourselves.

CHORUS: Phaedra, her words perform a useful service
in your current trouble, but it's you I praise.
And yet my praise creates more trouble
and more pain for you to hear than her words.

PHAEDRA: This is what destroys the fine cities
and homes of mortals: words spoken too well.
One must not speak words that please the ear
but ones that will make a good reputation.

NURSE: Why so pompous? You don't need   490
decorous words; you need the man.
Let's be clear now and speak the facts.
If your life were not in such crisis, if
you were a woman with self-control,
I wouldn't have brought you to this point

just to serve your pleasure in bed. But we're
struggling for your life. No one can blame us.

PHAEDRA: Terrible words! Seal your lips! Never
again utter these ugly words!

NURSE: Ugly perhaps, but better for you than   500
nice ones. Rather the act that saves you
than a name you take pride in and die.

PHAEDRA: Oh, please, no more, I beg you. You speak
what's ugly so well. Passion makes me ready
to hear: speak of ugliness with skill
and the very thing I flee will consume me.

NURSE: All right, no more of that. It would be best
if you hadn't gone wrong but, since you have,
give me your trust, a favor that's second best.
I have love potions in the house—   510
I've just remembered. They'll end your illness
without shame, without disturbing your mind,
if you're brave. We need a lock of hair,
a piece of clothing from the one you desire.
We'll take and mingle the two in a single blessing.

PHAEDRA: Is the potion an ointment or a drink?

NURSE: I don't know. It's help, not knowledge, you need, child.

PHAEDRA: I fear you'll be too clever for me.

NURSE: You fear everything; what scares you now?

PHAEDRA: You might reveal something to Theseus' son.   520

NURSE: Never fear, child. I'll put all to rights.

> *(The Nurse addresses the statue of Aphrodite at the entrance of the house as she prepares to go inside.)*

This once, Cypris, lady and mistress,
be my ally. As for what else I have in mind,
it'll be enough to tell our friends inside.

> *(The Nurse exits into the house, leaving Phaedra and the Chorus onstage. The Chorus sing and dance a hymn to Eros, god of love, son of Aphrodite and Zeus.)*

strophe 1

CHORUS: Eros, Eros, you make desire flow
from lovers' eyes, instill sweet pleasure
in the souls of those you attack.

Never come near to do me harm,
or break my life's rhythm.
No flash of fire, no starbeam is stronger   530
than the shaft of Aphrodite
the hand of Eros, son of Zeus, lets fly.

antistrophe 1

In vain, in vain the Greek land
slaughters bull upon bull by the river Alpheus,
or in the precinct of the Pythia, priestess of Apollo.*
To Eros we show no reverence.
He keeps the keys to Aphrodite's chamber;
he rules and ravages men,   540
hurls them, when he comes,
through every misfortune.

strophe 2

Young girl of Oechalia,†
filly untamed, no man
in her bed, no marriage.
Cypris yoked her, drove her from Eurytus' house,
like a nymph on the run, a Bacchant.   550
In the smoke and blood
of a deadly wedding
Cypris gave her to Alcmene's son,
a marriage to misery.

antistrophe 2

Walls of holy Thebes,
mouth of Dirce's spring,
you could tell a tale
of the coming of Cypris: she gave a bride‡
to lightning and thunder,   560
made her a bed of death,
mother of twice-born Bacchus.

---

* The Alpheus flows through Olympia, the sanctuary of Zeus in the Peloponnese. The precinct of the Pythia is Apollo's sanctuary at Delphi.

† Iole, daughter of Eurytus. Heracles, son of Alcmene (fathered by Zeus), sacked Iole's hometown, Oechalia, to win her as his mistress (and slave). Sophocles tells this story in his play *The Women of Trachis*.

‡ Semele, whom Zeus loved. When he granted her wish to see him in his true form, he appeared as a lightning bolt, striking and killing her. From her womb he snatched her fetal son, Dionysus (Bacchus), and gestated him in his thigh, thus making him "twice-born" (see the prologue to Euripides' *Bacchae* in this volume.

Cypris breathes terror on all,
like a bee she darts about here and there.
> *(Phaedra has moved to the entrance of the house and has been straining to hear what is happening inside.)*

PHAEDRA: Quiet, women! It's done; the end is here!

CHORUS: What is it, Phaedra? Something dreadful?

PHAEDRA: Wait. Let me hear what they're saying.

CHORUS: I'll say nothing, but this isn't a good beginning.
> *(After a pause while she listens, Phaedra cries out, and the Chorus respond in an excited song of dochmiacs. They continue to sing, while Phaedra responds in regular speech rhythms.)*

PHAEDRA: *iō moi, aiai*
oh, misery, what I suffer!   570

> CHORUS: What are you saying: what's this cry?
> Tell us the words that frighten you,
> that rush over your mind.
> *(Phaedra gestures to the Chorus to come and listen with her at the door of the* skēnē, *but the Chorus remain in the orchestra.)*

PHAEDRA: I'm destroyed. Stand here by the door;
listen to the din inside the house.

> CHORUS: You're there, by the door. *You* be the one
> to give us the news.
> Tell us, tell, what disaster has come.   580

PHAEDRA: Hippolytus, son of the Amazon, lover of horses,
is shouting cruel things at my nurse.

> CHORUS: I hear a voice, nothing clear,
> but his cry carries through the doors
> where it reaches you, there.*

PHAEDRA: What's clear now are the names he calls her,
"matchmaker of evil," "betrayer of her master's bed."   590

> CHORUS: *ōmoi*, so terrible! You are betrayed, dear one.
> What will I do to help?
> The secret is out, and you're destroyed,
> *aiai, e, e,* betrayed by one who loves you.

PHAEDRA: She has told my misfortune and ruined me;
from love she tried, but failed, to cure my sickness.

CHORUS: *(speaking)* What will you do now? There's no way out.

---

* The text is emended here.

PHAEDRA: I know only one way: to die right now.
  It's the only cure for the pain I feel.   600
            (Hippolytus bursts out from the house, followed by the Nurse.
            Phaedra remains hidden but able to hear throughout this
            encounter between Hippolytus and the Nurse.)
HIPPOLYTUS: Oh, Mother Earth, Sun in the open sky
  what words I've heard, unspeakable words!
NURSE: Quiet, child. Someone might hear.
HIPPOLYTUS: I can't hear terrible things and keep quiet.
            (The Nurse attempts to grasp Hippolytus' right arm in
            supplication.)
NURSE: Please, I beg you, by this right arm!
HIPPOLYTUS: Don't touch me! Don't grab my cloak!
            (The Nurse falls at his feet to grasp his knees in supplication,
            but Hippolytus moves away.)
NURSE: I beg you again, don't destroy me.
HIPPOLYTUS: Why fear? You claim you've said nothing bad.
NURSE: What I've told you isn't for all ears, child.
HIPPOLYTUS: (*with contempt*) Aren't good things better if *many* know
  them?   610
NURSE: Child, don't dishonor your oath.*
HIPPOLYTUS: My tongue swore, my mind did not.
NURSE: What, child? You'll destroy your dear ones?
HIPPOLYTUS: Vile thing! No one unjust is dear to me!
NURSE: Have pity, child. It's human to err.
HIPPOLYTUS: Oh, Zeus, why place in the light of the sun
  this fraud, this blight on human existence:
  women! If you wanted to sow the human race,
  you didn't need women to provide the means.
  Men could deposit bronze, silver, or gold   620
  in your temples and get in exchange a child,
  at a price determined by what he's worth.
  Then he'd live in his home, a free man—
  free of women. And here's the proof that *they*
  are pure disaster: the father of a girl
  raises her, and then pays out a dowry

---

* This line tells the audience that the Nurse had extracted from Hippolytus an oath to keep her information secret.

to be rid of her,* to house the evil far away.†

Then the groom takes the plague into his home   630
and adorns it, like a statue, to please his heart.
He gilds the ugliness and decks it with clothing—
and exhausts his family's wealth, poor wretch.‡
He has the easiest time who marries a nothing:
she sits there in the house, silly and useless.
But clever women I really hate. May I never have   640
a woman in my house who thinks more deeply
than a woman should. Cypris breeds wrongdoing
in smart women; the helpless ones are saved
from wantonness by their small minds.
We shouldn't allow a woman and her slave
in the same room. She should live with dumb
and vicious beasts, so that she can talk to no one
and no one talk to her. As it is,
women sit inside concocting evil plots,
which their slaves carry out for them.   650
That's why *you're* here, to seduce me into
my father's holy marriage bed, you filth.
I'll sluice my ears with fresh running water
to wash away your words. How could *I* do
wrong, when just to hear your words makes me
unclean! Be sure, woman, only my righteousness
saves you. If I hadn't been trapped, unsuspecting,
by an oath, nothing could stop me from telling
my father. So now I'll leave, while Theseus is away
from home, and I'll keep silent. But when he's back   660
and I with him, I'll be watching your every look,
you and your mistress. Die, both of you!§
I'll never have enough of hating women,

---

* A similar complaint from the woman's perspective is found in Euripides' *Medea* (lines 231–33 in this volume).

† Lines 625–26 have been deleted; they seem to be an interpolation referring to the custom of the bridegroom's payment of a sum to the bride's father: "and now to bring an evil into our house, / we pay out our wealth." This interpolation might have been an attempt to "correct" the anachronism of the dowry for the dramatic time of the play, when there were no dowries.

‡ Four lines following this one have been omitted. They are thought to be an interpolation, as they irrelevantly address the subject of in-laws.

§ The line following this has been omitted; it repeats the idea expressed in line 661.

not even if someone complains my words
go on forever—but so does women's evil.
So either let someone teach them self-control
or let me go on attacking them forever.

> *(Hippolytus leaves, using the exit that leads away from the town.*
> *Phaedra comes out of hiding and sings in dochmiacs, addressing*
> *the Chorus.)*

PHAEDRA: Ah, the sorry,
  ill-starred fate
  of women.
  What ways do we have, what words   670
  when things go wrong, to cut
  through the talk that binds us? I've met with justice.
  Oh, earth and light! Where can I go to escape?
  How will I hide this pain, friends?
  What god, what human
  might offer me help, might join
  in my unjust acts? My suffering passes
  beyond life's domain, a hard passage;
  Most unlucky of women am I.

CHORUS: *pheu, pheu,* it's all over; your nurse's designs   680
  have not set things right, lady; a bad ending.

> *(Phaedra addresses the Nurse.)*

PHAEDRA: What have you done to me, worst of the worst!
  Destroyer of those you love! May Zeus,
  my father's father, tear you up from the roots,
  strike you with fire. Didn't I read your mind,
  warn you to hide what now brings me shame?
  But you couldn't stop yourself. And now I'll die
  with my reputation in ruins. I need a new plan.
  This man, his mind sharpened with rage,
  will denounce me to his father—because of you!*   690
  He'll fill the land with his ugly talk.
  I curse you, you and anyone who's eager
  to do wrong for friends against their will!

NURSE: Mistress, you can blame me for this trouble

---

* The following line, claiming that Hippolytus will also tell Pittheus, has been omitted as an interpolation.

since its sting controls your judgment.
But I can answer your blame, if you'll let me.
I raised you; I want the best for you. I sought
a cure for your sickness but didn't find
what I wanted. Had I succeeded, I'd be called 700
wise: our wisdom depends on our success.
PHAEDRA: So this is your justice? I deserve this?
You wound me and then talk your way out?
NURSE: We're wasting time. I wasn't prudent, child,
but there's a way, even now, to be safe.
PHAEDRA: No more! You've given enough bad advice
already; you've taken enough wrong turns.
Leave me! Go, look after yourself,
and *I* will put my own affairs in order.
(The Nurse goes into the house; Phaedra addresses the Chorus.)
And you, noble daughters of Troezen, 710
give me this one thing I ask of you:
cover in silence what you've heard here.
CHORUS: I swear by holy Artemis, daughter of Zeus,
I'll never bring to light any trouble of yours.
PHAEDRA: I thank you; I'll tell you one thing more.
I've found a way out of my misfortune
that will preserve my children's good name
and benefit me, as far as events allow.
I'll not, to preserve one life, bring shame
to my Cretan home nor face Theseus 720
under the cloud of my disgraceful acts.
CHORUS: What irreparable harm are you about to do?
PHAEDRA: I'll die. But it's *how* I die I must devise.
CHORUS: Don't say such things!
PHAEDRA: Give only *good* advice!
I will give Cypris joy. She destroys me
and will rejoice today when my life is over.
I'll be the victim of bitter lust but
in death become disaster for another,
so he can know not to feel superior
about my plight. He'll share my sickness 730
and then he'll learn what self-control is about.
(Phaedra goes into the house.)

strophe 1

> CHORUS: I wish I were in the high hidden reaches
>   where a god might make me
>   a bird on the wing
>   flying with the flock.
>   I would rise high above the waves
>   striking the Adriatic shore
>   and the water of the river Eridanus.*
>   There the sad sisters of Phaethon
>   drop shining tears of amber
>   into the purple swell,   740
>   in their pity for a brother.

antistrophe 1

>   I wish for my journey's end on the shore
>   where the Hesperides†
>   sing among apple trees.
>   The lord of the purple sea allows
>   no passage there to sailors,
>   there he sets the sky's limit,
>   which Atlas shoulders.
>   Streams flow with ambrosia there
>   where Zeus made his bed of love,
>   where Earth with abundant gifts   750
>   swells the gods' happy state.

strophe 2

>   Oh, ship from Crete, your white sails flying,‡
>   you carried my mistress from her rich home
>   across the salt waves of the pounding sea,
>   swelling her delight
>   in a marriage to disaster.
>   She flew with ill omen from Minos' land,§

---

* In myth, the Eridanus is a river at the far western reaches of the known world, although here Euripides places it farther east, in the Adriatic. But the story he places there is that of Phaethon, the son of Helios (the Sun), who requests to drive his father's chariot across the heavens. He loses control and Zeus strikes him with a lightning bolt to save the world from being destroyed by the heat of the sun. Phaethon plunges to his death in the far west, where his sisters turn into poplar trees who weep tears of amber. The text has been slightly emended in the following lines.

† The Garden of the Hesperides, a kind of Eden, is also thought to be in the far western reaches of the world. Heracles travels to bring back golden apples from the trees there, and there also Atlas holds up the sky on his shoulders.

‡ The text in this stanza has been emended.

§ Crete.

with ill omen she reached famous Athens.   760
There they fastened twisted ropes
to the shore at Munychia*
and set their feet on mainland earth.

antistrophe 2

For this her mind was shattered by unholy passion,
the awful sickness of Aphrodite.
She's drained the bitter dregs of disaster,
and she will tie the rope
to her bedchamber's beams   770
and fit the noose on her white neck.†
Shamed by her hateful lot
she chooses to save her name
and free herself
from a passion that gives her pain.

      (The Chorus hear a voice crying out from inside the house.)

VOICE INSIDE: *iou, iou*

Call for help! Hurry, anyone nearby!
The lady, Theseus' wife, hangs in a noose.

CHORUS: *pheu, pheu,* it's done. The queen no longer
lives. She's hanging from the rope.

VOICE INSIDE: Hurry, won't you? Someone bring a sword!   780
Cut the knot tied fast around her neck.

      (The Chorus split into two groups to speak the following lines.)‡

CHORUS 1: Friends, what should we do? Should we go
into the house, undo the tight noose?

CHORUS 2: Why? Young servants are already there.
To interfere invites danger.

VOICE INSIDE: Straighten her poor body, lay it out.
A bitter task for the house's master.

CHORUS: I hear the poor woman is dead.
They're laying out her body now.

      (Theseus enters wearing a crown of leaves, customarily worn by
      those who have consulted the Delphic oracle and had a favorable
      response.)

THESEUS: Women, what's that noise in the house,   790

---

* Munychia is a hill in the port of Athens.

† The Chorus imagine Phaedra hanging herself, as that is the usual form that a woman's suicide took.

‡ When something terrible is happening inside the house, the Chorus in tragedy often debate what to do, as, by convention, they cannot leave the stage and run to help.

the heavy cry of slaves echoing in my ear?*
Something's wrong: no one has opened the doors
and welcomed me home, back from Delphi.
Is something wrong with Pittheus?
He's an old man, far on in life, but still
we'd grieve if he'd left these halls.

CHORUS: Your misfortune doesn't involve the old, Theseus.
The pain comes from the death of the young.

THESEUS: *oimoi*, it can't be my children's lives I've lost?

CHORUS: They live, but their mother's dead. Oh, the pain!   800

THESEUS: What are you saying? My wife dead?

CHORUS: She strangled herself, hung in a noose.

THESEUS: Numbed by sorrow? What happened to her?

CHORUS: I know only this. I, too, have just arrived,
Theseus, to mourn your misfortune here.†

(Theseus throws the crown off his head.)

THESEUS: *aiai*, why do I wear this leafy crown,
when my journey to the oracle ends like this?
Slaves, undo the locks, open the doors.
Let me see this bitter sight:
the death of my wife destroys me.   810

*(The doors of the house open, and the body of Phaedra is wheeled
out on the* ekkyklēma, *a movable platform. A writing tablet is
attached to her wrist. The Chorus break into a song of mourning
in dochmiacs.)*

CHORUS: *iō, iō*, poor woman, miserable misfortune!
You suffered so much, you did
so much, you stun this house—
aiai, your daring—
by dying in violence, in unholy
misfortune, the piteous wrestling
of your hand. Who blots out your unhappy life?

strophe

THESEUS:‡   *ōmoi*, my woes; wretched I've suffered
the worst blow. Oh, misfortune,

---

* The text is corrupt here.

† The Chorus keep their promise to Phaedra to reveal nothing of what they know.

‡ In his next two speeches, Theseus alternates between singing and speech, as indicated by indented (sung) lines.

heavy your tread on me, on the house,
some unseen avenger bringing defilement.   820
   The destruction of my life unlivable,
   the sea of trouble I see, I suffer,
so vast I'll never escape it,
never rise from misfortune's waves.
   What story can I tell, Phaedra,*
   what deadly suffering can I name?
You've gone like a bird, flown from my hand.
You rushed to leap, down to death.
   aiaiaiai, the pity of it, the piteous pain   830
sent by a god for a wrong long ago,
someone's errant past haunting me now.
CHORUS: (*speaking*) King, you're not alone in suffering disaster:
  like many others you've lost your loving wife.
antistrophe
   THESEUS: I long for the darkness below the earth, I long
     to die, to dwell in wretched darkness there,
now I've lost your precious company.
Destroying yourself you destroyed me.
   Who can tell me, who can say what deadly blow,†   840
   wretched wife, struck you to the heart?
Can anyone tell me what happened? Do I
keep slaves in this royal house for no purpose?
   ōmoi, from you, from you [...]‡
   what pain I've seen, unhappy house.
My ruin not to be borne, not to be spoken:
the house a desert, my children all alone.
   aiaiaiai, you left, you left dear one,
   best of all women the sunlight looks upon,
   and the night's shining stars.   850
CHORUS: (*singing*) Wretched man, such suffering this house holds.
  My eyes are wet
  with tears I shed for your misfortune,
  I tremble at the trouble yet to come.

---

* The text is uncertain here.
† The text is corrupt here.
‡ The text is corrupt here and cannot be securely emended.

THESEUS: (*crying out in surprise*): *eā, eā!*
What is this? This tablet fixed to her
dear hand? What news does it contain?
Did my poor wife write to ask me something
for the children? about a new wife?
Take heart, sad one. No bed of mine,   860
no house will take in another woman.
How the imprint of her golden seal
calls to me, though she lives no longer.
Let me undo the sealed binding, let me
see what this tablet wants to tell me.

    CHORUS:* *pheu pheu!* A new calamity
      the god sends to follow on
      the one that's here.
      pheu pheu! The house of my king
      lies in ruin; it is no more.†   870

    THESEUS: *ōmoi*, another horror! Such horror!
    CHORUS: What is it? Tell us, if we may share it.
    THESEUS: (*singing*) The tablet cries, it cries pain. Where
      can I escape calamity's weight? I go
      in ruins. What words I've seen,
      what song they sing to give me pain!   880
    CHORUS: *aiai*, your words are harbingers of ill.
    THESEUS: (*singing*) I can't contain this horror
      in my head! Its passage from my mouth
      is full of pain, it spells ruin. Oh, my city!

Hippolytus has dared to violate my wife
and desecrate the holy eye of Zeus.
So now, Father Poseidon, fulfill one
of the three curses you promised me: kill
my son. He should not live beyond this day,
if the curses you gave me hold fast.   890

CHORUS: King, take back your curse, I beg you.
    Believe me, you're making a mistake.
THESEUS: No, but I'll add this: I'll exile him
    from this land. One of these two fates

---

* The text of the Chorus's song is uncertain in various places, and some iambic lines seem to be a later
addition. The translation is therefore conjecture to some extent.

† Lines 871–73 and line 875 have been deleted as interpolations.

will finish him: either Poseidon will honor
my curse and send him to the house
of Death, or he'll wander in exile and drain
life's bitter dregs in a strange land.

CHORUS: But look, here's Hippolytus now, just in time.　　　　900
Cool your anger at your son, King Theseus.
Consider what's best for your household.

　　　　(Hippolytus rushes onto the stage. Theseus ignores him.)

HIPPOLYTUS: I heard you shout, Father, and came here
right away. I don't know what made you
cry out, but I wish you'd tell me.

　　　　(Hippolytus waits for Theseus' reply, but then sees Phaedra's body.)

eā! What's this? Father, this is the body
of your wife! I'm stunned. I can't believe it.
I was with her just now. I just left her.
Not long ago she was still alive and well.
What happened to her? How did she die?

　　　　(Theseus is silent.)

Father, I want to know! Tell me!　　　　910
You say nothing? Silence has no place*
in a time of trouble. From friends—and those
dearer than friends—it's wrong to hide your trouble.

THESEUS: Humankind! so wrong-headed and so useless!
Why teach countless skills, why invent,
why devise all things, but one thing
you don't know, you don't even search for:
how to teach mindless men to be wise.　　　　920

HIPPOLYTUS: A man *would* be very clever if he could
force those incapable of thought to think.
But, Father, it's not the time for subtlety.
You talk to excess from your pain, I fear.

THESEUS: *pheu!* There should be a clear mark on men:
a way to know friends' minds and hearts,
to tell which one is true and which is not.
A man should have two voices,
one saying what's just, the other whatever

---

* Two lines have been deleted as likely interpolations.

comes into his head, the just voice refuting   930
the other's unjust thoughts. Then we wouldn't be fooled.

HIPPOLYTUS: Has some friend been pouring slander
in your ears? Am I tainted, though innocent?
I'm shocked! Your words astound me.
They wander far from truth. They're mad!

THESEUS: *pheu*, the human mind—how far will it go?
What end is there to its bold insolence?
If it grows and grows through a man's life,
if one man exceeds his predecessor
in evil acts, the gods will have to form   940
another world to make room for those
whose natures are evil and unjust.
Look at this man here: I gave him life,
and he defiled my wife. In her death
she convicts him of pure villainy.

(Theseus speaks directly to Hippolytus at last.)
Come here to me, look me in the eye,
since I'm already polluted by your presence.*
You live with the gods because *you* are
a paragon, chaste and untouched by evil?
I'd never trust your boasts, be so deluded   950
that I'd attribute such ignorance to the gods.
Strut and swagger about your meatless diet! †
Claim Orpheus your lord! Celebrate his rites!
Honor the empty vapors of his written word!
You've been exposed, and I'll tell all to run
from men like you. They set their trap
with righteous words but plot disgrace.

(Theseus gestures to Phaedra's body.)
She's dead. Do you suppose that makes you safe?
This, more than anything, condemns you.
What oaths, what words have more power   960
than her death, to make you innocent?

---

* Theseus claims that merely being in Hippolytus' presence has exposed him to the danger of being polluted by his wrongdoing, and so he doesn't fear to approach him face to face. The Greeks believed that until a wrongdoer has been purified by certain rites, he can spread the consequences of his wrongdoing to others and therefore musn't be greeted or touched.

† Theseus lists characteristics of certain esoteric sects whose practices for purifying the soul, such as not eating meat, were unconventional. One of those sects was devoted to Orpheus. He isn't necessarily saying that Hippolytus belongs to such a sect but rather that he makes extraordinary claims for his own purity.

Will you claim she hated you, that the bastard
is naturally the enemy of the pure bred?
By that account she bartered poorly: she lost
her life, the dearest thing, for her hatred of you.
Or will you say that men aren't love-struck
fools, while women are? But I know
a young man is no more stable than a woman
when Cypris disturbs his youthful heart.
But his manhood gives him license.   970
Therefore,—but why do I debate with you
when this corpse's testimony is clear?
Leave this land, an exile! Go now!
Don't go near Athens, city built by gods;
don't enter any land ruled by my spear.
If I am weaker than you who wrong me,
then Sinis* won't bear witness that I killed him;
he'll call my boast an empty one. And the rocks
close by the sea, where Sciron lingered,
will deny that I am hard on wrongdoers.   980

CHORUS: I don't know how I could call
    any mortal happy, now the best have fallen.

HIPPOLYTUS: Father, the force and tension of your thoughts
    are fearsome. But the matter itself, stripped
    of the fine words you give it, isn't so fine.
    I have no skill at talking to a crowd.
    I'm better with just a few of my peers.
    That's natural, just as men who're worthless
    among the wise are eloquent before a crowd.
    That being said, I must loosen my tongue,   990
    since misfortune is upon me. I'll start
    with your first assault, which you assumed
    would destroy me irrefutably. You see
    this light, this earth? In it you'll find
    no man more chaste than I, deny it as you may.
    I know, above all, how to revere the gods.
    I choose friends with no interest in doing wrong;
    they'd be ashamed to ask for anything bad

---

* Sinis and Sciron were among the foes whom Theseus defeated in his youth. They plagued travelers on the road between Troezen and Athens. The latter kicked travelers over a cliff to rocks below when they were washing their feet at his command. Theseus gained his reputation as a heroic civilizer by such feats.

or acquiesce in another's evil request.
I do not mock my companions, Father.   1000
I'm the same if they're beside me or far away.
I've never touched what you condemn me for.
To this day my body is pure and innocent.
I know nothing of the act of love except
what I've heard or seen in pictures, and these
I have no desire to see. Mine is a virgin soul.
Yet my chastity does not convince you.
All right. Show me how I was corrupted.
Was *her* body more beautiful
than every other? Did I hope to acquire   1010
your household by taking its heiress to bed?*
Then I was not just foolish but out of my mind.
You'll say for a sane man power is sweet.
Not so, since ruling corrupts the minds
of those who find pleasure in it.
I want to be first in the Hellenic games†
but be second in the state and enjoy
prosperity with friends who are most noble.
That way I can be active without danger
and have more pleasure than if I'm king.   1020
I've one more thing to say; the rest you've heard.
If I had someone to testify to my character,
and Phaedra were alive as I pled my case,
the facts would've shown you the real culprit.
But as it is, I swear to you, by this earth
and Zeus who guards oaths, I never touched
your wife, would never think or want to.
May I die without name or fame,‡
may neither earth nor sea receive my corpse,   1030
if I am a man capable of evil.
          (*Hippolytus gestures to Phaedra's body.*)
I don't know why she was afraid and

---

* The text is questionable in various places in the next five lines.
† The Greeks held athletic contests at various sites, including Olympia and the Isthmus of Corinth. To compete and win in these games was a mark of great distinction.
‡ Line 1029 has been omitted as an interpolation.

took her own life. I may not say more.
She showed self-control though she had none,
while I had it and did not use it well.
CHORUS: You've said enough to avert blame:
this oath you swore is no paltry proof.
THESEUS: What a conjurer! A wizard!
He believes he can dishonor me
and then calm my fury with his serenity.   1040
HIPPOLYTUS: I'm equally amazed at you, Father.
If you were my child and I your father,
I'd kill you—not banish you—
if you'd presumed to touch my wife.
THESEUS: Your words match your worth. But you won't
die the way you've judged is right.
A quick death in misfortune would be easy.
You'll drink the last painful drop of life
in exile. You'll beg your way through foreign lands.*   1049
HIPPOLYTUS: *oimoi*, what do you intend? Won't you allow
time to reveal my guilt? You'll exile me now?
THESEUS: Further than the Black Sea or the Pillars
of Atlas,† if I could. I hate you.
HIPPOLYTUS: You'll exile me with no trial, with no test
of my testimony and oath, or the words of prophets?
                (Theseus holds up the tablet taken from Phaedra's wrist.)
THESEUS: This tablet needs no prophet; it condemns you
with utter certainty. I have no need
of bird-omens flying above my head.
HIPPOLYTUS: Why not break my oath and speak, you gods,   1060
if you allow my ruin though I revere you?
But no, I won't: I wouldn't convince the ones
I must convince; I'd break my oath‡ in vain.
THESEUS: *oimoi!* Your righteousness will kill me.
So go now from your ancestral land!
HIPPOLYTUS: Where can I go? What stranger's house
can I enter, banished on such a charge?

---

* Line 1050 has been omitted as an interpolation. It is very close in sense to line 1047.
† The extreme western and eastern limits of the world.
‡ The oath he gave the Nurse not to reveal what she tells him.

THESEUS: One which welcomes with pleasure strangers
  who defile women and commit adultery.
HIPPOLYTUS: *aiai*, my heart! I'm brought close to tears   1070
  if I appear evil, especially to you.
THESEUS: It was *then* you should have moaned and thought ahead,
  when you were boldly violating my wife.
      (Hippolytus gestures toward the palace.)
HIPPOLYTUS: Oh, house! I wish you could speak for me
  and testify if I'm a man capable of evil.
THESEUS: Your witnesses are mute: a clever defense.
  But the deed needs no speech to condemn you.
HIPPOLYTUS: *pheu*, I wish I could look at myself standing
  here. I'd weep then for the hardship I suffer.
THESEUS: You're much more practiced in self-worship   1080
  than in justice and reverence to your parents.
HIPPOLYTUS: My poor mother! Bitter my coming into the world!
  May no friend of mine know a foreign birth!*
THESEUS: Remove him, slaves! Didn't you hear me
  long ago declare this man an outcast?
HIPPOLYTUS: The slave who touches me will regret it.
  You throw me out, if that's what you want.
THESEUS: I will, if you don't obey my command.
  No pity for your exile steals over me.
      (Theseus enters the house.)
HIPPOLYTUS: It's over, then. What misery to know   1090
  the truth and not know how to tell it.
  Oh, daughter of Leto, dearest goddess,†
  partner and fellow hunter, I'm banned
  from glorious Athens. And so farewell,
  city and land of Erechtheus;‡ Troezen,
  farewell. What happiness to be young here
  on your soil. I see you and salute you
  for the last time.
  (*to his companions*) Now, friends of my youth,

---

* The word Hippolytus uses here, *nothos*, refers in Athenian law to someone whose father is a citizen but whose mother is foreign and who therefore doesn't have the rights of citizenship.

† Artemis.

‡ Erechtheus was the founding king of Athens. Hippolytus assumes his exile extends to Athens, since that, too, is Theseus' home.

bid me farewell and send me from this place.
You'll never see a man more self-controlled   1100
than me, no matter what my father thinks.
> (*Hippolytus exits with his followers away from the town.*)

strophe 1

    CHORUS: When I think of gods' care for man
        it lightens my pain, but understanding,
        concealed by hope, eludes me
        when I see what happens to men and what they do.
        From one place then another things come and go,
        men's lives shift about, wander here and there.   1110

antistrophe 1

        I pray: may it be my lot to have from god
        good luck and prosperity, a spirit no pain confounds.
        May my thinking be neither fixed nor false,
        may my easy ways alter one day to the next,
        may I share in happiness.

strophe 2

        I don't think clearly now, I don't see what I expect,   1120
        not since I watched Athens' brightest star,
        watched him propelled by his father's wrath
        to another land.
        O sands that lie on the city's shore,
        mountain woods where
        with swift hounds he killed wild beasts
        in holy Dictynna's* company!   1130

antistrophe 2

        No more will he yoke a Venetian pair†
        and race round the course by the Marsh;
        music from the lyre that never sleeps will cease
        in his father's house.
        No garlands in the resting places,
        the deep meadows sacred to Leto's daughter;‡
        the young girls' race for your marriage bed   1140
        ended by your flight.

---

* Another name for Artemis.
† See note to line 231.
‡ Artemis.

epode

I will bear my unhappy lot
with tears for your misfortune.
Wretched mother,
no joy from the son you bore.
I rage at the gods.
iō, iō
Band of Graces, why have you sent
this wretched man who deserves no ruin
from his father's land, from this house?   1150

CHORUS: What now? I see Hippolytus' attendant,
　looking grim and rushing toward the house.
　　　　(An attendant comes running from the direction of Hippolytus'
　　　　departure.)

MESSENGER: Women, where can I find Theseus,
　lord of this land? If you know,
　tell me. Is he inside this house?

CHORUS: There he is. He's coming out here now.
　　　　(Theseus enters from the house.)

MESSENGER: Theseus, my words deserve careful attention,
　yours and the citizens in the city
　of Athens and the land of Troezen.

THESEUS: What is it? Not new misfortune   1160
　for the two neighboring cities?

MESSENGER: Hippolytus lives no more—or barely so.
　He's breathing still, but his life is in the balance.

THESEUS: The cause? Someone's hatred caught up with him,
　someone whose wife, like his father's, he violated?

MESSENGER: His own chariot was his destruction,
　and the curse you uttered against your son
　in the name of your father, Lord of the Sea.

THESEUS: O gods! Poseidon! It's true you are
　my father. You heard the curse I made.   1170
　How did he die? Tell me, what trap did
　Justice set for him once he'd shamed me?

MESSENGER: At the place where the waves meet the shore
　we groomed the horses' manes with curry combs
　and wept. A messenger had come to tell us
　Hippolytus would walk the earth here
　no more: he faced miserable exile

at your command. Then Hippolytus himself came
with the same sad story. With him came
a large following of friends, a crowd of companions.   1180
After a while, when he'd stopped weeping,
he said: "Why am I so upset? I must obey
my father. Prepare the horse and chariot,
slaves. This is my city no longer."
Then every man there rushed to a task
and, quicker than you could say it, we brought
the mares in harness to our master's feet.
He took the reins from the chariot's rail
into his hands and fit his feet in the footholds.
Before leaving he raised his arms to the gods   1190
and prayed: "Zeus, may I live no longer
if I'm a man capable of evil. But whether
I live or die, may my father learn how
he dishonors me." At that he took the whip
in his hand and urged on the horses together.
We followed alongside, at the horses' heads,
along the road to Argos and Epidaurus.
We came to the lonely stretch beyond
this land's border where a headland juts
into the water there, the Saronic gulf. Just then   1200
a sound echoed from the earth, a deep rumbling
like Zeus' thunder. We shivered to hear it.
The horses lifted their heads, pricked up
their ears. Fear took hold of us: where
did the sound come from? We looked
to the surf-beaten shore and saw
a breath-taking wave towering to heaven,
so high it took from my sight the shore
of Sciron, the Isthmus, and Asclepius' rock.
The foam frothed, the sea spouted; swollen   1210
and churning the wave moved to shore,
where the chariot stood. From its surge
and heave the wave spewed out
a bull, a savage monster. All the earth
was filled with its roar and roared a response
that terrified us. The sight we saw eclipsed
our capacity to see. At once the mares

panicked and took flight. And our master,
skilled as he was from a lifetime with horses,
seized the reins in his two hands.   1220
Putting his whole body into it, like a boatman
at his oar, he pulled on the reins.
The mares took the bit firm between their teeth
and hauled him forward with all their force.
His commanding hand, their harness, the close-fitted
chariot, nothing diverted them. When he kept
control and steered to soft ground, the bull
appeared before them, drove the team insane
with fear and turned them back. But when the mares
raced in panic toward the rocks, the bull,   1230
in silence, drew close to the chariot's rail
and kept pace with it until it capsized:
a wheel hit the rocks, and the bull flipped it over.
Then there was chaos: the axle pins
and wheel hubs hurtled into the air,
with wretched Hippolytus tangled in the reins.
He's caught in knots he can't unloose
and dragged along. His head smashes on rocks,
his skin is shredded, his shouts terrible to hear.
"Stop! Mares I fed in my own stables!   1240
Don't demolish me! Father's wretched curse!
Who is there to save me, the best of men?"
Many wanted to, but we were far behind,
our feet too slow. He works free
from the reins—I don't know how—
and falls, alive still but breathing shallow breaths.
The horses vanished, the dreadful monster-bull
disappeared somewhere in the rocky land.
I am a slave in your household, lord,
but I will never be able to do this: 1250
believe that your son is evil.
Not even if the entire race of women
hang themselves and write all over Ida's*
pine forest. I know him to be noble.

---

* The Messenger imagines the dense pine forest on Mount Ida turned into tablets like the one on which
Phaedra wrote her accusation of Hippolytus. Mount Ida is probably the mountain near Troy spoken of
in the Homeric poems. It would be familiar to the audience as a vast mountain range.

CHORUS: *aiai*, this misfortune! This new disaster!
　There's no escaping the necessity of our lot.
THESEUS: My hatred for the man who's suffered so
　has given me pleasure in your words. But now,
　out of respect for the gods and him—my son—
　I'm neither pleased nor burdened by his ruin.　　　1260
MESSENGER: And so...? Should we bring him here? Or what
　does it please you to do with the wretched man?
　Take thought. If you follow my advice,
　you will not be harsh to your unlucky son.
THESEUS: Bring him here. I'll see him face to face,
　refute his denial of defiling my bed
　with the story of this misfortune, sent by god.
　　　　　(The Messenger exits the stage in the direction he came from.)

　　CHORUS: *(singing in dochmiacs)*
　　　Cypris, you lead the unbending minds
　　　of gods and men, and in your company
　　　the one with shimmering wings　　　　　1270
　　　encircles them in swift flight.
　　　Eros flies over the earth,
　　　over the sounding salt sea,
　　　and he enraptures whomever,
　　　heart-crazed, he swoops on, golden in flight:
　　　the mountains' and the seas' spawn,
　　　all that the earth feeds
　　　and the bright sun sees,
　　　and humankind. All these you rule,　　　1280
　　　Cypris, in solitary majesty.
　　　　　(The goddess Artemis appears and is lowered by the mēchanē
　　　　　*onto the roof of the house. She addresses Theseus, first chanting
　　　　　and then speaking.)*
　　ARTEMIS: I command you, noble son of Aegeus:
　　　Listen.
　　　I, daughter of Leto, Artemis, speak to you.
　　　Why do you feel joy in misery, Theseus?
　　　You've killed your son against heaven's law
　　　because you trusted your wife's false words,
　　　believed what you hadn't seen.
　　　But your ruinous blindness is evident to all.

How do you not cower deep below the earth 1290
in your shame?
or remove yourself from pain,*
take wing and fly away?
No part of a life among good men
can be yours.

Hear, Theseus, the account of your wrongdoing.
My words will improve nothing, but they'll give you pain.
I've come for this: to show that your son's mind
is just, so he may die with a good name,
and to show your wife's obsession or, in a way, 1300
her nobility. She was in love with your son,
goaded and stung by the goddess most hateful
to those of us who find pleasure in chastity.
She tried to conquer Cypris with strength of mind—
her nurse's unwanted scheme destroyed her.
Her nurse told your son under oath of silence
of her disease. As was right, he didn't give in
to her request; nor did reverence allow him
to abandon his oath, even when you abused him.
Phaedra, fearing exposure, wrote a false 1310
account. With this deceitful ruse she
persuaded you and destroyed your son.

THESEUS: *oimoi!*
ARTEMIS: This story hurts you, Theseus? Yet be still.
Listen to what follows; you'll weep more.
You know that you have from your father
three certain curses: one you used, evil man,
against your son, though you had
enemies to curse. Your father wished you well
but gave what his promise required of him.
You, however, wronged your son and me. 1320
You waited for neither proof nor prophesy.
You made no inquiry, gave no time for thought.
More quickly than you should, you hurled
curses at your son, and killed him.

---

* The text here is corrupt.

THESEUS: Lady, let me die!

ARTEMIS: You've done a terrible thing, yes,
    but even so you may find forgiveness yet.
    Cypris wanted all this to happen
    to sate her anger. We gods have this rule:
    No one wants to oppose the will
    of another god. We always stand aside.   1330
    Be sure, if I didn't fear Zeus, I'd never
    sink so far in disgrace as to allow
    the one mortal I love most of all
    to die. As for you, in the first place,
    your ignorance frees your error
    from evil intent. And then the death of your wife
    prevented any questions about her story
    that might have persuaded you. This disaster
    has hit you hardest. But it pains me, too.
    Gods don't enjoy the death of reverent men;   1340
    evil men we destroy: house, children, all.

        (*Hippolytus, supported by two slaves, enters, barely able to walk.*
        Both the Chorus and Hippolytus are chanting.)

  CHORUS: Here he comes now, wretched man,
    his blond head, his young flesh
    mangled. What grief,
    what twin troubles take hold of this house,
    the gods' doing.

  HIPPOLYTUS: *aiai, aiai*
    This desolation! My unjust father
    has blighted me with an unjust curse.
    I'm wretched, ruined, *oimoi moi.*   1350
    Pain shoots through my skull,
    my brain convulses.
    Wait! I must rest my failing body.

        (*After a pause, Hippolytus starts to move again and cries out*
        from the pain.)

    ē, ē
    You, my horses, fed by my hand,
    hateful now,
    you destroyed me, you killed me.
    pheu, pheu. I beg you, slaves,

lay gentle hands on my tattered flesh.
Who stands here, on my right? 1360
Hold me up with care, with sure strength
drag me forward, ill-fated and wrongfully cursed
by my father. Zeus, Zeus, do you see this?
I, reverent and god-fearing,
I, superior to all in self-control,
I go to Death; he's here before my eyes,
I've lost my life; all the effort
of decency, all in vain.

> (As the pain increases, Hippolytus shifts from chanting to singing.)

aiai, aiai
Now the pain, the pain engulfs me, 1370
let me go.
Let death come to heal my misery.
Kill me, give me an end.
I want a sharp sword
to slice me apart,
to put my life to rest.
Oh, father's wretched curse!
Bloody wrong done by ancestors
long ago is here now,*
it waits no more, 1380
it comes at me—why?
I am guiltless.
iō moi moi
What can I say? How
can I free myself from life,
free myself from suffering?
May the night-dark necessity
of Death come and take me,
wretched, to rest.

ARTEMIS: Poor man, what suffering has you under its yoke!
Your nobility of mind has destroyed you. 1390
> (Hippolytus hears but cannot see her.)

---

* Because Hippolytus knows himself to be innocent, he imagines that his suffering is in payment for some wrong done by a member of the family in earlier generations. Theseus makes a similar supposition at line 820.

HIPPOLYTUS: *eā!*

Divinely scented breath!* Even in suffering
I sense your presence and grow lighter.
Artemis, divine being, is here in this place.

ARTEMIS: Poor man, I'm here, your dearest goddess.

HIPPOLYTUS: Do you see my body, my wretched state?

ARTEMIS: I see, but the law of the gods forbids me tears.

HIPPOLYTUS: Your hunter and your servant is no more.

ARTEMIS: No, but even in death you're dear to me.

HIPPOLYTUS: Gone the keeper of your horses, your statue's guard.

ARTEMIS: Cypris in her villainy contrived it so.   1400

HIPPOLYTUS: *oimoi*, I understand! *That* goddess destroyed me!

ARTEMIS: She faulted your scorn and hated your chastity.

HIPPOLYTUS: On her own she destroyed three of us.

ARTEMIS: Yes: you, your father and his wife.

HIPPOLYTUS: I weep, then, for my father's misfortune.

ARTEMIS: The goddess plotted to deceive him.

HIPPOLYTUS: (*to Theseus*) Father, you've suffered great unhappiness.

THESEUS: I'm ruined, son. I have no joy in life.

HIPPOLYTUS: For your sake more than mine your error grieves me.

THESEUS: I wish I were the one dying, not you.   1410

HIPPOLYTUS: Bitter gift of your father Poseidon!

THESEUS: I wish the curse had never crossed my lips.

HIPPOLYTUS: You would've killed me anyway in your anger.

THESEUS: The gods deluded me; my judgment failed.

HIPPOLYTUS: *pheu.* Would that men could curse gods!

ARTEMIS: Leave it be. The rage Cypris visited
on your body won't go unavenged
even when you're in darkness below.
There will be recompense for your reverence and good heart.
I will exact payment with my own hand   1420
and these unerring arrows: some favorite of hers,
the one she loves most, will pay the penalty.
And you, poor man, will be honored above all
in Troezen, my gift in return for your suffering.
Unwed girls before they marry will cut

---

* Gods are often recognized by their scent, as in the Homeric hymn to Demeter or Aphrodite, for example.

their hair to honor you; you will reap
their tears of mourning through the ages.*
Maidens' songs will tell your story
for all time; Phaedra's passion for you
won't slip wordlessly into silence.   1430
And you, child of aged Aegeus, take
your son in your arms, draw him close.
In ignorance you killed him: men naturally
make mistakes when gods direct them to.
I counsel you, Hippolytus, not to hate
your father. This destruction is your lot.
And so farewell. I may not stay to watch
you die, be tainted by your dying breath.†
I see that you are near that end now.

HIPPOLYTUS: Farewell to you, blessed maiden! Go now.   1440
You leave our long acquaintance easily.
I fight my father no longer, as you ask.
Before this, too, I obeyed your command.

    (Artemis exits.)

aiai, now darkness covers my eyes.
Father, take hold of me; raise me up.

THESEUS: *oimoi*, child, what are you doing to me?

HIPPOLYTUS: I'm dying. I see the gates of death before me.

THESEUS: You leave me with my hands tainted?

HIPPOLYTUS: No, no. I absolve you of my murder.

THESEUS: You mean, you release me from bloodguilt?   1450

HIPPOLYTUS: As Artemis of the deadly arrows is my witness.‡

THESEUS: Dearest son, how good you are to your father!

HIPPOLYTUS: Pray you're treated so by sons born in wedlock.§

THESEUS: *oimoi*, your good and reverent heart! Farewell!

HIPPOLYTUS: Farewell, Father, again farewell.

---

* As is often the case at the end of a tragedy, Euripides connects the events of the play to a ritual known to or practiced by the audience. There was a cult practice in which young girls dedicated locks of hair to Hippolytus before their marriage. There was also a sanctuary honoring Hippolytus on the south slope of the Acropolis in Athens, but we know nothing about the ritual performed there.

† Sanctuaries of the gods, and the gods themselves, had to be kept apart from human death, which was considered unclean. Apollo makes the same point in *Alcestis*, lines 22–24.

‡ Lines 1452–56 have been slightly rearranged to make clearer sense.

§ Hippolytus refers here to his status as the child of a foreign mother (see note 74). In the play this illegitimacy is translated into his not having the same status as Phaedra's children.

THESEUS: Don't desert me, child. Be strong.

HIPPOLYTUS: My strength is gone; my death is here.
Father, cover my face quickly now.

THESEUS: Glorious Athens, land of Troezen,
such a man you've lost! In misery   1460
I'll recall the pain you've caused, Cypris.

CHORUS: (*chanting*) All citizens feel this new grief together.*
It wasn't foreseen.
There will be a torrent of tears.
Great men's stories, when they're told,
spread greater sorrow.

---

* These last lines of the Chorus are of uncertain origin. By convention the Chorus speaks the last lines of the play, but it is not clear whether this convention was Euripidean or a later development. These lines are particularly suspect.

Introduction to Euripides' *Electra*

Electra is the center of this play, as she was in Sophocles' *Electra*, and as with that Electra, her resentment and anger here propel Orestes to kill Aegisthus and Clytemnestra. Both this *Electra* and the one by Sophocles—perhaps written at about the same time, though neither can be securely dated—are recastings of Aeschylus' *Libation Bearers*, and both feature realistic characters who are not particularly laudable. In Euripides' drama, both Electra and Orestes are more interested in recovering their patrimony and their aristocratic way of life than in accomplishing the justice of Zeus. They spend more time plotting the murders than summoning Agamemnon's ghost, a reversal of the pattern by which Aeschylus had displayed the piety of *his* heroes.

Euripides introduces a new element into his *Electra* by giving his main character a husband—a peasant her mother has forced her to marry as a way of demoralizing and disempowering her. She is ashamed of the hovel where she lives, and she is obliged to keep house and fetch water, chores ordinarily performed by slaves. Her dirty hair is cropped short (long, carefully dressed hair was a luxury only noblewomen could afford). But her husband, a man so lowly he is not even given a name, treats her with kindness and honors her as a princess, in a marital relationship Euripides portrays with great tenderness.

When Orestes first sees his sister, he assumes she is a peasant, returning with her jug of water from the spring. She assumes he is a criminal, until he tells her that he has news about her brother. And in some ways Agamemnon's children *are* criminals, and the peasants to whom they feel superior seem more intelligent and honorable than they. Orestes is impressed by the noble nature of Electra's husband, who offers him such hospitality as he can. Suspense continues to build while the Chorus sing a long song about the Trojan War, glorious Achilles, and the leader of the army who was killed by Clytemnestra's adultery.

As Sophocles did in his drama, Euripides makes Orestes' old tutor an important agent in his plot, and he casts this man (rather than Electra) as the one who had taken young Orestes away from Argos long ago. The old tutor now enters and recognizes Orestes almost immediately. Electra, however, unable to believe that her brother has returned, rejects the tokens of recognition that had featured so prominently in Aeschylus' *Libation Bearers*: How could Orestes' locks of hair and footprints be similar to her own? How could he still be wearing cloth that she once wove for him—since she was only a child when he left, too young to weave? She accepts that the old tutor is right only when he points out a scar near Orestes' eyebrow, incurred when he fell while he and Electra were chasing a fawn.

The tutor now helps Electra and Orestes plot their revenge. Orestes and Pylades will go to the place where Aegisthus is sacrificing to the nymphs. Electra will send a message to Clytemnestra that she has given birth to a son (in fact her marriage is a chaste one, owing to the peasant's great reverence for her). The Chorus meanwhile sing of the quarrel between Atreus and Thyestes: Thyestes seduced Atreus' wife and stole a golden lamb from Atreus' flocks; Zeus reacted by reversing the course of the sun and depriving North Africa of rain. The Chorus react to the story with the kind of skepticism Euripides' characters often express about such traditional tales about miracles, but they insist that they have not lost their faith in the gods, even though the gods seem to have done nothing to stop the succession of crimes in the family.

A messenger brings the news that Orestes and Pylades have killed Aegisthus. But what he describes is not a heroic confrontation; rather, an ignoble ambush. Aegisthus was the perfect host, welcoming the two strangers to a sacrifice, and suspecting that something was wrong only when he discovered that the liver of the sacrificial victim had no lobe, an evil portent. As Aegisthus was bending over the entrails of the sacrificial animal, Orestes struck him from behind, smashing his vertebrae, leaving his body twitching. Nonetheless, Electra brings victory garlands to Orestes and Pylades as if they had won a fair and open victory in battle, and she delivers a long, triumphant speech over Aegisthus' dead body.

That leaves Clytemnestra for Orestes to deal with. Remarkably, the young man pauses to wonder whether the oracle he received at Delphi really was spoken by an avenging deity. But Electra will not allow him to shirk. The murder of Clytemnestra, as portrayed by Euripides, is a sordid affair, in that the victim is portrayed far more sympathetically than in other versions. Although Clytemnestra arrives at the peasant's humble dwelling in a chariot, accompanied by her Trojan slaves, she treats Electra with kindness, and she explains that she hated Agamemnon because he killed her daughter Iphigenia and came home with Cassandra as his concubine—behavior that even a model wife like Penelope could hardly have approved. When Electra dismisses these arguments, Clytemnestra seems almost to apologize to her: "I'm not too comfortable with what I've done. / Those plots and schemes I made! It was too much, / that rage against my husband. I regret it."

In Aeschylus' and Sophocles' versions of the story, the details of Clytemnestra's murder are not reported. But in this play, Electra and Orestes offer horrifying descriptions of how they killed their mother in the peasant's house. They saw her bare her breast and heard her plead with them not to kill her. Electra helped the hesitant Orestes thrust his sword through their mother's neck. Once the deed is done, they both express regret: Electra takes pity on Clytemnestra as she lies dead, putting the clothes back on the body of "our unkind kin, the enemy we loved."

As she prepares her mother's body for burial, Electra states: "This is the end of the sorrows of our house." But just at that moment, the twin gods Castor and Polydeuces (Pollux), Clytemnestra's divine brothers, appear atop the roof of the palace, and Castor (who speaks for both) makes it clear that those sorrows will continue:

> *... we saw*
> *your mother, and our sister's, ritual slaughter.*
> *Her death was right, but you were wrong to do it.*
> *Apollo—he's my master, so I must*
> *keep silence—. But he gave you bad advice,*
> *despite his wisdom. Still, now yield to Fate,*
> *and do what Destiny and Zeus command.* (1240–48)

Electra, they decree, is to marry Pylades and leave Argos (her unconsummated marriage to the Peasant is now considered annulled); Orestes must flee to Athens, pursued by the avenging deities known as Kēres (virtually synonymous with Aeschylus' Erinyes). There he will be acquitted of his mother's murder, as in the *Oresteia.* Then Orestes must go to Arcadia, where he will found a city that will be named after him. Pylades must take Electra's peasant ex-husband along with them and "reward him with a pile of wealth." When Orestes and Electra ask why the twin gods did nothing to prevent their sister's murder, the answer, as so often from gods in Euripides' dramas, only explains the obvious: it was fated, and Apollo had ordered it through his oracle; the curse on her family had made it inevitable. Electra and Orestes now realize that they will never see each other again, and Castor and Polydeuces depart, on their way to save mortals who love piety and justice—a painful contrast to their role in this play.

Interestingly, in this *deus ex machina* epilogue, Castor, who had been a mortal before Zeus raised him from the dead and made him divine, for a brief moment takes pity on Orestes and his suffering. But since he is now a god, he no longer feels the need to comfort his mortal niece and nephew. Like Apollo and the other gods, he and Polydeuces live at their ease and let humans do their dirty work for them. Agamemnon's death has been avenged, but Orestes must suffer before he can find happiness. In the realistic world depicted in Euripides' drama, a grim matricide brings no triumphant procession and no release from troubles.

As in the case of Sophocles' *Electra*, no definite date can be assigned to this drama. Because Euripides tended to use more short syllables in his lines of iambic dialogue as his style evolved, scholars have used the percentage of short syllables as a way to roughly date his plays, and this metric suggests that *Electra* was produced around 420 B.C. Perhaps the central role Euripides assigns to Electra was influenced by Sophocles' version of the story, but there is no way to know which play came first.

Euripides' *Electra* was the basis of a 1962 film by Michael Cacoyannis. An Academy Award nominee, it depicted vividly the harsh life led by farmers in the Greek countryside and the brutality of the murders of Agamemnon, along with those of Aegisthus and Clytemnestra. The film ended with Orestes and Electra both leaving the land they had sought to regain, but without the explanation given in Euripides' plays by the twin gods.

Electra

Translated by Emily Wilson

This translation is based on the text in J. Diggle, ed., *Euripidis Fabulae* (Oxford, Oxford University Press, 1994); I have also consulted M. J. Cropp, ed., *Euripides, Electra* (Ed.2; Oxford, Aris and Phillips, 2013) and H. M. Roisman and C.A.E. Luschnig, *Euripides, Electra: A Commentary* (Norman, OK, University of Oklahoma Press, 2011).

Cast of Characters (in order of appearance)

PEASANT, husband of Electra
ELECTRA, daughter of the dead king of Argos, Agamemnon, and
    the wife who murdered him, Clytemnestra
ORESTES, exiled brother of Electra
OLD MAN, loyal servant and long-ago tutor of Agamemnon
MESSENGER
CLYTEMNESTRA, mother of Electra
AEGISTHUS, lover of Clytemnestra and co-murderer of
    Agamemnon; in possession of the throne of Argos
CASTOR (with POLLUX, nonspeaking role), brothers of Helen and
    Clytemnestra, who have become gods
PYLADES, friend of Orestes (nonspeaking role)
CHORUS of women of Argos

Setting: The play takes place in rural Argos, outside the hut of the Peasant.

PEASANT: (*emerging from hut*)
Look! Here's ancient Argos, river Inachus,*
where Agamemnon raised the rage of War,†
sailing a thousand ships against great Troy.
He killed the king of Ilium, Lord Priam,
and took the famous city of the Dardans,
and came back here to Argos, where he filled
the lofty temples with the heaps of spoil,
taken from foreigners. So far, so good.
But then he died, at home, by his wife's tricks.
Yes, Clytemnestra and Aegisthus killed him.   10
He's gone, and left behind the ancient scepter
of Tantalus.‡ Aegisthus rules the land.
He's got the old king's wife, Tyndareus' daughter.§
As for the children left here when the king
set sail for Troy, Orestes and the girl,
Electra; well, his father's old attendant
saw that Aegisthus planned to kill the boy,
and took him to the king of Phocis, Strophius,¶
to care for. But Electra stayed at home
—her father's home. When she began to flower,
the best of Greece were eager for her hand.   20
But since Aegisthus didn't want her having

---

* The text of this line is problematic, but the general sense is not really in doubt.

† In the original, "War" is "Ares," the god of war. There is wordplay in the original, since "Ares" sounds like the word used for "raised" (*aras*).

‡ Tantalus was the father of Atreus, father of Agamemnon and Menelaus, and of Thyestes, father of Aegisthus. Aegisthus is thus Agamemnon's first cousin; hence his claim to the throne of Argos.

§ Clytemnestra and Helen were both supposed to have been the product of Zeus' rape of Leda, wife of Tyndareus, in the form of a swan. Here Clytemnestra's divine origin is downplayed, by the suggestion that she is the daughter of her mother's mortal husband.

¶ Strophius is the father of Orestes' friend Pylades, and was the guardian of Orestes during the boy's youth.

a child that might avenge dead Agamemnon,
he kept her home and wouldn't marry her
to any nobleman. Fear haunted him,
that she'd have babies with a lord in secret.
He planned to kill her; but her savage mother
was kind enough to save her from Aegisthus.
Her husband's murder was excusable,
but killing children might, she feared, look bad.
Aegisthus had to come up with a plan.   30
He promised money to whatever man
could kill Orestes—exiled from our land—
and gave Electra as a wife to *me*.
I am from Mycenean ancestry;*
no faulting me as far as that's concerned:
my blood is blue, but I am very poor.
In such a case, nobility is useless.
He hoped reducing her to such a husband
would help reduce his fear, since if a man
of status had her, he'd have woken up   40
the sleeping murder of dead Agamemnon;
then Justice would descend upon Aegisthus.
        But I—and Aphrodite is my witness!—
have never touched her. Yes, she's still a virgin.
I won't abuse a rich man's child; I'd feel
ashamed: I'm just not worthy of her class.
I'm sorry for my so-called brother-in-law,†
Orestes. If he ever comes to Argos,
poor man! He'll see his sister's dreadful marriage.
People may say I'm stupid, since I took   50
a virgin to my house, and didn't touch her.
But those who think such things should know the truth:
their values are corrupt, and they are, too!
        (Enter Electra, carrying a water pitcher.)‡
ELECTRA: Black Night! The nurse of all the golden stars!
    By night I'll take this pitcher on my head

---

* I.e. his family is not immigrant, but has been native to the land for several generations. In Athens, immigrants could not have full citizen rights.
† "So-called" because the marriage is unconsummated and therefore does not entirely count.
‡ Slave women commonly fetched the well water, carrying it on their heads.

down to the river streams to fetch the water,
and to the vastness of the sky I'll weep
for my dead father—not because I mind
my poverty, but just to show the gods   60
Aegisthus' wickedness. My monstrous mother
threw me from home to please him—her new husband.*
She's had new babies with him now—Orestes
and I will lose all status in our house!

PEASANT: Poor girl, you do not need to work so hard
for me, when you were raised for better things.

ELECTRA: You're a good friend to me, a godlike friend,
who didn't take advantage of my trouble.
Humans are very lucky when they find
healing in ruin: just as I found you.   70
So I should help you in your work, and lighten
your load as best I can, to make things easier
for you, and not because you told me to.
You have enough to do outside; the house
is up to me. It's nice for a man to find
everything neat when he comes home from work.

PEASANT: Well, it's your choice; go on then. After all,
the springs are not too far. And when day comes,
I'll take the oxen out to sow the furrows.
No point in prayer if you just sit there idle;   80
the only way to get your bread is work.

> *(Electra goes off to get the water. Enter Orestes and Pylades,*
> *wearing traveling clothes.)*

ORESTES: Ah, Pylades! My best, most loyal friend,
linked by both hospitality and blood.†
The only one who still respected me,
stuck by me when Aegisthus made me suffer.
He killed my father, with my monstrous mother.
I've been away, a visit to the god;‡

---

* The text is problematic here; the line ordering here reflects a rearrangement by the editor, Diggle.

† Pylades is Orestes' cousin, son of Agamemnon's sister Anaxibia. Pylades' father, Strophius, protected Orestes when he fled Argos after his father's death.

‡ Orestes says literally that he has been to the "rites" of the god—presumably a reference to his visit to Delphi, to consult the oracle of Apollo regarding what he should do about the murder of his father. Compared to other dramatic treatments of the myth, by Aeschylus and Sophocles, Euripides makes very little of this motif; nothing specific is mentioned about what the oracle said.

no one in Argos knows I've got back here,
to pay my father's killers death for death.
Last night I went to see my father's grave,   90
and wept for him, and gave a lock of hair,*
and killed a sheep, and poured blood on the fire,
in secret from the powers that be—those tyrants!
And I'm not setting foot inside the walls,
just coming to the borders of the land.   95
Two reasons: first, so I can get out fast,
if anybody sees me; secondly,
I'm looking for my sister, since they say
she's married now and living with a husband.
We'll team up: she will help me kill those two,   100
and help me understand what's going on
behind the walls.
                    Now white Dawn's face is up:
let's shift our footsteps from the beaten track,
so that a plowman, or a household slave
may tell us if my sister lives round here.
I need to find her!
            (He sees Electra approaching.)
                    But look now, here comes
a servant girl, whose hair is closely cropped,
carrying river water on her head,
a heavy load. Let's sit and listen here,
to this slave-girl, to see if we can hear   110
something about our quest, dear Pylades.
            *(Orestes and Pylades withdraw behind an altar but remain
            onstage.)*

strophe 1

   ELECTRA: (*singing*)† Faster, push your feet to dance; it's time!
        Onward, onward with your cries of grief.
        Ah, ah, ah!
        Agamemnon was my father,
        Clytemnestra bore me,
        that hateful child of Tyndareus.

---

* A traditional gesture of mourning.

† This section is a "monody," i.e. a single character, Electra, is singing in lyric meter, and presumably dancing at the same time.

My name among the citizens
is "Poor Electra."
Oh, what I've gone through! Nothing but pain.   120
Oh, what a horrible life!
Father, Agamemnon, you lie dead,
slaughtered by your wife,
and by Aegisthus.

*mesode 1**

Come on, wake up your tears!
It feels so good to cry.

antistrophe 1

Faster, push your feet to dance: it's time!
Onward, onward with your cries of grief.
Ah, ah, ah!
Where is your city, where is your home,   130
where are you wandering, my poor brother?
You left behind in our father's home
your poor sister,
to suffer the worst that could be.
If only you'd come home!
Set me free from my pain! Have pity on me!
And come for our father, remove the shame from his blood.
My own lost brother, make your way to shore
in Argos. O Zeus, Zeus!
    (Enter Servant, whom Electra addresses.)

strophe 2

Come take this pitcher from my head,   140
and set it down, so I can lift my voice
in a nocturnal song of grief for my dead father.
I'll wail, I'll sing, I'll chant,
for your death, Father.†
I'll send my lamentations down below the earth.
I spend all day melted away with tears,
tearing my own throat open with my nails,
beating my hands upon my shaven head,
because you're dead.

---

* This is a section of verse in between the main strophes.

† The text of these two lines may be corrupt.

mesode 2

> O, O! I'll rip out my hair!   150
> As the swan moans
> by the streams of the river,
> and calls to the father it loved,
> killed by treachery, caught in knotted nets,
> so I mourn you,
> my poor dear father.

antistrophe 2

> Washed in your last terrible bath,
> you lie there dead: what a way to die!
> How horrible! That axe
> slashed through you, Father. O, so horrible!   160
> What a return from Troy!
> Your wife didn't welcome you
> with garlands of glory;*
> she defiled your body and prepared it
> for Aegisthus with his two-edged sword to hack.
> So she got that trickster for a husband.
>
> > *(Enter Chorus of young women, inhabitants of the nearby countryside.)*

strophe

> CHORUS: Electra, Agamemnon's daughter! I have come
> to see you in your country cottage.
> Someone came to visit—yes, he did! A Mycenean,
> a mountain man, the kind that just drinks milk.   170
> He says in Argos they've announced
> a sacrifice, two days from now,
> and all unmarried girls
> will go in procession to Hera.
>
> ELECTRA: Friends, my heart is sad; it can't take flight
> for pretty things
> or golden necklaces.
> I can't lead the dance
> of Argive girls
> or twirl and stamp my feet.   180
> All night I cry, and crying is all I do,

---

* Wives were expected to wash the dusty feet of a husband returning from a journey (rather than kill them in the bath).

living in pain, day after day.
Look at my unwashed hair,
my dirty clothes.
Does this look right
for a princess,
King Agamemnon's daughter?
Even Troy is shamed by how I look:
that city still remembers being conquered by my father.

antistrophe

CHORUS: The goddess is mighty. Come now, I can lend you   190
fine woven clothes to wear,
and golden jewelry,
so fine and graceful.
Do you think you can neglect the gods
and still defeat your enemies? No, child:
your tears won't work: you need to pray and worship,
so that the gods will bring your day of joy.

ELECTRA: No god is listening to my voice
in my misfortune. No god long ago
heard, when they slaughtered my father.   200
Poor dead father!
Poor lost living brother,
who must be in another land—a wanderer,
living from job to job
and hearth to hearth,
despite his noble birth.
And as for me, I live in the house of a laborer,
wasting away my life,
an exile from my home, the home of my forefathers,
up in the mountain crags.   210
My mother lives there, married to that other man,
sleeping there with him on blood-soaked sheets.

CHORUS:* Your mother's sister Helen caused this trouble.†
She hurt the Greeks and hurt your family.

ELECTRA: Ah, yes! But, girls, I'll stop lamenting now.
          (*She sees Orestes and Pylades.*)
Look! There were some strangers lurking here

---

* The meter here reverts to the regular dialogue rhythm.

† Helen is blamed for the whole Trojan War, because her elopement with Paris prompted the conflict.

behind the altar by my house. They're coming!
Get away down the path, I'll run inside.
They're criminals, let's get away from them!
(Electra and the Chorus members try to flee.)

ORESTES: *(grabbing Electra)* Stop, wait! Poor girl! Don't run! Come, let me
   hold you!   220

ELECTRA: Apollo! Save me! Please don't let me die!

ORESTES: I'd rather kill the one I hate, not you!

ELECTRA: Away! Hands off a girl you shouldn't touch!

ORESTES: I have a right to touch you—no one more.

ELECTRA: Why did you lurk beside my house with swords?

ORESTES: Just wait and listen, then you'll say I'm right.

ELECTRA: I'll stay. You've got me anyway by force.

ORESTES: I've come to bring you news about your brother.

ELECTRA: My love! But is he still alive? Or dead?

ORESTES: Alive. So that's the good news. Start with that.   230

ELECTRA: Bless you! You deserve it! Such sweet news!

ORESTES: The gift's for both of us, good luck for both.

ELECTRA: But he's still lost, poor thing! So where is he?

ORESTES: He drifts from town to town. It's worn him out.

ELECTRA: You mean he doesn't have enough to eat?

ORESTES: He isn't starving, but he's weak from exile.

ELECTRA: What message did he send you with for me?

ORESTES: To see if you're alive, and how you are.

ELECTRA: Just look at me! I'm all dried up and skinny.

ORESTES: Wasted by grief. It makes me want to cry.   240

ELECTRA: You see I shaved my hair off with a blade.*

ORESTES: Stung by your brother's loss, and your dead father.

ELECTRA: Yes, oh, yes! They're all the world to me.

ORESTES: And what do you think your brother feels for you?

ELECTRA: We love each other, but he's far away.

ORESTES: Why are you living out here, far from town?

ELECTRA: Stranger, because I'm married. It's like death.

ORESTES: O, your poor brother!—to which Argive man?

ELECTRA: Not one my father hoped to give me to.

ORESTES: But tell me who it is; I'll tell your brother.   250

ELECTRA: This is my husband's house, out in the sticks.

---

* A traditional gesture of grief.

ORESTES: A farm-hand or a cowherd ought to live here!

ELECTRA: He's poor but noble, treats me with respect.

ORESTES: How does this husband show respect for you?

ELECTRA: He's never dared to touch me in my bed.

ORESTES: Out of religious scruple, or disgust?

ELECTRA: He doesn't want to disrespect my forebears.

ORESTES: But why was he not happy with this marriage?

ELECTRA: He thinks the man who gave me had no right.

ORESTES: He fears Orestes might come take revenge?   260

ELECTRA: Yes, that is part of it. Also, he's good.

ORESTES: Ah!

He does sound good. He must be treated right.

ELECTRA: He will be—if the missing man comes home.

ORESTES: But did your mother really let this happen?

ELECTRA: Yes, women love their men and not their children.

ORESTES: Why did Aegisthus do this wrong to you?

ELECTRA: To guarantee my children would be weak.

ORESTES: Not children who might rise to take revenge?

ELECTRA: That was his plan—and may he pay for it!

ORESTES: Does your stepfather know you're still a virgin?   270

ELECTRA: He doesn't. We have kept this from him, stranger.

ORESTES: So then, these women listening are friends?

ELECTRA: Yes, and they'll keep your secrets just like mine.

ORESTES: What should Orestes do if he comes home?

ELECTRA: How can you ask? For shame! The time is now!

ORESTES: Well, then: how could he kill his father's killers?

ELECTRA: With nerves of steel—like them against my father.*

ORESTES: But could you bear it if he killed your mother?

ELECTRA: Yes! With the very axe that killed my father!

ORESTES: Then shall I tell him? Is your mind made up?   280

ELECTRA: Yes, let me shed my mother's blood, then die!

ORESTES: O!

I wish Orestes could be here to hear you!

ELECTRA: I wouldn't recognize him if I saw him.

ORESTES: Of course: you two got separated young.

ELECTRA: There's only one of all our friends would know him.

ORESTES: The one that rescued him from being killed?

---

* The text is problematic in this line.

ELECTRA: Yes, our father's tutor, that old man.

ORESTES: And your dead father, has he got a tomb?

ELECTRA: It's what it is. They shoved him from his home.

ORESTES: That's terrible!—We humans feel the pain   290
    of suffering, even when it isn't ours.
    But tell me, so I can inform your brother,
    news that he will not like, but still must hear.
    The ignorant are not capable of pity;
    intelligent people are, though at a cost.
    A clever mind can understand too much.

CHORUS: I long for just the same thing in my heart.
    We're stuck out here, don't know what's going on
    inside the city, and I want to know.

ELECTRA: You're friends, and friends deserve the truth. I'll tell you.   300
    Things have been bad for me and for my father.
    But stranger, since you asked me for my story,
    I beg you, tell Orestes all my troubles.
    My pains are his. Tell him what clothes I wear;
    how I'm all caked with dirt; the peasant hut
    I live in—no more palaces for me!
    I have to labor, weaving wool for clothes,
    or I'd have none, nothing to wear at all.*
    I have to carry water from the stream;
    I am deprived of festivals and dances;   310
    I keep my distance from the married wives,
    since I'm a virgin. Also I feel embarrassed
    about my uncle Castor, who's a god now,
    but once my suitor.† Mother's on the throne,
    decked out spoils from Troy, with all the girls
    from Asia, whom my father took by war,
    their foreign dresses pinned with golden clasps.
    My father's blood is moldering in the house,
    black blood!—while he, the one who murdered him
    rides in his victim's chariot through the land,   320
    and proudly brandishes, in blood-stained hands,
    the scepter Father used to lead the troops.

---

* The text of this line is corrupt.

† Castor, brother of Electra's mother, Clytemnestra, apparently sought to marry her before becoming a god. This may be Euripides' invention. Athenian law allowed uncles and nieces to marry.

The tomb of Agamemnon gets no honor,
and no libations and no sprigs of myrtle;
his funeral mound is bare of offerings.
But he, this famous husband of my mother,
sodden with drink, leaps on the grave, they say,
and pelts my father's monument with rocks,
and dares to talk against us, saying this:
"Where is his son, Orestes? Is he here,   330
that fine protector of your grave?" Insulting
my absent brother!
     (*to Orestes*) Stranger, take this news.
It comes from many: I interpret them:
My hands, my tongue, my heavy-hearted mind,
my shaven head, and he—Orestes' father.
It looks bad, if his father conquered Troy
and he, young though he is, can't even kill
just this one man—his father was much better.
CHORUS: I see him coming! Him—I mean your husband.
He's finished work, and now he's coming home.   340
     (*Enter Peasant.*)
PEASANT: What's this? Who are these strangers at the house?
What do they want out here, in the countryside,
here at my house? Is it me they want to see?
A woman's shamed by standing out with men.
ELECTRA: Darling, please don't suspect the worst of me!
I'll tell you how it is. These strangers came
to bring me messages Orestes sent.
And, strangers, please forgive what he just said.
PEASANT: What did they tell you? Is he still alive?
ELECTRA: So goes their story, and I think it's true.   350
PEASANT: And does he think of you and your dead father?
ELECTRA: He hopes, but helplessly; an exile's weak.
PEASANT: What message did they bring you from Orestes?
ELECTRA: He sent them here to see how much I suffer.
PEASANT: Part they can see, and part, I guess, you told them?   355
ELECTRA: They understand. I have left out nothing.
PEASANT: Then why are they still waiting here outside?
     (*to the strangers*) Come in, come in! You've brought great news, you've earned
a welcome; all that's in my house is yours.

Servants, lift up the bags and take them in.* 360
No protests: you've come from a friend of ours,
so you're our friend. Although I was born poor
I'll never show an ill-bred attitude.
ORESTES: (*to Electra*) My god! Can this be your secret husband?
The one who doesn't want to shame my name?
ELECTRA: Yes, he's called my husband. It's no fun.
ORESTES: Gods! There's no art to tell a decent man,
since generations work haphazardly.
I have encountered worthless men, the sons
of noble fathers; good men born from bad; 370
and I've seen hunger in a rich man's mind,
a poor man's body housing thoughts sublime.
<How then should one distinguish them and judge?
By wealth? That standard's useless and corrupt.
Or by who has the least? But being poor
can make you sick, and teaches crime through need.
By force of arms? But who could testify
on moral worth, while staring down the spear?
Don't try to sort it out, just let it go.>†
This man, you see, is no great lord in Argos, 380
he's not puffed up by pride in family;
he's from the many, but a noble man.
So stop this foolishness, stop wandering round
in empty circles: judge nobility
by how a person acts with other people.
<This kind of person governs cities well,
and households, while those empty muscle-heads
look pretty in the market-place, that's all.
Strong arms withstand the spear no more than weak.
Courage and character, that's what it takes.>‡ 390
But as for me, I'm here and I'm deserving;
so is the absent son of Agamemnon

---

* This line is believed by many editors to be spurious, partly on the grounds that it seems like a social faux pas: the Peasant ought not to be giving instructions to Orestes' servants. But as Mastronarde has pointed out, there is no good reason why we ought to expect the Peasant to behave with perfect manners.

† This passage, bracketed, may not belong in the speech, though some editors defend it.

‡ Again, many editors suspect this passage is not genuine.

for whom I've come. So we'll accept this welcome.
Go, slaves, inside the house. I'd rather have
a poor but willing host than one who's rich.
I was impressed by how he welcomed us.
But still, I wish your brother had been here,
to lead us gladly to a house of joy.
Perhaps he'll come: Apollo's oracles
are sure, though mortal prophecy is not.

(Orestes and Pylades go into the house) 400

CHORUS: Electra, now, more than before, my heart
    grows warm with joy. Maybe, just maybe, now
    your fortune's rising; things may turn out well.

ELECTRA: *(to Peasant)* You silly man! You know how poor your house is;
    why did you ask these strangers in, your betters?

PEASANT: What's wrong? If they're as noble as they seem,
    won't they be happy with great men or small?

ELECTRA: Well, no. You got it wrong. You're lower class.
    So then: go find my father's dear old friend,
    the tutor, who lives down beside the river,
    the border cutting Argos off from Sparta. 410
    He's exiled from the town, his only friends
    are sheep. Tell him to come here, to our house,
    and bring some food to share for dinner-time.
    He will be glad and surely thank the gods,
    hearing the boy he saved is still alive.
    We wouldn't get a thing from Father's house,
    from my mean mother: she'd be pained to hear
    her son, Orestes, is alive and well.

PEASANT: Well, if you think it best, I'll take the news 420
    to that old man. But go, inside the house,
    quick as you can, and make things nice in there.
    If any woman wants to, she can find
    plenty to make a meal. We have at home
    enough to fill their bellies for today.

(Electra goes inside.)

Thinking of things like this, my mind soon turns
to money—what great power it has, to give
to guests, and buy the things you need to save
your life when you get sick. But daily food

costs little, and the same amount of bread   430
will fill your stomach, rich and poor alike.
> *(Peasant goes into the house.)*

strophe 1

CHORUS: Remember the famous ships that once embarked
    for Troy with countless oars
    that set the nymphs of the sea to dancing,
    and all the while the dolphin, lover of pipe music,*
    twists and turns around
    the sea-dark prows,
    taking Thetis' son,†
    so light on his springy feet,
    Achilles, along with Agamemnon   440
    to the shores of Troy.

antistrophe 1

    The Nereids left the headlands of Euboea
    and brought the labors of Hephaestus' anvil,‡
    bearing the shield, the golden arms,
    up over Pelion and the holy glens
    of craggy Ossa,§ where the nymphs keep watch,
    seeking girls.¶ And there the horseman father**
    raised a light for Greece,
    the child of the sea-goddess Thetis,   450
    quick-footed runner for Atreus' sons.

strophe 2

    I heard, in the harbor of Nauplia††
    from a man who came from Troy,

---

* It was common folk belief that dolphins love flute music.

† Achilles was son of the sea goddess Thetis.

‡ The armor of Achilles was made for him by Hephaestus, god of metalworking. The version of the story in the *Iliad* (book 18) tells that Achilles received the divine armor as a replacement, after Hector stripped his first set of armor from his friend Patroclus. Euripides seems to be working with a different version of the myth, in which sea nymphs bring Achilles the divinely crafted armor before the Trojan expedition begins.

§ Pelion and Ossa are mountains in central Greece—here the home of the Centaur Chiron, who tutored the young Achilles.

¶ The text seems to be corrupt in these lines.

** Presumably the Centaur Chiron, who was Achilles' tutor, although the lines are at least temporarily ambiguous, since his father, Peleus, is also known as a horse rider and charioteer.

†† Nauplia (modern Nafplio) is the port of Argos.

that on the circle of your famous shield,
O son of Thetis,
were worked these images
of fear for the Trojans:*
and on the part that ran around the rim,
Perseus over the sea, on flying sandals,
held up the Gorgon's head, throat-slit,†   460
with Hermes, messenger of Zeus,
boy born to Maia
in the countryside.‡

antistrophe 2

And in the middle of the shield there shone
the circle of the sun
with its winged horses
and choruses of dancing stars up in the sky,
the Pleiades, the Hyades, to turn
the eyes of Hector.§
On the helmet of beaten gold, in their talons   470
Sphinxes carry their prey, the prize of song.¶
And on the curving corslet round his ribs, with breath of fire
away rushed the lioness,
quick on her claws,
when she saw Pegasus, colt of Peirene.**

epode

And on his bloody sword the four-hoofed horses galloped,
black dust rose round their backs.
But the king of those men who suffered by the spear
was murdered,
daughter of Tyndareus,   480

---

* The text here is also problematic.

† The hero Perseus had magical sandals with wings; he used a mirror to kill and decapitate the monstrous snake-headed Gorgon, Medusa—a popular theme in art.

‡ Hermes, the messenger god, helped Perseus in his monster-slaying quests. His mother, the goddess Maia, gave birth to him secretly, in a countryside cave.

§ The text may be corrupt here. The idea seems to be that the shield will be so bright that it will dazzle Hector—perhaps like the mirror used by Perseus to dazzle the Gorgon.

¶ Sphinxes, like Sirens, were imagined to allure their victims by singing.

** The fire-breathing lioness is the monstrous Chimera, who was finally defeated by the hero Bellerophon riding on the winged horse Pegasus (with Perseus' help); hence, here, she is frightened of Pegasus. Pegasus supposedly emerged from the decapitated Gorgon. Bellerophon found and tamed Pegasus by the magical spring of Peirene.

by your affair, and by your wicked plans.*
For that, may those who live in heaven
one day send you death as punishment!
Blood, more blood,
I'll see more blood
dripping from your throat slashed through with iron.

> (*Enter Old Man, who makes his way up toward the hut of Electra, laden down with flowers, a lamb, wineskins, and other food supplies.*)

OLD MAN: My princess, my young mistress, where is she?
Where's Agamemnon's child, whom I helped raise?
What a steep trudge it is up to her house!
I'm old and bent, my wrinkled legs are shaking: 490
not sure if I can make it. But I must!
I'll drag these old bones up to see my friends.
      Daughter! I see you now, right by the house.
I've come to bring you this, a fat young lamb
—I stole it from the flock to give you: here!
And garlands, and this cheese I took from storage,
and vintage wine, the wealth of Dionysus:
the nose is excellent! Add just a cup,
no more, to some less alcoholic drink.†
Delicious! Now, go take this to the guests.   500
I want to use my ragged clothes to wipe
my eyes: my floods of tears have made them wet.

ELECTRA: You're crying, sir? Your face is soaked. But why?
Have I reminded you of painful things?
Or are you sad about my brother's exile,
and Father—whom you carried in your arms
and cared for as a boy—much good it did you!

OLD MAN: I know; but still I managed this: I took
a detour on my journey, by his tomb.
No one was there, and I lay down, and wept,   510
and from this flask I've brought your guests, I poured

---

* The primary reference is to Agamemnon, killed by Clytemnestra (daughter of Tyndareus) and her lover, Aegisthus. But the phrasing is ambiguous, allowing a secondary reminder that the other daughter of Tyndareus, Helen, was also responsible for an affair that caused the deaths of Agamemnon and many other men.

† The Greeks usually drank their wine diluted with water.

wine for the dead, and laid the myrtle round.
But on the pyre itself I saw a gift:
a sheep with black wool, with its blood just spilt,
and locks of yellow hair from someone's head.
So I was puzzled, child: who could have dared
approach the tomb? No Argive, that's for sure.
Maybe your brother came there secretly,
and honored his poor father's tomb like this.
Look at this hair, compare it to your own: 520
see if your color matches with the lock.
It's natural, those who share one father's blood
are physically alike in many ways.*

ELECTRA: Gosh, what a silly thing to say, old man!
You think my hero brother would sneak here
in secret? He's not frightened of Aegisthus!
And how can you expect the locks to match?
Blue-blooded men teach roughness to their hair
by wrestling. Female hair's acquired by combing.†
In any case, people who aren't related   530
often have matching hair color. You know that.

OLD MAN: Then step into the marks his boots have made;
see if your foot will match its size, my child.

ELECTRA: But how could there be any print at all
on stony ground? Or even if there were,
the man and woman's feet won't match together
even for siblings! Male is more than female.‡

OLD MAN: Well, if your brother has come to this land,§
wouldn't you recognize the cloth you wove,
in which I wrapped him when I saved his life?   540

ELECTRA: But I was still a child when he escaped.
I wasn't weaving. And, even if I had,

---

* In this scene, Euripides is alluding to (and mocking) Aeschylus' earlier treatment of the Orestes-Electra recognition scene, in the *Libation Bearers*. In Aeschylus, the brother and sister do indeed recognize each other by comparing their hair color and their footprints.

† I have tried to retain something of the odd language of the original, which implies that hair becomes male or female by means of its upbringing.

‡ Again, I have translated in such a way as to bring out the strikingly gendered language, which suggests not only that men's feet tend to be larger than women's feet, but more broadly or more abstractly, that "the male" is the winner in a putative competition over "the female."

§ A line seems to be missing after this one.

how could he still be wearing baby clothes?
Just use your head! His clothes grew, with his body.
Some stranger must have come and taken pity,
seeing his tomb, and left this lock of hair.*

OLD MAN: Well then, where are your guests? I'd like to see them
and ask them what they know about your brother.

(*Enter Orestes and Pylades, from the house.*)

ELECTRA: Here they are now, they're hurrying out to us.

OLD MAN: (*to Electra*) They look well-born, but you can't trust all that,   550
since lots of so-called noblemen are bad.

But never mind. (*to Orestes and Pylades*) Greetings and welcome, strangers!

ORESTES: The same to you, sir.—Tell me, please, Electra,
what's this old man's connection with your people?

ELECTRA: This is the man who brought my father up.

ORESTES: Really? The one who stole away your brother?

ELECTRA: The one who saved him—if he's still alive.

(*The Old Man stares at Orestes.*)

ORESTES: He's staring at me!
He looks as if he's checking out a coin.
But why? Is he comparing me to someone?

(*The Old Man walks around Orestes.*)

ELECTRA: He's glad to see a man who is so close ...   560

ORESTES: To Orestes? Yes, but why the circling?

ELECTRA: You know, I'm wondering the exact same thing.

OLD MAN: Princess Electra! Pray and praise the gods!

ELECTRA: But what am I supposed to pray about?

OLD MAN: The long lost treasure that the gods revealed!

ELECTRA: All right, "Ye gods!"—What do you mean, old man?

OLD MAN: (*pointing to Orestes*)
You're looking at your dearest love, my child!

ELECTRA: I've seen him.
(*to the Old Man*): Are you sure you're feeling well?

OLD MAN: Better than well! I'm looking at your brother!

ELECTRA: What are you saying? I despaired of this.   570

OLD MAN: He's here! Orestes! Son of Agamemnon!

ELECTRA: Have you seen some sign to prove this claim?

---

* There is a textual problem in this line. I have skipped the words "taking observers of this land," which seem to be corrupt.

OLD MAN: A scar along his eyebrow, which he got
chasing a fawn, with you, in your father's house.

ELECTRA: What's this? I see a fall has marked him. But—

OLD MAN: You hesitate to fall into his arms?

ELECTRA: No, no, no longer! This is evidence
to make my heart believe. (*to Orestes*)
     I've got you back,
beyond my hopes, after so long— **ORES.:** So long!

ELECTRA: I never thought— **ORES.:** And I, I never dreamed— 580

ELECTRA: And is it you? **ORES.:** It's me, your only ally.
To work: I'll enter, draw the latch, and then*
I'm sure I will succeed. There are no gods,
if evil triumphs over righteousness.

    CHORUS:† Now you've come, you've come, bright day has dawned!
      The day we waited for so long! The city sees the light!
      Here he is, our shining star, once lost,
      wandering long ago, in exile from his home.
      The fugitive returns!
      A god, a god is bringing us success. 590
      Be happy, dear Electra!
      Lift up your hands and raise your voice,
      pray to the gods for luck,
      good luck and fortune,
      as your brother first sets foot here in our city.

ORESTES: This loving welcome gives me so much joy.
I hope in time to pay back joy for joy.
But, old sir—glad you're here: now tell me, please,
how to take vengeance on my father's killer,
and his sinful partner, my own mother. 600
Do I have supporters here in Argos?
Or am I out of friends and out of luck?
Should I creep in by night, or look for help?
Tell me which way to turn on those I hate!

OLD MAN: Poor boy! You've got no friends. Your luck is bad.
It's rare to find a friend prepared to share

---

* Many editors believe there is a line missing here, perhaps specifying more precisely what would count as success.

† The Chorus are singing here, in lyric meter.

bad times and good, stick by you when you're down.
You left your friends no cause to hope: they saw
your life in ruins. Listen to me, then:
everything's up to you: use strength and luck   610
to claim your father's house and city back.

ORESTES: What should I do to get this good result?

OLD MAN: Kill him—Thyestes' son*—and kill your mother.

ORESTES: I came to win that crown. But how exactly?

OLD MAN: Don't think of getting past the city walls.

ORESTES: I guess he's posted lookouts armed with spears?

OLD MAN: He has. He's scared of you. He hardly sleeps.

ORESTES: All right: then guide me on what's best to do.

OLD MAN: Listen: a new idea just came to me.

ORESTES: May your advice and all my deeds be good.   620

OLD MAN: I saw Aegisthus on my journey here.

ORESTES: It must have been an omen. Whereabouts?

OLD MAN: Near to these fields, down where the horses graze.

ORESTES: My luck has changed! What was he doing there?

OLD MAN: Making the Nymphs a feast, or so it seemed.†

ORESTES: To bless his children, or a future child?

OLD MAN: I only know he had an ox to kill.

ORESTES: How many men were with him? Just his slaves?

OLD MAN: No Argives, just the people from his house.

ORESTES: No one who'd see and recognize me, then?   630

OLD MAN: Those household slaves have never seen your face.

ORESTES: But if we win, would they be on our side?

OLD MAN: Yes, that's the way of slaves: good news for you!

ORESTES: Then how should I approach him, do you think?

OLD MAN: Go where he'll see you while he kills the ox.

ORESTES: I guess the fields are right beside the road?

OLD MAN: Yes, he'll see you, and ask you to the feast.

ORESTES: A guest who'll hurt the host, if god sees fit.

OLD MAN: Watch how the dice may fall, then plan your move

ORESTES: Good! But my mother: where do you think she is?   640

OLD MAN: In Argos—but she'll join him for the meal.

ORESTES: Why did she not accompany him out?

---

* I.e. Aegisthus.

† The mountain nymphs, female deities associated with the mountains, are companions of Artemis and thus associated, like her, with childbirth and fertility.

OLD MAN: She was concerned about incurring gossip.

ORESTES: I see: she knows the citizens don't trust her.

OLD MAN: That's right—since people hate a sinful woman.

ORESTES: So should I kill them both at the same time?

ELECTRA: I will arrange the murder of my mother.

ORESTES: That's great! Good luck will surely guide our hands.

ELECTRA: But let this man give both of us advice.

ORESTES: Yes, fine. And what's your plan for killing Mother?   650

ELECTRA: (*to the Old Man*)

    Sir, go to Clytemnestra, please, and say*

    I've given birth: the baby is a boy.

OLD MAN: When was this birth? A while ago, or recent?

ELECTRA: Ten days ago, ten suns—I'm purified.†

ORESTES: But how does this bring on your mother's murder?

ELECTRA: Since when she hears I'm weak from birth, she'll come.

OLD MAN: Why? Do you think she loves you, cares for you?

ELECTRA: Yes; and she'll mourn the baby's lowly class.

OLD MAN: Maybe. But bring your story to its goal.

ELECTRA: It's obvious! She'll come here, and she'll die.   660

OLD MAN: She'll come right to your door, right to your house.

ELECTRA: From here, it's just a little step to Hades.

OLD MAN: Once I have seen this sight, my life's complete.

ELECTRA: Dear friend, first guide Orestes on his way.

OLD MAN: To where Aegisthus makes his sacrifice?

ELECTRA: Yes, and then tell my mother what I said.

OLD MAN: I'll make it seem as if you spoke the words.

ELECTRA: (*to Orestes*) Your turn to kill comes first: it's up to you.

ORESTES: If someone shows the way, I'm set to go.

OLD MAN: Then let me take you; it would be my pleasure.   670

ORESTES: O Zeus the god of Vengeance and of Fathers!

ELECTRA: O pity us! So pitifully we've suffered!

OLD MAN: Yes, Zeus, have mercy on your own descendants!

ORESTES: And Hera, goddess of Mycenae's altars.

ELECTRA: If what we pray is right, grant us the victory!

OLD MAN: Grant them the right of vengeance for their father!

ORESTES: Ah, Father! in your home beneath the earth!

---

* There may be a line missing after this one.

† Greek women traditionally stayed home for ten "holy days" after giving birth; after that time, the family celebrated the new baby.

ELECTRA: And Goddess Earth: I give my hands to you!
OLD MAN: Defend these children, whom you love so much!
ORESTES: Come out, and bring the dead to help us, Father!   680
ELECTRA: Yes, bring the men with whom you ruined Troy!
OLD MAN: And all who hate polluted, wicked people.
ELECTRA: My mother hurt you terribly, do you hear?
OLD MAN: Your father hears it all. It's time to go.
ELECTRA:* I know! So you must be a man, Orestes!
   I tell you that Aegisthus has to die.
   If he out-wrestles you and you should die,
   I'm dead as well—don't say I'm still alive.
   I'll take an axe and split my head in two.
   Now I'll go in the house and get set up.
   If good news comes from you, I know the house   690
   will ring with women's cries; but if you die
   —the opposite. That's all I'll say to you.
      (*to Chorus*) You girls, prepare to shout and spread the word
   about this contest. I'll be standing guard,
   sword drawn and at the ready in my hand.
   My enemies will never get to touch
   or violate my body, if I die.†

strophe 1

   CHORUS: It's an old, old story,
      but still worth the telling: 700
      how once upon a time
      the Lord of the Countryside, Pan,
      whose sweet music breathes from the pipes made of reed,
      brought a golden lamb with a fluffy fleece
      down from the hills, away from its gentle mother.
      High on the stony platform stood the herald:
      "Men of Mycenae," he cries:
      "Come gather, come to a meeting,
      come quickly to see
      this miracle! A wonderful, terrible sight!   710

---

* The order of the lines in the first section of this speech is debated; I am following the reconstructed numbering in Diggle/Cropp.

† The text is problematic in the last part of this speech; editors suspect that some lines may have been interpolated.

Come see this thing your lucky kings have got."
And bands of dancers glorified the house of Atreus.

antistrophe 1

The golden altars were prepared
and fires for sacrifice shone bright
throughout the town of the Argives.
The clarinets,* in service to the Muses,
sound beautiful notes,
enchanting songs rise up and up,
to praise the golden fleece
belonging to Thyestes.† Yes, he crept into the bedroom   720
to seduce his brother's precious wife,
and took the magic fleece back home with him.
Then out he comes
to the assembled crowd,
and shouts, "I've got it! In my house!
I've got the ram with golden wool!"

strophe 2

That was the moment—then—when Zeus exchanged
the shining orbits of the stars
for the sun's bright light
and the white face of dawn   730
and with hot flame divine
he drove across the west.‡
Toward the north the clouds are waterlogged;
in Libya, home of Ammon, the deserts are dry,
they parch and wither, wasted and deprived
of the beautiful showers Zeus sends from the sky.§

antistrophe 2

So goes the story: but to me
it's hardly plausible
that the sun, with its golden smile,
should turn from its fiery home   740

---

* Literally, "lotus": the wood of lotus trees was used for woodwind instruments.

† This golden fleece is different from the more famous mythical Golden Fleece that Jason and the Argonauts took from Colchis. It was associated with royal power in Mycenae: whoever had the fleece got to be king.

‡ The sun supposedly changed its course in horror at the crime of Thyestes in stealing the golden fleece.

§ Ammon (Amon) was the deity of Thebes, who became fused with the Egyptian sun god; his home is the oracle of Ammon in the Siwa oasis. Zeus is associated with rain.

to cause mortal misfortune
for mortal rights and wrongs.
But fairy tales that scare us humans
are useful for religion.
Because you put gods out of mind
you killed your husband, shaming your noble brothers.*

(A sound of shrieking from the house)

Wait! Wait!
Friends, did you hear that? Am I wrong? To me
it sounds like Zeus, a thunder in the earth.
The winds give hints of something—look!
Princess, Electra, come out, leave the house!   750

ELECTRA: Friends, what's the matter? Are we going to win?

CHORUS: I only know I heard a scream, like murder.

ELECTRA: I heard it, too, though faintly, from a distance.

CHORUS: The cry was audible from far away.

ELECTRA: Who was it shouting? Locals, or my family?

CHORUS: The noise is all mixed up, I just can't tell.

ELECTRA: Your words mean death for me. Why put it off?

CHORUS: Wait till you know your situation better!

ELECTRA: No, no: we've lost! Where are the messengers?

CHORUS: They'll come! It's no small thing to kill a king.   760

(Enter Messenger.)

MESSENGER: Congratulations, ladies of Mycenae!
  Good news for all our friends: Orestes won!
  Aegisthus, Agamemnon's murderer,
  is lying dead, and we must thank the gods.

ELECTRA: Who are you? What's my proof your words are true?

MESSENGER: Do you not know me? I'm your brother's man.

ELECTRA: Oh, yes! I was so frightened that I failed
  to recognize your face: but now I do.
  The man I hate, my father's killer: dead?

MESSENGER: Yes, dead! Shall I repeat the news? He's dead!   770

ELECTRA: O gods! All-seeing Justice, come at last!
  But how exactly did he kill Aegisthus?
  What was the pattern of the plot? Tell me!

MESSENGER: We left this cottage, setting out on foot,
  along a two-lane wagon path, and reached

---

* "You" is Clytemnestra, sister of the Dioscuri, Castor and Pollux.

this new king of Mycenae. He was walking
around an irrigated garden patch,
plucking soft myrtle sprays to make a wreath.
When he saw us, he shouted, "Greetings, strangers!
Who are you? Where'd you come from? From what land?"   780
Orestes said, "From Thessaly. We're off
to Alpheus, to sacrifice to Zeus."*
When he heard that, Aegisthus said, "Today
you'll have to join our feast and be our guests.
In service to the Nymphs, I have an ox
to kill today. So join us, and tomorrow
resume your journey. Let's all go inside!"
At that, he seized our hands and led us in,
insisting he would not take "no" for answer.
And when we got inside, here's what he said: 790
"Bring wash-bowls for these strangers, right away,
so they may stand beside the holy water."†
Orestes said, "No need: we've just got washed
with pure clean water from a rushing stream.
If guests and citizens may join together
in ritual, we are ready, King Aegisthus."
That's what he said, in front of everyone.
The slaves then put aside the spears they held
to guard their lord and set their hands to work.
Some brought the blood-bowl, some set out the baskets,   800
Others set pots around the hearth and lit
the fire. The building rang with sounds of work.
Your mother's partner took the grains and threw them
onto the altar, and he spoke these words:
"Nymphs of the rocks, may we, my wife and I,
live long to bring you many sacrifices.
Long last our luck, and curse our enemies!"
He meant you and Orestes. But my master
muttered a different prayer: that he would claim
his father's home. Aegisthus took a knife   810
out of the basket, cut the ox's forelock
with his right hand, and threw it on the fire.

---

* There was a sanctuary to Zeus at Olympia. The lines evoke a journey there from Thessaly through passes in the mountains (quicker in those days than the modern coastal route).

† One could not participate in a sacrifice without first being purified, by ritual washing in clean water.

Then as the servants held it on their shoulders,
he slit the ox's throat, and called your brother:
"In Thessaly, the greatest claim to fame
is skill in chopping oxen up, and skill
at breaking horses. Stranger, take the knife,
and prove the reputation of your people."
At once Orestes seized the well-wrought blade,
unpinned his cloak and threw it off his back,   820
and pushed away the slaves. As his assistant,
he chose just Pylades. He took the hoof,
stretched out his arm and stripped the white flesh bare.
Quicker than one could run two double laps*
he skinned the hide and opened up the flanks.
Aegisthus took the innards in his hands
and read the holy signs. The liver had
no lobe; the veins and gall bladder revealed
on close inspection, something very wrong.
He scowled. My master asked him, "Sir, what's wrong?"   830
"Stranger," he said, "I'm dreading being tricked
by some invader. My worst enemy
is Agamemnon's son—my nemesis."
Orestes answered, "Do you fear an exile,
when you're the king? Absurd! Let's make the feast.
Enough of this slim Doric knife;† bring me
a proper cleaver, let me smash that breast-bone!"
They brought it and he chopped. Meanwhile, Aegisthus
was hunching over, studying the entrails.
Your brother stood on tip-toe right behind him   840
and smashed his spine, shattered his vertebrae.
His body was all shaking and convulsed,
and heaving up and down in torturous death.
At this, the slaves were quickly grabbing spears,
many to fight with two. But brave Orestes
and Pylades stood firm, and grasped their weapons.
Orestes said, "I have not come to fight!
I'm not an enemy to you, my people.
I've come to take revenge for my dead father.

---

* I.e. about 1,600 yards: the time is therefore about four minutes (assuming a good sprinter).

† There is a distinction between two different instruments for cutting: the slim knife, associated with the Doric region of Greece, and the bigger cleaver, from Phthia (in southern Thessaly).

I am Orestes. Pity me, don't kill me!   850
You are my father's servants." When they heard,
they put their spears away, and one old man,
who'd been there many years, said, "Yes, I know him!"
At once they wreathed your brother's head, rejoicing,
shouting with joy. He's coming now to show you
the man you hate, Aegisthus: not a Gorgon.*
Blood shed is paid in blood, a bitter price
paid now with interest by this slaughtered man.

strophe

> CHORUS: Dance, dear Electra, put your feet to the dance like a deer,   860
>   leaping lightly to the sky in joy!
>   Your brother won a victory crown
>   greater than at the Olympics!
>   Come sing the song of triumph
>   accompanying my dance.
> ELECTRA: (*chanting*) O glorious dawn, bright chariots of the sun!
>   Till now I only saw the night and earth
>   but now my eyes are opened and I'm free!
>   The man who killed my father, he is fallen!
>   Come now, and let's congratulate my brother!   870
>   All the secret treasures in my home
>   I'll use to crown his victory, dear friends.

antistrophe

> CHORUS: Yes, do it now, bring out the gifts and wreathe his head!
>   But we will dance, the dance the Muses love.
>   Our favorite monarchs, those who used to rule us,
>   will take the throne again.
>   The good with righteousness cast down the wicked.
>   Come, let us shout our joy aloud, let pipes ring out!
>   (*Enter Orestes.*)

ELECTRA: Well done, Orestes!† Just as our father won   880
       the war of Troy and came in triumph home,

---

* I.e. not a sight to inspire terror, unlike the head of a Gorgon. Gorgons were a type of female monster of whom the most famous was Medusa, whose gaze could turn onlookers to stone. She was decapitated by Perseus. Some scholars have argued that the line suggests that Orestes is bringing Aegisthus' severed head, but it is more likely that he is bringing the whole mangled corpse (and has not necessarily chopped off the head).

† The original greeting (she calls him *kallinikos*, "glorious in victory") suggests the language used for a victorious athlete.

you've won! Now let me deck your hair with gold.
You've run the race successfully and come
home full of glory, having killed our enemy,
Aegisthus, killer of our poor dead father.

      And you, best friend, son of the best of friends,
Pylades, here: this garland is for you.
You shared the victory and you share the prize.
May fortune always bless you both, I pray!

ORESTES: Electra, first give glory to the gods,   890
the source of our success. I'm just the servant
of gods and fortune—but I've served them well.
I've killed Aegisthus, not in word but deed.
As certain proof that what I say is true,*
I bring the dead man here to you: you may
throw him out for wild beasts to devour,
or stick him on a post as spoil for birds,
children of heaven. You choose: he's now your slave,
the man whom once you had to call your master.

ELECTRA: I want to say something, but hesitate—   900

ORESTES: What for? Speak out! You've nothing now to fear.

ELECTRA: They may not like it if I curse the dead.

ORESTES: It's fine, no one could blame you if you did.

ELECTRA: Our city's critical and hard to please.

ORESTES: Still, Sister, if you want to, speak. We've vowed
a hatred everlasting with this man.

ELECTRA: All right. Where shall I start with all his crimes?
Where shall I end? And how to tell the tale?
(*to Aegisthus' corpse*)
I used to never tire of muttering,
each dawn, the things I hoped to say to you,   910
if ever I'd get free of my old fears.
And now I am! I'll give you all the curses
I wish I could have said to you in life.
You ruined me. You robbed me of my father,
you robbed us both—and we were innocent!
And then you dared—for shame!—to take our mother
as wife, and killed her man, the Greek commander:

---

* The text of this line is problematic.

and you a stay-at-home! You were so stupid,
you thought my mother'd make a decent wife
for you, though she'd betrayed my father's bed! 920
If you sneak into someone's house, seduce
or rape the wife, you'll suffer, you poor fool,
if you imagine she'll be true to you,
when she let down the man she had before.
Your life was misery, though you hid it well.
You knew your marriage was against religion,
and Mother knew how bad her lover was.
You were both wicked, and you took your chances
with one another, partners in evil ways.
The Argives talked about you in this way: 930
"This man's the wife, the woman is the man!"
It's shameful, if a woman leads the house,
and not the man. I also scorn the children,
who do not get their father's manly name;
instead the people know them by their mother.
This happens if a man marries too well:
they only talk of her, and he's forgotten.
Now here's where you deceived yourself the most:
you thought your wealth and power made you someone.
But money's nothing: here and gone again. 940
Trust nature, it's secure. Riches are not.
Nature remains forever, helps in trouble.
Prosperity that lives a while with fools
will briefly bloom with evil, then fly off.
As for your women—well, it isn't nice
for me to speak of it: I am a virgin.
I'll hint though. You did awful things, exploiting
your kingly power and looks. For me, I'd rather
a man for husband—you looked like a girl.
A real man's children know the arts of Ares; 950
others are only pretty in a chorus.
You still don't know that time caught up with you
and made you pay. May every criminal
see that he'll never win the race with Justice!
He may run quick at first, but play it out:
run on, right to the finish line of life.

CHORUS: He acted dreadfully, and dreadful, too,
   was what you did to him. Justice is strong.

ELECTRA: Now then, you slaves must take his corpse inside,
   hide it in darkness; when our mother comes   960
   she mustn't see it, till she's dead herself.

       (Enter Clytemnestra.)

ORESTES: (*to Electra*) We have to change the subject: look who's coming.

ELECTRA: What is it? Helpers for us from Mycenae?

ORESTES: No: it's my mother! Look, my mother's coming!

ELECTRA: That's good: she's stepping straight inside the trap.*
   Look at her sparkly clothes, her glittering chariot!

ORESTES: What shall we do? Can we really kill our mother?

ELECTRA: You're sorry for her now you see her? Really?

ORESTES: Yes! Oh, oh! How can I kill her? She raised me! Gave me birth!

ELECTRA: Easy! Kill her, the way she killed our father.   970

ORESTES: Apollo! What you prophesied was stupid!

ELECTRA: Who can be wise if Lord Apollo isn't?

ORESTES: (*addressing the unseen god*)
   You told me, "Kill your mother." But it's wrong!

ELECTRA: What's wrong with taking vengeance for our father?

ORESTES: I'll be a matricide! No longer pure!†

ELECTRA: If you fail your father, that's a sin.

ORESTES: I know, but won't I pay, for killing Mother?

ELECTRA: And if you fail to take revenge for Father?

ORESTES: Maybe a demon made that prophecy.

ELECTRA: Upon the holy tripod?‡ I don't think so.   980

ORESTES: I can't be sure those oracles were good.

ELECTRA: Don't be so cowardly! Up, be a man!
   Go on and trick her with the same deceit
   she and Aegisthus used to kill her husband.§

ORESTES: I'll go. I'll start to do this dreadful thing,
   this horror. Yes, I will. If it's the gods' will,
   I'll do it. But I take no joy in it.

---

* A line may be missing between 965 and 966, since it is unlikely that Electra would have two lines in a row.

† Orestes is worried about incurring pollution through the murder. The word for "pure" (*agnos*) connotes freedom from religious taint or pollution, as well as sexual chastity.

‡ The prophetess of Apollo used a special holy tripod to deliver prophecies that supposedly came right from the mouth of the god.

§ The text of this line is problematic.

CHORUS: (*to Clytemnestra*)
 Greetings, your majesty!
 Queen of the land of Argos,
 daughter of Tyndareus,
 sister of the hero twins,* the sons   990
 of Zeus, who live among the stars
 in fiery heaven, honored as the saviors
 of mortals in the crashing waves of the sea.
 Welcome! I worship you, just like a goddess,
 for your great happiness and wealth.
 It's right to pay due homage
 to your good fortune, Majesty.
CLYTEMNESTRA: (*to her attendants*) Women of Troy, get down, get out of the
 carriage
 and take my hand, so I may set my feet
 down on the ground. (*to the Chorus*) The temples of the gods 1000
 are gorgeously adorned with Trojan spoil.
 These girls are mine, to decorate my home;
 nice, but small recompense for my lost child.†
ELECTRA: Mother, this luckless place is where I live,
 a slave, in exile from my father's house.
 You're a fine lady; shall I take your hand?
CLYTEMNESTRA: Don't bother; look, the slaves are here to do it.
ELECTRA: But I'm the same as them! You shoved me out,
 occupied my home, had me enslaved,
 and left me here an orphan, fatherless.   1010
CLYTEMNESTRA: Thanks to your father's bad decisions, taken
 against the one he should have loved the most!
 I'll tell my side—although when women have
 bad reputations, no one wants to hear them.
 I say it's not my fault. Just listen, then
 hate me if it seems right; or if not, don't.
 My father gave me as a bride to yours,
 not meaning me to die! Nor yet my children—.
 But that man told my daughter she would marry

---

* I.e. Castor and Pollux.

† Iphigenia, killed by Agamemnon.

Achilles, just to get her from her home*— 1020
took her to Aulis, stretched her above the pyre,
and slit her dear white throat. Iphigenia!
If this had been to save his town from capture,
or help his house and save his other children,
by killing one, he could have been forgiven.
But as it is—since Helen was a slut
whose man did not know how to punish her
for her adultery—it was for that
he killed my child! And still despite these wrongs
I kept my cool. I didn't kill my husband. 1030
But he came back and brought into our bed
that crazy prophetess,† and tried to keep
two wives at once, in just a single house.
Women are silly, yes, I don't deny it.
But when, on top of that, a man does wrong,
and spurns the marriage bed, a woman will
do just the same, and take another man.
Then we're the ones who are notorious.
No one speaks ill of *them*, though they're to blame.
What if your father's brother had been kidnapped? 1040
Should I have killed Orestes, just to save
my sister's husband, Menelaus? No!
How would your father have put up with that?
Should he not die, for murdering my child,
if I must suffer tit for tat, for him?‡
I killed him and I turned for help to those
who were his enemies; I had no choice.§
What friend of his would help me kill your father?
Speak, if you want, and freely answer me.
How was your father's death not just and fair? 1050
CHORUS: You've spoken fairly, with an ugly fairness.

---

* As in *Iphigenia among the Taurians.*

† Cassandra, prophetess of Apollo and daughter of Priam and Hecuba, whom Agamemnon brought back from Troy as a concubine.

‡ There seems to be a line missing here.

§ Aegisthus and Agamemnon were ancestral enemies, since Aegisthus was the youngest son of Thyestes, who battled with Agamemnon's father, Atreus, over the throne. Thyestes had an affair with Atreus' wife, and Atreus took terrible revenge by tricking him into eating his own sons. Aegisthus was born later, the child of Thyestes by his own daughter.

Wives should obey their husbands all the time,
if they are sensible. Or if a woman
thinks differently, I put her out of mind.

ELECTRA: Remember, Mother, what you said just now,
that I could have free rein to speak against you.

CLYTEMNESTRA: Of course you may, my child, I won't deny you.

ELECTRA: Then you won't hurt me, if my words hurt you?

CLYTEMNESTRA: Certainly not; I only wish you well.*

ELECTRA: Then let me speak, and first I've this to say: 1060
if only, Mother, you'd had better sense!
Your looks are easy to admire, both yours
and Helen's. But your natures, not so much.
Both idiots! You're unworthy of your Castor.
She asked for it, she wanted to be raped,
while you destroyed the greatest man in Greece,
your husband, claiming it was for your child.
You fooled them: they don't know you—unlike me.
Before your daughter's sacrifice occurred,
as soon as your dear husband left the house,   1070
you took your mirror and began to comb
your long blond hair. A woman who's concerned
with beauty, when her husband is away
is wicked. If she wasn't hunting harm
she wouldn't want to look good for outsiders.
I also know that you, of all Greek women,
you were the one who smiled when Troy was doing well,
and frowned when they were doing worse—not wanting
Agamemnon to come home from Troy.
And yet you could have been a model wife!   1080
You had a husband whom all Greece had chosen
General-in-Chief, surely a better man
than that Aegisthus. And your sister's actions
gave you the chance for glory. Wicked news
provides a clear example for the good.
   You say our father killed his daughter—but
what harm had I done you? Or my poor brother?
After you killed your husband, why did you

---

* The text is problematic here.

not keep our property in trust for us?
You sold our house to buy yourself a husband!   1090
This husband should be exiled, not your son!
He ought to die—he's made my life a death.
My sister didn't suffer half as much.
If blood's the judge and one death pays another,
then with Orestes' help, I'll kill you. Just
revenge for Father. If you're right, we're right.*

CLYTEMNESTRA: Daughter, it's always been your way to love
    your father—so it goes. Some are like that,
    while others love their mothers more than fathers.
    I will forgive you, and I will admit
    I'm not too comfortable with what I've done.
    Those plots and schemes I made! It was too much,
    that rage against my husband. I regret it.   1100

ELECTRA: Too late to feel this way: there's no cure now.
    My father's dead. But why won't you bring back
    your son, who wanders exiled through the world?

CLYTEMNESTRA: I'm scared. I'm thinking not of him, but me.
    They say he's angry at his father's killing.

ELECTRA: But why'd you let your husband treat me so?

CLYTEMNESTRA: It's how he is. You're stubborn, too, you know.

ELECTRA: Because I'm suffering. But that will end.

CLYTEMNESTRA: In that case, he'll no longer trouble you.

ELECTRA: He's such a big-head! Living in my house! †   1120

CLYTEMNESTRA: Look at you! Still igniting arguments!

ELECTRA: I'll stop, but just because I'm scared of him.

CLYTEMNESTRA: Enough! But why'd you call me here, my child?

ELECTRA: I'm sure you've heard that I have given birth?
    Please make the usual tenth-night sacrifice
    to bless the newborn, since I don't know how.
    I've never had a child before, you see.

CLYTEMNESTRA: But this is what the midwife ought to do.

ELECTRA: I didn't have one; I gave birth alone.

---

* After this, five lines appear that are clearly an insertion by a later commentator, not part of the play. They read: "Whoever marries a bad woman based on wealth or birth is a fool. A lowly but thoughtful wife is better than great ones at home. Chorus: Luck is the presiding principle in marrying women. We see some do well, some badly."

† He is, of course, actually lying dead in the house.

CLYTEMNESTRA: You have no friends or neighbors near your house?   1130

ELECTRA: Nobody wants a pauper for a friend.

CLYTEMNESTRA: You're still unwashed, and in those awful clothes?
  Just getting up from after giving birth?
  All right, I'll help you; I will go and make
  the sacrifice for baby's safe arrival.
  Then I'll go meet my husband in the fields
  where he is sacrificing to the Nymphs.
  (*to her attendants*) Slaves! take the mules inside and give them food.
  Come back here when I've done my sacrifice,
  since then I'll have to go and help my husband.

ELECTRA: Go into my poor home. But please take care:
  it's thick with dirt, don't spoil your pretty clothes.   1140
  You'll soon be giving to the gods their due—
      (*Clytemnestra goes into the house.*)
  The basket's ready and the knife is sharp,
  which killed the bull, and you will lie beside him,
  battered to death. In Hades you'll stay married
  to him you chose in life. My gift to you!
  Your gift to me is justice for my father.

strophe

  CHORUS:* It's payback, fair and square: two wrongs make right.
    The breezes blowing on the house have turned.
    My master, my master, he fell long ago in the bath,†
    and the palace screamed, the stone walls shrieked, as he cried,   1150
    "You witch!
    You evil woman!
    Are you killing me now,
    after ten harvests,
    when I've only just got back home?"
    [...]‡

antistrophe

  The river of Justice is flowing upstream,

---

* This passage, including the utterances of Electra and Orestes as well as the Chorus, is in lyric meter.

† As described in Aeschylus' *Agamemnon*, Clytemnestra killed Agamemnon in his bath on his return home from Troy—a perversion of the wife's traditional welcome to the husband after a journey, which involved giving him a bath.

‡ A line is missing here.

to punish the woman who transgressed the bed.
She killed her husband with an ax,
she did it, when he was coming home,
after long years, to his giant sky-towering palace.
She did it! She took the weapon in her hands and struck. Poor man! 1160
I pity the husband, regardless
of the desperate woman's motives.
She acted like a lioness, down from the mountains,
prowling through the lush meadows.

CLYTEMNESTRA: (*voice heard from inside*)
O, children! By the gods! Don't kill your mother!

CHORUS: Do you hear her shouting in the house?

CLYTEMNESTRA: (*from inside, screaming*)
No! Don't! No!—

CHORUS: Poor woman, she's no more—her children killed her.
Sooner or later, justice comes from the god.
Poor woman, it's so dreadful, what happened to you!
But you also sinned   1170
against your man.

> (*Orestes and Electra come out of the palace with the bodies of
> Clytemnestra and Aegisthus, wheeled on a cart.*)

They're here! Soaked with blood from the mother
they just killed! They're marching out of the house!*

. . . .

With their prizes—the bodies are proof
of their terrible ritual slaughter.
No house in the whole of time has known such pain,
no family ever suffered as the Tantalids have done.†

strophe 1

ORESTES: Earth and Zeus, you see all human action.
Look at what we've done: pollution and blood:
two bodies:
we struck them and there they lie.   1180

---

* A line is missing here.

† Tantalus was the ancestor of the house of Orestes and Electra: he was the father of Pelops, who was father in turn of Atreus (father of Agamemnon and Menelaus) and of Thyestes (father of Aegisthus). Tantalus was cursed by Zeus, having tried to feed his son Pelops to the gods as food; he was condemned to constant hunger and thirst in the Underworld, with food and water always just beyond his grasp (hence the word "tantalizing").

I did it, I took revenge
for the pain they made me suffer.*
ELECTRA: Brother, this is so sad! It's all my fault!
I was on fire against my mother here,
the one who gave me birth. Oh, it's so awful!
CHORUS: Bad luck, terrible luck!
This poor mother!
You suffered horribly, worse than your children had done.
But still, it was right that you paid for killing their father.

antistrophe 1

ORESTES: Apollo, your oracles were riddles, but right,   1190
and now you've acted openly, to bring
pain, and for me, a future of exile
far from Greece, since I'm a murderer now.
What city can I go to?
Who'd be glad to welcome me?
Who could ever meet my eyes?
I killed my mother.
ELECTRA: What about me? Where can I go?
What group of girls will want to dance with me?
Who'd marry me? Who'd take me as a bride?   1200
CHORUS: Your minds have turned back
against the wind.
Now your thoughts are pure. Before they weren't.
Electra, friend, you did a dreadful thing
in persuading your brother to this.

strophe 2

ORESTES: Did you see what my poor mother did?
She took down her dress and showed us her breast†
while we were killing her: oh, oh, my god!
While her body, the source of our lives, collapsed! And I melted.
CHORUS: I know. You went through torture,   1210
hearing the wails
of the mother who gave you birth.

---

* Another line is missing here.

† The gesture recalls the moment in *Iliad* 22 when Hecuba, queen of Troy, pleads with her son Hector not to go and fight Achilles, and reminds him of their connection by showing her breast. Even closer is the moment in Aeschylus' *Choephoroe* when Clytemnestra begs Orestes not to kill her, showing him her breast from which he once suckled; in that play, Pylades is the one who maintains Orestes in his resolve.

antistrophe 2

ORESTES: She touched my cheek and cried to me,
"Child, my child, I'm begging you—"
She clutched at my face,
and my sword fell out of my hands.

CHORUS: Oh, the poor woman. How could you bear it,
watching with your own eyes
as your mother breathed out her life?   1220

strophe 3

ORESTES: I put up my cloak to cover my eyes,
then took up my sword to act out the rite,
and plunged it right in there, through my own mother's throat.

ELECTRA: I urged you on,
I held the sword with you.
I've done it: it's the worst that could happen.

antistrophe 3

ORESTES: Take this, cover Mother's body with this robe.
Bind up her wounds.
Mother, your own children were your murderers.

ELECTRA: Look, I'll put the cloth around her,   1230
our unkind kin, the enemy we loved.
This is the end of the sorrows of our house.
(Enter, on the roof over the palace, Castor and Pollux.)

CHORUS: But look! Up there, on the palace roof,*
spirits have come, or
maybe gods from heaven.
No mortal moves like that.
Why are they showing themselves
to humans?

CASTOR: Listen, Agamemnon's son. We two
are the Twins, your mother's brothers, sons of Zeus.
I'm Castor, and here is my brother, Pollux.   1240
We've just been warding off a bitter storm,
and now we visit Argos, since we saw
your mother, and our sister's, ritual slaughter.
Her death was right, but you were wrong to do it.
Apollo—he's my master, so I must

---

* The chorus begins to chant in anapests.

keep silence—but he gave you bad advice,
despite his wisdom. Still, now yield to Fate,
and do what Destiny and Zeus command.
Give Pylades Electra as a bride,
and you, leave Argos—you cannot set foot   1250
inside this city, having killed your mother.
The dreadful dog-faced Furies will pursue you,
wandering and whirling on the wheels of madness.
But go to Athens, kiss the holy image
of Pallas: she will stop those writhing Furies
and dreadful snakes from touching you. She'll spread
her rounded Gorgon shield above your head.
There is a Hill of Ares, first location
where gods sat casting votes on a murder charge,
when savage Ares killed Halirrothius,   1260
son of the ocean lord, in rage about
his daughter's evil rape.* Forever after
voting done here is sacred and secure.
That is the place you must be tried for murder.
The jury will be split, and this just process
will save your life: Apollo will acknowledge
himself to blame, since he told you to do it.
This law will be set down for times to come,
that when the votes are tied, defendants win.
The Furies will be struck with pain and sink   1270
into a chasm underneath the earth,
a holy oracle for pious people.
But you must found a city in Arcadia,
by River Alpheus, near a sanctuary,
of Zeus Lycaeus.†—Now, the Argive people
must lay Aegisthus' body in the earth.

---

* Ares killed Halirrothius, son of Poseidon, for raping his daughter Alcippe. The "hill of Ares" is the Areopagus in Athens, meeting place of a court that heard capital trials; it was also the setting of Aeschylus' *Eumenides*, in which Orestes is tried and acquitted for his mother's murder.

† The city is apparently Oresteion, located near the source of the river Alpheus; as the name suggests, it was mythically associated with Orestes. Euripides is probably inventing this alternative version of Orestes' future; in most versions, he establishes himself at Argos or Sparta rather than moving to Arcadia. The sanctuary of Zeus at Mount Lycaeon was actually about thirty miles from Oresteion; the cult to the god there was associated with human sacrifice and with wolves (Lycaeus means "wolfish," recalling the story of Lycaeus, a savage man in myth who turned into a wolf).

And Menelaus has at last arrived,
so long since he took Troy, at Nauplia.
Helen and he will bury her—your mother. 1280
Helen has come from Egypt, since in fact
she never went to Troy.* Zeus sent her image
to stir up strife and death for mortal men.
Then Pylades shall take his virgin bride
out of Achaea and back home with him,
to Phocis—with your sister's so-called husband;
let him reward him with a pile of wealth.
You, travel now on foot, across the neck
of Isthmia, to the glad Athenian hill.†
Fulfill your destiny, pay for this murder, 1290
and you'll find rest and peace and happiness.

   CHORUS:‡

      O Twins, double sons of Zeus,
      can you grant us permission
      to approach you and talk to you?

   CASTOR: Granted; you've suffered no taint from this killing.§

   CHORUS: Here is my question. Since you two are gods,
      the brothers of her who was killed,
      why didn't you keep the Furies away from the house? 1300

   CASTOR: Fate and Necessity brought us to this, what must be;
      and the words of Apollo, so foolish, are also to blame.

   ELECTRA: Tyndareus' sons, may I also join in the discussion?

   CASTOR: You may also. The blame for the murder
      I put upon Phoebus alone.

   ELECTRA: But what about me? What Apollo, what oracle,
      made me a murderer to my own mother?

   CASTOR: You shared in the action, you shared this destiny.
      One was the curse on the whole of your family,
      that was the thing that has torn you apart.

   ORESTES: Sister! I've only just seen you again, after long years,
      and now I'm deprived yet again of your love,
      so soon, I have lost you, you've lost me, so soon. 1310

---

* This alternate version of the myth is explored in Euripides' play the *Helen*.

† The final injunctions are addressed to Orestes again. The journey from Argos to Athens involves passing through Isthmia, a city on the eastern side of the Isthmus of Corinth.

‡ The last part of the play is in anapestic meter.

§ Polluted mortals could not approach gods.

CASTOR: She has a husband. She has a home.
    You don't need to pity her,
    but for the loss of her home, here in Argos.
ELECTRA: But what could be worse
    than leaving the home of one's fathers?
ORESTES: And me! I am leaving the house of my father,
    and going to stand on a trial for the killing
    of my mother, and judged by a jury of strangers.
CASTOR: Don't worry, you'll see: the city of Athens
    is holy. Be brave.   1320
ELECTRA: Now hug me, dear brother!
    Embrace me and hug me!
    My dearest, my brother.
    It's the curse of the murder of Mother
    that parts us from Father's home.
ORESTES: Embrace me and hold me and kiss me.
    Sing me a funeral song, as if I'm dead.
CASTOR: No, no, it is horrible! Terrible cry,
    even for gods to hear.
    It's possible even for me and the heavenly gods
    to pity you humans for so much pain.   1330
ORESTES: I never will see you again.
ELECTRA: I'll never be near you or look at your face.
ORESTES: This is the last time I'm talking to you.
ELECTRA: Goodbye to you, city!
    Goodbye and good wishes to you, dear women of Argos.
ORESTES: Sister, most loyal one, is it the end? Are you going already?
ELECTRA: I'm going. My face is soaked wet with my tears.
ORESTES: Goodbye to you, Pylades, good luck to you.   1340
    Best wishes to you, as the groom of Electra.
CASTOR: Yes, they should marry. But look out, Orestes:
    the dogs, they are coming.* Run, run off to Athens!
    Terrible creatures, they're tracking you down,
    they're right on your trail,
    snake-arms, their skin is black,
    sprouting with horrible stench.
    And we must hurry to the Sicilian Sea,

---

* Referring to the Erinyes of Furies, who punish kin murder.

to save the ships from the tempest.*
And as we weave along through the clear upper air
we cannot help the polluted: 1350
we help only those who love holiness
and justice. We hear them in trouble
and help them and save them from harm.
Let no one willingly do wrong,
nor sail with a man who breaks oaths.
I am god, and I say this to humans.

  (Castor and Pollux depart, drawn through the air on a pulley.
  The human characters leave the stage in separate directions.)

CHORUS: Goodbye! Good luck! If you can be,
  be lucky, steer clear of disaster.
  That's happiness for mortals.

---

* Castor and Pollux were the gods who protected sailors in storms.

Introduction to Euripides'

Trojan Women

Homer's *Iliad* was already some three hundred years old during the golden age of Athenian tragedy, but it remained the central literary text for the Greeks and colored all their thinking about war and loss. The downfall of the Trojans, made inevitable by the death of Prince Hector near the end of the *Iliad*, became the Greek paradigm for defeat of every kind, especially since Homer had explored so fully the pathos of the dying city. The Trojans of the *Iliad* are not "others" or enemies, and indeed are not even recognizably non-Greek. They are noble, heroic human beings, and it is their sufferings, rather than the imminent victory of the Greeks, that form the core of the poem's ending. The coda of the *Iliad* consists of a long dirge for the fallen Hector, as his corpse is lamented by his sister, Cassandra, his widow, Andromache, his mother, Hecuba, and even his sister-in-law, Helen—widely hated by the Trojans, who regard her as the cause of the war, but still honored and protected by Hector.

The funeral chants of these women struck a chord in Euripides, and he based his play *Trojan Women*, produced in 415 B.C., on the same four figures. Undoubtedly the events of his own times gave new meaning to their laments. Athens had by this time seen ten years of an immensely destructive war with Sparta, the so-called Peloponnesian War, and Greek cities caught in the fighting had suffered fates nearly as harsh as Troy's. Though a shaky truce still held in 415, Athens continued to expand its empire in an effort to gain advantage. Only months before this play was put on, the Athenians had destroyed tiny Melos, an Aegean island state guilty only of unwillingness to join their side. After besieging Melos and forcing its surrender, they put all the men to death and enslaved the women and children. Thucydides, the great historian of the Athens-Sparta conflict, explored the Melos episode in a now-famous dialogue; it later went down in history as one of the Greek world's worst war crimes.

We cannot know how Euripides felt about his city's aggressive imperialism, or whether he was, in any sense, "antiwar." Laments are not the same as protests, and no Greek of the fifth century B.C. would have opposed all warfare on grounds of principle. That said, there were many in Athens (as attested by the comedies of Aristophanes) who felt that the war with Sparta, dragging on without resolution and causing massive upheaval and hardship, was not worth the costs. In this play, as well as in two surviving ones that preceded it (*Hecuba* and *Andromache*, not in this volume), Euripides cataloged the sufferings of war's victims, an approach charged with meaning considering that his audience—Athenian males who had served in recent actions, or voted to support them, or both—had helped engineer those sufferings.

Another contemporary event may have been on Euripides' mind when he wrote this play, and it was certainly on the minds of its spectators. Right around the time of this production, Athenians opted to send a huge flotilla, filled with troops and supplies, to support their allies in Sicily and, if possible, to subjugate the island. The prologue to the *Trojan Women* must have been uncomfortable to watch for the audience that had voted (or was about to vote) to send the armada. In an unusual opening gambit—a dialogue between the gods Athena and Poseidon—Euripides allows the audience (but not the characters) to know that the Greek fleet sent to Troy will be wrecked by storms on its way home—the price of an impious rape committed by a minor Greek hero (Ajax, son of Oïleus, the "lesser Ajax"). For Athens in 415, then, words like these, spoken by Poseidon, could hardly be considered a good omen: "What fools these mortals are, to sack a city / with shrines and holy tombs of the departed. / Leaving ruin, they are lost themselves." Read with historical hindsight, the lines seem prophetic, for the Sicilian invasion force indeed came to great grief over the two years that followed this play, and few out of many returned.

The prologue also explores the causes of Troy's extinction and the sufferings of its women. Athena is credited with having brought the city down, presumably because of the slight Paris gave her when judging the beauty contest of the goddesses. But she has now changed allegiances and turned against the Greeks. "You hate too much, then love, for no good reason," Poseidon scolds her, and the charge seems to stick, even though the rape that occurred in her temple partly explains her shift. Meanwhile Poseidon, who has always sided with the Trojans and might now protect them, instead takes his leave of the city, foreseeing that it can no longer offer him sacrifices; his departure feels a bit like an abandonment (compare the swift exit of Artemis at the end of *Hippolytus*). These gods can offer mortals neither solace for nor insight into the causes of downfall, and their brief onstage appearance—unnoticed by Hecuba, who lies prone onstage while they converse—only underscores their distance from the sphere of human suffering.

Hecuba, the great *mater dolorosa* of Greek myth, arises as the gods leave the stage. She will provide the axis to what is otherwise an assortment of loosely connected episodes; she remains onstage throughout and vents her grief, or rage, to each of the other characters in turn. She has lost her sons, Hector and Paris, already; soon she will learn (as the audience learns in the prologue) that a daughter, Polyxena, is also dead. She goes now into slavery, along with her daughter Cassandra, her daughter-in-law Andromache, and the members of the Chorus. Cassandra, a virginal priestess of Apollo, will serve as concubine to Agamemnon, and mother and daughter lament her imminent violation (and the death that Cassandra knows will follow) with a grimly ironic marriage procession. Hector's widow, Andromache, for her part, will become a slave to Neoptolemus—the son of Achilles, who had slain her husband and desecrated his corpse. Hecuba, claiming to have surrendered her will just as a ship's crew surrenders to a storm (lines 686–95), advises Andromache to forget Hector and make the best of this new bond. She finds hope in Andromache's son, Astyanax, through whom Troy may someday rise again.

The simile of the ungoverned ship applies not just to Hecuba but to the entire disordered world of this drama, including the Greeks, who largely remain offstage, dispatching their herald Talthybius to do their bidding. We hear hardly anything of Agamemnon in this play, apart from his sexual predation. The leader who ought to be orchestrating the postwar order is nearly invisible. Instead, decisions are made by the casting of lots or by the will of an army "council," a democratic body (the Greek word used for it at line 721 emphasizes its universal membership). This council, urged on by the wily Odysseus, cruelly decrees that the infant Astyanax must die, hurled from whatever part of Troy's walls remains standing. Euripides may here be commenting (as he certainly did in two later plays, *Iphigenia in Aulis* and *Orestes*) on the state of the Athenian democracy in its post-Periclean phase, in which the Assembly, made up of all male citizens, often lacked direction or too quickly gave in to anger when it was thwarted, as it did in the case of the Melians.

At last one of the Greek chiefs does enter the scene, but only to make a decision that will not hold. Menelaus has been accorded the power of life and death over his errant wife, Helen, and a kind of trial now takes place, with Hecuba—her grief transformed momentarily into rage—playing the part of prosecutor. After hearing both Hecuba's denunciation and Helen's self-defense, Menelaus resolves that his wife must die, after traveling with him to Sparta. But Homer's *Odyssey* had long before this portrayed Helen living out her life happily in Sparta, so we know that Menelaus' resolve will weaken before he reaches home. As he leads the condemned woman away, Hecuba warns him not to sail in the same ship with her, prompting his weirdly out-of-tune comment—"Has she put on too much weight?" The peculiar exchange hints at what lies ahead.

Menelaus is clueless about the power his wife holds over him; she will escape her death sentence by means of seduction and sexual wiles.

Hecuba's fate, too, was known to this play's audience to be other than what is resolved here, namely, enslavement to Odysseus. Indeed, Euripides himself had described it in the *Hecuba* (not in this volume), produced perhaps ten years before the *Trojan Women*. Driven mad by grief over the murder of her son Polydorus, Hecuba will climb the mast of Odysseus' ship and drown herself in the sea, after being transformed by the gods into a barking, blazing-eyed dog. This strange, dehumanized death is touched on only lightly in the *Trojan Women*, when Cassandra puzzles over the seeming falsity of Apollo's oracle that her mother would die at Troy (lines 427–30). Cassandra herself, the last survivor among Hecuba's children, will soon die at the hands of Clytemnestra, as she foresees (lines 446–50) and as Aeschylus depicts in the *Agamemnon*. Her fated end, after the destruction of Astyanax that forms the final blow of this play, will extinguish the royal line, and the last hopes, of Hecuba.

TROJAN WOMEN

Translated by Emily Wilson

I have used the text of James Diggle (Oxford: Oxford University Press, 1984), and consulted the commentaries by Shirley A. Barlow (Warminster: Aris and Philips, 1986) and K. H. Lee (New York: St. Martin's Press, 1976), on particular points of interpretation.

CAST OF CHARACTERS (IN ORDER OF APPEARANCE)

POSEIDON

ATHENA

HECUBA, widow of Priam; queen of Troy

CHORUS of captured Trojan women

TALTHYBIUS, herald of the Greek army

CASSANDRA, Trojan prophetess; daughter of Hecuba and Priam, the late king of Troy

ANDROMACHE, Trojan noblewoman; widow of the Trojan hero Hector

ASTYANAX, young son of Andromache by Hector

MENELAUS, king of Sparta and co-leader of the Greek army

HELEN, wife of Menelaus, whom she left for the Trojan prince Paris (the cause of the Trojan War)

Setting: Troy, outside the tents of the Greeks, which are represented by the central stage building. Hecuba lies on the ground, motionless and unspeaking, while the gods discuss her city.

    (Enter Poseidon.)

POSEIDON: Here I am: Poseidon. I have left
    the salty depths of the Aegean sea,
    where sea-nymphs circle lovely feet in dance.
    Phoebus* and I constructed these stone walls
    round Troy, with careful measure; ever since
    I've always kept a fondness in my heart
    for this, the Phrygian city.† Now it lies
    in ruins, smoking, sacked by the Greek spear.
    A man from Mount Parnassus, Epeius,‡
    led by Athena's machinations, built   10
    a horse pregnant with arms, and sent it in
    to Troy, inside the walls—a deadly idol.
    <By men of future times it will be called
    the Wooden Horse, that holds wood spears within.>§
    Deserted now the sacred groves, the shrines
    flooded with blood. By Zeus' temple steps,
    Priam lies dead.¶ Now they are loading up
    a massive hoard of gold and Asian loot**
    on the Achaean ships.†† But they must wait
    until fair wind arrives to blow them home,   20

---

* Phoebus is another name for Apollo. Poseidon and Apollo built Troy's city walls together, at the request of the then king, Laomedon. Laomedon failed to keep his promise to reward the gods, and they sacked the city for the first time. The Trojan War thus marks the second destruction of the city.

† Phrygia was a region in Anatolia, modern Turkey, of which Troy was one of the most important cities.

‡ A Greek soldier, who was inspired by Athena in a dream to build the Trojan Horse.

§ Lines 13–14 are thought to be an "interpolation," a later addition to the text by a commentator or perhaps an actor, not written by Euripides.

¶ Priam was slaughtered by Achilles' son, Neoptolemus, in the temple of Zeus.

** By "Asian" is meant Phrygian.

†† Achaean=Greek.

to see their families after ten long harvests—
the Greeks who journeyed to attack this town.
But I shall leave this noble city, Troy,
and leave my altars. Hera and Athena
have won against me.* In such desolation
the bonds of men with gods are all diseased,
religion can no longer be respected.
Scamander† shrieks with wailing women captured
at spear-point, to be allocated masters.
Arcadian men got some, Thessalians others;   30
some taken by Athenians, Theseus' line;‡
those Trojan women not yet dealt to masters
wait in the tents, reserved for the top generals.
With them is Spartan Helen, Tyndareus' child—§
correctly classified a prize of war.
Look! if you want to see a wretched woman,
here Hecuba is lying by the entrance,
and weeping many tears, for many sorrows.
She doesn't know yet that her Polyxena—
poor child!—was slaughtered on Achilles' tomb.   40
Priam is gone. Their children, gone. The girl
the god Apollo left with mind run wild,
Cassandra, will be forced to share a bed
with Agamemnon—dark impiety.¶
O city, once so happy, I must leave
your well-constructed towers and firm foundations.
You'd still be standing firm, had not Athena,
daughter of Zeus, decided to destroy you.
      (Enter Athena.)
ATHENA: You are my father's nearest kin, a god

---

* Hera was hostile to Troy, which she saw as the source of several of her husband Zeus' infidelities (such as his affair with Ganymede, prince of Troy, who became cup-bearer to the gods).

† Scamander is the river of Troy.

‡ Arcadia and Thessaly are regions of Greece. Theseus is the legendary founder of Athens.

§ The usual myth is that Tyndareus' wife, Leda, was seduced or raped by Zeus (who had taken on the form of a swan), and she then gave birth to an egg, from which came Helen and her sister, Clytemnestra.

¶ Agamemnon, king of Argos, is the husband of Clytemnestra, sister of Helen. He took Cassandra as his concubine after the Trojan War, which was an "impiety" because she was supposed to have been left a virgin after Apollo could not have her.

great among gods and highly honored.* May I
abandon old hostilities, and speak?†   50
POSEIDON: Lady Athena, you may speak since ties
of kinship cast a spell upon my heart.
ATHENA: Thank you, my lord; so kind of you. I'd like
to speak of something that concerns us both.
POSEIDON: Do you bring news from any of the gods,
from Zeus or any other deity?
ATHENA: No; but I come to join your power with mine,
because of Troy, where we are walking now.
POSEIDON: But why? The city's burned to ashes now;
could that transform your hatred into pity?   60
ATHENA: First answer this. Will you team up with me,
and help me to achieve the things I want?
POSEIDON: Of course. But let me know your stake in this.
Have you come to side with Greeks, or Trojans?
ATHENA: I want to comfort my old foes, the Trojans,
and give the Greeks a bitter journey home.
POSEIDON: Why do you jump to change your mind like this?
You hate too much, then love, for no good reason.
ATHENA: Did you not know my shrine has been defiled?
POSEIDON: I know. When Ajax raped Cassandra there.   70
ATHENA: The Greeks said nothing! He is still unpunished!
POSEIDON: Though it was thanks to you they sacked the town!
ATHENA: That's why I want to hurt them, with your help.
POSEIDON: Ready for anything. So, what's the plan?
ATHENA: I want to make their journey home pure pain.
POSEIDON: While they remain on land, or on the sea?
ATHENA: When they set sail away from Ilium.‡
Rain will be sent by Zeus, unending hail,
and blasts of darkness bursting from the sky.
He promised me his thunderbolt, to hurl   80
at the Achaean fleet, to make it burn.
Your job will be to rouse the Aegean Sea;
and make it roar with massive waves and whirlpools,

---

* Poseidon and Zeus are brothers.

† Athena was on the side of the Greeks in the Trojan War because Paris (prince of Troy) had chosen Aphrodite over her and Hera as the goddess to whom he would give the golden apple.

‡ Ilium is an alternative name for Troy, from its legendary founder, Ilus.

fill up the curved Euboean bay with corpses,*
so in the future Greeks will honor me,
and my authority, and the other gods.

POSEIDON: So be it; I can help you, there's no need
of longer conversation. I'll stir up
the Aegean, and the coast of Mykonos,
rocky Delphi, Skyros, Lemnos, all 90
the cliffs of Caphereus will be filled
with bodies of the dead.† Go to Olympus,
and take the thunder from your father's hand;‡
and watch for when the Greeks let out their sails.
What fools these mortals are, to sack a city
with shrines and holy tombs of the departed.
Leaving ruin, they are lost themselves.

> *(Athena and Poseidon exit.)*

> *Scene: Hecuba lies on the ground in front of the stage building.*
> *The Chorus members gradually emerge from the tents to join her.*

HECUBA:§ Get up from the ground, get up! Lift up your head.
This is not Troy: Troy is no more.
I am no longer queen of Troy. 100
My luck has changed. Accept it.
Sail with the current, sail as fortune blows.
Don't set the prow of life
against the surging waters. My boat is blown by chance.
Unhappiness and pain—.
How can I ever stop crying? I have everything to weep for:
my homeland is gone, my children are gone, and my husband.
The rounded bellies of our forebears' ships
are flat. Reef in the sails; there's nothing there.¶

---

* Euboea is the long island strip on the eastern side of Greece.

† All places in Greece, on the way from Troy.

‡ Zeus carries the thunderbolt, which is sometimes borrowed by Athena.

§ This is a "monody," a song sung by a single actor. Hecuba's meter until she starts speaking to Cassandra is lyric, not the regular speaking meter of iambics; I have echoed this only by making the lines irregular in length. In the original performance, the actor would have sung these lines, while dancing in expression of Hecuba's grief.

¶ The image is of a ship's sail, which looks round when it is filled out with a strong breeze but flat when the wind goes down. There is a secondary suggestion of a mother's belly, once fertile, now empty. Metaphors from ships continue in the passage; the literal ships of the Greeks are met by the metaphorical ships of Hecuba's hopes, and of Troy, which are wrecked.

Why should I keep silence? But why speak?   110
What's the good of singing lamentation?
I am so unhappy. Now a heavy weight of fate
tosses my limbs around as I lie here,
stretched on my back on this hard bed.
Everything hurts. My head, my temples throb,
my ribs ache. I yearn to turn,
to switch my spine and roll back this way, that way,
listing my limbs to one side or the other,
making my way toward more songs of sorrow.
For someone in my state, this counts as music: 120
sobbing desolation: a noise no one can dance to.
The Greek ships swiftly rowed
across the dark blue sea
through welcoming Hellenic harbors
to holy Troy.
Pipes played a hateful song of triumph,
flutes chimed their horrible harmonic sound.
The ships, rigged out with woven ropes,
the craft of Egypt,*
pursued the hateful wife of Menelaus
into the bays of Troy, my Troy!   130
That woman brought disgrace upon her brothers,†
and shame to Sparta;‡
she killed my Priam, who fathered
a crop of fifty sons.§
And as for me, poor Hecuba:
that woman shipwrecked all my hopes.
Look where I'm sitting: by the tents
of Agamemnon!
I am a slave now, just a poor old woman,   140
taken from my home,

---

* I.e. ropes made from the papyrus plant.

† Helen's brothers are Castor and Pollux, twin demigods who protect sailors (equated with Gemini, the constellation).

‡ Helen is from Sparta.

§ Priam is said to have fathered fifty sons (or more by some accounts), and at least a dozen daughters, nineteen by Hecuba and the rest by concubines.

my hair all shorn.* I'm ruined, like my city.

Ah, we poor wives

of those Trojan warriors, whose bronze spears could not save us.

Poor girls, what terrible weddings for you!

Troy is smoking, slowly burning; we are crying.

I will lead the cries of lamentation,

like a mother bird with her squawking fledglings—

not with a song and dance

like those I used to lead,

feet tapping gladly   150

for the gods of Troy,

while Priam leaned upon his royal staff.

(Half the Chorus have now gathered around Hecuba.)

strophe 1

FIRST SEMI-CHORUS:† Hecuba, why are you shouting? What's all the
   commotion?

What are you trying to say? I heard from inside

your pitiful lamentations.

Fear shoots through our hearts,

all of us Trojan women in here,

crying about our loss of freedom.

HECUBA: Dear children, the men who row the Achaean ships

are starting now, their hands on the oars.   160

SEMI-CHORUS: Oh, no, what now? What do they want of me?

Will they take me from my home and over the sea?

HECUBA: I don't know, but I can guess. This means our ruin.

FIRST SEMI-CHORUS: Oh! Oh, no!

Poor women of Troy!

Come out from the tents to discover the pain you must suffer.

The Greeks are setting out for home.

HECUBA: Stop! No, no!

Don't send my poor Cassandra out,

crazy Cassandra, that the gods drove mad,   170

to be mocked by the Greeks! Don't add more pain

to my pain. Oh, no, no, no!

---

* Traditional expressions of grief in Greek society including cutting or shaving the hair, as well as beating one's breast and tearing the cheeks with one's nails.

† The Chorus are a group of Trojan women. "Semi-Chorus" means that they are divided into two groups for this passage: first, half of the women come out, then the second half.

O Troy, poor pitiable Troy! There's no more Troy.
We have to leave our home:
some of us alive, the dead already gone.
(Enter Second Semi-Chorus.)

antistrophe 1

SECOND SEMI-CHORUS: Ah, tell me! Shaking with fear, I left these
    tents,
the tents of Agamemnon, to hear from you,
my queen, what's going on. Do the Greeks
plan to kill me? Do they?
Or are the sailors getting ready   180
at the prows, to lift the oars?

HECUBA: Child,* I, too, was struck with terror, trembling: before dawn
my soul was wide awake, so I came here.

SECOND SEMI-CHORUS: Has there been any herald from the Greeks?
Do you know whose slave I'll be? I'm full of dread.

HECUBA: I think the time of drawing lots is near.

SECOND SEMI-CHORUS: Oh, no!
Will it be a man from Argos, or from Thessaly,
or will I have to travel to an island,
when I get taken from my home, far, far from Troy?

HECUBA: Ah, the pity of it!
I am a poor old woman; who will be my master?
Who must I serve, where will I go?
I am useless, I am old and weak,   190
I am like a corpse,
all I can do is honor the dead, and hardly that.
Oh! Think of it!
Will I have to serve them as a door-keeper,
or a nanny? When I was once a queen,
and had the glory of the throne of Troy?

strophe 2

CHORUS:† Ah! Ah! How can we find the words to wail
this degradation?
Now I shall no longer spin the shuttle
back and forth on my own native loom.   200

---

* Hecuba addresses a single member of the Chorus. Choruses often speak as if they are a single individual, while also serving as the voice of a collective.

† At this point, the Chorus becomes a united group of singers.

I will never see my parents' home again;
this is the last time, this is the end. And worse to come:
I'll either be forced to bed with a Greek
—a curse upon that night, that destiny!—
or else I'll be just a poor household slave,
drawing water from their holy spring, Pirene.*
I hope I go to the famous, happy land
of Theseus: Attica.†
But I never want to see the whirling Spartan river,   210
the Eurotas, or the home of hateful Helen;
may I never be a slave to Menelaus,
who sacked my town of Troy.

antistrophe 2

I've heard about the holy river-valley,
under Mount Olympus, Vale of Tempe.
They say it's thick with wealth,
weighted with fertile harvests.
That's my second choice of country; first is Athens,
holy, sacred country of the hero, Theseus.
Just north of Carthage there's another country,   220
home to Mount Etna, holy to Hephaestus,
Sicily, mother of mountains;‡
I hear it's famous for its victory-songs.§
And another land
lies near the Ionian Sea,¶
which the beautiful river Crathis
waters and nourishes
with holy streams that dye hair red or golden,**
and make the country rich and happy in its men.

---

* A fountain in Corinth, associated with inspiration.

† The region surrounding Athens.

‡ The island of Sicily, south of mainland Italy, was colonized by Greeks from the eighth century B.C. There may be an anachronistic reference here to the Athenian plan, during the Peloponnesian War, to send a naval expedition to Sicily and try to wrest control of the island (the expedition took place, with disastrous results). Sicily is "holy to Hephaestus" because the volcanic mountains of the island were said to be the result of the blacksmith god's technological workings beneath the earth.

§ The poet Pindar celebrated many victories of the Sicilian tyrant Hiero.

¶ There is a textual problem in this line. The transmitted text includes a word for "sailor," which does not make any sense and has been omitted here. The line may be referring to the Athenian colony of Thurii in the instep of the boot of Italy, another suggestion that the Trojan slaves would be better off in Athenian hands.

** The value of the river Crathis for dye is attested in other ancient authors, such as Pliny. Crathis is in southern Italy.

*(Enter Talthybius.)**

Look! Here comes the messenger from the Greek army,   230
to serve our share of news.

He's walking very fast, he's in a hurry.

What will he say? What news will he bring? We know already
that all of us are slaves to the land of Greece.

TALTHYBIUS:† So, Hecuba! We're old acquaintances.
I've often come from the Greek camp to Troy,
Talthybius the herald. Now, my lady,
I've come again with news to share with you.

HECUBA: This is it. Dear girls, this is what I feared. The moment I've long
been dreading.

TALTHYBIUS: Your lots have been assigned, if that's your fear.   240
HECUBA: Oh! Oh! Where? Where?
A city in Thessaly?
Will it be Thebes?

TALTHYBIUS: Each to a different man, not all together.
HECUBA: Who goes to whom then? Who's the lucky girl
that gets to stay in Troy?

TALTHYBIUS: Ask about each in turn, not all at once.
HECUBA: My child, my poor daughter,
who'll get her? Tell me, who'll get Cassandra?

TALTHYBIUS: King Agamemnon got her as his prize.
HECUBA: Oh, no! To make her serve as a slave to that Spartan wife?‡   250
No, no!

TALTHYBIUS: No, to be his secret second wife.
HECUBA: But she's a virgin of Apollo! Chastity was given to her as a
prize, by the god with golden hair!

TALTHYBIUS: Passion pierced the king for the god-struck girl.
HECUBA: Daughter, throw them down, your holy branches!
Take off your priestess clothes,
take off the wreaths you wear!

TALTHYBIUS: But isn't it great? The bed of a king is hers.
HECUBA: No, oh, no!—But tell me, what about my youngest?   260
The child you took from me? Where can I find her now?

TALTHYBIUS: Are you asking about Polyxena?

---

* Talthybius is the main messenger of Agamemnon's army in the *Iliad*.

† In this scene, Talthybius speaks in conversational meter, while Hecuba continues to sing or chant in less regular, lyric meter.

‡ I.e. Clytemnestra, Agamemnon's wife and Helen's sister; she was originally from Sparta.

HECUBA: Yes. How did her lot fall out? Who will she be yoked to?

TALTHYBIUS: It's set for her to serve Achilles' tomb.

HECUBA: O, O, O! My daughter, serve a tomb?

But what Greek law or custom is this?

How is this possible, my friend?

TALTHYBIUS: Count your daughter happy. She'll do well.

HECUBA: What do you mean?

Tell me, is she alive? Does she still see the sun? 270

TALTHYBIUS: She's in fate's hands; she'll be set free from pain.*

HECUBA: What about the wife of Hector, the brilliant bronze-armed

warrior?

Poor Andromache? What does her future hold?

TALTHYBIUS: Achilles' son has got her as his prize.

HECUBA: And I, who will I serve? I can't do much:

I need a stick as my third leg, grasped in my poor old hand.

TALTHYBIUS: Ithacan Lord Odysseus got you as his slave.

HECUBA: Ah! Ah!

I'll beat my shorn old head,

I'll tear both cheeks with my nails. 280

No, no, no!

I've been assigned to serve

a filthy liar,

an enemy to justice, a lawless monster,

who turns everything upside-down

and back again,

with his double tongue,

transforming friends to enemies and back.†

Mourn for me, women of Troy.

I am so unlucky: I am ruined.

What misery! I got 290

the worst of all the lots.

CHORUS: You know your fate, my lady. What of mine?

What man will take me? To which part of Greece?

  (Talthybius addresses the soldiers in attendance.)

---

* Hecuba does not yet know that Polyxena is dead, and Talthybius leaves it ambiguous here. In Euripides' *Hecuba*, the death of Polyxena plays a large part in the action.

† In Athenian tragedy, Odysseus is almost always presented in negative terms (the main exception being Sophocles' *Ajax*); he is usually envisioned as a trickster, too clever by half, and a prototype for the contemporary fifth-century figure of the sophistic rhetorician.

TALTHYBIUS: Go, you slaves, and bring Cassandra here,
    quick as you can, so I can hand her over
    to the general, then I'll take the other captives,
    and pass them out to their allotted masters.
    But hey! What is that light inside the tent?
    Those Trojan girls are up to something—burning
    their rooms,* to stop us taking them away   300
    to Greece? Are they attempting suicide,
    setting themselves on fire? Free people hate
    submitting to the yoke. Death may be best
    for them, but not the Greeks—and they'll blame me.
    So I must stop it: open up the doors!
HECUBA: There is no fire, no burning. My mad daughter
    Cassandra's rushing out here, with a torch.†

strophe

    CASSANDRA:‡ (*entering*) Bring the light! Hold it up!
      Oh, look! Look!
      I'll glorify this holy place with light. O marriage god!   310
      What joy for the bridegroom!
      What joy for me, my wedding day!
      My royal Argive wedding!
      Hymen,§ O Hymen, lord of marriage!
      Mother, since you're always weeping,
      and lamenting my dead father,
      and our beloved country,
      I myself will burn the torch
      for my own wedding,
      make it blaze with brightness, sparkling,   320
      offering you, Hymen,
      offering you, Hecate,¶

---

* The word for "rooms" suggests the innermost part of a house (the women's quarters); here it is obviously the tents assigned to the women.

† Torches were carried at weddings, usually by the bride's mother; Cassandra's torch symbolizes her marriage to Agamemnon. Note that this is the first time in the play that Hecuba speaks in dialogue meter: she is no longer singing or chanting, but speaking soberly.

‡ In the original, Cassandra speaks or sings in an excited, irregular meter called dochmiacs. Talthybius continues to speak in regular iambic meter, while Cassandra's and Hecuba's speech is in lyric rhythms.

§ Hymen is the god of marriage.

¶ Hecate is associated with the moon, witchcraft, and fire; the allusion to this sinister goddess may connote death as well as torchlight.

light for a young girl's wedding
in the traditional way.

antistrophe

Lift your feet to the sky! Lead the dance, lead the dance!
Cry aloud and sing "Hurrah, bravo!"*
As we did in those happy days
of my father's life. Dancing is holy.
Lead the dance, Lord Apollo. In the midst of your laurels,†
in your temple I'll sacrifice for you.   330
Hymen, O Hymen, O Hymen!
Dance, Mother, lead us in dancing,
Twirl your feet this way and that, with mine,
show us the steps we love!
Shout out the wedding song!
Celebrate the bride
with songs and calls of joy!
Come, girls of Troy, in your prettiest dresses,
sing for my wedding!
Sing for the husband destined
to share my bed.   340

CHORUS: Queen, will you not stop your daughter's frenzy?
She might go skipping off to the Greek camp!

HECUBA: Hephaestus,‡ you bless mortal marriages
with light; but this flame burning here is bitter.
I had high hopes for you, my child. All dashed.
I never thought you'd marry in this way:
forced by Greek soldiers with their swords and spears.
Give me the torch. You're whirling like a wild thing,
not carrying it straight. Your troubles, child,
have not restored your sanity. You're still   350
mad as you were. Women, take in the torches,
and change these wedding songs to tears of grief.

CASSANDRA: Mother, crown me! I have won the prize!
Be happy! I am marrying the king!
Send me to him: or, if I hesitate,

---

* In the original, the cries are *"Euhoi,"* an interjection associated with Bacchus, god of wine and frenzy.

† The laurel or bay tree is associated with Apollo. Cassandra may be wearing laurel wreaths; the reference may also be to the laurel trees that often surrounded temples to Apollo.

‡ Husband of Aphrodite, associated with fire and torches.

push me to him. If my prophetic god*
tells true, this famous Greek king, Agamemnon,
will have worse luck in his affair with me
than Helen had.† I'll kill him, sack his home,
revenge for my dead brothers and dead father. 360
Enough of that. I won't sing of the axe
to fall upon my neck and those of others,‡
the struggles of the matricide,§ begun
by this, my wedding, nor the overthrow
of all the house of Atreus. But I'll tell
how Troy is better off than all those Greeks.
I'll speak with inspiration, but quite calmly.¶
The Greeks destroyed thousands of men, in quest
of just one woman, Helen: one man's passion.
Their clever general killed the child he loved,** 370
for enemies he hated! Gave away
the joys of home and children, for his brother,††
for a wife who ran off freely, not abducted!
When they arrived here, by Scamander's banks,
they died and died, though no one made them leave
the citadels and borders of their home.
Those caught by Ares never got to see
their children, nor be wrapped in winding sheets
by their own wives. They lie in a foreign land.
The Greeks at home are doing just as badly.
Their wives are widowed, then they die. Their parents 380
die bereft, as if they'd had no children:
no one will come to bless their tombs with blood.‡‡
<This is the kind of praise that army earned!
Best not to talk of things that bring more shame:

---

* Apollo: literally referred to in the original by his epithet "Loxias," which connotes oracular riddling.

† "Than Helen had"—in her affair with Paris, which caused the Trojan war.

‡ Clytemnestra, Agamemnon's wife, will kill Cassandra and Agamemnon with an ax.

§ Orestes, Clytemnestra and Agamemnon's son, will kill his mother and will then be pursued by Furies and driven mad.

¶ Literally, she says she is temporarily "outside her madness."

** Agamemnon killed his daughter, Iphigenia, at Aulis as sacrifice to Artemis to bring wind for the Greek fleet to sail to Troy.

†† Menelaus.

‡‡ As a libation (liquid sacrifice) poured on the grave of the dead.

my Muse must not sing only of disaster.>*
As for the Trojans: well, first they won glory
by dying for their country. If the spear
took them, their kinsmen brought their corpses home.
The earth of home holds safe their bodies, buried
properly, by the hands of those that loved them.   390
And all those Trojans who weren't killed in battle
still went on living with their wives and children,
joys far distant from the Achaean soldiers.†
I know you mourn for Hector: but now hear
the truth. He's dead and gone, but he's a hero.
The Greek invasion gave him this great name.
His courage would be still unknown, if they
had stayed in Greece. If Paris hadn't taken
Helen, he'd have some unknown wife at home!
Sensible people should not wish for war,   400
but if it comes, be noble in defeat.
That saves us from disgrace, and wins us glory.
So, Mother, do not pity Troy, or me
for my new "husband," since I shall destroy
my enemy, and yours, by marrying him.

CHORUS: How merrily you laugh at your misfortune!
    So do your songs hold riddles you'll reveal?

TALTHYBIUS: (*to Cassandra*) If Lord Apollo had not made you mad,
    you would not get away with burdening
    my generals with bad omens for their journey.   410
    (*aside*) But even those who have the name of wise,
    the generals, are no better than these nothings.
    The king of all the Greeks, the son of Atreus,‡
    has chosen as his special concubine
    this crazy girl! I may be just a poor man,
    but I would never go to bed with her.
    (*to Cassandra*) Now, as for you, I know your mind's not right,
    so I'll consign your raving to the winds—
    your praises for the Trojans and your blame

---

* Editors suspect that these lines do not belong in the text, on stylistic grounds and also because they seem out of place; hence the angle brackets.

† "Achaean" is another term for Greek.

‡ Agamemnon.

of Greeks. No matter. But now follow me,
down to the ships, a fine bride for our leader.   420
(*to Hecuba*) And you: Laertes' son will come to get you;
follow him. You will serve a decent woman—
so say the men who marched against your city.

CASSANDRA: A clever servant! Why do heralds have
so much respect, when all humanity hates them,
underlings to kings and governments?
Do you say that Odysseus will bring
my mother to his house? What of Apollo?
His words to me foretell that she will die
right here at Troy. The rest is shame: I'll skip it.*   430
And he, poor man,† can't know what kind of pain
awaits him still. My sufferings, and those
of Troy, will seem like gold to him. He'll sail
ten years, then come alone to his own land.
[…]‡
He'll pass the narrow gorge where terrible
Charybdis lives, and in the hills he'll meet
the Cyclops who devours raw flesh, and Circe,
the witch, transforming men to pigs. Then shipwreck,
temptations of the Lotus, holy Cattle
of the Sun, whose bloody bodies moan
with sounds that will prove bitter for Odysseus.§   440
Briefly, he'll go to Hades, still alive;
escaping from the sea at last, he'll find
a thousand further troubles in his home.

Stop now. Why do I hurl these threats at Odysseus?¶
Hurry, Cassandra, marry your husband in Hades' house.
Greek commander, you think you did something great?

---

* She skips the fact that Hecuba will be transformed into a mad dog.

† Odysseus.

‡ A line seems to be missing in the original here.

§ This passage provides a brief synopsis of adventures told in the *Odyssey*. Odysseus has to pass between the devouring sea monster, Scylla, and the whirlpool, Charybdis; will meet the cannibalistic giant, the Cyclops Polyphemus; Circe, who turns many of Odysseus' men into pigs; the Lotus-Eaters, who tempt more of the crew to stay eating the numbing plant and forget the journey; and the Cattle of the Sun, which more crew members eat and are destroyed as a result. After consulting the dead, via the prophet Tiresias, Odysseus arrives home to find his home overrun by his wife's suitors.

¶ The meter changes here to trochaics.

Evil man, an evil death is coming, by night, not day.
Dead and naked, I'll be flung to the wild ravines,
floating down swollen creeks near the grave of my husband,
till animals eat my corpse. So ends Apollo's servant.   450
How I loved him! How I loved his worship!
Now no more of that. Off with my garland;
rip it from my body now! While I'm still virgin!
Off to the breezes. Take it, my prophet-master.
Where's the ship? I'm ready now to go:
first wind, first sail. Take me from my land,
a Fury, an avenger—one of three.*
Goodbye, Mother. Do not cry for me.
Troy, dear country, brothers, father beneath the earth;
soon I shall join the dead. I'll come victorious,   460
ruining the house that ruined us.†

CHORUS: Attendants! Aren't you watching? Look! Old Hecuba,
your mistress, fell! She's speechless, on the ground!
Give her a hand, you lazy girls! To leave
a poor old woman fallen! Lift her up!

HECUBA: Leave me. Kindness isn't kind if it's unwanted.
Let me lie here, girls. I have been felled
by suffering: past, present and to come.
You gods! I call on them, though they're poor helpers:
it sounds good, I suppose, to invoke the gods.   470
First, I want to sing of my good times;
so I'll increase the pity for my troubles.
I was a queen and married to a king,
and I bore children who were truly noble:
people of quality, the best of Phrygia.
No Trojan, Greek nor foreign woman ever
has felt as proud as I did of my children.
I saw them fall when Greek spears cut them down,
I cut my hair and mourned beside their tombs.   480
I wept, too, for their father, my own Priam.
I saw him die with my own eyes, I saw

---

* There are traditionally three Furies—the three spirits of vengeance. But Cassandra will also form another trio, along with Clytemnestra and Aegisthus, as joint devisers of Agamemnon's death (which avenges the death of Iphigenia and all his other innocent victims).

† I.e. the house of Atreus (the father of Agamemnon and Menelaus).

him slaughtered at the hearth of his own shrine;
I saw my city captured. And my girls
whom I raised up to make good marriages
—others took them, ripped them from my hands.
I'll never see my girls again, nor they
see me; never; no, no hope of that.
The cornerstone of all my misery
is that I'll go to Greece enslaved, and old.   490
They'll make me do things shameful for a woman
as old as I am; they'll make me keep the keys
and guard the door: I, Hecuba, Hector's mother!
Or bake the bread! I'll lay my poor old limbs
on the bare ground, after my royal bed,
with tattered rags on my poor tattered body—
rags, not the clothes a highborn lady wears.
I've lost so much. One woman's love affair
caused me such suffering, and it's not the end.
Cassandra, mad once with the gods' true frenzy,   500
you've lost your chastity in this disaster.
And you, where are you, my poor Polyxena?
None of my children—though I had so many!—
can help me now in times of need. Why then
bother to lift me up? What can I hope for?
I used to step so daintily through Troy.
Now I'm enslaved. Give me some straw, a stone
to rest my head. I'll fall and lie there weeping,
until my tears wear me away. Don't count
anyone happy till the day they die.   510

strophe

CHORUS: Troy! Sing for me, Muse,
    a funeral song for Troy,
    a song of tears,
    a strange and different kind of hymn.
    Now I'll lift my voice to sing for Troy,
    and for my sorrow: how I was destroyed,
    enslaved by Greek spears, when the Achaeans left
    the four-hoofed chariot at our gates,
    the Horse,

with its full armor clattering to the sky, 520
and shining cheeks of gold.*
The people stood upon the rock of Troy,
and called aloud,
"Come, all of you! Our troubles now are over!
Take this holy wooden statue to Athena,
the Trojan goddess, child of Zeus, the maiden."
What girl could miss that sight?
What old man could stay home?
But as they sang so happily,
disaster tricked them, took them. 530

antistrophe

All the Trojan race was rushing to the gates
to give the virgin goddess,
whose horses are immortal,†
the mountain pine-wood,
polished ambush of the Argives,
destruction for the Trojans.‡
They threw ropes of woven flax around it,
as one lifts the black hull of a ship,
and brought the killer of our country
to the marble temple floor 540
of Pallas.
But when the dark of night
arrived and came upon
their labor and their joy,
the Libyan pipes resounded,
along with Trojan songs,
and young girls leaped in unison,
toes tapping, shouting happy songs,
and in their homes, bright lights
of torches gave their darkened gleam
to the hours of sleep.§ 550

epode

I was one of those girls: in the palace,
I sang and danced with all the rest

---

* The wooden horse in which the Greeks were hiding to ambush Troy.
† Athena, as a war goddess, loved chariots and horses as instruments of battle.
‡ The "ambush" and the "destruction" are both references to the wooden horse.
§ The text of this line is doubtful.

for the mountain goddess,
the virgin child of Zeus. But then:
a bloody shout through the city
seized the citadel of Troy.*
Little children, dearly loved,
wrapped their shaking arms
around their mothers' dresses.
Ares leapt from his ambush.   560
This was the work of the Virgin, of Athena.
There was slaughter of the Trojans at the altars,
there was decapitation in the bedrooms—
desolation,
to win for Greece the prize
of girls to bear them children,
and for our land of Troy,
nothing but pain.

     (Andromache and Astyanax are led onstage, on a wagon or chariot.)

CHORUS: Hecuba, do you see Andromache?
    Taken on that foreign chariot?
    Her heart is pounding like a set of oars   570
    as she holds close her darling boy, Astyanax, Hector's son.
    Poor woman, where are they taking you on that carriage,
    along with the bronze arms of Hector,
    along with the spoils that they hunted from Troy with their spears,
    to take away, for Achilles' son
    to decorate his Phthian temples?†

strophe 1

ANDROMACHE:‡ Our Greek masters are taking me away.
HECUBA: Ah, no!
ANDROMACHE: Why do you sing my lament?
HECUBA: Sorrow!
ANDROMACHE: Mourn for our suffering.
HECUBA: O, Zeus!
ANDROMACHE: And our misfortune.   580
HECUBA: O, my children.
ANDROMACHE: So we were, once—.

---

* Named the Pergamon.

† Achilles' son is Neoptolemus (Pyrrhus), and their homeland is Phthia, a region of Thessaly.

‡ Andromache and Hecuba are singing in lyric meter throughout this exchange.

antistrophe 1

> HECUBA: Happiness is gone, and Troy is gone.
>
> ANDROMACHE: Nothing.
>
> HECUBA: My children were royalty once.
>
> ANDROMACHE: It's loss, pure loss.
>
> HECUBA: And the loss of my people!
>
> ANDROMACHE: Disaster.
>
> HECUBA: Yes, and the pity of it.
>
> ANDROMACHE: Our dear city.   590
>
> HECUBA: It's gone up in smoke.

strophe 2

> ANDROMACHE: Come back to me, husband!
>
> HECUBA: Poor girl, you're calling
>   a man who's in Hades. My son is dead.*
>
> ANDROMACHE: Hector, you're my defender,
>   and to the Greeks, you're ruin.

antistrophe 2

> HECUBA: To me, you're my firstborn,
>   first of all the sons I bore for Priam.
>
> ANDROMACHE: Take me to Hades.
>   How I long to die!

strophe 3

> HECUBA: Poor girl, this is what we suffer.
>
> ANDROMACHE: Gone is our city.   HEC.: Pain heaps onto pain.
>
> ANDROMACHE: The gods must have hated us. Your other son
>   escaped from death to ruin Troy, just for that cursed love affair.†
>   The bloody bodies of the dead are laid out before goddess Athena,
>   for vultures to take away. Paris set the yoke of slavery on Troy.   600

antistrophe 3

> HECUBA: O my beloved country. Such unhappiness.
>
> ANDROMACHE: I'm crying for you, left all alone.
>
> HECUBA: Now you see how it ends. Ah, the pity!
>
> ANDROMACHE: I'm leaving the home where my children were born.

---

* Hector, Hecuba's son and Andromache's husband, the best defensive fighter on the Trojan side, was killed by Achilles.

† Paris. Hecuba had a dream when Paris was a baby that was interpreted to mean that he would cause his city's downfall. But she and Priam could not bear to kill the child, so they exposed him on Mount Ida, where he was adopted by a herdsman and survived—to have his adulterous affair with Helen and cause the Trojan War. The story was the subject of the now lost *Alexandros*, by Euripides, part of the trilogy in which the *Trojan Women* was performed.

HECUBA: Children, your mother is left behind in a deserted city.
A time of weeping and of lamentation.
Tears pour from tears in our house.
The dead forget their pain.

CHORUS: When things are bad, it's very sweet to weep,
to wail in mourning and to sing your pain.

ANDROMACHE: Mother, do you see us? Think of Hector, your dear son,   610
whose spear destroyed so many Greeks. Do you see us now?

HECUBA: I see the gods at work. From nothing, they build up
high towers, but what seems something, they destroy.

ANDROMACHE: We're spoils of war, my child and I. I was
a queen, I'm now a slave. All overturned.

HECUBA: Necessity is a dreadful thing. Just now
they dragged Cassandra from me, took her away.

ANDROMACHE: Oh, no!
A second rape—Cassandra's second Ajax.*
You are plagued by more disasters, too.

HECUBA: So many I can't count them: there's no limit.   620
My sufferings are competing; worse on worst.

ANDROMACHE: Your daughter, Polyxena: she is dead,
slaughtered as a gift for dead Achilles.

HECUBA: Oh, no! This must be what Talthybius meant,†
speaking in riddles; now it all comes clear.

ANDROMACHE: I saw her corpse. I got down from this cart,
covered her with a dress, and mourned for her.‡

HECUBA: Oh, daughter! What a blasphemous sacrifice!
Oh! What a horror! What a way to die!

ANDROMACHE: She's dead and gone now. But, even in death,   630
she's luckier than me, still left alive.

HECUBA: Child, death isn't the same as seeing the light.
Death means nothing; where there's life, there's hope.

ANDROMACHE: Mother, here's the best that I can say;
listen and I'll try to cheer you up.§

---

* Cassandra was raped by Ajax (as mentioned in the prologue, line 70); now she faces rape by Agamemnon.

† In lines 268–70.

‡ Literally, "I cut myself (for) the corpse," i.e. Andromache made the traditional gestures of mourning, including beating her breast.

§ Some editors have suggested that these two lines should be cut from the text, on the grounds that Andromache's speech is not at all comforting for Hecuba.

I think that being born is not like death;
death is better, far, than painful life.
Their pains are gone, the dead feel no more pain.
But one who falls from fortune to disaster
is lost without the happiness she once had.   640
Polyxena's dead; her light's gone out,
and she knows nothing of her own misfortunes.
But I was shooting for a life of honor,
and hit the mark, but still missed happiness.
In Hector's house, I worked at all the things
considered right and proper for a woman.
First, I stayed in the house and put aside
all desire to leave and go elsewhere;
most scandals happen when girls leave the home,   650
whether or not there's any further wrong.
Inside my house, I wouldn't let the women
talk in clever, fancy ways; enough
to have my homegrown common sense as guide.
My tongue was silent and my eyes were calm
with Hector; I knew when to conquer him,
and when I ought to yield and let him win.
My reputation came to the Greek camp,
and has destroyed me. For, when I was captured,
Achilles' son desired me for his wife.
I will be a slave to murderers.   660
If I push darling Hector from my heart,
and roll it open to my present husband,*
I will betray the dead. But if I act
hostile, I'll be hated by my masters.
They say a woman's dislike for a man
will soften after just one night in bed.
But I spit on the wife who throws away
her former man and loves her new bed-partner.
If you divide a young horse from her partner,†
she'll no longer want to bear the yoke.   670

---

* "Roll it open" is a metaphor based on the unrolling of a scroll.
† The Greek contains a verbal repetition at the end of these lines, 678–79 *(diazugei ... zugon)*.

But animals can't speak or understand;
their nature is inferior to humans.
My darling Hector, you were my perfect man:
understanding, noble, rich and brave.
You took me from my father's home, untouched:
you were the first who came to join my bed.
Now you are dead; the ships are taking me
to Greece, a captive, to a life of slavery.
(*to Hecuba*) You mourn the death of Polyxena; think!
It's better than these losses that I suffer.   680
I've even lost what everybody has:
hope. My heart is not deceived. I know
it's sweet to dream, but nothing good will happen.
CHORUS: Your misfortune matches mine; in weeping
for yours, you teach me what my pain is like.
HECUBA: Although I've never yet been on a ship,
I have seen pictures and heard tales of them.
If sailors meet a storm they can endure,
they strive to get away from all their troubles;
one takes the rudder, one goes to the sails,   690
another pumps the water from the ship.
But if the sea swells up and overwhelms them,
then they surrender to the waves and Fate.
In the same way, I have so much to mourn,
I just give up. I have no more to say,
defeated by the gods' disastrous storm.
But, darling daughter, no more now of Hector.
You can't save him with tears. He's dead. Let be.
Be deferential to your present master;
behave so charmingly the man will love you.   700
If you do this, you'll make your people happy,
and raise my grandson here, this little child,
to be Troy's greatest hope, so that one day,
your children may again inhabit Troy:
the city may continue to exist.
        (*Enter Talthybius.*)
But time has come to talk of other things:
who's this I see? The herald of the Greeks,
coming back here with some more news to tell?

TALTHYBIUS: (*to Andromache*) Former wife of Hector, Trojan hero,
　please do not hate me. It was not my wish　　　　　　　　　710
　to bring this news of what the Greeks are planning.
ANDROMACHE: What's this? Your words suggest you've brought bad news.
TALTHYBIUS: Your son here—well, they plan … how can I say it?
ANDROMACHE: Won't he come with me, serve the same master?
TALTHYBIUS: No Greek will ever make your son his slave.
ANDROMACHE: Will they leave him here as Troy's last remnant?
TALTHYBIUS: I don't know how to tell you this. It's bad.
ANDROMACHE: What do you mean? Bad news? Tell me the truth!
TALTHYBIUS: They're going to kill your child. So now you know.
ANDROMACHE: Oh, no! No, no! This is worse than that marriage!　　720
TALTHYBIUS: The assembly was persuaded by Odysseus.
ANDROMACHE: No! No! This is beyond what I can bear!
TALTHYBIUS: He said we must not raise a hero's son.
ANDROMACHE: I hope the same thing happens to his children!
TALTHYBIUS: He said we have to throw him from the walls.
　Be sensible: you have to let it happen.
　Don't resist: be noble in disaster.
　You have no power here, just realize that.
　You can't do anything. You have to think.
　Your city and your husband, both are gone.　　　　　　　730
　You're beaten, we can easily prevail
　against a single woman. Do not fight.
　Don't do anything to provoke or shame
　the Greeks: no, please don't hurl your curse at them.
　If you say anything to enrage the army,
　your child will get no burial, no pity.
　If you keep quiet and bear misfortune well,
　you need not leave his body here unburied,
　and you yourself will find the Greeks more gentle.
ANDROMACHE: (*to Astyanax*) My sweet, sweet child! They fear you far
　　too much.　　　　　　　　　　　　　　　　　740
　You'll die! They'll kill you! I'll be left without you!
　Your father's heroism means your death,
　though it saved so many other Trojans.*
　For you, his nobleness became a curse.

---

* Many editors think these two lines, 742–43, are inserted by a later commentator.

My marriage brought me nothing but disaster.
When I came to Hector's house, I thought
the son I'd bear would rule this fertile land—
not be a victim slaughtered by the Greeks.
Child, are you crying? Do you understand?
Why are you clinging, clutching at my dress,   750
like a baby bird beneath my wings?
Hector will not rise up from the earth,
his famous spear in hand, to come and save you.
Your family can't help, nor can your city.
You'll fall from a terrible height, down to your death.
Neck broken, no more breath in you. The pity!
My sweetest baby, nestled in my arms!
Your soft skin smells so good! Was it for nothing
I fed you at my breast when you were tiny?
For nothing that I wore myself to shreds,   760
in looking after you? Now, kiss your mother,
hug me one last time, nuzzle close to me,
kiss me and hold me tight, my own sweet baby …
How can you act with such barbarity?*
You think you're civilized! Why kill this child?
He did no harm! And Helen, you're no daughter
of Zeus.† No, you had many fathers: Vengeance,
then Envy, Murder, Death, and all the evils
that Mother Earth is nursing. I am sure
Zeus never fathered you—to be a curse   770
on foreigners and Greeks alike.‡ Die, Helen!
I hate those pretty eyes of yours, that ruined
the famous plains of noble Troy. Disgusting!

    Well, go on, then: take him and hurl him down!
You want to do it? Why not eat him, too?
The gods are killing us. I can't protect

---

* The word used here, *barbaroi*, usually connotes "non-Greek"; there is a paradox that the supposedly civilized Greeks are not acting in a civilized manner.

† Helen and Clytemnestra's mother, Leda, wife of the Spartan king Tyndareus, was seduced by Zeus in the form of a swan, and gave birth to two eggs, from which hatched her four children. Helen was thus supposed to be semidivine, the only female child of Zeus (since her sister, Clytemnestra, was the daughter of the mortal Tyndareus).

‡ "Foreigners" is the same word translated above as "barbarity." It is, of course, paradoxical in the mouth of Andromache (who is herself a "foreigner" from a Greek perspective).

my child from death. So hide me, cover me up,
throw me on board the ship. Congratulations!
Time to get married! With my sweet child lost ...

CHORUS: Poor Troy! So many people now destroyed   780
for just one woman and that cursed affair.*

TALTHYBIUS:† Come on, boy, leave the arms of your mother—
poor woman! March to the crown, to the peak
of your family's citadel. There you'll let go
of breath: so we've decreed by vote.
(to the guards) Seize him!
(aside) This is the kind of message
a man without pity should bring;
a man with a heartless mind—
but mine is not that way.

(Talthybius and the guards march the child away. Andromache
in the cart is led off in a different direction.)

HECUBA: Child, son of my poor dead son,   790
your mother and I are robbed
of your life. It's wrong! What now for me? What
can I do for you, my poor child? I'll give
these blows to my head and my chest for you.
That's all I can do. O my city!
Oh, poor little boy! Is there no end?
What can prevent us from rushing
to instant and total destruction?

strophe 1

CHORUS: Telamon, king of Salamis, land of the bees,‡
you lived in that island in the midst of the sea,   800
across from the holy Acropolis. There first Athena
made the gray olive tree sprout,

---

* The elopement of Paris and Helen.

† The original meter shifts here to anapests—a rhythm associated with military marching, and therefore a clue that Talthybius and his guardsmen are beginning to escort Astyanax away. I have not written
English anapests (two short syllables followed by one long), but I have tried to echo the effect with
shorter lines and more syncopated rhythm.

‡ Telamon was prince of Aegina, who was banished to Salamis for killing his half brother and then
joined Heracles in his quest to sack Troy after the Trojan king Laomedon failed to reward him with the
horses he'd promised as payment for building the city walls. Salamis was one of the main areas in Greece
where honey was produced—hence the bees.

the heavenly crown and the glory of Athens,
shining with oil.* You came, you came,
along with the archer, Heracles, heroes together,
to sack Troy, our Troy, our city
—ours in former times
when you came from Greece.†

antistrophe 1

The hero, insulted at being deprived of his horses,
roused up the flower of Greek manhood, and led them   810
by seafaring oar to the plain of the flowing Simois,‡
fastened the ships, and from the deck, he let fire with sure aim,
to slaughter Laomedon. With the purple breath of flame
he wrecked the walls Apollo built so straight,
and sacked the land of Troy.
Twice the bloody spear, in two fell swoops,
flattened the walls of Dardania.§

strophe 2

What good does it do,
that Laomedon's son   820
tiptoes on delicate feet
to pour the wine from the golden cups,
to fill the cup of Zeus, that glorious service?¶
Ganymede!
the city of your birth
is now on fire.
The shores of the sea
resound like a bird
who cries for her chicks: 830
one woman weeps for her husband, another her child,
another for her old mother.
Boy, the baths where you washed in the dew,
and the race-tracks you ran on

---

* Athena and Poseidon had a contest to see which god was more beneficial to the city of Athens. Poseidon, god of the sea, made a spring of salt water burst forth, but Athena made the olive grow, and won the prize.

† The text of this line is likely to be wrong.

‡ A river of Troy.

§ Troy is also called Dardania, after its legendary founder, Dardanus.

¶ Ganymede, a Trojan youth famous for his beauty, was taken by Zeus to be his cup-bearer in heaven.

are gone; but you keep the beautiful calm
of your young face, as you serve
the throne of Zeus as his favorite.
The spear of Greece has ruined the land of Priam.

antistrophe 2

Love, Love,*
the pet of the heavenly goddesses,   840
you came once to the palace of Troy,
and built the city up,
so high,
by joining us in marriage
to the gods.
But now? I will never put the blame on Zeus.
White-winged Day,
beloved by humans,
shed the light of destruction
as she looked down on Troy.   850
She looked down at the ruin of our Pergamum,
though she had in her bedroom a husband,
father of her children,
who came from our land:†
her golden chariot of stars
led by four horses,
snatched him and took him,
a great source of hope for his home.
But Troy has no more love-charms for the gods.‡
(Enter Menelaus, with his attendants.)

MENELAUS: What a glorious day this is! A happy dawn!   860
Today I'll lay my hands on my own wife,
Helen. I'm the one who worked to get her—
with the army's help. I'm Menelaus.§
I came from Troy, but not for what they think:

---

* Love (Eros) is personified: he is the ever-young child of Aphrodite (equivalent to Cupid).

† Tithonus, a Trojan, abducted in her chariot by the dawn goddess, Eos, to be her husband. He lived with her forever, immortal but not ageless. They had two sons, Memnon and Emathion.

‡ I.e. now that Ganymede and Tithonus are gone, there are no more Trojans left whose beauty might bewitch the gods and thus save the city.

§ These two lines, 862–63, may be an actor's interpolation. Note the discrepancy between the use of the name Helen at 862 and the refusal to say the name at 870.

not for the woman, but that man, that traitor,
the guest who tricked me, took away my wife,
from my own home! And now, thanks to the gods,
he's got his punishment, he and his land.
Greek spears have laid them low. But I have come
to get Miss Sparta:* I won't say the name—   870
my former wife. She's in detention here
with the Trojan girls, the prisoners.
The men who fought with spears to capture her
gave her to me to kill, or if I'd rather,
to take back home with me to the land of Argos.
I decided not to intervene
with Helen's fate in Troy, but take her back
by ship to Hellas. Let them kill her there,
as retribution for those lost at Troy.
(*to his attendants*) But go now, men, and get her from the tent!   880
Drag that woman here, bring her to me
by her blood-guilty hair! When fair winds come,
we'll take her back with us to the land of Greece.†

HECUBA: Sustainer of the earth, in heaven above,
whoever you may be, Divine Unknown,
Zeus, Fate of Nature, or the Mind of Man,
I pray to you: you come with silent tread
and bring some justice to the affairs of mortals.

MENELAUS: What's this? What a strange new way to pray.‡

HECUBA: Menelaus, I approve your plan   890
to kill your wife. But flee her hellish sight!§
She'll trap you with desire. She traps men's eyes,
ruins cities, burns up homes: she has such charms!
I know her. So do you, so do her victims.

(*The guards bring Helen out.*)

HELEN: Menelaus, what a scary opening!
Your guards marched in and laid their hands on me

---

* Literally, "that Spartan woman."

† The Spartans are to be given the pleasure of executing Helen.

‡ Hecuba's prayer reflects contemporary fifth-century philosophical speculation about the true nature of the gods.

§ There is a pun in the original on the name Helen, which sounds like the verb "to trap."

and dragged me here outside by force! So rough!
Well, I suppose that you must hate me; still
I want to speak. What have you all decided,
you and the Greeks, about my life or death?   900
MENELAUS: We didn't need a vote count; the whole army
sent me to kill you, since you did me wrong.
HELEN: All right. May I say something in reply,
explaining why it isn't fair to kill me?
MENELAUS: I didn't come to talk: I came to kill you.
HECUBA: No, Menelaus, listen! Don't deprive her
of this before she dies. And grant to me
the chance to speak against her. You know nothing
of what we've borne in Troy. If all is told
my words will kill her. She cannot escape.   910
MENELAUS: It slows things down; but yes, if you want to, speak.
Just so you know, I grant this gift to her,
not for her sake, but so that you may speak.
HELEN: Perhaps you see me in such hostile terms
you won't reply even if my speech is good.
But I'll set out an answer to the charges
that I anticipate you'll make against me,
giving replies for every accusation.*
First: this woman mothered this whole mess
by bearing Paris. Second, her old husband   920
ruined both Troy and me. He failed to kill
the infant—nightmare image of a torch,
that Alexander.† Listen, I have more.
He judged the trio, those three goddesses.‡
Athena promised him that he would lead
the Trojans to defeat the Greeks in war.
Hera swore, if he picked her, she would give him
empire from Asia to the shores of Europe.

---

* This line may be spurious.

† Hecuba dreamed when pregnant with Paris that she was about to give birth to a firebrand surrounded by snakes; the dream was interpreted to mean the child would cause the fall of Troy. Hecuba and Priam did not have the heart to kill their baby, so they exposed him on the mountain by Troy, Mount Ida, where he was adopted by shepherds, who named him Alexander (Paris being his non-Greek name).

‡ In the Judgment of Paris, Zeus was asked to adjudicate which of the three goddesses should be awarded the golden apple of Discord. The god deferred the judgment to Paris, who picked Aphrodite because she promised him in return the most beautiful woman in the world: Helen.

But Aphrodite had been thunderstruck
by me—my beauty. She said if she won   930
the beauty contest, she would give him me.
Now see what follows. Cypris beat the others,*
and my new marriage benefited Greece.
No foreign power has conquered you in war
or politics—you're free. But Greek delight
cost me my ruin: sold for my beauty, loathed
by those who should have blessed and crowned my head.
    You'll say I'm not yet at the central issue:
how could I sneak in secret from your house?
The curse on Hecuba, a mighty goddess,†   940
was with that man—call him what name you will:
That Alexander—also known as Paris.
That's who you left at home—you idiot!
—when you sailed from Sparta off to Crete.‡
Well, next?
I won't ask you this one: I'll ask myself.
What was I thinking, going with a stranger,
betraying my own home and native land?
Punish the goddess; outstrip Zeus in power,
who dominates the other gods, but slaves
for Aphrodite. So I should be pardoned.   950
Now you might raise a specious point against me:
when Paris died and went beneath the earth,
when that god-gotten union was dissolved,
I should have left and gone to the Greek ships.
I tried to! Be my witness, guards: I did!
The watchmen from the towers and from the walls
often found me slipping out in secret,
dropping from the battlements on ropes.
But my new husband forced me to his side,
Deiphobus, despite the Trojans' will.§   960

---

* Cypris is a title of Aphrodite.
† I.e. Aphrodite.
‡ Catreus, king of Crete, had died (killed mistakenly by his own son), and Menelaus went to his funeral, leaving his wife alone with Paris.
§ Deiphobus, a brother of Paris and an excellent warrior, was given Helen as a prize of war after the death of Paris. Some editors believe these lines are spurious.

So, husband, how could I deserve to die,
when I was forced to that affair, and when
I suffered bitter slavery in that house,
not victory? But if you want to win
against the gods, you don't know what to want.

CHORUS: (*to Hecuba*) Your majesty, protect your land and children
    by undermining her: she speaks so well,
    plausibly, but she's bad. A terrible thing.

HECUBA: First, let me defend the goddesses,
    and show this woman's words were simply wrong.   970
I don't believe that Hera and the Maiden,
Athena, could have ever been so stupid—
Hera, to sell her Argos to barbarians,
Athena making Athens slave to Troy!
They didn't go to Ida to play games
or have a beauty pageant! Why would Hera
yearn to be beautiful? She is a goddess!
Married to Zeus—could she improve her status?
Or was Athena on the hunt to marry
some god—Athena, who implored her father   980
to let her be a virgin? Don't make gods
seem fools, to prettify your faults; you won't
persuade the wise. You said that Aphrodite
went with my son to Menelaus' house.
Ridiculous! She could have stayed in heaven,
resting, and transported you to Troy
and all of Sparta, too.* No, no. My son
was very handsome: glimpsing him, your mind
caused your desire. Humans are such fools,
they're Aphro-dotty—hence the goddess' name.†   990
When you saw Paris in his flashy gold,
dressed so exotic, well, you lost your mind.
You didn't have much when you lived in Argos;
you hoped to trade your Sparta for our city,
our Troy which flows with gold, and floods the town

---

* The original refers to a city in Sparta called Amyclae, site of a special cult of Aphrodite.

† There is an untranslatable pun in the original, between the name of the goddess, Aphrodite, and the word for folly (*aphrosyne*). Hecuba is suggesting a connection between the two words, implying that it's appropriate that the word "folly" and the name of the sex goddess sound alike.

with luxury. Already you'd run riot
living it up in Menelaus' palace.
But still you wanted more.

                    Now then. You say
my son took you by force. Who saw you go?
Did any Spartan woman know about it?*
What Spartan heard you? Didn't you shout? If so,
why didn't Castor and his brother hear you?   1000
They were still on earth, not turned to stars.†
And when you came to Troy, and Greeks pursued you,
hot on your heels, when spears were falling fast,
if you heard news your husband might be winning,
you sang his praises to upset my son,
with all the greatness of his sexual rival.
But if the men of Troy were doing better,
that man was nothing. You were always acting
with an eye to fortune, never virtue.
Now then: you claim you stole away on ropes   1010
down from the towers; you didn't want to stay.
Were you ever found hung from a noose,
or having stabbed yourself? A decent woman
would do that if she missed her former husband.
But I was always giving you advice:
"Daughter, go! And let my sons be free
to marry other wives. I'll take you safely
down to the ships. So you can stop the fighting
of Greece and Troy." But you hated that idea.
You got so grand and uppity in his palace,   1020
you wanted foreigners prostrate before you.‡
That's what you valued. Now, after such behavior,
you come out here dolled up, and dare to share
the sky your husband sees? Disgusting monster!
You should have come here humbly, dressed in rags,

---

* Since women lived in shared apartments, it would have been unlikely for a woman to be abducted without the other women hearing anything.

† Helen's twin brothers, Castor and Pollux, eventually were catasterized (turned to stars).

‡ Prostration—lying down in front of a ruler as a gesture of reverence—was considered by Greeks a mark of "oriental" servility.

trembling with fear, your hair all snipped and shaved.
That would be decent, given what you've done,
so many wicked actions. You are shameless!

    Menelaus, here's my final word:
Crown Greece with glory, glorify yourself,   1030
by killing her. So set the rule for others:
a woman who betrays her man must die.*

CHORUS: King, take revenge on her! Show even Troy
    you're worthy of your birth, and show the Greeks
    they need not blame you for effeminate ways.

MENELAUS: (*to Hecuba*)
    Your opinion matches mine; she went
    willingly from my house to the stranger's bed.
    Her talk of Aphrodite's meaningless.
    (*to Helen*) Go! Let them stone you! Die, and with your death,
    pay back the ten-year sufferings of the Greeks.   1040
    Then you'll know better than to dishonor me.

HELEN: (*kneeling*)
    I beg you, do not kill me! All this plague
    came from the gods; you have to pity me.

HECUBA: (*also kneeling*)
    Do not betray the friends this woman killed.
    I beg you, too, for them and for my children.

MENELAUS: Hush, old woman. I'm going to take no notice
    of her. I'll tell the slaves to take her down
    onto the ships; we'll take her off by sea.

HECUBA: You must not let her share a ship with you!

MENELAUS: Why not? Has she put on too much weight?†   1050

HECUBA: Lovers feel affectionate forever.

MENELAUS: Some do, some don't; their attitude depends.
    But as you wish. I won't let her embark
    in my ship; what you say does make some sense.
    But when she gets to Argos she will die;
    she'll come to the bad end that she deserves,
    to teach all women decency. Not easy,

---

* Under Athenian law, women who had committed adultery were to be excluded from public activity, but the law specified that they should not be killed.

† It is rare in tragedy to find characters making actual jokes, like this one.

but Helen's death will stop their nasty ways,
through fear, although they'll still be just as shameless.
    (Helen and Menelaus exit together.)

strophe 1

   CHORUS: How could you, Zeus, abandon   1060
       your Trojan temple and its smoking altar
       to the Achaeans?
       You left the burning honey cake,*
       the myrrh that smoked so high,
       and holy Pergamum,
       and the ivy-covered valleys
       of mount Ida.
       Ida! where rivers run with melted snow,
       where the horizon is first struck by dawn,
       that radiant, most sacred place.†   1070

antistrophe 1

       Gone are your sacrifices, gone the sweet songs
       of dancing choirs, and gone the festivals
       where gods were worshipped all night long, in thick of darkness.
       Gone are the wooden statues set with gold,
       gone the Trojans holiest holy,
       the moon-cakes, numbering twelve.‡
       Do you even care, my lord? I feel so worried:
       did you just go back to sit in heaven,
       up there in the sky while Troy is ruined,
       devastated by the rush of flaming fire?   1080

strophe 2

       My darling dearest husband,
       you're dead, and wandering in the Underworld,
       without the rites of washing, or a tomb.§ Meanwhile,

---

* A reference to the sacrificial burning of a glutinous mixture of honey, oil, and meal.

† There was a myth that Ida, the mountain overlooking Troy, collected rays of light from the sea and formed them into a new sun each day.

‡ Apparently these were crescent-shaped cakes used for sacrificial offerings. It is quite possible that the reference was obscure to Euripides' audience also—an evocation of an exotic and alien religious practice.

§ Greek funeral practices involved a ritual washing of the dead body (which of course cannot be performed for those killed in battle); hence, the husband's dead spirit is wandering, lost, in the Underworld.

I have to cross the sea,
on a swift-winged ship,
to Argos, home of horses, where the people live
in stone walls raised to heaven by the Giants.*
Hordes of children at the gates
are crying, clinging to their mother's necks,
and wailing,   1090
"Mother, the Greeks are taking me away alone, all by myself,
they're taking me away from you! I need your face.
I'm just a little girl. They're taking me somewhere
on their dark ship
rowing over the sea—
maybe to holy Salamis
or the Isthmus where the peak looks out
on double seas, the gate
of Pelops' palace."†

antistrophe 2

May sacred fire, the flash of lightning,   1100
hurled with two fists, blast Menelaus' ship
right in the midst of the oars
as it crosses the Aegean.
I can't stop crying. He's taking me away
to Greece to be a slave, my home is gone.
Meanwhile, she gets all the things a girl could want:
golden mirrors for the child of Zeus.
May he never reach his Spartan home   1110
or his ancestral hearth,
nor come to Pitane
with its bronze-gated temple of Athena,‡
after taking that curse of a wife,
that shame to mighty Greece,
and the cause of so much pain
by the banks of the Simois.

---

* The stone walls of the palaces at Mycenae and Argos were supposedly built by the Cyclopes.

† A reference to the Acrocorinth, the upper palace or citadel of Corinth, which was on a peak above two harbors, the Saronic and Corinthian gulfs. Pelops, a mythical king, originally came from Phrygia or Lydia (near Troy) but then moved to mainland Greece (the Peloponnese); he was the grandfather of Agamemnon and Menelaus.

‡ Pitane is a district in the city of Sparta.

(*Enter Talthybius and his men with the body of Astyanax on a shield.*)

CHORUS: Oh, no, no, no!
New troubles, always more and always worse for Troy.
Poor women, look at this body.
It is Astyanax: he's dead.   1120
A horrible death. The Greeks just tossed him down
like a discus from the ramparts; so they killed him.

TALTHYBIUS: The last ship, Hecuba, is set with oars,
ready to take the final spoils of Pyrrhus,*
Achilles' son, back to the shores of Phthia.
Neoptolemus is gone already.
He heard new trouble's come to Peleus:
Acastus exiled him from his own land.†
That's why he's gone so quick, no time to waste,
and with him went Andromache. I wept,   1130
I couldn't help it, when she left her country,
when she was crying for her home, and calling
to Hector's tomb. She begged that Pyrrhus bury
this corpse, this boy, who fell down from the walls
and lost his life: the child of your son Hector.
She also asked him not to take with him
to Peleus' house, the place she must submit
to him as bride, this shield of bronze, which Hector
carried when he terrified the Greeks.
<So sad: Andromache, the dead boy's mother.>‡   1140
"Instead of cedar coffin and stone tomb,
bury the boy on this!" she said, and begged me
to set it in your arms, to shroud the corpse
in clothes and coverings, as best you can.
She had to go; her master's haste has robbed her
of giving burial rites to her own son.
But I myself, when you have dressed the corpse,
will bury it, then lift our oars and go.

---

* Also known as Neoptolemus (the name used in the original); son of the now-dead Achilles. Phthia is the homeland of both Achilles and Pyrrhus.

† Acastus, son of Pelias, drove Peleus, father of Achilles, out of his home; he tried to meet up with his grandson Neoptolemus, but was shipwrecked and died.

‡ Editors believe this line to be an ancient commentator's gloss, not part of the original.

Quick as you can, do as you have been told.
But there's one job I've done for you already: 1150
I crossed the river Scamander, right there,
taking the body, and I washed his wounds.
And now I'll go and dig the boy a grave.
You work, I work, we'll work on this together,
then we'll be done and row our ships back home.

HECUBA: Lay on the ground the rounded shield of Hector,
terrible sight! I can't bear looking at it.
O, Greeks! Your weapons had more force than sense:
why did you feel afraid of this young boy?
Strange and unnatural killing. Did you fear   1160
he'd one day raise up fallen Troy? You're worthless!
We were losing even then, when Hector
stood strong against your hundred thousand spears.
Now this city's taken and we Trojans
ruined: and this tiny body frightened you!
Don't be afraid unless you've got a reason.

         Oh, sweetheart, what bad luck you had in death!
If you'd grown up, got married, and obtained
this godlike kingdom, and then died for it,
your life would have been good; that's happiness.   1170
But as it is, you glimpsed a happy future,
but never knew it or enjoyed your birthright.
Poor boy, how horribly your own home's walls,
the ramparts of Apollo, crushed your head
and ripped the curls your mother doted on;
she often used to kiss you there—where blood
laughs out between the broken bits of skull.
I won't hide the horror. Your sweet hands,
so like your father's, lie there dislocated,
broken. And your lovely mouth is dead,
that made false promises as you tugged my dress,   1180
saying, "Grandma, at your funeral,
I'll cut my hair for you and bring my friends
to say goodbye and tell how much we loved you."
You didn't bury me, I buried you,
so young, and I'm so old: citiless, childless.
Poor little body! How I used to hold you,

and watch you as you slept: now what's the use?
What could a poet write upon your tomb?
"The Greeks once killed this boy because they feared him"?   1190
That is an epitaph to shame all Greece!
You didn't get your father's legacy,
but you will have his shield—to be your coffin.
O shield! You kept safe Hector's fine strong arms,
then lost your own best guardian and protector.
How sweet to see his imprint in your handle,
his sweat left on your smooth, well-rounded rim,
dripping from Hector's forehead when he pressed
his chin against you, laboring in war.
(*to the Chorus*) Come here, bring what we've got, let's try to dress   1200
the corpse as best we can. God does not grant
the chance to make it beautiful. I'll give you
this, what I have, not much. People are fools
to trust in happiness when luck is theirs.
Fate lunges back and forth, like one struck mad,
and no one ever gets to choose good fortune.
       (Hecuba's women bring out clothes to adorn the boy's body.)
CHORUS: Here are the women, bringing from the spoils
    of Troy, some ornaments for the little corpse.
HECUBA: Here, child: your grandma has some gifts for you,
    from things that once were yours—not as a prize   1210
    for winning in a horse race, nor at archery—
    sports the Trojans treat with proper honor.
    No: that woman that the gods abhor,
    Helen, has robbed you, even of your life!
    She's killed you, and our whole house is destroyed.
      CHORUS:* Oh, oh, oh! You touched my heart,
        my heart, Astyanax! You were once a mighty prince,
        in this my city.
HECUBA: I'll dress you in the best of Trojan clothes,
    the ornaments you should have worn for marriage
    to the best princess in the whole of Asia.   1220
    And shield, dear shield of Hector, you once won

---

* This and other choral interventions in this final scene are in lyric meter, which is intermingled with
sections of iambic dialogue meter. Hecuba switches between lyric and iambic meters.

so many victories, a thousand triumphs,
mother of glory, take this crown. You die
with this corpse, but live forever. Better honor you
than the weapons of that wicked, sharp Odysseus.

> CHORUS: No, no, no!
>> Pain and lamentation! O, little boy,
>> the earth will take you now.
>> Mourn him, Mother!

> HECUBA: Ah, ah, ah!   1230

> CHORUS: Weep for the dead.

> HECUBA: Oh, oh, oh!

CHORUS: Ah, your suffering goes beyond bearing.

HECUBA: I'll bandage up your wounds for you and nurse them.
I'm a bad nurse. I cannot make you well.
Your father will look after you in Hades.

> CHORUS: Beat your head, beat it,
>> pound at your body.
>> Shout: O, O, O, O!

> HECUBA: Dear girls—

> CHORUS: Hecuba, tell it: what do you want to say?

HECUBA: <The gods were nothing then. There's only pain,>*   1240
and Troy was hated more than any city.
I gave them sacrifices; it was pointless.
But if god hadn't overturned our world,†
we'd be invisible; no bard would sing
our story to the future generations.
Well, go, bury the corpse in his poor grave.
He has the garlands that the dead should have.
I think it matters little to the dead,
whether they get riches in the grave.
This is an empty gesture of the living.   1250

> CHORUS: O, O, O!
>> Poor mother! And poor baby! Such great hopes
>> you had for life, all mangled and ripped up.
>> Child, you were born with so much wealth,
>> such noble birth, but you died such a terrible death.

---

* This line is corrupt. The general sense is that the gods meant nothing but pain to Hecuba, or did nothing but make her suffer.

† The singular "god" (without definite article) could be Zeus, or some other unnamed deity; Hecuba cannot know which god or gods are responsible.

(Enter Talthybius, accompanied by soldiers.)
> But what is this? Who are these people on the citadel,
> their hands afire with burning torches,
> scooping the air like oars?
> It looks as if there's more bad news for Troy.

TALTHYBIUS: Captains, you have orders to set light   1260
> to Priam's city here: don't let the flame
> sit idle in your hands, but fire, fire, fire!
> Once we've razed Ilium, burned it to the ground,
> we'll go home safe and sound away from Troy.
>
> Now here's the other side of my instructions:
> you women, Trojan daughters, when the generals
> give the signal with the trumpet, echoing high,
> go to the ships, where you'll be taken off.
> *(to Hecuba)* You, too, old woman—poor unlucky thing!
> go with these men; they'll take you to Odysseus,   1270
> whose exiled slave the ballot says you are.

HECUBA: I'm finished, then. It's over now, the end,
> the final terminus of all my sorrow.
> I'm leaving home; my city's set on fire.
> Up, you old feet, and hurry the best you can:
> let me pay my respects to wretched Troy.
> Troy, once the flower of Asia, redolent
> with glory, soon you'll lose your famous name.
> They're burning you, and taking us away
> as slaves. O gods! But why call on the gods?   1280
> They didn't listen last time they were called.
> Come then, let's rush into the flames! It's best
> for me to die here, in my burning home.

TALTHYBIUS: Poor woman, you've gone crazy from your troubles.
> But men, take her away; do not hold back.
> Give her to Odysseus as his prize.

strophe 1
> HECUBA:* Ruin!
> Zeus, Lord of Phrygia,
> father of the Dardan race,†
> do you see our suffering? We don't deserve this!   1290

---

* The last part of the play is all in lyric meter.

† Zeus was the father of Dardanus, founder of Troy. The text of these lines is mangled, though the general sense seems clear.

CHORUS: He has seen it all; and yet our mighty city
is no city now; it's ruined, and Troy does not exist.

antistrophe 1

HECUBA: Disaster!
Troy shines bright,
the buildings of our citadel are all ablaze with flame,
the city and the summits of our walls.

CHORUS: Like smoke on the wing of the wind,
our land falls to the spear, and now it's gone.
Buildings are set alight with raging flame   1300
and enemy spears.

HECUBA: My country, that fed and raised my children!

strophe 2

CHORUS: Ah, ah, ah!

HECUBA: Children listen, hear your mother's cry!

CHORUS: You're calling lamentations to the dead.

HECUBA: (*kneeling*) I lay my old limbs down upon the ground
and beat the earth with my two fists.

CHORUS: (*kneeling*) I, too, in turn, will kneel upon the earth
and call to my poor husband
in the earth below.

> (*Talthybius' men begin to lay hands on Hecuba and the Chorus
> members.*)

HECUBA: They're taking us away!

CHORUS: It's agony. Tell it loud! Agony!   1310

HECUBA: Taking us to a house of slavery.

CHORUS: Away from our family home.

HECUBA: Oh, Priam, Priam,
you had no grave, you died without a friend,
and you don't know my ruin.

CHORUS: Black death closed his eyes,
holy in unholy slaughter.*

antistrophe 2

HECUBA: O, temples of the gods, O my dear city!

CHORUS: O, dear city!

HECUBA: Ruin of fire and force of spear possessed you.

---

* Priam was killed by Achilles' son Pyrrhus, at the altar of Zeus—hence, it was an unholy death.

CHORUS: So soon, you'll lose your name and fall to our dear earth.

HECUBA: Like smoke winging up to the sky, the dust   1320
will soon blind me to my own home.

CHORUS: The name of the country will be lost. And everything,
everything everywhere gone,
and poor Troy is no more.

(Loud crashing noises are heard offstage.)

HECUBA: Did you hear, do you know what it is?

CHORUS: It's the crash of the towers.

HECUBA: Earthquake, earthquake everywhere!

CHORUS: Waves engulf the town.

HECUBA: O, o, o! My poor old shaking legs,
carry me off
to my day of slavery.   1330

CHORUS: Weep for our city! But we have to go
onto the ships of the Greeks.

(All leave the stage.)

Introduction to Euripides' *Helen*

Euripides took greater interest in the figure of Helen than did his fellow tragedians. Indeed, he was the only tragic playwright, to our knowledge, to put her
on the stage, not only in this play but in the *Trojan Women* and *Orestes* as well.
His unique focus on a woman who, conventionally, had few heroic dimensions
reveals much about his innovative, genre-bending technique. Ever since Homer's *Iliad*, Helen had been associated in the Greek mind with beauty, sexual allure, and a faithlessness and cunning born of these two qualities. To build a
tragedy around such a woman—the polar opposite, in terms of stature, of Antigone or Medea—as Euripides did in 412 B.C. was a daring move, almost certain
to produce a play that was not, in fact, tragic.

So it is with *Helen*, a play that has been classed as comedy, romance, or melodrama, even though it was produced as part of the traditional tragic tetralogy.
As he did in other plays—the *Alcestis* is a prominent example in this volume—
Euripides here pushes the boundaries of the Athenian dramatic forms that had
come down to him little changed in half a century of development. The central
problem he deals with in *Helen* is not one of justice or the social order of the
polis; after all, he sets his scene in Egypt, a long way from the nearest Greek
city-state. Instead, the play is centrally concerned, like many a modern thriller
or action movie, with the mechanics of getting away from someone who wants
to do you grave harm.

The same problem dominates another Euripidean play, *Iphigenia among the
Taurians*, probably written at about the same time as *Helen*. The plots of the two
plays are nearly identical. Both cast a Greek wayfarer—Menelaus, in the case
of *Helen*—onto the shores of a ruthless foreign king who despises Greeks. The
wayfarer miraculously meets a long-lost loved one who is in the king's power.
Together the two plan a ruse that will allow them to sail back to the safety of
Hellas. The ending of both plays takes the form of a taut, tense chase, narrated
by a messenger since it could not be enacted onstage, followed by the arrival of
gods—in this play, the Dioscuri, Helen's divine brothers—who quell the tyrant's rage and head off further violence.

Nowhere else in the surviving corpus of Greek tragedy do we find two such
closely correlated dramas. It seems likely, moreover, that both were written

during the period of Athens's enormous naval invasion of the island of Sicily, a part-Greek, part-barbarian realm that became an Athenian military target at the midpoint of the Peloponnesian War. The relationship between these two escape dramas and the unfolding crisis in Sicily, where an enormous Athenian-led force became fatally entrapped and unable to escape, is unclear, but some relationship surely exists. *Helen*, it should be noted, was put on only a few months after the devastating news reached Athens of its armada's destruction in Sicily.

Though they might have been puzzled by *Helen*'s novelty of form, the Athenians who attended the original production would have been familiar with its back story. The bizarre plot conceit by which Helen had lain hidden in Egypt while the Greek army fought for her *eidolon*, or phantom, at Troy was not original to Euripides; a poet named Stesichorus had promulgated this "alternative history" more than a century earlier, and Herodotus, Euripides' close contemporary, had in part endorsed it (though without mentioning the phantom). An Egyptian king named Proteus, Herodotus claims, had detained Helen, keeping her safe for Menelaus, after the ship in which Paris was abducting her was driven onto his shores. With coldly pragmatic logic, Herodotus reasons that Helen could not really have been in Troy, since the Trojans would never have waged a grinding war for ten long years, as Homer's *Iliad* says that they did, rather than surrender her and gain peace in an instant.

Euripides framed his *Helen* as a kind of sequel to Herodotus' account. Proteus, protector of Helen, is now dead, and his son, Theoclymenus, is on the Egyptian throne—a less noble ruler than his father, especially in his lust to have Helen for his own. But Euripides also makes use here of Stesichorus' *eidolon*, and indeed amplifies its unsettling implications. In Euripides' version, the phantom, still taken to be the real Helen, has accompanied Menelaus and his crew on their homeward voyage, until—*poof!*—it melts into thin air (as a servant describes, lines 605–15), revealing in a parting speech that the Greeks and Trojans had fought for nothing. This idea must have disquieted Athenians who not only revered Homer's more heroic account of the Trojan War—scenes from it were at this moment being carved for their new temple of Athena Nike—but had suffered enormous losses in their own war against Sparta, a conflict that by this time had stretched out twice as long as the Trojan one. A meditation by *Helen*'s Chorus (1151–65), probably inspired by Herodotus' idea that the Trojans and Greeks could have avoided bloodshed and negotiated their differences, has often been seen as an object lesson for contemporary Athens and Sparta, in line with Aristophanes' war-weary comedy *Lysistrata*, produced less than a year after *Helen*.

But Euripides leaves implicit the question raised by the phantom's disappearance: that of whether the Trojan War—or any subsequent war—had any point that could justify its terrible cost. He focuses instead on the joyous, passionate reunion of husband and wife, a reunion sweetened by a wholly unexpected twist: Helen is here portrayed as a fiercely loyal wife who has steadfastly resisted Theoclymenus' attempts to possess her by taking refuge at Proteus' tomb (where the play is set). One can almost see the mischievous smile on Euripides' face as he contemplated the inversion by which he made Helen, the most notorious tramp of Greek mythology, tenaciously chaste. Helen's sexual fidelity, and Menelaus' relief at learning of it, looks back to the story of Penelope in the *Odyssey*, but it also looks ahead to the New Comedies that would dominate the Athenian stage in the century after *Helen*, and to the romance novels that circulated through the Greek world thereafter. These genres eschew the public concerns of the *polis* for those of a domestic realm in which ardent love and happy pair-bonding are the supreme marks of divine favor. With its emphases on these personal, familial objectives, *Helen* has been termed a romance, set at the start of a Greek literary trend that would continue to evolve for centuries.

That is not to say that the larger cosmos of classical Greek tragedy has been left behind in this play. Thanks to the remarkable Theonoë, a seer who knows all things, we learn that the Olympian gods are, at the moment the play takes place, deciding among themselves the fates of Helen and Menelaus—even if her report of their deliberations (lines 878–886) is so brief, and focused on such petty concerns, as to be nearly parodic. At the play's end, the appearance *ex machina* of Helen's divine brothers, the Dioscuri, frames the preceding action as the working out of the will of Zeus, similar to the closing epiphanies in other Euripidean dramas (compare, in this volume, *Bacchae* and *Hippolytus*). The old questions posed by Greek tragic poets throughout the fifth century are voiced again here, as urgently as ever, by the Chorus of Greek maidens:

> *What mortal can think it all through and explain*
> *what is god, what is not god . . . ?* (1138–39)

But the hope of obtaining answers seems to be increasingly remote:

> *The most one can hope is to glimpse how their works*
> *leap around, back and forth and around,*
> *in a world of surprises and self-contradiction.* (1140–42)

Thus the lives of Helen and Menelaus, proceeding from helplessness and near-destruction to salvation, restored happiness, and, as forecast by the Dioscuri, redemption from death, reveal the vicissitudes of ever-changing Fortune more than they do the triumph of a coherent moral order.

Helen is one of nine plays that have survived not because they were selected by Byzantine schoolmasters as exemplary texts, but as part of a single papyrus scroll, preserved by random chance, from an alphabetically arranged collection of Euripides' plays. It stands today as a reminder that Athenian "tragedy" had many different tones, timbres, and techniques. In some cases, especially in the late plays of Euripides, the pity and fear that (according to Aristotle) gave the highest tragic pleasure took a backseat to other kinds of enjoyment: exotic locales, reunions of long-parted lovers, and the timeless thrill of a narrow escape from peril.

HELEN

Translated by Emily Wilson

I have used the text printed in William Allen's edition (Cambridge: Green and Yellow, 2008) and have been much helped by his commentary; I have also consulted the edition by Peter Burian (Aris and Philips, 2007).

CAST OF CHARACTERS (IN ORDER OF APPEARANCE)

HELEN, wife of Menelaus
TEUCER, a Greek hero from Salamis
CHORUS of Greek maidens
MENELAUS, king of Sparta
SERVANT
THEONOË, priestess and sister of Theoclymenos
THEOCLYMENUS, ruler of Egypt
MESSENGER
CASTOR and POLLUX, semidivine brothers of Helen (also known as the Dioscuri)

Setting: The play takes place in front of the palace of Theoclymenos, ruler of
Egypt.

HELEN: So beautiful, so chaste! This river Nile
    waters the plain of Egypt with white snow
    instead of rain from heaven. Long ago
    when Proteus was alive, he ruled this land,
    <—living in Pharos, but the king of Egypt—>*
    and married one of the maidens of the sea,
    Psamathe, when she left Aeacus' bed.†
    She bore two children in this house: a boy,
    named Theoclymenos,‡ and a noble girl,   10
    named Belle§—her mother's joy when she was small.
    But since she's reached the age when girls get married,
    they call her Theonoë, since she knows
    the gods, and all that is and is to come,¶
    a power inherited from Nereus.**

        And as for me, my country, too, is famous.
    I come from Sparta; Tyndareus was my father.
    There is another story—if it's true,
    that Zeus became a swan and flew disguised,
    chased by an eagle, into my mother's bed,   20
    and tricking Leda, he achieved his end.
    I am named Helen. I would like to tell
    the things I've suffered. Once, for the sake of beauty,

---

* This line is probably an interpolation, inserted by somebody who wanted to reconcile this play with the *Odyssey*, in which Proteus lives on Pharos (*Odyssey* 4.354–57). Proteus in Homer is a shape-shifting sea god, but here, as in Herodotus, he is depicted as a human king.

† The marriage of Psamathe to a mortal hero, Aeacus, is attested in Hesiod (*Theogony* 1003–5); her later marriage to Proteus may be Euripides' invention (and hints at the fact that other wives are not necessarily as loyal to their first husbands as Helen herself).

‡ There is an interpolated clause here that reads "because he lived his life honoring the gods."

§ Or "Beauty."

¶ The name suggests "divine knowledge."

** Nereus, a sea god and father of Psamathe, was known for his justice and his skill in prophecy.

three goddesses met Paris in the cave
on Ida, so that he could judge their looks:
Hera, Aphrodite, and Athena.*
My beauty was what Aphrodite offered—
if curses count as beauty—and she won,
by promising him me. So Paris left
his cowsheds and arrived in Sparta, seeking   30
my bed.† But Hera, hating having lost,
turned my affair with Paris into wind.
She gave king Priam's son an empty image,
not me but something like me, made of air
but breathing. So he thought that he had me,
but it was just an empty false appearance.
The plans of Zeus in turn brought further trouble.
He set the Greeks at war with those poor, suffering
people of Troy. He hoped to lighten earth,
our mother, weighted down by all these humans,   40
and bring renown to the best man of Greece.
So "I"—not I, my name—was made the prize,
a gift for Greeks, a test for Trojan valor.
Hermes concealed me in the folds of air,
with clouds for blankets, since Zeus cared for me.
He set me in this house of Proteus,
picking the most self-disciplined of humans,
to save the purity of my marriage-bed
for Menelaus. That is why I'm here,
while my poor husband's gathered up an army,   50
to hunt for my abduction off in Troy.‡
And by Scamander's streams, so many souls
have died for me. I'm cursed: it looks as if
I cheated on my husband and I caused
a massive war for Greece! That's what I suffer.
Why am I still alive? Because I heard
Hermes—who knew I never went to Troy—
say I would live again in famous Sparta

---

* Athena is not named in the original, but defined as "the Zeus-born virgin."
† The word for "bed" also connotes marriage.
‡ The odd phrasing whereby Menelaus hunts for Helen's "abduction" rather than "Helen" is in the original.

with my own man—if I keep faith with him.*
As long as Proteus saw the light of day,   60
my bed was safe. But now he's dead, dark earth
covers his body, and his son is hunting
to marry me. I'm here to throw myself
on Proteus' tomb. I'm praying to save myself
for my original husband, whom I honor.
Even if my name is smirched through Greece,
my body never will be tainted here.

TEUCER: Who has control of this strong citadel?
This is a regal palace, fit for Plutus,†
with all its splendid cornices and walls.   70
        (seeing Helen)
Hey!
O gods, what's this? It looks like that most hated
murderess, of me and all the Greeks.
May the gods curse you, counterfeit of Helen!
If I were not on foreign earth, you'd die
by my unerring arrow,‡ as reward
for looking so much like that child of Zeus.

HELEN: Poor man! Who are you? Why do you turn from me,
and hate me for that woman's circumstances?

TEUCER: Sorry! I lost my temper, I was wrong.   80
You know all Greece hates Zeus's daughter, lady.
So please forgive me for the things I said.

HELEN: Where did you travel from? And who are you?

TEUCER: I'm one of those most wretched Greeks, my lady.

HELEN: It's not surprising, then, that you hate Helen.
But who exactly are you? What's your name?

TEUCER: I'm Teucer, the son of Telamon; the country
that bore and nourished me was Salamis.

HELEN: Then why did you come here, beside the Nile?

TEUCER: I'm wandering in exile from my home.   90

HELEN: Poor you! Who drove you from your fatherland?

TEUCER: My father, Telamon! My next of kin!

---

* Literally, "if I do not make the bed for anybody," a euphemism for sharing another man's bed.

† The god of wealth. But there is also a hint of Pluton (Pluto), an alternative name for Hades, god of the Underworld; the two are often confused.

‡ Teucer was known for his skill in archery.

HELEN: But why? What kind of trouble made this happen?

TEUCER: My brother Ajax' death in Troy destroyed me.

HELEN: You surely didn't kill him with your sword?

TEUCER: No, no, he leapt on his own sword, himself.

HELEN: Had he gone mad? No sane man would do this.

TEUCER: Well—do you know of someone named Achilles?

HELEN: Yes!

He once came courting Helen—so I've heard.

TEUCER: In death, his friends competed for his arms.* 100

HELEN: But why did that hurt Ajax? TEUCER: Someone else
attained the armor, and he killed himself.

HELEN: So you are sick because of what he suffered.

TEUCER: Yes, and because I did not die with him.

HELEN: Stranger, did you go to Troy? TEUCER: I did
but I myself was ruined, when we sacked it.

HELEN: Is Troy already burned down to the ground?

TEUCER: Yes, you could hardly see a trace of walls.

HELEN: Poor Helen! It's through you the Trojans died.

TEUCER: And through the Greeks! Great wrongs have been committed. 110

HELEN: When was the city sacked? How long ago?

TEUCER: It's almost seven harvest-times since then.

HELEN: And how much more time did you spend in Troy?

TEUCER: So many moons! We stayed there ten long years.

HELEN: And did you ever take the Spartan woman?

TEUCER: Yes, Menelaus dragged her by the hair.

HELEN: Did you see that poor girl, or is it rumor?

TEUCER: I saw her face to face, as I see you.

HELEN: Was it an apparition from the gods?

TEUCER: Let's change the subject—no more talk of her! 120

HELEN: But can you trust this sighting? Was it her?

TEUCER: I saw her with my own eyes, and my mind.

HELEN: Is she already home with Menelaus?

TEUCER: No, he's not yet in Argos, nor in Sparta.

HELEN: Oh, no! This is bad news, for some at least.

TEUCER: They say he's disappeared, with his wife.

HELEN: But didn't all the Greeks sail back together?

---

* After Achilles' death, his mother, Thetis, proposed that his allies should compete to win his armor
(which had been forged by the god Hephaestus). Odysseus won. The story was dramatized by Aeschylus.

TEUCER: Yes, but a storm sent them all different ways.
HELEN: In which particular part of the salty sea?
TEUCER: Just as they crossed the middle of the Aegean.　　　　130
HELEN: And since then, no one's heard of Menelaus?
TEUCER: No, and the word in Greece is that he's dead.
HELEN: I'm done for!—What about the child of Thestius?
TEUCER: Leda, you mean? She's definitely dead.
HELEN: Was it—I hope not!—Helen's shame that killed her?
TEUCER: It was. She wound a noose around her neck.
HELEN: And what about her sons? Alive, or dead?
TEUCER: They're dead, and not dead. There's a double story.*
HELEN: How terrible! Which story is the best?
TEUCER: They say they're gods, transformed to look like stars.†　　140
HELEN: That's good! But what about the other story?
TEUCER: They killed themselves for what their sister did.
　　Enough! I have no wish to weep again.
　　I traveled to this palace here to see
　　the prophetess: her name is Theonoë.
　　Please introduce me, so she can divine
　　which way I ought to turn my sails to catch
　　a fair wind on to Cyprus, where Apollo
　　foretold that I should live, and name the island
　　in honor of my homeland: Salamis.‡　　　　150
HELEN: Stranger, the journey will reveal itself.
　　But you must leave this land, before you're seen
　　by Proteus' son, the king. He is away,
　　hunting wild animals with his faithful hounds.
　　He kills all Greeks that come here, if he finds them.
　　Don't ask the reason why: I will not tell you,
　　since if I did, what good could it do you?
TEUCER: Thank you, my lady. May the gods reward
　　your kindness with the gifts that you deserve.
　　Your body is like Helen's, but your heart　　160

---

* Helen's brothers, Castor and Pollux, the sons of Leda and Tyndareus (one of whom, Pollux, is sometimes said to have been the son of Zeus) are the Dioscuri, who were sometimes represented as mortal, sometimes as immortal, and often as taking turns with having immortality—one would be alive while the other was dead, and then they would trade.

† The brothers became the constellation Gemini (the Twins).

‡ The idea is that Cypriot Salamis is named for the Salamis in Attica.

is very different, not at all alike.
May she die, and never reach the banks
of the Eurotas. But to you, good luck!
HELEN: I'm overwhelmed by grief. How can I sing
to match my pain? What muse can I discover
for wails and keening, tears and lamentation?

strophe 1

Fly to me on your wings
young daughters of the Earth,
Sirens, bring to my cries of mourning
a Libyan oboe or pipes   170
to harmonize with my grief.
Tune your tears to mine and sing my songs,
match your melody to my lament,
so that the Queen of Death, Persephone,
may gain a gift from me
of a tearful hymn
to the dead.

antistrophe 1

CHORUS: Beside the dark blue water   180
I was drying purple clothes
out on the tangled grasses
in the golden sunlight
by the sprouting reeds.
There I heard a dreadful wailing,
a sad song that no lyre could play,
that once a girl was screaming,
wailing like a Naiad,
crying a song of grief
as she runs away across the mountains,
then screeches in the rocky caves,
as Pan is raping her.   190

strophe 2

HELEN: Women of Greece!
Hunted and captured by the oars of barbarians!
Somebody came, an Achaean, a sailor,
and brought to me tears and more tears.
The ruins of Troy
now belong to the enemy's fire,

and I am the killer of many,
my name is the cause of the pain,
and Leda is dead,
she hung from a noose,   200
in despair at my shame.
And my husband has wandered all over the sea,
and is finally dead and gone,
and the light of my homeland, my brothers the twins,
Castor and Pollux,
are not to be seen, they have vanished,
leaving the plains that once shook with their horse-hoofs,
leaving the training arena beside the reedy Eurotas,
where they exercised once in their youth.   210

antistrophe 2

CHORUS: My lady, what you have suffered,
from the griefs caused by fate and the gods!
The life you received is like no life at all.
Down through the air, Zeus dazzled on wings
of a snowy white swan, and he fathered you.
You've had every misfortune,
endured every pain life could bring.
Your mother is gone,
your beloved twin brothers, the children of Zeus,   220
have no happiness,
and you can't see your homeland.
It's rumored, my lady, all through the cities
that you will be handed to barbarian beds,
and your own man is dead
in the salt and the waves,
and he'll never again bring joy to the palace
of home, or bronze-plated Athena.*

epode

HELEN: (*weeping*)
What man of Asia
or who from the country of Greece   230
cut the pine

---

* The temple of Athena in Sparta was plated with bronze.

that brought tears to Troy?
From that wood Priam's son
made the boat of destruction
and sailed with barbarian oarsmen
to my home and my hearth
on a quest for the curse of my beauty,
to take me as wife,
and with him sailed Aphrodite, the trickster, the killer,
who brought death to the Greeks.
I've had so much bad luck!   240
But Hera, Queen Hera, whom Zeus holds in his arms,
on her golden throne
sent swift-footed Hermes,
the child of Maia.
I was gathering fresh roses
in my dress, to go
to bronze-plated Athena.
He seized me and took me
through the air to this bad land,
and created the conflict, the war and the misery,
setting the Greeks against the children of Priam.
So my name has a false reputation   250
by the streams of the Simois.

CHORUS: You're suffering. I know that. Still you should
bear life's necessities as best you can.

HELEN: Why am I partnered with bad luck? Dear friends,
since birth I've been an odd anomaly.
A woman who was neither Greek nor foreign,
Leda, produced an egg, with Zeus as father,
or so they say: a pouch of chicks, all white.
A weird beginning! My whole life's been strange,
because of Hera, and because of beauty.   260
I wish I could go back to being ugly,
my beauty wiped away from me like paint.
I wish the Greeks forgot my misadventures
and only kept good thoughts of me in mind.
It's hard to face it when the gods have hurt us
even one time—but once is bearable.
I'm tangled up in multiple misfortunes.
First, I'm dishonored—though I've done no wrong.   270

It's worse than really being bad, to suffer
the punishment for things you never did.
Second, the gods transferred me from my country,
into this alien culture. Now deprived
of friends, I've lost my freedom: I'm a slave!
Among barbarians, all are slaves but one.
My fortunes hung upon a single anchor:
my husband, who might someday come to save me.
But now he's dead and I have no more hope.
My mother's dead, and I her murderer—   280
wrongly so called, and yet that wrong is mine.
My daughter, too, our household's pride and mine,
is growing gray without a man, still virgin,
and my twin brothers, so-called sons of Zeus
are dead. I've had bad luck of every kind
and died in circumstance, though not in fact.
The worst of all is this: if I went home
to Sparta, they would bolt the gates against me,
thinking that I was Helen back from Troy
without my Menelaus. If he'd lived
we would have known each other by the signs   290
that no one else knows. That won't happen now:
he's lost forever. Why do I go on living?
What is my future? Shall I escape my troubles
by marriage with a foreigner, and sit
at his rich table? No! A husband who
disgusts his wife, makes even her body revolting.
<It's best to die; but how can I die well?
It's shameful to suspend yourself in air,
by hanging—even slaves look down upon it.   300
Cutting your throat is dignified and fine,
and quick—it doesn't take too long to die.>*
This is how far I've sunk in suffering!
Since other women benefit from beauty,
but beauty is the thing that ruined me.

CHORUS: Helen, do not assume this man, this stranger,
whoever he may be, told all the truth.

HELEN: Well, but he clearly said my husband's dead.

---

* These lines, though enjoyably inappropriate in context, are generally believed to be an interpolation.

CHORUS: Clear declarations often turn out false.

HELEN: And conversely, sometimes those words are true.   310

CHORUS: You always seem to be expecting trouble.

HELEN: Yes: dread surrounds me and I fear the worst.

CHORUS: What is your attitude to those inside?

HELEN: All friends—except the one who hunts my hand.

CHORUS: Here's what you do: first leave the tomb's protection.

HELEN: What are you telling me? Where is this going?

CHORUS: Go in the house and ask Theonoë,
    the sea-nymph's daughter, who knows everything,
    about your husband—if he's still alive
    or if he's left the light. And when you know,   320
    rejoice or weep, according to the facts.
    Until you know the truth, what is the use
    of grieving? No, just do as I have said.
    <So leave this tomb and go to meet the girl
    who'll tell you everything. When you can see
    the truth inside the house, why look elsewhere?>*
    I also want to go inside with you,
    and hear the priestess speak, along with you,
    since women always ought to work together.

        (The dialogue now switches to lyric meter.)

    HELEN: Friends, I accept your advice.   330
        Come in, come into the house,
            to see what adventures
            I'll meet in these halls.

CHORUS: I want to! You don't need to tell me.

    HELEN: Oh, what a day! Oh, what I've been through!
        And after all this, what will I be told?
        A story of tears.

CHORUS: Don't grieve in advance, my love:
        no need to be prophet of pain.

    HELEN: What has my poor husband endured?   340
        Is he still seeing the light and the chariot of the sun,
        and the pathways of stars?
        Or has his time arrived at last, and does he lie
        among the dead, below the earth?

---

* These lines, which merely repeat what has already been said, are probably an interpolation.

CHORUS: Just hope for the best,
   whatever that is.
HELEN: I call on you, I swear by you,
   Eurotus, green with water reeds,   350
   if this report is true,
   my husband's really dead,
   then what's so difficult to understand?
   I'll stretch a noose of death
   around my neck,
   or with a sword I'll seek to die,
   slaughtered as the blood pours from my throat:
   I'll drive the iron inside my flesh, to win
   the game of death—a sacrifice to them,
   that triple team of goddesses, and to the son of Priam,   360
   who sat there on that day, beside his cattle-pens
   beneath Mount Ida.
CHORUS: May your troubles turn away!
   I wish you better luck.
HELEN: O, Troy! Unhappy city, ruined
   through deeds that were not done: how terribly you suffered.
   My gifts from Aphrodite bore
   so much blood, so much weeping,
   grief on grief and pain on pain.
   Mothers lost their children,
   girls cut their hair
   for their dead brothers
   beside the waters of the Scamander.
   The land of Greece cried out and keened   370
   with wails and lamentation.
   They beat their faces, and ripped their tender cheeks
   with fingernails that scraped
   till they were wet with blood.
   You lucky girl, Callisto! Long ago
   you left the bed of Zeus on all four paws, a bear!
   More fortunate than me,*
   since you got free of sorrow

---

* I omit line 379, which is a nonsensical interpolation reading "with violent eye the shape of a lioness."

through the shape of that shaggy bear.*
Lucky, too, the Titan child of Merops.†   380
Artemis drove her from the dance, transformed
into a doe with golden horns—because of her beauty.
But mine: my lovely body ruined, yes, it ruined
the citadel of Troy, and those damned Greeks.

    (Enter Menelaus.)

MENELAUS: O Pelops! In that famous chariot race
    in Pisa, when you raced with Oenomaus,
    <after you served as food to feast the gods,>‡
    if only you had died that very day,
    before you fathered Atreus, my father,   390
    who had two famous sons by Aerope:
    Menelaus—me!—and Agamemnon.
    I think, and I'm not boasting here, I led
    the greatest army in that fleet to Troy.
    I was no tyrant leading them by force;
    I led those Greek young men as volunteers.
    Now we can count the numbers of the dead,
    and those who made it safely from the sea
    are bringing home the names of those who died.
    But I've been lost upon the surging waves   400
    of gray and salty ocean, since the time
    I sacked the towers of Troy. I long for home,
    but I don't think the gods will grant my wish.
    I've sailed to all the ports of Libya
    and found no welcome. When I'm near my country
    winds always blow me back; no friendly breeze
    puffs in my sail to let me reach my homeland.
    And now I'm shipwrecked. I have lost my friends.
    I've washed up here; against the rocks, my ship
    was smashed to millions of smithereens.   410
    Only the keel was left of that fine structure,
    on which I barely managed to survive
    along with Helen—whom I dragged from Troy.

---

* Callisto was a human girl who was seduced or raped by Zeus and then transformed into a bear.

† This story is only attested here. Apparently the daughter of Merops was changed into a deer by Artemis.

‡ This line is likely an interpolation.

I do not know the name of where I am,
or who lives here—I am ashamed to meet them,
because they'll see the shabby clothes I'm wearing.
I want to hide my history: I'm embarrassed.
It's worse to fall from happiness to pain
than always be unlucky—then it's normal.
But I'm in desperate straits. I have no food   420
and nothing good to wear. That's obvious,
since I am wrapped in rags ripped from the wreck.
The ocean seized my clothes: my bright white cloak
and royal robes are gone. I hid my wife,
who started all this trouble, in a cave.
I forced my comrades, those that still survived,
to guard my marriage bed from further harm.
I'm traveling alone; I hope to find
provisions I can take back to my friends.
Look at this palace! What fine walls and friezes!   430
What splendid gates! A rich man must live here.
From such a wealthy house it seems quite likely
that I'll get something for my men. The poor
can't help me even if they wanted to.
       Hey there! Is there a guard? Come out, and tell
the people in the house about my troubles!
       (Enter Old Woman.)
OLD WOMAN: Who's at the gate? Be off, don't linger there,
     beside our courtyard entrance! You'll annoy
     my masters. If you stay, you'll die! You're Greek.
     No Greeks are welcome in my masters' home.   440
MENELAUS: Old woman, there's no need to talk so roughly.
     I'm listening to you. Don't get riled up.
OLD WOMAN: Away with you, you foreigner! My job
     is to keep Greeks from coming near this house.
MENELAUS: Whoa there! Don't threaten me! No fists! Don't shove me!
OLD WOMAN: It's your fault. You're not listening to me.
MENELAUS: Just go inside and say this to your masters—
OLD WOMAN: If I did that it would be worse for you.
MENELAUS: A shipwrecked stranger should be seen as sacred.
OLD WOMAN: Go to another house! You can't stay here.   450
MENELAUS: I need to get inside. Do what I say!
OLD WOMAN: You are a nuisance! We'll soon shove you out.

MENELAUS: I'm lost! Where is my famous army now?

OLD WOMAN: Were you important somewhere? Here, you're not.

MENELAUS: Oh, god! It isn't fair, this disrespect!

OLD WOMAN: Why are you crying? Who would pity you?

MENELAUS: Because I used to have so much good luck.

OLD WOMAN: Then why not leave? Your friends can watch you cry.

MENELAUS: What is this place? Is this a royal palace?

OLD WOMAN: The house of Proteus. The land is Egypt.   460

MENELAUS: Egypt? Oh, no! Is that where I have sailed to?

OLD WOMAN: The sparkling Nile: what's wrong with it, to you?

MENELAUS: I wasn't criticizing. I'm just sad.

OLD WOMAN: Well, so are lots of people, not just you.

MENELAUS: Is there a person here that you call master?

OLD WOMAN: This is his tomb. His son now rules the land.

MENELAUS: Where might he be? Inside, or is he out?

OLD WOMAN: He's out. And anyway, he hates all Greeks.

MENELAUS: Then might I learn the reason for this hatred?

OLD WOMAN: Helen the child of Zeus is in this house.   470

MENELAUS: She what? What do you mean? Say that again!

OLD WOMAN: The child of Tyndareus, the girl from Sparta.

MENELAUS: But when? My wife was stolen from the cave?

OLD WOMAN: It was before the Greeks arrived in Troy.
　　Now, stranger, leave the house. We're busy here—
　　there's trouble in the palace at the moment.
　　You came at a bad time, and if the master
　　catches you, you'll be killed. And there's your welcome!   480
　　I personally am friendly to the Greeks;
　　I spoke like this because I fear my master.
　　　　　(Exit Old Woman.)

MENELAUS: What shall I say? Or do? I'm hearing things
　　that pile on top of all my former pain.
　　Since if I seized my wife from Troy, and brought her
　　with me and kept her guarded in a cave,
　　some other woman must be living here,
　　who's not my wife, but just the same in name.
　　The woman said she was the child of Zeus.
　　Is there some man who has the name of Zeus   490
　　beside the Nile? There's only one in heaven.
　　Is there a Sparta somewhere else, not just

beside the reedy waters of Eurotas?
There's only one man named Tyndareus.
Is there another country that's called Sparta,
and Troy? I don't know what to say! I guess
the world is large, and many men must have
the same names. Also cities. Also women.
There's nothing so surprising about that.
I won't be put off by that slave's threats;   500
no man is so barbaric in his mind
as not to give me food, hearing my name.
My name is known across the world, because
of Troy's great fire—that Menelaus lit.
I'll wait to see the king. I have two ways
of staying safe. If he's a savage man
I'll hide myself and go back to the wreck.
But if he's gentle I will ask for things
to help me in my present time of need.
This is the lowest depth of all my troubles: 510
being a king, to have to beg for food
to stay alive, from other kings. I have to!
There is a saying, not mine but it's good:
nothing is stronger than necessity.

    CHORUS: I heard from the oracle girl
        what I hoped I would learn when I went to the palace:
        Menelaus has not yet
        been covered in earth.
        He has not gone down through the shadows of darkness;
        he's still on the waves of the sea.   520
        He hasn't yet come to the harbors
        of his homeland, exhausted
        by wandering, begging,
        unhappy and friendless,
        traveling to all kinds of places,
        as he rows on the ocean
        away from the land of Troy.
        (Enter Helen.)

HELEN: Here I am, back beside this tomb. I've got
    good news from Theonoë: and she always
    knows the whole truth. She says he's still alive!   530

My husband sees the light! It shines on him!
She says he's drifted over many seas,
all over everywhere, worn out by wandering,
but when his trouble's over, he'll come here.
One thing she didn't say: if he'll survive.
I didn't ask if she could clarify;
I was too happy hearing he'd survived.
She said he's somewhere near this land; he's shipwrecked,
with just a few companions. O, my husband!
When will you come? I'd be so glad to see you!   540
     (She sees Menelaus.)
But who is this? Has that unholy son
of Proteus made plans to ambush me?
I'll canter like a foal or like a maenad
to clutch the altar! This man looks so rough,
so wild, as if he's on the hunt to seize me.

MENELAUS: You there! Wait up! Stop all that desperate struggle
   to reach the base and pillars of the tomb
   and its burnt offerings! Why are you running?
   Your looks gave me a shock. In fact, I'm speechless!

HELEN: Women! It's criminal! He's keeping me   550
   from getting to the tomb! He wants to give me
   in marriage to that tyrant! I don't want it!

MENELAUS: I'm not a kidnapper. Nor sent by bad guys.

HELEN: And anyway, your clothes are very dirty.

MENELAUS: Stop, don't be scared, no need to dart away.

HELEN: I'll stand here, since I'm touching this safe tomb.

MENELAUS: Who are you, woman? Who is this I see?

HELEN: And who are you? Our questions are the same.

MENELAUS: I never saw a woman more like her.

HELEN: Gods! It's a god, to recognize one's love!   560

MENELAUS: Are you a Hellene? Or a native here?

HELEN: I am Hellenic. And what about you?

MENELAUS: I never saw a woman so like Helen!

HELEN: And you're like Menelaus! I can't speak.

MENELAUS: You're right, I am that poor, unlucky man.

HELEN: At last you're here! Come here, to your wife's arms!

MENELAUS: What kind of "wife"? Get your hands off my cloak.

HELEN: My father Tyndareus gave me to you.

MENELAUS: Light-bearing Hecate, send gentle ghosts!

HELEN: I'm not a nightmare vision. You can see me!　570
MENELAUS: But surely I'm not husband to *two* wives?
HELEN: What other woman has you as her husband?
MENELAUS: The one I brought from Troy. She's in the cave.
HELEN: You have no other wife. It's only me.
MENELAUS: I can't be thinking straight. It's mental illness.
HELEN: Look at me. Don't you see? I am your wife!
MENELAUS: Your body's similar, but nothing's certain.
HELEN: Just look! What could be clearer proof than this?
MENELAUS: You do look like her. I won't argue there.
HELEN: What better teacher for you than your eyes?　580
MENELAUS: I don't get this: I have another wife!
HELEN: I didn't go to Troy. That was a phantom.
MENELAUS: Who manufactures living, seeing bodies?
HELEN: The gods made you a woman out of air.
MENELAUS: Which god? Your story is improbable.
HELEN: Hera, so Paris wouldn't take me, swapped me.
MENELAUS: But how? So you were here, and in Troy, too?
HELEN: Names can be everywhere. A body, not.
MENELAUS: I've had enough of trouble. Let me go!
HELEN: You're leaving me? For It? That emptiness?　590
MENELAUS: Yes. Have a good one, since you look like Helen.
HELEN: Disaster! I found you, but not as husband.
MENELAUS: My pain at Troy persuades me. You do not.
HELEN: Oh, who has ever suffered more than me?
 My loved ones leave me, and I'll never come
 to my own country, where the Hellenes live.
   (Enter Servant.)
SERVANT: I've found you, Menelaus! I've been searching
 all over this here foreign land for you,
 sent by your men, the ones you left behind.
MENELAUS: What? Did barbarians rob you? No!　600
SERVANT: It's a mistake. That word's too small for this.
MENELAUS: Tell me. Your haste suggests you bring big news.
SERVANT: I'll tell you how your work was all for nothing.
MENELAUS: Those are old tears. But what's the news you bring?
SERVANT: Your wife is gone, into the folds of sky.
 She's taken. She's invisible. She's hidden,
 in heaven. She has left the holy cave
 where we were guarding her. She said: "Poor Trojans!

and Greeks who died for me beside the banks
of the Scamander, all through Hera's schemes.   610
Paris, you thought, had Helen. He did not.
I stayed as long as I was meant to stay,
and now I'm going back, to Sky, my father.
I've served my destiny." Poor Helen got a
bad reputation she did not deserve.

> *(Seeing Helen)*

    Oh, hello, Leda's daughter. So you're here?
I was just telling how you'd gone away
to nestle with the stars! I didn't know
that you could fly. But you won't trick us twice!
I won't allow it! You've caused trouble enough,   620
at Troy, both for your husband and his allies.

MENELAUS: Well, what do you know! Her words have turned out true!
    This is the day of happiness I longed for,
    when I can take my Helen in my arms.*

HELEN: (*singing*)† Oh, my darling! My dearest of men, Menelaus!
    It's been such a long time! But now what a joy!
    Women, I'm so happy! I have my husband back.
    I get to wrap my loving arms around him,
    after so many suns have spent their light.

MENELAUS: Me, too! I have so many things to say!   630
    I don't know where to start right now.

HELEN: I am so glad, my eyes are wet with tears.
    My hair is prickling up on end like feathers!
    Husband, what joy it is
    to throw my arms around you.

MENELAUS: It's so good to see you! I can't blame you!
    I have you, my own wife, the child of Zeus and Leda.‡

HELEN: Beneath the marriage torches, my brothers, on white horses,
    blessed me, yes, they blessed me.   640

MENELAUS: The past is gone. The god once took you away from me,

---

* There is a partial pun in the original, since the word for "arms" sounds a little like "Helen."

† The dialogue now switches to lyric meter, primarily dochmiac. This passage is unique in Greek tragedy in featuring a male singer participating in a lyric duet: in other cases, the female character sings while the male character speaks.

‡ The text of this line is corrupt.

but leads you now to a different life,
a better future.

HELEN: A piece of good bad luck brought us together,
husband. It took a while. But now, let me enjoy it!

MENELAUS: Yes, be happy! I pray the same as you.
We two are a team: if one is sad, so is the other.

HELEN: (*to the Chorus*) Friends! Friends!
No longer will I grieve or cry about the past.
I have him! I've got him! My husband! My husband!   650
I waited and waited so many long years for him to come back from
    Troy.

MENELAUS: You have me and I have you. I have lived through
so many dawns of suffering, but now I see the light:
it was the goddess. Now my tears
are more for joy than sorrow.

HELEN: What can I say? Whoever would have guessed it!
So unexpectedly, I hold you close.

MENELAUS: And I hold you: the wife I thought had gone
to Ida's city and to poor Troy's towers.
But by the gods, how did you leave my house?   660

HELEN: Don't, no! You're going back to the terrible beginning.
No, don't! You're asking for a story that hurts too much.

MENELAUS: Tell me! I have to hear. This all comes from the gods.

HELEN: Curse that story
which I'm about to tell.

MENELAUS: But tell it anyway! It's sweet to hear of sorrow.

HELEN: The ship didn't fly to the bed
of that foreign young man.
My desire didn't fly to adultery.

MENELAUS: What spirit or what fate took you from your homeland?

HELEN: Husband, it was the child of Zeus and Maia   670
who brought me here to the Nile.

MENELAUS: Amazing! Who sent him? An extraordinary story!

HELEN: I cannot stop crying, my eyes are a flood of tears,
since I was destroyed by the wife of Zeus.

MENELAUS: Hera? But what was her motive in doing us harm?

HELEN: A curse on the baths and the springs
where the goddesses sparkled their beauty,
then went to the Judgment!

MENELAUS: But why did that Judgment cause Hera to hurt you?*

HELEN: To take me from Paris—

MENELAUS: But why? Tell me that.   680

HELEN: Because Aphrodite had promised me to him.

MENELAUS: Oh, poor you!

HELEN: Poor me indeed! So that's why she brought me to Egypt.

MENELAUS: I hear what you're saying: she gave me a phantom in
     exchange.

HELEN: And Mother! What you've suffered!
     O, my home!

MENELAUS: What's this?

HELEN: My mother is dead. She hanged herself, twisting
     the rope round her neck, in shame at my ruined marriage.

MENELAUS: I'm sorry. And is there news of our daughter, Hermione?

HELEN: Husband, she is unmarried, she has no children.
     She's mourning for my marriage—my non-marriage.   690

MENELAUS: Paris sacked my whole house, top to bottom.

HELEN: The situation ruined you, and countless
     bronze-armored Greeks.
     God cast me out from my home, away from my city, away from you,
     accursed and doomed,
     when I left my house and my bed—though I didn't leave!—
     for that wicked adultery.

CHORUS:† If in the future all your luck is good,
     that would be recompense for this bad past.

SERVANT: You two! Menelaus! Give me, too,   700
     the joy I see but don't yet understand.

MENELAUS: Yes, old man! You can share the news with us.

SERVANT: This woman didn't cause the war in Troy?‡

MENELAUS: No. The gods tricked us. In our arms we held
     an image made of cloud—the source of ruin.

SERVANT: We suffered for no reason? For a *cloud*?

MENELAUS: Yes. Hera did it, and that goddess contest.

SERVANT: Then is this really her? Is this your wife?

---

* The Greek text of this line is problematic, but its general sense seems clear.

† The meter reverts now to regular iambic trimeter, the dialogue rhythm.

‡ The word used for "one who causes"—*brabeus*—is here used in a unique sense: it usually suggests the umpire of a contest or competition.

MENELAUS: It's her. Believe me when I tell you this.   710
SERVANT: Daughter! How complicated, hard to read
 the gods are; how they turn things upside-down!
 They whirl things round, I guess. One person suffers,
 another doesn't, but then gets destroyed.
 There's never constancy in present luck.
 You and your husband had your share of troubles:
 he suffered from the war, and you from words.
 His work was all for nothing. Now he's got
 the greatest blessings, with no work at all.
 You didn't shame your father or your brothers,   720
 or do the things that you were said to do.
 I'm thinking of your wedding songs again,
 remembering the torches that I held,
 running beside the four-horsed chariot.
 As this man's bride you left your happy home.
 A servant who won't share his masters' lives,
 joy in their joy and suffer in their pain,
 is bad! By birth I'm just a hired hand;
 but count me with the slave gentility.
 My mind is free although my name is not.   730
 Better to have one evil thing than both:
 either be base and wicked in your heart,
 or be obedient to other people.
MENELAUS: Old man, we've been through many things together:
 shields side by side we stood, we strove, we suffered.
 Now share my good luck, too: go tell my comrades,
 the ones who still survive, what I've discovered,
 and my good fortune. Tell them to wait there
 beside the shore, to see how things turn out
 in all the challenges that I still face,   740
 trying to steal this woman out of Egypt.
 Watch for a way that we can get together
 and manage to escape these foreigners.
SERVANT: I will, my master.—As for prophecy,
 it's useless, full of lies! I see that now.
 There's nothing solid in the flash of fire
 or in the cries of birds. In fact, it's stupid
 even to think that birds would help us humans.

Calchas said nothing, made no sign at all,
when he could see us dying for a cloud. 750
Neither did Helenus. The town was sacked
for nothing. You may say, it was Zeus's will.
Then why do we prophesy? We ought to pray
only for blessings. Give up divination!
It's all a trick! No one gets rich from sitting
beside the prophet's fire and doing nothing.
Forethought and brains can tell the future best.

CHORUS: You're right. If you can keep the gods as friends,
that's the best kind of omen for the house. 760

HELEN: All right then: things so far are going well.
But my poor husband, how did you escape
from Troy? It does no good to know. And yet,
in love we crave to learn our loved one's pain.

MENELAUS: Your single question has so many answers.
Why tell who drowned in the Aegean Sea,
when Nauplius set the beacon-fires to wreck us?*
I trekked from Crete to Libya and on,
to Perseus' Tower.† Were I to fill you full
of words, I'd suffer as I told my troubles 770
as when I felt them—they'd hurt me twice over.

HELEN: You told me more already than I asked for.
So leave the rest aside: just tell me this—
how long you drifted on the salty sea.

MENELAUS: I spent ten years in Troy, and in addition
sailed round and round the sea for seven more.

HELEN: Oh, what a long time! You poor thing! And now,
escaping that, you've come here to your death.

MENELAUS: What's that? What did you say? You're killing me!

HELEN: Hurry and leave this land, quick as you can! 780
The master of the house is going to kill you.

---

* Nauplius was a Greek hero whose son, Palamedes, was killed by the Greeks through the machinations of Odysseus (since Palamedes had exposed the feigned madness whereby Odysseus tried to escape going to Troy). In retaliation against the Greeks as they returned from war, Nauplius lit fires on the rocky cliffs of Euboea, to lure their ships to be wrecked.

† The location of this watchtower is unknown. There was a Tower of Perseus in Egypt (Herodotus 2.15), but this is likely a different place, since Menelaus is supposed not to have been to Egypt before. The reference makes a link between this play and the *Andromeda*, which was performed in the same trilogy and which has Perseus as a main character.

MENELAUS: What did I do to earn this punishment?
HELEN: Your sudden coming here impedes my wedding.
MENELAUS: Who planned to marry you? This bed is mine!
HELEN: A rapist! I'd have had to suffer rape!
MENELAUS: A private citizen? Or this land's tyrant?
HELEN: The master of the land, the son of Proteus.
MENELAUS: That woman at the door—I get her riddle!
HELEN: What door? Which foreign gate excluded you?
MENELAUS: This one, when I was wandering as a beggar.   790
HELEN: Asking for food? Oh, no! Oh, this is awful!
MENELAUS: That's what I did, but let's not call it that.
HELEN: Now you know everything about my wedding.
MENELAUS: I don't know if you've stayed out of his bed.
HELEN: I'll tell you: I have kept my bed untouched.
MENELAUS: What proof is there? Though if it's true, I love it—
HELEN: You see my squalid camp beside this tomb?
MENELAUS: I see some nasty straw. What's that to you?
HELEN: It's where I'm praying, to escape his bed.
MENELAUS: Is there no altar? Is this a foreign custom?
HELEN: The tomb protected me just like a temple.   800
MENELAUS: So I can't take you home with me by ship?
HELEN: Your future is a sword, not bed with me.
MENELAUS: If so, I am the unhappiest of mortals!
HELEN: Then run away! You need not be embarrassed.
MENELAUS: And leave you? When I just sacked Troy for you?
HELEN: Better than let my marriage kill us both!
MENELAUS: It's cowardly! Unworthy of great Troy!
HELEN: Maybe you want to kill the king? You can't!
MENELAUS: Then can his body not be pierced by iron?   810
HELEN: Daring the impossible is stupid!
MENELAUS: I should say nothing, let my hands be bound?
HELEN: You're in a tricky place. You need a plan.
MENELAUS: Better to die in action than do nothing.
HELEN: There's just one possibility that might save us.
MENELAUS: Does it take money, courage, or smart words?
HELEN: If the king doesn't know that you've arrived—
MENELAUS: No one knows who I am! So who would tell him?
HELEN: He has inside an ally like a god.
MENELAUS: A voice that's nestled there inside the house?   820

HELEN: No, it's his sister. She's called Theonoë.

MENELAUS: A priestly name.* So tell me what she does.

HELEN: Well, she's omniscient. She'll tell him you're here.

MENELAUS: I'm dead then! It's impossible to hide!

HELEN: Perhaps if we beseech her, we'll persuade her!

MENELAUS: To do what? What's this hope you're building up to?

HELEN: Just not to tell her brother that you're here.

MENELAUS: If we persuade her, could we cross the border?

HELEN: Yes, easily, with her. In secret, never.

MENELAUS: You talk to her! One woman to another.   830

HELEN: Of course I'll do it, and I'll touch her knees.

MENELAUS: But if she turns us down, rejects our pleas?

HELEN: You'll die. And I'll be forced to marry him.

MENELAUS: Traitor! Your talk of force is all excuses!

HELEN: I swear a holy oath, on your own life!

MENELAUS: To what? To die? And never to remarry?

HELEN: I'll die by that same sword and lie beside you.

MENELAUS: On these conditions take my hand: let's shake!

HELEN: I promise, if you die, I'll leave the light.

MENELAUS: And if I lose you, I will end my life.   840

HELEN: How can we die an honorable death?

MENELAUS: I'll kill you on the tomb, then kill myself.
But first we'll struggle in a mighty contest.
The prize is: bed with you. Come one and all!
I will not shame the glory won from Troy,
nor when I come to Greece will I be shamed
—I who robbed Thetis of her son Achilles,
and watched when Ajax killed himself, and Nestor
losing his son.† Then shall I flinch to die,   850
for my own wife? I will not! If the gods
are wise, they will embrace with gentle earth
and burial, the man who dies with courage
in battle. But the coward they'll reject,
hurling him from the earth to barren rock.

---

* The name Theonoë suggests "god-mind" or "god-knowledge."

† Achilles was killed by Paris, by an arrow to the heel. Ajax killed himself after losing the armor of Achilles to Odysseus and being afflicted by madness in which he killed a flock of sheep under the delusion that they were Greeks (the subject of Sophocles' *Ajax*). Antilochus, son of Nestor, the oldest hero at Troy, was killed while trying to save his father's life in battle.

CHORUS: Gods, may the House of Tantalus, one day,
　　be happy! May their suffering have an end!
HELEN: It's just my luck! I seem to be accursed!
　　We're finished, Menelaus! Here she comes,
　　the priestess, Theonoë. I can hear
　　the clang of doors unlocking. Run away! 860
　　But what's the use? She must already know
　　that you are here, whether she comes or not.
　　Though you survived barbarian Troy, you'll die
　　upon a barbarous sword right here. I'm done for!
　　　(Enter Theonoë, with female attendants.)
THEONOË: *(to one of her servants)* You, lead the way, carry the burning lamp,
　　and fumigate the corners of the air,
　　our holy ritual, so we breath pure sky.
　　(to another servant) And you, make clean the path with fire, wherever
　　someone has marked it with unholy feet;
　　and tap the torch in front, so I may pass. 870
　　When we have paid the gods our usual service
　　take back the fire to the palace hearth.
　　(to Helen) So, Helen, what about my prophecies?
　　Your husband, Menelaus, is right here,
　　without his ships, without your replica.
　　Poor man! You've been through so much pain already,
　　and still don't know if you'll get home or not.
　　Today the gods will argue: they'll debate
　　about your future at the throne of Zeus.
　　Hera, who was your enemy before, 880
　　is kindly now, and wants your safe return
　　with Helen, so that Greece may know that Paris
　　was only falsely married by the gift
　　of Aphrodite. Aphrodite wants
　　to spoil your journey home, to save her face,
　　if it's revealed she bought the prize for beauty
　　for weddings with no pay-off, and no Helen.
　　It's up to me, whether she gets her wish:
　　either I tell my brother you are here,
　　and ruin you, or else I side with Hera,
　　and save your life by hiding you from him,
　　although his orders are that I must tell him 890

if ever you should travel to this land.

(*to one of the servants*) <Go tell my brother that this man is here,

so I can keep myself from any danger.>*

HELEN: (*kneeling in front of Theonoë and clasping her knees*)

Maiden! I fall as suppliant at your knees!

My situation here is miserable,

since I'm about to watch this poor man die,

when I just got him back after so long.

Don't tell your brother that my darling husband

is here and in my arms. Save him, I beg you!

Do not betray your holy piety,   900

buying your brother's favor at the price

of evil and injustice. God detests

brute force, and tells us all we must not sieze

possessions that belong to other people.†

The sky belongs to every human being,

as does the earth. We must not rob or steal

to fill our homes with other people's things.

Hermes whisked me up in time of need

and gave me to your father, to keep safe   910

for my own husband, who is here, and wants

to get me back. How can he, if he's dead?

And how can Proteus pay back living debts

to dead men? Think now of the gods, and think

of your father's wishes. Would they want

to give back neighbors' property, or not?

I think they would. Do not pay greater heed

to your rough brother than your noble father.

You are a priestess; you believe in gods.

If you betray your father's moral code   920

to please your wicked brother, it's a shame!

For you to know so much about religion,

the future and the present, yet not know

what's right and wrong! And as an extra favor,

---

* Many editors believe these two lines are an interpolation, since they seem out of character for the selfless Theonoë and do not seem to fit well with the lines before (when she is still undecided) and the lines after (when Helen does not react as if the revelation is definite).

† Line 905 in the original is skipped here since it is presumably an interpolation, being irrelevant and unmetrical. It reads: "If riches are not righteous, let them go!"

protect me! I am in most dreadful danger.
There's nobody who doesn't hate poor Helen.
In Greece they call me an adulteress,
who cheated on her husband and now lives
in Trojan palaces bedecked with gold.
But if I can go back, set foot in Sparta,
when people hear and see that all those deaths
were caused by machinations of the gods,   930
and that I never did betray my friends,
they'll give my good name back to me again!
I'll organize a wedding for my daughter
whom no one wants to marry now. No more
of grief and poverty. I'll get the goodness
of my own property in my own home.
If he'd been burnt to ash upon a pyre
in distant lands, I would have been content
to weep for him. How can I lose him now,
when he's alive and safe? No, maiden, please,
I beg you! Grant me this, and imitate   940
your worthy father's ways. The greatest honor
a child of a true nobleman can have
is to turn out exactly like the father.

CHORUS: The subject of your speech arouses pity,
and so do you. Now what will Menelaus
say, for his life? That's what I want to know.

MENELAUS: I will not kneel to supplicate, or weep.
I would not stoop to it, since it would shame
Troy, if I suddenly turned coward now.
They say it's proper for a well-born hero   950
to let his eyes shed tears in times of crisis.
This may be fine, but I refuse to do it:
I will maintain my fortitude instead.
I am a stranger and a guest: I ask
for my own wife back—as is right and proper.
If you agree, return her and save me.
If not, it would be nothing new to me:
I've suffered many times. But you'll reveal
your wickedness! I fall upon the tomb
of your own father, and I'll tell him what   960

will touch your heart: the justice I deserve.
(*addressing the tomb*) Old man, inhabitant of this stone grave,
I beg you, give me back my wife, whom Zeus
sent here to you, to keep her safe for me.
I know you'll never give her back: you're dead.
But still, I call on you below the earth:
your daughter's in control, and she will shrink
to taint her noble father's reputation.
And Hades down below, I call on you
to be my ally. With my sword I gave you   970
a wealth of fallen corpses, killed for Helen.
Either give back those men, alive again,
or make this girl give back my wife to me,
showing herself more pious than her father.
But if you rob me of my wife, I'll tell you
what Helen's speech left out. Just so you know,
priestess, we're bound by promises: the first
is that I'll fight a duel with your brother:
one of us two must die. Simple as that.
If he will not step up to fight, but hunts   980
by starving us, poor suppliants at this tomb,
we have a plan: I'll kill my wife, then drive
this sharp sword through my liver, on this mound,
so that our streams of blood may soak the grave.
Upon the polished marble we will lie,
coupled in death at least. We'll give you pain
forever, and bring shame upon your father.
Your brother's never going to marry her,
and nor is any other man. If I
can't bring her home, I'll take her down to death.   990
        (*He begins to cry.*)
No, I must stop this! If I start to cry,
just like a woman, I'll be pitiful,
not active. If you want to kill us, do it!
We'll die as heroes. Better yet, obey me,
then you'll be good, and I will get my wife.
CHORUS: Maiden, it's up to you to judge their words.
    Make a decision that will please us all.
THEONOË: Piety is my nature and my wish.

I care about myself, nor would I taint
my father's name. I will not help my brother 1000
with favors that dishonor me. I have
a mighty temple in my character,
to Justice, left to me by Nereus.
I'll always try to keep that temple safe.
If Hera wants to do you good, I add
my vote to hers. May Aphrodite look
gently on me, though I'm not on her team.
I hope to stay a virgin all my life.
I say the same to that aggressive speech
you hurled at Father's tomb. I would be wrong 1010
if I refused to give her back, since Father,
were he alive, would give you her, her you.
Everyone, those below and up on earth,
is punished when they sin. When people die
their mind is dead, but has an understanding
that lives forever in the immortal air.
In brief, I'll keep your prayers to me a secret;
I'll never join my brother in his folly.
I'll do him good, though he will not believe it, 1020
converting him to piety from sin.
You find a way to get out for yourselves;
I'll stand aside, and I will keep your secret.
Start with the gods, first pray to Aphrodite
to let this woman go back to her homeland;
pray Hera that her mind remain the same,
to save you and your husband. My dead father!
You have the noble name of holiness.
You'll never lose it, if it's up to me.

CHORUS: Justice never guarantees good fortune, 1030
but justice holds out hope of our salvation.

HELEN: The girl has done her part to save us, husband.
Now you must think things through and make a plan,
for both of us so we can get away.

MENELAUS: Then listen. You've been in that house a while,
and got to know the servants of the king.

HELEN: Why do you say this? What do you hope to do
that may be advantageous to us both?

MENELAUS: Could you persuade one of the men who drive
   the four-horse chariots, to give us one?   1040

HELEN: I'll try. But how would that help us escape?
   We do not know the land; it's foreign to us.

MENELAUS: That won't work then. What if I hide inside
   and kill the king with this, my sharp edged sword?

HELEN: His sister wouldn't stand for it—she'd talk,
   if you were making plans to kill her brother.

MENELAUS: But there's no ship in which we could escape.
   The one I used to have is out at sea.

HELEN: Listen, in case a woman can be smart.
   Do you want to die in word, but not in fact?   1050

MENELAUS: An evil omen! Still, if it brings me gain,
   yes, I will die in word but not in fact.

HELEN: I'll cut my hair in mourning and I'll wail,
   as widows do, to that blaspheming king.

MENELAUS: How could doing that help us escape?
   This whole idea just seems a bit cliché.

HELEN: I'll tell the Egyptian tyrant that you died
   at sea, and ask if I can bury you.

MENELAUS: If he says yes, still, how can we escape,
   without a ship, by empty burial?   1060

HELEN: I'll say he has to give a boat, so I
   can take your grave gifts to the sea's embrace.

MENELAUS: There's just one problem: this pretense is useless
   if he tells you to build my tomb on land.

HELEN: I'll say it's not the way it's done in Greece,
   for those who died at sea to rest in earth.

MENELAUS: You solved that, too! Then I will sail with you
   and help you make the offerings from the boat.

HELEN: Of course you have to be there, and your men,
   those of the crew who have survived the wreck.   1070

MENELAUS: If I can have an anchored ship, my men
   will stand close ranked together, swords in hand.

HELEN: You be in charge of everything. Let's hope
   fair winds will fill our sails and stir the ship.

MENELAUS: They will. The gods will end my suffering.
   Who will you say told you about my death?

HELEN: You! Tell him you sailed out with Menelaus,
   and saw him die. You were the sole survivor.

MENELAUS: These rags I'm dressed in will confirm your story,   1080
   since they bear witness I was in a shipwreck.
HELEN: Bad at the time but now it's turned out well.
   Your suffering may soon turn into good.
MENELAUS: Should I go with you now inside the palace,
   or sit here quietly beside this tomb?
HELEN: Stay here. If he tries anything aggressive,
   this tomb will surely save you. And your sword.
   I'll go inside and cut my curly hair,
   and scratch my cheeks all bloody with my nails.
   A lot's at stake in this. I see two endings: 1090
   either I'm caught, and then I'll have to die,
   or else I'll save you, and I'll go back home.

      Queen Hera, you who share a bed with Zeus,
   set free two wretched mortals from our toils.
   We beg you, as we lift our hands to heaven—
   your home among the spangles of the stars.
   And you, who sold my marriage for your beauty,
   Cypris, Dione's daughter, don't destroy me.
   You've hurt me quite enough before. You gave
   my name if not my body, to barbarians.   1100
   But if you want to kill me, let me die
   in my own country. Why are you never sated
   with wickedness: deceit and tricks and lust,
   and charms that spill the blood of families?
   You'd be the sweetest of the gods to humans
   if you were less excessive. That's the truth.
      (Exit Helen into the palace.)

strophe 1

   CHORUS: I'll call to you, up through the tangles of forest,
      up where you nest in some melodious plot,
      poet of birds,
      singing sweet music of tears:*   1110
      join with me now in the labor of lamentation,
      trilling from your trembling tawny throat,
      as I sing of the sorrows of Helen,
      and weep for the fate
      of Troy, laid low

---

* The "poet of birds" is the famously sweet-voiced nightingale.

by the spears of the Greeks.
The barbarian man in barbarian ship swooped away
over the rushing gray waves, far distant from Sparta,
bringing the sorrows of sleeping with Helen, with you,
to the people of Priam. Destroyer of marriage, destructive in
    marriage,   1120
it was Paris. He was led by Aphrodite.

antistrophe 1

The Achaeans hurled lances and rocks that sent many men
down to the bleakness of Hades; they breathed out their last.
Their wives were bereaved and in grief cut their hair,
and their homes became empty of marriage.
The solitary oarsman ignited the Cape of Euboea
with his fiery flare, and killed many Achaeans,*
hurling their ships
at the rocks of Caphereus,
shining his star of deceit   1130
on the cliffs of the sea, the Aegean.
And then Menelaus took away in his ships
that prize that was no prize, the source of the struggle,
the phantom, the image, the icon of Hera.
The breath of the storm blew him far from his homeland,
to sad harborless borders, where the costumes are strange.

strophe 2

What mortal can think it all through and explain
what is god, what is not god, and what's in between?
The most one can hope is to glimpse how their works   1140
leap around, back and forth and around,
in a world of surprises and self-contradiction.
Helen, descendent of Zeus, Zeus' daughter:
your father turned to a swan and he flew
to between Leda's thighs and there fathered you.
Then all through the country of Greece you were labeled,
treacherous, trustless, immoral and godless.
I don't know for sure what truth I can find
of the gods among mortals.   1150

---

* Nauplius lighted false flares in order to lure the Greek ships to be wrecked, in revenge for the death of his son Palamedes.

antistrophe 2

> They're fools who win glory in war
> by stabbing and thrusting with spears,
> stupidly seeking an end to their labors in death.
> If the contest of blood is the judge, there will never
> be an end to the conflicts between cities, between humans.
> What they won by the fighting was a bed to lie down in, beneath
>   Priam's earth,
> when they could have resolved it with words,
> all that wrangling for Helen.   1160
> Like lightning from Zeus, the fire of killing fell down on the walls,
> and you must bear pain upon pain,
> poor suffering woman. We pity your life.
>   *(Enter Theoclymenus.)*

THEOCLYMENUS: Hail to my father's tomb, hail, Proteus!
I set you at the entrance of my house,
so that whenever I go in or out
I greet you. I am Theoclymenos,
your son. Now slaves, take in my hounds, and these,
my hunting nets, inside the royal palace.   1170
I've often had occasion to regret
failures to punish criminals with death.
I've just now learnt a man came to this land,
clearly a Greek, yet he got through the guards.
Either a spy, or on the hunt for Helen:
a kidnapper. He'll die, if I can catch him.
        (He sees that Helen is gone.)
Hey!
Helen has left her place beside the tomb!
It's empty! She's been whisked away by sea!
Unlock the gates! Open the stables up!   1180
Servants, bring out my chariot! I'll work
to stop the wife I want from being abducted.
        (He notices Menelaus and his companions and Helen.)
But wait! I see the men I'm hunting down
right at my house—they haven't run away.
(to Helen) And you! Why have you changed from your white dress
into this black one? Why did you chop off
your hair so roughly from your noble head?

Are your cheeks wet with tears? Have you been crying?
Have you been having visions in the night,   1190
or did you hear some message from your country
that made you mourn and broke your heart with grief?
HELEN: Master—since I must call you that already—
   I'm done for. My life's over. I am dead.
THEOCLYMENUS: What's happening to you? What is your trouble?
HELEN: My Menelaus is—just say it!—dead.
THEOCLYMENUS: I'm sorry. Though for me, this news is lucky.
   How do you know? Did Theonoë tell you?
HELEN: Yes, and one who was present when he died.
THEOCLYMENUS: Did someone come and give a full report?   1200
HELEN: Yes. And may that man go where I would wish!*
THEOCLYMENUS: Who is he? Where? I need to find out more.
HELEN: This man who's cowering beneath the tomb.
THEOCLYMENUS: Apollo! What disgusting clothes he's wearing!
HELEN: My husband must be in the same sad plight.
THEOCLYMENUS: This fellow who arrived, where is he from?
HELEN: He is a Greek, one of my husband's shipmates.
THEOCLYMENUS: How does he say that Menelaus died?
HELEN: A dreadful death beneath the salty waves.
THEOCLYMENUS: Where was he sailing? In which foreign sea?   1210
HELEN: The man was cast away on Libyan rocks.
THEOCLYMENUS: How did he live, when Menelaus died?
HELEN: Sometimes the better man is not as lucky.
THEOCLYMENUS: Where did he leave the fragments of the wreck?
HELEN: Somewhere—oh, curse that ship! But bless my husband!
THEOCLYMENUS: He's dead. But in what boat did this man come?
HELEN: He says some random sailors picked him up.
THEOCLYMENUS: Where is that bad thing sent to Troy for you?
HELEN: You mean the cloudy image? In the sky.
THEOCLYMENUS: Priam and Troy! Your ruin was for nothing.   1220
HELEN: I shared in Priam's people's suffering.
THEOCLYMENUS: And did he lay your husband in the earth?
HELEN: No! Such a dreadful thing! He is not buried.
THEOCLYMENUS: And this is why you cut your golden curls?

---

* There is dramatic irony here: Theoclymenus is supposed to hear the line as a curse ("May he go to hell!"), but Helen can mean it in a good way ("May he, Menelaus, go to Greece!").

HELEN: Yes, since I loved him once, and he's still dear.*

THEOCLYMENUS: But is it right that you should weep for him?

HELEN: Yes. Do you think your sister makes mistakes?

THEOCLYMENUS: No. But what now? Will you stay by this tomb?

HELEN: Yes, I'll be true to him, and run from you.   1230

THEOCLYMENUS: Why do you tease me? He's dead; let him go.

HELEN: All right, no more. Begin the wedding plans.†

THEOCLYMENUS: About time, too! But good, I'm glad you're ready.

HELEN: Then here's what you must do: forget the past.

THEOCLYMENUS: One good deserves another: tell your terms.

HELEN: Let's make a truce, forgive me and make friends.

THEOCLYMENUS: I hold no grudge against you. Let it go!

HELEN: (*kneeling and grasping his legs in supplication*)

    If you're a friend, I beg you, at your knees—

THEOCLYMENUS: Why are you stretching out your arms in prayer?

HELEN: Because I want to bury my dead husband.

THEOCLYMENUS: Can absent shadows get a burial?   1240

HELEN: It's the Greek custom, when one dies at sea—

THEOCLYMENUS: Your culture has so much sophistication!

HELEN: —to "bury" them, in an empty winding cloth.

THEOCLYMENUS: Do it, and choose the spot to build the mound.

HELEN: That's not the way we bury those that drown.

THEOCLYMENUS: How then? I don't know much about Greek culture.

HELEN: We take the trappings for the corpse to sea.

THEOCLYMENUS: What stuff must I provide, to serve the dead?

HELEN: This man knows that; I don't. It's my first loss.

THEOCLYMENUS: (*to Menelaus*)

    Stranger, you came with happy news for me!   1250

MENELAUS: But not for me, and not for him who's dead.

THEOCLYMENUS: How do you bury those who died at sea?

MENELAUS: As best each person's riches will allow.

THEOCLYMENUS: Have all the wealth you want—for Helen's sake.

MENELAUS: First blood must spill, an offering to the dead.

THEOCLYMENUS: What animal? Just tell me and I'll do it.

---

* The transmitted text of this line is problematic; I have translated one of a number of posssible reconstructions.

† Lines 1226–27 are difficult to interpret in the original, and lines 1228–30 are out of order in the manuscript tradition; this translation reflects a scholarly conjecture of how the lines should be ordered.

MENELAUS: You can decide, since any gift is fine.

THEOCLYMENUS: Barbarians usually give a horse or ox.

MENELAUS: Just make sure what you give is not malformed.

THEOCLYMENUS: I have a wealth of good ones in my herds.   1260

MENELAUS: A bier without a body must be brought.

THEOCLYMENUS: Yes. Then what else is it the norm to bring?

MENELAUS: Weapons of bronze, since war was what he loved.

THEOCLYMENUS: I'll give him arms, worthy of Pelops' people.

MENELAUS: And all the finest produce from the earth.

THEOCLYMENUS: Of course. And how do you take it out to sea?

MENELAUS: We need a ship, and a crew of skillful oarsmen.

THEOCLYMENUS: How far away from shore must this boat go?

MENELAUS: So you can scarcely see its wake from land.

THEOCLYMENUS: Why's that? Why do the Greeks perform this rite?   1270

MENELAUS: So tides won't wash pollution back to shore.

THEOCLYMENUS: You'll have a swift Phoenician ship, with oars.

MENELAUS: That's good, and Menelaus will be pleased.

THEOCLYMENUS: But can't you do these rituals without Helen?

MENELAUS: No: it's the job of mother, child or wife.

THEOCLYMENUS: She has to lay her husband to his rest?

MENELAUS: It's pious not to rob the dead's last rites.

THEOCLYMENUS: Then let her go. I want a pious wife.

Go in the house and take things for the corpse.

And when you leave, you'll not go empty-handed,   1280

since you've helped Helen, and brought me good news.

I'll give you proper clothes instead of rags,

and food, to make the journey to your country.

I see how badly off you are right now.

(*to Helen*) And you: I'm sorry for your loss. But do not waste

your life on useless mourning.* Menelaus

has passed away, and grief won't bring him back.

MENELAUS: (*to Helen*) Your job, young lady, is to let go the husband

who isn't here, and love the one who is.

That's best for you, given the situation.   1290

If I survive and make my way to Greece,

I'll stop them blaming you, if you can treat

the man who shares your bed the way you should.

---

* There is a short lacuna here, including a missing verb.

HELEN: I will. I'll never speak ill of my husband.
    You'll be beside me and you'll know the truth.
    But you, poor traveler, go in and wash,
    and change your clothes. I want, without delay,
    to do you favors, since you will perform
    the duties owed to darling Menelaus
    more lovingly if I've done right by you.   1300

strophe 1

    CHORUS: Once long ago, the Lady of the Mountains,
        the Mother of Gods, came running and rushing
        through glades thick with forest
        and gushing of rivers
        and the deep-sounding wave of the ocean.
        She longed for her daughter, the lost girl,
        whose name is unspeakable.
        The cymbals that clashed like the thunder
        screamed to a din to resound far and wide,
        when the goddess first yoked up her chariot   1310
        with a team of wild beasts,
        and rode out to hunt for the one who was taken
        from the dancing circles of girls:
        for the Maiden.*
        With feet like the stormwind they came:
        Artemis, bearing her bow,
        Athena, full-armed with her spear, her eyes glaring.
        Zeus the all-seeing one trained his bright gaze
        from his throne up in heaven
        and altered their destiny.

antistrophe 1

        The Mother was out of her mind: she ran wandering, everywhere,
        searching and suffering, seeking her daughter,   1320
        tracking the tricks of the rape.
        When she gave up her labors she climbed
            up the crags to the Nymphs
        on the peaks of Mount Ida, fed by the snow-drifts,
        and hurled herself down in her grief

---

* There are a couple of words missing in this line.

on the rocks in the snow-covered brush.
She offered no harvest for humans
and the fields of the earth lay sproutless and barren.
She brought death to the races of people.
She sent forth no fodder for flocks,   1330
no luscious tendrils of rich leafy vines.
Life was gone from the cities.
No rites were performed for the gods.
The offerings lay on the altars unburnt.
She stopped the dewy streams
of clear bright water,
in her bitter grief for her child.

strophe 2

But when she stopped all kinds of banquets
for gods and the human race,
Zeus softened the hatred
and rage of the Mother, by speaking: 1340
"Go, holy Graces,
go to Demeter; with shouting and chanting
take from her angry heart
grief for her daughter.
Muses, go heal her with singing and dancing."
Then the most beautiful one of the blessed gods,
Cyprian Aphrodite,
took up the bronze that speaks like an earthquake
and drums made of skin stretched taut.
The goddess laughed
and took in her hands   1350
the deep-rumbling hornpipe
and was glad at the noise.

antistrophe 2

You burnt offerings down in the chambers of earth*
that were wrong and unholy,
and, daughter, because you dishonored
the rites of the mighty Mother,
her wrath is upon you.

---

* There are textual problems in this line and the next. The Chorus seem to be saying that Helen has somehow failed to offer proper sacrifice to the goddess and that her sufferings are a result of this.

Great power lies in the colorful clothes
of the fawnskin
and greenness of ivy   1360
as crown for the holy fennel stalks
and the whirling and shaking up high in the air
of the rhombus revolving
and the hair that dances for Bacchus,*
and the all-night rites for the goddess.
Ah, Helen, the beautiful moon
rode her chariot far up above you,
but you prided yourself on your beauty alone.†

HELEN: My friends, we've had good luck with things inside.
When Theonoë's brother questioned her   1370
about my husband, she said he's not here.
She helped me to conceal him, since she claimed
he's dead and can no longer see the sunlight.
My husband seized upon his lucky strike.
The weapons he'd been meant to sink at sea
were his: he thrust his arm into a shield,
and lifted it. His right hand grabbed a spear,
as if to join in service to the dead.
He'd armed himself in readiness for battle,
prepared, when we've embarked upon the ship,   1380
to triumph over countless foreigners.‡

I got him changed out of his shipwreck clothes,
gave him a bath, the first for quite some time,
in pure fresh riverwater, and I dressed him.
But hush, don't tell! The man who thinks he has
definite prospects that I'll be his bride
is coming from the palace. I implore you,
here on my knees, be kind and hold your tongue,
so we'll escape, and save you, too, someday.
        (Enter Theoclymenus.)

---

* The fawnskin, fennel stalk, and ivy are all associated with the worship of Dionysos (Bacchus).

† The transmitted text of this line is problematic; I have translated one of a number of posssible reconstructions.

‡ The original suggests literally that Menelaus will put up trophies to gloat about his victories over the dead barbarians, presumably when he returns to Greece.

THEOCLYMENUS: Slaves! Come at once, just as the stranger ordered.   1390
  Bring out the oceanic funeral gifts.
  (*to Helen*) and Helen, if you think my words are sound,
  do as I say: stay here. You give your husband
  the same respect whether you're there or not.
  I am afraid you'll get a sudden urge
  to hurl yourself into the swelling waves,
  struck by affection for your former husband.
  You mourn too much for him, though he's not here.

HELEN: Oh, my new husband! No, I have to honor
  the marriage bed where I was first a bride.   1400
  And yes, I'd like to lie beside that husband
  for love of him. But what good would it do him,
  if I shared in his death? Just let me go
  so I can pay his funeral gifts myself.
  So may the gods grant you what I would wish,
  and bless this stranger, since he shares the task.
  You'll find me just the kind of wife I should be,
  when you've done this good turn to Menelaus
  and me. Yes, everything will turn out well.
  Now as your final kindness, get somebody   1410
  to bring a ship in which we'll take this cargo.

THEOCLYMENUS: (*to a slave*) You! Go and get a ship with fifty oars,
  and fifty oarsmen, a Phoenician one.

HELEN: I hope the funeral leader can be captain?

THEOCLYMENUS: Of course. My sailors must obey this man.

HELEN: Tell them again, be sure they understand.

THEOCLYMENUS: I will, and three times over, if you wish.

HELEN: Bless you! And may my plans bless me, as well.

THEOCLYMENUS: Don't spoil your pretty skin with too much weeping.

HELEN: Today will show how much I'll do for you.   1420

THEOCLYMENUS: It's useless labor, caring for the dead.

HELEN: It matters, here and there. I'm telling you.*

THEOCLYMENUS: I'll be as good a husband as your first.

HELEN: There's nothing wrong with you. I just need luck.

---

* Some editors believe this line and the next are nonsensical and do not belong in the text; the line is certainly somewhat obscure. If genuine, it seems to create an ironic double meaning: she is saying both that funeral rites matter for the living and the dead, and also that her fake funeral for Menelaus will have important consequences both in Egypt and in Greece.

THEOCLYMENUS: It's up to you, if you'll be kind to me.

HELEN: I don't need teaching how to love my loved ones.

THEOCLYMENUS: Do you want me to come, too, and help with things?

HELEN: No, master! Don't be slave to your own slaves.

THEOCLYMENUS: All right. I'll let your old Greek customs go.

My house is pure, since it was not the place   1430
that Menelaus died. Go, slave, and tell
my chieftains they should bring my wedding presents
here to my palace. Let all Egypt ring
with wedding songs and shouts of happiness,
and may our marriage be admired and envied.
(*to Menelaus*) And stranger, when you've gone to give these gifts
to Helen's former husband, deep in ocean,
then take my wife and hurry her back home.
You are invited to my wedding feast,
then you may go back home, or stay, with pleasure.   1440

MENELAUS: Zeus! You're called the Father, God of Wisdom!
Look on us now and save us from our troubles.
We're dragging up our fortunes to the clifftop;
come join us! Quick! If just your fingertip
brushes us, we will reach the goal we seek.
Our former sufferings are quite enough.
Gods, I have often called on you to listen
to prayers of pain that went unanswered. But
my luck can change, my feet can forge ahead.
Just grant me this! You'll make me glad forever!   1450

strophe 1

CHORUS: Sidonian ship, with your oars rowing swiftly,
Ship of Phoenicia, beloved by the waves,
of Nereus, lord of the Ocean!
You lead in the chorus of beautiful dancers,
the dolphins. Whenever
the waters are windless,
the blue-flashing child of the deep sea,
Galaneia, says this:
"Come now, let down your sails;
don't think of sea breezes,   1460
but take up your oars made of fir,

sailors, O sailors,
and take Helen back to the harbors
of Perseus' home."

antistrophe 1

    I think she will come to Leucippus' daughters,
    by the rush of the river
    or in front of the temple to the Maiden,*
    and finally she will join in with the dancing,
    or join the festivities, joy in the night time,
    for dead Hyacinthus,
    killed by Apollo when he was competing   1470
    with the infinite circle, the discus.†
    The god, son of Zeus, commanded the Spartans
    to honor a day when the oxen are sacrificed.
    May she <rejoin her daughter Hermione>,‡
    the young heifer she left in her home,
    who has not yet been lit by the blazing of torches for marriage.

strophe 2

    I wish we could fly through the air
    where the Libyan birds come flocking,   1480
    leaving the rainstorms of winter,
    led by the pipe
    of their eldest, their shepherd,
    who cries as he flies
    over waterless plains
    over lands rich in harvest.
    O long-necked cranes,
    who share in the race of the clouds,
    swoop under the midst of the Pleiades,
    under Orion and on through the night   1490
    and land in Eurotas
    and pass on the message:

---

* The Chorus imagine Helen's arrival in Sparta. The daughters of Leucippus were the wives of Helen's brothers, Castor and Pollux, who were objects of cult worship in Sparta. The river is the Eurotas, the river of Sparta, and the Maiden is Athena, who had a temple on the Spartan acropolis.

† Apollo accidentally killed his young boyfriend Hyacinthus with a discus in a competition. In grief he instituted a festival cult, practiced in Sparta in Euripides' time, called the Hyacinthia, involving festivities and animal sacrifice.

‡ There is a line missing here; the words in angle brackets supply the sense.

Menelaus has captured the city of Troy
and he will be coming back home.

antistrophe 2

Now come, Dioscuri, twin sons of Tyndareus,
rush to us riding on horseback
through the sky
from your home in the heavens
beneath whirling bright stars.
Saviors of Helen   1500
dash over the green sea waves,
and over the blue-gray surging
of the dark salt water,
send fresh fair gusts,
to blow for the sailors,
and take from your sister her shame
for barbarian beds,
the shame that she got
through the strife on Mount Ida,
though she never went to the city of Troy   1510
and the towers of Apollo.

(Enter Messenger.)

MESSENGER: Master, there's been disaster for your house!*
I have some shocking news to share with you.
THEOCLYMENUS: What? MESS.: You've been working hard to gain the hand
of someone else's wife. Helen is gone!
THEOCLYMENUS: Did she fly off? Or walk, feet on the ground?
MESSENGER: Her Menelaus took her from our land.
He came here bringing news of his own death.
THEOCLYMENUS: No! This is bad! What ship took them from Egypt?
This makes no sense. Your story can't be true.   1520
MESSENGER: The ship you gave the stranger. He has gone
with your own sailors. That, in brief, is that.
THEOCLYMENUS: I need to understand! I'd never guess
one man could get the better of so many:
of all those sailors that I sent them off with!

---

* The text is problematic here: the original is unmetrical, and it suggests, absurdly, that the disaster has occurred actually inside the king's house.

MESSENGER: When Zeus' daughter left this royal palace,
and set out to the sea, mincing along,
she cried for her dead husband—clever tricks,
since he was at her side! He wasn't dead.
Arriving at the corral of your dock,   1530
we launched the ship out for her maiden voyage,
with space for fifty seats and fifty oars.
We got to work, first one task then the next.
One set the mast in place, one fixed the oars,
spreading them out. The white sails were unfurled,*
and rudders lowered down to sea on ropes.
In all the bustle, Menelaus' Greeks,
who, I suppose, were watching for this moment,
came to the waterfront, dressed in the clothes
of shipwreck victims. Handsome men, but dirty.   1540
When Menelaus saw that they'd arrived,
he called aloud with a pretense of pity:
"Poor men! Your vessel must have smashed to pieces.
What was your ship? I'm guessing you're Achaeans.
So join the funeral of dead Menelaus,
whom Helen's burying, though he's not here."
They started crying—all pure fabrication!—
and went on board deck carrying the gifts
for Menelaus. We were quite suspicious,
and muttered to each other at the crowd   1550
of passengers. But following your instructions
we held our tongues. You ordered that the stranger
should have command on board. You caused this mess!
We packed most of the cargo in the ship,
easily—it was light. The bull, however,
refused to put his hoof upon the gangway.
He bellowed out and rolled his eyes around,
arching his back and glaring beneath his horns.
We couldn't touch him. Helen's husband shouted,
"Soldiers! You sacked the town of Ilium!   1560
So can't you hoist the weight of this big bull
on your strong backs, seizing him up Greek-style,

---

* This line is corrupt in the original.

and hurl him on the prow as sacrifice
for this dead man?" At that, he drew his sword.
The men obeyed. They came and seized the bull
and lifted it and put it on the ship.
Then Menelaus stroked the horse's neck
and nose, persuading it to come on board.
Finally everything was on the ship.
Then Helen set her shapely foot and ankle   1570
to climb the ladder. She sat on the quarter deck
with her so-called-dead husband at her side.
The men sat down in pairs, one by another,
along the boat walls, left and right. They kept
swords hidden underneath their clothes. The bo'sun
gave signal and the sea was full of shouting.
When we were not too far from land, and not
too near, the helmsman asked, "Stranger, should we
keep rowing on, or is this far enough?
You are in charge of everything on board."   1580
He said, "This is enough!" In his right hand
he held his sword, and stepped into the prow
to sacrifice the bull. He did not speak
about the dead, but as he slit the throat,
he prayed: "Poseidon, Dweller of the Deep,
and holy maidens, daughters of Nereus,
let me escape from here to Nauplia,
and save my wife!" The stream of blood gushed out
into the sea, good omens for the stranger.
One person said, "This trip is all a trick!
Let's row back home. Give orders to the crew   1590
and turn the rudder round." But Menelaus
stood where he'd killed the bull and called his comrades:
"Heroes of Greece! Why do you hesitate
to kill, to slaughter those barbarians
and hurl them from the ship?" The bo'sun called
orders to your crew, King, on fighting back:
"Some of you, go, get planks to use as spears.
Smash up the benches! Pull oars from their sockets!
Bloody the skulls of these invading foreigners!"
They all leaped up—one side was only armed   1600

with timbers, and the other side, with swords.
Blood flowed all through the ship, and from the prow
Helen cheered on the fighting. She called out,
"Where's Trojan glory now? Show these barbarians!"
They battled. Some fell, some got up, some lay
as corpses. Menelaus, in full armor,
checked where his comrades might be suffering,
and reached his arm out there, and thrust his sword
so your men cleared the benches as they jumped
overboard. Then he went up to the helmsman   1610
and told him he should steer the boat to Greece.
They raised the mast and fair winds blew the sails.
They've left the country. I survived the slaughter
and scaled down to the water on the anchor.
I drifted in exhaustion, till a fisherman
lifted me up and brought me back to land,
to tell you this. And nothing is more useful
for mortals, than clear-minded skepticism.

CHORUS: I never would have thought it! Menelaus
was here, and we had no idea, my lord!   1620

THEOCLYMENUS:* No, no, no! I've been caught by the schemes of the
women!
My bride has escaped! No more marriage for me! If the ship
could have been followed and taken, I'd have hastened to catch them.
But now, I will punish my sister, the one who betrayed me,
who saw Menelaus was here in my house, and said nothing.
She'll never fool anyone else with her lies and her prophecies!

CHORUS: Wait, master! What is your intention? What violent action?

THEOCLYMENUS: I'm going where Justice commands me. Stand out of the
way.

CHORUS: I will not let go of your clothes! What you're planning is evil!

THEO.: Can a slave be the boss of the master?   CHOR.: I can if I'm
right!   1630

THEO.: You're not if you will not allow me—   CHOR.: I will not allow you!

THEO.: That woman betrayed me!   CHOR.: A noble betrayal! She did the
right thing.

---

* The meter switches here in the original to trochaics, a rhythm associated with dancing, excitement,
and high energy.

THEO.: She gave my own bride to another man! CHOR.: One with more
right to her.

THEO.: Who had more right than myself? CHOR.: He who took her from
her father.

THEO.: Chance gave her to me! CHOR.: And Necessity took her away.

THEO.: You ought not to dictate to me what to do. CHOR.: Yes, I should, if
I'm right!

THEO.: But I am the king! I have power! CHOR.: To act piously. Not to do
wrong.

THEO.: It sounds like you're eager to die. CHOR.: So then kill me. I'll
never consent

to your killing your sister. Just kill me instead. It's heroic   1640
for slaves who are noble to die on behalf of their masters.

> *(Helen's twin brothers, Castor and Pollux, the Dioscuri, appear
> over the roof of the palace.)*

CASTOR:[*] Restrain your rage, don't get too carried away,
King Theoclymenus. My name is Castor,
and this is Pollux. We're the sons of Leda,
brothers of Helen who escaped your house.
This marriage was not meant to be for you.
The daughter of the sea nymph, Theonoë,
your sister, did not wrong you. She fulfilled
your father's just commands and those of the gods.   1650
It was that woman's destiny to live
with you in your house till the present time.
But now that Troy's foundations have been sacked,
and now she's given her name to the gods,
she must be yoked again in her old marriage,
and go back home and live with her same husband.
Don't hurt your sister with your blackened sword.
Just understand, she acted with good conscience.
We would have saved our sister long ago
if Zeus had made us gods. We were too weak
against Necessity, and against the gods,   1660
who had decided things would go like this.
That's what I say to you. (*to Helen*) Now to my sister:
sail with your husband. You will have good winds.

---

[*] The meter for the rest of the play switches back to regular iambics.

We, your twin brothers, will ride on beside you
over the sea and guide you safe to home.
And when you reach the final goal of life,
you'll be a goddess and receive libations
along with us, and share in gifts from humans.
This is the will of Zeus. The place where Hermes   1670
first set you down, when he'd flown off with you
from Sparta, so that Paris wouldn't get you,
I mean the island sheltering Attica,*
will have the name of Helen in the future,
because it took you in when you were stolen.
The gods decree that wandering Menelaus
will also live in the Islands of the Blest.
The gods do not despise those who are noble,
although they suffer more than the masses do.

THEOCLYMENUS: O sons of Leda and of Zeus, I'll set   1680
aside my quarreling about your sister.
Let her go home, if that's the will of the gods,
and I no longer wish to kill my sister.
Let me say this to you: your own dear sister
is the most chaste of women. She's the best.
I wish you well for Helen's sake: she is
a truly decent woman—unlike most.

   CHORUS: Spirits take on many forms,
          and gods create a multitude of surprises.
          Things we expect don't come to pass,   1690
          and god finds ways toward the unexpected.
          That's how this story went.

---

* The island of Makronissus, called Helen in antiquity.

INTRODUCTION TO EURIPIDES' *BACCHAE*

Dionysus is unlike the other deities in the Olympian pantheon. He was the product of Zeus' union with a mortal woman, the Theban princess Semele; mixed parentage would ordinarily have made him mortal, but, in part because Zeus gestated the fetus in his own thigh after Semele's death—she was blasted apart when Zeus visited her in the form of a thunderbolt—his divine nature prevailed. He was raised in the East, on the legendary Mount Nysa, and was therefore thought to have entered the Greek world from outside, after first teaching his arts, including the making of wine, to the barbarian peoples of Asia. Greek artists loved to depict him arriving in Europe as a beautiful young man, followed by a train of Asian women clad in animal skins, playing music on exotic instruments and tossing their heads back in frenzied dances—the *bakkhai*, or female worshippers of Dionysus, also sometimes called maenads, who form the chorus of Euripides' celebrated tragedy. Since the procession has journeyed overland through Anatolia and Thrace, the first mainland Greek city it reaches is Thebes, the place of Dionysus' birth, and it is here, shortly after his arrival, that the action of the *Bacchae* takes place.

Dionysus played a far different role in Greek religious practice than did Zeus and his other children. His worship had broader social reach, including especially women and the poor, in part since his power manifested itself in wine and frenzied dancing, the most widely available routes the Greeks had toward out-of-self experience. But this populist appeal, together with his perceived foreignness and legendary late arrival among the Hellenes, made Dionysus anomalous, perhaps even dangerous, within the hierarchies of the Greek *polis*. Thus his shrines tended to be placed outside city walls, and his rites often took place in the wild, in unpeopled mountain vales. The Athenians, the most democratic of Greek peoples, devised a special ceremony to make this rural god at home in their city: in the grand festival called the Greater or City Dionysia, held in the spring, a cult statue of Dionysus was carried in from the country and installed in a temple on the south slope of the Acropolis. This was the occasion, as has often been stressed in this volume, for annual performances of tragedy at Athens, since drama, another route toward out-of-self experience, was thought to be an invention of Dionysus and was held sacred to that god.

But Thebes, at the time that Euripides' *Bacchae* takes place, has no such ritual for making Dionysus welcome. Indeed, its ruler, Pentheus, holds a deep antipathy to the new cult that has drawn the women of his city, and even some old men, into the wilds of Mount Cithaeron, dressed in animal skins rather than "civilized" Greek wool garments. He does not even believe Dionysus to be divine; Semele, his aunt, might easily (as he thinks) have claimed Zeus as her lover merely to explain an embarrassing out-of-wedlock pregnancy. His belief system, like his monarchic line, is hierarchical and aristocratic. The idea that new gods can suddenly emerge on the scene, and new rites can spread like wildfire among the disenfranchised, threatens both his most deeply held convictions and the basis of his political power. That power is made visible onstage, as often in Greek theater, by a backdrop representing the strong wall of his royal palace; in this case, however, those walls are fated to crumble.

The sphere in which Dionysus operates extends far beyond the intoxications of wine and the transformations of theater. His presence is felt wherever the forces of nature are strongest: in the rapid growth of vines, the might of bulls, the quick, light movements of deer and leopards. His followers assimilate themselves to such darting creatures by wearing their skins or, in a rite described in myth but perhaps never put into practice, by tearing them apart and devouring their flesh raw, absorbing the blood that animates them. Union with natural forces, for *polis*-dwellers normally far removed from them, offers an ecstasy as powerful as that of dancing or drunkenness. The sex drive is of course one such force, and goat-footed satyrs and Sileni, embodying the power of that drive with their erect phalluses, were depicted in Greek art as Dionysus' principal followers, along with the bacchae, women who have surrendered themselves, in nonsexual ways, to Dionysiac experience.

When he chose to explore that experience in a tragedy, Euripides was living far from Athens, at the court of the Macedonian king Archelaus. Perhaps he was influenced by the strange rites he saw there, for the Macedonians apparently gave freer rein to Dionysus than did their southerly neighbors. Whatever inspired him, he created in the *Bacchae* the most intense and harrowing of his surviving dramas, in recent decades the most influential and most frequently produced of all the plays in this volume. Unfortunately, the *Bacchae* has not survived intact; its ending is marred by a long gap, between lines 1329 and 1330 of the existing text, where an entire page was lost from an early manuscript.

At the heart of the play stands the tense, psychologically complex duel between Dionysus and Pentheus, cousins and agemates—both around twenty years old, to the extent that gods can be said to have ages—now locked in a struggle for control of Thebes. Throughout this contest, Dionysus operates in disguise, pretending to be only a priest of the newly imported cult rather than the deity it serves. He knows, and the audience knows, that he can make a mockery of all Pentheus' blusters, threats, and armed guards. When he is finally imprisoned in the palace strongholds, an earthquake levels the walls and an unruffled Dionysus steps into freedom. Euripides seems to have based his portrayal on an archaic poem in which a disguised Dionysus, taken captive on board a pirate ship, coolly bides his time before unleashing his powers and terrifying the crew into jumping overboard. The mixture of mischievousness, malevolence, and adolescent brashness in this god's character makes him fascinating to watch.

Pentheus struggles blindly against this "stranger," whose curling locks and feminine manner he deeply mistrusts and who, as he imagines, has led the women of Thebes into a debased sex romp. Yet behind his disgust lie covert desires to experiment himself with androgyny and voyeurism. In a mysterious moment of transformation, perhaps begun by Dionysus casting a kind of spell, Pentheus allows those desires to emerge and take control, to the extent of putting on women's clothes and going out as a spy to Mount Cithaeron. This moment (beginning at line 810) leaves some readers puzzled, but to others it makes perfect sense; directors have adopted various approaches when putting it onstage. Pentheus, now in a kind of trance, sees two suns in the sky and a two-horned bull where the stranger stands; he has crossed over into Dionysus' world, but the journey will lead, in the horrific episodes that follow, to his destruction.

As Pentheus' transformation takes place, the Chorus, made up of Asian women who have accompanied Dionysus from the East, sing one of Euripides' most haunting and mysterious odes, asking "What is wisdom?" Their philosophical question is immediately followed by a violent, vengeful one, that seems to anticipate Pentheus' coming demise: "What better gift / can gods give to mortals than to hold / an upper hand / above the enemy's head?" The ode then moves through various meditations on the power of the gods and the vanity of human endeavors, ending with a couplet that seems to sum all up: "A truly happy life / is happiness day by day." This resigned yet hopeful assertion— that joy, if it ever comes, should not be taken for granted in the present nor counted on in the future—is perhaps the final message of Athenian tragedy, given gorgeous expression here in the final play of our collection and, quite possibly, the final work of Euripides' career.

Euripides was in fact already dead at the time his *Bacchae* was put onstage, in 405 B.C. According to stories that circulated later, he had passed away the previous year in Macedonia, and this play, along with his *Iphigenia in Aulis* and one other tragedy, were found among his papers and staged by a relative. The playwright Sophocles, himself very near death, reportedly wore a black cloak of mourning in the festal procession that preceded that year's tragic festival, drawing tears from onlookers. After the performances, Euripides was posthumously awarded first prize, only the fourth time he achieved that honor.

Athens was by that time nearly exhausted from its long war against Sparta and its allies; the very next year saw the city's defeat and surrender. Athens' power would partly recover in the decades that lay ahead, but the energies that had given rise to its golden age of tragic drama had dissipated. Though tragedies continued to be written during subsequent decades, none of these later ones were thought to have reached the fifth century's high levels of sublimity, and none of them has survived into modern times.

BACCHAE

Translated by Emily Wilson

I follow the text in E. R. Dodds's edition (Oxford: Clarendon, 1960). Important variants or textual problems are marked in the notes. I have also benefited from Richard Seaford's edition (Aris and Phillips, 1996, reprinted 2011).

CAST OF CHARACTERS (IN ORDER OF APPEARANCE)

DIONYSUS, a god (son of Zeus by the mortal woman Semele), in disguise as a mortal; his alternative name is Bacchus, so his followers are known as Bacchants

PENTHEUS, king of Thebes

AGAVE, mother of Pentheus

CADMUS, father of Agave; previous king and founder of Thebes

TIRESIAS, old prophet

SERVANT

MESSENGER

SECOND MESSENGER

CHORUS of maenads,* female worshippers of Dionysus, or Bacchus, who have accompanied him from the East; also known as Bacchants or, in Latin, Bacchae—hence the play's title

---

* "Maenad" suggests a woman who is stricken by madness or frenzy; it comes from the verb *mainomai*, "to rave," "to be raging."

Setting: The play takes place at Thebes, in front of the palace of Cadmus, by the river Dirce. There is an ever-smoldering tomb marking the place where Dionysus' mother, Semele, died from Zeus' lightning bolt.*

DIONYSUS: Here: I am come to Thebes: I, Dionysus,
son of Zeus and son of Cadmus' daughter,
Semele, midwifed by the lightning's fire.
Shifting my shape to mortal from divine,
I am here at Dirce's spring, Ismenos' river.†
I see my thunder-blasted mother's tomb,
here, near the palace, and the smoking ruins:
her home, destroyed by Zeus' flame, still burning:
the mark of Hera's everlasting hate.
Cadmus did well, in making here a shrine   10
for his dead daughter. I surrounded it
with luscious grapes and green vines intertwined.
    I journeyed from the golden Lydian fields,
from Phrygia and through Persia's sunny slopes,
to Bactrian towns and to the colder country
where the Medes live, to rich Arabia,
and all the Ionian coast, by the salty sea,
where Greeks and foreigners are mixed together,
in crowded cities crowned with handsome towers.‡
At last I have come to Greece—this city first.   20
Already I've made Asia dance and serve me,

---

* After Zeus impregnated Semele, princess of Thebes, daughter of Cadmus, she was persuaded by Hera, Zeus' jealous wife, to ask to see him in his true form, as a god, armed with his thunderbolts. The sight killed her, but Zeus took the unborn child, Dionysus, and sewed him up in his thigh until it was time for him to be born.

† Stream and river in center of Thebes. Dirce, wife of Lycus, was killed by her great-nephews by being tied to the horns of a bull and dragged apart, as punishment for having been unkind to their mother, Antiope. Dirce had been a devoted worshipper of Dionysus, and he rewarded her loyalty by making a spring well up in the location of her death.

‡ The place names mark a journey from the more distant East, through Asia Minor, to the Greek-speaking cities of Ionia (in modern Turkey), and finally to Greece itself. Phrygia was in modern Turkey; Bactria overlapped with modern Afghanistan.

to show all mortals that I am a god.*

In Greece the Thebans are the first I've roused
to ululations, wrapped in fawn-skin cloaks,
thyrsus and darts of ivy in their hands,†
since my mother's sisters, my own aunts,
denied that I was born the son of Zeus!
They said that Semele‡ slept with some man,
got pregnant, and pretended it was Zeus.
Cadmus' smart idea, they snickered: Zeus   30
killed her for lying, saying I was his.
For that, I stung them till I buzzed them mad:
I made them homeless, crazy, mountain-dwellers.
I made them wear the uniform of my cult:
out of their homes, out of their minds, I drove
all of the female Theban population.
Regular women mix with royalty
out on the roofless rocks beneath green pines.
This city has to learn, by force if need be,
what comes of its resistance to my rites.§   40
And I must save the honor of my mother,
by showing humans I am son of Zeus.

Cadmus has handed over royal power
to Pentheus, the son his daughter bore.¶
He fights with gods, and shoves me from my rites,
and never thinks to praise me in his prayers.
For that, I'll show him I was born a god,
and Thebes will see. Once I have fixed things here,
I'll lead the dance away, to show myself
in yet another land. But if Thebes tries   50
to march in violent anger up the mountains,
then I will lead my maenads into war.
That is the reason I took mortal shape

---

* Dionysus, more than other gods, has to demonstrate his divinity, since his mother was mortal.

† The traditional dress of maenads, worshippers of Dionysus, often mentioned in this play. The "thyrsus" is a stick of giant fennel, usually wound round with ivy, carried by worshippers of the god.

‡ "Semele" has three syllables, with a long "e" at the end.

§ There is an implication here that Dionysus' rites are like a mystery religion; the city has refused to be initiated into the cult.

¶ Pentheus is the son of Cadmus' daughter, Agave. No explanation is given for Cadmus' abdication, beyond that he is old and feeble.

transformed to human nature in my looks.
(*to the Chorus*) Women, holy sisterhood, who left
barbarian lands and Lydian mountain peaks
for me, companions, helpers, fellow-travelers,
take up your tambourines—which I invented
with the Great Mother Rhea's help, in Phrygia.*
Come, beat your rhythms all around this palace,   60
the place of Pentheus: let the whole town see.
But I will go to deep Cithaeron's folds†
to find the Bacchants and to dance with them.

CHORUS:‡

    We came from the East,
    from holy Mount Tmolus,§
    to work the sweet work
    for the Lord of Rumbling Thunder.¶
    Praise to Lord Bacchus!
    Who stops us, who, who, who?
    Go now, away with you, indoors, go.
    Keep your words sacred, keep your mouth clean.   70
    We will sing the eternal ritual song
    for Dionysus.

strophe 1

    O,
    the happiness! To know
    the worship of the gods,
    to live the holy life,
    twining yourself with others,
    as a mountain maenad,
    blessed and sanctified,

---

* Rhea is identified in Roman mythology with Cybele, the Great Mother (Magna Mater), a mother goddess associated with an ecstatic cult, originating in the east, that involved wine, dancing, and drumming.

† Cithaeron is the mountain above Thebes.

‡ The meter of this passage in the original is *ionics a minore*, a rhythm associated with Dionysiac cult hymns.

§ In Lydia.

¶ I use this phrase to translate Bromios, a cult title of Dionysus that connotes a loud, manic noise used of drums, thunder, whinnying horses, crackling fires, or earthquakes. The title was associated with the thunder at the god's birth.

honoring the mystery rites
of the mighty Mother,*
and whirling high the thyrsus,   80
wearing ivy garlands,
to worship Dionysus!
Come, Bacchants, come, come, come,
take up the god, resounding god, son of god,
bring back Bacchus, down from the mountains,
back home to Greece, to the streets broad for dancing,
Lord of the Rumbling Thunder.

antistrophe 1

Long ago lightning
flew forth from Zeus
to the woman, pregnant, a mother,   90
forcing her painful birth-pangs:
she bore the tiny child before his time,
and left her life, struck by the blow of thunder.
But right away Zeus, son of Cronus,
took him and hid him in chambers of birthing,
tucking the baby inside his thigh,
fastened together with golden pins
to hide him from Hera.
And when the Fates fulfilled the time,
Zeus gave birth to a bull-horned god,   100
and crowned him with snakes for a crown.†
That's why the maenads wear wreaths on their hair
from the spoil they have caught in the wilderness,
nurse of the wild things.

strophe 2

Glory, Thebes, for suckling Semele!
Wear wreaths of ivy,
luxuriant city,
with lovely berries of greenbriar vines!
Deck yourselves in garlands: oak or fir,
turning to Bacchants, worshippers of Bacchus.   110
Dress in dappled fawn skin, knotted up

---

* Another reference to Cybele, the Great Mother, whose cult was similar to that of Dionysus and often associated with it.

† Cult associated Dionysus closely with the bull and the snake.

with tufts of white-haired wool.
Be reverent as you wave the wild wand.*
Now the whole world will dance together:
any leader of the dance is god.
To the mountain! To the mountain! Every woman in the land
has left her shuttle, left her loom, infected
by the sting of gadfly Dionysus.

antistrophe 2

Secret caves,   120
home to the Spirit Boys,†
holy Cretan haunts where Zeus was born,‡
where the triple-turbaned frenzied crowd
discovered how to play the kettledrum,
tapping the round of tight-stretched skin for me.§
Taut with ecstasy, they mix the beat
with the sweet exhalation of the pipe:
give Mother Earth the drum, and let her mark
the rhythm for the Bacchants' shrieks of joy.
Here are the wild Goat Men, gone mad,   130
performing in the mother goddess' cult.¶
All the women join the dance,
the ritual every other year:**
all the women Dionysus loves.

epode

Sweet delight! when from among the cantering crowd,
down to the ground a worshipper collapses,
wearing the holy deerskin tunic,
hunting the blood of the slaughtered goat, the loveliness
of eating fresh raw flesh, new-killed,††

---

* Again, the wand is the thyrsus, made from a fennel stalk, used by worshippers of Dionysus.

† The Spirit Boys (Kouretes) were deities appointed by Rhea, mother of Zeus, to watch over the baby. Their name comes from the word *kouros* (or *koros*), meaning "boy."

‡ Rhea gave birth to Zeus in a secret cave of the nymphs, on the island of Crete, to avoid having his father, Cronos, find him and eat him. The priests of Rhea used rhythmic drumming, in rituals closely associated with those of Cybele (with whom Rhea is sometimes identified).

§ The passage refers to a number of instruments closely associated with Bacchic cult, including the kettle drum and the flute. The "triple-turban" is obscure: it may refer to some kind of exotic hat.

¶ The Goat Men are satyrs, part man, part goat, with huge phalluses.

** In classical Athens, Dionysus was worshipped every year, but in other cities the rituals may have been biennial.

†† Maenads supposedly hunted animals with their bare hands and ate them raw.

and rushing to the eastern mountains,
and our leader is the Lord of the Rumbling Thunder! Shout his
    name!   140
Earth flows with milk, earth flows with wine,
earth flows with honeyed nectar.*
Bacchus lifts aloft and shakes
the fiery flare of the pine-wood torch
from the giant fennel wand,
like smoke from Syrian incense,
herding the ones who are lost from the circle
with running and dancing
and weaving and wailing,
tossing his delicate hair in the sky.   150
Now amid the maenads' wailing, hear him roar:
Come to me, Bacchants,
Come to me, Bacchants,
with glittering gold, from Lydian rivers,†
sing to the glory of Lord Dionysus,
beat on your timpani, deep-booming kettledrums,
call glory to him, god of joy, god of noise, cry triumph!
as they do in Phrygia, call and shout and whoop,
as sonorous flutes ring out the holy music,   160
a sound of holy joy
that rises with us
as we rush to the hills,
to the hills! ‡
Like a filly running
beside her mother in the pasture,
we maenads leap and bound,
kicking our feet in our joy.
    (*Enter Tiresias, blind and hobbling on a stick, led by a boy.*)

TIRESIAS: Open the door! Call Cadmus from the house: 170
   Cadmus, Agenor's son, who came from Sidon,

---

* The god's fertility makes the earth flow with all liquids, not only wine but also milk and honey.

† Apparently the maenads are using golden shakers or castanets to accompany their drumbeat. The gold comes from the river Pactolus, in Lydia (in modern Turkey), which lay beneath the gold mines of Mount Tmolus and carried electrum (an amalgam of gold and silver) in its waters (the source of the famous Lydian wealth).

‡ The numbering in Dodds's text leaves only one line between 160 and 165, and two between 165 and 170. I have spaced the lines out to avoid confusion.

to found this citadel, the town of Thebes.*
Go in, boy, tell him that Tiresias
is here for him. He knows why I have come.
     (The boy goes in.)
I am old and he is older, but we plan
to carry wands and dress ourselves in skins
and wrap fresh ivy wreaths around our heads.
     (Cadmus emerges from the palace.)

CADMUS: My dearest friend! Here at my house! What pleasure
to hear your voice; your words always make sense.
Look, I have my costume on already,   180
for Dionysus—since he is my grandson,
and has revealed himself a god on earth.
We must give him glory, all we can.
Where should I go and dance and stamp my feet,
and shake my gray old hair? We both are old;
Tiresias, teach me. You have deeper knowledge.
I'll never tire, by night or day, of tapping
my Bacchic stick on the ground. In all our joy,
we have forgotten we are old.   TIRESIAS: I feel
the same. I too feel young; I'll try to dance.   190

CADMUS: Shall we take a chariot to the mountain?

TIRESIAS: That's not the way to glorify the god.†

CADMUS: Then shall I nanny you—though we're both old?‡

TIRESIAS: With magic ease the god will lead us there.

CADMUS: Are we the only citizens to worship?

TIRESIAS: Yes: only we have sense. The rest have none.

CADMUS: We're wasting time. Come on now, take my hand.

TIRESIAS: Look here, take mine, let's link our arms together.

CADMUS: Since I am human, I respect the gods.

TIRESIAS: Our cleverness is nothing to their power.   200
We have traditions from our ancestors,
as old as time itself, immune to reason,

---

* Cadmus originated from the Phoenician city of Sidon (in modern Lebanon). After his sister Europa was abducted, he was sent by his father to look for her. In the course of his wanderings, an oracle at Delphi told him to abandon the quest and instead to follow a special cow and build a city where she first lay down. The cow led Cadmus to Boeotia ("cow country"), where he founded the city of Thebes.

† It is important for all the followers of Dionysus to be equal before him: hence, the royal family should not claim the special privilege of riding in a chariot, as Cadmus lazily hopes they can do.

‡ The verb for "nanny" in the original implies an old male slave employed to take care of a young boy.

however cleverly you try to argue.
Why, you may ask, am I so unembarrassed
to wear a wreath and dance, in my old age?
The god makes no distinction. Young and old
must dance together, everyone the same.
He wants us all to honor him together,
and no one is excused from joining in.

CADMUS: (*looking offstage*)
Tiresias, I'll be your eyes for you,   210
interpreting my vision into words.
I see Pentheus rushing to the palace,
Echion's son,* whom I made king of Thebes.
He looks so flustered. What is going on?

        (Enter Pentheus.)

PENTHEUS: I happened to be out of town; I'm back.
I hear strange news, new trouble in our city.
They say our womenfolk have left their homes
for these fake Bacchic rites. They skip and dance
up on the shady mountains, worshipping
this whatshisname, this new "god," Dionysus.   220
Apparently their gatherings involve
huge vats of wine,† and one by one, those girls
slink off alone to serve some man with sex.
They say this craziness is for the god,
but they like Aphrodite more than Bacchus.‡
I have arrested some of them; my men
have them in chains, hands bound, in the common jail.
The ones that got away, I'll hunt them down,
out of the mountain: Ino and Agave,
and cousin Actaeon's mother, Autonoë.§   230

---

* Echion was one of the Spartoi, the sons of the dragon's teeth sown by Cadmus in founding Thebes. When Cadmus, as an exile from Phoenicia, first arrived at the site of Thebes, he killed a dragon and was instructed by Athena to sow its teeth in the ground. They sprang up as armed men, who began killing each other. The five who survived became the first lords of the new city; one of them, Echion, married Cadmus' daughter Agave and was the father of Pentheus. It is not clear how he died.

† The original is *krateres*, a vessel used to mix up a large quantity of wine and water.

‡ Aphrodite is the goddess associated with sex.

§ Actaeon, a hunter, inadvertently saw Artemis bathing naked in the woods, and she took revenge by making his own dogs tear him apart and eat him. Ino and Autonoë are the sisters of Agave, mother of Pentheus. These lines may be an addition by a later commentator, noting the names of the women. Note that the name Agave has three syllables, and Autonoë has four; also note that the name Autonoë suggests self-will.

I'll dress them up in nets of iron, and stop
all of this Bacchic wickedness, right now.

    They say a stranger has arrived in town,
a wizard of some kind, from Lydia,
with perfume in his hair and yellow curls,
eyes dark as wine—his aphrodisiac charms.
He spends all day and night with teenage girls
making them perform his ritual chants.
If I catch him here, inside this house,
I'll stop him waving wands and tossing his hair: 240
I'll slice his neck and cut his head right off.
This fellow says that he's that Dionysus
who once got sewn up into Zeus's thigh,
when thunderbolts had burnt him, with his mother,
because she lied that she had lain with Zeus.
Whoever he is, this foreigner deserves
to hang for such outrageous wickedness.

    But here's another strange surprise: Tiresias
the prophet, dressed in multicolored skins,
and my mother's father—what a laugh!   250
—acting all Bacchic with a fennel-wand.
Father, it's embarrassing to see you
old but not wise. Why not shake off that ivy?
Make your hand free, Grandfather! Drop the wand!

    You talked him into this, Tiresias.
You want to introduce this new divinity
to profit from new trade in prophecies.
Your white hair saves you; were it not for that
I'd chain you up with all those maenad women,
for introducing wicked mystery rites.   260
Festivals with sparkling wine and women
are an unhealthy cult, in my opinion.

CHORUS: What blasphemy! Have you no shame, strange Greek,*
    before the gods, and Echion, your father,
    and Cadmus, who once sowed the earth-born men?

TIRESIAS: If a clever man has solid facts,
    it isn't hard to speak impressively.
    Your tongue is fluent and you sound so smart,

---

* The Chorus members are of course non-Greeks, from Asia Minor; Greeks are strangers to them.

but there is no true wisdom in your words.
Authority and rhetoric may come   270
from pride; but only wise men help their city.
      And he, this new divinity you laugh at:
no words can tell how great he will become
throughout the land of Greece. Young man, there are
two basic human needs. Goddess Demeter
—in fact the earth, but call her what you like—
feeds mortal men on dry and solid food.*
Then came the son of Semele, who found
the liquid counterpart, the juice of grapes,
his gift of pain-relief to suffering souls.   280
The flowing vine, drunk to the full, provides
sleep and forgetfulness from daily pain,
nor is there any other cure for trouble.
This god is poured as offering to the gods,
so through this god comes human happiness.
      And yet you mock him, laughing at the tale
that he was sewn inside the thigh of Zeus?
Let me enlighten you. Zeus caught him up,
the fetus-god out of the thunder's fire.
Hera yearned to throw him out of heaven,   290
but Zeus outwitted her; gods make smart plans.
He pulled a piece of the encircling sky,
a pawn to save his spawn from Hera's envy.†
As time went by, humans began to say
he was sewn up in Zeus's leg—a story
developed from a pun, because he served
as pledge to Hera—god to goddess captive! ‡
      This god can tell the future, too. Inspired
by Bacchic madness, frenzy brings foreknowledge.
Possessed in body by the god's full power,   300
the maddened worshippers tell what's to come.

---

* Demeter is the goddess associated with the harvest.
† There may be a line missing after 293.
‡ There is a series of puns on the original (slightly echoed here by the "pawn ... spawn" and "pledge ...
leg" wordplay), on the Greek words for "part," "thigh," and "hostage"/"pledge." The implication is that
the myth is based on an etymological mistake, as well as a mistake about the relative power of male and
female divinities.

He also has affinities with Ares.*
For even troops drawn up by rank and armed
are seized by fear before hand touches lance.
This, too, is frenzy brought by Dionysus.

     One day you'll see him on the rocks of Delphi,†
leaping across the plain between the hills,
pine torch in hand and brandishing the thyrsus,
all over Greece. Believe me, Pentheus,
be not so sure that force rules human lives,   310
or that your thoughts make sense. No, understand:
accept the god into your land and pour
libations, wear his wreath, belong to him.
The god will not force women to be chaste:
Chastity always lies within one's nature.
It is inside us. Look to that. For even
in Bacchic ecstasy a temperate woman
will keep her purity still undefiled.

     Remember, you yourself are glad when crowds
throng at the gates to magnify the name   320
of Pentheus. He, too, in my opinion,
delights in being honored. Cadmus and I,
though mocked by you, will dance in ivy crowns,
a pair of grays but ready still to dance;
You can't tell me to fight against the god.
Such insanity! Your mind seems drugged,
but now no drug could cure your mental illness.

CHORUS: Old man, your words show due respect to Phoebus,‡
and also honor the great God of Thunder.

CADMUS: Dear boy, Tiresias gives good advice.   330
Stay home with us, don't live outside our ways.
You're drifting up into the air; your senses
make no sense. What if you're right, and he
is not a god? You still should say he is.
White lies can bring our Semele the glory
of having borne a god, which glorifies

---

* God of war.

† Location of the most famous Greek oracle, sacred to Apollo, and supposedly the center of the world.

‡ Apollo, to whom Tiresias, as a prophet, owes his primary allegiance.

us all. Remember Actaeon, how he died?
His darling dogs, whom he himself had fed,
ripped him apart in the hills, and ate him raw,
because he boasted he could hunt with hounds   340
better than Artemis. Don't share his fate!
Come, here's an ivy wreath. Praise god with us.

PENTHEUS: Get your hands off me! Do your raving elsewhere!
Don't smear your silliness on me. I'll find
that man, the one who taught you this stupidity
and punish him.
(*to the slave attendants*) One of you, run, go quickly
to his headquarters where he watches birds:*
Pry it up with tridents, levers, crowbars,
turn the whole thing upside down, destroy it,
and cast his garlands to the wind and air.   350
That's the way I'll sting him most of all.
The rest of you, quick, run through town and catch
the girly foreigner, who brings that new
infection to our women, taints our beds.
If you catch him, bring him here in chains:
let him be stoned! He'll see a bitter end
to introducing Bacchus into Thebes.

TIRESIAS: You don't know what you're saying. You have turned
from craziness to total loss of wits.

　　　　Well, Cadmus, let us go, and let us pray,   360
for this man's sake, despite his savage ways,
and for the city: may the god refrain
from action. Bring your ivy staff, and come;
try to help me get up there, and I'll help you.
If we old men fall down, it's a disgrace;
but still, let's go; Bacchus is son of Zeus
and we must be his slaves. Cadmus, I hope
Pentheus will not bring sorrow to your house
despite his name.† This is not prophecy,
but based on facts. A fool says foolish things.

---

* Augurs divined the future by observing the flight of birds.

† There is a pun in the original on Pentheus and *penthos*, "sorrow."

(Cadmus and Tiresias exit, leaving Pentheus onstage alone.)

strophe 1

CHORUS:* Holiness, queen of the gods,   370
Holiness, gliding on golden wings
above the earth,
do you see what Pentheus is doing?
Do you see his unholy
blasphemy to Bacchus, God of Rumbling Thunder,
son of Semele, the first of godly powers,
first of the blessed gods for pure, sweet joy?
His worshippers are crowned with loveliness. This is his gift:
uniting us in dancing,
laughing as the wild pipes play,   380
taking all our pains away,
when grape clusters sparkle
at the feasts of gods,
or men in ivy garlands
gather at their festivals:
the wine-bowl circles sleep around the men.

antistrophe 1

Misfortune is the end
of tongues unbridled
and thoughtless folly.
But lives of quietness
and common sense   390
are stable and unswayed;
they keep homes safe.
Those who live in far-off heaven, above the air,
still see what mortals do.
Thinking thoughts above the human,
acting wise—that isn't wisdom.
Life is short. If, in our little span,
we seek ambitious goals,
we'll miss what lies to hand.
These are the habits of insanity,   400
the plots of wickedness,
in my opinion.

---

* The meter is again ionics, the rhythm associated with Dionysiac song.

strophe 2

> If only I could go to Cyprus,
> Aphrodite's Island,
> home of Desires, that cast a spell
> on mortal hearts,
> or Paphos, which the hundred mouths
> of the distant foreign Nile
> make fruitful without rain.*
> Or take me to Pieiria, the Muses' lovely home,   410
> holy slope of Mount Olympus,†
> take me there, Lord of the Rumbling Thunder.
> Lord of our rituals, Lord of our worshipping cries,
> there live the Graces, there is the home of Longing.
> There, by right, we acts as maenads,
> performing celebration.

antistrophe 2

> The god, the son of Zeus,
> delights in festivals,
> loves Peace that brings prosperity,
> protector of our children, nurturing goddess.   420
> To rich and poor alike
> he gives the joy of wine,
> the cure for pain.
> Our god hates those who do not share our goals:
> we aim for happiness our whole life long,
> by light of day and lovely night, and we reject
> people who act too wise, the arrogance
> of those who try to be superior.
> As the masses, simple people,   430
> think and act and live:
> so let me be.
>> (*Enter Servant with the god Dionysus in disguise, captured and bound.*)

---

* Both Cyprus and Paphos are sacred to Aphrodite, goddess of sex. The part about "make fruitful without rain" is puzzling: it may suggest an idea that the Nile current is strong enough to fertilize Paphos at a distance, by pushing its rich mud onto the island's shores; or else that the river's waters pass under the sea, to well up in the island's springs (a belief attested in twentieth-century Cypriot natives: see Dodds, p. 125).

† Pieria is where the spring of poetic inspiration was located.

SERVANT: The hunt is over, Pentheus! We caught
 the prey you sent us for, we got our prize.
 This animal is tame, he has not tried
 to run; he held his hands out willingly.
 His face looks just the same, not pale but bright
 like wine. He smiled and let us tie him up
 and lead him here. His patience made my job   440
 so easy I felt bad, and I said, "Stranger,
 I didn't want to catch you. I'm obeying
 Pentheus' orders." And the maenads, whom
 you caught and chained up in the public jail,
 are gone! They skipped off freely to the hills,
 calling on their god, the Lord of Thunder.
 The chains around their ankles just dissolved,
 the bolts released the doors, without the touch
 of human hand. This man's a miracle worker.
 Well, it's for you to tell what's best to do.   450
PENTHEUS: Untie his hands. He's trapped inside my net.
 He can't run from me now. He's not so quick.
   (Attendants untie Dionysus.)
 Well, stranger, I can see you are attractive,
 to women anyway—that's why you came here.
 Your hair is long, unsuitable for wrestling:
 it ripples down your cheek so alluringly.
 Your skin is white: you must take care of it,
 avoiding sunlight, staying in the shade,
 hunting Aphrodite with your beauty.*
 Tell me first, what family do you come from?   460
DIONYSUS: No need to boast.† It's easy to tell this:
 no doubt you've heard of Tmolus, rich in flowers?
PENTHEUS: I know it: it surrounds the town of Sardis.
DIONYSUS: I come from there; I am a Lydian.
PENTHEUS: And why do you bring these rituals into Greece?
DIONYSUS: Dionysus sent me, son of Zeus.

---

* Athenian elite women spent most of their time indoors and did not get suntanned; white skin is therefore closely associated with being ladylike.

† I have tried to reproduce the original syntax here, since there is an important ambiguity. The stranger can be heard as saying that he himself will not boast about his ancestry, and presumably Pentheus takes it that way. But on another level, Dionysus is giving an insidious reproach to Pentheus for boasting about his successful hunt.

PENTHEUS: Is there a new Zeus there, who breeds new gods?

DIONYSUS: No, the same Zeus who married Semele here.

PENTHEUS: Was it in dreams he pushed you to this quest?

DIONYSUS: No, to my waking eyes he taught the rites. 470

PENTHEUS: These rites of yours, what are they like exactly?

DIONYSUS: The uninitiated must not know.*

PENTHEUS: What profit do those celebrating get?

DIONYSUS: A good one, but not right for you to hear.

PENTHEUS: What a smart trick! You want to make me curious.

DIONYSUS: Impiety is hateful to our god.

PENTHEUS: You mean you saw this "god"? What was he like?

DIONYSUS: It's not for me to say. He chose his look.

PENTHEUS: Again, you side-stepped with an empty phrase!

DIONYSUS: It looks like folly to talk sense to fools. 480

PENTHEUS: Is this the first place you have brought this "god"?

DIONYSUS: All of the Easterners dance to these rites.†

PENTHEUS: Foreigners are much sillier than us.

DIONYSUS: Their customs aren't the same. In this, they're smart.

PENTHEUS: Are your rites done at night, or in the day?

DIONYSUS: Mostly at night. Darkness is magical.

PENTHEUS: Dirty tricks, just to seduce our women!

DIONYSUS: People act badly in the daylight, too.

PENTHEUS: You'll have to pay the price for your smart tongue!

DIONYSUS: And you for ignorant blasphemy to the god. 490

PENTHEUS: What bare-faced brashness! What a practiced sophist!‡

DIONYSUS: Tell me: how do you plan to punish me?

PENTHEUS: First I will cut this pretty hair of yours.

DIONYSUS: My locks are holy, sacred to the god.

PENTHEUS: Then, give me that thyrsus that you hold.

DIONYSUS: Take it yourself. I carry it for the god.

PENTHEUS: I'll lock you up in prison and post guards.

DIONYSUS: The god himself will free me, when I wish.

PENTHEUS: When you stand with your maenads, calling him?

DIONYSUS: Yes. He's near, and knows my situation. 500

---

* Many ritual practices in Greek religion were to be kept secret from all but the initiate, most famously the Eleusinian Mysteries.

† The "Easterners" or "foreigners" are literally the "non-Greeks," the *barbaroi*.

‡ The language of this exchange closely recalls contemporary debates about the new forms of "wisdom" taught by the new "wisdom-teachers," or sophists, who were hired by Athenian fathers, at a price, to educate their adolescent sons.

PENTHEUS: Where is he, then? I certainly can't see him!

DIONYSUS: With me. Impiety has made you blind.

PENTHEUS: (*to attendants*) Seize him! He's mocking me, and mocking Thebes.

DIONYSUS: Do not bind me. I am sane, you are not.

PENTHEUS: I tell you, bind him! I'm the master here.

> (*Attendants prepare to bind Dionysus.*)

DIONYSUS: You do not know yourself, or what you're doing.

PENTHEUS: I am Agave's son, and Echion's:

    Pentheus.   **DION.:** A name that means misfortune.*

PENTHEUS: Go! (*to attendants*) Shut him in the stables with the horses,

Let him see only darkness. Dance in the dark!   510

As for those women you brought with you here,

accomplices, we'll sell them,† or we'll stop

their hands from beating noisy time on drums:

set them to work the loom as household slaves.

DIONYSUS: I'll go. No need for needless suffering.

The god whom you declare does not exist

is after you; he'll punish your abuses.

By wronging me, you chained the god himself.

> (*Attendants and Servant lead Dionysus to the stables. Pentheus returns to the palace.*)

strophe

    CHORUS:‡ Pure River Dirce, our lady, our princess,§

        child of the ancient waterways,   520

        long ago you welcomed to your springs

        the infant child of Zeus,

        when his father snatched him

        from the immortal flaming thunder

        to hide him in his thigh, and called aloud:

        "Come, Twice Born,¶ and enter

        this, my manly womb.

---

* Another pun on the name Pentheus, connoting *penthos*, "pain."

† I.e. as slaves; or else they will be kept in Pentheus' own household, also as domestic slaves.

‡ Again (as at lines 64ff. and 370ff.) *ionics a minore*, the Dionysiac rhythm.

§ On Dirce, see note to line 5.

¶ The word "dithyramb" was the name for a type of poetic choral performance associated with Dionysus. Ancient etymologists explained the title as coming from *dis*, "twice," and *thyra*, "gate": Dionysus came twice from the gates of life, since he was first in the womb of Semele, and then in the thigh of Zeus.

I will proclaim to all of Thebes
that this shall be your name: the Lord of Dithyramb, the Double
    Gate!'"*
But Holy Dirce, you reject me   530
and my revels on your banks,
with my garlanded companions.
Why do you spurn me? Why do you run from me?
I'm sure of it, I swear, even by the clusters
of joy that Dionysus' grapes can bring,
you truly care about our Lord, the Rumbling Thunder.

antistrophe

What rage, what passionate rage
the earth-born race is showing,
and Pentheus, descendent of the dragon's teeth,
the son of Echion, the earth-born,   540
that savage monster, not a mortal man.
Like a murderous giant,
he attacked the gods.
Now look! He plans to tie me up—
me, a follower of the Thunder Lord!
Already he has taken
my fellow celebrant,
chained him up and hidden him away,
in darkness, inside the house.
Do you see, Dionysus, son of Zeus,   550
how those who speak your glory
are in trial and tribulation, forced to yield?
Come, Lord, come, down from mount Olympus,
holding high your thyrsus, smiling golden;
stop this violent, red-handed man.

epode

Dionysus, are you dancing on Mount Nysa,
where wild animals are nourished,
or on the crags of the Corycian Cave,
waving high your wand above your worshippers?†

---

* See note to line 526.

† Nysa was the mythical mountain where the young Dionysus was nursed by the nymphs. The Corycian Cave, on Mount Parnassus, was haunted by other nymphs; the Athenian worship of Dionysus was held on this mountain in the wintertime.

Or are you hiding in the forest, dense with trees, 560
on Mount Olympus, where once Orpheus played,
plucking his lyre, and by his music
gathered the trees together,
and gathered the wild beasts?*
Pieria, you are blessed:†
the Lord of Ululation honors you;
he will come and bring his dances
and his rites of holy joy;
he will cross swift-flowing Axius,
bringing us, his whirling maenads, 570
over Father Lydias,
whose lovely streams
bring wealth to mortals,
which makes rich the Land of Horses,
Macedonia.‡

(*Dionysus calls to the Chorus from offstage.*)

DIONYSUS: Cry triumph!§
Hear me, maenads! Hear me, maenads!
Hear my voice!

CHORUS: Who is this? Where did it come from,
the joyful call of our Lord, a cry of triumph?

DIONYSUS: Cry *triumph*! I call again! 580
I am Dionysus, son of Semele.

CHORUS: Cry triumph, Master, Master!
Come to us, join our company,
now, O Lord of the Rumbling Thunder!

DIONYSUS: Spirit of Earthquakes, shake up the flat of the earth!

CHORUS: O my Lord, O my Lord,
the palace of Pentheus
shakes on its pediments, soon it will fall!

---

* Orpheus, son of Apollo by one of the Muses, played the lyre so beautifully that even the animals and plants and stones were enchanted. Mount Olympus was the home of the Twelve Gods, who include Dionysus.

† Pieria is in central Macedonia; in mythology it is associated with Orpheus and the Muses (and hence, with the music and song that also play an essential part in Dionysiac worship).

‡ These rivers (Axius and Lydias) are in Macedonia. There may be an implied compliment to Euripides' hosts, since the poet spent his last years at the royal court of Macedonia.

§ During this earthquake scene (lines 576–603), the Chorus and the god are both singing in lyric meters, not speaking.

—Honor him.

—We honor him!* 590

Did you see? The lintels of stone on the columns

have broken apart!

—Now our Lord of the Thunder

shrieks in triumph in the house!

DIONYSUS: (*still from offstage*) Light the fiery torch of lightning!

Burn it all, burn it down, burn the whole house of Pentheus!

CHORUS: Oh, look! Did you see?

Do you see the fire, do you see what's happening?

The flame of Zeus's lightning burns again around the tomb of

Semele,

thunderbolt that struck her long ago!

Throw yourselves to the ground, 600

trembling maenads, throw your bodies down.

Our lord the son of Zeus

has come upon this house;

he turns it downside up and upside-down.

(*Dionysus enters, disguised as the Stranger.*)

DIONYSUS:† Women of Asia, why be so alarmed?

Why are you falling to the ground? Because

Bacchus is making Pentheus' palace quake?

Stand up, be confident, no need to tremble!

CHORUS: Light of my life, my ecstasy, my joy!

We were alone, but now you're here, you're safe!

DIONYSUS: Did you despair, when I was taken in 610

to Pentheus' dark dungeons, in his snares?

CHORUS: Of course! Who could protect me, if you fell?

How did you free yourself from that blasphemer?

DIONYSUS: Easily. I saved myself; no trouble.

CHORUS: Did Pentheus not tie your hands with ropes?

DIONYSUS: That made me laugh! He thought that he could trap me.

He couldn't touch me, all his hopes were foiled.

In the stable where he took and bound me,

he found a bull, and panting, dripping sweat,

grinding his teeth with effort, he was striving 620

---

* The lines are divided between different individual members of the Chorus.

† The lyric section ends here. The meter used in lines 604–41 is trochaic trimeter, suggesting the excited tone of the section; it may have been accompanied by dancing or marching by the Chorus.

to shove his shackles round its legs. But I
sat quietly watching what he did. Just then,
Bacchus came and shook the house, set fire
to Semele's tomb. When he saw this, he thought
his house was burning, and ran here and there,
calling his slaves for water.* So much work,
and useless. Once he saw I had escaped,
he stopped, grabbed his black sword, and ran inside.
Then the Lord of Thunder—as I guess—
made a phantom† in the courtyard, which the man   630
dashed at, stabbing shining air, thinking
he was killing me! And more: the god
has hurt him more: his house is razed, all ruined.
Now he sees what comes of jailing me!
He's exhausted, and has dropped his sword.
This mortal man dared challenge god to fight.
But I came quietly out of the house, to you.
I didn't worry about Pentheus.

      I hear his boots inside the house—it seems
he's coming out to the front. What will he say?
No matter how he huffs, I'll keep my calm.   640
Wise men are gentle and have self-control.
        (Enter Pentheus.)
PENTHEUS:‡ Terrible news! The foreigner escaped me!
  I'd only just managed to chain him up.
  (He sees Dionysus.) But look! He's here!
  This is the man! What's this? Has he got out?
  Is this really him outside the house?
DIONYSUS: Stop there, calm down, enough of this emotion.
PENTHEUS: How on earth did you escape and get here?   650
DIONYSUS: Didn't I say someone would set me free?
  Didn't you listen? PENT.: Who? You talk so strangely.
DIONYSUS: The one who makes thick-clustered vines for mortals.
PENTHEUS: <Wine makes people act indecently.>§

---

* The word for "water" is here Achelous, literally the name of a river—a poetic usage.
† Or "light": the manuscripts read "light" (*phos*), while the word for "phantom" is an emendation.
‡ The meter shifts back to iambic trimester here.
§ There seems to be a line missing here, in which Pentheus says something derogatory about wine; I have supplied this sentence, which is not in the text, to suggest the kind of thing he would have said.

DIONYSUS: You sneer at Dionysus' greatest glory.

PENTHEUS: (*to attendants*) Block up all gates into the garrison!

DIONYSUS: Why? Can't gods leap over any walls?

PENTHEUS: You know it all, but you know nothing real.

DIONYSUS: I've always known whatever I need to know.

      (*Enter Messenger.*)

  Now listen to this messenger from the mountains,

  and find out what he has to say to you.

  I'll wait for you, I will not run away.

MESSENGER: Ruler of this land of Thebes, King Pentheus,   660

  I have come from Mount Cithaeron, shining

  with coverings of white snow that keep on falling.

PENTHEUS: Have you come with some important news?

MESSENGER: I saw the holy women in their frenzy:

  like spears their snow-white bodies flew, stung mad.

  I came because I wished to tell you and the city,

  master, what miracles they do, and more.

  Also, please tell me if I may speak freely,

  or check my tongue about what happened there.

  I fear the quickness of your temper, lord,   670

  your passion: you are all too much a king.

PENTHEUS: Just speak! I promise not to punish you;

  one must not lose one's temper with the innocent.

  But the more terrible the things you say

  about the maenad women, so much more

  I'll punish him who taught them all these tricks.

MESSENGER: My herd of cattle was just climbing up

  to pasture at the summit, as the sun

  was sending out its warmest rays to earth.

  I saw three choruses of women dancers: 680

  one led by Autonoë, and the second

  your mother led; the third was led by Ino.

  They all were fast asleep, bodies relaxed,

  some resting on the boughs of silver fir,

  while others used the oak leaves as a pillow,

  down on the ground, in careless innocence:

  not drunk with wine, as you said, or with music

  of pipes, nor hunting Eros in the wild.

      You mother stood up in the midst of them

and called, "Wake up! Stand up!" She'd heard the lowing 690
of the long-horned cattle coming near.
The women rubbed the deep sleep from their eyes
and stood right up: what an amazing sight!
So beautiful! Young girls, old women, virgins.
First they let their hair down to their shoulders,*
then fastened on their fawnskins, if they'd loosened
from their knots, and belted the brindled furs
with snakes whose tongues stuck out to lick their cheeks.
Those whose breasts were full from giving birth,
who'd left their babies back at home, were cradling 700
deer or wolf-cubs in their arms, which sucked
their white milk. On their heads, they set their wreaths
of ivy, oak, or flowering greenbriar.
When one taps her thyrsus on the rock,
a stream of dewy water rushes out.
Another strikes her fennel on the ground,
and there, right there, the god makes wine pour forth.
If any girl was thirsty for some milk,
she scratched the earth with just her fingertips,
and out spurt jets of gushing white. Their wands 710
of ivy dripped with honey, flowing sweet.
If you had been there, you, too, would have worshipped
the god you now despise—if you had seen it.

We joined together, shepherds and cowherds both,
arguing with each other and debating
about the marvelous miracles we saw.
A man from town who had a way with words
said to us all: "Come now, inhabitants
of these holy mountain valleys, shall we
hunt Agave, Pentheus' mother, drive her 720
out from these Bacchic rites, and please the king?"
We liked his plan, and hid in the tufty thickets,
ready to pounce. At the appointed hour
they raised their wands to start the Bacchic rites,

---

* The costume is echoed by contemporary vase painting of maenads, which usually shows them with hair let down loose. Respectable women would keep their hair braided up.

calling the lord of Thunder, "Praise the lord!,"
calling the son of Zeus, and with their worship
all the mountain, all the beasts were dancing.

    Just then Agave leapt right next to me.
I jumped to catch her—so I hoped: I left
the bushes I had made my hiding place.   730
But she called out, "Swift hunting dogs of mine,
let's hunt these men! Come on now, follow me,
carrying the thyrsus as our weapon."

    We made a quick retreat—we didn't want
those maenads tearing us apart. The women,
holding no swords, attacked a grazing herd
of cattle. Here a heifer, fat with milk
bellows as a woman seizes her
and rips her open. Others shred the calves:
ribs and cloven hooves are flung around,   740
up and down; you should have seen it! Pieces
hung from the firs, bespattered, dripping blood.
Proud butting bulls whose horns were thick with rage
now tumbled to the ground, laid low by girls;
many little hands drag down their bulk.
The flesh that clothed their bodies got torn off
quicker than you could blink your royal eyes.
They swoop like birds uplifted by their speed
through valleys down below, beside the river
that nourishes the fertile Theban harvests.   750
Like soldiers they invade the villages
that lie beneath Cithaeron's rocky crags:
creating chaos everywhere, they turn
Erythrae upside down;* they kidnap babies
out of their homes, and grab bronze pots and iron;
balanced on their shoulders; not one topples
however high the pile. Around their hair,
flames lick but never burn them. Villagers
grew angry and began to arm themselves
against the maenads; terrible, my lord!   760
The men's sharp swords got not a drop of blood;

---

* This is a village in the foothills of Cithaeron. In the original, another village, Hysiae, is also mentioned.

the women hurled their thyrsuses, and hit,
wounding their enemies and routing them.
Such things could not have happened without a god.
Returning to the place from which they came,
they used the streams the god had sent for them
to wash away the blood. Snakes came and licked
the last drops clean away from their bright cheeks.

      So then, my lord, whoever this god may be,
accept him into Thebes. He has great powers,   770
including this, as I have heard: they say
he gives us wine which takes away our pain.
Without the gift of wine, there'd be no sex,
nor any other pleasure for mankind.

CHORUS: I'm frightened to speak freely to a king;
    but still, I will speak out. This Dionysus
    is just as good as any other god.

PENTHEUS: The maenads' shocking actions catch like fire:
    they're spreading closer, to the shame of Greece.
    No time to hesitate. Go, and assemble   780
    all of our troops beside the southern gate:
    the infantry with heavy shields and light,
    the cavalry on their fleet-footed horses,
    the archers, fingers poised upon the string;
    we'll run those Bacchants down. It's just too much
    that I be treated in this way by women!

DIONYSUS: Though you hear my words, you still ignore them,
    Pain-theus.* Though you did me wrong, I'll speak.
    Do not raise your arms against the god.
    Peace, now. Don't try to move the holy women   790
    out of the hills. The Thunderlord won't let you.

PENTHEUS: Still scolding me? You just escaped from jail:
    be careful or I'll punish you again!

DIONYSUS: Better to worship him, that's my advice.
    A mortal ought to sacrifice to god,
    rather than rage and kick when you're spurred on.

PENTHEUS: I'll sacrifice by slaughtering the women;
    I'll wreak havoc on the mountain. They deserve it!

---

* There is again a pun in the original on the name Pentheus with *penthos*, "pain."

DIONYSUS: You'll end up running, all of you: you'll blush
    to see the maenads' wands defeat bronze shields.
PENTHEUS: The stranger is impossible! We tussle,   800
    But still, no matter what, he won't be quiet.
DIONYSUS: Well, sir, you have the chance to make things right.
PENTHEUS: Should I enslave myself to my own slave girls?
DIONYSUS: I'll bring the women here; no need of arms.
PENTHEUS: No end to it! He keeps on trying to trick me.
DIONYSUS: A trick? What if I'm using brains to save you?
PENTHEUS: You plotted with them, to preserve your rites.
DIONYSUS: I plotted, yes; I plotted with the god.
PENTHEUS: Slaves, bring weapons here. And you: be quiet!
DIONYSUS: Wait!   810
    You want to see them gathered on the hill?
PENTHEUS: I'd pay a pile of gold to see that sight.
DIONYSUS: Really? Why do you have this sudden craving?
PENTHEUS: I would be shocked to see them drunk—so awful!
DIONYSUS: But you would like to see what may disgust you?
PENTHEUS: Well, yes, if I can hide behind the fir trees.
DIONYSUS: They'll track you down, even if you try to hide.
PENTHEUS: You're absolutely right, that's clearly true.
DIONYSUS: Then shall I lead you? Do you want to try it?
PENTHEUS: Yes, please: right away! I just can't wait.   820
DIONYSUS: Quick then: here's a dress. You put it on.
PENTHEUS: What? Will my status change, from man to woman?
DIONYSUS: If they catch you as a man, they'll kill you.
PENTHEUS: You're right. You've always had such good ideas.
DIONYSUS: Yes, Dionysus taught me everything.
PENTHEUS: How can I best follow your advice?
DIONYSUS: Come inside with me, I'll get you dressed.
PENTHEUS: Dressed—in a woman's dress? I feel ashamed.
DIONYSUS: Don't you want to watch the maenad show?
PENTHEUS: I do! But how exactly must I dress?   830
DIONYSUS: I'll pull a flowing wig over your head.
PENTHEUS: What is the second item in my outfit?
DIONYSUS: A floor-length dress, and band around your hair.
PENTHEUS: And what accessories will you add to these?
DIONYSUS: A spotty deerskin cape, and a thyrsus wand.
PENTHEUS: But I could never put on women's clothes.

DIONYSUS: If you fight the Bacchants, blood will spill.
PENTHEUS: That's true. I first must go and spy on them.
DIONYSUS: Smarter than hunting wrong by doing wrong.
PENTHEUS: What if I should be seen when leaving town? 840
DIONYSUS: We travel secret paths. I'll lead the way.
PENTHEUS: Anything, just don't let the maenads mock me.
    We'll go inside. I'll plan things for the best.
DIONYSUS: So be it. Anyway, I'm all prepared.
PENTHEUS: I'll go inside, I guess. Maybe I'll arm
    and march against them, or adopt your plans.
        (Exit Pentheus.)
DIONYSUS: *(to the Chorus)*
    The man is heading for the net: he'll go
    to where the maenads are, where he will die.
        Lord Bacchus, now the work is yours. You're near.
    We'll make him pay: but you first drive him mad, 850
    out of his mind; insert a dizzy madness.
    If he were sane, he'd never do it; veering
    away from sanity, he'll strip for me.
    I want him to be laughed at by the Thebans:
    I'll lead him through the city in a dress,
    after those dreadful threats he made before.
    But I will fashion Pentheus in the dress
    he'll wear to go to death, a trip to slaughter,
    killed at his mother's hands. He'll recognize
    the true god, Dionysus, son of Zeus, 860
    most dreadful and most gentle to mankind.

strophe

    CHORUS: Will my white feet ever dance
        in the night-long Bacchic dances?
        Will I throw my head back, neck exposed,
        to the night air wet with dew,
        like a fawn, leaping, laughing,
        in the green joy of the meadow,
        when she discovers freedom from the terror of the hunt,
        escapes the guards around the woven nets,* 870

---

* Nets were commonly used in hunting, to trap the animal before going in for the kill.

and the huntsman barks, "Hold back!"
to hounds that strain to run.
Struggling, swift she dashes, like the storm-winds; out she bursts,
over the meadow down there by the river,
full of joy in the wild with no people, and joy at the lushness
of the shadows in the woods.
What is wisdom? Or what better gift
can gods give mortals than to hold
an upper hand
above the enemy's head?   880
We always want the best.*

antistrophe

The strength of gods
is slow but sure.
It straightens out the kinks
of human folly, human pride,
human madness, failure
to worship the divine.
Cunningly they hide
as Time runs his slow race.
They hunt the heretic.   890
Never set your plans or thoughts above the laws.
Small the price
of faith in the power
of whatever is holy.
Believe in tradition,
both lawful and natural.
What is wisdom? Or what better gift
can gods give mortals than to hold
an upper hand
above the enemy's head?   900
We always want the best.

epode

One kind of happiness is to survive
a storm at sea, and reach the shore in safety.
Another is to triumph over hardship.
Another is surpassing other people,

---

* The original phrase is proverbial, suggesting, more literally, "A thing of beauty is dear forever."

moving up in wealth and strength and power.
Or one can hope; there are so many hopes.
Some human hopes succeed
and others fail.
But a truly happy life   910
is happiness day by day.

DIONYSUS: (*calling to the palace*)
You there! So keen to see, so keen to get
things you should never ask for: Pentheus!
Come out before the palace, let me see you,
dressed as a woman, as a frenzied maenad,
the mirror image of your aunt and mother.
   (*Pentheus comes out, dressed in women's clothes.*)
Ah, it's you. Just like a Theban princess!
PENTHEUS: I seem to see two suns, and Thebes itself,
the seven-gated citadel, looks double,
and you, my leader, you look like a bull: 920
I think I see horns growing on your head.
You've changed into a bull—or were you always?
DIONYSUS: The god is near now: earlier he was hostile,
but now he's on our side. Now you can see.
PENTHEUS: How do I look? How is my posture? Is it
like my aunt's or mother's way of standing?
DIONYSUS: When I look at you, it's them I see.
But this curl of yours is out of place,
slipped from where I fixed it in your headband.
PENTHEUS: I dislodged it when I tossed my hair back,   930
dancing in the palace, maenad-style.
DIONYSUS: Then let me fix it. I'll take care of you.
I'll put your hair in place. Lift up your head.
PENTHEUS: I'm all yours now: go on, you can arrange it.
DIONYSUS: Your belt needs tightening, your pleats are crooked;
so let me straighten them, down to your ankles.
PENTHEUS: I think it's rumpled here, by my right foot;
but on the other side, my skirt hangs smooth.
DIONYSUS: You'll say I am your best friend, when you see
to your astonishment, the maenads sane.   940
PENTHEUS: Should I lift my thyrsus in my right hand,
or the left, to look more like a Bacchant?

DIONYSUS: The right, and stamp your right foot keeping time.
   I'm glad you've lost the mind you used to have.
PENTHEUS: Then can I lift the peaks of Mount Cithaeron
   upon my shoulders with the maenad girls?
DIONYSUS: You could, should you so wish. Your former thoughts
   were sick, but now you're thinking as you should.
PENTHEUS: Shall I bring crowbars? Or just set my back   950
   to lift the mountain up with my bare hands?
DIONYSUS: No: do not destroy the holy places,
   caves of the nymphs, and grottoes sweet with Pan-pipes.
PENTHEUS: Yes; brute force is not the way to win
   against these girls. I'll hide behind the trees.
DIONYSUS: You'll find the perfect place to hide and spy,
   sneaking to watch the maenads secretly.
PENTHEUS: Yes! I can see them in the bushes now,
   like mating birds, enmeshed in nets of love.
DIONYSUS: No wonder that you want to go and watch.
   Perhaps you'll catch them: or they'll catch you first.   960
PENTHEUS: Parade me through the midst of Thebes in triumph;
   I am the only man who dares to go.
DIONYSUS: Alone you suffer for your town, alone;
   there are indeed more toils awaiting you.
   Follow me: I will guide you there in safety,
   but someone else will bring you back.   PENT.: My mother!
DIONYSUS: They'll watch you, like a show.   PENT.: That's why I'm going.
DIONYSUS: You will be carried—   PENT.: Ah, you'll make me soft!
DIONYSUS: In your mother's arms.   PENT.: You're spoiling me!
DIONYSUS: A kind of spoiling.   PENT.: Well, I do deserve it.   970

   (Exit Pentheus.)
DIONYSUS: Terrible man: your sufferings will be terrible,
   a tale whose fame will stretch to heaven's height.
   Agave and your sisters, Cadmus' daughters,
   reach out your arms! I bring you this young man
   for a great competition,* which I'll win,
   as will the Thunder god. Now time will tell.

---

* The word for "competition," *agōn*, implies struggle; it was also used for the competitions between the tragic playwrights at the City Dionysia.

strophe

CHORUS: Go! Go! Go to the mountains, swift she-dogs of Frenzy,
go where the daughters of Cadmus are gathered
for their rituals, and sting them to madness;
rouse them against this maddened man who spies   980
on maenads—this fake woman in a dress.
As he watches from the smooth or craggy rock
his mother first will see him
and call out to the women:
"Who is following our footsteps, maenads?
Who is coming to the mountain, to the mountain?
We are Cadmus' daughters, we are mountain runners. Who is he?
Who is his mother? Not a woman made of blood.
He's the child of a lioness
or a Libyan Gorgon's son.   990
Let Justice walk in brightness with a sword
to stab right through the throat
of the man who has no god, no law, no righteousness,
the earth-born son of Echion.

antistrophe

The man of unjust mind and lawless passion
sets out with crazy cunning and perverted purpose
against your worship, Bacchus,
and your mother's.   1000
Death waits for no excuse. It teaches us restraint,
and how to moderate our minds to things divine.
If you want a painless life, live as a mortal should.
I have no quarrel with cleverness; I love
to hunt it down. But other things are greater;
plain to see. What a life, to live for beauty
by day and through the night
in piety and reverence, rejecting
law without morality. Honor the gods.   1010
Let Justice walk in brightness with a sword
to stab right through the throat
of the man who has no god, no law, no righteousness,
the earth-born son of Echion.

epode

Come, Bacchus! Show yourself to us,

as bull or many-headed snake,
or fire-breathing lion.
Come with smiling face, and throw   1020
a net around that maenad hunter,
a net of death to make him fall
at the hands of the herd of your people.

SECOND MESSENGER: Long ago, the old king came from Sidon
   to sow the earth-born serpent sons: this house
   was happy once, as every Greek could say.
   But now, although I am a slave, I weep for you.*

CHORUS: What is the news? Is it about the maenads?

MESSENGER: Pentheus is dead, the son of Echion.   1030

   CHORUS: O Lord of Thunder, now you are revealed a mighty God!†

MESSENGER: What are you saying? What's this? Woman, surely
   you can't be happy at my master's downfall?

   CHORUS: Ah, joy, cry freedom! I am a foreign woman and I sing a
       foreign song.
       Cry freedom! I need no longer tremble at my bonds!

MESSENGER: You don't think Thebes has men <who could enslave you>?‡

   CHORUS: My lord is Dionysus, Dionysus!
       Thebes has no power over me.

MESSENGER: I can understand your feelings, women:
   but it's ugly to take pleasure in misfortune.   1040

   CHORUS: The wicked man is dead! He died on his wicked quest!
       Tell me, tell me, tell me, how did he die?

MESSENGER: We left the settlements of Thebes behind,
   and crossed the streaming river Asopus.
   We reached the craggy slopes of Mount Cithaeron,
   the king and I—I followed Pentheus,
   but the stranger was our guide to find the sight.
       First we settled in a grassy valley
   just creeping quietly and saying nothing,
   so as to see but not be seen ourselves.   1050
   The glen was bound by cliffs and wet with streams;

---

* Line 1028 is skipped because it is an interpolated line, borrowed from the *Medea* (54) and inserted here by a later commentator. It runs, "The masters' fortunes [affect] good slaves."

† The meter of the Chorus becomes lyrical, a mark of their excitement. The Messenger continues to speak in iambics, the normal dialogue meter.

‡ The bracketed phrase represents an incomplete line; after 1036, a line seems to be missing.

the pine trees cast thick shadows. There the maenads
sat working with their hands, quite happily.
Some were twining ivy round their sticks
to make them into magic wands again.
Others were singing rounds of Bacchic songs,
like glad young ponies free from painted yokes.
A crowd of women! But poor Pentheus
could hardly see them, and he said, "From here,
stranger, I cannot see these maenad fakes.   1060
I need to get up higher, into the pine tree,
to see exactly what disgusting things
they're doing now." The stranger then performed
a miracle! I saw it! Reaching up
he took a pine tree's highest branch, and brought it
down, down to the shadowy earth, curved in a circle
like a bow or wheel or measuring compass.
So the stranger bent the mountain tree trunk,
round to the earth—a superhuman deed.
He settled Pentheus in a bough of the tree,   1070
and smoothly, so the rider would not fall,
let go: the branch swept up between his hands,
towering straight and high to upper heaven,
with my master sitting on its back.
But hoping to see them, he himself was seen.
At first, he was invisible up high.
The stranger vanished, but there was a voice
shouting from the sky; in my opinion
it was Dionysus. "Girls, I bring you
the man who mocked both you and me, and laughed   1080
at these, my holy rituals. Take revenge!"
No sooner said, than light of magic fire
shot up and stretched between the earth and heaven.
The air was silent; in the woody glade
not a leaf stirred, no creature made a sound.
The women heard the voice, but not distinctly,
so up they stood and looked around again.
He called again, and when the women heard
the clear command of Dionysus, off they shot
quick as a flock of doves, their feet a whir   1090

of running motion: all of them, Agave
his mother, and her sisters, Cadmus' daughters,
and all the maenads. Over the gushing brooks
and crags they leaped, inspired by the god.
When they saw my master in the tree,
first they climbed a towering rock, then hurled
stones at him with all their might, and branches
of fir trees, which they used as javelins.
Others tossed their thyrsus through the air
at Pentheus, their poor target. But they missed.   1100
For he was higher than their zeal could reach;
poor man, his seat had now become a trap.
At last they struck the tree roots with a blast
like thunder, but with crowbars made of wood.
They struggled mightily, to no avail.
Then called Agave: "Maenads, join in a circle!
Seize the trunk and we will catch this beast
that climbs up there, this spy that wants to tell
the secret ways we dance to please the god."
Hands without number grasped the tree and felled it.   1110
From high aloft, high up, down to the ground
he fell, with desperate, infinite cries of loss:
Pentheus. He knew now the end was near.
His mother, priestess of the sacrifice,
was first to fall on him. He hoped to show her
who he was: he ripped his headband off,
to stop her killing him: poor, poor Agave.
Touching her cheek, "Mother," he said, "I am
your child, Pentheus, son of Echion.
Mother, pity me! Don't kill me, Mother.   1120
I made mistakes, but I am still your child."
        But she was foaming at the mouth, her eyes
rolled all around; her mind was mindless now.
Held by the god, she paid the man no heed.
She grabbed his left arm just below the elbow:
wedging her foot against the victim's ribs
she ripped his shoulder off—not by mere force;
the god made easy everything they touched.
On his right arm worked Ino, ripping flesh;

Autonoë and the mob of maenads gripped him,   1130
screaming as one. While he had breath, he cried,
but they were whooping victory calls. One took
an arm, a foot another, boot and all.
They stripped his torso bare, staining their nails
with blood, then tossed the balls of flesh around.
Pentheus' body lies in fragments now:
on the hard rocks, and mingled with the leaves,
buried in woodland, hard to find. His mother
stumbled across his head: poor head! She grabbed it,
and fixed it on her thyrsus, like a lion's,   1140
to wave in joyful triumph at her hunt.
Sad triumph! She ran all across the mountain,
down through Cithaeron, leaving there her sisters
dancing with maenads. Now she has arrived
inside the city walls. She's shouting: "Bacchus!
You shared the hunt with me, you share the prize!
Together we have won this victory!"
Tears are the prize the god has won for her.
I'm leaving this disaster scene before
Agave's homecoming. Respect religion   1150
and practice self-restraint; that is, I think,
the best and wisest thing for any mortal.

    CHORUS:*   Let us dance together for the god!
        Let us shout together for the fall
        of Pentheus, the son of dragon seed.
        He wore the women's dress,
        he took the fennel wand, the lovely thyrsus,
        as the bull was guiding him to doom.
        Daughters of Cadmus, worshippers with us,   1160
        you have turned our song of triumph
        to cries of grief, to tears.
        Here's a good game: try to embrace your child
        when your hands are dripping with his blood.
    But now I see Agave, running to the palace,†
    Pentheus' mother, with her rolling eyes:

---

* A brief song in an excitable lyric meter, dochmiacs.
† Lyrics end here, and the Chorus speak in iambics.

Welcome the celebrants of the Lord of Noise!

    (Enter Agave.)

strophe

AGAVE:* Maenads from the East!   CHOR.: No, don't push me to look!

AGAVE: Look: I've brought down something from the hills,

    fresh-killed, a curling sprout: what a lucky hunt!   1170

  Here's a lovely present for our house.

CHORUS: I see it, and I'll take you as my partner in the dance; a

  celebration.

AGAVE: I caught this cub without even a net,

  this wild young lion cub.

  Just look at it!†

CHORUS: Where did you get it? Out in the wilds?

AGAVE: Cithaeron.   CHOR.: Cithaeron?

AGAVE: I killed him.

CHORUS: Who struck the blow?   AGAVE: I was the first, the first to

                        win the prize.

  Lady Luck's my title, all the dancers call me that.   1180

CHORUS: Who else?   AGAVE: You know Cadmus?

CHORUS: What about Cadmus?   AGAVE: All his daughters

  grabbed the animal. But I was first!

  Yes, this was a lucky, lucky hunt!

antistrophe

Now share the feast!   CHOR.: What, me? Me, share? What horror!

AGAVE: The calf is young: look, his cheeks

  have only just begun to sprout soft hair.

CHORUS: Yes, that hair does look just like a wild beast's fur.

AGAVE: Dionysus is a master hunter:

  wisely he hurled his maenads

  at this beast.   1190

CHORUS: Yes, the Lord is a hunter.

AGAVE: So, you praise me?   CHOR.: Yes, I praise you.

AGAVE: And soon the Thebans—

CHORUS: And your child, Pentheus—?   AGAVE: —will praise his

                             mother!

  For catching this lion cub, my hunting prize.

---

* The dialogue in the first part of this scene, until line 1200, is in lyric meter and was presumably accompanied by dancing—a mark of its intense emotional pitch.

† The text in these lines is doubtful.

CHORUS: No ordinary prize.   AGAVE: No ordinary hunt!
CHORUS: Are you happy?   AGAVE: I am full of joy.
    In this hunt, I have achieved
    things great beyond great, and plain to see.
CHORUS:* Then, poor Agave, show the citizens   1200
    the victory prize you've carried from this hunt.
AGAVE: Beautiful Thebes, with such majestic towers!
    Citizens, you've come to see the beast
    we caught, we daughters of the old king Cadmus,
    not using the thonged javelins of Thessaly,†
    or nets, but just the sharp and pointed nails
    of our white hands. After this deed of ours,
    no hunter armed with spears can boast his kill.
    I caught this creature with my hands alone,
    and with bare hands I tore his limbs apart.   1210
    Where is my father? Go, slaves, call him here.
    And where is Pentheus, my son? He must
    set up a ladder firm against the house,
    and nail this lion's head up there on the frieze,
    this prize of mine, the spoils of my hunt.
        (Enter Cadmus, accompanied by slaves carrying a covered
        stretcher.)
CADMUS: What a wretched burden: here's the corpse
    of my poor Pentheus. Slaves, come, bring it here,
    set it before the house. I labored hard
    searching and searching for the pieces, scattered
    on Mount Cithaeron's slopes and in the woods: 1220
    no easy search, they lay so far apart.
    I heard the dreadful things my daughters did,
    when I had left the maenads and returned
    through the town walls, with old Tiresias.
    Then I turned back, back to the hills, to get
    the body of the boy the maenads killed.
    I saw there Autonoë, who once bore
    poor Actaeon; and I saw Ino, too,
    hovering by the trees, still stung to frenzy.

---

* The meter now reverts to iambics, the normal dialogue meter.
† The people of Thessaly commonly used javelins for hunting.

Poor things! Then someone told me that Agave   1230
was running here, still crazy. It was true.
> (*Sees Agave.*)
I see her now. It's not a happy sight.
AGAVE: You must be very proud of us now, Father!
Your daughters are the best by far, the best
of all humanity—especially me!
I left the loom and shuttle, and I rose
to greater things: I hunt with my bare hands.
Now, as you see, I'm carrying in my arms
this prize I've caught. I'll hang it on your house.
But first, dear Father, wouldn't you like to hold it?   1240
Feel the joy of my successful hunt,
and call our friends to feast. Yes, you are lucky!
You're blessed by these accomplishments of mine.
CADMUS: Pain! This passes bearing.* I can't look:
poor daughter, you hold slaughter in your arms.
You've made a lovely killing for the gods,
and call the Thebans to a feast, and me.
I have to weep, for you and for myself.
The god, the Lord of Thunder, our own kinsman,
was just, too just: he has destroyed us all.   1250
AGAVE: Old men are always grumpy, full of scowls.
I hope my son will grow up good at hunting,
taking after me, his huntress mother,
when he joins Theban youths to go in quest
of animals in the wild. All he can do
is fight the gods.† Father, it's your job
to give him good advice. Go, someone, call him!
Bring him to see me, see my happiness!
CADMUS: Ah, daughter! When you see what you have done,
your grief will pass all grief. But if you stay   1260
forever in this state of mind you're in,
you can't be happy, but you're not unhappy.
AGAVE: What's wrong with how things are? What isn't good?
CADMUS: First, turn your head and look up at the sky.

---

* He uses the word *penthos* for "pain," suggestive of Pentheus' name.

† She wishes he would fight animals, in the natural way of the hunter, rather than only "fighting" gods.

AGAVE: All right. But why do you want me to look there?

CADMUS: Does it seem the same to you, or different?

AGAVE: It's brighter than before, it's clearer now.

CADMUS: Do you still feel troubled and excited?

AGAVE: I don't know what you mean. But I suppose
   I am aware; my mind is somehow changing.   1270

CADMUS: Can you listen then, and answer clearly?

AGAVE: Yes, Father. What were we saying? I forget.

CADMUS: What household did you come to as a bride?

AGAVE: You gave me to the so-called Snake-Son: Echion.

CADMUS: You had a baby with your husband: named?

AGAVE: Pentheus, he's the son we had together.

CADMUS: Whose head, then, are you holding in your arms?

AGAVE: A lion's head; the hunters told me so.

CADMUS: Now look more closely; easy enough to look.

AGAVE: Oh, what's this I see? What's this I'm holding?   1280

CADMUS: Look carefully, you'll understand it better.

AGAVE: I see horror—agony. I see my ruin.

CADMUS: You don't see a lion anymore?

AGAVE: No, I am holding my own Pentheus' head.

CADMUS: I've been in mourning long before you knew.

AGAVE: Who killed him? How did he get here, in my hands?

CADMUS: The truth is painful when the time is wrong.

AGAVE: Tell me! My heart is thumping. Tell me now!

CADMUS: You killed him, and your sisters. You're the one.

AGAVE: What? Where did he die? At home, or where?   1290

CADMUS: Where once the hounds ripped Actaeon between them.

AGAVE: But why did this poor man go to Cithaeron?

CADMUS: He went to mock your maenads and your god.

AGAVE: How did we flock there? What was going on?

CADMUS: You were possessed; all Thebes was in a frenzy.

AGAVE: Bacchus destroyed us. Now I understand.

CADMUS: He had been insulted: you denied him.

AGAVE: Where is the body of my darling boy?

CADMUS: Here's what there is; I searched as best I could.

AGAVE: Is it all laid out nicely, limb to limb?   1300

   [...

   ...

   ...]

AGAVE: What did my folly have to do with Pentheus?

CADMUS: He was like you: not worshipping the god.
That's why the god blamed all of you alike,
you and this boy; so he destroyed our house,
and me. Now I, who have no son, have seen
my only male descendant—from your womb,
poor daughter—seen him killed, so horribly.
Boy, you gave our darkened house its light,
pillar of our family, my grandson;
you terrified the city. No one dared   1310
insult me in old age, when they saw you.
You took revenge on anyone who tried.
But now I shall be exiled from my home:
I, great Cadmus, who once founded Thebes,
who sowed and harvested that splendid crop.*
My dearest, darling boy—even now you're dead,
child, you're still the one I love the most.
Now you will no longer stroke my beard,
and hold me in your arms, child, saying, "Grandpa,
Who has hurt you, who has done you wrong?   1320
Who has troubled your old heart? Tell me,
so I can punish anyone who hurts you,
Grandpa"—Now: what pain for me, and you,
and for your wretched mother; our poor family!
If anyone does not respect the gods,
look at the death of Pentheus, and believe.

CHORUS: I'm sorry for you, Cadmus. Your child's son
deserved this; it was just—but sad for you.

AGAVE: Father, do you see? My life is overturned—
[…]
[…]
[…]*

DIONYSUS: (*no longer in disguise, speaking from
the palace roof after entering from above*)
[…]†

---

* Another reference to the men born from the dragon's teeth after the founding of Thebes (see note to line 213).

† There is an extensive missing section here, at least fifty lines, because a whole page was lost from an early copy of the text. The missing part apparently included Agave desperately begging to bury the

You will become a serpent, and your wife   1330
will also change her shape and be a snake,
your wife Harmonia, human child of Ares.*
And as the prophecy of Zeus foretold,
you and your wife will drive an oxcart, leading
tribes of barbarians. With your vast army
you'll sack a set of cities. But when they
reach Delphi, they are doomed: no journey home.†
But Ares will protect you and Harmonia,
and make you live forever with the gods.‡
I speak not as a mortal, but the son   1340
of Zeus. If you had not refused to see
what wisdom means, you could have had a god,
the son of Zeus, as ally, and been happy.

CADMUS: I beg you, Dionysus! We did wrong.

DIONYSUS: Too late you've known me; earlier, you failed.

CADMUS: I recognize it. Still, you are too harsh.

DIONYSUS: I was insulted—I, who was born a god.

CADMUS: In anger gods should not resemble mortals.

DIONYSUS: My father Zeus long since decided this.

AGAVE: (*to Cadmus*) Ah, Father, now we have no choice but exile.   1350

DIONYSUS: Then why delay the things that are decreed?

CADMUS: Daughter, what a terrible disaster
for all of us, poor girl, you and your sisters,
and me, poor me: I must, in my old age,

---

body. Cadmus consented; Agave accused herself (as the ancient commentator tells us) and embraced each limb in turn, lamenting over it. Then the god Dionysus appeared from above the palace (on the pulley, the *mēchanē*) in his true form, no longer as the Stranger. The mask and costume of the actor may have changed. Dionysus announced the establishment of his cult at Thebes, which had been his purpose in coming to the city, as he announces in the Prologue. He then blamed the Thebans in general for rejecting him. He then turned to predict the fate of each individual affected by his cult. Agave and her sisters, he said, would have to leave Thebes. When our preserved text resumes, he is delivering a strange prophecy to Cadmus.

* The prophecy was, as Dodds notes, as puzzling to ancient mythologers as to modern readers. The problem is twofold: first, that it does not seem to fit other mythological accounts of the life of Cadmus; and second, that it seems deeply unfair that Cadmus—who has, one might think, done everything right by Dionysus—should be punished in this way. The story seems to be based on Theban legends and ritual practices current at the time of Euripides; in Thebes, Harmonia was once a central household goddess, who seems to have taken snake form.

† There was an ancient tradition, mentioned in Herodotus (9.42–43), that there was an oracle about an army that would come to Greece, sack Delphi, and then be destroyed.

‡ Harmonia, Cadmus' wife, is the daughter of Ares and Aphrodite; hence Ares' special favor toward the couple.

go live with strangers. And, the god foretells,
I'll lead a motley army of barbarians
to Greece, and as a snake, I'll bring my wife,
Harmonia, Ares' daughter, also turned
into a snake, against the tombs and altars
of the Greeks; so says the oracle.   1360
Nor will my suffering cease: I will not cross
Acheron;* I'll find no peace in death.

AGAVE: Father, I, too, have lost my home, and you!

CADMUS: Poor child, why do you cling to me and hold me?
You're like the swan that shelters its white father.

AGAVE: I'm exiled from my home; where can I turn?

CADMUS: I don't know, my child. Your father is no help.

    AGAVE:† Goodbye to my home. Goodbye to my house,
      goodbye to the town of my father.
      Unlucky I leave you, expelled from the rooms where I lived.‡   1370

    CADMUS: Go now, my child, go to Lord Aristaeus.§

    AGAVE: I weep for you, Father.   CAD.: And I for you, child.
      And I weep for your sisters.

AGAVE: Our master, our lord Dionysus
    has brought terrible pain
    on your house.

DIONYSUS: Yes, since I suffered such terrible pain at your hands:
    the Thebans were giving no honor to me and my name.

    AGAVE: Goodbye, Father.   CAD.: Goodbye to you also, poor
                   daughter.
    But there is nothing good about your future.   1380

AGAVE: Take me away, help me and guide me,
    to my poor sisters, companions in exile.
    May I come to a place
    where polluted Cithaeron will never see me
    and my eyes will never see that dreadful mountain,
    and where no thyrsus will bring back the memory.

---

* River of pain in the Underworld.

† The meter shifts to anapests, a marching meter often used when characters enter or—as here—prepare to leave the stage.

‡ The women in a Greek house lived in separate quarters from the men.

§ There seems to be a line missing here; "go" is supplied speculatively. Aristaeus is the husband of Autonoë, Agave's sister; perhaps Agave is told to go and join him in some foreign land.

Those things are for other maenads, not for me.
> *(Agave and Cadmus leave the stage, in different directions.*
> *Dionysus exits above, carried upward by the* mēchanē*)*

CHORUS: Spirits divine take many shapes, and many
are the unexpected actions of the gods.
Our predictions do not come to pass;   1390
the god finds a way for what we don't expect.
This is what has happened here today.

APPENDICES

Appendix A

"Saving the City": Tragedy in Its Civic Context
Daniel Mendelsohn

At the climax of Aristophanes' comedy *Frogs*, a tartly affectionate sendup of Greek tragedy that premiered in 405 B.C., Dionysus, the god of wine and theater, is forced to judge a literary contest between two dead playwrights. Earlier in the play, the god had descended to the Underworld in order to retrieve his favorite tragedian, Euripides, who'd died the previous year; without him, Dionysus grumpily asserts, the theatrical scene has grown rather dreary. But once he arrives in the land of the dead, he finds himself thrust into a violent literary quarrel: at the table of Pluto, god of the dead, the newcomer Euripides has claimed the seat of Best Tragic Poet—a place long held by the revered Aeschylus, author of the *Oresteia*, who's been dead for fifty years. A series of competitions ensues, during which excerpts of the two poets' works are rather fancifully compared and evaluated—scenes replete with the kind of in-jokes still beloved of theater lovers. (At one point, lines from various plays by the occasionally bombastic Aeschylus are "weighed" against verses by the occasionally glib Euripides: Aeschylus wins, because his diction is "heavier.") None of these contests is decisive, however, and so Dionysus establishes a final criterion for the title of Best Tragic Poet. The winner, he asserts, must be the one who offers to the city the most useful advice—the one whose work can "save the city."

Today, the idea that a work written for the theater could "save" a nation—for this was what Aristophanes' word *polis*, "city," really meant: Athens, for the Athenians, was their country—seems odd, even as a joke. For us, theater and politics are two distinct realms. We think of theater as a form of entertainment, and of theatergoing as a leisure-time activity, something cordoned off from our workaday lives and even more from public life and political action. In the contemporary theatrical landscape, overtly political dramas that seize the public's imagination and garner critical acclaim (Arthur Miller's *The Crucible*, say, with its thinly veiled parable about McCarthyism, or Tony Kushner's AIDS epic *Angels in America*) are the exception rather than the rule; we rarely expect even the most trenchant of such works to have any effect on national policy or politics (let alone to "save the city"). The segregation of theater from civic concerns is, of course, only more pronounced in the case of plays that eschew overtly political subjects for psychological or familial or social themes—which is to say, most of the "serious" drama that we see. The lessons that *A Streetcar Named Desire* has to teach about beauty and vulnerability and madness are lessons we learn as private people, not as voters.

The circumstances in which we attend theatrical performances today underscore the segregation between our theater and what Aristophanes would call "the city." We attend plays in the evening, when the workday is over, or on weekends, at the end of the working week. When we attend a performance of a drama or a musical comedy, we do so as private persons expressing personal preferences: from a wide array of choices we choose the play we happen to be interested in at the moment; we select the date and the time that suit us; we order our tickets so as to be sure to have the kind of seats we prefer. When we enter the theater itself, however, the "selves" that we have expressed in making these choices disappear: we assume a kind of willed anonymity, exchanging the familiar world of lights and activity and noise for an uncanny, hushed darkness. In this blackness we sit, invisible and unrecognizable to one another until such time as the play is over, at which point the lights come up and we shuffle out of the theater to assume our public identities once more.

Private, personal, anonymous, invisible: it would be hard to think of a theatergoing experience less like the one familiar to the ordinary Athenian citizen during the 400s B.C. This—the so-called "Athenian century," the hundred-year period of Athens' political and cultural dominance, from the establishment of her democratic government in 509 B.C. to her humiliating defeat at the end of the three-decade-long Peloponnesian War in 404—was also the century, not coincidentally, in which the dramatic masterpieces collected in this volume were composed, produced, and first performed. I say "not coincidentally" because what we think of as "Greek tragedy" was, properly speaking, "Athenian tragedy": invented at Athens, this uniquely Athenian genre flourished in tandem with the Athenian state—and withered and died with it, too.

That the fates of Athens and of tragedy were so closely entwined suggests a profound organic connection between the polity and the genre. For us, the children of Freud, great drama is often most satisfying when it enacts the therapy-like process by which the individual psyche is stripped of its pretensions or delusions to stand, finally, exposed to scrutiny—and, as often as not, to the audience's pity or revulsion. (One thinks again of *Streetcar*.) But even though there are great Greek plays that enact that same process—Sophocles' *Oedipus*, most notably—it would appear, given the strange twinning of Athenian drama and

Athenian political history, that for the Athenians, tragedy was just as much about "the city" as it was about the individual. Indeed, the notion of "the individual" in our sense of the word was foreign to the Greeks: when the philosopher Aristotle famously says that "the human is a political animal," he didn't mean that we are all like Lyndon Baines Johnson but, rather, that the human species is naturally social and civic—by nature suited to live in a *polis*, a "city."

In fact, both the structure of the Greek plays and the context in which they were originally performed (the latter in particular being unimaginably foreign to our way of experiencing the theater, as will soon be clear) emphasized the political aspect of life—that is, political in Aristotle's sense, "having to do with the *polis*." As a result, tragedy became the ideal literary vehicle for exploring, and often questioning, the political, social, and civic values of Athens herself.

In his treatise *Poetics*, the first extended work of theater criticism in the Western tradition, Aristotle, writing in the mid-300s B.C. and looking back to the great century of Athenian drama and, beyond that, to the dim origins of drama itself, suggests that tragedy grew out of a kind of ritual chorus known as dithyramb, sung in honor of the god Dionysus. (We know that in the fifth century—perhaps a century and a half after the primal moment that Aristotle was trying to reconstruct—dithyrambs were sung at public festivals by choruses of fifty singers, men or boys. These were led by an *exarchon*, a performer who "led off" the singing.) The philosopher asserts that tragedy grew out of an instant of "improvisation" on the part of these chorus leaders who, evidently, decided at a certain point that instead of simply feeding the opening bars of the chorus to their fellow singers, they were going to sing a few lines of their own.

Whether this notion was based on hard evidence known to the author and since lost, or simply a shrewd surmise, the theory has an obvious appeal: its narrative—of the leader who sets himself apart from the group, the individual who is willing to stand isolated from others—is, in embryo, the narrative of most Greek tragedies. Every one of the thirty-two Athenian tragedies that have survived from antiquity to the present day enacts the process whereby someone makes a decision to take an oppositional stance; every one of these plays, moreover, consists of a series of arguments about that decision, speeches that are delivered in the presence of a Chorus that never leave the stage and that, at intervals, sing songs that comment on, or are thematically related to, the controversy at the heart of the play. What is noteworthy in all this, what contributes the "political" element (in Aristotle's sense), is the constant presence of the Chorus: the group that, like the city itself, is always watching, listening, observing.

These relatively simple formal components—the pointed debates between characters or between a character and the Chorus, the rhythmic alternations between individual utterance and choral song—allowed Athenian dramas to explore with particular incisiveness the city's great social and civic preoccupations. Many people know that Athens in the fifth century B.C. was a radical democracy, in which all citizens voted directly on most matters of pressing public concern and in whose day-to-day workings all citizens were, at least theoretically, expected to participate. (Certain offices were assigned by lot.) What is less well known is that the great aristocratic families of an earlier era in the city's history continued to hold and to covet power, manipulating the ostensibly democratic system in order to preserve their prestige and privileges; Pericles, for instance, belonged to a family that might well be compared to the Vanderbilts or the Rockefellers of a later age. Unsurprisingly, the tensions between glamorous, charismatic, and powerful leaders—"heroes," in a word—and the masses, who are simultaneously susceptible to and suspicious of those heroes' allure, often make themselves felt in Greek tragedy, where uneasy dynamics between protagonists and Choruses are a central feature in many works. Whatever else Sophocles' *Oedipus* is about, the arc that it traces from the Chorus's worshipful adulation of the hero at the beginning of the play to the revulsion and pity they feel for him by the play's final revelation of his true identity reminds us that our relationship to great leaders is often unstable.

This opposition between individual and group, which forms one strand of tragedy's DNA, allows it to dramatize with particular elegance certain kinds of political conflicts and, indeed, to examine certain kinds of polities. Aeschylus' *Agamemnon* begins with the Watchman hinting darkly at the smoldering resentment felt by the people toward the queen, Clytemnestra, who has seized power illicitly with her paramour, Aegisthus; by the end of the play this tension has erupted into open confrontation between the queen and the Chorus leader, a dire instability that is resolved only at the end of the final play of the trilogy to which the *Agamemnon* belongs, when the rule of law is enshrined at last. In the same playwright's *Persians*, the Chorus of Persian elders is pointedly reminded by another queen—the mother of the emperor, Xerxes, who has failed in his attempt to invade Greece—that although the foolish ruler has been defeated, he will return from his campaign to reign with impunity in Persia. Monarchs, we are reminded—unlike elected leaders—are not subject to political scrutiny or review.

The other strand of tragedy's DNA—the theater's ability to enact confrontations between entire worldviews by placing two individuals with opposing convictions across from each other onstage and letting them argue—allowed the genre both to articulate and to investigate other kinds of tension that surged through the Athenian polity. The best-known example occurs in Sophocles' *Antigone*, which features a stark confrontation between two characters who are mouthpieces of very different views about the individual's relation to the state: one character insists on the authority of the state and on obedience to its laws, whereas the other insists on adherence to religious custom and allegiance to family and clan. In real life, these two realms were and are, of necessity, interdependent; the staged conflict in Sophocles' play literally dramatizes the difficulties of finding equilibrium between them.

It is, indeed, no accident that so many tragedies explore the fatal consequences of a failure to maintain a healthy balance—often among the disparate elements of a single individual's nature, which, in some plays, becomes a microcosm for "the city" as a whole. In Euripides' *Bacchae*, the protagonist, an overly rigid young king whose obsessive interest in maintaining political control (and what we would call psychological "boundaries"; he's very anxious about sexuality, among other things) leads him, as it does the king in *Antigone*, to ignore certain social and religious priorities at terrible cost to his city. This political failing is enacted in the play's highly symbolic finale, a scene of astonishing violence in which the youthful ruler is literally torn to pieces, no longer in control of anything, unable to maintain the boundaries even of his own body. The *Bacchae*, it's worth pointing out, was produced in 405 B.C., a year after its author's death, a year before the fall of Athens itself: a polity whose inability to maintain its own balance, one might say, led to its "tragic" fall from the heights of political and cultural supremacy. And 405 was also the year that saw the first performance of *Frogs*, the comedy that expressed the forlorn hope that a play could save the city.

The circumstances under which the Athenian citizen took in these dramas, followed these plots, and analyzed these conflicts further emphasized the theater's public and civic concerns. All Greek tragedies were composed for and performed as part of a grand annual religious and civic ceremonial known as the City (or Great) Dionysia, held each spring in honor of Dionysus (a deity who, as the timing of the festival suggests, also presided over vegetative fertility and growth). The climax of this celebration, which went on for five days and featured magnificent processions and sacrifices, was the theatrical performances. Each year, three dramatists were selected to present four plays each: three tragedies (sometimes linked by plot or theme as a trilogy) plus one so-called "satyr play," a short comedy whose ribald humor was, presumably, meant to alleviate the intense emotionality of the serious dramas that preceded it.

This brings me back to our typical Athenian of the 400s B.C. and why he would have found our theatergoing practices incomprehensible: for the performances he attended had almost nothing in common with the ones we are familiar with today. Whereas our theaters plunge us into darkness as a necessary condition for the "suspension of disbelief," Greek plays were performed in broad daylight, the performances starting at dawn and ending at sundown. This meant, among other things, that the citizens who attended the plays were not anonymous, as we are, but as plainly visible to one another as the actors and Chorus on the stage were. Those Chorus members, it's worth mentioning, were not professionals but ordinary Athenians: the audience was mirrored therefore on the stage. This must have given audiences a thrilling sense of connection to the dramas that were unfolding before them (particularly, you can't help feeling, those in which the Choruses stood up to kings and tyrants). The audience members didn't choose their seats, as we do, but were seated according to "tribes," the ten subcommunities into which all Athenian citizens were divided as part of the city's political structuring. All citizens were expected to attend: by Aristotle's time, a fund had been established to help poorer Athenians pay to attend the theatrical and civic festivals.

The *polis*-oriented organization of the audience was reflected in the elaborate pre-performance ceremonials. Before the performances began, the city's ten leading generals, the *stratēgoi*, solemnly poured libations before the vast audience. (The Theater of Dionysus could hold as many as eighteen thousand spectators.) Following that rite, the tribute that had been amassed that year from Athens' subject-allies was paraded around the theater precinct; afterward, the names of citizens who had greatly benefited the city in some way were recited by heralds, each civic benefactor receiving an honorary garland or crown. Finally, the sons of Athenian soldiers who had died in the city's wars—boys who had since been raised at the state's expense—were paraded before the vast audience. The official proclamation that was recited by a herald during this portion of the ceremonies underscored the elaborate connections between the city, its citizens, and the theater, connections that lay at the heart of the entire festival:

> These young men, whose fathers showed themselves brave men and
> died in war, have been supported by the state until they have come
> of age; and now clad thus in full armor by their fellow citizens, they
> are sent out with the prayers of the city, to go each his way; and they
> are invited to seats of honor in the theater.

The daylight, the fanfare, the solemn rites and loud proclamations: we are very far here from the private, anonymous vacuums in which we today absorb the theater and its lessons. The vast and impressive buildup to the performance of Athenian dramas, so many of which focused on conflicts between individuals and their societies, emphasized above all the authority and might of the city: the dignity of its military leaders and institutions, the extent of its predominance over other city-states, the honors that attached to civic service and to military self-sacrifice.

To be aware of all this is, often, to be forced to rethink our customary responses to some of the most familiar Greek tragedies, many of which are collected in this volume. To take an example mentioned already: to us, Sophocles' *Antigone* can seem like a straightforward parable about the virtue of individual resistance to state oppression. In the play, the headstrong young Theban princess Antigone defies a decree issued by the city's new ruler, her uncle Creon (to whom, as the play opens, she pointedly refers as "the general"), that forbids anyone to bury the body of her traitorous brother, Polynices, who has been slain while trying to invade the city. She opposed Creon's decree in the name of family ties and of religious law (which insists that bodies must be interred with due ritual). In her defiance, we have traditionally liked to see an unambiguously heroic act of conscience—an admirable act of individual resistance to the state. It is this aspect of the play that has made it a favorite of later adapters with a pointedly political agenda: for instance, the French writer Jean Anouilh, whose *Antigone* premiered in Paris in 1944 and was clearly intended as a parable of resistance to the Nazi occupation.

But it is hard not to wonder how, precisely, the play's original audience would have considered the act of resistance to military and political authority that is the fulcrum of Sophocles' drama. How would her contempt for "the general" and his decree have struck an audience that, only minutes before the actor playing Antigone uttered this speech, had witnessed a moving ceremony presided over by the city's greatest generals and honoring its civic leaders, a rite during which they beheld the poignant sight of young men who had been raised by "the state": the orphaned children of soldiers who, unlike Antigone, had unquestioningly followed the decrees of their commanding officers, at the cost of their own lives?

So, too, with many other plays. There is a wrenching moment early in Aeschylus' *Agamemnon* when the Chorus recall the long-ago crime that has triggered this play's action: Agamemnon's sacrifice of his daughter Iphigenia at the beginning of the Trojan War, a rite performed in order to win fair winds for the Greek armada as it sailed for Troy. It is in revenge for this infanticide—a crime evoked by the Chorus in poignant detail, down to the way in which the gagged girl pleaded with her eyes for mercy—that Clytemnestra murders Agamemnon at the climax of Aeschylus' play. (Like Antigone, Agamemnon's queen sees herself as the champion of family interests that have been eclipsed by those of the state.) And yet here again, an awareness of the tribal and patriotic energies that must have animated the audience members as they watched this play for the first time makes it difficult to dismiss Agamemnon's decision, as modern audiences tend to do, as crass military opportunism or political self-interest. The Iphigenia myth symbolizes, and the play dramatizes, a far more complicated and vexing reality: that whenever a city goes to war, every family, every private household, must "sacrifice" its children. For Americans, who do not have to perform compulsory military service (a political choice that betrays our conviction that citizen participation in war is not a civic duty), the obvious choice, increasingly, is to save the child—the "individual." For the Greeks, to whom warfare, like attendance at the theater, was a civic obligation, the opposite choice—to "save the city," prioritize the community—was just as obvious, although of course no less agonizing. It is this agony that plays such as the *Agamemnon* explore.

The few examples cited thus far are notable for another crucial feature in Greek tragedy, the nuances and ramifications of which are also best appreciated in light of the realities of Athenian culture and society. The conflict between ideologies, between competing allegiances, that animates the plays written for the Athenian stage is often dramatized as a conflict between a man and a woman: Clytemnestra versus Agamemnon, Antigone versus Creon, and many more. Looking at the titanic heroines of Greek drama—not only Clytemnestra and Antigone but Sophocles' Electra and Euripides' Phaedra, Hecuba, and Helen—it can be easy to forget that in classical Greek society, women were meant to be largely invisible, confined, at least in theory, to the women's quarters of their houses, compelled to wear veils in public, unable to own property, and denied any role in political life. (There is still debate as to whether women even attended the tragic performances.) We cannot know the precise extent to which these social conventions were observed in day-to-day life, but certainly the women and girls in Greek tragedy were aware of them. "Silence is the adornment of women," a character in Sophocles declares; in a drama by Euripides called the *Sons of Heracles*, a young girl who volunteers to be a human sacrifice in order to save the city of Athens makes her entrance by apologizing for having violated feminine decorum by speaking in public.

Yet despite the limitations imposed on them in real life—or perhaps because of them—women as represented on the tragic stage could serve as mouthpieces for values and concerns that were too easily trampled by men, or had been left out of their agendas. In Euripides' *Medea*, the heroine is, to be sure, outraged that her husband has abandoned her for a younger woman (this all-too-familiar story being the focus of many a modern production); but attentive readers will notice that what bothers her even more than this blow to her vanity is the fact that Jason has broken the oath he took when he married her. It is this betrayal— the betrayal of words and their connection to action—that she incredulously refers to throughout the play. There is an irony here that, it is hard not to suspect, would have struck the original audience of the play in 431 B.C.—the year in which the Peloponnesian War began—with uncomfortable force. For here, it's the woman (and, indeed, a non-Greek) who champions the integrity of language, the connection between words and deeds, while her Greek husband—a legendary hero, no less!—is portrayed as a glib opportunist whose mortifying sophistries ("I'm leaving you for your own good and the good of the children!") convince no one.

Similarly, in the same playwright's *Trojan Women*, produced only months after Athens carried out a brutal reprisal against a rebellious ally during the course of the Peloponnesian War, the mothers, wives, and daughters of the brutally conquered Trojans of myth become, in abject defeat, triumphant symbols of civilization itself. As Cassandra, the prophetess daughter of the murdered Trojan king, Priam, reminds the Greek "winners" of the great war have in fact lost, because they have abandoned the moral, ethical, and cultural values that make humans civilized. By contrast, she observes, the defeated Trojans have maintained their values and traditions and are thus, in some larger sense, the real victors. The fact that this moving case is made by an unmarried young woman—which is to say, a member of Athenian society who was unable to participate in the political decisions that set great wars in motion in the first place—lends a complexity, even an irony, to the *Trojan Women*'s pronouncements about war and civilization.

Complexity; irony. I don't want to suggest that a lively awareness of the social and civic conditions that produced Greek drama should lead us to exchange one reductive kind of reading (Antigone is a moral heroine, Creon is a political villain) for another (Antigone's resistance would have been frowned on and Creon's edict would have been unambiguously applauded by the original audience, who were, after all, watching these plays as part of a patriotic festival). Rather, the considerations highlighted above should deepen and complicate our readings of Greek tragedy. The tension between the celebratory civic ceremonial that preceded the plays and the acts of defiance and opposition to authority and social norms that furnish so many of those plays' plots surely created a space for fruitful consideration of the complexities of life as a citizen.

Every polity, to recur once again to the example of *Antigone*, must find a way to balance the concerns of the state with the concerns of individuals and their families: the point of Sophocles' play—one that emerges more crisply when we give due consideration not only to the play's text, but to its context—is not that Antigone is "right" and that Creon is "wrong," that the individual and the family are valuable and state control is pernicious, but rather that each character has a valid point to make. The problem—and the source of interest to a great playwright like Sophocles—is that each character's preoccupation with the value of his or her own viewpoint prevents him from seeing the value of the other's. Each is mistaking the part for the whole.

This consideration takes us very close to what it is that makes Greek tragedy "tragic." A play about an unambiguously heroic young woman, someone's mother or sister or daughter, squaring off against an unambiguously villainous general or king, a man greedy for military renown or for power, is a melodrama, not a tragedy. What gives the *Antigone* and *Agamemnon* and the other plays collected here their special and unforgettable force, a force that can still be felt after twenty-five centuries, is that they present the irresistible spectacle of two worldviews, each with its own validity, harrowingly locked in irreducible conflict. And yet while the characters in these plays are unable to countenance, let alone accept, their opponents' viewpoints, the audience is being invited to do just that—to weigh and compare the principles the characters adhere to, to reflect on the necessity of seeing the whole and on the difficulties of keeping the parts in equilibrium. Or at least to appreciate the costs of sacrificing some values to others when the occasion demands.

It is in this way—by sensitizing its audience to the dreadful ironies and irreducible complexities, the agonizing choices and painful prioritizations, that come with being both an individual and a citizen—that Athenian tragedy strove to educate the members of its audience. For this reason, it was indeed a genre that could, at least in theory, "save the city." As we know, tragedy failed in the end to save Athens. But during the great century of its efflorescence, we cannot doubt that the astonishing invention that was Athenian drama provided many thousands of citizens with opportunities to reflect on themselves and their remarkable city.

Appendix B

Material Elements and Visual Meaning
David Rosenbloom

Drama enjoyed widespread popularity in antiquity. In towns and cities throughout the ancient world, theaters were landmarks essential to the idea of community. Stone theaters cropped up throughout the Greek-speaking world from the fourth century B.C. onward; towns and cities in the Hellenistic and Roman periods built, remodeled, and expanded their theaters. As a result, many surviving theaters date from a much later time than their original construction and over the years were adapted for spectacles and uses besides drama. The reconstruction of theaters as they were in the fifth century B.C. presents challenges.

Some painted, sculpted, and molded images provide useful indices of what a production might look like; but most of these postdate the fifth century, and their creators were uninterested in accurately representing dramatic performances. The stuff of fifth-century theater—the appearance of the stage house and its decoration, the shape of the orchestra, the color and texture of the costumes, the look of the masks, the gestures and vocal delivery of the actors, the choreography of the dances, the melodies of the songs, the composition of the audiences—are either lost to us or have been reconstructed from a small body of evidence.

Tragedies also survive as texts of the words and lyrics composed for performance. These manuscripts were copied and recopied for as many as nineteen centuries before they were printed in books. In some cases, they contain interpolations from later productions. And while they offer no stage directions or blocking instructions, the texts do tend to signal entrances and exits and to give indications, however ambiguous, of what is visible to the audience. We need not endorse the fourth-century B.C. philosopher Aristotle's view that reading and watching a tragedy are essentially the same thing; something is lost and something is gained by reading tragedy. But we need all available evidence, including later performances and adaptations, to take the full measure of Greek tragedy, both as evanescent sensory experiences and as enduring documents of an extraordinary verbal art.

Tragedy at Athens was performed in the Theater of Dionysus, dedicated to the god of wine, evergreen vegetation, mysteries, madness, and illusion. Situated in the god's precinct just north of his temple and altar, this open-air theater was dug into the southeastern slope of the Acropolis, an outcrop of limestone some five hundred feet above sea level that functioned as citadel and location of the community's most cherished property—temples, treasuries, commemorations. The theater's position sheltered spectators from northwesterly winds that blow across the Acropolis; its shape retained the sun's warmth. These were important considerations, for in the fifth century the Athenians staged tragedies in the months of Gamelion (January) and Elaphebolion (March/April) at festivals honoring Dionysus. The preeminent of these festivals was the City Dionysia. Held annually after the vernal equinox, when the seas were navigable, the festival attracted spectators from all over the Greek-speaking world. Around 440 B.C., tragedies were also presented at a winter festival celebrating Dionysus, the Lenaea.

The Greek word for theater, *theatron*, literally means a "place for viewing." Throughout the fifth century, the city hired *theatropōlai*, "sellers of theater seats," to furnish wooden planks for spectators to sit on during dramatic festivals. A stone theater seating as many as seventeen thousand would not be completed in Athens until the Lycurgan period (338–324 B.C.). The plays in this volume (with the possible exception of the *Prometheus Bound*) were produced in a theater that could seat between four and six thousand spectators. Front row seating, *prohedria*, was reserved for the priest of Dionysus and other dignitaries. In front of them, at the edge of the orchestra, sat the ancient wooden statue of Dionysus brought to the theater in ritual procession from Eleutherae in Boeotia. The god was the theater's most honored spectator. Precisely in what proportions the rest of the audience was comprised—rich and poor, male citizens, resident foreigners, visitors, slaves—is unknown. Whether women attended performances of tragedy in the theater is controversial but impossible to ascertain given our evidence. Each reader may well ask how women's presence or absence might affect the meaning and reception of a play.

By all accounts, audiences in ancient Athens and throughout the Greek-speaking world were passionate spectators of tragedy. They signaled their appreciation of playwrights and performers by applauding vigorously. But they were also exacting critics, and they tolerated nothing short of excellence. Athenians insisted that the subject of tragedy be distanced from them in time and place—tragedy is about other people's suffering, not the audience's. An early fifth-century production of a historical event—the Persian sack of Miletus, a city in Asia Minor that was an ally of Athens, ending a war the Athenians helped to start but were unable to finish—cut too close to the bone and reduced the audience to tears. The Athenians decreed that this play never be performed again.

Technical errors could pique an audience's ire, as when a tragedian had a character exit from a side entrance and then return to acting space through the stage house: his production was hissed from the stage. Bored audiences showed their displeasure by clucking and hissing, putting an abrupt end to a performance, especially if the playwright tried to cram too much narrative into a play. Aristotle notes that it was at times such as these—when a play dragged on—that theatergoers, unruly in the best of times, increased their consumption of food and drink while watching. Ever sensitive to the effect of the masses upon culture, the philosopher Plato termed the role of the audience in the theater *theatrokratia*, "the rule of the spectator."

The orchestra, a "place for dancing," was the centerpiece of the fifth-century theater. Here actors performed, choruses sang and danced, and musicians played the *aulos*, a double-reed pipe that accompanied actors' monodies and the choruses' singing and dancing. Whether the orchestra of the fifth-century theater was circular or polygonal is uncertain. A theater with wooden planks for seating could not form the arc of a circle; joining rows of planks would impose a polygonal form. A polygonal orchestra would suit such a theater better than a circular one; and this is the shape of orchestras found in village theaters such as the one at Thorikos.

Most scholars agree that the fifth-century theater had no stage raised above the orchestra; the orchestra was the acting space. It was entered and exited via two side routes (*parodoi*), one to and from the east (stage right) and the other to and from the west (stage left). An altar or hearth, called a *thymelē*, may have stood in the orchestra in the fifth century; we do not know when or why it came to be there. The *aulos* player took up a position at it. Later uses of the adjective "thymelic" to designate "musical" and "non-dramatic" contests may indicate that the *thymelē* originated in competitions among musicians.

The fifth-century theater had no permanent buildings or scenery, but the visual dimension of tragedy imposed a degree of verisimilitude upon staging. Achilles, as Aristotle remarks, could not chase Hector around Troy in an orchestra the way he does in the *Iliad*. However, a messenger arriving from offstage could narrate such action; and tragedies constructed vivid offstage worlds to complement their staging. Indeed, pivotal and catastrophic events—murders, battles, shipwrecks, political assemblies—transpire outside the gaze of the audience. The locations in which the dramatic action occurs are typically places prominent in Greek myth such as Troy, Thebes, or Argos, but the range of locations is extensive. Sometimes they are outlandish: a tragedy could be set in Hades or at the ends of the earth.

A simple and versatile solution to problems of space and setting was to erect a temporary wooden stage house (*skēnē*, literally "tent") at the rear of the orchestra as needed. The date of the *skēnē*'s introduction in the theater is debated. Some believe that it was in use by the time of the *Persians* in 472, arguing that the *skēnē* represents a council house and the tomb of Darius. Many contend that the theater did not employ the *skēnē* until the *Oresteia* in 458. In the *Agamemnon*, the house of Atreus functions as a kind of mute character, encompassing in silence a history of adultery, murder, cannibalism, curse, and pollution.

The *skēnē* provided a façade and interior space for actors to change costumes and masks. It could be entered and exited through one or more doors at orchestra level and a hatch on the roof. Most of the time, the *skēnē* represented a palace or temple; but it also depicted humbler structures, such as hovels and tents, and natural formations, such as caves or groves. The pairing of *skēnē* and tomb or altar in the orchestra became common, as the *Libation Bearers* and *Helen* attest. Aristotle states that Sophocles introduced *skēnographia*, or "scene-painting." "Scene" refers to the *skēnē* (source of our word "scene," via Latin *scaena*): *skēnographia* denotes the art of painting the *skēnē* to depict features with the illusion of depth. It is unlikely that the fifth-century theater used painted backdrops.

As performed in the fifth century, tragedy required few technical devices. A wooden platform on wheels, an *ekkyklēma*, could be rolled out of the *skēnē* to disclose what had taken place in its interior—typically tableaux of murder scenes featuring corpses and killer. The *Eumenides*, however, employs the *ekkyklēma* to stage the appearance of Clytemnestra's ghost in the Erinyes' dream. Another important theatrical device was the *mēchanē*, an apparatus that enabled dramatic characters, particularly gods, to enter and exit through the air. The Latin phrase *deus ex machina*, "god from a machine," derives from its use, mainly from the late fifth century onward, to bring on a god or gods at the end of a tragedy to resolve seemingly insoluble impasses in the plot. Medea makes her shocking and awesome exit from the top of the *skēnē* via the *mēchanē* as the granddaughter of the Sun. *Prometheus Bound* seems to use the *mēchanē* for the Chorus's arrival on winged creatures and for Ocean's entry and exit on a griffin.

The heart and soul of tragic performances were the actors and choruses. In the first half of the fifth century, the state funded two actors to perform in tragedies. Aeschylus' *Persians* requires two speaking actors, as does the *Prometheus Bound*. The *Libation Bearers* briefly employs three speaking actors, while the *Eumenides* (Apollo, Athena, Orestes) makes extensive use of three actors, as do the rest of plays in this volume. Aristotle in the *Poetics* credits Sophocles with introducing the third actor. This may have happened sometime between Sophocles' debut in 468 and the *Oresteia* in 458. Aeschylus used a chorus of twelve; Sophocles increased its number to fifteen. Actors were professionals, but choruses were amateurs recruited for their talent. Their upkeep, costumes, and training were paid for by a wealthy citizen assigned to be "producer" (*chorēgos*) of the plays produced at the festival. From the time prizes were awarded for acting at the City Dionysia (c.449) to the time of Aristotle's *Poetics* (c.330), actors became a dominant theatrical force and plays were written as vehicles for their talents. During this period, the importance of amateur choruses diminished.

Actors and choruses wore ornate costumes and linen masks styled to differentiate gender, age, status, and comportment. Males played both male and female parts. Masks linked their wearers to Dionysus, who was worshipped as a mask atop a clothed pillar; but they also permitted individuals to play multiple roles—a benefit in three-actor drama—and to assume identities incompatible with their actual gender, age, and appearance. The fixed expression of the mask made voice, delivery, and gesture paramount in tragic acting. Performers' bodies were vehicles of visual meaning. Hecuba's body lies in an agonized heap in the orchestra at the beginning of the *Trojan Women*, just like her city and fortunes. In the *Eumenides*, the terrified Pythia exits the oracle of Delphi on all fours when she sees the Erinyes sleeping in the temple; but when the audience sees them in this position, it senses the waning of their power.

Entrances and exits on cars or chariots indicate characters' statuses and circumstances. Andromache and Astyanax enter in the *Trojan Women* on a cart to signify their reduction to property as spoils of war. Chariots symbolized conquest and the wealth derived from it, as they do in the queen's first arrival and exit in the *Persians* (compare her second entry) and Agamemnon's entrance with Cassandra and other spoils from Troy in the *Agamemnon*.

Texts of the plays and images on painted pottery indicate the use of movable props, such as the urn holding Orestes' "ashes" in Sophocles' *Electra* or Hector's shield, which serves as Astyanax' makeshift casket in the *Trojan Women*. Such props often condense complex verbal meanings and potent emotions in a single visual image. Cassandra enters carrying a marriage torch in the *Trojan Women*: this image indicates the baleful unity of Paris' birth and marriage to Helen, Cassandra's rape and "vengeance," and the razing of Troy that concludes the play.

Dyed and decorated fabrics were likewise essential components of tragic spectacle. Scenes of robing and disrobing—such as Cassandra's contemptuous removal and trampling of her mantic costume in the *Trojan Women* or Dionysus' ritual dressing of Pentheus as a maenad prior to his *diasparagmos* (being torn limb from limb) in the *Bacchae*—constitute major moments in the plays. Dramatic poets sought to make emotion visible. The *Persians* repeats the gesture of tearing linen robes in sorrow and shame multiple times in song and narrative before enacting it at the end of the play in the onstage lament between Xerxes and the Chorus. In the *Oresteia*, Agamemnon's trampling of crimson-dyed tapestries reenacts before the audience the crimes he committed at Aulis and Troy. The precious ooze that dyes the fabrics suggests the blood that stains Agamemnon's hands, sullies his wealth, and pollutes his house; the fine fabrics resemble the nets of delusion and divine punishment that bind mortals in disaster. Agamemnon's royal mantle, which Clytemnestra uses to render him powerless before the kill, extends the imagery. Orestes reveals the mantle to the Sun after he avenges Agamemnon, addressing it as his father and decrying it as an instrument of vicious criminality.

Finally, tragedies and satyr plays were not the only spectacles audiences watched in the Theater of Dionysus. Immediately before tragedies were performed in the theater, the city of Athens staged a pageant of its wealth, power, and military resolve. Athens exacted monetary tribute from numerous subject city-states, and functionaries carried this tribute, which was due at the time of festival, into the orchestra of the theater for the audience to view with awe. The names of benefactors of Athens were read aloud, and they were presented with golden crowns as a token of the city's gratitude and to encourage further contributions to the city. Children whose fathers died in war (Athens was at war continuously during the period in which the tragedies in this volume were presented) were raised by the state. Upon coming of age, they were presented with an infantry soldier's arms and armor in the Theater of Dionysus before the performance of tragedies. The city thus made a spectacle of its generosity while also displaying the determination of the sons of the war dead to avenge their fathers. It is well worth contemplating the dissonance between individual tragedies, which typically stage the moral and religious liabilities of wealth, power, and multigenerational vengeance, and the pre-play ceremonies, which extravagantly display Athens' riches, power, and ambition.

APPENDIX C

PLATO AND TRAGEDY
Joshua Billings

Plato grew up in an Athens in which public performances of tragedy were among the most important forms of collective culture. Born around 425, he could have been in the audience for the late masterpieces of Sophocles and Euripides. The fact of poetry's central role in the life of the city is essential to understanding Plato's critique of poetry in general and tragedy in particular. For Plato was operating not with conceptions of "high art" or aesthetic autonomy, but with a view of poetry as a civic institution with a role to play in the formation of citizens. The writings of poets formed a central part of Athenian education, and performing in a chorus was one of the important ways that young men were socialized into their role as citizens. Wisdom was often sought in poetry, and dramatists were regarded as teachers of the populace. Against this traditional reverence for poets and centrality of poetry to Athenian life, Plato responds with a biting critique of tragedy.

The late fifth century was a time of intellectual upheaval, as new currents of thoughts associated with the "sophists" (teachers of philosophy and rhetoric) were making themselves felt in Athenian culture and casting doubt on received ideas of wisdom and morality. Among these intellectuals was Socrates, who was well known for his eccentric investigations of nature and virtue as well as for his somewhat suspect friendliness toward the young men of the city. Plato became one of a group of followers of Socrates—many of them, like Plato, from aristocratic families. There is a story—probably apocryphal—that in his youth, Plato aspired to be a tragedian, but after hearing Socrates speak, he burned his tragedies and turned himself wholly to philosophy.

The legend of Plato's turn from tragedian to philosopher illustrates the proximity and distance between literature and philosophy in Plato's writing. Plato consistently sees poetry as the antagonist of philosophy, a rival genre that philosophy must interrogate, critique, and ultimately subsume. Though there are many passages in the Platonic corpus that invoke tragedy or use it as a metaphor, the central question surrounding the genre is whether a well-ruled city should admit performances of tragedy. The *Republic* contains the most sustained critique of tragedy, staged as a dialogue between Socrates a small group of interlocutors. In two separate discussions, Socrates addresses the value of poetry for the city and for the individual. Though we should be wary of equating the views expressed by the character Socrates with Plato's own (and likewise of assuming that Plato held a single view throughout his career), the *Republic* at least makes a case for a sharp condemnation of poetry in general and of tragedy most of all.

Beginning in books II and III of the *Republic*, in which Socrates addresses the role of poetry in education, and continuing in book X, in which he discusses the value of poetry to the city in general, the critique of tragedy follows two broad strands: an ethical critique, which considers the effect of tragic performance first on the performer (in the earlier books) and then on the spectator (in book X); and a metaphysical critique, which investigates the way that tragic poetry, as an imitation of reality (*mimēsis*), relates to ultimate truths. *Mimēsis* could be translated "imitation" or "representation," and it seems to describe the ways that poetry creates an appearance of reality without actually being the reality it represents. At the most basic level, Plato fears that we will be misled by appearances to lose sight of reality, and that this will make us worse citizens and philosophers.

Books II and III lay the groundwork for the ethical critique of tragedy. Socrates is considering how the young should be educated in an ideal city, and particularly, what kinds of stories they should hear as children. He suggests that the young are particularly impressionable and can easily be led astray by the kinds of stories they are exposed to (a concern we can recognize even today). The myths of the Greeks regularly portrayed gods and heroes acting in morally reprehensible ways, and Socrates fears that such stories perpetuate an impious and false view of divinity (an unusual and even radical view, given that most Greeks of this time seem to have considered the gods subject to human shortcomings). Even more deleterious seems to be the way that poetry depicts humans—even largely admirable ones—as acting and faring in ways contrary to reason. When we view a hero lamenting, or a bad man prospering, we are led to believe that the world is such that people fail to live up to the moral ideals that the *Republic* outlines. The poetic depiction of gods and humans, Socrates says, should present positive models for emulation, so that the young who witness them gain a sense of the good and just. This entails rejecting the majority (though not all) of serious poetry for the education of the young, because "poets and prose-writers speak badly about the most important matters concerning human beings" (392a).

This specific charge against *mimēsis*—that it confuses proper ethical understanding—is developed, in book X, into the even more general and damning metaphysical claim that all artistic *mimēsis* presents a false and misleading image of true reality. Socrates sets up a three-tiered hierarchy beginning with "forms" (perfect and immaterial templates for everything that exists), below that some material copy of the form, and at the bottom an artistic imitation of the material. A bed, for example, exists first and most fully as a form in the mind of the carpenter, then, less perfectly, as an actual bed made by the carpenter, and then, still less adequately, in a pictorial representation of a bed. At each level, something is lost from the previous one, to the point that the work of art corresponds to the fullest reality in only a vague and derivative sense. Applying this logic from the visual arts to poetry reveals that, insofar as it strives to imitate excellence, poetry—unlike philosophy, it is implied—cannot imitate the form of the good, but only its earthly manifestations. All poets are therefore merely "imitators of images of excellence" (600e), and their products cannot be considered philosophically serious. On this point, Aristotle will most strongly—if implicitly—disagree with Plato and elaborate a theory of *mimēsis* that does not rely on such hierarchies.

The famous charge that *mimēsis* is "third from the king and the truth" (597e) relates to all artistic representation, and it condemns aesthetic *mimēsis* generally as a faulty path to knowledge. But there is a more specific problem with tragedy, which has to do with the way that it speaks to our baser impulses (returning to the ethical strand of argument). Socrates finds that tragedy creates a conflict between reason, which urges us to restrain our emotions, and our natural desire to express our feelings. While in everyday life, we control the emotional parts of our soul with reason, the stories depicted in tragedy allow and even encourage these emotions to gain the upper hand, and thus they make us more prone to them in everyday life. The imitative poet, then, "arouses, nourishes, and makes the [inferior] part of the soul stronger, and so destroys the rational part" (605b).

Socrates' final argument, the "greatest charge" against tragedy, goes a step further, by considering how and why tragedy is so compelling. It is, he finds, precisely *because* tragedy addresses these lower parts of our soul that we enjoy it so much. The pleasure of tragedy is an inherently irrational one, and so any exposure to tragedy will have a corrupting influence, even on the most rational people. Tragic poetry, by depicting intense emotional experience, unbalances our soul, giving way to pleasurable but ultimately destructive emotional responses. We can become so caught up in the enjoyment of tragedy that we fail to evaluate it rationally. If we allow it into our city, "pleasure and sorrow will rule in the city instead of law and reason" (607a). Tragedy threatens the effort of the *Republic* as a whole to construct a city on the basis of reason, for it places at the center of civic life an experience that is fundamentally contrary to rational thought. Socrates' attack is directed against the entire Athenian way of life, typefied by the centrality it grants to poetry. In the well-ordered city, philosophy must replace poetry as the source of wisdom and education.

Plato never again addresses tragedy at such length, but the genre's role as an antagonist of philosophy remains potent in his later writings. In the late dialogue *Laws*, an Athenian imagines addressing tragedians as a city legislator: "Most excellent of strangers, we are ourselves to the best of our ability the poets of the finest and most excellent tragedy. For our entire constitution has been set up as an imitation [*mimēsis*] of the finest and most excellent life, which we say at any rate is actually the truest tragedy" (817b). The passage points to an inevitable competition between the legislator and the tragic poet, both of whom produce *mimēseis*, tragedians in their plays and legislators in their constitutions. Both aim at the same goal—imitating "the finest and most excellent life"—but only a properly ordered city is capable of succeeding. "The truest tragedy" is not the one played onstage, but the one lived every day by citizens guided by philosophy.

It is, then, no accident that Plato's dialogues themselves have a dramatic form: they aspire to replace one imitation of life with another. There is an irony to Plato's project of displacing the false tragedies that he saw onstage with the "true tragedy" of civic order. Plato aims for a complete reorientation of the sources of civic value and prestige from the empty appearances of poetry to the secure truths of philosophy—but he sees both, at least metaphorically, as forms of tragedy. In turning to philosophy, Plato could burn his tragedies without ceasing to be a tragedian.

Appendix D

Aristotle's *Poetics* and Greek Tragedy
Gregory Hays

A view of Greek tragedy still encountered with some frequency runs something like this: Greek tragedies center on a single protagonist—the "tragic hero." While generally noble and admirable, this person has a tragic flaw that brings about his or her destruction. Often the flaw in question is excessive pride, which the Greeks called *hybris*. The play depicts the hero's downfall, which plays out over the course of a single day and in a single location. At intervals a Chorus of observers sing and dance and provide commentary expressing the playwright's view of events. The audience members who witness the play feel various emotions, predominantly pity and fear, but they emerge from the experience with a sense of moral uplift.

This farrago of half-truths and misunderstandings has proved remarkably tenacious; generations of students have dutifully debated whether Creon or Antigone is the real hero of Sophocles' play or tried to identify Medea's tragic flaw. Whether they or their teachers realized it, many of this distorted picture's components can be traced back to a treatise by Aristotle known as the *Poetics*, an examination of the Homeric epics, some related works, and especially tragedy. Apart from the surviving plays themselves (and perhaps the comedies of Aristophanes), no ancient source about tragedy is more valuable. Yet none is more frustrating and potentially misleading.

Aristotle was born in 384 B.C., at Stagira, on the north rim of the Aegean. His father was a doctor with connections to the Macedonian court—both facts potentially relevant to the philosopher's later career. At the age of seventeen he entered Plato's scholarly community at Athens, the Academy. Departing after Plato's death in 348 or 347, he investigated marine biology in Asia Minor and Lesbos and was employed, famously but briefly, as tutor to the son of King Philip II of Macedon, the future Alexander the Great. Returning to Athens in 335, he founded his own school, the Lyceum. Following Alexander's death in 323, Athens became uncomfortable for those with Macedonian connections, and Aristotle thought it safest to leave the city. He died the following year.

The *Poetics* is often presented as a central monument of ancient literary criticism, alongside Horace's *Ars Poetica* and the treatise *On the Sublime* that goes under the name of "Longinus." But its importance is very much a product of the late middle ages and Renaissance. For much of antiquity, there is little evidence that the work was read by much of anybody. It did continue to be studied by philosophical commentators in the late Roman empire; like other Aristotelian works it was translated into Syriac, and from Syriac into Arabic. By this point, the second book, on comedy, appears to have become detached (the imagined survival of a single copy provides a plot point in Umberto Eco's novel *The Name of the Rose* but has no basis in reality). The Arabic translation and the twelfth-century commentary on it by the great Islamic scholar Averroes (Ibn Rushd) were translated into Latin in the thirteenth century; a slightly later but less widely read version was made from the original Greek. Once it was available in Latin, however, its survival and influence were assured. In the late middle ages Aristotle was a superstar, often cited simply as "the Philosopher" (just as we speak of Shakespeare as "the Bard"). The work's impact only grew after the invention of printing, notably through an influential commentary by the Italian poetic theorist Lodovico Castelvetro (c.1505–1571). Profoundly influential on European drama, the *Poetics* also played a crucial role in the development of opera.

It is important to emphasize what the *Poetics* is not. As we have seen, Aristotle was not a contemporary of the great tragedians. When he arrived at the Academy, Euripides had been dead for forty years. Obviously the great fifth-century tragedians had not read the *Poetics*; and their observable practice is often at variance with Aristotle's prescriptions. Nor does Aristotle offer us a reliable guide to how fifth-century Athenians (let alone "the Greeks" in general) interpreted or responded to the plays. He represents only himself: an intelligent and enthusiastic reader, roughly as distant in time from the *Oresteia* as modern students are from *Tosca* or *The Cherry Orchard*.

The *Poetics* provides some material (though not as much as we would like) on the early history and development of tragedy. Some comments are suggestive but difficult to assess. Nietzsche was famously inspired by the remark that tragedy grew out of an earlier type of performance called the dithyramb, a genre of which we know little other than it appears to have had to do with Dionysiac celebrations. Other information is interesting and perhaps accurate: that it was Aeschylus who introduced a second actor, for example, or that Sophocles invented stage scenery. Without Aristotle we would not know that Agathon's *Antheus* was not based on a preexisting myth but had an entirely invented plot. The *Poetics* also gives us a sense of how partial our picture of tragedy is. Familiar plays—*Oedipus the King, Iphigenia among the Taurians, Medea*—sit side by side with offhand references to works that are now just names to us: "Dicaeogenes's *Cyprians*, where the character wept at the painting" or "the use of the boat in the *Tyro*." Yet it is clear that the survival of the "big three" tragedians is not accidental; Sophocles and Euripides between them make up the majority of the examples, though many are from plays now lost.

If the *Poetics* preserves useful information, it has also generated much confusion. Some of this stems from the work's nature and origins. Aristotle left behind a large number of polished literary works, many in the dialogue form pioneered by Plato; none of these so-called "exoteric" works have survived. The treatises we know today as Aristotle's are more informal texts, which initially circulated only among his followers. Some of these "esoteric" works look like lecture notes, made either by Aristotle himself or by students at his lectures. It follows that they do not necessarily represent Aristotle's final thoughts, or even a clear snapshot of his thoughts at any single time. They are likely to contain loose ends, points inadequately thought through, or placeholder notes used as cues to oral expansion. Some passages appear to contradict others. Notoriously, *Poetics* chapter 13 tells us that the best tragedies are those, like *Oedipus the King*, that end in disaster, while in chapter 14, Aristotle appears to prefer narrow-escape plots like that of *Iphigenia among the Taurians*.

The nature of the treatise probably also accounts for several frustrating passages. Notable among these is Aristotle's famous definition of tragedy as "the reproduction of a weighty, self-contained action of some consequence ... which through pity and fear achieves the *katharsis* of such emotions" (chapter 6). The final clause has proved inexhaustibly fascinating to critics despite—or because of—its deep obscurity. Elsewhere in the treatise, Aristotle speaks of the production of pity and fear as the goals of tragedy. But what is meant by *katharsis*, a word that generally denotes cleansing or purgation of a ritual sort? Does tragedy cleanse us of these feelings, leaving us "calm of mind, all passion spent"? Or does it somehow purify the emotions themselves? How does it do this? It is as if we have missed a previous lecture, or are hearing a teaser for a future one.

An equally intractable problem confronts us in chapter 13, in which Aristotle asserts that the best tragedies depict protagonists who are not "outstanding in virtue and justice" and who do not come to grief "through wickedness or viciousness, but through some *hamartia*." This passage is ultimately responsible for the tenacious myth of the "tragic flaw" from which tragic protagonists are thought to suffer. Yet the word *hamartia* does not normally imply a character defect or weakness; it connotes an "error" or "mistake" of some sort. Aristotle's own examples are Oedipus and Thyestes. The former certainly errs in believing his parentage to be other than it is. Thyestes is a murkier case; we do not know what play Aristotle had in mind, but the mutual vendetta he wages with his brother Atreus involves plenty of wickedness and vice. And how would the term apply to extant revenge plays like the *Medea* or *Hecuba?* The answer may be that such plays simply do not meet Aristotle's standards for the ideal tragedy. For when Aristotle discusses actual plays, his goals are not purely descriptive; he seeks to define the characteristics of the "best" tragedies (as he sees them). His definition does not fit—was never intended to fit—the full range of surviving dramas.

For Aristotle, plot is central, "the soul of tragedy" (chapter 6). Character is subsidiary. Still less important are style, versification, and staging. This focus on the mechanics of storytelling makes him the father of what we would now call narratology. Critical to a good plot, in Aristotle's view, is unity of action; a play should depict a coherent and self-contained sequence of events. (In modern terms, it should resemble a well-crafted sitcom episode, not the nightly news.) Purely episodic plots stem either from incompetence on the playwright's part or from a desire to curry favor with actors. An example of such a play would be the *Prometheus Bound*, whose entire action consists of Prometheus receiving a succession of visitors. Another is Euripides' *Phoenician Women*, a play riddled with actors' additions, which manages to condense almost the whole Theban cycle into a single drama. A mess by Aristotelian standards, it was one of the ten Euripidean plays selected for canonization by later critics, and one of the three most studied in the Byzantine period—a reminder that Aristotle's preferences are not necessarily representative even of ancient audiences and readers.

For Aristotle the best tragic plot is complex. Often it will involve a surprising reversal of fortune (*peripeteia*) and scenes of discovery or recognition (*anagnorisis*). Dorothy L. Sayers is not the only reader to have noted the affinity of this "best plot" with that of the detective novel. Indeed, one of the two plays Aristotle cites most frequently, *Oedipus the King*, is a kind of whodunit in which a murder is committed, an investigation undertaken, witnesses questioned, and the identity of the killer finally revealed—even if the solution violates one of the commandments laid down by Sayers's fellow novelist Ronald Knox ("The detective must not himself commit the crime"). Indeed, in talking about his "best" tragedy, Aristotle frequently reminds one of the modern mystery critic, not only in his prescriptive tone and his fascination with the nuts and bolts of plotting, but also in his sense that tragedy, like the detective novel, is a fundamentally moral genre, despite the often horrific events it represents. In some ways the work's truest descendants are not Dryden's *Essay of Dramatick Poesie* or Wellek and Warren's *Theory of Literature*, but W. H. Auden's "The Guilty Vicarage" and Raymond Chandler's "The Simple Art of Murder."

But detective stories, of course, are not the only kind of story. It is no indictment of *The Adventures of Huckleberry Finn* that it is not *The Murder of Roger Ackroyd*. The limitations of Aristotle's prescriptions can be seen by trying to apply them to some of the plays included in this volume. The *Trojan Women*, for example, is a play with no single protagonist—a true ensemble piece. Nor is it easy to charge the leading characters with errors or mistakes (other than being Trojan and women). The play is not complex (in the Aristotelian sense); it is a series of episodes that could be reordered, reduced, or added to without fundamentally affecting the plot. Yet the large number of modern productions testifies to the play's enduring emotional power; if this is a poor tragedy, then there is something wrong with our—or Aristotle's—criteria.

Aristotle's analysis also ignores a number of aspects of tragedy that have seemed important to later observers. One is religion. Whatever its exact origins, tragedy was a religious ritual, performed as part of a religious festival, and it remained so throughout its classic period. Religion is incidental to some plays (the *Helen*, for example), but one cannot make sense of the *Oedipus at Colonus* without understanding the Greek institution of the "hero cult," through which favored mortals become protective guardians of a particular place after their death.

Likewise neglected is the political side of tragedy. Tragedy was a primarily (though not uniquely) Athenian art form; its public performance at a state festival provided a venue in which the *polis* could talk to itself, about itself. Sometimes the political message is explicit, as it is in Aeschylus' *Persians*. More often it is present by implication. As many modern critics have noted, the dysfunctional monarchic households of tragedy (Thebes, the House of Atreus, and the rest) serve as implicit foils for democratic Athens. They also supply a kind of mental arena in which familiar tensions (between individuals and society, state and household, men and women) can be played out.

Worth noting, finally, is Aristotle's lack of interest in the *theatrical* side of theater. It is this indifference to performance that led the French scholar Florence Dupont to describe him as a "vampire" sucking the lifeblood of Western drama. His exaltation of the script at the expense of production is perhaps not surprising. Athenian tragedies originally enjoyed only one performance; while some of the fifth-century classics were revived in Aristotle's day, he may never have seen many of the plays he discusses in performance. This perhaps helps explain his relative neglect of Aeschylus, the master of impressive stagecraft among the Big Three tragedians. Readers trained by the *Poetics* may be able to poke holes in the recognition scene in the *Libation Bearers*, but they will miss the stunning tableaux of Aeschylean theater: Agamemnon walking up a trail of blood-red carpets into the house where he will die, the apparition of Darius' ghost in the *Persians*, the torchlit procession that welcomes the Furies to their new role as Eumenides. (Aristotle's apparent indifference to these elements contrasts with the loving parodies of the tragedians' stagecraft in Aristophanes' comedies, notably the *Frogs* and *Women Celebrating the Thesmophoria*.)

No one would deny that the *Poetics* provides us with some useful tools for thinking about drama. Indeed, many of these are now so familiar to us that we may not recognize them as innovations: the distinction between plot and character (and between plot, story, and myth), the concept of the "recognition scene," or the idea that works of art should be integral wholes with a beginning, middle, and end. Aristotle was a great critic writing about a genre he clearly loved, and what he has to say deserves our careful attention. But he cannot provide a shortcut to the interpretation of tragedy, or a substitute for our own experience of it. In this respect as in others, the plays themselves remain their own best introduction.

FURTHER READING

Translations of the *Poetics* are numerous and vary in reliability. Readers will be in good hands with the Penguin version by Malcolm Heath (London, 1996), the Focus/Hackett translation by Richard Janko (Indianapolis, 1987), the World's Classics version by Anthony Kenny (Oxford, 2013), or Stephen Halliwell's version in the Loeb Classical Library (Cambridge, MA: Harvard University Press, 1995); the last includes a facing Greek text. Halliwell's *The "Poetics" of Aristotle* (London and Chapel Hill: University of North Carolina Press, 1987) is closer to paraphrase than translation and omits some of the more technical passages, but it is equipped with a helpful commentary. Even Greekless readers can benefit from the edition and commentary by D. W. Lucas, *Aristotle: Poetics* (Oxford: Oxford University Press, 1968).

The modern literature on the work is vast. The most significant book-length study is Stephen Halliwell, *Aristotle's "Poetics"* (London and Chapel Hill: University of North Carolina Press, 1986), which includes a chapter on the work's later influence. A number of useful studies are collected in Amélie Oksenberg Rorty, ed., *Essays on Aristotle's "Poetics"* (Princeton: Princeton University Press, 1992). Dorothy L. Sayers's "Aristotle on Detective Fiction" can be found in her *Unpopular Opinions* (New York: Harcourt, Brace, 1947).

APPENDIX E

THE POSTCLASSICAL RECEPTION OF GREEK TRAGEDY
Mary-Kay Gamel

Theater and Literature. More Greek drama is being produced now than at any time in history—on the stage, in musical renditions, in film, and in other genres. There are many reasons for this remarkable interest—the plays are both exotically different from contemporary life and hauntingly familiar; they raise significant moral and ethical issues; they offer magnificent roles to actors and great opportunities to directors; in a post-Freudian age, when the unconscious is much on our conscious minds, they offer ways to access primal emotions and impulses; their perspectives on power, gender, and sexuality are often provocative and disturbing; their tragic vision of life may seem truer than the optimistic visions offered by monotheistic religions; their established reputations, like that of Shakespeare, may more easily attract audiences—and more.

Yet for a thousand years the plays of Aeschylus, Sophocles, and Euripides were little known. After the fall of the Roman Empire, knowledge of Greek declined in Europe, but libraries in the eastern part of the former empire guarded Greek manuscripts. When Constantinople was conquered by Ottoman troops in 1453, Greek scholars fled to the West, and the rediscovery of Greek helped to fuel the Renaissance ("rebirth") of classical texts and humanistic thought. Greek tragedies were first printed in the early sixteenth century. In the same century there were academic productions in Latin translation at various European universities, but the most celebrated performance was a staging of *Oedipus the King* at the Teatro Olimpico in Vicenza (1585). The play was chosen because of its prominence in Aristotle's *Poetics* (see appendix D in this volume). A stone theater modeled on Roman theater design was built, music was composed for the choral songs, and the performance was regarded as a triumph.

Such an attempt at recreating ancient stagings of Greek tragedy was not typical. In the seventeenth and eighteenth centuries, productions typically featured free adaptations, adding subplots that often included love stories to soften the harshness of tragedy and make it more appropriate for female audiences. Jean de Rotrou's *Antigone* (1638) amplifies the relationship between Antigone and

Hémon so tenuously sketched in Sophocles' play. In Jean Racine's *Phèdre* (1677), Hippolyte is not a misogynist, as in Euripides' play named for him, but loves the daughter of his father's enemy, and all the characters try to resist their passions—without success. In their *Oedipus* (1678), John Dryden and Nathaniel Lee add a myriad of new characters (including the ghost of Laius) plus love interests and subplots, and they conclude with the stage full of dead bodies. John Milton took another tack, combining biblical subject matter with classical form (as its name indicates) in *Samson Agonistes* (1671).

Sometimes changes in plots were made to avoid offending audiences. Medea's murder of her children was especially problematic. Pierre Corneille's version (1635, based on Seneca as well as Euripides) includes the infanticide, but British authors delete it: in Charles Gildon's version, called *Phaeton; or, The Fatal Divorce* (1698), the locals murder the children without Medea's knowledge; after learning of their deaths she goes insane and commits suicide. In Richard Glover's *Medea* (1767), Jason's abandonment of his wife is a momentary lapse; he begs her pardon, but the protagonist kills the children in a fit of madness. The need to treat female behavior carefully was surely influenced by King Charles II's 1662 decree that female roles on the British stage be played by actual women.

In eighteenth-century Europe, the work of Johann Joachim Winckelmann, a pioneering art historian and archaeologist, sparked new interest in Greek art. In the nineteenth century, archaeological discoveries in Greece, and the Greek war of independence that began in 1821, aroused further attention, leading to the hugely influential neoclassical movement in visual arts, literature, music, architecture, and theater. In 1841, Ludwig Tieck aimed to revive Greek tragedy by staging *Antigone*, sponsored by the king of Prussia. In addition to using the latest knowledge about Greek theater, this production included music by Felix Mendelssohn. Opening in Potsdam and going on to Paris, London, Edinburgh, and Dublin, its influence was felt all over Europe. Its success did not keep Edward Leman Blanchard from burlesquing the play in *Antigone Travestie* (1845), which featured a single actor as the Chorus performing "monopolylogues," patter songs in which he took all the parts. The success of this burlesque led to many others of all three Greek playwrights, usually written in doggerel verse with lots of alliteration, bad puns, anachronisms, song parodies (familiar tunes with changed lyrics), and dance featuring cross-dressed actors of both genders. In 1850, Frank Talfourd wrote a burlesque of *Alcestis* with the subtitle *The Original Strong-Minded Woman* that was performed in New York, while Robert Brough produced *Medea; or, The Best of Mothers with a Brute of a Husband* in 1856, each against the background of a debate about divorce legislation. Despite their mockery these burlesques increased non-elite audiences' awareness of Greek drama.

Another very influential nineteenth-century production was Jules Lacroix's *Oedipus the King*, first staged in Paris (1858) and frequently thereafter, including a performance in 1881 with the powerful actor Jean Mounet-Sully as the lead and the young Sigmund Freud in the audience. Only five years later, Sophocles' play was prohibited in Britain because of its incest theme; in 1910, Gilbert Murray, Regius Professor of Greek at Oxford, who had recently completed his own translation of the play, led a successful appeal to lift the ban. His translation was staged in London in 1912, directed by the Austrian Max Reinhardt. This production was remarkable, featuring a vast acting space with a chorus of three hundred, eliminating the usual distance between audience and actors so that the audience was immediately involved in the events. This was a bold step forward in the staging of Greek tragedy.

Besides these commercial ventures there were academic productions—relatively few in the seventeenth and eighteenth centuries, more in the nineteenth, in both Britain and the United States. In 1881 *Oedipus the King* was performed in Sanders Theater at Harvard in a lavish production with original music that attracted six thousand spectators over its five-night run. Many other colleges and universities followed suit; some of these productions were in ancient Greek, and some universities have continued the tradition of the annual Greek play up to the present day. Some also aimed to recreate ancient Athenian performance, including outdoor settings, and a number of theaters were built on the model of ancient theaters. One prominent example is the Hearst Greek Theatre (1908) at the University of California, Berkeley, which was modeled on the ancient theater at Epidaurus and holds 8,900 spectators. This theater saw performances by the remarkable actress Margaret Anglin in *Antigone* (1909), Sophocles' *Electra* (1913), and a triple bill of *Iphigenia in Aulis*, *Electra*, and *Medea* (1915). Anglin was very influential in bringing naturalism to the performance of Greek tragedy.

The twentieth century saw an explosion of Greek tragedies in performance—more productions of more plays in more ways and in more places than ever before. Here are a few especially significant productions of some of the plays in this volume, with suggestions on what made them significant:

Aeschylus' *Oresteia* directed by Max Reinhardt opened in Munich 1911 and toured throughout Europe; like his *Oedipus*, it was characterized by strong interaction between actors and audience. Eugene O'Neill's three-play adaptation *Mourning Becomes Electra*, set in New England, was staged in New York in 1931, offering a strikingly dark and Freudian vision in the midst of anti-Depression whoopee. Mabel Whiteside staged the trilogy in Greek with an all-female cast in a stone outdoor theater at Randolph-Macon College, Virginia, in 1954; this venue is currently used for "original practices" Greek productions by Amy

Cohen. In London (1981), Peter Hall directed Tony Harrison's version in Anglo-Saxonese verse (four-beat lines, use of compound words such as "bloodclan" for "family," "she-child" for "daughter," etc.); this production, with an all-male cast in masks and a strong score by composer Harrison Birtwhistle, is available on video. In Ariane Mnouchkine's *Les Atrides* (1992), a ten-hour extravaganza, a large company of actors using a variety of multicultural performance styles and much music and dance played in Paris and on tour to great acclaim. Mnouchkine's inclusion of Euripides' *Iphigenia in Aulis* as a "prequel" and her sympathetic portrayal of Clytemnestra gave a strong feminist tone to the production.

Sophocles' *Oedipus at Colonus* is rarely staged, but *The Gospel at Colonus*, a musical version by Bob Telson and Lee Breuer set in an African American church with a gospel choir as the Chorus, was performed in New York in 1993 and subsequently around the United States; it is available on video. The challenging lead role of the furious grieving daughter in Sophocles' *Electra* has attracted famous actresses such as Margaret Anglin (Berkeley 1913, San Francisco 1915, New York 1918), Blanche Yurka (Boston 1931, New York 1932), and in London, Fiona Shaw 1989 and Zoë Wanamaker 1997.

Because of its depiction of the sufferings caused by war, Euripides' *Trojan Women* was one of the most frequently staged tragedies in the war-filled twentieth century. Michael Cacoyannis, who had directed *Elektra* (based on Euripides) in 1962, cast Katharine Hepburn as Hecuba in his 1971 film. Ellen McLaughlin's 1996 version was deeply influenced by the Balkan conflict. Charles L. Mee's bold adaptations always include non-Greek material; on his website he states that he creates plays that are "broken, jagged, filled with sharp edges, filled with things that take sudden turns, career into each other, smash up, veer off in sickening turns." His *Trojan Women: A Love Story* (1994) combines Euripides with Berlioz's *Les Troyens*; the second half focuses on Dido and Aeneas. An *Oresteia* in Berlin in 1936 was explicitly propagandistic, suggesting that the trilogy's movement from barbarism to enlightenment demonstrated the superiority of National Socialism. Jean Anouilh's adaptation of *Antigone*, staged in Paris in 1944, was acclaimed for what audiences perceived as its support for the French Resistance. In 1993, the director Peter Sellars staged Robert Auletta's version of the *Persians* in Los Angeles as an explicit critique of the 1991 American attack on Iraq. Xerxes was depicted as a still-defiant Saddam Hussein, while the Chorus called the enemy "terrorists" trying to grab Iran's oil. Enraged audiences walked out in droves.

Euripides' *Bacchae* has been very popular from the 1960s on. The conflict between Dionysus and Pentheus evoked contemporary debates in the United States about drug use, gender roles, and sexual freedom. Richard Schechner's version *Dionysus in '69* (1968) used nudity, sexual allusions and acts, ritual, music, and improvisation to involve the audience; it is available on video. The Nigerian poet Wole Soyinka's *Bacchae: A Communion Rite*, staged in London (1973), focused on themes of slavery and anticolonialism.

Many distinguished twentieth-century writers have been inspired by Greek tragedy. H.D. (Hilda Doolittle), an important American imagist poet, studied Greek literature at Bryn Mawr and published free translations of Euripides including choruses from various plays, *Hippolytus Temporizes* (1927), and *Helen in Egypt* (1961). T. S. Eliot used a Greek-like chorus to comment on the assassination of Thomas Becket in *Murder in the Cathedral* (1935) and based *The Cocktail Party* (1949) on *Alcestis*. In 1943, Jean-Paul Sartre wrote *The Flies*, a play based on the *Oresteia* influenced by World War II and Sartre's existentialist philosophy. A number of Irish authors turned to Greek tragedy during the country's fierce political and social struggles. Derek Mahon produced the *Bacchae* (1996), Marina Carr created an Irish Medea in *By the Bog of Cats* (1998), and Tom Paulin, Brendan Kennelly, and Seamus Heaney (Nobel Prize winner 1995) each created versions of *Antigone*; Heaney's *The Burial at Thebes* (2004) contains beautiful poetry that is also speakable. Two Japanese artists have created significant stagings of Greek tragedy by combining Japanese and Western theater traditions. One is Tadashi Suzuki, who writes his own scripts; he staged the *Trojan Women* 1974, the *Bacchae* in 1978 (a bilingual production with Japanese and American actors, none of whom spoke the others' language), and *Clytemnestra* (based on the *Oresteia* and Sophocles' and Euripides' *Electra*) in 1983. The other is Yukio Ninagawa, who staged *Medea* in 1978 and 2002 and *Oedipus the King* in 1986 and 2002. Each of these directors has toured his productions around the world.

Fiction and Greek tragedy may seem radically different forms, yet some modern writers have combined them: Kate Cicellis in *The Way to Colonos* (1960); Nancy Bogen in *Klytaimnestra Who Stayed at Home* (1979); Christa Wolf in *Medea* (1998). An exciting new form of fiction is the graphic novel, combining art and text. Mike Carey and John Bolton's *The Furies* (2002) and Eric Shanower's *Age of Bronze* (a series begun in 2001 and still ongoing) make fascinating use of Greek tragedy along with other classical sources.

A number of festivals of Greek tragedy arose in the twentieth century, many on ancient sites. One of the first was the Delphic Festival founded by Greek poet/director Angelos Sikelianos and his American wife Eva Palmer. They staged an outdoor *Prometheus Bound* in 1927 complete with a chorus of fifty. The Syracuse Festival at the ancient theater in Sicily started in 1914 and has staged two Greek dramas every two years, attracting many spectators. The severely damaged Theater of Dionysus in Athens is currently being restored, but the

Roman theater of Herodes Atticus, also on the slopes of the Acropolis, has housed the Festival of Athens since 1955. In 1938, Sophocles' *Electra* was the first play staged at the theater of Epidaurus, and since 1954 there has been an annual festival there; the summer of 2015 will see presentations in modern Greek of the *Prometheus Bound, Philoctetes, Helen,* and *Bacchae.*

One of the most important manifestations of Greek tragedy's intellectual influence is the work of significant philosophers. In his *Aesthetics* (1820–29), G.W.F. Hegel argues that tragedy reconciles opposing moral claims both of which have value. *Antigone* is a prime example, which results, Hegel argues, not in the vindication of either Antigone's or Creon's position, but a reconciliation of the two (too late, of course, for the protagonists). In *The Birth of Tragedy* (1872, 1886), Friedrich Nietzsche outlines a dichotomy between the Apollonian and the Dionysiac, or idealistic art and disorderly revelry, and argues that Greek tragedy mixes these elements. Aeschylus and Sophocles, he thinks, understood and employed this mixture, but it was undermined by Euripides' and Socrates' excessive rationalism. More recent discussions by the psychoanalyst Jacques Lacan (1959), the feminist Judith Butler (2000), and the political philosopher Slavoj Žižek (2002–2005) indicate that *Antigone* continues to arouse philosophical questions.

The first fifteen years of the twenty-first century have seen many strong productions of Greek tragedy around the world. Three representative versions: Yaël Farber adapted the *Oresteia* into *Molora* ("ash" in Sesotho) in the context of post-apartheid South Africa, where "reconciliation" took on new meaning. First staged in Johannesburg 2003, it featured harsh violence and traditional Xhosa music. Luis Alfaro's *Oedipus el Rey*, set in California with Oedipus as an ex-convict, was first performed in San Francisco in 2010. Increasing awareness of the problems faced by soldiers returning from war has led to productions of Greek tragedy intended to provide therapy for them and others suffering from PTSD, addiction, imprisonment, and other crises (http://www.outsidethewire llc.com). The success of all these productions suggests that experimentation into the meanings ancient Greek plays can hold for modern audiences will continue unabated.

Screen. Greek tragedies provided subjects for the very earliest films. A number of silent films, most quite brief, based on *Oedipus the King* were produced in France (1908), Italy (1910), England (1912, 1913), and the Netherlands (1913), but no prints of these are available.

Some films are based on drama performances, such as Tyrone Guthrie's production of *Oedipus Rex* in W. B. Yeats's translation, staged at the Stratford Festival in Ontario, Canada, in 1956, with actors in masks and stylized costumes. George Tzavellas directed *Antigone*, starring the wonderful Greek actress Irene Papas, in 1961. Don Taylor staged and filmed for the BBC modern-dress productions of his own translations of *Antigone, Oedipus the King*, and *Oedipus at Colonus* (1986). The poet and translator Tony Harrison wrote and directed *Prometheus* (1998), commenting eloquently on the decline of the working class in England and the collapse of socialism in Eastern Europe.

Distinguished directors have included Greek tragedy in their oeuvre: Pier Paolo Pasolini directed *Edipo Re* (1967), using a provocative mixture of ancient and modern settings, and *Medea* (1969) with the opera star Maria Callas in her only film role. Jules Dassin's *Phaedra* (1962) modernized *Hippolytus*, with Theseus as a Greek shipping magnate; in his *A Dream of Passion* (1978) starring Melina Mercouri and Ellen Burstyn, an actress preparing to play Medea onstage forms a relationship with a woman who has killed her own children. Hungarian director Miklós Jancsó set *Elektra, My Love* (1974) on the broad Hungarian plain, using the Greek framework to comment on contemporary politics. Lars von Trier made a 1988 TV film of *Medea* making magnificent use of northern Danish scenery and creating an unforgettable depiction of the infanticide.

There is at least one contemporary film that, though not explicitly based on Greek drama, uses one of its basic elements (discovery of a family secret) with tremendous force: the Canadian *Incendies* (2010), in which twins, following their mother's last wishes, journey to the Middle East.

Music. Before 1600, Europe had known combinations of music and drama in Christian liturgy and court entertainments. But then a movement arose to reform music by emphasizing the words. Greek tragedy, which many believed had musical accompaniment throughout, provided a model for *dramma per musica*, involving libretti with a real dramatic structure. The earliest operas took their subjects from Greek myth; one of the most frequent is the story of Orpheus, a great musician who, after losing his bride, Eurydice, goes to the Underworld and by singing convinces the gods of the Lower World to give her back, only to lose her again. Monteverdi's *Favola d'Orfeo* (1607), though not based on a particular tragedy, has a tragic structure and tone.

Later come works more closely based on particular Greek tragedies. Some fifty composers wrote operas based on *Medea*; Cavalli's *Giasone* (1649) was the first, and other composers include Marc-Antoine Charpentier (1693), Luigi Cherubini (1797), and Aribert Reimann (2010). In John Fisher's metatheatrical *Medea: The Musical* (1994), a director has rewritten the play to comment on contemporary gay issues, but things go awry when the gay actor playing Jason falls in love with the actress playing Medea, a straight feminist. The musical dimension was provided by song parodies (popular songs with lyrics changed). *Alcestis* has been very popular, no doubt partly because of its apparently happy ending when Herakles brings the wife who sacrificed herself for her husband back to him. Jean-Baptiste Lully's *Alceste* (1674) is a very free adaptation with various supernatural forces at work. Handel's version *Admeto* (1727) adds many extra characters and complicated love plots. Christoph Willibald Gluck's *Alceste* (1767) is the second of his "reform" operas, in which he rejected the dominant model for music drama (the overly complicated plots, extra characters, repetition, improvisation, elaboration so clearly seen in Handel's version), focusing instead on plot and character. A little-known example of the musical reception of Greek tragedy is Wagner's *Ring* cycle of four operas, which premiered in 1876. Though the obvious source is German myth and literature, Wagner was deeply influenced by Greek literature, especially the *Oresteia*. While most late nineteenth-century Russian composers focus on Russian history and literature, Sergey Taneyev created an *Oresteia* trilogy (1895).

Twentieth-century musical works that use Greek tragedy include two operas by Richard Strauss, each with a libretto by the distinguished poet Hugo von Hoffmansthal. *Elektra* (1909), based on Sophocles, is thrillingly dark, concentrating on Electra's obsession with her father's death and including an ending in which Electra's joy at the murder of Agamemnon's killers leads her to dance herself to death. *Egyptian Helen* (1928) is a very free adaptation of Euripides' *Helen* with many added characters including an omniscient seashell. But the boldest musical version of the Helen story is unquestionably Jacques Offenbach's *La belle Hélène* (1864), which is not a tragedy but a comic spoof that mocks Menelaus and ends with Paris and Helen sailing off to erotic happiness.

Igor Stravinsky's *Oedipus Rex* (1928) is an oratorio that can be presented either fully or partly staged. In the libretto by Jean Cocteau, a narrator speaking Latin, "a medium not dead but turned to stone," mediates between audience and performance, providing a definite alienation effect. Julie Taymor's 1992 production in Japan is available on video. Carl Orff, most famous for his *Carmina Burana*, used Hölderlin's translation in creating his *Antigonae* (1949).

Three modern operas are based on Euripides' *Bacchae*. Karol Szymanowski's *King Roger* (1926) focuses on a twelfth-century Christian king of Sicily who is deeply upset by meeting a shepherd with pagan beliefs. In the final act, the shepherd's followers dance and the shepherd is transformed into Dionysus; instead of Euripides' tragic ending, Roger is transformed and grateful. Egon Wellesz's *Die Bakchantinnen* (1931) similarly uses biblical imagery to suggest that

Dionysus is Christ, while Hans Werner Henze's *The Bassarids*, with an English libretto by W. H. Auden and Chester Kallman (1966), follows Euripides' play. Most recently, John Eaton has composed three operas based on Greek tragedy, including *The Cry of Clytemnestra* (1980) and *Antigone* (1999); Judith Weir composed music for a production of *Oedipus the King* directed by Peter Hall (1996); and Andrew Simpson created an *Oresteia* consisting of three one-act operas (2003).

All the evidence suggests that translators, adapters, directors, composers, and filmmakers will continue to create exciting productions, films, and music based on Greek tragedy.

FURTHER READING

Good overviews of the theatrical reception of tragedy are Helene P. Foley, *Reimagining Greek Tragedy on the American Stage* (Berkeley and Los Angeles: University of California Press, 2012) and Robert Garland, *Surviving Greek Tragedy* (London: Duckworth, 2004), which focuses on British productions and also includes musical and film reception. *Dionysus Since 1969: Greek Tragedy at the Dawn of the Third Millennium*, edited by Edith Hall, Fiona Macintosh, and Amanda Wrigley (Oxford: Oxford University Press, 2004) discusses various productions in the late twentieth century. Studies on individual plays include *Agamemnon in Performance: 458 BC to AD 2004*, edited by Fiona Macintosh, Pantelis Michelakis, Edith Hall, and Oliver Taplin (Oxford: Oxford University Press, 2005); George Steiner, *Antigones: How the Antigone Legend Has Endured in Western Literature, Art, and Thought* (New York and Oxford: Oxford University Press, 1984); Erin B. Mee and Helene P. Foley, *Antigone on the Contemporary World Stage* (Oxford: Oxford University Press, 2011); and *Medea in Performance 1500–2000*, edited by Edith Hall, Fiona Macintosh, and Oliver Taplin (Oxford: Legenda, 2000).

On tragedy in film, see Pantelis Michelakis, *Greek Tragedy on Screen* (Oxford: Oxford University Press, 2013) for an extensive (though not comprehensive) guide with excellent theoretical perspectives. In *Opera from the Greek: Studies in the Poetics of Appreciation* (Farnham: Ashgate, 2007), Michael Ewans discusses five operas based on Greek tragedy. *Ancient Drama in Music for the Modern Stage*, edited by Peter Brown and Suzana Ograjenšek (Oxford: Oxford University Press, 2010), provides in-depth discussions of works from the late sixteenth century to the present day.

An indispensable aid is the Archive of Performances of Greek and Roman

Drama at Oxford (www.apgrd.ox.ac.uk), which includes archival, digital, and bibliographic resources on productions of ancient texts from 1450 to the present. Most useful for Americans is the online searchable database of productions (www.apgrd.ox.ac.uk/research-collections/performance-database/productions), which is constantly seeing the addition of new material.

About the Contributors

JOSHUA BILLINGS is Assistant Professor of Classics at Princeton University. His research focuses on tragedy and intellectual history, and he has published one monograph, *Genealogy of the Tragic: Greek Tragedy and German Philosophy* (Princeton, 2014).

MARY-KAY GAMEL has worked as translator, adaptor, director, dramaturg, and/ or producer on more than thirty fully staged productions of ancient drama, including Aeschylus, Sophocles, Euripides, and Aristophanes, in the U.S., Canada, the U.K., and New Zealand. She has also written widely on issues involved in such "subsequent performances," including what constitutes "authentic stagings."

GREGORY HAYS is Associate Professor of Classics at the University of Virginia. He has published articles and reviews in journals ranging from *Classical Quarterly* to *The New York Review of Books*. His translation of Marcus Aurelius's *Meditations* is available from the Modern Library.

RACHEL KITZINGER is professor emerita of the Department of Greek and Roman Studies at Vassar College. In addition to a book on Sophoclean choruses and articles on Sophoclean tragedy, she has directed a number of productions of Greek tragedy, including Sophocles' *Oedipus at Colonus*, using the translation she collaborated on with the poet Eamon Grennan.

MARY LEFKOWITZ is Andrew W. Mellon Professor in the Humanities, emerita, at Wellesley College. A recipient of several honorary degrees and a National Humanities Medal for her teaching and writing, her books include *The Lives of the Greek Poets; Greek Gods, Human Lives; Euripides and the Gods;* and the sourcebook *Women's Life in Greece and Rome.*

DANIEL MENDELSOHN, an author and critic, writes frequently for *The New York Review of Books* and *The New Yorker*. His books include the international bestseller *The Lost: A Search for Six of Six Million;* a translation of the complete poems of Cavafy; and two collections of essays and criticism, most recently *Waiting for the Barbarians: Essays from the Classics to Pop Culture* (2012). He teaches at Bard College.

FRANK NISETICH is Professor of Classics, emeritus, the University of Massachusetts in Boston. He has translated Pindar (*Pindar's Victory Songs*), Euripides (*Orestes*), Callimachus (*The Poems of Callimachus*), and Posidippus. In addition to *Pindar and Homer* (1989), he has published articles on Pindar, Euripides, Callimachus, and the influence of Pindar on modern poetry.

JAMES ROMM is the James H. Ottaway Jr. Professor of Classics at Bard College and the author of several books, including *Ghost on the Throne: The Death of Alexander the Great and the War for Crown and Empire*. He has edited and annotated translations of numerous Greek texts, most recently a collection of Plutarch's Roman lives entitled *The Age of Caesar*.

DAVID ROSENBLOOM is Chair of the Ancient Studies Department at the University of Maryland, Baltimore County. He is author of *Aeschylus: Persians* and co-editor of *Greek Drama IV: Texts, Contexts, Performance*, as well as numerous articles and chapters on Athenian drama, oratory, and history.

SARAH RUDEN (Harvard Ph.D., Johns Hopkins Writing Seminars M.A.), an award-winning poet, has published five previous books of translation from Greek and Roman literature, most recently *The Golden Ass of Apuleius* and Augustine's *Confessions*, as well as *The Face of Water: A Translator on Beauty and Meaning in the Bible*.

EMILY WILSON is Associate Professor in Classical Studies at the University of Pennsylvania. Her work includes *Mocked with Death: Tragic Overliving from Sophocles to Milton; The Death of Socrates: Hero, Villain, Chatterbox, Saint; Seneca: A Life; Seneca: Six Tragedies;* and a new translation of the *Odyssey*.

ABOUT THE TYPE

The principal text of this Modern Library edition was set in a digitized version of Janson, a typeface that dates from about 1690 and was cut by Nicholas Kis (1650–1702), a Hungarian working in Amsterdam. The original matrices have survived and are held by the Stempel foundry in Germany. Hermann Zapf (b. 1918) redesigned some of the weights and sizes for Stempel, basing his revisions on the original design.

Copyrights for Play Translations